# DICTIONARY
## of the
# TURKIC LANGUAGES

## ENGLISH: AZERBAIJANI, KAZAKH, KYRGYZ, TATAR, TURKISH, TURKMEN, UIGHUR, UZBEK

Kurtuluş Öztopçu
Zhoumagaly Abuov - Nasir Kambarov
Youssef Azemoun

ROUTLEDGE
ROUTLEDGE
Taylor & Francis Group

London and New York

First published 1996
by RoutledgeFalmer
2 Park Square, Milton Park, Abingdon, Oxon, OX14 4RN

Simultaneously published in the USA and Canada by RoutledgeFalmer
270 Madison Ave, New York NY 10016
First published in paperback 1999

RoutledgeFalmer is an imprint of the Taylor & Francis Group

Reprinted 1999

Transferred to Digital Printing 2006

© 1996 Kurtuluş Öztopçu

Set in
METimes: Gürel/Sayed, Cambridge, MA, USA
Anatoliano, and Uzbekkazakh: Geoffrey Graham, Berkeley, CA, USA
Uighur: M. Rıza Bekin, Doğu Turkistan Vakfı , İstanbul, Türkiye
Database was designed using 4th Dimension for Macintosh.
Layout was done with Word 5.1 for Macintosh.
Customized multilingual database and camera ready copy: Interactive Media and Geographic
Information Systems, Oxnard, CA, USA.

*British Library Cataloguing in Publication Data*
A catalogue record for this book is available from the British Library

*Library of Congress Cataloguing in Publication Data*
A dictionary of the Turkic languages: English, Azerbaijani, Kazakh, Kyrgyz, Tatar, Turkish,
Turkmen, Uighur, Uzbek/Kurtuluş Öztopçu... et. al.
1. English language - Dictionaries - Turkic      I. Öztopçu, Kurtuluş, 1950-.
PL26.D53 1996
423'.943-dc20   96-5893

ISBN 0–415–14198–2 (hbk)
ISBN 0–415–16047–2 (pbk)

# DICTIONARY
## of the
# TURKIC LANGUAGES

For Mr Hikmet Aksan and Mrs Belkıs Aksan

# Contents

Preface ix

Alphabets and Transcription Systems x

Guide to Pronunciation xi

Table of Alphabets and Transcriptions xii

Notes on Entry Selection and Style xiv

Abbreviations xv

Acknowledgments xvi


Dictionary 1

Azerbaijani - English Index 171

Kazakh - English Index 195

Kyrgyz - English Index 217

Tatar - English Index 239

Turkish - English Index 263

Turkmen - English Index 285

Uighur - English Index 309

Uzbek - English Index 339

# Preface

This is the first English - Turkic languages dictionary to include all the eight major Turkic languages in their official alphabets, together with a convenient transcription system for those without an official Latin alphabet. It is also the first dictionary to use the new Latin alphabets for the Turkmen and Uzbek languages.

The dictionary is followed by eight Turkic language - English indices, one for each of the Turkic languages included. The dictionary and the indices together fulfill an urgent need for a multilingual guide to these languages, which are spoken by approximately 150 million people.

The new official Latin alphabets for Azerbaijani, Turkmen and Uzbek, employed in this dictionary, were adopted during the past three years as Azerbaijan, Turkmenistan and Uzbekistan became independent. They will, however, probably not be fully implemented for some time.

Responsibility for the content and editing of the individual languages was undertaken as follows:
Azerbaijani, Turkish and Uighur: Kurtuluş Öztopçu, Visiting Assistant Professor of Turkic Languages at the University of California, Los Angeles, and Visiting Lecturer for Turkish at the University of California, Berkeley.
Kazakh and Kyrgyz: Zhoumagaly Abuov, Kazak State Law Institute.
Uzbek and Tatar: Nasir Kambarov, Uzbek State World Languages University.
Turkmen: Youssef Azemoun, Turkmen expert.

The duties of the editor included the following: Compiling the basic English word list; incorporating all the changes in the official scripts that have occurred since the project began; determining the requirements of a suitable database; editing, organizing and inputting all of the data; checking for accuracy; finding attractive and workable fonts; coordinating the translations, the work of the authors and reviewers; preparing indices for all languages; and producing the final copy.

# Alphabets and Transcription Systems

- Turkish is given only in the official Latin alphabet, in use since 1928.

- Azerbaijani, Turkmen and Uzbek are given in both their official Cyrillic and Latin scripts. In the following table of alphabets and transcriptions the Azerbaijani Latin alphabet is in its official alphabetical order, however the Cyrillic alphabet has been reordered to create a one to one correspondance with the Latin. For Turkmen and Uzbek since there is no one to one correspondance between their official Latin and Cyrillic alphabets these are provided simply in their official alphabetical order.

- Kazakh, Kyrgyz, and Tatar, which have no official Latin-based scripts, are given in their official Cyrillic alphabets and in our Latin transcriptions in parenthesis. While the Latin transcriptions of these different languages are almost identical, there is no absolute one-to-one correspondence between the Cyrillic letters and the Latin transcription because one sound in one language may be rendered by a different Cyrillic letter in another.

- Uighur is given in its official Arabic script and in our Latin transcription in parenthesis.

# Guide to Pronunciation

In the Turkic languages most words are pronounced as they are written, and each character usually has the same pronunciation no matter where in a word it occurs. In this dictionary we have provided either an official Latin script or a Latin transcription for each Turkic language. In the transcriptions we have preferred generally understood signs that reflect pronunciation rather than less well known, more scholarly symbols. Several different characters in the official Latin scripts and in the transcriptions correspond to either the same or similar sounds in English.

One character may be pronounced differently in different languages. Thus "ğ" is pronounced slightly differently in Azerbaijani and Turkish. The characters in the following chart should be noted because either they do not exist in the English alphabet, or because they may not be pronounced in the Turkic languages as they are in English.

| Latin alphabet or transcription | English equivalent | Appears in these languages... |
|---|---|---|
| c | as in gentleman | Azerbaijani, Turkish |
| ç | as in child | Azerbaijani, Turkish, Turkmen |
| ə | as in dad | Azerbaijani |
| e | as in say | Turkish |
| e | as in bet | all Turkic languages except Turkish |
| ä | as in dad | Kazakh, Tatar, Turkmen, Uighur |
| ğ | /gh/ | Azerbaijani and Turkish |
| g' | /gh/ | Uzbek |
| ı | as in serial | Azerbaijani, Kazakh, Kyrgyz, Tatar, Turkish |
| j | as in measure | Azerbaijani and Turkish |
| ñ | as in song | Turkmen |
| o | as in qualm | Uzbek |
| o' | as in boy | Uzbek |
| ö | as in turn | all Turkic languages except Uzbek |
| q | as in guard or /kh/ | Azerbaijani |
| ş | as in shirt | Azerbaijani, Turkish, Turkmen |
| ü | like German ü | all Turkic languages except Uzbek |
| x | /kh/ | Azerbaijani, Uzbek |
| ſ | as in measure | Turkmen |
| y | as in serial | Turkmen |
| ÿ | as in yes | Turkmen |

# Table of Alphabets and Transcriptions

| Azerbaijani Latin | Azerbaijani Cyrillic | Kazakh Cyrillic | Kazakh Trans. | Kyrgyz Cyrillic | Kyrgyz Trans. | Tatar Cyrillic | Tatar Trans. |
|---|---|---|---|---|---|---|---|
| a | а | а | (a) | а | (a) | а | (a) |
| b | б | ә | (ä) | б | (b) | б | (b) |
| c | ч | б | (b) | в | (v) | в | (v) |
| ç | ч | в | (v) | г | (g) | г | (g) |
| d | д | г | (g) | д | (d) | д | (d) |
| e | е | ғ | (gh) | е | (e) | е | ([y]e) |
| ə | ə | д | (d) | ё | (yo) | ё | (yo) |
| f | ф | е | ([y]e) | ж | (j) | ж | (zh) |
| g | к | ё | (yo) | з | (z) | з | (z) |
| ğ | ғ | ж | (zh) | и | (i) | и | (i) |
| h | h | з | (z) | й | (y) | й | (y) |
| x | х | и | (i[y]) | к | (k) | к | (k) |
| ı | ы | й | (y) | л | (l) | л | (l) |
| i | и | к | (k) | м | (m) | м | (m) |
| j | ж | қ | (q) | н | (n) | н | (n) |
| k | к | л | (l) | ң | (ng) | о | (o) |
| q | г | м | (m) | о | (o) | п | (p) |
| l | л | н | (n) | ө | (ö) | р | (r) |
| m | м | ң | (ng) | п | (p) | с | (s) |
| n | н | о | (o) | р | (r) | т | (t) |
| o | о | ө | (ö) | с | (s) | у | (u) |
| ö | ө | п | (p) | т | (t) | ф | (f) |
| p | п | р | (r) | у | (u) | х | (kh) |
| r | р | с | (s) | ү | (ü) | ц | (ts) |
| s | с | т | (t) | ф | (f) | ч | (ch) |
| ş | ш | у | ([u]w) | х | (kh) | ш | (sh) |
| t | т | ұ | (u) | ц | (ts) | щ | (shch) |
| u | у | ү | (ü) | ч | (ch) | ъ | (') |
| ü | Y | ф | (f) | ш | (sh) | ы | (ı) |
| v | в | х | (kh) | щ | (shch) | ь | (') |
| y | j | һ | (h) | ъ | (') | э | (e) |
| z | з | ц | (ts) | ы | (ı) | ю | (yu) |
| ' | ' | ч | (ch) | ь | (') | я | (ya) |
| | | ш | (sh) | э | (e) | ә | (ä) |
| | | щ | (shch) | ю | (yu) | ө | (ö) |
| | | ъ | (') | я | (ya) | Y | (ü) |
| | | ы | (ı) | | | җ | (j) |
| | | і | (i) | | | ң | (ng) |
| | | ь | (') | | | һ | (h) |
| | | э | (e) | | | | |
| | | ю | (yu) | | | | |
| | | я | (ya) | | | | |

| Turkish Latin | Turkmen Cyrillic | Turkmen Latin | Uighur Arabic | Uighur Trans. | Uzbek Cyrillic | Uzbek Latin |
|---|---|---|---|---|---|---|
| a | а | a | ﺍ | (a) | а | a |
| b | б | b | ﻪ | (ä) | б | b |
| c | в | ç | ﺏ | (b) | в | d |
| ç | г | d | پ | (p) | г | e |
| d | д | e | ﺕ | (t) | д | f |
| e | е | ä | ﺝ | (j) | е | g |
| f | ё | f | ﭺ | (ch) | ё | h |
| g | ж | g | ﺥ | (kh) | ж | i |
| ğ | җ | h | ﺩ | (d) | з | j |
| h | з | i | ﺭ | (r) | и | k |
| ı | и | j | ﺯ | (z) | й | l |
| i | й | ʃ | ﮊ | (zh) | к | m |
| j | к | k | ﺱ | (s) | л | n |
| k | л | l | ﺵ | (sh) | м | o |
| l | м | m | ﻍ | (gh) | н | p |
| m | н | n | ﻑ | (f) | о | q |
| n | ң | ñ | ﻕ | (q) | п | r |
| o | о | o | ﻙ | (k) | р | s |
| ö | ө | ö | ﮒ | (g) | с | t |
| p | п | p | ﯓ | (ng) | т | u |
| r | р | r | ﻝ | (l) | у | v |
| s | с | s | ﻡ | (m) | ф | x |
| ş | т | ş | ﻥ | (n) | х | y |
| t | у | t | ﻩ | (h) | ц | z |
| u | ү | u | ﺋﻮ | (o) | ч | o' |
| ü | ф | ü | ﯗ | (u) | ш | g' |
| v | х | w | ﺋﯚ | (ö) | ъ | sh |
| y | ц | y | ﺋﯜ | (ü) | ь | ch |
| z | ч | ÿ | ﯞ | (v) | э | ng |
|  | ш | z | ﺋﻰ | (e) | ю |  |
|  | щ |  | ﺋﻰ | (i) | я |  |
|  | ъ |  | ﻯ | (y) | ÿ |  |
|  | ы |  | ﺋ | (') | қ |  |
|  | ь |  |  |  | ғ |  |
|  | э |  |  |  | ҳ |  |
|  | ю |  |  |  |  |  |
|  | я |  |  |  |  |  |

# Notes on Entry Selection and Style

• The English corpus of approximately 800 words was selected from several lists of "most frequently used words." The remainder were added to meet the needs of the most likely users: students, businessmen, linguists, and tourists.

• Since an eight-language dictionary cannot be both portable and comprehensive, an English entry is defined with the single most common Turkic equivalent from each Turkic language, unless two Turkic words are needed for a full definition. Thus under the entry "brother" the reader will find both the Uzbek "aka" and "uka" because the first means "older brother," the second "younger brother." An exception was also made for some Tatar words, where two equivalents are provided. The reason for this is that Tatar has uniquely been under Russian influence for more than four centuries so that colloquial Tatar has come to include a substantial number of borrowed Russian words.

• Since this work is also, by way of its indices, a Turkic languages - English dictionary, some English entries were selected not because they are in common use in English but because of the frequent use of their Turkic equivalents. Thus we included such entries as "(be) bored," "(be) born" and words for objects common in the Turkic world such as "mulberry," "pomegranate," and "quince."

• To indicate that an entry word is being defined in a restricted sense, it is followed either by a subject category marker (e.g. "branch *bot.*", thus not a "branch of a bank"), by an abbreviation for a grammatical category (e.g. *n.*, *adj.*, *adv.*), or, if these do not suffice, by an explanation in parenthesis (e.g. "bright (=full of light)", thus not "intelligent").

• The grammatical category designations that follow the English entry word apply only to that entry word, as the Turkic equivalents may not belong in the same grammatical category.

• If the transitive and intransitive forms of an English verb are both in common use, they are entered separately and marked *vt.* or *vi.*

• Verbs are entered by verb stem followed by a dash indicating the infinitive suffix, rather than the traditional practice in single-language dictionaries in which verbs are entered in their infinitive form.

# Abbreviations

| | | | | |
|---|---|---|---|---|
| *adj.* | adjective | | *med.* | medicine |
| *adv.* | adverb | | *mil.* | military |
| *ag.* | agriculture | | *mus.* | music |
| *art.* | arts | | *n.* | noun |
| *ast.* | astronomy | | *num.* | numeral |
| *bot.* | botany | | *phy.* | physics |
| *clo.* | clothing | | *phys.* | physiology |
| *conj.* | conjunction | | *pol.* | politics |
| *cul.* | culinary, food & utensils | | *pre.* | press |
| *econ.* | economics & finance | | *prep.* | preposition |
| *geo.* | geography | | *pro.* | pronoun |
| *geol.* | geology | | *rel.* | religion |
| *geom.* | geometry | | *spor.* | sports, games & physical educ |
| *interj.* | interjection | | *tech.* | technology & tools |
| *jud.* | judiciary | | *v.* | verb |
| *ling.* | linguistics & grammar | | *vi.* | verb intransitive |
| *lit.* | literature | | *vt.* | verb transitive |
| *math.* | mathematics | | *zool.* | zoology |

Signs:

| | |
|---|---|
| = | synonym |
| ~ | similar in meaning |
| x | antonym |
| * | additional information about entry word |
| - | used to indicate the infinitive suffix after Turkic verb stem |

# Acknowledgments

My co-authors and I would like to acknowledge the help of the following, without whose help this project would not have been realized: Jala Garibova, Ralph Jaeckel, Agnes Kefeli-Clay, Kamran M. Khakimov, Elmira Kochumkulova, Gulbahar Mamut, Aynur Öztopçu, Gönenç Öztopçu, Özden Öztopçu, Seda Öztopçu, Mehmet M. Tulum, Ibadulla Zakhirov, Nadirbek Zheerenchiev, and Rakhmanova M. Zhumabekovna for checking various sections of the dictionary; Andreas J. E. Bodrogligeti and Güliz Kuruoğlu for their continuous support; my dear friend Suha Ülgen for designing a flexible, multilingual, multiscript and multimedia database; Marla A. Petal, my agent, for recognizing the importance of this work and finding the right publisher; and last but not least, Simon Bell, senior editor at Routledge, a Turkophile and an enthusiastic supporter of the project from its inception. All shortcomings of the dictionary are, of course, the responsibility of the authors.

Kurtuluş Öztopçu
Editor

# DICTIONARY

ENGLISH: AZERBAIJANI, KAZAKH, KYRGYZ,
TATAR, TURKISH, TURKMEN, UIGHUR, UZBEK

## about *adv.*

1. тэхминəн təxminən
2. шамамен (shamamen)
3. чамасы менен (chaması menen)
4. чамасы (chaması)
5. tahminen
6. такмынан takmynan
7. تخمنن (täkhminän)
8. тахминан taxminan

## about *prep.*

1. һаггында haqqında
2. туралы (tuwralı)
3. тууралуу (tuuraluu)
4. хакында (khakında)
5. hakkında
6. барада barada
7. ھەققىدە (häqqidä)
8. хақида haqida

## above *adv.*

1. jухарыда yuxarıda
2. жоғарыда (zhogharıda)
3. жогорудо (jogorudo)
4. югарыда (yugarıda)
5. yukarıda
6. ёкарда ÿokarda
7. يۇقىرىدا (yuqirida)
8. юқорида yuqorida

## above *prep.*

1. үстүндə üstündə
2. үстінде (üstinde)
3. үстүндө (üstündö)
4. өстендə (östendä)
5. üstünde
6. үстүнде üstünde
7. ئۈستىدە (üstidä)
8. устида ustida

## abstract *adj.*

1. мүчəррəд mücərrəd
2. абстракт (abstrakt)
3. абстрактуу (abstraktuu)
4. абстракт (abstrakt)
5. soyut
6. абстракт abstrakt
7. ئابستراكت (abstrakt)
8. мавхум mavhum

## accept *v.*

1. гəбул ет- qəbul et-
2. қабылда- (qabılda-)
3. кабыл ал- (kabıl al-)
4. кабул ит- (kabul it-)
5. kabul et-
6. кабул əт- kabul et-
7. قوبۇل قىل (qobul qil-)
8. қабул қил- qabul qil-

## accident (*traffic) *n.*

1. гəза qəza
2. авария (avariya)
3. авария (avariya)
4. авария (avariya)
5. kaza
6. авария awariÿa
7. قازا (qaza)
8. авария avariya

## account *n.*

1. һəсаб hesab
2. есеп (yesep)
3. эсеп (esep)
4. исəп (isäp)
5. hesap
6. хасап hasap
7. ھېسابات (hesabat)
8. хисоб hisob

## add *v.*

1. əлавə ет- əlavə et-
2. қос- (qos-)
3. кош- (kosh-)
4. куш- (kush-)
5. ekle-
6. гош- goş-
7. قوش (qosh-)
8. қўш- qo'sh-

## addition *math. n.*

1. топлама toplama
2. қосу (qosuw)
3. кошуу (koshuu)
4. кушу (kushu)
5. toplama
6. гошма goşma
7. قوشۇش (qoshush)
8. қўшиш qo'shish

## address *n.*

1. үнван ünvan
2. адрес (adres)
3. адрес (adres)
4. адрес (adres)
5. adres
6. адрес adres
7. ئادرېس (adres)
8. адрес adres

## adjective *ling. n.*

1. сифəт sifət
2. сын есім (sın yesim)
3. сын атооч (sın atooch)
4. сыйфат (sıyfat)
5. sıfat
6. сыпат sypat
7. سۈپەت (süpät)
8. сифат sifat

---

**admire** *v.*
1. һejpaн oл- heyran ol-
2. таңдан- (tangdan-)
3. таңдан- (tangdan-)
4. сокланып карап тор-
   (soklanıp karap tor-)
5. hayran ol-
6. тәсин гал- täsin gal-
7. قايل بول (qayil bol-)
8. қойил қол- qoyil qol-

**adult** *n.*
1. һәдди-бұлуға чатмыш
   həddi-büluğa çatmış
2. ер жеткен (yer zhetken)
3. бойго жеткен
   (boygo jetken)
4. буйга җиткән
   (buyga jitkän)
5. yetişkin
6. яшы етен ÿaşy ÿeten
7. بويغا يەتكەن ئادەم
   (boyigha yätkän adäm)
8. балоғатга еттан одам
   balog'atga yetgan odam

**adverb** *ling. n.*
1. зәрф zərf
2. үстеу (üstew)
3. тактооч (taktooch)
4. рәвеш (rävesh)
5. zarf
6. хал hal
7. رەۋىش (rävish)
8. равиш ravish

**advertisement** *n.*
1. реклам reklam
2. хабарландыру
   (khabarlandıruw)
3. жарыя (jarıya)
4. реклама (reklama)
5. reklam
6. реклама reklama

7. ئېلان (elan)
8. реклама reklama

**advice** *n.*
1. мәсләһәт məsləhət
2. ақыл-кеңес (aqıl-kenges)
3. кеңеш (kengesh)
4. мәслихәт (mäslikhät)
5. öğüt
6. маслахат maslaxat
7. نەسىھەت (näsihät)
8. маслахат maslahat

**afraid: be afraid** *v.*
1. горх- qorx-
2. қорқ- (qorq-)
3. корк- (kork-)
4. курк- (kurk-)
5. kork-
6. горк- gork-
7. قورق (qorq-)
8. қўрқ- qo'rq-

**after** *prep.*
1. соңра sonra
2. соң (song)
3. кийин (kiyin)
4. соң (song)
5. sonra
6. соңра soñra
7. كېيىن (keyin)
8. кейин keyin

**afternoon** *n.*
1. күнортадан соңра
   günortadan sonra
2. түс (tüs)
3. түш (tüsh)
4. төштән соңгы вакыт
   (töshtän songgı vakıt)
5. öğleden sonra
6. өйле öyle

7. چۈشتىن كېيىن
   (chüshtin keyin)
8. тушки пайт tushki payt

**again** *adv.*
1. јенидән yenidən
2. қайтадан (qaytadan)
3. кайтадан (kaytadan)
4. тагы(н) (tagı[n])
5. tekrar
6. ене ÿene
7. يەنە (yänä)
8. яна yana

**against** *prep.*
1. гаршы qarşı
2. қарсы (qarsı)
3. каршы (karshı)
4. каршы (karshı)
5. karşı
6. гаршы garşy
7. قارشى (qarshi)
8. қарши qarshi

**age** *n.*
1. јаш yaş
2. жас (zhas)
3. жаш (jash)
4. яшь (yash')
5. yaş
6. яш ÿaş
7. ياش (yash)
8. ёш yosh

**ago** *adv.*
1. өнчә öncə
2. бұрын (burın)
3. мурда (murda)
4. элек (elek)
5. önce
6. озал ozal
7. بۇرۇن (burun)
8. аввал avval

---

## agree *v.*
1. разы ол- razı ol-
2. келіс- (kelis-)
3. макулдаш- (makuldash-)
4. риза бул- (riza bul-)
5. razı ol-
6. ылалаш- ylalaş-
7. ‫توشۇل‬ (qoshul-)
8. рози бўл- rozi bo'l-

## agreement *n.*
1. мүтавилэ müqavilə
2. келісім (kelisim)
3. келишим (kelishim)
4. килешү (kileshü)
5. sözleşme
6. ылалашык ylalaşyk
7. ‫كېلىشىم‬ (kelishim)
8. битим bitim

## agriculture *n.*
1. кэнд тэсэррүфаты
   kənd təsərrüfatı
2. ауыл шаруашылық
   (awıl sharwashılıq)
3. дыйканчылык
   (dıykanchılık)
4. авыл хужалыгы
   (avıl khujalıgı)
5. tarım
6. оба хожалыгы
   oba hojalygy
7. ‫يېزا ئىگىلىكى‬ (yeza igiliki)
8. қишлоқ хўжалиги
   qishloq xo'jaligi

## air *n.*
1. һава hava
2. ауа (awa)
3. аба (aba)
4. һава (hava)
5. hava
6. хова howa
7. ‫ھاۋا‬ (hava)
8. хаво havo

## airline *n.*
1. һава јолу hava yolu
2. ауа жолы (awa zholı)
3. аба жолу (aba jolu)
4. һава юлы (hava yulı)
5. hava yolu
6. хова ёлы howa ÿoly
7. ‫ھاۋا يولى‬ (hava yoli)
8. хаво йўли havo yo'li

## airmail *n.*
1. һава почту hava poçtu
2. авиапочта (aviapochta)
3. авиапочта (aviapochta)
4. авиапочта (aviapochta)
5. uçak postası
6. авиапочта awiapoçta
7. ‫ھاۋا پوچتىسى‬
   (hava pochtisi)
8. авиапочта aviapochta

## airplane *n.*
1. тәјјарә təyyarə
2. самолёт (samolyot)
3. самолёт (samolyot)
4. самолёт, очкыч
   (samolyot, ochkıch)
5. uçak
6. учар uçar
7. ‫ئايروپىلان‬ (ayropilan)
8. тайёра tayyora

## airport *n.*
1. тәјјарә лиманы
   təyyarə limanı
2. аэропорт (aeroport)
3. аэропорт (aeroport)
4. аэропорт (aeroport)
5. havaalanı
6. аэропорт aeroport
7. ‫ئايروپورت‬ (ayroport)
8. тайёрагох̦ tayyoragoh

## algebra *n.*
1. чәбр cəbr
2. алгебра (algebra)
3. алгебра (algebra)
4. алгебра (algebra)
5. cebir
6. алгебра algebra
7. ‫ئالگېبرا‬ (algebra)
8. алгебра algebra

## alike *adj.*
1. охшар oxşar
2. ұқсас (uqsas)
3. окшош (okshosh)
4. охшаш (okhshash)
5. benzer
6. мензеш meñzeş
7. ‫ئوخشاش‬ (okhshash)
8. ўхшаш o'xshash

## alive *adj.*
1. чанлы canlı
2. тірі (tiri)
3. түрүү (türüü)
4. жанлы (janlı)
5. canlı
6. дири diri
7. ‫تىرىك‬ (tirik)
8. тирик tirik

## all *adj.*
1. бүтүн bütün
2. бәрі (bäri)
3. баары (baarı)
4. һәммә (hämmä)
5. bütün
6. эхли ähli
7. ‫ھەممە‬ (hämmä)
8. хамма hamma

---

1. Azerbaijani  2. Kazakh  3. Kyrgyz  4. Tatar  5. Turkish  6. Turkmen  7. Uighur  8. Uzbek

## all *pron.*

1. һамы hamı
2. бәри (bäri)
3. баары (baarı)
4. барлық (barlık)
5. hepsi
6. хеммеси hemmesi
7. بارلىق (barliq)
8. ҳамма hamma

## almond *bot. n.*

1. бадам badam
2. миндаль (mindal')
3. миндаль (mindal')
4. бадам (badam)
5. badem
6. бадам badam
7. بادام (badam)
8. бодом bodom

## almost *adv.*

1. демәк олар ки demәk olar ki
2. дерлік (dyerlik)
3. дәәрлик (deerlik)
4. диярлек (diyarlek)
5. hemen hemen
6. диен ялы diyen ÿaly
7. دېيەرلىك (deyärlik)
8. деярли deyarli

## alone *adj.*

1. јалғыз yalqız
2. жалғыз (zhalghız)
3. жалгыз (jalgız)
4. ялгыз (yalgız)
5. yalnız
6. еке ÿeke
7. يالغوز (yalghuz)
8. ёлғиз yolg'iz

## alphabet *n.*

1. әлифба әlifba
2. алфавит (alfavit)
3. алфавит (alfavit)
4. әлифба (älifba)
5. alfabe
6. әлипбий elipbiÿ
7. ئېلىپبە (elipbä)
8. алифбо alifbo

## also *adv.*

1. да, дә da, dә
2. тағы да (taghı da)
3. дагы да (dagı da)
4. да, дә (da, dä)
5. da, de
6. хем, да, де hem, da, de
7. ـمۇ (-mu)
8. ҳам ham

## always *adv.*

1. һәмишә hәmişә
2. әрқашан (ärqashan)
3. ар дайым (ar dayım)
4. һәрвакыт (härvakıt)
5. daima
6. хемише hemişe
7. ھەمىشە (hämishä)
8. доим doim

## ambassador *n.*

1. сәфир sәfir
2. елші (yelshi)
3. элчи (elchi)
4. илче (ilche)
5. elçi
6. илчи ilçi
7. ئەلچى (älchi)
8. элчи elchi

## ambulance *med. n.*

1. тә'чили јардым машыны tә'cili yardım maşını
2. жедел жәрдем (zhedel zhärdem)
3. тез жардам (tez jardam)
4. тиз ярдәм күрсәту машинасы (tiz yardäm kürsätü mashinası)
5. ambulans
6. тиз көмек машыны tiz kömek maşyny
7. قۇتقۇزۇش ماشىنىسى (qutquzush mashinisi)
8. тез тиббий ёрдам машинаси tez tibbiy yordam mashinasi

## amount *n.*

1. мигдар miqdar
2. сан (san)
3. сан (san)
4. микъдар (mik'dar)
5. miktar
6. мукдар mukdar
7. مىقدار (miqdar)
8. микдор miqdor

## anarchy *pol. n.*

1. анархија anarxiya
2. анархия (anarkhiya)
3. анархия (anarkhiya)
4. анархия (anarkhiya)
5. anarşi
6. анархия anarhiÿa
7. ئانارخىزم (anarkhizm)
8. анархия anarxiya

---

1. Azerbaijani  2. Kazakh  3. Kyrgyz  4. Tatar  5. Turkish  6. Turkmen  7. Uighur  8. Uzbek

## and *conj.*
1. вә və
2. және (zhäne)
3. жана (jana)
4. һәм (häm)
5. ve
6. ве we
7. وه (vä)
8. ва va

## angel *rel. n.*
1. мәләк mәlәk
2. періште (perishte)
3. periшte (perishte)
4. фәрештә (färeshtä)
5. melek
6. перишде perişde
7. پرشته (pärishtä)
8. фаришта farishta

## anger *n.*
1. гәзәб qәzәb
2. ашу (ashuw)
3. ачуу (achuu)
4. ачу (achu)
5. öfke
6. гахар gahar
7. غزهپ (ghäzäp)
8. жахл jahl

## angle *math. n.*
1. бучаг bucaq
2. брыш (burish)
3. бурч (burch)
4. почмак (pochmak)
5. açı
6. бурч burç
7. بۇلۇڭ (bulung)
8. бурчак burchak

## angry *adj.*
1. ачыглы acıqlı
2. ашулы (ashuwlı)
3. ачуулуу (achuuluu)
4. ачулы (achulı)
5. kızgın
6. гахарлы gaharly
7. خاپا (khapa)
8. жахли чиккан
jahli chiqqan

## animal *n.*
1. һејван heyvan
2. айуан (aywan)
3. айбан (ayban)
4. хайван (khayvan)
5. hayvan
6. хайван haÿwan
7. هايۋان (hayvan)
8. ҳайвон hayvon

## anniversary *n.*
1. илдөнүмү ildönümü
2. жылдық мереке
(zhıldıq mereke)
3. жылдык (jıldık)
4. еллык (yellık)
5. yıldönümü
6. юбилей ÿubileÿ
7. يىللىق (yilliq)
8. йиллик yillik

## another *adj.*
1. башга başqa
2. баска (basqa)
3. башка (bashka)
4. башка (bashka)
5. başka
6. башга başga
7. باشقا (bashqa)
8. бошка boshqa

## answer *v.*
1. чаваб вер- cavab ver-
2. жауап бер- (zhawap ber-)
3. жооп бер- (joop ber-)
4. җавап бир- (javap bir-)
5. cevap ver-
6. җогап бер- jogap ber-
7. جاۋاب بەر- (javab bär-)
8. жавоб бер- javob ber-

## answer *n.*
1. чаваб cavab
2. жауап (zhawap)
3. жооп (joop)
4. җавап (javap)
5. cevap
6. җогап jogap
7. جاۋاب (javab)
8. жавоб javob

## ant *zool. n.*
1. гарышга qarışqa
2. құмырсқа (qumırsqa)
3. кумурска (kumurska)
4. кырмыска (kırmıska)
5. karınca
6. гарынҗа garynja
7. چۈمۈله (chümülä)
8. чумоли chumoli

## antenna *tech. n.*
1. антенна antenna
2. антенна (antenna)
3. антенна (antenna)
4. антенна (antenna)
5. anten
6. антенна antenna
7. ئانتېننا (antenna)
8. антенна antenna

---

**any** *pron.*
1. həp һaнсы hər hansı
2. әр, әр кім, әр бір
   (är, är kim, är bir)
3. ар. нерсе (ar, nerse)
4. теләсә нинди
   (teläsä nindi)
5. herhangi
6. ислендик islendik
7. ﻫﻪﺭﻗﺎﻧﺪﺍﻕ (härqandaq)
8. ҳар қандай har qanday

**anybody** *pron.*
1. кимсә, һәр кәс
   kimsə, hər kəs
2. әр кім, біреу
   (är kim, birew)
3. бирөө, ар ким
   (biröö, ar kim)
4. һәркем, кемдер
   (härkem, kemder)
5. kimse, herkes
6. хер ким her kim
7. ﺑﯩﺮ ﻛﯩﻢ، ﺑﯩﺮﻩﯞ
   (bir kim, biräv)
8. ҳамма, ҳар ким
   hamma, har kim

**anything** *pron.*
1. һәр һaнсы бир шей
   hər hansı bir şey
2. бір нәрсе (bir närse)
3. бир нерсе (bir nerse)
4. берәр нәрсә (berär närsä)
5. herhangi bir şey
6. хайсы хем болса бир зат
   haÿsy hem bolsa bir zat
7. ﺑﯩﺮﻩﺭ ﻧﻪﺭﺳﻪ (birär närsä)
8. бирор нарса biror narsa

**apartment** *n.*
1. мәнзил mənzil
2. пәтер (päter)
3. батир (batir)
4. фатир, квартира
   (fatir, kvartira)
5. apartman dairesi
6. квартира kwartira
7. ﺑﯩﻨﺎ ﺋﯚﻱ (bina öy)
8. квартира kvartira

**apologize** *v.*
1. үзр истә- üzr istə-
2. кешірім сұра-
   (keshirim sura-)
3. кечирим сура-
   (kechirim sura-)
4. гафу сора- (gafu sora-)
5. özür dile-
6. өтүнч сора- ötünç sora-
7. ﻛﻪﭼﯜﺭﯛﻡ ﺳﻮﺭﺍ (kächürüm sora-)
8. узр сўра- uzr so'ra-

**apology** *n.*
1. үзр üzr
2. кешірім (keshirim)
3. кечирим (kechirim)
4. кичерү (kicherü)
5. özür
6. өтүнч сорама
   ötünç sorama
7. ﺋﻪﭘﯘ (äpu)
8. узр uzr

**appear** *v.*
1. көрүн- görün-
2. көрін- (körin-)
3. көрүн- (körün-)
4. күрен- (küren-)
5. görün-
6. гөрүн- görün-

7. ﭘﻪﻳﺪﺍ ﺑﻮﻝ (päyda bol-)
8. пайдо бўл- paydo bo'l-

**apple** *bot. n.*
1. алма alma
2. алма (alma)
3. алма (alma)
4. алма (alma)
5. elma
6. алма alma
7. ﺋﺎﻟﻤﺎ (alma)
8. олма olma

**apply**
(=make a request) *v.*
1. мүрачиәт ет- müraciət et-
2. өтін- (ötin-)
3. өтүн- (ötün-)
4. мөрәҗәгать ит-
   (möräjägat' it-)
5. baş vur-
6. арза бер-, йүз тут-
   arza ber-, ÿüz tut-
7. ﺋﯩﻠﺘﯩﻤﺎﺱ ﻗﯩﻞ (iltimas qil-)
8. мурожаат қил-
   murojaat qil-

**appointment**
(=engagement) *n.*
1. тә'ин олунмуш көрүш
   tə'yin olunmuş görüş
2. кездесу (kezdesuw)
3. кездешүү (kezdeshüü)
4. очрашу (ochrashu)
5. randevu
6. душушык duşuşyk
7. ﺋﯘﭼﺮﯨﺸﯩﺶ (uchrishish)
8. учрашув uchrashuv

---

1. Azerbaijani   2. Kazakh   3. Kyrgyz   4. Tatar   5. Turkish   6. Turkmen   7. Uighur   8. Uzbek

**appointment** (=assigning
to a position) *n.*
1. тә'јин tə'yin
2. тағайындау (taghayındaw)
3. дайындоо (dayındoo)
4. тәгаенләү (tägayenläü)
5. atama
6. беллеме belleme
7. تەيينلەش (täyinläsh)
8. тайинлаш tayinlash

**approach** *v.*
1. јахынлаш- yaxınlaş-
2. жақында- (zhaqında-)
3. жакында- (jakında-)
4. якынлаш- (yakınlash-)
5. yaklaş-
6. чемелеш- çemeleş-
7. يېقىنلاش- (yeqinlash-)
8. яқинлаш- yaqinlash-

**approval** *n.*
1. тәсдиг етмә təsdiq etmə
2. мақұлдау (maquldaw)
3. макулдау (makuldau)
4. хуплау (khuplau)
5. onaylama
6. макуллама makullama
7. ماقۇللاش (maqullash)
8. тасдиқлаш tasdiqlash

**apricot** *bot. n.*
1. әрик, гајсы ərik, qaysı
2. өрiк (örik)
3. өрүк (örük)
4. өрек, абрикос
(örek, abrikos)
5. kayısı
6. эрик erik
7. ئۆرۈك (örük)
8. ўрик o'rik

**April** *n.*
1. апрел aprel
2. көкек (kökek)
3. апрель (aprel')
4. апрель (aprel')
5. nisan
6. апрель aprel
7. ئاپرېل (aprel)
8. апрель aprel'

**architect** *n.*
1. ме'мар me'mar
2. сәулетші (säwletshi)
3. архитектор (arkhitektor)
4. архитектор (arkhitektor)
5. mimar
6. архитектор arhitektor
7. ئارخىتېكتور (arkhetektor)
8. меъмор me'mor

**argue** *v.*
1. мүбаhисә ет-
mübahisə et-
2. талас- (talas-)
3. талаш- (talash-)
4. бәхәсләш- (bäkhäsläsh-)
5. tartış-
6. давалаш- dawalaş-
7. تالاش-تارتىش قىل- 
(talash-tartish qil-)
8. баҳслаш- bahslash-

**argument** *n.*
1. мүбаhисә mübahisə
2. талас (talas)
3. талаш-тартыш
(talash-tartısh)
4. бәхәс (bäkhäs)
5. münakaşa
6. дава dawa
7. تالاش-تارتىش 
(talash-tartish)
8. баҳс bahs

**arm** *phys. n.*
1. гол qol
2. қол (qol)
3. кол (kol)
4. кул (kul)
5. kol
6. гол gol
7. بىلەك (biläk)
8. қўл qo'l

**armchair** *n.*
1. кресло kreslo
2. кресло (kreslo)
3. отургуч (oturguch)
4. кресло, кәнәфи
(kreslo, känäfi)
5. koltuk
6. кресло kreslo
7. يۆلەنچۈكلۈك ئورۇندۇق
(yölänchüklük orunduq)
8. кресло kreslo

**army** *mil. n.*
1. орду ordu
2. армия (armiya)
3. армия (armiya)
4. гаскәр (gaskär)
5. ordu
6. гошун goşun
7. ئارمىيە (armiyä)
8. қўшин qo'shin

**arrival** *n.*
1. кәлиш gəliş
2. келу (keluw)
3. келүү (kelüü)
4. килү (kilü)
5. varış
6. гелиш geliş
7. كېلىش (kelish)
8. келиш kelish

---

1. Azerbaijani   2. Kazakh   3. Kyrgyz   4. Tatar   5. Turkish   6. Turkmen   7. Uighur   8. Uzbek

**arrive** *v.*
1. чат-, jетиш- çat-, yetiş-
2. кел-, жет- (kel-, zhet-)
3. кел-, жет- (kel-, jet-)
4. кил-, җит- (kil-, jit-)
5. gel-, var-
6. бар-, гел- bar-, gel-
7. يه تـ، كـالـ (käl-, yät-)
8. кел-, етиб бор- kel-, yetib bor-

**arrow** *mil. n.*
1. ox ox
2. жебе (zhebe)
3. жебе (jebe)
4. ук (uk)
5. ok
6. яйынң окы ÿaÿyñ oky
7. نوق (oq)
8. ўқ o'q

**art** *n.*
1. инчәсәнәт incəsənət
2. өнер (öner)
3. искусство (iskusstvo)
4. сәнгать (sängat')
5. sanat
6. сунгат sungat
7. سـه نئـه ت (sän'ät)
8. санъат san'at

**article**
    (*in a periodical) *n.*
1. мәгалә məqalə
2. мақала (maqala)
3. макала (makala)
4. мәкалә (mäkalä)
5. makale
6. макала makala
7. ماقال (maqalä)
8. мақола maqola

**artificial** *adj.*
1. сүн'и sün'i
2. жасанды (zhasandı)
3. жасалма (jasalma)
4. ясалма (yasalma)
5. yapay
6. ясама ÿasama
7. سـۇنئـی (sün'iy)
8. сунъий sun'iy

**artillery** *mil. n.*
1. артиллерija artilleriya
2. артиллерия (artilleriya)
3. артиллерия (artilleriya)
4. артиллерия (artilleriya)
5. top
6. артиллерия artilleriÿa
7. زه مبیره ك (zämbiräk)
8. артиллерия artilleriya

**artist** *n.*
1. рәссам rəssam
2. суретши (suwretshi)
3. сүрөтчү (sürötchü)
4. рәссам (rässam)
5. ressam
6. художник hudoⵏnik
7. ره ســام (rässam)
8. рассом rassom

**as if** *conj.*
1. санки sanki
2. сияқты (siyaqtı)
3. сыяктуу (sıyaktuu)
4. гүя(ки) (güya[ki])
5. sanki
6. хамала hamala
7. خۇددی (khuddi)
8. худди xuddi

**ash** *n.*
1. күл kül
2. күл (kül)
3. күл (kül)
4. көл (köl)
5. kül
6. күл kül
7. كۆل (kül)
8. кул kul

**ashamed:**
    **be ashamed** *v.*
1. утан- utan-
2. ұял- (uyal-)
3. уял- (uyal-)
4. оял- (oyal-)
5. utan-
6. утан-, уял- utan-, uÿal-
7. ئۇیال (uyal-)
8. уял- uyal-

**ask** *v.*
1. соруш- soruş-
2. сұра- (sura-)
3. сура- (sura-)
4. сора- (sora-)
5. sor-
6. copa- sora-
7. سورا (sora-)
8. сўра- so'ra-

**assignment**
    (=school task) *n.*
1. вәзифә vəzifə
2. тапсырма (tapsırma)
3. тапшырма (tapshırma)
4. бирем (birem)
5. ödev
6. табшырык tabşyryk
7. تاپشۇرۇق (tapshuruq)
8. вазифа vazifa

---

1. Azerbaijani   2. Kazakh   3. Kyrgyz   4. Tatar   5. Turkish   6. Turkmen   7. Uighur   8. Uzbek

## assist v.

1. көмәк ет- kömək et-
2. жәрдемдес- (zhärdemdes-)
3. жардамдаш- (jardamdash-)
4. ярдәм ит- (yardäm it-)
5. yardım et-
6. көмек бер- kömek ber-
7. ياردەم قىل (yardäm qil-)
8. кўмаклаш- ko'maklash-

## assistance n.

1. көмәк kömək
2. көмек (kömek)
3. көмөк (kömök)
4. ярдәм (yardäm)
5. yardım
6. ярдам ÿardam
7. ياردەم (yardäm)
8. ёрдам yordam

## at prep.

1. -да, -дә -da, -dә
2. -да, -де, -та, -те
(-da, -de, -ta, -te)
3. -да, -де, -та, -те, -до, -дө,
-то, -тө (-da, -de, -ta, -te,
-do, -dö, -to, -tö)
4. -да, -дә, -та, -тә
(-da, -dä, -ta, -tä)
5. -da, -de, -ta, -te
6. -да, -де -da, -de
7. ـدا، ـدە، ـتا، ـتە
(-da, -dä, -ta, -tä)
8. -да -da

## attack v.

1. hүчум ет- hücum et-
2. шабуылда- (shabuwılda-)
3. чабуул кой-
(chabuul koy-)
4. hөжүм ит- (höjüm it-)
5. hücum et-
6. чоз- çoz-

7. ـهۇجۇم قىل (hujum qil-)
8. хужум қил- hujum qil-

## attack n.

1. hүчум hücum
2. шабуыл (shabuwıl)
3. чабуул (chabuul)
4. hөжүм (höjüm)
5. hücum
6. хүжүм hüjüm
7. هۇجۇم (hujum)
8. хужум hujum

## attempt n.

1. тәшәббүс tәşәbbüs
2. әрекет (äreket)
3. аракет (araket)
4. тырышу (tırıshu)
5. teşebbüs
6. сынанышык synanyşyk
7. تىرىششش (tirishish)
8. харакат қилиш
harakat qilish

## attention n.

1. дигтәт diqqət
2. назар (nazar)
3. назар (nazar)
4. дикъкать (dik'kat')
5. dikkat
6. үнс üns
7. دىققەت (diqqät)
8. диккат diqqat

## attraction n.

1. чазибә cazibә
2. тартымдылық
(tartımdılıq)
3. сүйкүмдүүлүк
(süykümdüülük)
4. сөйкемлелек
(söykemlelek)
5. cazibe
6. гөрмегейлик görmegeÿlik

7. جەلپ (jälp)
8. жозиба joziba

## August n.

1. август avqust
2. тамыз (tamız)
3. август (avgust)
4. август (avgust)
5. ağustos
6. август awgust
7. ئاۋغۇست (avghust)
8. август avgust

## aunt n.

1. хала, биби xala, bibi
2. апа (apa)
3. тай әже, әже (tay eje, eje)
4. апа, тәтәй (apa, tätäy)
5. teyze, hala
6. дайза, әҗеке daÿza, ejeke
7. هامما (hamma)
8. хола, амма xola, amma

## author n.

1. јазычы yazıçı
2. автор (avtor)
3. автор (avtor)
4. автор (avtor)
5. yazar
6. автор awtor
7. ئاپتور (aptor)
8. муаллиф muallif

## automobile n.

1. автомобил avtomobil
2. автомобиль (avtomobil')
3. автомобиль (avtomobil')
4. автомобиль (avtomobil')
5. otomobil
6. машын maşyn
7. ئاپتوموبىل (aptomobil)
8. автомобиль avtomobil'

---

1. Azerbaijani  2. Kazakh  3. Kyrgyz  4. Tatar  5. Turkish  6. Turkmen  7. Uighur  8. Uzbek

## autonomy *pol. n.*
1. мухтарижјәт muxtariyyət
2. автономия (avtonomiya)
3. автономия (avtonomiya)
4. узидарә (üzidarä)
5. özerklik
6. автономия awtonomiÿa
7. مۇختاريبەت (mukhtariyät)
8. мухторият muxtoriyat

## autumn *n.*
1. пајыз payız
2. күз (küz)
3. күз (küz)
4. көз (köz)
5. sonbahar
6. гүйз güÿz
7. كوز (küz)
8. куз kuz

## avenue *n.*
1. хијабан xiyaban
2. проспект (prospekt)
3. проспект (prospekt)
4. проспект (prospekt)
5. bulvar
6. проспект prospekt
7. چوڭ كوچا (chong kocha)
8. хиёбон xiyobon

## awake *vi.*
1. ојан- oyan-
2. оян- (oyan-)
3. ойгон- (oygon-)
4. уян- (uyan-)
5. uyan-
6. оян- oÿan-
7. ئويغان (oyghan-)
8. уйғон- uyg'on-

## awake *vt.*
1. ојат- oyat-
2. оят- (oyat-)
3. ойгот- (oygot-)
4. уят- (uyat-)
5. uyandır-
6. ояр-, оят- oÿar-, oÿat-
7. ئويغات (oyghat-)
8. уйғот- uyg'ot-

## axe *tech. n.*
1. балта balta
2. балта (balta)
3. балта (balta)
4. балта (balta)
5. balta
6. палта palta
7. پالتا (palta)
8. болта bolta

## baby *n.*
1. көрпә körpə
2. бөбек (böbek)
3. бөбөк (böbök)
4. яңа туган бала, бәби (yanga tugan bala, bäbi)
5. bebek
6. бөбек bäbek
7. بوۋاق (bovaq)
8. чақалоқ chaqaloq

## back *phys. n.*
1. арха arxa
2. арқа (arqa)
3. арка (arka)
4. арка (arka)
5. sırt
6. арқа arka
7. دۈمبە (dümbä)
8. орқа orqa

## bad *adj.*
1. пис pis
2. жаман (zhaman)
3. жаман (jaman)
4. начар (nachar)
5. kötü
6. эрбет erbet
7. يامان (yaman)
8. ёмон yomon

## bag *n.*
1. чанта çanta
2. сөмке (sömke)
3. сомке (somke)
4. сумка (sumka)
5. çanta
6. сумка sumka
7. خالتا (khalta)
8. сумка sumka

## baggage *n.*
1. јүк yük
2. жүк (zhük)
3. жүк (jük)
4. йөк (yök)
5. yük
6. йүк ÿük
7. يۈك‑تاق (yük-taq)
8. юк yuk

## baker *n.*
1. чөрәкчи çörəkçi
2. наубайшы (nawbayshı)
3. наабайчы (naabaychı)
4. икмәк пешеруче (ikmäk pesherüche)
5. fırıncı
6. чөрекчи çörekçi
7. ناۋاي (navay)
8. новвой novvoy

---

1. Azerbaijani  2. Kazakh  3. Kyrgyz  4. Tatar  5. Turkish  6. Turkmen  7. Uighur  8. Uzbek

**bakery** *n.*
1. чөрәкхана çörәkxana
2. наубайхана (nawbaykhana)
3. гөнкө (göngkö)
4. икмәк кибете (ikmäk kibete)
5. fırın
6. чөрекхана çörekhana
7. ناۋايخانا (navaykhana)
8. новвойхона novvoyxona

**balcony** *n.*
1. балкон balkon
2. балкон (balkon)
3. балкон (balkon)
4. балкон (balkon)
5. balkon
6. балкон balkon
7. بالكون (balkon)
8. балкон balkon

**bald** *adj.*
1. кечәл keçәl
2. таз (taz)
3. таз (taz)
4. пеләш (peläsh)
5. kel
6. такыр келле takyr kelle
7. تاقىر (taqir)
8. кал kal

**ball** *spor. n.*
1. топ top
2. доп (dop)
3. топ (top)
4. туп (tup)
5. top
6. пөкги, топ pökgi, top
7. توپ (top)
8. тўп to'p

**ballet** *n.*
1. балет balet
2. балет (balet)
3. балет (balet)
4. балет (balet)
5. bale
6. балет balet
7. بالت (balet)
8. балет balet

**banana** *bot. n.*
1. банан banan
2. банан (banan)
3. банан (banan)
4. банан (banan)
5. muz
6. банан banan
7. بانان (banan)
8. банан banan

**bandage** *med. n.*
1. бинт bint
2. бинт (bint)
3. бинт (bint)
4. бинт (bint)
5. sargı bezi
6. бинт bint
7. تبكتى (tengiq)
8. бинт bint

**bank** *econ. n.*
1. банк bank
2. банк (bank)
3. банк (bank)
4. банк (bank)
5. banka
6. банк bank
7. بانكا (banka)
8. банк bank

**banquet** *n.*
1. зијафәт ziyafәt
2. банкет (banket)
3. банкет (banket)
4. банкет (banket)
5. ziyafet
6. банкет banket
7. زيياپەت (ziyapät)
8. зиёфат ziyofat

**bare** *adj.*
1. чылпаг çılpaq
2. жалаңаш (zhalangash)
3. жыланач (jılangach)
4. ялан (yalan)
5. çıplak
6. ялаңач ÿalañaç
7. يالىڭاچ (yalingach)
8. яланг yalang

**bark** *bot. n.*
1. габыг qabıq
2. қабық (qabıq)
3. кабык (kabık)
4. кабык (kabık)
5. kabuk
6. габык gabyk
7. قوۋزاق (qovzaq)
8. пўстлоқ po'stloq

**barley** *bot. n.*
1. арпа arpa
2. арпа (arpa)
3. арпа (arpa)
4. арпа (arpa)
5. arpa
6. арпа arpa
7. ئارپا (arpa)
8. арпа arpa

---

1. Azerbaijani  2. Kazakh  3. Kyrgyz  4. Tatar  5. Turkish  6. Turkmen  7. Uighur  8. Uzbek

**barometer** *n.*
1. барометр barometr
2. барометр (barometr)
3. барометр (barometr)
4. барометр (barometr)
5. barometre
6. барометр barometr
7. بارومېتر (barometr)
8. барометр barometr

**basket** *n.*
1. сәбәт səbət
2. кәрзінкә (kärzinkä)
3. корзина (korzina)
4. кәрҗин (kärjin)
5. sepet
6. себет sebet
7. سېۋەت (sevät)
8. сават savat

**basketball** *n.*
1. баскетбол basketbol
2. баскетбол (basketbol)
3. баскетбол (basketbol)
4. баскетбол (basketbol)
5. basketbol
6. баскетбол basketbol
7. ۋاسكېتبول (vasketbol)
8. баскетбол basketbol

**bathroom** *n.*
1. ванна отағы vanna otağı
2. ванна бөлмесі (vanna bölmesi)
3. ванна (vanna)
4. ванна, юыну бүлмәсе (vanna, yuınu bülmäse)
5. banyo
6. ванна отагы wanna otagy
7. مۇنچا (muncha)
8. ванна vanna

**battle** *mil. n.*
1. мүһарибә müharibə
2. ұрыс (urıs)
3. уруш (urush)
4. сугьш (sugısh)
5. savaş
6. сөвеш söweş
7. جەڭ (jäng)
8. жанг jang

**bay** *geo. n.*
1. көрфәз körfəz
2. шығанак (shıghanaq)
3. булуң (bulung)
4. култык (kultık)
5. körfez
6. айлаг aÿlag
7. دېڭىز قولتۇقى (dengiz qoltuqi)
8. кўрфаз ko'rfaz

**be** *v.*
1. ол- ol-
2. бол- (bol-)
3. бол- (bol-)
4. бул- (bul-)
5. ol-
6. бол- bol-
7. بول- (bol-)
8. бўл- bo'l-

**beach** *n.*
1. чимәрлик çimərlik
2. пляж (plyazh)
3. пляж (plyaj)
4. пляж (plyazh)
5. plaj
6. пляж plÿa∫
7. دېڭىز بويى (dengiz boyi)
8. пляж plyaj

**beak** *zool. n.*
1. димдик dimdik
2. тұмсық (tumsıq)
3. тумшук (tumshuk)
4. томшык (tomshık)
5. gaga
6. чүңк çüñk
7. تۇمشۇق (tumshuq)
8. тумшуқ tumshuq

**bean** *bot. n.*
1. пахла, лобја paxla, lobya
2. бұршак (burshaq)
3. буурчак (buurchak)
4. фасоль (fasol')
5. fasulye
6. нойба noÿba
7. پۇرچاق (purchaq)
8. ловия loviya

**bear** *zool. n.*
1. ајы ayı
2. аю (ayu)
3. аюу (ayuu)
4. аю (ayu)
5. ayı
6. айы aÿu
7. ئېيىق (eyiq)
8. айиқ ayiq

**beard** *phys. n.*
1. саггал saqqal
2. сақал (saqal)
3. сакал (sakal)
4. сакал (sakal)
5. sakal
6. сакгал sakgal
7. ساقال (saqal)
8. соқол soqol

## beautiful *adj.*
1. көзәл gözəl
2. әдемі (ädemi)
3. сулуу (suluu)
4. матур (matur)
5. güzel
6. овадан owadan
7. چىرايلىق (chirayliq)
8. чиройли chiroyli

## beauty *n.*
1. көзәллик gözəllik
2. сҰлулық (suluwlıq)
3. сулуулук (suluuluk)
4. матурлык (maturlık)
5. güzellik
6. оваданлык owadanlyk
7. گۈزەللىك (güzällik)
8. гўзаллик go'zallik

## because *conj.*
1. ЧҮНКИ çünki
2. сондықтан (sondıqtan)
3. ошондуктан (oshonduktan)
4. чөнки (chönki)
5. çünkü
6. ЧҮНКИ çünki
7. چۈنكى (chünki)
8. ЧҮНКИ chunki

## become *v.*
1. ол- ol-
2. бол- (bol-)
3. бол- (bol-)
4. бул- (bul-)
5. ol-
6. бол- bol-
7. بول (bol-)
8. бўл- bo'l-

## bed *n.*
1. јатаг yataq
2. кереует (kerewet)
3. керебет (kerebet)
4. каравaт, урын
(karavat, urın)
5. yatak
6. кравать krawat
7. كارىۋات (karivat)
8. каравот karavot

## bedroom *n.*
1. јатаг отағы yataq otağı
2. Ұйықтайтын бөлме
(uyıqtaytın bölme)
3. жата турган бөлмө
(jata turgan bölmö)
4. йокы бүлмәсе
(yokı bülmäse)
5. yatak odası
6. ятылян отаг ÿatylÿan otag
7. ياتاق ئۆيى (yataq öyi)
8. ётоқхона yotoqxona

## bee *zool. n.*
1. ары арı
2. ара (ara)
3. аары (aarı)
4. бал корты (bal kortı)
5. arı
6. бал арысы bal arysy
7. ھەرە (härä)
8. ари ari

## beef *cul. n.*
1. мал әти ınal əti
2. сиыр еті (siyır yeti)
3. уй эти (uy eti)
4. сыер ите (sıyer ite)
5. sığır eti
6. сыгыр әти sygyr eti
7. كالا گۆشى (kala göshi)
8. мол гўшти mol go'shti

## beer *cul. n.*
1. пивә pivə
2. сыра (sıra)
3. пиво (pivo)
4. сыра (sıra)
5. bira
6. пиво piwo
7. پىۋا (piva)
8. пиво pivo

## before *prep.*
1. әввәл əvvəl
2. бҰрын (burın)
3. мурда (murda)
4. борын (borın)
5. önce
6. өҢ öñ
7. بۇرۇن (burun)
8. олдин oldin

## begin *v.*
1. башла- başla-
2. баста- (basta-)
3. башта- (bashta-)
4. башла- (bashla-)
5. başla-
6. башла- başla-
7. باشلا (bashla-)
8. бошла(н)- boshla[n]-

## behave *v.*
1. давран- davran-
2. өзін Ұста- (özin usta-)
3. өзүн алып жүр-
(özün alıp jür-)
4. үзен тот- (üzen tot-)
5. davran-
6. өзүҢи алып бар-
özüñi alyp bar-
7. ئۆزىنى تۇت- (özini tut-)
8. ўзини тут- o'zini tut-

---

1. Azerbaijani　2. Kazakh　3. Kyrgyz　4. Tatar　5. Turkish　6. Turkmen　7. Uighur　8. Uzbek

**behavior** *n.*
1. давраныш davranış
2. тәртіп (tärtip)
3. тартип (tartip)
4. холық (kholık)
5. davranış
6. гылық gylyk
7. يۇرۇش-تۇرۇش
(yürüsh-turush)
8. хулқ xulq

**behind** *adv.*
1. архада arxada
2. артта (artta)
3. артта (artta)
4. артта (artta)
5. arkada
6. аркада arkada
7. ئارقىدا (arqida)
8. орқада orqada

**belief** *rel. n.*
1. инам inam
2. сеніM (senim)
3. ишеним (ishenim)
4. ышану (ıshanu)
5. inanç
6. ынанч ynanç
7. ئىشەنچ (ishänch)
8. ишонч ishonch

**believe** *v.*
1. инан- inan-
2. сен- (sen-)
3. ишен- (ishen-)
4. ышан- (ıshan-)
5. inan-
6. ынан- ynan-
7. ئىشەن- (ishän-)
8. ишон- ishon-

**bell** *n.*
1. зәнк zəng
2. қоңырау (qongıraw)
3. коңгуроо (kongguroo)
4. звонок (zvonok)
5. zil
6. җаң jañ
7. توڭغۇراق (qongghuraq)
8. қўнғироқ qo'ng'iroq

**belly** *phys. n.*
1. гарын qarın
2. қарын (qarın)
3. карын (karın)
4. эч (ech)
5. karın
6. гарын garyn
7. قورساق (qorsaq)
8. қорин qorin

**below** *adv.*
1. ашағыда aşağıda
2. төменде (tömende)
3. төмөндө (tömöndö)
4. түбәндә (tübändä)
5. aşağıda
6. ашакда aşakda
7. تۆۋەندە (tövändä)
8. пастда pastda

**belt** *clo. n.*
1. кәмәр kəmər
2. белбеу (belbew)
3. бел боо (bel boo)
4. билбау (bilbau)
5. kemer
6. гушак guşak
7. بەلباغ (bälbagh)
8. камар kamar

**bend** *v.*
1. әј- əy-
2. бүг- (büg-)
3. ий- (iy-)
4. ий- (iy-)
5. eğ-
6. әг- eg-
7. ئەگ- (äg-)
8. әг-, бук- eg-, buk-

**benefit** *n.*
1. фајда fayda
2. пайда (payda)
3. пайда (payda)
4. файда (fayda)
5. fayda
6. пейда peÿda
7. پايدا (payda)
8. фойда foyda

**beside** *prep.*
1. јанында yanında
2. жанында (zhanında)
3. жанында (janında)
4. янында (yanında)
5. yanında
6. янында ÿanynda
7. يېنىدا (yenida)
8. ёнида yonida

**besides** *prep.*
1. башга başqa
2. басқа (basqa)
3. башка (bashka)
4. башка (bashka)
5. başka
6. башга-да başga-da
7. تاشقىرى (tashqiri)
8. ташқари tashqari

---

1. Azerbaijani   2. Kazakh   3. Kyrgyz   4. Tatar   5. Turkish   6. Turkmen   7. Uighur   8. Uzbek

**best** *adj.*
1. əн jaxшы ən yaxşı
2. eң жақсы (yeng zhaqsı)
3. эң жакшы (eng jakshı)
4. иң яхшы (ing yakhshı)
5. en iyi
6. иң говы iň gowy
7. ﺋﻪﯓ ﻳﺎﺧﺸﻰ (äng yakhshi)
8. энг яхши eng yaxshi

**better** *adj.*
1. даһа jaxшы daha yaxşı
2. жақсырақ (zhaqsıraq)
3. жакшыраак (jakshıraak)
4. яхшы (yakhshı)
5. daha iyi
6. говырак gowyrak
7. ﻳﺎﺧﺸﻴﺮﺍﻕ (yakhshiraq)
8. яхшироқ yaxshiroq

**between** *prep.*
1. арасында arasında
2. арасында (arasında)
3. арасында (arasında)
4. арасында (arasında)
5. arasında
6. арасында arasynda
7. ﻧﺎﺭﺩﺳﺪﺍ (arisida)
8. орасида orasida

**beverage** *n.*
1. ички içki
2. ішімдік (ishimdik)
3. суусундук (suusunduk)
4. эчемлек (echemlek)
5. içecek
6. ичги içgi
7. ﺋﯩﭽﯩﻤﻠﯩﻚ (ichimlik)
8. ичимлик ichimlik

**bicycle** *n.*
1. велосипед velosiped
2. велосипед (velosiped)
3. велосипед (velosiped)
4. велосипед (velosiped)
5. bisiklet
6. велосипед welosiped
7. ﻭﺑﻠﺴﻴﭙﻴﺖ (velisipit)
8. велосипед velosiped

**big** *adj.*
1. бөjүк böyük
2. үлкен (ülken)
3. чоң (chong)
4. зур (zur)
5. büyük
6. улы uly
7. ﺟﻮﻟﻚ (chong)
8. катта katta

**bill** (=a statement of account) *n.*
1. һесаб hesab
2. есеп (yesep)
3. эсеп (esep)
4. счёт (schyot)
5. hesap
6. счёт sçÿot
7. ﻫﺴﺎﺑﺎﺕ (hesabat)
8. хисоб-китоб варақаси hisob-kitob varaqasi

**billion** *num.*
1. милjард milyard
2. миллиард (milliard)
3. миллиард (milliard)
4. миллиард (milliard)
5. milyar
6. миллиард milliard
7. ﻣﻠﻴﺎﺭﺩ (milyard)
8. миллиард milliard

**bird** *zool. n.*
1. гуш quş
2. құс (qus)
3. куш (kush)
4. кош (kosh)
5. kuş
6. гуш guş
7. ﻗﯘﺵ (qush)
8. қуш qush

**birth** *n.*
1. доғум doğum
2. туылу (tuwıluw)
3. туулуш (tuulush)
4. туу (tuu)
5. doğum
6. догулма dogulma
7. ﺗﻮﻏﯘﺕ (tughut)
8. туғилиш tug'ilish

**birthday** *n.*
1. ад күнү ad günü
2. туған күн (tuwghan kün)
3. туулган күн (tuulgan kün)
4. туган көн (tugan kön)
5. doğum günü
6. доглан гүн doglan gün
7. ﺗﯘﻏﯘﻟﻐﺎﻥ ﻛﯚﻥ (tughulghan kün)
8. туғилган кун tug'ilgan kun

**bite** *v.*
1. дишлə- dişlə-
2. тісте- (tiste-)
3. тиште- (tishte-)
4. тешлə- (teshlä-)
5. ısır-
6. дишле- dişle-
7. ﺟﯩﺸﻠﻪ (chishlä-)
8. тишла- tishla-

---

## bitter adj.
1. ачы асı
2. ащы (ashchı)
3. ачуу (achuu)
4. ачы (achı)
5. acı
6. аҗы ajy
7. ئاچچىق (achchiq)
8. аччиқ achchiq

## black adj.
1. гара qara
2. қара (qara)
3. кара (kara)
4. кара (kara)
5. siyah
6. гара gara
7. قارا (qara)
8. қора qora

## blanket n.
1. аджал adyal
2. одеял (odeyal)
3. жууркан (juurkan)
4. юрган (yurgan)
5. battaniye
6. одеял odeÿal
7. ئەدىيال (ädiyal)
8. адёл adyol

## bleed v.
1. гана- qana-
2. қана- (qana-)
3. кана- (kana-)
4. кана- (kana-)
5. kana-
6. гана- gana-
7. قانا_ (qana-)
8. қона- qona-

## blind adj.
1. кор kor
2. соқыр (soqır)
3. сокур (sokur)
4. сукыр (sukır)
5. kör
6. көр kör
7. قارىغۇ (qarighu)
8. кўр ko'r

## blindness n.
1. корлуг korluq
2. соқырлық (soqırlıq)
3. сокурлук (sokurluk)
4. сукырлык (sukırlık)
5. körlük
6. көрлүк körlük
7. قارىغۇلۇق (qarighuluq)
8. кўрлик ko'rlik

## blood phys. n.
1. ган qan
2. қан (qan)
3. кан (kan)
4. кан (kan)
5. kan
6. ган gan
7. قان (qan)
8. қон qon

## blood pressure med. n.
1. ган тəзйиги qan təzyiqi
2. қан қысымы (qan qısımı)
3. кан басымы (kan basımı)
4. кан басымы (kan basımı)
5. tansiyon
6. давление dawleniÿe
7. قان بىسمى (qan besimi)
8. қон босими qon bosimi

## blouse clo. n.
1. блуз bluz
2. блузка (bluwzka)
3. көйнөк (köynök)
4. блуза (bluza)
5. bluz
6. блузка bluzka
7. كۆڭلەك (köngläk)
8. блуза bluza

## blue adj.
1. көj göy
2. көк (kök)
3. көк (kök)
4. зəнгəр (zänggär)
5. mavi
6. гөк gök
7. كۆك (kök)
8. кўк ko'k

## boast v.
1. өjүн- öyün-
2. мақтан- (maqtan-)
3. мактан- (maktan-)
4. мактан- (maktan-)
5. övün-
6. өвүн- öwün-
7. ماختان_ (makhtan-)
8. мақтан- maqtan-

## boat n.
1. гајыг qayıq
2. қайық (qayıq)
3. кайык (kayık)
4. каек (kayek)
5. kayık
6. гайык gaÿyk
7. قبىـق (qeyiq)
8. қайиқ qayiq

---

## body *phys. n.*
1. бәдән bədən
2. дене (dene)
3. дене (dene)
4. гәүдә (gäüdä)
5. beden
6. беден beden
7. بدن (bädän)
8. бадан badan

## boil *v.*
1. гајна- qayna-
2. қайна- (qayna-)
3. кайна- (kayna-)
4. кайна- (kayna-)
5. kayna-
6. гайна- gaÿna-
7. قاينا (qayna-)
8. қайна- qayna-

## bomb *mil. n.*
1. бомба bomba
2. бомбы (bombı)
3. бомбу (bombu)
4. бомба (bomba)
5. bomba
6. бомба bomba
7. بومبا (bomba)
8. бомба bomba

## bone *phys. n.*
1. сүмүк sümük
2. сүйек (süyek)
3. сөөк (söök)
4. сөяк (söyak)
5. kemik
6. сүңк süñk
7. سۇڭگەك (söngäk)
8. суяк suyak

## book *n.*
1. китаб kitab
2. кітап (kitap)
3. китеп (kitep)
4. китап (kitap)
5. kitap
6. китап kitap
7. كتاب (kitab)
8. китоб kitob

## bookcase *n.*
1. китаб шкафы kitab şkafı
2. кітап шкафы (kitap shkafı)
3. текче (tekche)
4. этажерка (etazherka)
5. kitaplık
6. китап шкафы kitap şkafy
7. كتاب جازيسى (kitab jazisi)
8. китоб жавони kitob javoni

## bookseller *n.*
1. китаб сатан kitab satan
2. кітап сатушы (kitap satuwshı)
3. китеп сатуучу (kitep satuuchu)
4. китап сатучысы (kitap satuchısı)
5. kitapçı
6. китап сатыжысы kitap satyjysy
7. كتابپۇرۇش (kitabpurush)
8. китоб сотувчи kitob sotuvchi

## bookshop *n.*
1. китаб мағазасы kitab mağazası
2. кітап дүкені (kitap dükeni)
3. китеп дүкөнү (kitep dükönü)
4. китап кибете (kitap kibete)
5. kitapçı
6. китап магазини kitap magazini
7. كتابخانا (kitabkhana)
8. китоб дўкони kitob do'koni

## boot *clo. n.*
1. (узунбоғаз) чәкмә [uzunboğaz] çəkmə
2. етік (yetik)
3. өтүк (ötük)
4. итек (itek)
5. çizme
6. әдик ädik
7. ئۆتۈك (ötük)
8. этик etik

## border *pol. n.*
1. сәрһәд sərhəd
2. шекара (shekara)
3. чек ара (chek ara)
4. чик (chik)
5. sınır
6. серхет serhet
7. چېگرا (chegra)
8. чегара chegara

## bored: be bored *v.*
1. дарых- darıx-
2. зерігі- (zerig-)
3. зерик- (zerik-)
4. ямансула- (yamansula-)
5. sıkıl-
6. ир- ir-
7. زېرىك (zerik-)
8. зерик- zerik-

---

## boring *adj.*

1. дарыхдырычы darıxdırıcı
2. зеріктіретін (zeriktiretin)
3. жадатма (jadatma)
4. кызыксыз (kızıksız)
5. sıkıcı
6. иргинч irginç
7. زېرىكەرلىك (zerikärlik)
8. зериктирадиган zeriktiradigan

## born: be born *v.*

1. доғул- doğul-
2. туыл- (tuwıl-)
3. туул- (tuul-)
4. ту- (tu-)
5. doğ-
6. доғул- dogul-
7. توغۇل (tughul-)
8. туғил- tug'il-

## borrow *v.*

1. борч ал- borc al-
2. қарыз ал- (qarız al-)
3. карыз ал- (karız al-)
4. бурычка ал- (burıchka al-)
5. ödünç al-
6. карз ал- karz al-
7. ئۆتنە ئال (ötnä al-)
8. қарз ол- qarz ol-

## both ... and *conj.*

1. һəм ... һəм дə həm ... həm də
2. да ... да (da ... da)
3. да ... да (da ... da)
4. həm ... həm (häm ... häm)
5. hem ... hem
6. хем... хем hem... hem
7. ھەم ... ھەم (häm ... häm)
8. ҳам ... ҳам ham ... ham

## bother *v.*

1. нараһат ет- narahat et-
2. мазала- (mazala-)
3. тынчсыздандыр- (tınchsızdandır-)
4. тыныycызла- (tınıchsızla-)
5. rahatsız et-
6. биынҗалык эт- biynjalyk et-
7. ئاۋارە قىل (avarä qil-)
8. ташвишландир- tashvishlandir-

## bottle *n.*

1. шүшə şüşə
2. шиша (shiysha)
3. бөтөлкө (bötölkö)
4. шешə (sheshä)
5. şişe
6. чүйше çüÿşe
7. بوتۇلكا (botulka)
8. шиша shisha

## bow *mil. n.*

1. jaj yay
2. садақ (sadaq)
3. саадак (saadak)
4. жəя (jäya)
5. yay
6. яй ÿaÿ
7. يا (ya)
8. камон kamon

## bowl *cul. n.*

1. каса kasa
2. кесе (kese)
3. кесе (kese)
4. касə (kasä)
5. kâse
6. окара okara
7. قاچا (qacha)
8. коса kosa

## box *n.*

1. гуту qutu
2. жəшiк (zhäshik)
3. жашик (jashik)
4. кечкенə əрҗə (kechkenä ärjä)
5. kutu
6. гуты guty
7. قۇتا (quta)
8. қути quti

## boy *n.*

1. оғлан oğlan
2. ұл бала (ul bala)
3. эркек бала (erkek bala)
4. ир бала (ir bala)
5. oğlan
6. оглан oglan
7. ئوغۇل بالا (oghul bala)
8. ўғил бола o'g'il bola

## brain *phys. n.*

1. бejин beyin
2. ми (miy)
3. мээ (mee)
4. ми (mi)
5. beyin
6. бейни beÿni
7. مېڭگە (mengä)
8. мия miya

## branch *bot. n.*

1. будаг budaq
2. бұтақ (butaq)
3. бутак (butak)
4. ботак (botak)
5. dal
6. шаха şaha
7. شاخ (shakh)
8. шох shox

---

1. Azerbaijani   2. Kazakh   3. Kyrgyz   4. Tatar   5. Turkish   6. Turkmen   7. Uighur   8. Uzbek

**brave** *adj.*
1. чәсур cəsur
2. батыл (batıl)
3. кайраттуу (kayrattuu)
4. батыр (batır)
5. cesur
6. батыр batyr
7. جەسۇر (jäsur)
8. мард mard

**bread** *cul. n.*
1. чөрәк çörək
2. нан (nan)
3. нан (nan)
4. икмәк (ikmäk)
5. ekmek
6. чөрек çörek
7. نان (nan)
8. нон non

**break** *vt.*
1. сындыр- sındır-
2. сындыр- (sındır-)
3. сындыр- (sındır-)
4. сындыр- (sındır-)
5. kır-
6. дөв- döw-
7. سۇندۇر ـ (sundur-)
8. синдир- sindir-

**breakfast** *n.*
1. сәһәр јемәји
  səhər yeməyi
2. таңертеңгі ас
  (tangyertenggi as)
3. таңкы аш (tangkı ash)
4. иртәнге аш (irtänge ash)
5. kahvaltı
6. эртирлик ertirlik
7. ئەتىگەنلك تاماق
  (ätigänlik tamaq)
8. нонушта nonushta

**breast** *phys. n.*
1. дөш döş
2. емшек (yemshek)
3. әмчек (emchek)
4. имчәк (imchäk)
5. göğüs
6. гөвүс göwüs
7. كۆكس (köks)
8. кўкрак ko'krak

**breath** *n.*
1. нәфәс nəfəs
2. дем (dem)
3. дем (dem)
4. тын (tın)
5. nefes
6. дем dem
7. نەپەس (näpäs)
8. нафас nafas

**brick** *n.*
1. кәрпич kərpic
2. кірпіш (kirpish)
3. кыш (kısh)
4. кирпеч (kirpech)
5. tuğla
6. керпич kerpiç
7. خىش (khish)
8. ғишт g'isht

**bride** *n.*
1. кәлин gəlin
2. қалындық (qalıngdıq)
3. келин (kelin)
4. килен (kilen)
5. gelin
6. дурмуша чыкян гыз
  durmuşa çykyan gyz
7. كېلىن (kelin)
8. келин kelin

**bridegroom** *n.*
1. бәј bəy
2. күйеу (küyew)
3. күйөө (küyöö)
4. кияу (kiyaü)
5. güvey
6. өйленйән йигит
  öylenyän yigit
7. كۈيوغۇل (küyoghul)
8. куёв kuyov

**bridge** *n.*
1. көрпү körpü
2. көпір (köpir)
3. көпүрө (köpürö)
4. купер (küper)
5. köprü
6. көпри köpri
7. كۆۋرۈك (kövrük)
8. кўприк ko'prik

**bright** (=full of light) *adj.*
1. парлаг parlaq
2. жарық (zharıq)
3. жарык (jarık)
4. якты (yaktı)
5. aydınlık
6. ягты ýagty
7. يورۇق (yoruq)
8. ёрқин yorqin

**bring** *v.*
1. кәтир- gətir-
2. әкел- (äkel-)
3. алып кел- (alıp kel-)
4. алып кил- (alıp kil-)
5. getir-
6. гетир- getir-
7. ئېلىپ كەلـ (elip käl-)
8. олиб кел- olib kel-

---

## broad *adj.*
1. кениш geniş
2. кең (keng)
3. кең (keng)
4. кин (king)
5. geniş
6. гиң giñ
7. كەڭ (käng)
8. кенг keng

## broken *adj.*
1. гырыг qırıq
2. сынық (sınıq)
3. сынык (sınık)
4. ватылган (vatılgan)
5. kırık
6. дөвүк döwük
7. سۇنۇق (sunuq)
8. синиқ siniq

## broom *n.*
1. сүпүркә süpürgə
2. сыпырғыш (sıpırghısh)
3. шыпыргы (shıpırgı)
4. себерке (seberke)
5. süpürge
6. сүбсе sübse
7. سۈپۈرگە (süpürgä)
8. супурги supurgi

## brother *n.*
1. гардаш qardaş
2. аға, іні (agha, ini)
3. ага, ини (aga, ini)
4. абый, эне (abıy, ene)
5. erkek kardeş
6. доган dogan
7. ئاكا، ئۇكا (aka, uka)
8. ака, ука aka, uka

## brown *adj.*
1. рәһвәји qəhvəyi
2. қоңыр (qongır)
3. күрөң (küröng)
4. кызгылт көрөн (kızgılt körän)
5. kahverengi
6. гоңур goñur
7. قوڭۇر (qongur)
8. жигар ранг jigar rang

## brush *n.*
1. фырча fırça
2. щётка (shchyotka)
3. щётка (shchyotka)
4. щётка (shchyotka)
5. fırça
6. чотта çotga
7. چوتكا (chotka)
8. чўтка cho'tka

## bucket *n.*
1. ведрә vedrə
2. шелек (shelek)
3. чака (chaka)
4. чиләк (chiläk)
5. kova
6. бедре bedre
7. چەلەك (cheläk)
8. челак chelak

## budget *econ. n.*
1. будчә büdcə
2. бюджет (byudzhet)
3. бюджет (byudjet)
4. бюджет (byudzhet)
5. bütçe
6. бюжет büyüʃet
7. بۇدجت (budjet)
8. бюджет byudjet

## build *v.*
1. тик- tik-
2. қҰр- (qur-)
3. кур- (kur-)
4. кор- (kor-)
5. inşa et-
6. сал-, гур- sal-, gur-
7. قۇر_ (qur-)
8. қур- qur-

## building *n.*
1. бина bina
2. қҰрылыс (qurılıs)
3. курулуш (kurulush)
4. бина (bina)
5. bina
6. бина bina
7. بنا (bina)
8. бино bino

## bull *zool. n.*
1. буға buğa
2. бҰқа (buqa)
3. бука (buka)
4. үгез (ügez)
5. boğa
6. буга buga
7. بۇقا (buqa)
8. бұқа buqa

## burglar *n.*
1. оғру oğru
2. үй тонаушы (üy tonawshı)
3. үй тоноочу (üy tonoochu)
4. карак (karak)
5. hırsız
6. огры ogry
7. ئوغرى (oghri)
8. ўғри o'g'ri

---

1. Azerbaijani   2. Kazakh   3. Kyrgyz   4. Tatar   5. Turkish   6. Turkmen   7. Uighur   8. Uzbek

## burn *vi.*
1. jaн- yan-
2. жан- (zhan-)
3. жан- (jan-)
4. ян- (yan-)
5. yan-
6. ян- ÿan-
7. كزيـ (köy-)
8. ён- yon-

## burn *vt.*
1. jaндыр- yandır-
2. жағ- (zhagh-)
3. жак- (jak-)
4. яндыр- (yandır-)
5. yak-
6. як- ÿak-
7. كزيدۇر (köydür-)
8. ёқ- yoq-

## bury *v.*
1. басдыр- basdır-
2. köм- (köm-)
3. köм- (köm-)
4. күм- (küm-)
5. göm-
6. гөм- göm-
7. كزمـ (köm-)
8. күм- ko'm-

## bus *n.*
1. автобус avtobus
2. автобус (avtobus)
3. автобус (avtobus)
4. автобус (avtobus)
5. otobüs
6. автобус awtobus
7. ئاپتوبۇس (aptobus)
8. автобус avtobus

## business *n.*
1. тичарәт ticarət
2. іc (is)
3. иш, бизнес (ish, biznes)
4. сәүдә (säüdä)
5. ticaret, iş
6. сөвда söwda
7. سودا (soda)
8. савдо, иш savdo, ish

## businessman *n.*
1. бизнесмен biznesmen
2. іскер (isker)
3. ишкер (ishker)
4. бизнесмен, сәүдәгәр (biznesmen, säüdägär)
5. iş adamı
6. бизнесмен biznesmen
7. سودىگەر (sodigär)
8. ишбилармон ishbilarmon

## busy *adj.*
1. мәшғул məşğul
2. бос емес (bos yemes)
3. бош эмес (bosh emes)
4. мәшгуль (mäshgul')
5. meşgul
6. мешгул meşgul
7. ئالدىراش (aldirash)
8. банд band

## but *conj.*
1. амма amma
2. бірақ (biraq)
3. бирок (birok)
4. әмма (ämma)
5. ama
6. эмма emma
7. ئەمما (ämma)
8. бироқ biroq

## butcher *n.*
1. гәссаб qəssab
2. қасапшы (qasapshı)
3. касапчы (kasapchı)
4. итче (itche)
5. kasap
6. гассап gassap
7. قاساپ (qassap)
8. қассоб qassob

## butcher shop *n.*
1. әт дүканы ət dükanı
2. ет дүкені (yet dükeni)
3. эт дүкөнү (et dükönü)
4. ит кибете (it kibete)
5. kasap dükkânı
6. эт дүканы et dükany
7. گۆش دۇكانى (gösh dukani)
8. гўшт дўкони go'sht do'koni

## butter *cul. n.*
1. кәрә jaғы kərə yağı
2. сары май (sarı may)
3. май (may)
4. сары май (sarı may)
5. tereyağı
6. месге яг mesge ÿag
7. سېرىق ماي (seriq may)
8. сариёғ sariyog'

## butterfly *zool. n.*
1. кәпәнәк kəpənək
2. көбелек (köbelek)
3. көпөлөк (köpölök)
4. күбәләк (kübäläk)
5. kelebek
6. кебелек kebelek
7. كېپىنەك (kepinäk)
8. капалак kapalak

---

**button** *clo. n.*
1. дүјмә düymə
2. түйме (tüyme)
3. түймө (tüymö)
4. төймә (töymä)
5. düğme
6. илик ilik
7. تۈگمە (tügmä)
8. тугма tugma

**buy** *v.*
1. сатын ал- satın al-
2. сатып ал- (satıp al-)
3. сатып ал- (satıp al-)
4. сатып ал- (satıp al-)
5. satın al-
6. сатын ал- satyn al-
7. سېتىۋال_ (setival-)
8. сотиб ол- sotib ol-

**buyer** *n.*
1. алычы alıcı
2. сатып алушы
   (satıp aluwshı)
3. сатып алуучу
   (satıp aluuchu)
4. сатып алучы (satıp aluchı)
5. alıcı
6. алыҗы alyjy
7. خېرىدار (kheridar)
8. харидор xaridor

**by** *prep.*
1. илә, тәрәфиндән
   ilə, tərəfindən
2. мен, арқылы (men, arqılı)
3. менен, аркалуу
   (menen, arkaluu)

4. бeлән, аркылы
   (belän, arkılı)
5. ile, tarafından
6. билен, тарапындан
   bilen, tarapyndan
7. بىلەن، تەرىپىدىن (bilän, täripidin)
8. билан, орқали
   bilan, orqali

**bye-bye** *interj.*
1. худаһафиз xudahafiz
2. қош болыңыз
   (qosh bolıngız)
3. кош болуңуз
   (kosh bolunguz)
4. хуш, хушығыз
   (khush, khushıgız)
5. allahaısmarladık
6. хош hoş
7. خەير_خوش (khäyr-khosh)
8. хайр xayr

**cab**    see taxi

**cabbage** *bot. n.*
1. кәләм kələm
2. капуста (kapusta)
3. капуста (kapusta)
4. кәбестә (käbestä)
5. lahana
6. келем kelem
7. كاللەكبەسەي (kalläkbäsäy)
8. карам karam

**café** *n.*
1. кафе kafe
2. кафе (kafe)
3. кафе (kafe)
4. кафе (kafe)
5. kafeterya
6. кафе kafe
7. قەهۋەخانا (qähväkhana)
8. кафе kafe

**cake** *cul. n.*
1. пирожна pirojna
2. торт (tort)
3. торт (tort)
4. бәлеш, пирог
   (bälesh, pirog)
5. pasta
6. торт tort
7. تورت (tort)
8. пирожное pirojnoye

**calculate** *v.*
1. һесабла- hesabla-
2. есепте- (yesepte-)
3. эсепте- (esepte-)
4. хисапла- (khisapla-)
5. hesapla-
6. хасапла- hasapla-
7. هېسابلا_ (hesabla-)
8. ҳисобла- hisobla-

**calendar** *n.*
1. тәгвим təqvim
2. календарь (kalendar')
3. календарь (kalendar')
4. календарь (kalendar')
5. takvim
6. календарь kalendar
7. كالېندار (kalendar)
8. календарь kalendar'

**call** (=shout for) *v.*
1. чағыр- çağır-
2. шақыр- (shaqır-)
3. чакыр- (chakir-)
4. чакыр- (chakır-)
5. çağır-
6. чагыр- çagyr-
7. چاقىر_ (chaqir-)
8. чақир- chaqir-

**calm** *adj.*
1. сакит sakit
2. тыныκ (tınıq)
3. тынч (tınch)
4. тыныч (tınıch)
5. sakin
6. юваш ÿuwaş
7. تىنچ (tinch)
8. осойишта osoyishta

**camel** *zool. n.*
1. дәвә dəvə
2. түйе (tüye)
3. төө (töö)
4. дөя (döya)
5. deve
6. дуе düye
7. تۆگە (tögä)
8. туя tuya

**camera** *n.*
1. фотоапарат fotoaparat
2. фотоаппарат (fotoapparat)
3. фотоаппарат (fotoapparat)
4. фотоаппарат (fotoapparat)
5. fotoğraf makinası
6. фотоаппарат fotoapparat
7. فوتو ئاپپارات (foto apparat)
8. фотоаппарат fotoapparat

**canal** *n.*
1. канал kanal
2. канал (kanal)
3. канал (kanal)
4. канал (kanal)
5. kanal
6. канал kanal
7. قانال (qanal)
8. канал kanal

**cancer** *med. n.*
1. хәрчәнк xərçəng
2. рак (rak)
3. рак (rak)
4. рак (rak)
5. kanser
6. рак rak
7. راك (rak)
8. рак rak

**candle** *n.*
1. шам şam
2. шырак (shıraq)
3. шам (sham)
4. шәм (shäm)
5. mum
6. шем şem
7. شام (sham)
8. шам sham

**candy** *cul. n.*
1. конфет konfet
2. кәмпит (kämpit)
3. кемпут (kemput)
4. кәнфит (känfit)
5. şeker
6. сүйҗи süÿji
7. كەمپۈت (kämpüt)
8. конфет konfet

**cannon** *mil. n.*
1. топ top
2. зеңбірек (zengbirek)
3. замбирек (zambirek)
4. туп (tup)
5. top
6. топ top
7. زەمبىرەك (zämbiräk)
8. түп to'p

**capital** (*city) *n.*
1. пајтахт paytaxt
2. астана (astana)
3. борбор (borbor)
4. башкала (bashkala)
5. başkent
6. пайтагт paÿtagt
7. پايتەخت (paytäkht)
8. пойтахт poytaxt

**captain** *n.*
1. капитан kapitan
2. капитан (kapitan)
3. капитан (kapitan)
4. капитан (kapitan)
5. kaptan
6. капитан kapitan
7. كاپىتان (kapitan)
8. капитан kapitan

**car** *n.*
1. машын maşın
2. машина (mashina)
3. машина (mashina)
4. машина (mashina)
5. araba
6. машын maşyn
7. ماشىنا (mashina)
8. машина mashina

## careful *adj.*
1. дигтəтли diqqətli
2. абай (abay)
3. абайла (abayla)
4. сак (sak)
5. dikkatli
6. əтиячлы ätiÿaçly
7. ئەھتىياتچان (ehtiyatchan)
8. эхтиёткор ehtiyotkor

## cargo *n.*
1. jʏк yük
2. жʏк (zhük)
3. жʏк (jük)
4. йөк (yök)
5. yük
6. йʏк ÿük
7. يۈك (yük)
8. юк yuk

## carnation *bot. n.*
1. гəрəнфил qərənfil
2. қалампыр (qalampır)
3. калемпир (kalempir)
4. канəфер чəчəк (kanäfer chächäk)
5. karanfil
6. гвоздика gwozdika
7. قەلەمپۇر (qälämpur)
8. чиннигул chinnigul

## carpet *n.*
1. халы xalı
2. кілем (kilem)
3. килем (kilem)
4. келəм (keläm)
5. halı
6. халы haly
7. گىلەم (giläm)
8. гилам gilam

## carrot *bot. n.*
1. jеркөкʏ yerkökü
2. сəбіз (säbiz)
3. сабиз (sabiz)
4. кишер (kisher)
5. havuç
6. кəшир käşir
7. سەۋزە (sävzä)
8. сабзи sabzi

## carry *v.*
1. дашы- daşı-
2. тасы- (tası-)
3. ташы- (tashı-)
4. ташы- (tashı-)
5. taşı-
6. чек- çek-
7. توشۇ (toshu-)
8. таши- tashi-

## cart *n.*
1. араба araba
2. арба (arba)
3. араба (araba)
4. арба (arba)
5. at arabası
6. араба araba
7. ھارۋا (ḥarva)
8. арава arava

## cartoon *n.*
1. карикатура karikatura
2. карикатура (karikatura)
3. карикатура (karikatura)
4. карикатура (karikatura)
5. karikatür
6. карикатура karikatura
7. ھەجۋىي رەسىم (häjviy räsim)
8. карикатура karikatura

## cash *n.*
1. нəгд пул nəqd pul
2. нақты ақша (naqtı aqsha)
3. нак акча (nak akcha)
4. кулда булган акча (kulda bulgan akcha)
5. nakit
6. нагт nagt
7. نەق پۇل (näq pul)
8. нақд пул naqd pul

## cashier *n.*
1. кассир kassir
2. кассир (kassir)
3. кассир (kassir)
4. кассир (kassir)
5. veznedar
6. кассир kassir
7. كاسسىر (kassir)
8. кассир kassir

## cassette *n.*
1. касет kaset
2. кассет (kasset)
3. кассет (kasset)
4. кассета (kasseta)
5. kaset
6. касета kaseta
7. ئۈنئالغۇ لېنتىسى (ün'alghu lentisi)
8. кассета kasseta

## cat *zool. n.*
1. пишик pişik
2. мысық (mısıq)
3. мышық (mıshıq)
4. песи (pesi)
5. kedi
6. пишик pişik
7. مۈشۈك (müshük)
8. мушук mushuk

## catch *v.*
1. jaxala- yaxala-
2. ұста- (usta-)
3. карма- (karma-)
4. тот- (tot-)
5. yakala-
6. тут- tut-
7. تۇت (tut-)
8. тут- tut-

## cattle *n.*
1. мал-гара mal-qara
2. қара мал (qara mal)
3. кара мал (kara mal)
4. мал-туар (mal-tuar)
5. sığır
6. гара мал gara mal
7. قارا مال (qara mal)
8. қорамол qoramol

## cause *n.*
1. сәбәб səbəb
2. себеп (sebep)
3. себеп (sebep)
4. сәбәп (säbäp)
5. sebep
6. себәп sebäp
7. سەۋەب (säväb)
8. сабаб sabab

## ceiling *n.*
1. таван tavan
2. төбе (töbe)
3. шып (shıp)
4. түшәм (tüshäm)
5. tavan
6. потолок potolok
7. توروس (torus)
8. шип ship

## celebrate *v.*
1. бајрам ет- bayram et-
2. мерекеле- (merekele-)
3. майрамда- (mayramda-)
4. бәйрәм ит- (bäyräm it-)
5. kutla-
6. байрам әт- bаÿram et-
7. تەبریكلە (täbriklä-)
8. нишонла- nishonla-

## celebration *n.*
1. бајрам етмә bayram etmə
2. мейрамдау (meyramdaw)
3. майрамдоо (mayramdoo)
4. котлау (kotlau)
5. kutlama
6. байрам әтме bаÿram etme
7. قۇتلۇقلاش (qutluqlash)
8. нишонлаш nishonlash

## celery *bot. n.*
1. кәрәвиз kərəviz
2. селдерей (selderey)
3. селдерей (selderey)
4. сельдерей (sel'derey)
5. kereviz
6. селдерей selderеÿ
7. چىڭساي (chingsäy)
8. сельдерей sel'derey

## cement *n.*
1. семент sement
2. цемент (tsement)
3. цемент (tsement)
4. цемент (tsement)
5. çimento
6. цемент tsement
7. سېمونت (semont)
8. цемент tsement

## cemetery *n.*
1. гәбиристан qəbiristan
2. зират (ziyrat)
3. көрүстөн (körüstön)
4. каберлек (kaberlek)
5. mezarlık
6. мазарчылык mazarçylyk
7. مازارلىق (mazarliq)
8. қабристон qabriston

## censorship *pre. n.*
1. сензура senzura
2. цензура (tsenzura)
3. цензура (tsenzura)
4. цензура (tsenzura)
5. sansür
6. цензура tsenzura
7. تەكشۈرۈش (täkshürüsh)
8. цензура tsenzura

## center
(=a central point) *n.*
1. мәркәз mərkəz
2. орталық (ortalıq)
3. борбор (borbor)
4. үзәк (üzäk)
5. merkez
6. меркез merkez
7. مەركەز (märkäz)
8. марказ markaz

## century *n.*
1. әср əsr
2. ғасыр (ghasır)
3. кылым (kılım)
4. гасыр (gasır)
5. yüzyıl
6. асыр asyr
7. ئەسىر (äsir)
8. аср asr

---

## ceremony  *n.*
1. тәнтәнә təntənə
2. мейрам (meyram)
3. салтанат (saltanat)
4. тантана (tantana)
5. tören
6. дабара dabara
7. تَنتَنه (täntänä)
8. тантана tantana

## chair  *n.*
1. стул stul
2. орындық (orındıq)
3. орундук (orunduk)
4. урындык (urındık)
5. sandalye
6. стул stul
7. ئورۇندۇق (orunduq)
8. курси kursi

## change (=alter)  *vt.*
1. дәјишдир- dəyişdir-
2. өзгерт- (özgert-)
3. өзгөрт- (özgört-)
4. узгәрт- (üzgärt-)
5. değiştir-
6. үйтгет- üytget-
7. ئۆزگەرت_ (özgärt-)
8. ўзгартир- o'zgartir-

## change (=small coins)  *n.*
1. хырда пул xırda pul
2. майда ақша (mayda aqsha)
3. майда акча (mayda akcha)
4. вак акча (vak akcha)
5. bozuk para
6. овнук пул ownuk pul
7. پارچه پۇل (parchä pul)
8. майда пул mayda pul

## channel (*TV, radio)  *n.*
1. канал kanal
2. канал (kanal)
3. канал (kanal)
4. канал (kanal)
5. kanal
6. канал kanal
7. قانال (qanal)
8. канал kanal

## chase  *v.*
1. излә- izlə-
2. ізге түс- (izge tüs-)
3. изге түш- (izge tüsh-)
4. ку- (ku-)
5. kovala-
6. ковала- kowala-
7. توغلا_ (qoghla-)
8. кув(ла)- quv[la]-

## cheap  *adj.*
1. учуз ucuz
2. арзан (arzan)
3. арзан (arzan)
4. арзан (arzan)
5. ucuz
6. арзан arzan
7. ئەرزان (ärzan)
8. арзон arzon

## check  *econ. n.*
1. чек çek
2. чек (chek)
3. чек (chek)
4. чек (chek)
5. çek
6. чек çek
7. چەك (chäk)
8. чек chek

## cheek  *phys. n.*
1. јанаг yanaq
2. бет (bet)
3. бет (bet)
4. яңак (yangak)
5. yanak
6. яңак ÿañak
7. مەگز (mängz)
8. ёноқ yonoq

## cheese  *cul. n.*
1. пендир pendir
2. ірімшік (irimshik)
3. сыр (sır)
4. сыр (sır)
5. peynir
6. пейнир peÿnir
7. پىشلاق (pishlaq)
8. пишлоқ pishloq

## cherry  *bot. n.*
1. ҝилас gilas
2. шие (shiye)
3. арча (archa)
4. чия (chiya)
5. kiraz
6. үлҗе ülje
7. گىلاس (gilas)
8. олча olcha

## chess  *spor. n.*
1. шаһмат şahmat
2. шахмат (shakhmat)
3. шахмат (shakhmat)
4. шахмат (shakhmat)
5. satranç
6. күшт küşt
7. شاھمات (shahmat)
8. шахмат shaxmat

## chest *phys. n.*
1. синə sinə
2. көкiрек (kökirek)
3. көкүрөк (kökürök)
4. күкрəк (kükräk)
5. göğüs
6. дөш döş
7. كۆكرەك (kökräk)
8. кўкрак ko'krak

## chestnut *bot. n.*
1. шабалыд şabalıd
2. каштан (kashtan)
3. каштан (kashtan)
4. кəстəнə (kästänä)
5. kestane
6. каштан kaştan
7. كاشتان (kashtan)
8. каштан kashtan

## chew *v.*
1. чејнə- çeynə-
2. шайна- (shayna-)
3. чайна- (chayna-)
4. чəйнə- (chäynä-)
5. çiğne-
6. чейне- çeÿne-
7. چاينا‎ (chayna-)
8. чайна- chayna-

## chicken *cul. n.*
1. тоjуг əти toyuq əti
2. тауық еті (tawıq yeti)
3. тоок эти (took eti)
4. тавык ите (tavık ite)
5. tavuk eti
6. товук əти towuk eti
7. تورخۇ گۆشى (tokhu goshi)
8. товуқ гўшти tovuq go'shti

## child *n.*
1. ушаг uşaq
2. бала (bala)
3. бала (bala)
4. бала (bala)
5. çocuk
6. чага çaga
7. بالا (bala)
8. бола bola

## chimney *n.*
1. бача baca
2. мүржа (murzha)
3. мор (mor)
4. моржа (morja)
5. baca
6. түссечыкар tüsseçykar
7. تۇرخۇن (turkhun)
8. мүри mo'ri

## chin *phys. n.*
1. чəнə çənə
2. иек (iyek)
3. ээк (eek)
4. ияк (iyak)
5. çene
6. əңек eñek
7. ئەڭگەك (engäk)
8. ияк iyak

## choose *v.*
1. сеч- seç-
2. таңда- (tangda-)
3. танда- (tanda-)
4. сайла- (sayla-)
5. seç-
6. сайла- saÿla-
7. تاللا (talla-)
8. танла- tanla-

## Christian *rel. n.*
1. христиан xristian
2. христиан (khristiyan)
3. христиан (khristian)
4. христиан (khristian)
5. Hıristiyan
6. христиан hristian
7. خرىستىئان (khristi'an)
8. христиан xristian

## church *rel. n.*
1. килсə kilsə
2. шiркеу (shirkew)
3. чиркөө (chirköö)
4. чиркəү (chirkäü)
5. kilise
6. бутхана buthana
7. چېركاۋ (cherkav)
8. черков cherkov

## cigarette *n.*
1. сигарет siqaret
2. темекi (temeki)
3. тамеки (tameki)
4. сигарет (sigaret)
5. sigara
6. чилим çilim
7. تاماكا (tamaka)
8. сигарет sigaret

## cinema *n.*
1. кинотеатр kinoteatr
2. кино (kino)
3. кино (kino)
4. кинотеатр (kinoteatr)
5. sinema
6. кинотеатр kinoteatr
7. كىنوخانا (kinokhana)
8. кинотеатр kinoteatr

---

**circle** *geom. n.*
1. дaирə dairə
2. шeнбер (shengber)
3. тeгерек (tegerek)
4. түгəрəк (tügäräk)
5. daire
6. тeгелек tegelek
7. دائره (da'irä)
8. доира doira

**circulation** *pre. n.*
1. тираж tiraj
2. тираж (tirazh)
3. тираж (tiraj)
4. тираж (tirazh)
5. tiraj
6. тираж tiraſ
7. تراژ (tirazh)
8. тираж tiraj

**circus** *n.*
1. сирк sirk
2. цирк (tsirk)
3. цирк (tsirk)
4. цирк (tsirk)
5. sirk
6. цирк tsirk
7. سېرك (serk)
8. цирк tsirk

**citizen** *n.*
1. вəтəндаш vətəndaş
2. азамат (azamat)
3. граждан (grajdan)
4. граждан (grazhdan)
5. vatandaş
6. граждан graſdan
7. گراژدان (grazhdan)
8. фуқаро fuqaro

**city** *n.*
1. шəhəр şəhər
2. қала (qala)
3. шаар (shaar)
4. шəhəр (shähär)
5. şehir
6. шəхер şäher
7. شەھەر (shähär)
8. шаҳар shahar

**clap** *v.*
1. əл чал- əl çal-
2. шапалақта- (shapalaqta-)
3. кол чап- (kol chap-)
4. кул чап- (kul chap-)
5. alkışla-
6. əл чарп- el çarp-
7. چاۋاق چال- (chavaq chal-)
8. чапак чал- chapak chal-

**classroom** *n.*
1. синиф sinif
2. класс (klass)
3. класс (klass)
4. класс (klass)
5. sınıf
6. клас klas
7. سىنىپ (sinip)
8. синф sinf

**clay** *geol. n.*
1. кил gil
2. балшық (balshıq)
3. топурак (topurak)
4. балчык (balchık)
5. kil
6. тоюн toÿun
7. سېغىز لاي (seghiz lay)
8. лой loy

**clean** *adj.*
1. тəмиз təmiz
2. таза (taza)
3. таза (taza)
4. таза (taza)
5. temiz
6. арасса arassa
7. تازا (taza)
8. тоза toza

**clean** *vt.*
1. тəмизлə- təmizlə-
2. тазала- (tazala-)
3. тазала- (tazala-)
4. тазарт- (tazart-)
5. temizle-
6. арассала- arassala-
7. تازىلا- (tazila-)
8. тозала- tozala-

**clever** *adj.*
1. ағыллы ağıllı
2. ақылды (aqıldı)
3. акылдуу (akılduu)
4. акыллы (akıllı)
5. akıllı
6. акыллы akylly
7. ئەقىللىق (äqillliq)
8. ақлли aqlli

**climate** *n.*
1. иглим iqlim
2. ауа райы (awa rayı)
3. аба ырайы (aba ırayı)
4. климат (klimat)
5. iklim
6. климат klimat
7. ئىقلىم (iqlim)
8. иқлим iqlim

## climb *v.*
1. дырман- dırman-
2. өрмеле- (örmele-)
3. жөрмөлөп чык-
(jörmölöp chık-)
4. үрмәләп мен-
(ürmäläp men-)
5. tırman-
6. дырмаш- dyrmaş-
7. ‫ياماش‬ (yamash-)
8. тирмашиб чиқ-
tirmashib chiq-

## clinic *med. n.*
1. клиника klinika
2. емхана (yemkhana)
3. эмкана (emkana)
4. клиника (klinika)
5. klinik
6. клиника klinika
7. ‫دوختۇرخانا‬ (dokhturkhana)
8. клиника klinika

## clock *n.*
1. дивар сааты divar saatı
2. сағат (saghat)
3. дубал саат (dubal saat)
4. стена сәгате (stena sägate)
5. duvar saati
6. дивар сагады
diwar sagady
7. ‫تام سائتى‬ (tam sa'iti)
8. девор соати devor soati

## close *vt.*
1. бағла- bağla-
2. жаб- (zhab-)
3. жап- (jap-)
4. яп- (yap-)
5. kapa-
6. яп- ÿap-
7. ‫ياپ‬ (yap-)
8. ёп- yop-

## closed *adj.*
1. бағлы bağlı
2. жабық (zhabıq)
3. жабык (jabık)
4. ябык (yabık)
5. kapalı
6. япык ÿapyk
7. ‫يېپىق‬ (yepiq)
8. ёпиқ yopiq

## clothes *n.*
1. палтар paltar
2. кийм (kiyim)
3. кийим (kiyim)
4. кием (kiyem)
5. elbise
6. эгин-эшик egin-eşik
7. ‫كىيىم‬ (kiyim)
8. кийим-кечак
kiyim-kechak

## cloud *n.*
1. булуд bulud
2. бұлт (bult)
3. булут (bulut)
4. болыт (bolıt)
5. bulut
6. булут bulut
7. ‫بۇلۇت‬ (bulut)
8. булут bulut

## club (=a social
organization) *n.*
1. клуб klub
2. клуб (klub)
3. клуб (klub)
4. клуб (klub)
5. klüp
6. клуб klub
7. ‫كۇلۇب‬ (kulub)
8. клуб klub

## coal *geol. n.*
1. көмүр kömür
2. көмір (kömir)
3. көмүр (kömür)
4. күмер (kümer)
5. kömür
6. көмүр kömür
7. ‫كۆمۈر‬ (kömür)
8. кўмир ko'mir

## coast *geo. n.*
1. саһил sahil
2. жаға (zhagha)
3. жээк (jeek)
4. яр буе (yar buye)
5. sahil
6. яка ÿaka
7. ‫دېڭىز قىرغىقى‬
(dengiz qirghiqi)
8. денгиз соҳили
dengiz sohili

## coffee *cul. n.*
1. рәһвә qəhvə
2. кофе (kofe)
3. кофе (kofe)
4. кофе (kofe)
5. kahve
6. кофе kofe
7. ‫قەھۋە‬ (qähvä)
8. қаҳва qahva

## coin *n.*
1. дәмир пул dəmir pul
2. тиын (tiyın)
3. тыйын (tıyın)
4. тәңкә (tängkä)
5. madeni para
6. шайы пул şaÿy pul
7. ‫تەڭگە‬ (tänggä)
8. танга tanga

---

1. Azerbaijani  2. Kazakh  3. Kyrgyz  4. Tatar  5. Turkish  6. Turkmen  7. Uighur  8. Uzbek

## cold *adj.*
1. cojyг soyuq
2. суық (suwıq)
3. суук (suuk)
4. суык (suık)
5. soğuk
6. совук sowuk
7. سوغوق (soghuq)
8. совуқ sovuq

## cold *med. n.*
1. cojyгдәјмә soyuqdəymə
2. тұмау (tumaw)
3. тумоо (tumoo)
4. томау (tomau)
5. soğuk algınlığı
6. дүмев dümew
7. زوكام (zukam)
8. шамоллаш shamollash

## collar *clo. n.*
1. jaxa yaxa
2. жаға (zhagha)
3. жака (jaka)
4. яка (yaka)
5. yaka
6. яка ÿaka
7. ياقا (yaqa)
8. ёқа yoqa

## collect *v.*
1. топла- topla-
2. жина- (zhiyna-)
3. жыйна- (jıyna-)
4. җы- (jı-)
5. topla-
6. йыгна- ÿygna-
7. ينغ (yigh-)
8. йиг- yig'-

## color *n.*
1. рәнк rəng
2. түс (tüs)
3. түс (tüs)
4. төс (tös)
5. renk
6. реңк reñk
7. رەڭ (räng)
8. ранг rang

## comb *v.*
1. дара- dara-
2. тара- (tara-)
3. тара- (tara-)
4. тара- (tara-)
5. tara-
6. дара- dara-
7. تارا (tara-)
8. тара- tara-

## comb *n.*
1. дараг daraq
2. тарақ (taraq)
3. тарак (tarak)
4. тарак (tarak)
5. tarak
6. дарак darak
7. تارغاق (targhaq)
8. тароқ taroq

## come *v.*
1. кәл- gəl-
2. кел- (kel-)
3. кел- (kel-)
4. кил- (kil-)
5. gel-
6. гел- gel-
7. كەل (käl-)
8. кел- kel-

## comedy *art. n.*
1. комедија komediya
2. комедия (komediya)
3. комедия (komediya)
4. комедия (komediya)
5. komedi
6. комедия komediÿa
7. كومېدىيە (komediyä)
8. комедия komediya

## comfortable *adj.*
1. раһат rahat
2. ыңғайлы (ıngghaylı)
3. ыңгайлуу (ınggayluu)
4. уңайлы (ungaylı)
5. rahat
6. җайлы jaÿly
7. راھەتلىك (rahätlik)
8. қулай qulay

## comma *ling. n.*
1. веркүл vergül
2. үтір (ütir)
3. үтүр (ütür)
4. өтер (öter)
5. virgül
6. отур otur
7. پەش (päsh)
8. вергуль vergul'

## command *v.*
1. әмр ет- əmr et-
2. бұйрық бер- (buyrıq ber-)
3. буйрук бер- (buyruk ber-)
4. боерык бир- (boyerık bir-)
5. emret-
6. буйрук бер- buÿruk ber-
7. بۇيرۇ (buyru-)
8. буйруқ бер- buyruq ber-

## communication  n.
1. əlaqə əlaqə
2. байланыс (baylanıs)
3. байланыш (baylanısh)
4. багланыш (baglanısh)
5. iletişim
6. арагатнашык aragatnaşyk
7. قاتناش (qatnash)
8. алоқа aloqa

## company  econ. n.
1. ширкәт şirkət
2. компания (kompaniya)
3. компания (kompaniya)
4. компания (kompaniya)
5. şirket
6. фирма firma
7. شركت (shirkät)
8. ширкат shirkat

## comparison  n.
1. мүгајисə müqayisə
2. салыстыру (salıstıruw)
3. салыштыруу (salıshtıruu)
4. чагыштыру (chagıshtıru)
5. karşılaştırma
6. дeнeшдирме deñeşdirme
7. سېلىشتۇرۇش (selishturush)
8. қиёслаш qiyoslash

## competition  econ. n.
1. рəгабəт rəqabət
2. жарыс (zharıs)
3. атаандаштык (ataandashtık)
4. ярышучылык (yarıshuchılık)
5. rekabet
6. бəсдешлик bäsdeşlik
7. رىقابەت (riqabät)
8. рақобат raqobat

## complain  v.
1. шикајəт ет- şikayət et-
2. арыздан- (arızdan-)
3. арыздан- (arızdan-)
4. шикаять ит- (shikayat' it-)
5. şikâyet et-
6. шикаят əт- şikaÿat et-
7. شكايەت قىل (shikayät qil-)
8. шикоят қил- shikoyat qil-

## complaint  n.
1. шикајəт şikayət
2. арыз (arız)
3. арыз (arız)
4. зар (zar)
5. şikâyet
6. шикаят şikaÿat
7. شكايەت (shikayät)
8. шикоят shikoyat

## complete  adj.
1. там tam
2. түгел (tügel)
3. түгөл (tügöl)
4. тулы (tulı)
5. tam
6. долы doly
7. تولۇق (toluq)
8. тугал tugal

## composer  mus. n.
1. бəстəкар bəstəkar
2. композитор (kompozitor)
3. композитор (kompozitor)
4. композитор (kompozitor)
5. besteci
6. композитор kompozitor
7. كومپوزىتور (kompozitor)
8. композитор, бастакор kompozitor, bastakor

## composition  mus. n.
1. мусиги əсəри musiqi əsəri
2. шығарма (shıgharma)
3. чыгарма (chıgarma)
4. композиция (kompozitsiya)
5. beste
6. саз əсери saz eseri
7. مۇزىكا (muzika)
8. композиция kompozitsiya

## computer  n.
1. компүтер kompüter
2. компьютер (komp'yuter)
3. компьютер (komp'yuter)
4. компьютер (komp'yuter)
5. bilgisayar
6. компьютер kompÿuter
7. ھېسابلاش ماشىنىسى (hesablash mashinisi)
8. компьютер komp'yuter

## concert  mus. n.
1. консерт konsert
2. концерт (kontsert)
3. концерт (kontsert)
4. концерт (kontsert)
5. konser
6. концерт kontsert
7. كونسېرت (konsert)
8. концерт kontsert

## concrete  adj.
1. конкрет konkret
2. нақты (naqtı)
3. так (tak)
4. анық (anık)
5. somut
6. конкрет konkret
7. كونكرېت (konkret)
8. аниқ aniq

---

## condition
(=a requisite)   *n.*
1. шәрт şərt
2. шарт (shart)
3. шарт (shart)
4. шарт (shart)
5. şart
6. шерт şert
7. شەرت (shärt)
8. шароит sharoit

## condition (=state)   *n.*
1. һал hal
2. жағдай (zhaghday)
3. жагдай (jagday)
4. хәл (khäl)
5. hal
6. ягдай ÿagdaÿ
7. هال (hal)
8. аҳвол ahvol

## confidence   *n.*
1. е'тимад e'timad
2. сенім (senim)
3. ишеним (ishenim)
4. ышаныч (ıshanıch)
5. güven
6. ынам ynam
7. ئىشەنچ (ishänch)
8. ишонч ishonch

## congratulate   *v.*
1. тәбрик ет- təbrik et-
2. құттықта- (quttıqta-)
3. куттукта- (kuttukta-)
4. котла- (kotla-)
5. tebrik et-
6. гутла- gutla-
7. تەبرىكلە (täbriklä-)
8. табрикла- tabrikla-

## congratulation   *n.*
1. тәбрик təbrik
2. құттықтау (quttıqtaw)
3. куттуктоо (kuttuktoo)
4. котлау (kotlau)
5. tebrik
6. гутлама gutlama
7. تەبرىك (täbrik)
8. табриклаш tabriklash

## conscience   *n.*
1. вичдан vicdan
2. ар (ar)
3. ар (ar)
4. вөҗдан (vöjdan)
5. vicdan
6. выждан wyĵdan
7. ۋىجدان (vijdan)
8. виждон vijdon

## consonant   *ling. n.*
1. самит samit
2. дауыссыз (dawıssız)
3. үнсүз тыбыш
    (ünsüz tıbısh)
4. тартык (tartık)
5. ünsüz
6. чекимсиз çekimsiz
7. ئۈزۈك تاۋۇش (üzük tavush)
8. ундош undosh

## constipation   *med. n.*
1. гәбизлик qəbizlik
2. iш қату (ish qatuw)
3. ич катуу (ich katuu)
4. эч кату (ech katu)
5. kabızlık
6. ичиң гатама içiñ gatama
7. ئىچ قەتىش (ich qetish)
8. қабзият qabziyat

## consumer   *n.*
1. истеһлакчы istehlakçı
2. тұтынушы (tutınuwshı)
3. керектөөчү (kerektööchü)
4. кулланучы (kullanuchı)
5. tüketici
6. алыжы alyjy
7. ئىستەمالچى (istemalchi)
8. истеъмолчи iste'molchi

## continue   *v.*
1. давам ет- davam et-
2. ұлас- (ulas-)
3. улан- (ulan-)
4. дәвам ит- (dävam it-)
5. devam et-
6. довам эт- dowam et-
7. داۋام قىل (davam qil-)
8. давом эт- davom et-

## convenient   *adj.*
1. әлверишли əlverişli
2. қолайлы (qolaylı)
3. жарамдуу (jaramduu)
4. уңайлы (ungaylı)
5. elverişli
6. аматлы amatly
7. ئوڭاي (ongay)
8. қулай qulay

## cook   *n.*
1. ашпаз aşpaz
2. аспаз (aspaz)
3. ашпоз (ashpoz)
4. аш пешерүче
    (ash pesherüche)
5. aşçı
6. ашпез aşpez
7. ئاشپەز (ashpäz)
8. ошпаз oshpaz

---

## cook  vi.

1. биш- biş-
2. піс- (pis-)
3. бьш- (bısh-)
4. пеш- (pesh-)
5. piş-
6. биш- biş-
7. پش (pish-)
8. пиш- pish-

## cook  vt.

1. бишир- bişir-
2. пісір- (pisir-)
3. бышыр- (bıshır-)
4. пешер- (pesher-)
5. pişir-
6. бишир- bişir-
7. پشور (pishur-)
8. пишир- pishir-

## cookie  cul. n.

1. печење peçenye
2. печенье (pechen'ye)
3. печенье (pechen'ye)
4. печенье (pechen'ye)
5. kurabiye
6. көке köke
7. پرهنك (piränik)
8. печенье pechen'ye

## cool  adj.

1. сәрин sərin
2. салқын (salqın)
3. салкын (salkın)
4. салкын (salkın)
5. serin
6. салкын salkyn
7. سالقين (salqin)
8. салқин salqin

## copper  geol. n.

1. мис mis
2. мыс (mıs)
3. жез (jez)
4. бакыр (bakır)
5. bakır
6. мис mis
7. مس (mis)
8. мис mis

## corn  bot. n.

1. гарғыдалы qarğıdalı
2. жүгері (zhügeri)
3. жүгөрү (jügörü)
4. кукуруз (kukuruz)
5. mısır
6. мекгежөвен mekgejöwen
7. قوناق (qonaq)
8. маккажўхори makkajo'xori

## corner  n.

1. күнч künc
2. бұрыш (burısh)
3. бурч (burch)
4. почмак (pochmak)
5. köşe
6. бурч burç
7. بولوڭ (bulung)
8. бурчак burchak

## correct  v.

1. дүзәлт- düzəlt-
2. түзет- (tüzet-)
3. түзөт- (tüzöt-)
4. төзәт- (tözät-)
5. düzelt-
6. дүзет- düzet-
7. توغریلا (toghrila-)
8. тўғрила- to'g'rila-

## correct  adj.

1. дүз düz
2. тура (tuwra)
3. туура (tuura)
4. дөрес (döres)
5. doğru
6. догры dogry
7. توغرا (toghra)
8. тўғри to'g'ri

## corruption  n.

1. коррупсија korrupsiya
2. коррупция (korruptsiya)
3. коррупция (korruptsiya)
4. ришвәтчелек (rishvätchelek)
5. irtikâp
6. коррупция korruptsiÿa
7. چرىكلىشىش (chiriklishish)
8. порахўрлик poraxo'rlik

## cost  (=price)  n.

1. гијмәт qiymət
2. баға (bagha)
3. куну (kunu)
4. кыйммәт (kıymmät)
5. paha
6. баха baha
7. باها (baha)
8. нарх narx

## cotton  bot. n.

1. памбыг pambıq
2. мақта (maqta)
3. пахта (pakhta)
4. мамык (mamık)
5. pamuk
6. пагта pagta
7. پاختا (pakhta)
8. пахта paxta

---

## cough *med. n.*
1. өскүрәк öskürәk
2. жөтел (zhötel)
3. жөтөл (jötöl)
4. ютәл (yutäl)
5. öksürük
6. үсгүлевүк üsgülewük
7. يۆتەل (yötäl)
8. йүтал yo'tal

## count *v.*
1. сај- say-
2. сана- (sana-)
3. сана- (sana-)
4. сана- (sana-)
5. say-
6. сана- sana-
7. سانا‍ (sana-)
8. сана- sana-

## countryside *n.*
1. кәнд kәnd
2. ауыл (awıl)
3. айыл (ayıl)
4. кыр (kır)
5. kır
6. оба ери oba ÿeri
7. سەھرا (sähra)
8. қишлоқ жой qishloq joy

## courage *n.*
1. чәсарәт cәsarәt
2. батылдық (batıldıq)
3. кайраттану (kayrattanu)
4. йөрәклелек (yöräklelek)
5. cesaret
6. эдерменлик edermenlik
7. جاسارەت (jasarät)
8. мардлик mardlik

## courageous *adj.*
1. чәсур cәsur
2. батыл (batıl)
3. кайраттуу (kayrattuu)
4. батыр (batır)
5. cesur
6. батыр batyr
7. جەسۈر (jäsur)
8. жасур jasur

## course: of course *adv.*
1. әлбәттә әlbәttә
2. әрине (äriyne)
3. албетте (albette)
4. әлбәттә (älbättä)
5. elbette
6. әлбетде elbetde
7. ئەلۋەتتە (älvättä)
8. албатта albatta

## court *jud. n.*
1. мәһкәмә mәhkәmә
2. сот (sot)
3. сот (sot)
4. суд (sud)
5. mahkeme
6. суд sud
7. سوت مەھكىمىسى
   (sot mähkimisi)
8. суд sud

## courtyard *n.*
1. һәјәт hәyәt
2. аула (awla)
3. короо (koroo)
4. ишегалды (ishegaldı)
5. avlu
6. ховлы howly
7. ھويلا (hoyla)
8. ховли hovli

## cover *v.*
1. өрт- ört-
2. жаб- (zhab-)
3. жап- (jap-)
4. яп- (yap-)
5. örp-
6. өрт- ört-
7. ياپ‍ (yap-)
8. ёп- yop-

## cow *zool. n.*
1. инәк inәk
2. сыыр (siyır)
3. уй (uy)
4. сыер (sıyer)
5. inek
6. сыгыр sygyr
7. كالا (kala)
8. сигир sigir

## coward *adj.*
1. горхаг qorxaq
2. қорқақ (qorqaq)
3. коркок (korkok)
4. куркак (kurkak)
5. korkak
6. горкак gorkak
7. قورقاق (qorqqaq)
8. қўрқоқ qo'rqoq

## cowardice *n.*
1. горхаглыг qorxaqlıq
2. қорқақтық (qorqaqtıq)
3. коркоктук (korkoktuk)
4. куркаклык (kurkaklık)
5. korkaklık
6. горкаклык gorkaklyk
7. قورقاقلىق (qorqqaqliq)
8. қўрқоқлик qo'rqoqlik

---

1. Azerbaijani  2. Kazakh  3. Kyrgyz  4. Tatar  5. Turkish  6. Turkmen  7. Uighur  8. Uzbek

**crazy** *adj.*
1. чылғын çılğın
2. жынды (zhındı)
3. жинди (jindi)
4. ақылдан язған (akıldan yazgan)
5. çılgın
6. дәли däli
7. تەلۋە (tälvä)
8. жинни jinni

**cream** *cul. n.*
1. гајмаг qaymaq
2. қаймақ (qaymaq)
3. каймак (kaymak)
4. каймак (kaymak)
5. kaymak
6. гаймак gaymak
7. قايماق (qaymaq)
8. қаймоқ qaymoq

**credit** *econ. n.*
1. кредит kredit
2. кредит (kredit)
3. кредит (kredit)
4. кредит (kredit)
5. kredi
6. кредит kredit
7. كرېدت (kredit)
8. қарз qarz

**crescent** *n.*
1. ајпара aypara
2. жарты ай (zhartı ay)
3. жарым ай (jarım ay)
4. яңа ай (yanga ay)
5. hilal
6. ярымай ÿarymaÿ
7. يېڭى ئاي (yengi ay)
8. хилол hilol

**crime** *n.*
1. чинајәт cinayət
2. қылмыс (qılmıs)
3. кылмыш (kılmısh)
4. җинаять (jinayat')
5. suç
6. гүнә, женаят günä, jenaÿat
7. جنايەت (jinayät)
8. жиноят jinoyat

**criminal** *n.*
1. чинајәткар cinayətkar
2. қылмыскер (qılmısker)
3. кылмышкер (kılmıshker)
4. җинаятьче (jinayat'che)
5. suçlu
6. гүнәли, женаятчы günäli, jenaÿatçy
7. جنايەتچى (jinayätchi)
8. жиноятчи jinoyatchi

**crocodile** *zool. n.*
1. тимсаһ timsah
2. крокодил (krokodil)
3. крокодил (krokodil)
4. крокодил (krokodil)
5. timsah
6. крокодил krokodil
7. تىمساھ (timsah)
8. тимсох timsoh

**crop** *ag. n.*
1. мәһсул məhsul
2. егін (yegin)
3. эгин (egin)
4. уңыш (ungısh)
5. ekin
6. экин ekin
7. ھوسۇل (hosul)
8. хосил hosil

**crosswalk** *n.*
1. пијада кечиди piyada keçidi
2. жолдың қиылысы (zholdıng qiyılısı)
3. жолдуң кыйылычы (joldung kıyılıchı)
4. юл чаты (yul chatı)
5. yaya geçidi
6. гечелге geçelge
7. پىيادىلەر ئۆتىش يولى (piyadilär ötish yoli)
8. чорраха chorraha

**crow** *zool. n.*
1. гарға qarğa
2. қарға (qargha)
3. карга (karga)
4. карга (karga)
5. karga
6. гарга garga
7. قاغا (qagha)
8. қарға qarg'a

**crowd** *n.*
1. издиһам izdiham
2. көп халық (köp khalıq)
3. калың эл (kalıng el)
4. халык төркеме (khalık törkeme)
5. kalabalık
6. мәреке märeke
7. ئادەملەر توپى (adämlär topi)
8. оломон olomon

**cruel** *adj.*
1. залым zalım
2. қатал (qatal)
3. катаал (kataal)
4. мәрхәмәтсез (märkhämätsez)
5. zalim
6. залым zalym
7. رەھىمسىز (rähimsiz)
8. рақмсиз rahmsiz

---

1. Azerbaijani  2. Kazakh  3. Kyrgyz  4. Tatar  5. Turkish  6. Turkmen  7. Uighur  8. Uzbek

**crush** *vt.*
1. әз- әz-
2. ез- (yez-)
3. зз- (ez-)
4. из- (iz-)
5. ez-
6. оврат- owrat-
7. ‫ئەز‬ (äz-)
8. зз- ez-

**cry** *v.*
1. ағла- ağla-
2. жыла- (zhıla-)
3. ыйла- (ıyla-)
4. ела- (yela-)
5. ağla-
6. агла- agla-
7. ‫يىغلا‬ (yighla-)
8. йиғла- yig'la-

**cucumber** *bot. n.*
1. хијар xiyar
2. қияр (qiyar)
3. бадыраң (badırang)
4. кыяр (kıyar)
5. hıyar
6. хыяр hyÿar
7. ‫تەرخەمەك‬ (tärkhämäk)
8. бодринг bodring

**cultivation** *ag. n.*
1. јетишдирмә yetişdirmә
2. культивация (kultivatsiya)
3. культивация (kultivatsiya)
4. культивациялэу (kultivatsiyaläü)
5. tarım
6. экин экме ekin ekme
7. ‫تېرىقچىلىق‬ (teriqchiliq)
8. дехқончилик dehqonchilik

**culture** *n.*
1. мәдәнијјәт mәdәniyyәt
2. мәдениет (mädeniyet)
3. маданият (madaniyat)
4. мәдәният (mädäniyat)
5. kültür
6. медениет medeniyet
7. ‫مەدەنيەت‬ (mädäniyät)
8. маданият madaniyat

**cup** *cul. n.*
1. финчан fincan
2. шыныаяқ (shınıayaq)
3. чыны аяк (chını ayak)
4. чынаяк (chınayak)
5. fincan
6. чашка çaşka
7. ‫پىيالە‬ (piyalä)
8. пиёла piyola

**cupboard** *n.*
1. долаб dolab
2. шкаф (shkaf)
3. шкаф (shkaf)
4. шкаф (shkaf)
5. dolap
6. шкаф şkaf
7. ‫ئىشكاپ‬ (ishkap)
8. шкаф shkaf

**cure** *med. v.*
1. мүаличә ет- müalicә et-
2. емде- (yemde-)
3. дарыла- (darıla-)
4. дәвала- (dävala-)
5. tedavi et-
6. бежер- bejer-
7. ‫داۋالا‬ (davala-)
8. давола- davola-

**cure** *med. n.*
1. мүаличә müalicә
2. ем (yem)
3. эм (em)
4. дәвалау (dävalau)
5. tedavi
6. эм em
7. ‫داۋالاش‬ (davalash)
8. даволаш davolash

**currency** *econ. n.*
1. пул pul
2. ақша (aqsha)
3. акча (akcha)
4. акча (akcha)
5. para
6. пул pul
7. ‫پۇل‬ (pul)
8. пул pul

**curtain** *n.*
1. пәрдә pәrdә
2. перде (perde)
3. парда (parda)
4. пәрдә (pärdä)
5. perde
6. перде perde
7. ‫پەردە‬ (pärdä)
8. парда parda

**cushion** *n.*
1. јастығ yastıq
2. жастық (zhastıq)
3. жастык (jastık)
4. мендәр (mendär)
5. minder
6. яссык ÿassyk
7. ‫كۆرپە‬ (körpä)
8. кўрпача ko'rpacha

1. Azerbaijani  2. Kazakh  3. Kyrgyz  4. Tatar  5. Turkish  6. Turkmen  7. Uighur  8. Uzbek

## custom *n.*
1. адәт adət
2. әдет-ғұрып (ädet-ghurıp)
3. урп-адат (urp-adat)
4. гореф-гадәт (goref-gadät)
5. gelenek
6. дәп-дессур däp-dessur
7. ‎عادەت (adät)
8. урф-одат urf-odat

## customer *n.*
1. мүштәри müştəri
2. сатып алушы (satıp aluwshı)
3. сатып алуучу (satıp aluuchu)
4. сатып алучы (satıp aluchı)
5. müşteri
6. мүшдери müşderi
7. ‎خریدار (kheridar)
8. харидор xaridor

## customs *n.*
1. көмрүк gömrük
2. таможня (tamozhnya)
3. бажыкана (bajıkana)
4. таможня (tamozhnya)
5. gümrük
6. гүмрүк gümrük
7. ‎تاموژنا (tamozhna)
8. божхона bojxona

## cut *v.*
1. кәс- kəs-
2. кес- (kes-)
3. кес- (kes-)
4. кис- (kis-)
5. kes-
6. кес- kes-
7. ‎کەس (käs-)
8. кес- kes-

## dagger *n.*
1. хәнчәр xəncər
2. қанжар (qanzhar)
3. канжар (kanjar)
4. хәнҗәр (khänjär)
5. hançer
6. гама gama
7. ‎خنجر (khänjär)
8. ханжар xanjar

## daisy *bot. n.*
1. гызчичәји qızçiçəyi
2. ромашка (romashka)
3. ромашка (romashka)
4. ак чәчәк (ak chächäk)
5. papatya
6. маргаритка margaritka
7. ‎دە ستارگۆل (dästargül)
8. дасторгул dastorgul

## dam *n.*
1. бәнд bənd
2. бөгет (böget)
3. бөгөт (bögöt)
4. буа (bua)
5. baraj
6. бент bent
7. ‎توسما (tosma)
8. тўғон to'g'on

## damage *n.*
1. зијан ziyan
2. зиян (ziyan)
3. зыян (zıyan)
4. зыян (zıyan)
5. ziyan
6. зыян zyÿan
7. ‎زیان (ziyan)
8. зиён ziyon

## damp *adj.*
1. нәм nəm
2. дымқыл (dımqıl)
3. нымдуу (nımduu)
4. дымлы (dımlı)
5. nemli
6. чыглы çygly
7. ‎نەم (näm)
8. нам nam

## dance *v.*
1. рәгс ет- rəqs et-
2. биле- (biyle-)
3. бийле- (biyle-)
4. би- (bi-)
5. dans et-
6. танс әт- tans et-
7. ‎ئۇسسۇل ئۇينا (ussul oyna-)
8. рақсга туш- raqsga tush-

## dancer *n.*
1. рәггас(ә) rəqqas[ə]
2. биши (biyshi)
3. бийчи (biychi)
4. биюче (biyuche)
5. dansör, dansöz
6. тансчы tansçy
7. ‎ئۇسسۇلچی (ussulchi)
8. рақкос(а) raqqos(a)

## danger *n.*
1. тәһлүкә təhlükə
2. қауіп (qawip)
3. коркунуч (korkunuch)
4. хәтәр (khätär)
5. tehlike
6. ховп howp
7. ‎خەتر (khätär)
8. хавф xavf

---

## dangerous *adj.*
1. тәһлүкәли təhlükəli
2. қауіпті (qawipti)
3. коркунучтуу (korkunuchtuu)
4. хәтәрле (khätärle)
5. tehlikeli
6. ховплы howply
7. خەتەرلىك (khätärlik)
8. хавфли xavfli

## dark (=with no light) *adj.*
1. гаранлыг qaranlıq
2. қараңғы (qarangghı)
3. караңгы (karanggı)
4. караңгы (karanggı)
5. karanlık
6. гараңкы garañky
7. قاراڭغۇ (qarangghu)
8. қоронғи qorong'i

## darkness *n.*
1. гаранлыг qaranlıq
2. қараңғылық (qarangghılıq)
3. караңгылык (karanggılık)
4. караңгылык (karanggılık)
5. karanlık
6. гараңкылык garañkylyk
7. قاراڭغۇلۇق (qarangghuluq)
8. қоронғилик qorong'ilik

## data *n.*
1. мә'лумат mə'lumat
2. мәлімет (mälimet)
3. маалымат (maalımat)
4. мәгълүматлар (mäg'lümatlar)
5. veri
6. маглуматлар maglumatlar
7. مەلۇمات (mälumat)
8. маълумот ma'lumot

## date *bot. n.*
1. хурма xurma
2. құрма (qurma)
3. курма (kurma)
4. хөрмә (khörmä)
5. hurma
6. хурма hurma
7. خورما (khorma)
8. хурмо xurmo

## date (*time) *n.*
1. тарих tarix
2. уақыт (waqıt)
3. дата (data)
4. тарих (tarikh)
5. tarih
6. сене sene
7. ۋاقىت (vaqit)
8. сана sana

## daughter *n.*
1. гыз qiz
2. қыз (qız)
3. кыз (kız)
4. кыз (kız)
5. kız
6. гыз gyz
7. قىز (qiz)
8. қиз qiz

## dawn *n.*
1. дан dan
2. таң (tang)
3. таң (tang)
4. таң (tang)
5. tan
6. даң dañ
7. تاڭ (tang)
8. тонг tong

## day *n.*
1. күн gün
2. күн (kün)
3. күн (kün)
4. көн (kön)
5. gün
6. гүн gün
7. كۈن (kün)
8. кун kun

## daytime *n.*
1. күндүз gündüz
2. күндіз (kündiz)
3. күндүз (kündüz)
4. көндез (köndez)
5. gündüz
6. гүндиз gündiz
7. كۈندۈز (kündüz)
8. кундуз kunduz

## dead (x alive) *adj.*
1. өлу ölü
2. өлік (ölik)
3. өлүк (ölük)
4. үле (üle)
5. ölü
6. өли öli
7. ئۆلۈك (ölük)
8. ўлик o'lik

## deaf *adj.*
1. кар kar
2. керең (kereng)
3. дүлөй (dülöy)
4. саңгырау (sanggırau)
5. sağır
6. кер ker
7. پاڭ (pang)
8. гаранг garang

---

1. Azerbaijani   2. Kazakh   3. Kyrgyz   4. Tatar   5. Turkish   6. Turkmen   7. Uighur   8. Uzbek

## deafness  *n.*
1. карлыг karlıq
2. керендік (kerengdik)
3. дүлөйлүк (dülöylük)
4. саңгыраулык (sanggıraulık)
5. sağırlık
6. керлик kerlik
7. پاڭلىق (pangliq)
8. гаранглик garanglik

## dear  *adj.*
1. севимли sevimli
2. қымбатты (qımbattı)
3. кымбаттуу (kımbattuu)
4. газиз (gaziz)
5. sevgili
6. әзиз eziz
7. قەدىرلىك (qädirlik)
8. азиз aziz

## death  *n.*
1. өлүм ölüm
2. өлім (ölim)
3. өлүм (ölüm)
4. улем (ülem)
5. ölüm
6. өлүм ölüm
7. ئۆلۈم (ölüm)
8. ўлим o'lim

## debt  *n.*
1. борч borc
2. қарыз (qarız)
3. карыз (karız)
4. бурыч (burıch)
5. borç
6. берги bergi
7. قەرز (qärz)
8. қарз qarz

## December  *n.*
1. декабр dekabr
2. желтоқсан (zheltoqsan)
3. декабрь (dekabr')
4. декабрь (dekabr')
5. aralık
6. декабрь dekabr
7. دېكابر (dekabr)
8. декабрь dekabr'

## decide  *v.*
1. гәрара кәл- qərara gəl-
2. ұйғар- (uyghar-)
3. чеч- (chech-)
4. карар ит- (karar it-)
5. karar ver-
6. карара гел- karara gel-
7. قارار قىل (qarar qil-)
8. қарор қил- qaror qil-

## decision  *n.*
1. гәрар qərar
2. шешім (sheshim)
3. чечим (chechim)
4. карар (karar)
5. karar
6. карар karar
7. قارار (qarar)
8. қарор qaror

## decrease  *vi.*
1. азал- azal-
2. азай- (azay-)
3. азай- (azay-)
4. ким- (kim-)
5. azal-
6. азал- azal-
7. ئازاي (azay-)
8. камай- kamay-

## deep  *adj.*
1. дәрин dərin
2. терең (tereng)
3. терең (tereng)
4. тирән (tirän)
5. derin
6. чуңңур çuññur
7. چوڭغۇر (chongqur)
8. чуқур chuqur

## deer  *zool. n.*
1. марал maral
2. бұғы (bughı)
3. бугу (bugu)
4. болан (bolan)
5. geyik
6. кейик keyik
7. بۇغا (bugha)
8. буғу bug'u

## defeat  *v.*
1. мәглуб ет- məğlub et-
2. жең- (zheng-)
3. жең- (jeng-)
4. җиң- (jing-)
5. yen-
6. ең- yeñ-
7. يەڭ (yäng-)
8. тор-мор қил- tor-mor qil-

## defeat  *n.*
1. мәглубијјәт məğlubiyyət
2. жеңіліс (zhengilis)
3. жеңилүү (jengilüü)
4. җиңелу (jingelü)
5. yenilgi
6. еңлиш yeñliş
7. مەغلۇبىيەت (mäghlubiyät)
8. мағлубият mag'lubiyat

---

1. Azerbaijani  2. Kazakh  3. Kyrgyz  4. Tatar  5. Turkish  6. Turkmen  7. Uighur  8. Uzbek

## defend   v.

1. мүдафиә ет- müdafiə et-
2. қорға- (qorgha-)
3. корго- (korgo-)
4. сақла- (sakla-)
5. savun-
6. гора- gora-
7. مۇداپىئە قىل‍ـ (mudapi'ä qil-)
8. ҳимоя қил himoya qil-

## defense   n.

1. мүдафиә müdafiə
2. қорғау (qorghaw)
3. коргонуу (korgonuu)
4. оборона (oborona)
5. savunma
6. горанма goranma
7. مۇداپىئە (mudapi'ä)
8. мудофаа mudofaa

## degree   (=measurement of heat)   n.

1. дәрәчә dərəcə
2. градус (gradus)
3. градус (gradus)
4. градус (gradus)
5. derece
6. градус gradus
7. گرادۇس (gradus)
8. даража daraja

## delay   n.

1. jубанма yubanma
2. кейінге қалу (keyinge qaluw)
3. кармалуу (karmaluu)
4. соңа калу (songa kalu)
5. gecikme
6. эгленме eglenme
7. كېچىكىش (kechikish)
8. кечиктириш kechiktirish

## delicious   adj.

1. ләззәтли ləzzətli
2. дәмди (dämdi)
3. даамдуу (daamduu)
4. тәмле (tämle)
5. lezzetli
6. тагамлы tagamly
7. تەملىك (tämlik)
8. мазали mazali

## democracy   pol. n.

1. демократиja demokratiya
2. демократия (demokratiya)
3. демократия (demokratiya)
4. демокрая (demokratiya)
5. demokrasi
6. демократия demokratiÿa
7. دېموكراتىيە (demokratiyä)
8. демократия demokratiya

## demon   rel. n.

1. шеjтан şeytan
2. демон (demon)
3. демон (demon)
4. иблис (iblis)
5. şeytan
6. шейтан şeÿtan
7. شەيتان (shäytan)
8. иблис iblis

## demonstration   pol. n.

1. нүмаjиш nümayiş
2. демонстрация (demonstratsiya)
3. демонстрация (demonstratsiya)
4. демонстрация (demonstratsiya)
5. gösteri
6. демонстрация demonstratsiÿa
7. نامايىش (namayish)
8. намойиш namoyish

## dentist   n.

1. диш һәкими diş həkimi
2. тіс дәрігері (tis därigeri)
3. тиш дарыгери (tish darıgeri)
4. теш врачы (tesh vrachı)
5. dişçi
6. диш догторы diş dogtory
7. چىش دوختۇرى (chish dokhturi)
8. тиш доктори tish doktori

## deny   v.

1. инкар ет- inkar et-
2. мойындама- (moyındama-)
3. тан- (tan-)
4. инкярь ит- (inkyar' it-)
5. inkar et-
6. инкәр эт- inkär et-
7. ئىنكار قىل‍ـ (inkar qil-)
8. инкор қил- inkor qil-

## depart   v.

1. jола дүш- yola düş-
2. кет- (ket-)
3. кет- (ket-)
4. кит- (kit-)
5. kalk-
6. угра- ugra-
7. يولغا چىق‍ـ (yolgha chiq-)
8. жүнаб кет- jo'nab ket-

## department   n.

1. шө'бә şö'bə
2. бөлім (bölim)
3. бөлүм (bölüm)
4. бүлек (bülek)
5. bölüm
6. бөлүм bölüm
7. بۆلۈم (bölüm)
8. бўлим bo'lim

---

## department store *n.*
1. универмаг univermaq
2. универмаг (univermag)
3. универмаг (univermag)
4. универмаг (univermag)
5. büyük mağaza
6. универмаг uniwermag
7. سودا سارای (soda saray)
8. универмаг univermag

## departure *n.*
1. јола дүшмә yola düşmə
2. кету (ketuw)
3. кетүү (ketüü)
4. киту (kitü)
5. kalkış
6. уграма, гитме
   ugrama, gitme
7. يولغا چىقىش
   (yolgha chiqish)
8. жўнаб кетиш jo'nab ketish

## depth *n.*
1. дәринлик dərinlik
2. терендік (terengdik)
3. терендик (terengdik)
4. тирәнлек (tiränlek)
5. derinlik
6. чуңлук çuñluk
7. چوڭقۇرلۇق (chongqurluq)
8. чуқурлик chuqurlik

## describe *v.*
1. тәсвир ет- təsvir et-
2. суретте- (suwrette-)
3. сүрөттө- (süröttö-)
4. тасвирла- (tasvirla-)
5. tarif et-
6. бәян эт- beÿan et-
7. تەسۋىرلە (täsvirlä-)
8. тасвирла- tasvirla-

## description *n.*
1. тәсвир təsvir
2. суреттеу (suwrettew)
3. сүрөттөө (süröttöö)
4. тасвирлау (tasvirlau)
5. tasvir
6. васп этме wasp etme
7. تەسۋىر (täsvir)
8. тасвирлаш tasvirlash

## desert *geo. n.*
1. чөллүк çöllük
2. шөл (shöl)
3. чөл (chöl)
4. чүл (chül)
5. çöl
6. чөл çöl
7. چۆل-بايا ۋان (chöl-bayavan)
8. чўл cho'l

## desire *n.*
1. арзу arzu
2. қалау (qalaw)
3. каалоо (kaaloo)
4. теләк (teläk)
5. arzu
6. арзув arzuw
7. ئارزۇ (arzu)
8. хохиш xohish

## desk *n.*
1. парта parta
2. парта (parta)
3. парта (parta)
4. парта (parta)
5. sıra
6. парта parta
7. پارتا (parta)
8. парта parta

## dessert *cul. n.*
1. ширнијјат şirniyyat
2. тәтті тағам (tätti tagham)
3. таттуу тамак
   (tattuu tamak)
4. десерт (desert)
5. tatlı
6. десерт desert
7. تاتلىق يېمەكلىك
   (tatliq yemäklik)
8. ширинлик shirinlik

## destroy *v.*
1. дағыт- dağıt-
2. бұз- (buz-)
3. кыйрат- (kıyrat-)
4. җимер- (jimer-)
5. tahrip et-
6. йык- ÿyk-
7. بۇز- (buz-)
8. буз- buz-

## development *n.*
1. инкишаф inkişaf
2. даму (damuw)
3. өнүгүү (önügüü)
4. алга барыш (alga barısh)
5. gelişme
6. өсүш ösüş
7. راۋاجلىنىش (ravajlinish)
8. ривожланиш rivojlanish

## diamond *geo. n.*
1. ромб romb
2. ромбы (rombı)
3. ромб (romb)
4. ромб (romb)
5. baklava biçimi
6. ромб romb
7. ئالماس (almas)
8. ромб romb

---

**diarrhea** *med. n.*
1. исһал ishal
2. iш өту (ish ötuw)
3. ич өтүү (ich ötüü)
4. эч киту (ech kitü)
5. ishal
6. ичгечме içgeçme
7. ئـچ سـۇرۇش (ich sürüsh)
8. ич кетиш ich ketish

**dictionary** *n.*
1. лүғәт lüğət
2. сөздiк (sözdik)
3. сөздүк (sözdük)
4. сүзлек (süzlek)
5. sözlük
6. сөзлук sözlük
7. لۇغـت (lughät)
8. луғат lug'at

**die** *v.*
1. өл- öl-
2. өл- (öl-)
3. өл- (öl-)
4. үл- (ül-)
5. öl-
6. өл- öl-
7. ئۆل_ (öl-)
8. ўл- o'l-

**difference** *n.*
1. фәрг fərq
2. айырма (ayırma)
3. айырма (ayırma)
4. аерымлык (aerımlık)
5. fark
6. тапавут tapawut
7. پـەرق (pärq)
8. фарқ farq

**different** *adj.*
1. фәргли fərqli
2. басқа (basqa)
3. башка (bashka)
4. башка (bashka)
5. farklı
6. үйтгешик üytgeşik
7. پـەرقلىك (pärqlik)
8. турли turli

**difficult** *adj.*
1. чәтин çətin
2. қиын (qiyın)
3. кыйын (kıyın)
4. авыр (avır)
5. zor
6. кын kyn
7. تـەس (täs)
8. қийин qiyin

**dig** *v.*
1. газы- qazı-
2. қаз- (qaz-)
3. каз- (kaz-)
4. каз- (kaz-)
5. kaz-
6. газ- gaz-
7. قـاز (qaz-)
8. ковла- kovla-

**diligent** *adj.*
1. чалышган çalışqan
2. ықыласты (ıqılastı)
3. адептүү (adeptüü)
4. хезмәт сөючән
   (khezmät söyuchän)
5. çalışkan
6. ыхласлы yhlasly
7. تـرىـشچـان (tirishchan)
8. тиришқоқ tirishqoq

**dining room** *n.*
1. jeмәк отағы yemək otağı
2. ас iшетiн бөлме
   (as ishetin bölme)
3. ашкана (ashkana)
4. аш бүлмәсе (ash bülmäse)
5. yemek odası
6. наһар ийилйән отаг
   nahar iyilyän otag
7. تـامـاق يـەيـيـدىغـان ئـۆي
   (tamaq yeyidighan öy)
8. ошхона oshxona

**dinner** *n.*
1. наһар nahar
2. кешкі ас (keshki as)
3. кечки тамак
   (kechki tamak)
4. кичке аш (kichke ash)
5. akşam yemeği
6. агшамлык наһар
   agşamlyk nahar
7. كـەچكى تـامـاق (kächki tamaq)
8. кечки овқат kechki ovqat

**diploma** *n.*
1. диплом diplom
2. диплом (diplom)
3. диплом (diplom)
4. диплом (diplom)
5. diploma
6. диплом diplom
7. دىپلوم (diplom)
8. диплом diplom

**direction** (~way) *n.*
1. истигамәт istiqamət
2. бағыт (baghıt)
3. бағыт (bagıt)
4. як (yak)
5. yön
6. угур ugur
7. يـۆنـىلـىش (yönilish)
8. йўналиш yo'nalish

---

**dirty** *adj.*
1. чирк(ли) çirk[li]
2. лас (las)
3. кир (kir)
4. пычрак (pıchrak)
5. kirli
6. хапа hapa
7. پاسكنا (paskina)
8. ифлос iflos

**disappear** *v.*
1. jox ол- yox ol-
2. жоғал- (zhoghal-)
3. жогол- (jogol-)
4. югал- (yugal-)
5. kaybol-
6. гөздэн гайып бол- gözden gaÿyp bol-
7. يوقال (yoqal-)
8. йўкол- yo'qol-

**discount** *econ. n.*
1. күзэшт güzəşt
2. арзандату (arzandatuw)
3. арзандатуу (arzandatuu)
4. төшеру (tösherü)
5. indirim
6. арзанлатма arzanlatma
7. باهاسنى چۈشۈرۈش (bahasini chüshürüsh)
8. арзонлаштириш arzonlashtirish

**discover** *v.*
1. кэшф ет- kəşf et-
2. аш- (ash-)
3. ач- (ach-)
4. ач- (ach-)
5. keşfet-
6. тап- tap-
7. كەشپ قىل (käshp qil-)
8. кашф кил- kashf qil-

**discussion** *n.*
1. мүзакирэ müzakirə
2. талқылау (talqılaw)
3. талкылоо (talkıloo)
4. моназара (monazara)
5. müzakere
6. маслахатлашма maslahatlaşma
7. مۇزاكىرە (muzakirä)
8. музокара muzokara

**disgust** *n.*
1. нифрэт nifrət
2. жийркену (zhiyirkenuw)
3. жийиркенүү (jiyirkenüü)
4. нэфрэт (näfrät)
5. nefret
6. йигренч ÿigrenç
7. نەپرەت (näprät)
8. нафрат nafrat

**dish** (=meal) *n.*
1. jемэк yemək
2. тамак (tamaq)
3. тамак (tamak)
4. ашамлык (ashamlık)
5. yemek
6. нахар nahar
7. تائام (ta'am)
8. таом taom

**dish** (=plate) *n.*
1. бошгаб boşqab
2. табак (tabaq)
3. тарелка (tarelka)
4. тэлинкэ (tälinkä)
5. tabak
6. межме mejme
7. تەخسە (tähsä)
8. идиш idish

**dishwasher** *n.*
1. габjyjан машын qabyuyan maşın
2. ыдыс жуғыш (ıdıs zhuwghısh)
3. идиш жуугуч (idish juuguch)
4. савыт юучы машина (savıt yuuchı mashina)
5. bulaşık makinesi
6. гап-гач ювма машыны gap-gaç ÿuwma maşyny
7. قاچا يۇيۇش ماشىنسى (qacha yuyush mashinisi)
8. идиш ювадиган машина idish yuvadigan mashina

**distance** *n.*
1. мэсафэ məsafə
2. ара қашықтық (ara qashıqtıq)
3. аралык (aralık)
4. ара (ara)
5. mesafe
6. аралык aralyk
7. ئارىلىق (ariliq)
8. масофа masofa

**distribute** *v.*
1. паjла- payla-
2. бөл- (böl-)
3. бөл- (böl-)
4. бүл- (bül-)
5. paylaştır-
6. пайла- paÿla-
7. تەقسىم قىل (täqsim qil-)
8. тақсимла- taqsimla-

## disturb *v.*
1. нараһат ет- narahat et-
2. бҰз- (buz-)
3. буз- (buz-)
4. тынычсызла-
   (tınıchsızla-)
5. rahatsız et-
6. ынжалыксызландыр-
   ynjalyksyzlandyr-
7. ناۋ اره قلــ (avarä qil-)
8. безовта қил- bezovta qil-

## dive *v.*
1. баш вур- baş vur-
2. сҮңгі- (sünggi-)
3. сҮңгҮ- (sünggü-)
4. чум- (chum-)
5. dal-
6. чҮм- çüm-
7. شۇكگنو (shungghu-)
8. шӰнғи- sho'ng'i-

## divide *v.*
1. бөл- böl-
2. бөл- (böl-)
3. бөл- (böl-)
4. бҮл- (bül-)
5. böl-
6. бөл- böl-
7. بزل (böl-)
8. бӱл- bo'l-

## division *math. n.*
1. бөлмә bölmə
2. бөлу (böluw)
3. бөлу (bölü)
4. бҮлу (bülü)
5. bölme
6. бөлмек bölmek
7. بزلزش (bölüsh)
8. бӱлиш bo'lish

## divorce *n.*
1. бошанма boşanma
2. ажырасу (azhırasuw)
3. ажырашуу (ajırashuu)
4. аерылышу (ayerılıshu)
5. boşanma
6. айрылма aÿrylma
7. ناجرــشــش (ajrishish)
8. ажралиш ajralish

## divorce *vi.*
1. бошан- boşan-
2. ажырас- (azhıras-)
3. ажыраш- (ajırash-)
4. аерыл- (ayerıl-)
5. boşan-
6. айрылыш- aÿrylyş-
7. ناجراشــ (ajrash-)
8. ажраш- ajrash-

## do *v.*
1. ет- et-
2. қыл- (qıl-)
3. кыл- (kıl-)
4. кыл- (kıl-)
5. yap-
6. эт- et-
7. قلــ (qil-)
8. қил- qil-

## doctor *med. n.*
1. һәким həkim
2. дәрігер (däriger)
3. дарыгер (darıger)
4. доктор (doktor)
5. doktor
6. врач wraç
7. دوختۇر (dokhtur)
8. доктор doktor

## dog *zool. n.*
1. ит it
2. ит (iyt)
3. ит (it)
4. эт (et)
5. köpek
6. ит it
7. ىت (it)
8. ит it

## donkey *zool. n.*
1. ешшәк eşşək
2. есек (yesek)
3. әшек (eshek)
4. ишәк (ishäk)
5. eşek
6. әшек eşek
7. ىشهك (eshäk)
8. эшак eshak

## door *n.*
1. гапы qapı
2. есік (yesik)
3. эшик (eshik)
4. ишек (ishek)
5. kapı
6. гапы gapy
7. ىشىك (ishik)
8. эшик eshik

## doubt *n.*
1. шҮбһә şübhə
2. кҮмән (kümän)
3. шектенҮҮ (shektenüü)
4. шөбһә (shöbhä)
5. şüphe
6. шубхе şübhe
7. گۇمان (guman)
8. шубха shubha

---

**down** *adv.*
1. ашағы aşağı
2. төмен (tömen)
3. төмөн (tömön)
4. түбән (tübän)
5. aşağı
6. ашак aşak
7. تۆۋەن (tövän)
8. паст past

**dozen** *n.*
1. дүжүн düjün
2. дюжина (dyuzhiyna)
3. он эки дана (on eki dana)
4. дюжина (dyuzhina)
5. düzine
6. он ики on iki
7. دوژنا (dozhna)
8. дюжина dyujina

**drama** *art. n.*
1. драм әсәри dram әsәri
2. драма (drama)
3. драма (drama)
4. драма (drama)
5. piyes
6. пьеса piyesa
7. دراما (drama)
8. драма drama

**drawing** *art. n.*
1. шәкил şәkil
2. сызу (sızuw)
3. сызуу (sızuu)
4. сызым (sızım)
5. çizim
6. сурат чекме surat çekme
7. ره سم (räsim)
8. чизиш chizish

**dream** *n.*
1. jyxy yuxu
2. түс (tüs)
3. түш (tüsh)
4. төш (tösh)
5. rüya
6. дүйш düÿş
7. چۈش (chüsh)
8. туш tush

**dress** *clo. n.*
1. палтар paltar
2. көйлек (köylek)
3. кийим (kiyim)
4. күлмәк (külmäk)
5. elbise
6. аял көйнеги aÿal köynegi
7. ئاياللار كىيىمى (ayallar kiyimi)
8. кўйлак ko'ylak

**drill** *tech. n.*
1. бурғу burğu
2. бұрғы (burghı)
3. бургу (burgu)
4. борау (borau)
5. matkap
6. бурав buraw
7. بۇرغا (burgha)
8. пармадаста parmadasta

**drink** *v.*
1. ич- iç-
2. іш- (ish-)
3. ич- (ich-)
4. эч- (ech-)
5. iç-
6. ич- iç-
7. ئىچ (ich-)
8. ич- ich-

**drink** (*alcoholic) *n.*
1. ички içki
2. ішімдік (ishimdik)
3. ичимдик (ichimdik)
4. исерткеч әчемлек (isertkech echemlek)
5. içki
6. ичги içgi
7. هاراق (haraq)
8. спиртли ичимлик spirtli ichimlik

**drive** *v.*
1. сүр- sür-
2. айда- (ayda-)
3. айда- (ayda-)
4. йөрт- (yört-)
5. sür-
6. сүр- sür-
7. ھەيدە (häydä-)
8. хайда- hayda-

**driver** *n.*
1. сүрүчү sürücü
2. шофёр (shofyor)
3. айдоочу (aydoochu)
4. шофер (shofyer)
5. sürücü
6. шофёр şofÿor
7. شوپۇر (shopur)
8. хайдовчи haydovchi

**drop** (*of liquid) *n.*
1. дамчы damcı
2. тамшы (tamshı)
3. тамчы (tamchı)
4. тамчы (tamchı)
5. damla
6. дамжа damja
7. تامچ (tamchä)
8. томчи tomchi

---

**drought** *n.*
1. гураглыг quraqlıq
2. құрғақшылық (qurghaqshılıq)
3. кургакчылык (kurgakchılık)
4. корылык (korılık)
5. kuraklık
6. гуракчылык gurakçylyk
7. قۇرغاقچىلىق (qurghaqchiliq)
8. қурғоқчилик qurg'oqchilik

**drown** *vi.*
1. боғул- boğul-
2. бат- (bat-)
3. чөгүп кет- (chögüp ket-)
4. бат- (bat-)
5. boğul-
6. гарк бол- gark bol-
7. چۆك- (chök-)
8. чўк- cho'k-

**drug** *med. n.*
1. дәрман dərman
2. дәрі (däri)
3. дары (darı)
4. дару (daru)
5. ilaç
6. дерман derman
7. دورا (dora)
8. дори dori

**drunk** *adj.*
1. мәст məst
2. мас (mas)
3. мас (mas)
4. исерек (iserek)
5. sarhoş
6. серхош serhoş
7. مەست (mäst)
8. маст mast

**dry** *adj.*
1. гуру quru
2. құрғақ (qurghaq)
3. кургак (kurgak)
4. коры (korı)
5. kuru
6. гуры gury
7. قۇرۇق (quruq)
8. қуруқ quruq

**dry** *vi.*
1. гуру- quru-
2. құрға- (qurgha-)
3. кургa- (kurga-)
4. кор- (kor-)
5. kuru-
6. гура- gura-
7. قۇرۇ- (quru-)
8. қури- quri-

**duck** *zool. n.*
1. өрдәк ördək
2. үйрек (üyrek)
3. өрдөк (ördök)
4. үрдәк (ürdäk)
5. ördek
6. өрдек ördek
7. ئۆردەك (ördäk)
8. ўрдак o'rdak

**dusk** *n.*
1. торанлыг toranlıq
2. ымырт (ımırt)
3. күүгүм (küügüm)
4. әнгер-менгер (engger-mengger)
5. akşam karanlığı
6. инрик iňrik
7. گۈگۈم (gügüm)
8. оқшом oqshom

**dust** *n.*
1. тоз toz
2. шаң (shang)
3. чаң (chang)
4. тузан (tuzan)
5. toz
6. тозан tozan
7. چاڭ توزان (chang-tozan)
8. чанг chang

**duty** (=task) *n.*
1. вэзифэ vəzifə
2. міндет (mindet)
3. милдет (mildet)
4. бурыч (burıch)
5. görev
6. везипе wezipe
7. ۋەزىپە (väzipä)
8. бурч burch

**dye** *vt.*
1. боja- boya-
2. боя- (boya-)
3. боё- (boyo-)
4. буя- (buya-)
5. boya-
6. боя- boÿa-
7. بويا- (boya-)
8. бўя- bo'ya-

**eagle** *zool. n.*
1. гартал qartal
2. бүркіт (bürkit)
3. бүркүт (bürküt)
4. бөркет (börket)
5. kartal
6. бүргүт bürgüt
7. بۈركۈت (bürküt)
8. бургут burgut

**ear** *phys. n.*
1. гулаг qulaq
2. қ¥лақ (qulaq)
3. кулак (kulak)
4. колак (kolak)
5. kulak
6. гулак gulak
7. قولاق (qulaq)
8. қулоқ quloq

**early** *adv.*
1. еркән erkən
2. ерте (yerte)
3. әрте (erte)
4. иртә (irtä)
5. erken
6. ир ir
7. ەرتىگن (ätigän)
8. эрта erta

**earth** (=the world) *n.*
1. јер yer
2. жер (zher)
3. жер (jer)
4. җир (jir)
5. dünya
6. ер ÿer
7. يەر شارى (yär shari)
8. ер yer

**earth** (~soil) *n.*
1. торпаг torpaq
2. топырак (topıraq)
3. топурак (topurak)
4. туфрак (tufrak)
5. toprak
6. топрак toprak
7. توپراق (tupraq)
8. тупроқ tuproq

**earthquake** *n.*
1. зәлзәлә zəlzələ
2. жер сілкініс (zher silkinis)
3. жер титирөө (jer titiröö)
4. җир тетрәу (jir teträü)
5. deprem
6. ер титремеси
   ÿer titremesi
7. يەر تەۋرەش (yär tävräsh)
8. ер қимирлаш
   yer qimirlash

**east** *n.*
1. шәрг şərq
2. шығыс (shıghıs)
3. чыгыш (chıgısh)
4. көнчыгыш (könchıgısh)
5. doğu
6. гүндогар gündogar
7. شەرق (shärq)
8. шарқ sharq

**easy** *adj.*
1. асан asan
2. оңай (ongay)
3. оңой (ongoy)
4. ансат (ansat)
5. kolay
6. аңсат añsat
7. ئاسان (asan)
8. осон oson

**eat** *v.*
1. је- ye-
2. же- (zhe-)
3. же- (je-)
4. аша- (asha-)
5. ye-
6. ий- iÿ-
7. يە- (yä-)
8. е- ye-

**economics** *n.*
1. игтисадијјат iqtisadiyyat
2. экономика (ekonomika)
3. экономика (ekonomika)
4. экономика (ekonomika)
5. ekonomi
6. экономика ekonomika
7. ئىقتىساد (iqtisad)
8. иқтисод iqtisod

**edge** *n.*
1. кәнар kənar
2. шет (shet)
3. чет (chet)
4. чит (chit)
5. kenar
6. гыра gyra
7. چەت (chät)
8. қирра qirra

**education** *n.*
1. тәһсил təhsil
2. білім (bilim)
3. билим (bilim)
4. тәрбия (tärbiya)
5. eğitim
6. билим bilim
7. تەلىم-تەربىيە (tälim-tärbiyä)
8. таълим ta'lim

**effect** *n.*
1. тә'сир tə'sir
2. әсер (äser)
3. таасир (taasir)
4. тәэсир (täesir)
5. etki
6. тәсир täsir
7. تەسىر (täsir)
8. таъсир ta'sir

---

1. Azerbaijani   2. Kazakh   3. Kyrgyz   4. Tatar   5. Turkish   6. Turkmen   7. Uighur   8. Uzbek

**egg** *cul. n.*
1. jумурта yumurta
2. жұмыртқа (zhumırtqa)
3. жумуртка (jumurtka)
4. йомырка (yomırka)
5. yumurta
6. юмуртга ÿumurtga
7. تۇخۇم (tukhum)
8. тухум tuxum

**eggplant** *bot. n.*
1. бадымчан badımcan
2. баклажан (baklazhan)
3. баклажан (baklajan)
4. баклажан (baklazhan)
5. patlıcan
6. бадамжан badamjan
7. چەيزە (chäyzä)
8. баклажон baqlajon

**eight** *num.*
1. сәккиз səkkiz
2. сегіз (segiz)
3. сегиз (segiz)
4. сигез (sigez)
5. sekiz
6. секиз sekiz
7. سەككىز (säkkiz)
8. саккиз sakkiz

**eighteen** *num.*
1. он сәккиз on səkkiz
2. он сегіз (on segiz)
3. он сегиз (on segiz)
4. унсигез (unsigez)
5. on sekiz
6. он секиз on sekiz
7. ئون سەككىز (on säkkiz)
8. ўн саккиз o'n sakkiz

**eighty** *num.*
1. сәксән səksən
2. сексен (seksen)
3. сексен (seksen)
4. сиксән (siksän)
5. seksen
6. сегсен segsen
7. سەكسەن (säksän)
8. саксон sakson

**either ... or** *conj.*
1. ja ... ja (да) ya ... ya [da]
2. не ... не (ne ... ne)
3. же ... же (je ... je)
4. я ... я (ya ... ya)
5. ya ... ya [da]
6. я... я(-да) ÿa... ÿa [-da]
7. يا(كى)...يا(كى) (ya[ki] ... ya[ki])
8. ё ... ё yo ... yo

**elbow** *phys. n.*
1. дирсәк dirsək
2. шынтақ (shıntaq)
3. чыканак (chıkanak)
4. терсәк (tersäk)
5. dirsek
6. тирсек tirsek
7. جەينەك (jäynäk)
8. тирсак tirsak

**elect** *vt.*
1. сеч- seç-
2. сайла- (sayla-)
3. шайла- (shayla-)
4. сайла- (sayla-)
5. seç-
6. сайла- saÿla-
7. سايلا (sayla-)
8. сайла- sayla-

**election** *n.*
1. сечки seçki
2. сайлау (saylaw)
3. шайлоо (shayloo)
4. сайлау (saylau)
5. seçim
6. сайлав saÿlaw
7. سايلام (saylam)
8. сайлов saylov

**electricity** *n.*
1. електрик elektrik
2. электр (elektr)
3. электр (elektr)
4. электричество (elektrichestvo)
5. elektrik
6. электрик тогы elektrik togy
7. ئېلېكتر (elektr)
8. электр elektr

**elephant** *zool. n.*
1. фил fil
2. піл (pil)
3. пил (pil)
4. фил (fil)
5. fil
6. пил pil
7. پىل (pil)
8. фил fil

**elevator** *n.*
1. лифт lift
2. лифт (lift)
3. лифт (lift)
4. лифт (lift)
5. asansör
6. лифт lift
7. لىفت (lift)
8. лифт lift

## eleven *num.*
1. он бир on bir
2. он бір (on bir)
3. он бир (on bir)
4. унбер (unber)
5. on bir
6. он бир on bir
7. ئون بىر (on bir)
8. ўн бир o'n bir

## embrace *v.*
1. гучагла- qucaqla-
2. құшақта- (qushaqta-)
3. кучакта- (kuchakta-)
4. кочакла- (kochakla-)
5. kucakla-
6. гужакла- gujakla-
7. توچاتلا_ (quchaqla-)
8. қучоқла- quchoqla-

## empty *adj.*
1. бош boş
2. бос (bos)
3. бош (bosh)
4. буш (bush)
5. boş
6. бош boş
7. بوش (bosh)
8. бўш bo'sh

## empty *vt.*
1. бошалт- boşalt-
2. босат- (bosat-)
3. бошот- (boshot-)
4. бушат- (bushat-)
5. boşalt-
6. бошат- boşat-
7. بوشات_ (boshat-)
8. бўшат- bo'shat-

## end *n.*
1. сон son
2. соң (song)
3. соңку (songku)
4. соң (song)
5. son
6. соңы soñy
7. ئاخىر (akhir)
8. охир oxir

## enemy *mil. n.*
1. дүшмəн düşmən
2. жау (zhaw)
3. жоо (joo)
4. дошман (doshman)
5. düşman
6. душман duşman
7. دۇشمەن (düshmän)
8. душман dushman

## engine *tech. n.*
1. мотор motor
2. мотор (motor)
3. мотор (motor)
4. мотор (motor)
5. motor
6. мотор motor
7. ماتور (mator)
8. мотор motor

## engineer *n.*
1. мүһəндис mühəndis
2. инженер (inzhener)
3. инженер (injener)
4. инженер (inzhener)
5. mühendis
6. инженер inʃener
7. ئىنژېنېر (inzhener)
8. мухандис muxandis

## enjoy *v.*
1. зөвг ал- zövq al-
2. рақаттан- (raqattan-)
3. көңүл ач- (köngül ach-)
4. ləззəтлəн- (läzzätlän-)
5. zevk al-
6. хезил эт- hezil et-
7. هۇزۇرلان_ (huzurlan-)
8. роҳатлан- rohatlan-

## enmity *n.*
1. дүшмəнчилик düşmənçilik
2. дұшпандық (dushpandıq)
3. душмандык (dushmandık)
4. дошманлык (doshmanlık)
5. düşmanlık
6. душманчылык duşmançylyk
7. دۇشمەنلىك (düshmänlik)
8. душманлик dushmanlik

## enough *adv.*
1. кифајəт гəдəр kifayət qədər
2. жеткілікті (zhetkilikti)
3. жеткиликтүү (jetkiliktüü)
4. җитəрлек (jitärlek)
5. yeteri kadar
6. етерлик ẏeterlik
7. يېتەرلىك (yetärlik)
8. етарли yetarli

## enter *v.*
1. кир- gir-
2. кір- (kir-)
3. кир- (kir-)
4. кер- (ker-)
5. gir-
6. гир- gir-
7. كىر_ (kir-)
8. кир- kir-

---

1. Azerbaijani　2. Kazakh　3. Kyrgyz　4. Tatar　5. Turkish　6. Turkmen　7. Uighur　8. Uzbek

## entertainment  *n.*
1. әјләнчә әylәncә
2. ойын-сауық (oyın-sawıq)
3. оюн шоок (oyun shook)
4. юаныч (yuanıch)
5. eğlence
6. гүйменме güymenme
7. ئويۇن_تاماشا

   (oyun-tamasha)
8. томоша tomosha

## entrance  *n.*
1. кириш giriş
2. кіру (kiruw)
3. кируу (kirüü)
4. керу (kerü)
5. giriş
6. гирелге girelge
7. كىرىش (kirish)
8. кириш kirish

## envelope  *n.*
1. зәрф zәrf
2. конверт (konvert)
3. конверт (konvert)
4. конверт (konvert)
5. zarf
6. букжа bukja
7. كونۋېرت (konvert)
8. конверт konvert

## envy  *v.*
1. гибтә ет- qibtә et-
2. көре алма- (köre alma-)
3. кызган- (kızgan-)
4. кызык- (kızık-)
5. kıskan-
6. гөзи гит- gözi git-
7. ھەسەتخورلۇق قىل_

   (hәsätkhorluq qil-)
8. хасад кил- hasad qil-

## envy  *n.*
1. һәсәд hәsәd
2. іш тарлық (ish tarlıq)
3. ичи тардык (ichi tardık)
4. көнчелек (könchelek)
5. haset
6. гөриплик göriplik
7. ھەسەتخورلۇق (hәsätkhorluq)
8. хасад hasad

## epic  *lit. n.*
1. дастан dastan
2. эпик (epik)
3. эпик (epik)
4. эпос, дастан (epos, dastan)
5. destan
6. дессан dessan
7. داستان (dastan)
8. достон doston

## equal  *adj.*
1. бәрабәр bәrabәr
2. тең (teng)
3. тең (teng)
4. тиң (ting)
5. eşit
6. дең deñ
7. تەڭ (täng)
8. тенг teng

## equipment  *n.*
1. аваданлыг avadanlıq
2. құрал (qural)
3. курал (kural)
4. жиһазлар (jihazlar)
5. teçhizat
6. энжамлар enjamlar
7. قورال سايمان

   (qoral-sayman)
8. асбоб-ускуна
   asbob-uskuna

## era  *n.*
1. дөвр dövr
2. дәуір (däwir)
3. доор (door)
4. әра (era)
5. devir
6. әра era
7. دەۋر (dävr)
8. давр davr

## erase  *v.*
1. сил- sil-
2. өшip- (öshir-)
3. өчүр- (öchür-)
4. сөрт- (sört-)
5. sil-
6. боз- boz-
7. ئۆچۈر_ (öchür-)
8. ўчир- o'chir-

## eraser  *n.*
1. позан pozan
2. өшіргіш (öshirgish)
3. өчүргүч (öchürgüch)
4. бетергеч (betergech)
5. silgi
6. бозгуч bozguç
7. ئۆچۈرگۈچ (öchürgüch)
8. ўчиргич o'chirgich

## escape  *v.*
1. гач- qaç-
2. қаш- (qash-)
3. кач- (kach-)
4. кач- (kach-)
5. kaç-
6. гачып гит- gaçyp git-
7. قاچ_ (qach-)
8. қочиб кет- qochib ket-

---

## especially *adv.*
1. хүсусилə xüsusilə
2. ерекше (yerekshe)
3. айрыкча (ayrıkcha)
4. аеруча (ayerucha)
5. özellikle
6. ылайта-да ylaÿta-da
7. خۇسۇسەن (khususän)
8. айникса ayniqsa

## eternity *n.*
1. əбəдијjəт əbədiyyət
2. мəнгілік (mänggilik)
3. түбөлүк (tübölük)
4. мəнгелек (mänggelek)
5. ebediyet
6. əбедилик ebedilik
7. مەڭگۈلۈك (mänggülük)
8. мангулик mangulik

## even *adv.*
1. həттa hətta
2. тіпті (tipti)
3. ал тургай (al turgay)
4. хəтта (khätta)
5. hatta
6. хатда hatda
7. ھەتتا (hätta)
8. хатто hatto

## evening *n.*
1. ахшам axşam
2. кеш (kesh)
3. кеч (kech)
4. кич (kich)
5. akşam
6. агшам agşam
7. ناخشام (akhsham)
8. окшом oqshom

## event *n.*
1. hадисə hadisə
2. оқиға (oqiygha)
3. окуя (okuya)
4. вакыйга (vakıyga)
5. olay
6. хадыса hadysa
7. ۋەقە (väqä)
8. воқеа voqea

## every *adj.*
1. həp hər
2. əр (är)
3. ар (ar)
4. həp (här)
5. her
6. хер her
7. ھەر (här)
8. хар har

## everybody *pron.*
1. həp кəс hər kəs
2. əр кiм (är kim)
3. ар ким (ar kim)
4. həpкем (härkem)
5. herkes
6. хер ким her kim
7. ھەركىم (här kim)
8. хар ким har kim

## everything *pron.*
1. həp шеj hər şey
2. бəрi (beri)
3. баары (baarı)
4. həpнəрсə (härnärsä)
5. herşey
6. хер зат her zat
7. ھەر بىر نەرسە
   (här bir närsä)
8. хар нарса har narsa

## everywhere *adv.*
1. həp jердə hər yerdə
2. барлык жерде
   (barlıq zherde)
3. ар жерде (ar jerde)
4. həркайда (härkayda)
5. her yerde
6. хер ерде her ÿerde
7. ھەر يەردە (här yärdä)
8. хар ерда har yerda

## examination *n.*
1. имтаhан imtahan
2. емтихан (yemtiykhan)
3. сынoo (sınoo)
4. имтихан (imtikhan)
5. sınav
6. экзамен ekzamen
7. ئىمتىھان (imtihan)
8. имтихон imtihon

## example *n.*
1. нүмунə nümunə
2. мысал (mısal)
3. мисал (misal)
4. мисал (misal)
5. örnek
6. мысал mysal
7. مىسال (misal)
8. мисол misol

## excitement *n.*
1. həjəчан həyəcan
2. қозу (qozuw)
3. толкундоo (tolkundoo)
4. дулкынлану (dulkınlanu)
5. heyecan
6. җошгун joşgun
7. ھاياجان (hayajan)
8. хаяжон hayajon

---

1. Azerbaijani   2. Kazakh   3. Kyrgyz   4. Tatar   5. Turkish   6. Turkmen   7. Uighur   8. Uzbek

### excuse *n.*
1. бәһанә bəhanə
2. сылтау (sıltaw)
3. тиричилик (tirichilik)
4. сылтау (sıltau)
5. bahane
6. бахана bahana
7. باهانه (bahanä)
8. баҳона bahona

### exhibition *n.*
1. сәрки sərgi
2. көрме (körme)
3. көргөзмө (körgözmö)
4. күргәзмә (kürgäzmä)
5. sergi
6. серги sergi
7. كۆرگەزمە (körgäzmä)
8. кўргазма ko'rgazma

### existence *n.*
1. варлыг varlıq
2. барлық (barlıq)
3. барлык (barlık)
4. барлык (barlık)
5. varlık
6. бар болмаклык bar bolmaklyk
7. مەۋجۇدىيەت (mävjudiyät)
8. мавжудлик mavjudlik

### exit *v.*
1. чых- çıx-
2. шыг- (shıgh-)
3. чык- (chık-)
4. чык- (chık-)
5. çık-
6. чык- çyk-
7. چىق (chiq-)
8. чиқ- chiq-

### exit *n.*
1. чыхыш çıxış
2. шыгу (shıghuw)
3. чыгуу (chıguu)
4. чыгу (chıgu)
5. çıkış
6. чыкалга çykalga
7. چىقىش (chiqish)
8. чиқиш chiqish

### expense *n.*
1. хәрч xərc
2. шығын (shıghın)
3. чыгым (chıgım)
4. чыгым (chıgım)
5. gider
6. чыкдажы, харажат çykdajy, harajat
7. خىراجەت (khirajät)
8. харажат xarajat

### expensive *adj.*
1. баһа baha
2. қымбат (qımbat)
3. кымбат (kımbat)
4. кыйммәт (kıymmät)
5. pahalı
6. гыммат gymmat
7. قىممەت (qimmät)
8. қиммат qimmat

### experience *n.*
1. тәчрүбә təcrübə
2. тәжірибе (täzhiriybe)
3. тажрыйба (tajrıyba)
4. тәжрибә (täjribä)
5. tecrübe
6. тежрибе tejribe
7. تەجرىبە (täjribä)
8. тажриба tajriba

### explain *v.*
1. изаһ ет- izah et-
2. түсіндір- (tüsindir-)
3. түшүндүр- (tüshündür-)
4. ачыкла- (achıkla-)
5. açıkla-
6. дүшүндир- düşündir-
7. چۈشەندۈر (chüshändür-)
8. тушунтир- tushuntir-

### explanation *n.*
1. изаһат izahat
2. түсіндіру (tüsindiruw)
3. түшүндүрүү (tüshündürüü)
4. аңлатма (anglatma)
5. açıklama
6. дүшүндириш düşündiriş
7. ئىزاھات (izahat)
8. тушунтириш tushuntirish

### extinguish *v.*
1. сөндүр- söndür-
2. өшір- (öshir-)
3. өчүр- (öchür-)
4. сүндер- (sünder-)
5. söndür-
6. сөндүр- söndür-
7. ئۆچۈر (öchür-)
8. ўчир- o'chir-

### eye *phys. n.*
1. көз göz
2. көз (köz)
3. көз (köz)
4. күз (küz)
5. göz
6. гөз göz
7. كۆز (köz)
8. кўз ko'z

## eyebrow *phys. n.*
1. гаш qaş
2. қас (qas)
3. каш (kash)
4. каш (kash)
5. kaş
6. гаш gaş
7. قاش (qash)
8. қош qosh

## eyelash *phys. n.*
1. киприк kiprik
2. кірпік (kirpik)
3. кирпик (kirpik)
4. керфек (kerfek)
5. kirpik
6. кирпик kirpik
7. كرپيك (kirpik)
8. киприк kiprik

## face *phys. n.*
1. үз üz
2. бет (bet)
3. бет (bet)
4. бит (bit)
5. yüz
6. йүз ÿüz
7. چيراي (chiray)
8. юв yuz

## factory *n.*
1. фабрик fabrik
2. фабрика (fabrika)
3. фабрика (fabrika)
4. фабрика (fabrika)
5. fabrika
6. фабрик fabrik
7. زاۋۇت (zavut)
8. завод zavod

## faint *v.*
1. һушуну итир- huşunu itir-
2. талып қал- (talıp qal-)
3. талып кал- (talıp kal-)
4. һуштан яз- (hushtan yaz-)
5. bayıl-
6. өзүнден гит- özünden git-
7. هوشىدىن كەت (hushidin kät-)
8. хушдан кет- xushdan ket-

## faith *rel. n.*
1. е'тигад e'tiqad
2. сенім (senim)
3. ишеним (ishenim)
4. дин (din)
5. itikat
6. иман iman
7. ئېتىقاد (etiqad)
8. эътиқод e'tiqod

## fall *vi.*
1. дүш-, jыхыл- düş-, yıxıl-
2. құла- (qula-)
3. кула- (kula-)
4. төш- (tösh-)
5. düş-
6. йыкыл- ÿykyl-
7. چۈش (chüsh-)
8. туш-, йиқил- tush-, yiqil-

## false *adj.*
1. сахта saxta
2. жалған (zhalghan)
3. жалган (jalgan)
4. ясалма (yasalma)
5. sahte
6. яландан ÿalandan
7. ساختا (sakhta)
8. қалбаки qalbaki

## family *n.*
1. аилә ailə
2. семья (sem'ya)
3. үй-бүлө (üy-bülö)
4. гаилә (gailä)
5. aile
6. машгала maşgala
7. ئائىله (a'ilä)
8. оила oila

## famine *n.*
1. ачлыг aclıq
2. ашаршылық (asharshılıq)
3. ачарчылык (acharchılık)
4. ачлык (achlık)
5. açlık
6. ачлык açlyk
7. ئاچارچىلىق (acharchiliq)
8. очарчилик ocharchilik

## famous *adj.*
1. мәшһур məşhur
2. атақты (ataqtı)
3. атактуу (ataktuu)
4. атаклы (ataklı)
5. meşhur
6. мешхур meşhur
7. مەشھۇر (mäshhur)
8. машхур mashhur

## far *adj.*
1. узаг uzaq
2. алыс (alıs)
3. алыс (alıs)
4. ерак (yerak)
5. uzak
6. даш daş
7. ئۇزاق (uzaq)
8. узоқ uzoq

## fare *n.*
1. јол пулу  yol pulu
2. жол ақы (zhol aqı)
3. жол кире (jol kire)
4. түләү (tüläü)
5. yol parası
6. ёл кирейи ÿol kireÿi
7. يول ھەقىی (yol häqqi)
8. йўл хақи  yo'l haqi

## farm *n.*
1. тәсәрруфат təsərrüfat
2. ферма (ferma)
3. ферма (ferma)
4. ферма (ferma)
5. çiftlik
6. ферма ferma
7. دېھقانچىلىق مەیدانی (dehqanchiliq mäydani)
8. хўжалик xo'jalik

## fashion *clo. n.*
1. мода moda
2. мода (moda)
3. мода (moda)
4. мода (moda)
5. moda
6. мода moda
7. مودا (moda)
8. мода moda

## fast *rel. n.*
1. оруч oruc
2. ораза (oraza)
3. орозо (orozo)
4. ураза (uraza)
5. oruç
6. ораза oraza
7. روزا (roza)
8. рўза ro'za

## fast (=rapid) *adj.*
1. чәлд cəld
2. жылдам (zhıldam)
3. тез (tez)
4. тиз (tiz)
5. hızlı
6. чалт çalt
7. تېز (tez)
8. тез tez

## fasten *v.*
1. бағла- bağla-
2. бекіт- (bekit-)
3. бекит- (bekit-)
4. бәйлә- (bäylä-)
5. bağla-
6. даң- daň-
7. باغلا_ (baghla-)
8. боғла- bog'la-

## fat *adj.*
1. көк kök
2. семіз (semiz)
3. семиз (semiz)
4. юан (yuan)
5. şişman
6. семиз semiz
7. سېمىز (semiz)
8. семиз semiz

## fat *cul. n.*
1. јағ yağ
2. май (may)
3. май (may)
4. май (may)
5. yağ
6. яг ÿag
7. یاغ (yagh)
8. ёғ yog'

## fate *rel. n.*
1. тале tale
2. тағдыр (taghdır)
3. тагдыр (tagdır)
4. язмыш (yazmısh)
5. kader
6. ықбал ykbal
7. تەقدىر (täqdir)
8. тақдир taqdir

## father *n.*
1. ата ata
2. әке (äke)
3. ата (ata)
4. ата, әти (ata, äti)
5. baba
6. кака kaka
7. دادا (dada)
8. ота ota

## faucet *n.*
1. кран kran
2. кран (kran)
3. кран (kran)
4. кран, борын (kran, borın)
5. musluk
6. кран kran
7. جۆمەك (jümäk)
8. кран kran

## fault *n.*
1. хәта xəta
2. қате (qate)
3. ката (kata)
4. хата (khata)
5. hata
6. ялңышлык ÿalñyşlyk
7. ئەیىب (äyib)
8. айб ayb

---

## fear *n.*
1. горху qorxu
2. қорқыныш (qorqınısh)
3. коркуу (korkuu)
4. курку (kurku)
5. korku
6. горкы gorky
7. ڤەھىم (vähimä)
8. қўрқув qo'rquv

## feather *n.*
1. гуш түкү quş tükü
2. құс жүні (qus zhüni)
3. куш канаты (kush kanatı)
4. кәләм (kaläm)
5. kuştüyü
6. елек ÿelek
7. پەي (päy)
8. пат pat

## February *n.*
1. феврал fevral
2. ақпан (aqpan)
3. февраль (fevral')
4. февраль (fevral')
5. şubat
6. февраль fewral
7. فېۋرال (fevral)
8. февраль fevral'

## feel *v.*
1. һисс ет- hiss et-
2. сез- (sez-)
3. сез- (sez-)
4. сиз- (siz-)
5. hisset-
6. дуй- duÿ-
7. ھېس قىل (hes qil-)
8. ҳис қил- his qil-

## feeling *n.*
1. дуйғу duйğu
2. сезім (sezim)
3. сезим (sezim)
4. тойғы (toygı)
5. duygu
6. дуйғы duÿgy
7. تۇيغۇ (tuyghu)
8. ҳис his

## fence *n.*
1. чәпәр çəpər
2. шарбақ (sharbaq)
3. кашаа (kashaa)
4. койма (koyma)
5. çit
6. гермев germew
7. چىت (chit)
8. панжара panjara

## fertilizer *ag. n.*
1. күбрә gübrə
2. тыңайтқыш (tıngaytqısh)
3. кык (kık)
4. тирес (tires)
5. gübre
6. дөкүн dökün
7. ئوغۇت (oghut)
8. ўғит o'g'it

## festival *n.*
1. фестивал festival
2. мереке (mereke)
3. фестиваль (festival')
4. фестиваль (festival')
5. şenlik
6. байрамчылык bayramçylyk
7. بايرام (bayram)
8. фестиваль festival'

## fever *med. n.*
1. гыздырма qızdırma
2. қызу (qızuw)
3. температура (temperatura)
4. температура (temperatura)
5. ateş
6. гызгын gyzgyn
7. قىزىتما (qizitma)
8. иситма isitma

## few *adj.*
1. аз az
2. аз (az)
3. аз (az)
4. аз (az)
5. az
6. аз az
7. ئاز (az)
8. кам kam

## field *ag. n.*
1. тарла tarla
2. егін даласы (yegin dalası)
3. талаа (talaa)
4. кыр (kır)
5. tarla
6. мейдан meÿdan
7. ئېتىز (etiz)
8. дала dala

## fifteen *num.*
1. он беш on beş
2. он бес (on bes)
3. он беш (on besh)
4. унбиш (unbish)
5. on beş
6. он бәш on bäş
7. ئون بەش (on bäsh)
8. ўн беш o'n besh

---

1. Azerbaijani  2. Kazakh  3. Kyrgyz  4. Tatar  5. Turkish  6. Turkmen  7. Uighur  8. Uzbek

**fifty** *num.*
1. әлли әlli
2. елу (yeluw)
3. әлҮҮ (elüü)
4. илле (ille)
5. elli
6. элли elli
7. ئەللىك (ällik)
8. эллик ellik

**fig** *bot. n.*
1. әнҹир әncir
2. інжір (inzhir)
3. инжир (injir)
4. инҗир (injir)
5. incir
6. инҗир injir
7. ئەنجۈر (änjür)
8. анжир anjir

**fight** *v.*
1. дөјҮш- döyüş-
2. кҮрес- (küres-)
3. кҮрөш- (kürösh-)
4. көрәш- (köräsh-)
5. kavga et-
6. уруш- uruş-
7. سوقۇش (soqush-)
8. кураш- kurash-

**file** *tech. n.*
1. әјә әyә
2. егеу (yegew)
3. өгөө (ögöö)
4. игәҮ (igäü)
5. eğe
6. иге ige
7. ئېكەك (ekäk)
8. эгов egov

**fill** *v.*
1. долдур- doldur-
2. толтыр- (toltır-)
3. толтур- (toltur-)
4. тутыр- (tutır-)
5. doldur-
6. долдур- doldur-
7. تولدۇر (toldur-)
8. тўлдир- to'ldir-

**film** (*for camera) *n.*
1. лент lent
2. пленка (plyonka)
3. пленка (plenka)
4. пленка (plyonka)
5. film
6. пленка plÿonka
7. لېنتا (lenta)
8. пленка plyonka

**find** *v.*
1. тап- tap-
2. таб- (tab-)
3. тап- (tap-)
4. тап- (tap-)
5. bul-
6. тап- tap-
7. تاپ (tap-)
8. топ- top-

**fine** (=good) *adj.*
1. көзәл gözәl
2. жақсы (zhaqsı)
3. жакшы (jakshı)
4. яхшы (yakhshı)
5. güzel
6. оңат oňat
7. ياخشى (yakhshi)
8. яхши yaxshi

**fine** (=thin) *adj.*
1. инчә incә
2. жҰқа (zhuqa)
3. жука (juka)
4. юка (yuka)
5. ince
6. инче inçe
7. ئىنچىكە (inchikä)
8. ингичка ingichka

**finger** *phys. n.*
1. бармаг barmaq
2. саусақ (sawsaq)
3. манжа (manja)
4. бармак (barmak)
5. parmak
6. бармак barmak
7. بارماق (barmaq)
8. бармоқ barmoq

**finish** *vt.*
1. гуртар- qurtar-
2. бітір- (bitir-)
3. бҮтҮр- (bütür-)
4. бетер- (beter-)
5. bitir-
6. гутар- gutar-
7. پۈتتۈر (püttür-)
8. тугат- tugat-

**fir** *bot. n.*
1. кҮкнар küknar
2. шырша (shırsha)
3. балаты (balatı)
4. чыршы (chırshı)
5. köknar
6. пихта pihta
7. ئاق قارىغاي (aq qarighay)
8. қорақарағай qoraqarag'ay

**fire** (=a destructive burning) *n.*
1. jaнғын yanğın
2. өрт (ört)
3. өрт (ört)
4. янгын (yangın)
5. yangın
6. янгын ÿangyn
7. يانغـن (yanghin)
8. ёнғин yong'in

**fire** (=burning) *n.*
1. од od
2. от (ot)
3. от (ot)
4. ут (ut)
5. ateş
6. от ot
7. ئوت (ot)
8. ўт o't

**firm** *econ. n.*
1. фирма firma
2. компания (kompaniya)
3. компания (kompaniya)
4. компания (kompaniya)
5. şirket
6. фирма firma
7. شـركت (shirkät)
8. ширкат shirkat

**fish** *zool. n.*
1. балыг balıq
2. балық (balıq)
3. балык (balık)
4. балык (balık)
5. balık
6. балык balyk
7. بـلـق (beliq)
8. балиқ baliq

**fisherman** *n.*
1. балыгчы balıqçı
2. балықшы (balıqshı)
3. балыкчы (balıkchı)
4. балыкчы (balıkchı)
5. balıkçı
6. балыкчы balykçy
7. بـلـتچى (beliqchi)
8. баликчи baliqchi

**five** *num.*
1. беш beş
2. бес (bes)
3. беш (besh)
4. биш (bish)
5. beş
6. бәш bäş
7. بـش (bäsh)
8. беш besh

**flag** *n.*
1. бајраг bayraq
2. жалау (zhalaw)
3. желек (jelek)
4. байрак (bayrak)
5. bayrak
6. байдак baÿdak
7. بايراق (bayraq)
8. байроқ bayroq

**flame** *n.*
1. алов alov
2. жалын (zhalın)
3. жалын (jalın)
4. ялкын (yalkın)
5. alev
6. ялын ÿalyn
7. يالغۇن (yalqun)
8. аланга alanga

**flea** *zool. n.*
1. бирə birə
2. бүрге (bürge)
3. бүргө (bürgö)
4. борча (borcha)
5. pire
6. бүре büre
7. بۈرگ (bürgä)
8. бурга burga

**flee** *v.*
1. гач- qaç-
2. қаш- (qash-)
3. кач- (kach-)
4. кач- (kach-)
5. kaç-
6. гач- gaç-
7. قاچ- (qach-)
8. қочиб қутул- qochib qutul-

**flight** (=travel by air) *n.*
1. учуш uçuş
2. рейс (reys)
3. рейс (reys)
4. рейс (reys)
5. uçuş
6. рейс reÿs
7. ئۇچۇش (uchush)
8. рейс reys

**flood** *n.*
1. сел sel
2. су ағыны (suw aghını)
3. су агымы (su agımı)
4. ташкын (tashkın)
5. sel
6. сув дашгыны suw daşgyny
7. سـل (säl)
8. сув тошқини suv toshqini

---

**floor** (*of a room) *n.*
1. дөшәмә döşəmə
2. еден (yeden)
3. пол (pol)
4. идән (idän)
5. döşeme
6. пол pol
7. پول (pol)
8. пол pol

**flour** *cul. n.*
1. ун un
2. ҰН (un)
3. ун (un)
4. он (on)
5. un
6. ун un
7. ئۇن (un)
8. ун un

**flow** *v.*
1. ax- ax-
2. аг- (agh-)
3. ак- (ak-)
4. ак- (ak-)
5. ak-
6. ак- ak-
7. ئاق_ (aq-)
8. оқ- oq-

**flower** *bot. n.*
1. күл gül
2. ГҮЛ (gül)
3. ГҮЛ (gül)
4. гөл (göl)
5. çiçek
6. гүл gül
7. گۈل (gül)
8. гул gul

**flu** *med. n.*
1. грип qrip
2. грипп (gripp)
3. грипп (gripp)
4. грипп (gripp)
5. grip
6. грип grip
7. يۇقۇملۇق زۇكام (yuqumluq zukam)
8. грипп gripp

**fly** *vi.*
1. уч- uç-
2. ҰШ- (ush-)
3. уч- (uch-)
4. оч- (och-)
5. uç-
6. уч- uç-
7. ئۇچ_ (uch-)
8. уч- uch-

**fly** *zool. n.*
1. милчәк milçək
2. шыбын (shıbın)
3. чымын (chımın)
4. чебен (cheben)
5. sinek
6. синек siñek
7. چىۋىن (chivin)
8. пашша pashsha

**fog** *n.*
1. думан duman
2. ТҰМАН (tuman)
3. туман (tuman)
4. томан (toman)
5. sis
6. үмүр, думан ümür, duman
7. تۇمان (tuman)
8. туман tuman

**fold** *vt.*
1. гатла- qatla-
2. қатта- (qatta-)
3. катта- (katta-)
4. бөк- (bök-)
5. katla-
6. әпле- eple-
7. قاتلا_ (qatla-)
8. букла- bukla-

**folklore** *n.*
1. фолклор folklor
2. фольклор (fol'klor)
3. фольклор (fol'klor)
4. фольклор (fol'klor)
5. folklor
6. фольклор folklor
7. فولكلور (folklor)
8. фольклор fol'klor

**folktale** *n.*
1. нағыл nağıl
2. ертек (yertek)
3. жомок (jomok)
4. халык әкияте (khalık äkiyate)
5. halk hikâyesi
6. халк дессаны halk dessany
7. چۆچەك (chöchäk)
8. халқ әртаги xalq ertagi

**follow** *v.*
1. изла- izlə-
2. ер- (yer-)
3. әәрчи- (eerchi-)
4. артыннан бар- (artınnan bar-)
5. izle-
6. ызарла- yzarla-
7. ئەگەش_ (ägäsh-)
8. эргаш- ergash-

---

1. Azerbaijani   2. Kazakh   3. Kyrgyz   4. Tatar   5. Turkish   6. Turkmen   7. Uighur   8. Uzbek

## food *n.*
1. гида qida
2. азық-түлік (azıq-tülik)
3. тамак-аш (tamak-ash)
4. аш (ash)
5. yiyecek
6. иймит iÿmit
7. يبمەك (yemäk)
8. озиқ-овқат oziq-ovqat

## foot *phys. n.*
1. ajar ayaq
2. аяқ (ayaq)
3. аяк (ayak)
4. аяк (ayak)
5. ayak
6. аяк aÿak
7. پۇت (put)
8. оёқ oyoq

## for *prep.*
1. үчүн üçün
2. үшін (üshin)
3. үчүн (üchün)
4. өчен (öchen)
5. için
6. үчин üçin
7. ئۇچۈن (üchün)
8. учун uchun

## forbid *v.*
1. гадаған ет- qadağan et-
2. тый- (tıy-)
3. тый- (tıy-)
4. тый- (tıy-)
5. yasakla-
6. гадаган эт- gadagan et-
7. مەنئى قىل (män'i qil-)
8. ман эт- man et-

## force *n.*
1. күч güc
2. күш (küsh)
3. күч (küch)
4. көч (köch)
5. güç
6. гүйч güÿç
7. كۈچ (küch)
8. куч kuch

## forehead *phys. n.*
1. алын alın
2. маңдай (mangday)
3. маңдай (mangday)
4. маңгай (manggay)
5. alın
6. маңлай mañlaÿ
7. پىشانە (peshanä)
8. пешана peshana

## foreigner *n.*
1. харичи xarici
2. шет елдік (shet yeldik)
3. чет эдлик (chet eldik)
4. чит ил кешесе (chit il keshese)
5. yabancı
6. дашары юртлы daşary ÿurtly
7. چەت ەللىك (chät ällik)
8. чет эллик chet ellik

## forest *n.*
1. меша meşə
2. орман (orman)
3. токой (tokoy)
4. урман (urman)
5. orman
6. токай tokaÿ
7. ئورمان (orman)
8. ўрмон o'rmon

## forget *v.*
1. унут- unut-
2. ұмыт- (umıt-)
3. унут- (unut-)
4. оныт- (onıt-)
5. unut-
6. унут- unut-
7. ئۇنتۇ (untu-)
8. унут- unut-

## forgive *v.*
1. бағышла- bağışla-
2. кешір- (keshir-)
3. кечир- (kechir-)
4. гафу ит- (gafu it-)
5. affet-
6. багышла- bagyşla-
7. كەچۈر (kächür-)
8. кечир- kechir-

## fork *cul. n.*
1. чәнкәл çəngəl
2. шаңышқы (shanıshqı)
3. вилка (vilka)
4. чәнечке (chänechke)
5. çatal
6. вилка wilka
7. ۋىلكا (vilka)
8. санчқи sanchqi

## form
(~paper document) *n.*
1. бланк blank
2. бланк (blank)
3. бланк (blank)
4. бланк (blank)
5. form
6. бланка blanka
7. قەغەز (qäghäz)
8. бланка blanka

---

**forty** *num.*
1. гырх qırx
2. қырық (qırıq)
3. кырк (kırk)
4. кырык (kırık)
5. kırk
6. кырк kyrk
7. قىرىق (qiriq)
8. қирқ qirq

**forward** *adv.*
1. ирәли irəli
2. алға (algha)
3. алга (alga)
4. алга (alga)
5. ileri
6. өңе öñe
7. ئالغا (algha)
8. олға olg'a

**fountain** *n.*
1. фонтан fontan
2. фонтан (fontan)
3. фонтан (fontan)
4. фонтан (fontan)
5. çeşme
6. фонтан fontan
7. فونتان (fontan)
8. фонтан fontan

**four** *num.*
1. дөрд dörd
2. төрт (tört)
3. төрт (tört)
4. дүрт (dürt)
5. dört
6. дөрт dört
7. تۆت (töt)
8. түрт to'rt

**fourteen** *num.*
1. он дөрд on dörd
2. он төрт (on tört)
3. он төрт (on tört)
4. ундүрт (undürt)
5. on dört
6. он дөрт on dört
7. ئون تۆت (on töt)
8. ўн түрт o'n to'rt

**fox** *zool. n.*
1. түлку tülkü
2. түлкі (tülki)
3. түлку (tülkü)
4. төлке (tölke)
5. tilki
6. тилки tilki
7. تۆلكە (tülkä)
8. тулки tulki

**fraction** *math. n.*
1. кәсир kəsir
2. бөлшек (bölshek)
3. бөлчөк (bölchök)
4. вакланма (vaklanma)
5. kesir
6. дробь drob
7. كەسىر (käsir)
8. каср kasr

**frame** (*for pictures) *n.*
1. чәрчивә çərçivə
2. жақтау (zhaqtaw)
3. рамка (ramka)
4. рамка (ramka)
5. çerçeve
6. рамка ramka
7. رامكا (ramka)
8. рамка ramka

**free** *pol. adj.*
1. азад azad
2. азат (azat)
3. эркин (erkin)
4. иркен (irken)
5. özgür
6. азат azat
7. ئەركىن (ärkin)
8. эркин erkin

**free** (=gratis) *adj.*
1. пулсуз pulsuz
2. тегін (tegin)
3. бекер (beker)
4. түләүсез (tüläüsez)
5. bedava
6. мугт mugt
7. پۇلسىز (pulsiz)
8. текин tekin

**freedom** *pol. n.*
1. азадлыг azadlıq
2. азаттық (azattıq)
3. эркиндик (erkindik)
4. иркенлек (irkenlek)
5. özgürlük
6. азатлык azatlyk
7. ئەركىنلىك (ärkinlik)
8. эркинлик erkinlik

**freeze** *vi.*
1. дон- don-
2. тоң- (tong-)
3. тоң- (tong-)
4. туң- (tung-)
5. don-
6. доң- doñ-
7. تۇڭلا- (tongla-)
8. музла- muzla-

---

1. Azerbaijani   2. Kazakh   3. Kyrgyz   4. Tatar   5. Turkish   6. Turkmen   7. Uighur   8. Uzbek

## fresh *adj.*
1. тәзә təzə
2. жаңа (zhanga)
3. жаңы (jangı)
4. яңа (yanga)
5. taze
6. тәзе täze
7. يڭگى (yengi)
8. янги yangi

## Friday *n.*
1. чүмә cümə
2. жұма (zhuma)
3. жума (juma)
4. жомга (jomga)
5. cuma
6. анна anna
7. جۇمه (jümä)
8. жума juma

## friend *n.*
1. дост dost
2. дос (dos)
3. дос (dos)
4. дус (dus)
5. arkadaş
6. дост dost
7. دوست (dost)
8. дўст do'st

## friendship *n.*
1. дослуг dostluq
2. достық (dostıq)
3. достук (dostuk)
4. дуслык (duslık)
5. arkadaşlık
6. достлук dostluk
7. دوستلۇق (dostluq)
8. дўстлик do'stlik

## frog *zool. n.*
1. гурбага qurbağa
2. құрбақа (qurbaqa)
3. бака (baka)
4. бака (baka)
5. kurbağa
6. гурбага gurbaga
7. پاقا (paqa)
8. құрбақа qurbaqa

## from *prep.*
1. -дан, -дән -dan, -dən
2. -тан, -тен, -дан, -ден, -нан, -нен (-tan, -ten, -dan, -den, -nan, -nen)
3. -дан, -ден, -дон, -дөн, -тан, -тен, -тон, төн (-dan, -den, don, -dön, -tan, -ten, -ton, -tön)
4. -дан, -дән, -тан, -тән, -нан, -нән (-dan, -dän, -tan, -tän, -nan, -nän)
5. -dan, -den, -tan, -ten
6. -дан, -ден -dan, -den
7. ـدىن ، ـتىن (-din, -tin)
8. -дан -dan

## front: in front of *prep.*
1. өнүндә önündə
2. алдында (aldında)
3. алдында (aldında)
4. алда (alda)
5. önünde
6. өнүнде öñünde
7. ئالدىدا (aldida)
8. олдида oldida

## frost *n.*
1. шахта şaxta
2. аяз (ayaz)
3. тоң (tong)
4. суык (suık)
5. don
6. аяз aÿaz

7. قىراۋ (qirav)
8. совук sovuq

## fruit *n.*
1. мејвә meyvə
2. жеміс (zhemis)
3. жемиш (jemish)
4. җимеш (jimesh)
5. meyve
6. миве miwe
7. مېۋه (mevä)
8. мева meva

## fruit juice *n.*
1. мејвә ширәси meyvə şirəsi
2. шырын (shırın)
3. шире (shire)
4. су (su)
5. meyva suyu
6. миве сувы miwe suwy
7. شىرنه (shirnä)
8. шарбат sharbat

## full *adj.*
1. долу dolu
2. толы (tolı)
3. толо (tolo)
4. тулы (tulı)
5. dolu
6. долы doly
7. تولۇق (toluq)
8. тўла to'la

## fur *n.*
1. хәз xəz
2. тері (teri)
3. тери (teri)
4. мех (mekh)
5. kürk
6. багана bagana
7. تېره (terä)
8. мўйна mo'yna

---

1. Azerbaijani  2. Kazakh  3. Kyrgyz  4. Tatar  5. Turkish  6. Turkmen  7. Uighur  8. Uzbek

**furniture** *n.*
1. мебел mebel
2. мебель (mebel')
3. эмерек (emerek)
4. җиһаз (jihaz)
5. mobilya
6. мебелъ mebel
7. ئۆي جاھازلىرى
   (öy jahazliri)
8. жиҳоз jihoz

**future** *n.*
1. кәләчәк gələcək
2. болашақ (bolashaq)
3. келечек (kelechek)
4. киләчәк (kilächäk)
5. gelecek
6. гелҗек geljek
7. كەلگۈسى (kälgüsi)
8. келажак kelajak

**game** *n.*
1. ojуn oyun
2. ойын (oyın)
3. оюн (oyun)
4. уен (uyen)
5. oyun
6. оюн oÿun
7. ئويۇن (oyun)
8. ўйин o'yin

**game** (*hunting) *n.*
1. ов ov
2. аң (ang)
3. аң (ang)
4. ау (au)
5. av
6. ав aw
7. ئوۋ (ov)
8. ов ov

**garage** *n.*
1. гараж qaraj
2. гараж (garazh)
3. гараж (garaj)
4. гараж (garazh)
5. garaj
6. гараж garaʃ
7. گاراژ (garazh)
8. гараж garaj

**garden** *n.*
1. баг bağ
2. бақша (baqsha)
3. бакча (bakcha)
4. бакча (bakcha)
5. bahçe
6. баг, бакжа bag, bakja
7. باغچە (baghchä)
8. бог bog'

**gardener** *n.*
1. багбан bağban
2. багбан (baghban)
3. бакчы (bakchı)
4. бакчачы (bakchachı)
5. bahçıvan
6. багбан bagban
7. باغۋەن (baghvän)
8. богбон bog'bon

**garlic** *bot. n.*
1. сарымсаг sarımsaq
2. сарымсақ (sarımsaq)
3. сарымсак (sarımsak)
4. сарымсак (sarımsak)
5. sarmısak
6. сарымсак sarymsak
7. سامساق (samsaq)
8. саримсоқ sarimsoq

**gas** *phy. n.*
1. газ qaz
2. газ (gaz)
3. газ (gaz)
4. газ (gaz)
5. gaz
6. газ gaz
7. گاز (gaz)
8. газ gaz

**gasoline** *n.*
1. бензин benzin
2. бензин (benzin)
3. бензин (benzin)
4. бензин (benzin)
5. benzin
6. бензин benzin
7. بېنزىن (benzin)
8. бензин benzin

**gate** *n.*
1. дарваза darvaza
2. қақпа (qaqpa)
3. дарбаза (darbaza)
4. капка (kapka)
5. kapı
6. дервезе derweze
7. دەرۋازا (därvaza)
8. дарвоза darvoza

**general** *adj.*
1. умуми ümumi
2. жалпы (zhalpı)
3. жалпы (jalpı)
4. гомуми (gomumi)
5. genel
6. умумы umumy
7. ئومۇمىي (omumiy)
8. умумий umumiy

---

## generous *adj.*
1. әлиачыг әliaçıq
2. жомарт (zhomart)
3. жоомарт (joomart)
4. юмарт (yumart)
5. cömert
6. сахы sahy
7. سبخي (sekhiy)
8. сахий saxiy

## gentle *adj.*
1. мүлајим mülayim
2. нәзік (näzik)
3. назик (nazik)
4. назлы (nazlı)
5. nazik
6. мәхирли mähirli
7. ياۋاش (yavash)
8. нозик nozik

## gentleman *n.*
1. чәнаб cәnab
2. мырза (mırza)
3. мырза (mırza)
4. әфәнде (äfände)
5. efendi
6. җентльмен jentlmen
7. ئەپەندى (äpändi)
8. жаноб janob

## geography *n.*
1. чоғрафиja coğrafiya
2. география (geografiya)
3. география (geografiya)
4. география (geografiya)
5. coğrafya
6. география geografiÿa
7. جۇغراپىيە (jughrapiyä)
8. жўғрофия jo'g'rofiya

## geology *n.*
1. кеолокиja geologiya
2. геология (geologiya)
3. геология (geologiya)
4. геология (geologiya)
5. jeoloji
6. геология geologiÿa
7. گېئولوگىيە (ge'ologiyä)
8. геология geologiya

## geometry *n.*
1. hәндәсә hәndәsә
2. геометрия (geometriya)
3. геометрия (geometriya)
4. геометрия (geometriya)
5. geometri
6. геометрия geometriÿa
7. گېئومېترىيە (ge'ometriyä)
8. геометрия geometriya

## get off *v.*
1. дүш- düş-
2. түс- (tüs-)
3. түш- (tüsh-)
4. төш- (tösh-)
5. in-
6. дүш- düş-
7. چۇش (chüsh-)
8. туш- tush-

## get on *v.*
1. мин- min-
2. мін- (min-)
3. мин- (min-)
4. утыр- (utır-)
5. bin-
6. мүн- mün-
7. چىق (chiq-)
8. чик- chiq-

## get up (=arise) *v.*
1. галх- qalx-
2. тұр- (tur-)
3. тур- (tur-)
4. тор- (tor-)
5. kalk-
6. тур- tur-
7. تۇر (tur-)
8. тур- tur-

## ghost *n.*
1. кабус kabus
2. жын (zhın)
3. шайтан (shaytan)
4. өрәк (öräk)
5. ruh
6. арвах arwah
7. جن (jin)
8. арвох arvoh

## giant *n.*
1. див div
2. дәу (däw)
3. дөө (döö)
4. дию (diyu)
5. dev
6. дөв döw
7. دۆھ (divä)
8. дев dev

## girl *n.*
1. гыз qız
2. қыз бала (qız bala)
3. кыз (kız)
4. кыз бала (kız bala)
5. kız
6. гыз gyz
7. قىز (qiz)
8. қиз qiz

---

**give** *v.*
1. вер- ver-
2. бер- (ber-)
3. бер- (ber-)
4. бир- (bir-)
5. ver-
6. бер- ber-
7. بەر_ (bär-)
8. бер- ber-

**glad** *adj.*
1. шад şad
2. риза (riyza)
3. ыраазы (ıraazı)
4. канәгатъ (kanägat')
5. memnun
6. шат şat
7. خۇشال (khushal)
8. хурсанд xursand

**glass** (*material) *n.*
1. шуша şüşə
2. шыны (shını)
3. айнек (aynek)
4. пыяла (pıyala)
5. cam
6. айна aÿna
7. ئەينەك (äynäk)
8. шиша shisha

**glass** (~cup) *n.*
1. стәкан stəkan
2. ыстакан (ıstakan)
3. ыстакан (ıstakan)
4. стакан (stakan)
5. bardak
6. стакан stakan
7. ئىستاكان (istakan)
8. стакан stakan

**glasses** *n.*
1. көзлүк gözlük
2. көзілдірік (közildirik)
3. көз айнек (köz aynek)
4. күзлек (küzlek)
5. gözlük
6. әйнек äÿnek
7. كۆزەينەك (közäynäk)
8. кўзойнак ko'zoynak

**glove** *clo. n.*
1. әлчәк əlcək
2. қолғап (qolghap)
3. кол кап (kol kap)
4. бияләй (biyaläy)
5. eldiven
6. эллик ellik
7. پەلەي (päläy)
8. қўлқоп qo'lqop

**glue** *n.*
1. јапышған yapışqan
2. желім (zhelim)
3. желим (jelim)
4. җилем (jilem)
5. zamk
6. елим ÿelim
7. يەلىم (yelim)
8. елим yelim

**go** *v.*
1. кет- get-
2. бар- (bar-)
3. кет- (ket-)
4. бар- (bar-)
5. git-
6. гит- git-
7. بار_ (bar-)
8. бор- bor-

**goat** *zool. n.*
1. кечи keçi
2. ешкі (yeshki)
3. эчки (echki)
4. кәжә (käjä)
5. keçi
6. гечи geçi
7. ئۆچكە (öchkä)
8. эчки echki

**God** *rel. n.*
1. танры tanrı
2. құдай (quday)
3. кудай (kuday)
4. алла (alla)
5. Tanrı
6. танры tañry
7. تەڭرى (tängri)
8. худо xudo

**gold** *geo. n.*
1. гызыл qızıl
2. алтын (altın)
3. алтын (altın)
4. алтын (altın)
5. altın
6. гызыл gyzyl
7. ئالتۇن (altun)
8. олтин oltin

**good** *adj.*
1. јахшы yaxşı
2. жақсы (zhaqsı)
3. жакшы (jakshı)
4. әйбәт (äybät)
5. iyi
6. говы gowy
7. ياخشى (yakhshi)
8. яхши yaxshi

---

1. Azerbaijani  2. Kazakh  3. Kyrgyz  4. Tatar  5. Turkish  6. Turkmen  7. Uighur  8. Uzbek

## goods *n.*
1. мал mal
2. бүйым (buyım)
3. буюм (buyum)
4. товар (tovar)
5. mal
6. харытлар harytlar
7. مال (mal)
8. мол mol

## goose *zool. n.*
1. газ qaz
2. қаз (qaz)
3. каз (kaz)
4. каз (kaz)
5. kaz
6. газ gaz
7. غاز (ghaz)
8. ғоз g'oz

## government *pol. n.*
1. һөкумәт hökumət
2. үкімет (ükimet)
3. өкмөт (ökmöt)
4. хөкүмәт (khökümät)
5. hükûmet
6. хөкүмет hökümet
7. ھۆكۈمەت (hökümät)
8. хукумат hukumat

## gradually *adv.*
1. тәдричән tədricən
2. біртіндеп (birtindep)
3. бара бара (bara bara)
4. акрынлап (akrınlap)
5. tedricen
6. юваш-ювашдан
   ÿuwaş-ÿuwaşdan
7. بارا ـ بارا (bara-bara)
8. аста-секин asta-sekin

## graduation *n.*
1. мәктәб битирмә
   məktəb bitirmə
2. бітіру (bitiruw)
3. окууну бүтүрүү
   (okuunu bütürüü)
4. укуны бетерү
   (ukunı beterü)
5. mezuniyet
6. окув гутарма
   okuw gutarma
7. ئوقۇشنى پۈتۈرۈش
   (oqushni pütürüsh)
8. тугатиш tugatish

## grain *ag. n.*
1. тохум, дән toxum, dən
2. дән, үрық (dän, urıq)
3. урук, дан (uruk, dan)
4. ашлық, орлық
   (ashlık, orlık)
5. tane, tohum
6. дәне, тохум däne, tohum
7. ئاشلىق، دان (ashliq, dan)
8. дон don

## grandchild *n.*
1. нәбә nəvə
2. немере (nemere)
3. небере (nebere)
4. оныk (onık)
5. torun
6. агтык agtyk
7. نەۋرە (nävrä)
8. невара nevara

## grandfather *n.*
1. баба baba
2. ата (ata)
3. чоң ата (chong ata)
4. бабай (babay)
5. dede
6. ата ata

7. بوۋا (bova)
8. бобо bobo

## grandmother *n.*
1. нәнә nənə
2. әже (äzhe)
3. чоң эне (chong ene)
4. әби (äbi)
5. nine
6. эне, мама ene, mama
7. موما (moma)
8. буви buvi

## grape *bot. n.*
1. үзүм üzüm
2. жүзім (zhüzim)
3. жүзүм (jüzüm)
4. йөзем (yözem)
5. üzüm
6. үзүм üzüm
7. ئۈزۈم (üzüm)
8. узум uzum

## grass *bot. n.*
1. от, чәмән ot, çəmən
2. шөп (shöp)
3. чөп (chöp)
4. үлән (ülän)
5. ot, çimen
6. от ot
7. ئوت (ot)
8. ÿр o't

## grasshopper *zool. n.*
1. чәјирткә çəyirtkə
2. шегіртке (shegirtke)
3. чегиртке (chegirtke)
4. чикерткә (chikertkä)
5. çekirge
6. чекиртге çekirtge
7. چىكەتكە (chekätkä)
8. чигиртка chigirtka

---

1. Azerbaijani  2. Kazakh  3. Kyrgyz  4. Tatar  5. Turkish  6. Turkmen  7. Uighur  8. Uzbek

## gratitude  *n.*
1. миннәтдарлыг minnətdarlıq
2. алғыс (alghıs)
3. алкыш (alkısh)
4. рәхмәт (räkhmät)
5. minnettarlık
6. миннетдарлык minnetdarlyk
7. مننەتدارلىق (minnätdarliq)
8. миннатдорчилик minnatdorchilik

## great (=large)  *adj.*
1. бөјүк böyük
2. үлкен (ülken)
3. чоң (chong)
4. зур (zur)
5. büyük
6. улы uly
7. كاتتا (katta)
8. катта katta

## green  *adj.*
1. јашыл yaşıl
2. жасыл (zhasıl)
3. жашыл (jashıl)
4. яшел (yashel)
5. yeşil
6. яшыл ÿaşyl
7. يېشىل (yeshil)
8. яшил yashil

## greet  *v.*
1. саламлаш- salamlaş-
2. амандас- (amandas-)
3. амандаш- (amandash-)
4. исәнләш- (isänläsh-)
5. selamlaş-
6. саламлаш- salamlaş-
7. سالام بەر (salam ber-)
8. саломлаш- salomlash-

## grey  *adj.*
1. боз boz
2. сүр (sur)
3. сур (sur)
4. соры (sorı)
5. gri
6. чал çal
7. كۆلرەڭ (külräng)
8. кул ранг kul rang

## grind  *v.*
1. үјүт- üyüt-
2. үгіт- (ügit-)
3. майдала- (maydala-)
4. тарт- (tart-)
5. öğüt-
6. үвe- üwe-
7. تارتـ (tart-)
8. майдала- maydala-

## grow  *vi.*
1. бөјү- böyü-
2. өс- (ös-)
3. өс- (ös-)
4. үс- (üs-)
5. büyü-
6. өс- ös-
7. ئۆس (ös-)
8. ўс- o's-

## growth  *n.*
1. бөјүмә böyümə
2. өсу (ösuw)
3. өсүү (ösüü)
4. үсү (üsü)
5. büyüme
6. өсүш ösüş
7. ئۆسۈم (ösüm)
8. ўсиш o'sish

## guess  *v.*
1. зәнн ет- zənn et-
2. болжа- (bolzha-)
3. болжо- (boljo-)
4. уйла- (uyla-)
5. tahmin et-
6. чакла- çakla-
7. تەخمىن قىلـ (täkhmin qil-)
8. тусмолла- tusmolla-

## guest  *n.*
1. гонаг qonaq
2. қонақ (qonaq)
3. конок (konok)
4. кунак (kunak)
5. misafir
6. мыхман myhman
7. مىهمان (mehman)
8. меҳмон mehmon

## guilty  *adj.*
1. күнаһкар günahkar
2. айыпты (ayıptı)
3. күнөөкөр (künöökör)
4. гаепле (gayeple)
5. suçlu
6. гүнәкәр günäkär
7. ئەيىبدار (äyibdar)
8. айбдор aybdor

## gun  *mil. n.*
1. силаһ, топ silah, top
2. қару (qaruw)
3. курал-жарак (kural-jarak)
4. корал (koral)
5. silah
6. яраг ÿarag
7. قورال (qoral)
8. қурол qurol

---

1. Azerbaijani  2. Kazakh  3. Kyrgyz  4. Tatar  5. Turkish  6. Turkmen  7. Uighur  8. Uzbek

## habit *n.*
1. адәт adət
2. әдет (ädet)
3. адат (adat)
4. гадәт (gadät)
5. adet
6. адат adat
7. ئادەت (adät)
8. одат odat

## hail *n.*
1. долу dolu
2. бұршақ (burshaq)
3. мөндүр (möndür)
4. боз (boz)
5. dolu
6. долы doly
7. مۆلدۈر (möldür)
8. дүл do'l

## hair (*on head) *phys. n.*
1. сач saç
2. шаш (shash)
3. чач (chach)
4. чәч (chäch)
5. saç
6. сач saç
7. چاچ (chach)
8. соч soch

## hairdresser *n.*
1. бәрбәр, дәлләк bərbər, dəllək
2. шаштараз (shashtaraz)
3. чачтарач (chachtarach)
4. парикмахер (parikmakher)
5. berber, kuaför
6. деллек dellek
7. ساتىراش (satirash)
8. сартарош sartarosh

## half *adj.*
1. јарым yarım
2. жарты (zhartı)
3. жарым (jarım)
4. ярты (yartı)
5. yarım
6. ярым ÿarym
7. يېرىم (yerim)
8. ярим yarim

## hammer *tech. n.*
1. чәкич çəkic
2. балға (balgha)
3. балка (balka)
4. чүкеч (chükech)
5. çekiç
6. чекич çekiç
7. بولغا (bolqa)
8. болға bolg'a

## hand *phys. n.*
1. әл əl
2. қол (qol)
3. кол (kol)
4. кул (kul)
5. el
6. әл el
7. قول (qol)
8. қўл qo'l

## handbag *n.*
1. әл чантасы əl çantası
2. қол сөмке (qol sömke)
3. кол сөмкө (kol sömkö)
4. сумка, букча (sumka, bukcha)
5. el çantası
6. әл сумкасы el sumkasy
7. قول سومكىسى (qol somkisi)
8. сумкача sumkacha

## handkerchief *n.*
1. дәсмал dəsmal
2. қол орамал (qol oramal)
3. кол аарчы (kol aarchı)
4. күлъяулық (kul'yaulık)
5. mendil
6. эл яглык el ÿaglyk
7. قول ياغلىق (qol yaghliq)
8. рўмолча ro'molcha

## handle *n.*
1. дәстәк dəstək
2. тұтқа (tutqa)
3. тутка (tutka)
4. сап (sap)
5. sap
6. сап sap
7. ساپ (sap)
8. соп sop

## handsome *adj.*
1. гәшәнк qəşəng
2. әдеми (ädemi)
3. сүйкүмдүү (süykümdüü)
4. күркәм (kürkäm)
5. yakışıklı
6. гөрмегей görmegeÿ
7. كېلىشكەن (kelishkän)
8. ёқимли yoqimli

## hang *vt.*
1. ас- as-
2. іл- (il-)
3. ил- (il-)
4. ас- (as-)
5. as-
6. ас- as-
7. ئاس (as-)
8. ос- os-

**hanger** *n.*
1. асгы asqı
2. ілгіш (ilgish)
3. илгич (ilgich)
4. кием әлгеч (kiyem elgech)
5. askı
6. вешалка weşalka
7. کیم ئاسقۇچ (kiyim asquch)
8. илгак ilgak

**happen** *v.*
1. ол- ol-
2. болып қал- (bolıp qal-)
3. болуп кал- (bolup kal-)
4. бул- (bul-)
5. ol-
6. бол- bol-
7. يۈز بەر_ (yüz bär-)
8. юз бер- yuz ber-

**happy** *adj.*
1. хошбәхт xoşbəxt
2. бақытты (baqıttı)
3. бактылуу (baktıluu)
4. шат (shat)
5. mutlu
6. багтлы bagtly
7. بەختیار (bäkhtiyar)
8. бахтиёр baxtiyor

**harbor** *n.*
1. лиман liman
2. гавань (gavan')
3. гавань (gavan')
4. гавань (gavan')
5. liman
6. порт port
7. پورت (port)
8. порт port

**hard** (x easy) *adj.*
1. чәтин çətin
2. қиын (qiyın)
3. кыйын (kıyın)
4. авыр (avır)
5. zor
6. кын kyn
7. تەس (täs)
8. қийин qiyin

**hard** (x soft) *adj.*
1. бәрк bərk
2. қатты (qattı)
3. катуу (katuu)
4. нык (nık)
5. katı
6. гаты gaty
7. قاتتىق (qattiq)
8. қаттиқ qattiq

**harm** *n.*
1. зәрәр zərər
2. залал (zalal)
3. залал (zalal)
4. зарап (zarar)
5. zarar
6. зыян zyÿan
7. زەرەر (zärär)
8. зарап zarar

**harmful** *adj.*
1. зәрәрли zərərli
2. зиянды (ziyandı)
3. зыяндуу (zıyanduu)
4. зарарлы (zararlı)
5. zararlı
6. зелелли zelelli
7. زىيانلىق (ziyanliq)
8. зарарли zararli

**harmony** *mus. n.*
1. аһәнк ahəng
2. гармония (garmoniya)
3. гармония (garmoniya)
4. гармония (garmoniya)
5. uyum
6. сазлашма sazlaşma
7. ئاھاڭداشلىق (ahangdashliq)
8. хамоханглик hamohanglik

**harvest** *ag. n.*
1. бичин biçin
2. егін ору (yegin oruw)
3. оруу (oruu)
4. уру (uru)
5. hasat
6. орак orak
7. هوسۇل (hosul)
8. хосил hosil

**haste** *n.*
1. тәләсиклик tələsiklik
2. асығыстық (asığhıstıq)
3. ашыгуу (ashıguu)
4. ашыгу (ashıgu)
5. acele
6. ховлукмачлык howlukmaçlyk
7. ئالدىراشلىق (aldirashliq)
8. шошиш shoshish

**hat** *clo. n.*
1. папаг papaq
2. қалпақ (qalpaq)
3. калпак (kalpak)
4. эшләпә (eshläpä)
5. şapka
6. папак papak
7. باش كىيىم (bash kiyim)
8. шляпа shlyapa

**hate** *v.*
1. нифрэт ет- nifrət et-
2. жек көр- (zhek kör-)
3. жек көр- (jek kör-)
4. дошман күр-
   (doshman kür-)
5. nefret et-
6. йигрен- ÿigren-
7. نپرهتلن_ (näprätlän-)
8. нафратлан- nafratlan-

**hazelnut** *bot. n.*
1. фындыг fındıq
2. орман жаңғак
   (orman zhangghaq)
3. ормон жаңгак
   (ormon janggak)
4. фундук (funduk)
5. fındık
6. фундук хозы funduk hozy
7. نۇرمان ياگشتى
   (orman yangiqi)
8. ўрмон ёнғоғи
   o'rmon yong'og'i

**he** *pron.*
1. о о
2. ол (ol)
3. ал (al)
4. ул (ul)
5. o
6. ол, о ol, o
7. ئۇ (u)
8. y u

**head** *phys. n.*
1. баш baş
2. бас (bas)
3. баш (bash)
4. баш (bash)
5. baş
6. келле kelle

7. باش (bash)
8. бош bosh

**headache** *n.*
1. баш ағрысы baş ağrısı
2. бас ауруы (bas awruwı)
3. баш ооруу (bash ooruu)
4. баш авыруы (bash avıruı)
5. baş ağrısı
6. келлагыры kellagyry
7. باش ئاغرىقى (bash aghriqi)
8. бош оғриғи bosh og'rig'i

**health** *n.*
1. сағламлыг sağlamlıq
2. денсаулық (densawlıq)
3. ден соолук (den sooluk)
4. саулык (saulık)
5. sağlık
6. саглык saglyk
7. سالامەتلك (salamätlik)
8. соғлик sog'lik

**healthy** *adj.*
1. сағлам sağlam
2. сау (saw)
3. соо (soo)
4. сау (sau)
5. sağlıklı
6. сагат sagat
7. ساغلام (saghlam)
8. соғлом sog'lom

**hear** *v.*
1. ешит- eşit-
2. есіт- (yesit-)
3. ук- (uk-)
4. ишет- (ishet-)
5. duy-
6. эшит- eşit-
7. ئاڭلا_ (angla-)
8. эшит- eshit-

**heart** *phys. n.*
1. үрәк ürək
2. жүрек (zhürek)
3. жүрөк (jürök)
4. йөрәк (yöräk)
5. kalp
6. йүрек ÿürek
7. يۈرەك (yüräk)
8. юрак yurak

**heat** *n.*
1. һәрарәт hərarət
2. ыстықтық (ıstıqtıq)
3. ысыктык (ısıktık)
4. кызу (kızu)
5. ısı
6. йылылык ÿylylyk
7. ئىسسىقلىق (issiqliq)
8. иссиқлик issiqlik

**heavy** *adj.*
1. ағыр ağır
2. ауыр (awır)
3. оор (oor)
4. авыр (avır)
5. ağır
6. агыр agyr
7. ئېغىر (eghir)
8. оғир og'ir

**height** *n.*
1. јүксәклик yüksəklik
2. биіктік (biyiktik)
3. бийиктик (biyiktik)
4. биеклек (biyeklek)
5. yükseklik
6. бейиклик beÿiklik
7. ئېگىزلك (egizlik)
8. баландлик balandlik

## helicopter *n.*
1. вертолјот vertolyot
2. вертолёт (vertolyot)
3. вертолёт (vertolyot)
4. вертолёт (vertolyot)
5. helikopter
6. вертолёт wertolÿot
7. تك ئوچار ئايروپىلان (tik uchar ayropilan)
8. вертолёт vertolyot

## hell *rel. n.*
1. чәһәннәм cəhənnəm
2. тозақ (tozaq)
3. тозок (tozok)
4. тәмугъ (tämug')
5. cehennem
6. довзах dowzah
7. دوزاخ (dozakh)
8. дўзах do'zax

## hello *interj.*
1. салам salam
2. сәлем (sälem)
3. салам (salam)
4. исәнмесез (isänmesez)
5. merhaba
6. салам salam
7. ياخشىمۇسز (yakhshimusiz)
8. салом salom

## help *v.*
1. көмәк ет- kömək et-
2. көмектес- (kömektes-)
3. көмөктөш- (kömöktösh-)
4. ярдәм бир- (yardäm bir-)
5. yardım et-
6. ярдам әт- ÿardam et-
7. ياردەم قىل (yardäm qil-)
8. ёрдамлаш- yordamlash-

## help *n.*
1. көмәк kömək
2. көмек (kömek)
3. жардам (jardam)
4. ярдәм (yardäm)
5. yardım
6. ярдам ÿardam
7. ياردەم (yardäm)
8. ёрдам yordam

## hen *zool. n.*
1. тојуг toyuq
2. тауық (tawıq)
3. тоок (took)
4. тавык (tavık)
5. tavuk
6. товук towuk
7. مىكيان (mekiyan)
8. товуқ tovuq

## her *adj.*
1. онун onun
2. оның (onıng)
3. анын (anın)
4. аның (anıng)
5. onun
6. онуң onuñ
7. ئۇننڭ (uning)
8. унинг uning

## her *pron.*
1. ону onu
2. оны (onı)
3. аны (anı)
4. аны (anı)
5. onu
6. оны ony
7. ئۇنى (uni)
8. уни uni

## herb *bot. n.*
1. от, битки ot, bitki
2. ем шөп (yem shöp)
3. ем чөп (em chöp)
4. дару үләне (daru üläne)
5. ot, bitki
6. дерман өсүмлиги derman ösümligi
7. دورا ئوسۇملۇكلەر (dora ösümlüklär)
8. доривор ўсимлик dorivor o'simlik

## herd *n.*
1. сүрү sürü
2. отар (otar)
3. отор (otor)
4. көтү (kötü)
5. sürü
6. сүри süri
7. پادا (pada)
8. пода poda

## here *adv.*
1. бурада, бураја burada, buraya
2. осында, мұнда (osında, munda)
3. мында, бул жерде (mında, bul jerde)
4. монда (monda)
5. burada, buraya
6. бу ерде bu ÿerde
7. بۇ يەردە، مۇشۇ يەردە (bu yärdä, mushu yärdä)
8. бу ерда, бу ерга bu yerda, bu yerga

---

**hers** *pron.*
1. онунку onunku
2. оніकі (oniki)
3. анықы (anıkı)
4. анықы (anıkı)
5. onunki
6. онунқы onuñky
7. ئۇنىڭكى (uningki)
8. уники uniki

**herself** *pron.*
1. өзү özü
2. өзі (özi)
3. өзү (özü)
4. үзе (üze)
5. kendisi
6. өзи özi
7. ئۆزى (özi)
8. ўзи o'zi

**hide** *vt.*
1. кизләт- gizlət-
2. жасыр- (zhasır-)
3. жашыр- (jashır-)
4. яшер- (yasher-)
5. sakla-
6. гизле- gizle-
7. يوشۇر- (yoshur-)
8. яшир- yashir-

**high** *adj.*
1. уча uca
2. биік (biyik)
3. бийик (biyik)
4. биек (biyek)
5. yüksek
6. бейик beÿik
7. ئېگىز (egiz)
8. баланд baland

**hill** *geo. n.*
1. тәпә təpə
2. төбе (töbe)
3. дөбө (döbö)
4. калкулык (kalkulık)
5. tepe
6. депе depe
7. دۆڭ (döng)
8. тепа tepa

**him** *pron.*
1. ону onu
2. оны (onı)
3. аны (anı)
4. аны (anı)
5. onu
6. оны ony
7. ئۇنى (uni)
8. уни uni

**himself** *pron.*
1. өзү özü
2. өзі (özi)
3. өзү (özü)
4. үзе (üze)
5. kendisi
6. өзи özi
7. ئۆزى (özi)
8. ўзи o'zi

**his** *adj.*
1. онун onun
2. оның (onıng)
3. анын (anın)
4. аның (anıng)
5. onun
6. онуң onuñ
7. ئۇنىڭ (uning)
8. унинг uning

**his** *pron.*
1. онунку onunku
2. онікі (oniki)
3. анықы (anıkı)
4. анықы (anıkı)
5. onunki
6. онунқы onuñky
7. ئۇنىڭكى (uningki)
8. уники uniki

**historian** *n.*
1. тарихчи tarixçi
2. тарихшы (tariykhshı)
3. тарыхчы (tarıkhchı)
4. тарихчы (tarikhchı)
5. tarihçi
6. тарыхчы taryhçy
7. تارىخشۇناس (tarikhshunas)
8. тарихчи tarixchi

**history** *n.*
1. тарих tarix
2. тарих (tariykh)
3. тарых (tarıkh)
4. тарих (tarikh)
5. tarih
6. тарых taryh
7. تارىخ (tarikh)
8. тарих tarix

**hit** *v.*
1. вур- vur-
2. ұр- (ur-)
3. ур- (ur-)
4. сук- (suk-)
5. vur-
6. ур- ur-
7. ئۇر- (ur-)
8. ур- ur-

---

1. Azerbaijani   2. Kazakh   3. Kyrgyz   4. Tatar   5. Turkish   6. Turkmen   7. Uighur   8. Uzbek

**hold** *v.*
1. тут- tut-
2. ұста- (usta-)
3. карма- (karma-)
4. тот- (tot-)
5. tut-
6. тут- tut-
7. توت (tut-)
8. ушла- ushla-

**hole** *n.*
1. дәлик dəlik
2. тесік (tesik)
3. тешик (teshik)
4. тишек (tishek)
5. delik
6. дешик deşik
7. تۆشۈك (töshük)
8. тешик teshik

**holiday**
(~commemoration) *n.*
1. бајрам bayram
2. мейрам (meyram)
3. майрам (mayram)
4. бәйрәм (bäyräm)
5. bayram
6. байрам baýram
7. بايرام (bayram)
8. байрам bayram

**holiday** (~vacation) *n.*
1. тә'тил tə'til
2. демалыс (demalıs)
3. дем алыш (dem alısh)
4. ял (yal)
5. tatil
6. дынч алыш dynç alyş
7. تەتىل (tätil)
8. дам олиш dam olish

**home** *n.*
1. ев ev
2. үй (üy)
3. үй (üy)
4. өй (öy)
5. ev
6. өй öý
7. ئۆي (öy)
8. уй uy

**honest** *adj.*
1. дүрүст dürüst
2. адал (adal)
3. чынчыл (chınchıl)
4. намуслы (namuslı)
5. dürüst
6. догручыл dogruçyl
7. سەمىمى (sämimiy)
8. виждонли vijdonli

**honey** *cul. n.*
1. бал bal
2. бал (bal)
3. бал (bal)
4. бал (bal)
5. bal
6. бал bal
7. ھەسەل (häsäl)
8. асал asal

**honeymoon** *n.*
1. бал ајы bal ayı
2. бал ай (bal ay)
3. бал ай (bal ay)
4. ширбәт ae (shirbät aye)
5. balayı
6. бал айы bal aÿy
7. شېرىن ئاي (sherin ay)
8. асал ойи asal oyi

**honor** *n.*
1. шәрәф şərəf
2. намыс (namıs)
3. намыс (namıs)
4. намус (namus)
5. şeref
6. хормат hormat
7. شەرەپ (shäräp)
8. шараф sharaf

**hope** *n.*
1. үмид ümid
2. үміт (ümit)
3. үмүт (ümüt)
4. өмет (ömet)
5. umut
6. умыт umyt
7. ئۈمىد (ümid)
8. умид umid

**hope** *v.*
1. үмид ет- ümid et-
2. үміттен- (ümitten-)
3. үмүт кыл- (ümüt kıl-)
4. өметлән- (ömetlän-)
5. um-
6. умыт эт- umyt et-
7. ئۈمىد قىل (ümid qil-)
8. умид кил- umid qil-

**horizon** *n.*
1. үфүг üfüq
2. көк жиек (kök zhiyek)
3. горизонт (gorizont)
4. офык (ofık)
5. ufuk
6. горизонт gorizont
7. ئۇپۇق (upuq)
8. уфк ufq

---

**horn** *zool. n.*
1. бујнуз buynuz
2. мүйіз (müyiz)
3. мүйүз (müyüz)
4. мөгез (mögez)
5. boynuz
6. шах şah
7. مۇڭگۈز (mönggüz)
8. шох shox

**horse** *zool. n.*
1. ат at
2. ат (at)
3. ат (at)
4. ат (at)
5. at
6. ат at
7. ئات (at)
8. от ot

**hospital** *n.*
1. хәстәхана xəstəxana
2. аурухана (awruwkhana)
3. оорукана (oorukana)
4. шифахәнә (shifakhänä)
5. hastane
6. кеселхана keselhana
7. دوختۇرخانا (dokhturkhana)
8. касалхона kasalxona

**hospitality** *n.*
1. гонагсевәрлик qonaqsevərlik
2. меймандостық (meymandostıq)
3. меймандостук (meymandostuk)
4. кунакчыллык (kunakchıllık)
5. konukseverlik
6. мыхмансөерлик myhmansöyerlik

7. مىھماندوستلۇق (mehmandostluq)
8. мехмондўстлик mehmondo'stlik

**host** *n.*
1. ев саһиби ev sahibi
2. қожайын (qozhayın)
3. кожоюн (kojoyun)
4. хуҗа (khuja)
5. ev sahibi
6. өй әеси öy eÿesi
7. ئۆي ئىگىسى (öy igisi)
8. мезбон mezbon

**hot** *adj.*
1. исти isti
2. ыстық (ıstıq)
3. ысык (ısık)
4. әссе (esse)
5. sıcak
6. ыссы yssy
7. ئىسسىق (issiq)
8. иссик issiq

**hotel** *n.*
1. меһманхана mehmanxana
2. қонақ үйі (qonaq üyi)
3. мейманкана (meymankana)
4. кунакханә (kunakkhänä)
5. otel
6. мыхманхана myhmanhana
7. مىھمانخانا (mehmankhana)
8. мехмонхона mehmonxona

**hour** *n.*
1. саат saat
2. сағат (saghat)
3. саат (saat)
4. сәгатъ (sägat')
5. saat
6. сагат sagat

7. سائەت (sa'ät)
8. соат soat

**house** *n.*
1. ев ev
2. үй (üy)
3. үй (üy)
4. йорт (yort)
5. ev
6. өй öÿ
7. ئۆي (öy)
8. уй uy

**how** *adv.*
1. нечә necə
2. қалай (qalay)
3. кандай (kanday)
4. ничек (nichek)
5. nasıl
6. нәхили nähili
7. قانداق (qandaq)
8. қандай qanday

**how much** (=what amount) *adv.*
1. нә гәдәр nə qədər
2. қанша (qansha)
3. канча (kancha)
4. ничә (nichä)
5. ne kadar
6. нәче näçe
7. نەچچە (nächchä)
8. неча necha

**how much** (=what price) *adv.*
1. нечәјә neçəyə
2. қанша (qansha)
3. канча (kancha)
4. ничә (nichä)
5. kaça
6. нәче näçe
7. قانچە (qanchä)
8. қанча qancha

**huge** *adj.*
1. чох бөjүк çox böyük
2. үлкен (ülken)
3. чоң (chong)
4. бик зур (bik zur)
5. kocaman
6. әгирт улы ägirt uly
7. ناھايىتى چوڭ
(nahayiti chong)
8. каттакон kattakon

**human being** *n.*
1. инсан insan
2. адам (adam)
3. адам (adam)
4. адәм (adäm)
5. insan
6. ынсан ynsan
7. ئادەم (adäm)
8. одам odam

**hundred** *num.*
1. jүз yüz
2. жүз (zhüz)
3. жүз (jüz)
4. йөз (yöz)
5. yüz
6. йүз yüz
7. يۈز (yüz)
8. юз yuz

**hunger** *n.*
1. ачлыг aclıq
2. аштық (ashtıq)
3. ачтык (achtık)
4. ачыгу (achıgu)
5. açlık
6. ачлык açlyk
7. ئاچلىق (achliq)
8. очлик ochlik

**hungry** *adj.*
1. ач ac
2. аш (ash)
3. ач (ach)
4. ач (ach)
5. aç
6. ач aç
7. ئاچ (ach)
8. оч och

**hunt** *vt.*
1. овла- ovla-
2. аң аула- (ang awla-)
3. аң уула- (ang uula-)
4. аула- (aula-)
5. avla-
6. авла- awla-
7. ئوۋلا- (ovla-)
8. овла- ovla-

**hurry** *v.*
1. тәләс- tәlәs-
2. асық- (asıq-)
3. ашык- (ashık-)
4. ашык- (ashık-)
5. acele et-
6. ховлук- howluk-
7. ئالدىرا- (aldira-)
8. шошил- shoshil-

**husband** *n.*
1. әр әr
2. күйеу (küyew)
3. күйөө (küyöö)
4. ир (ir)
5. koca
6. әр är
7. ئەر (är)
8. эр er

**I** *pron.*
1. мән mәn
2. мен (men)
3. мен (men)
4. мин (min)
5. ben
6. мен men
7. مەن (män)
8. мен men

**ice** *n.*
1. буз buz
2. мұз (muz)
3. муз (muz)
4. боз (boz)
5. buz
6. буз buz
7. مۇز (muz)
8. муз muz

**ice cream** *cul. n.*
1. дондурма dondurma
2. балмұздак (balmuzdaq)
3. балмуздак (balmuzdak)
4. туңдырма (tungdırma)
5. dondurma
6. мароженое maroʃenoÿe
7. مارۇژنى (marozhni)
8. музкаймок muzqaymoq

**idea** *n.*
1. фикир fikir
2. ой (oy)
3. ой (oy)
4. фикер (fiker)
5. fikir
6. пикир pikir
7. ئوي (oy)
8. ўй o'y

---

1. Azerbaijani  2. Kazakh  3. Kyrgyz  4. Tatar  5. Turkish  6. Turkmen  7. Uighur  8. Uzbek

## idiom *ling. n.*
1. ифадә ifadә
2. идиома (idioma)
3. идиома (idioma)
4. идиома (idioma)
5. deyim
6. идиома idioma
7. ئدىئوم (idi'om)
8. ибора ibora

## if *conj.*
1. әкәр әgәr
2. егер (yeger)
3. әгерде (egerde)
4. әгәр (ägär)
5. eğer
6. әгер eger
7. ئەگەر (ägär)
8. агар agar

## ill *med. adj.*
1. хәстә xәstә
2. аýру (awruw)
3. ооруу (ooruu)
4. авыру (avıru)
5. hasta
6. сыркав syrkaw
7. كېسەل (kesäl)
8. касал kasal

## illness *med. n.*
1. хәстәлик xәstәlik
2. аýру (awruw)
3. оору (ooru)
4. авыру (avıru)
5. hastalık
6. кесел kesel
7. كېسەللىك (kesällik)
8. касаллик kasallik

## immediately *adv.*
1. дәрһал dәrhal
2. дереу (derew)
3. дароо (daroo)
4. хәзер ук (khäzer ük)
5. hemen
6. деррев derrew
7. دەرھال (därhal)
8. дархол darhol

## important *adj.*
1. мүһүм mühüm
2. маңызды (mangızdı)
3. маанилүү (maanilüü)
4. мөһим (möhim)
5. önemli
6. мөхүм möhüm
7. مۇھىم (muhim)
8. ахамиятли ahamiyatli

## impossible *adj.*
1. имкансыз imkansız
2. мүмкін емес (mümkin yemes)
3. мүмкүн эмес (mümkün emes)
4. чарасыз (charasız)
5. imkânsız
6. мүмкин дәл mümkin däl
7. مۇمكىن بولمىغان (mumkin bolmighan)
8. иложсиз ilojsiz

## in *prep.*
1. -да, -дә -da, -dә
2. -да, -де, -та, -те (-da, -de, -ta, -te)
3. -да, -де, -до, -дө, -та, -те, -то, -тө (-da, -de, -do, -dö, -ta, -te, -to, -tö)
4. -да, -дә, -та, -тә (-da, -dä, -ta, -tä)
5. -da, -de, -ta, -te
6. -да, -де -da, -de
7. ـدا، ـدە، ـتا، ـتە (-da, -dä, -ta, -tä)
8. -да -da

## income *n.*
1. кәлир gәlir
2. кіріс (kiris)
3. киреше (kireshe)
4. килер (kiler)
5. gelir
6. гирдежи girdeji
7. كىرىم (kirim)
8. даромад daromad

## increase *vi.*
1. арт- art-
2. көбей- (köbey-)
3. көбөй- (köböy-)
4. арт- (art-)
5. art-
6. арт- art-
7. كۆپەي- (köpäy-)
8. кўпай- ko'pay-

## independence *pol. n.*
1. мустәгиллик müstәqillik
2. тәуелсіздік (täwelsizdik)
3. эркиндик (erkindik)
4. мөстәкыйльлек (möstäkıyl'lek)
5. bağımsızlık
6. гарашсызлык garaşsyzlyk
7. مۇستەقىللىك (mustäqillik)
8. мустақиллик mustaqillik

## infection *med. n.*
1. инфексиjа infeksiya
2. инфекция (infektsiya)
3. инфекция (infektsiya)
4. инфекция, йогыш (infektsiya, yogısh)
5. enfeksiyon
6. инфекция infektsiÿa
7. ياللۇغ (yallugh)
8. инфекция infektsiya

## inflation *econ. n.*
1. инфлjасиjа inflyasiya
2. инфляция (inflyatsiya)
3. инфляция (inflyatsiya)
4. инфляция (inflyatsiya)
5. enflasyon
6. инфляция inflÿatsiÿa
7. پۇل پاخاللىقى (pul pakhalliqi)
8. инфляция inflyatsiya

## influence *n.*
1. тә'сир tə'sir
2. әсер (äser)
3. таасир (taasir)
4. тәэсир (täesir)
5. etki
6. тәсир täsir
7. تەسىر (täsir)
8. таъсир ta'sir

## inform *v.*
1. хәбәр вер- хәbər ver-
2. айт- (ayt-)
3. кабарла- (kabarla-)
4. белдер- (belder-)
5. haber ver-
6. хабар бер- habar ber-
7. ئۇقتۇر- (uqtur-)
8. хабар қил- xabar qil-

## information *n.*
1. мә'лумат mə'lumat
2. информация (informatsiya)
3. информация (informatsiya)
4. информация (informatsiya)
5. bilgi
6. информация informatsiÿa
7. مەلۇمات (mälumat)
8. хабар xabar

## ink *n.*
1. мүрәккәб mürəkkəb
2. сия (siya)
3. сыя (sıya)
4. кара (kara)
5. mürekkep
6. сыя syÿa
7. سىيا (siya)
8. сиёх siyoh

## innocence *n.*
1. күнаһсызлыг günahsızlıq
2. күнәсіздік (künäsizdik)
3. күнөөсүздүк (künöösüzdük)
4. гөнаһсызлык (gönahsızlık)
5. masumiyet
6. бигүнәлик bigünälik
7. ئەيىبسىزلىك (äyibsizlik)
8. бегуноҳлик begunohlik

## innocent *adj.*
1. күнаһсыз günahsız
2. айыпсыз (ayıpsız)
3. күнөөсүз (künöösüz)
4. гаепсез (gayepsez)
5. suçsuz
6. бигүнә bigünä
7. ئەيىبسىز (äyibsiz)
8. бегуноҳ begunoh

## insanity *n.*
1. дәлилик dəlilik
2. жындылық (zhındılıq)
3. жиндилик (jindilik)
4. тилелек (tilelek)
5. delilik
6. дәлилик dälilik
7. سارا گلىق (sarangliq)
8. жиннилик jinnilik

## insect *zool. n.*
1. бөчәк böcək
2. қурт-қумырсқа (qurt-qumırsqa)
3. курт-кумурска (kurt-kumurska)
4. бөжәк (böjäk)
5. böcek
6. мөр-мөжек mör-möjek
7. قۇرت_قوڭغۇز (qurt-qongghuz)
8. ҳашарот hasharot

## inside *adv.*
1. ичәридә içəridə
2. ішінде (ishinde)
3. ичинде (ichinde)
4. эчтә (echtä)
5. içeride
6. ичерде içerde
7. ئىچىدە (ichidä)
8. ичкарида ichkarida

## instrument *mus. n.*
1. чалғы аләти çalǧı aləti
2. аспап (aspap)
3. аспап (aspap)
4. музыкаль инструмент (muzıkal' instrument)
5. çalgı aleti
6. саз гуралы saz guraly
7. چالغۇ ئەسۋابلىرى (chalghu äsvabliri)
8. асбоб asbob

---

1. Azerbaijani  2. Kazakh  3. Kyrgyz  4. Tatar  5. Turkish  6. Turkmen  7. Uighur  8. Uzbek

## insurance  *n.*
1. сығорта sığorta
2. сақтандыру (saqtandıruw)
3. камсыздоо (kamsızdoo)
4. страховка (strakhovka)
5. sigorta
6. страхование strahowaniÿe
7. سۇغۇرتا (sughurta)
8. суғурта sug'urta

## intellectual  *n.*
1. зијалы ziyalı
2. зиялы (ziyalı)
3. интелигент (inteligent)
4. укымышлы (ukımıshlı)
5. aydın
6. интеллектуал intellektual
7. زىيالى (ziyaliy)
8. зиёли ziyoli

## intelligent  *adj.*
1. ағыллы ağıllı
2. зерек (zerek)
3. зеендүү (zeendüü)
4. акыллы (akıllı)
5. zeki
6. акыллы akylly
7. ئەقىللىق (äqilliq)
8. ақлли aqlli

## intention  *n.*
1. нијјәт niyyət
2. ниет (niyet)
3. ниет (niet)
4. ният (niyat)
5. niyet
6. ниет niÿet
7. نىيەت (niyät)
8. ният niyat

## interest  *n.*
1. мараг maraq
2. қызығу (qızıghuw)
3. кызыгуу (kızıguu)
4. кызыксыну (kızıksınu)
5. ilgi
6. хөвес höwes
7. قىزىقىش (qiziqish)
8. қизиқиш qiziqish

## interest  *econ. n.*
1. фаиз faiz
2. пайда (payda)
3. пайда (payda)
4. процент (protsent)
5. faiz
6. процент protsent
7. ئۆسۈم (ösüm)
8. фойда foyda

## interesting  *adj.*
1. мараглы maraqlı
2. қызық (qızıq)
3. кызык (kızık)
4. кызыклы (kızıklı)
5. ilginç
6. гызыклы gyzykly
7. قىزىق (qiziq)
8. қизиқарли qiziqarli

## international  *adj.*
1. бејнәлхалг beynəlxalq
2. халықаралық (khalıqaralıq)
3. эл аралык (el aralık)
4. халыкара (khalıkara)
5. uluslararası
6. халкара halkara
7. خەلقئارا (khälq'ara)
8. халқаро xalqaro

## intestine  *phys. n.*
1. бағырсаг bağırsaq
2. ішек (ishek)
3. ичеги (ichegi)
4. эчэк (echäk)
5. bağırsak
6. ичеге içege
7. ئۈچەي (üchäy)
8. ичак ichak

## introduce  (*person)  *v.*
1. таныш ет- tanış et-
2. таныстыр- (tanıstır-)
3. тааныштыр- (taanıshtır-)
4. таныштыр- (tanıshtır-)
5. tanıştır-
6. таныштыр- tanyşdyr-
7. تونۇشتۇر- (tonushtur-)
8. таништир- tanishtir-

## investigation  *n.*
1. тәдгигат tədqiqat
2. тергеу (tergew)
3. тергөө (tergöö)
4. тикшеру (tiksherü)
5. araştırma
6. дернеw derñew
7. تەكشۈرۈش (täkshürüsh)
8. текшириш tekshirish

## investment  *econ. n.*
1. капитал гојулушу
   kapital qoyuluşu
2. қаржыландыру
   (qarzhılandıruw)
3. каржыландыруу
   (karjılandıruu)
4. капитал салу
   (kapital salu)
5. yatırım
6. мая гоюш maÿa goÿuş
7. توشقان سەرمايە
   (qoshqan särmayä)
8. ташаббус tashabbus

---

1. Azerbaijani  2. Kazakh  3. Kyrgyz  4. Tatar  5. Turkish  6. Turkmen  7. Uighur  8. Uzbek

**invitation** *n.*
1. дә'вәт də'vət
2. шақыру (shaqıruw)
3. чакыруу (chakıruu)
4. чакыру (chakıru)
5. davet
6. чакылык çakylyk
7. تەكلىپ (täklip)
8. таклиф taklif

**invite** *v.*
1. дә'вәт ет- də'vət et-
2. шақыр- (shaqır-)
3. чакыр- (chakır-)
4. чакыр- (chakır-)
5. davet et-
6. чагыр- çagyr-
7. تەكلىپ قىل- (täklip qil-)
8. таклиф қил- taklif qil-

**iron** *geol. n.*
1. дәмир dəmir
2. темір (temir)
3. темир (temir)
4. тимер (timer)
5. demir
6. демир demir
7. تۆمۈر (tömür)
8. темир temir

**iron** *tech. n.*
1. үтү ütü
2. үтік (ütik)
3. үтүк (ütük)
4. үтүк (ütük)
5. ütü
6. үтүк ütük
7. دەزمال (däzmal)
8. дазмол dazmol

**island** *geo. n.*
1. ада ada
2. арал (aral)
3. арал (aral)
4. утрау (utrau)
5. ada
6. ада ada
7. ئارال (aral)
8. орол orol

**it** *pron.*
1. о o
2. ол (ol)
3. ал (al)
4. ул (ul)
5. o
6. ол, о ol, o
7. ئۇ (u)
8. у u

**its** *adj.*
1. онун onun
2. оның (onıng)
3. анын (anın)
4. аның (anıng)
5. onun
6. онуң onuñ
7. ئۇنىڭ (uning)
8. унинг uning

**its** *pron.*
1. онунку onunku
2. онікі (oniki)
3. аныкы (anıkı)
4. аныкы (anıkı)
5. onunki
6. онуңкы onuñky
7. ئۇنىڭكى (uningki)
8. уники uniki

**itself** *pron.*
1. өзү özü
2. өзі (özi)
3. өзү (özü)
4. үзе (üze)
5. kendisi
6. өзи özi
7. ئۆزى (özi)
8. ўзи o'zi

**jacket** *clo. n.*
1. жакет jaket
2. жәкет (zhäket)
3. жакет (jaket)
4. жакет (zhaket)
5. ceket
6. куртка kurtka
7. چاپان (chapan)
8. камзул kamzul

**jail** *n.*
1. һәбсхана həbsxana
2. түрме (türme)
3. түрмө (türmö)
4. төрмә (törmä)
5. hapishane
6. түрме türme
7. تۈرمە (türmä)
8. қамоқхона qamoqxona

**jam** *cul. n.*
1. мүрәббә mürəbbə
2. қайнатпа (qaynatpa)
3. варенье (varen'e)
4. варенье (varen'ye)
5. reçel
6. мүрепбе mürepbe
7. مۇرابىا (murabba)
8. мураббо murabbo

---

## January *n.*
1. jaнвар yanvar
2. қаңтар (qangtar)
3. январь (yanvar')
4. гыйнвар (gıynvar)
5. ocak
6. январь ÿanwar
7. يانۋار (yanvar)
8. январь yanvar'

## jar *n.*
1. банка banka
2. банка (banka)
3. банка (banka)
4. банка (banka)
5. kavanoz
6. банка banka
7. ئىدىش (idish)
8. банка banka

## jealous *adj.*
1. гысганч qısqanc
2. қызғаншақ (qızghanshaq)
3. кызганчаак (kızganchaak)
4. көнче (könche)
5. kıskanç
6. габанжаң gabanjañ
7. ھەسەتخور (häsätkhor)
8. хасадчи hasadchi

## Jew *rel. n.*
1. jәһуди yәhudi
2. еврей (yevrey)
3. еврей (evrey)
4. еврей (yevrey)
5. Musevi
6. еврей ÿewreÿ
7. يەھۇدى (yähudiy)
8. яхудий yahudiy

## jeweler *n.*
1. зәркәр zәrgәr
2. зергер (zerger)
3. зергер (zerger)
4. зәркән (zärkän)
5. kuyumcu
6. зергәр zergär
7. زەرگەر (zärgär)
8. заргар zargar

## job *n.*
1. иш iş
2. жұмыс (zhumıs)
3. иш (ish)
4. эш (esh)
5. iş
6. иш iş
7. ئىش (ish)
8. иш ish

## joke *n.*
1. зарафат zarafat
2. әзіл (äzil)
3. азил (azil)
4. шаярту (shayartu)
5. şaka
6. дегишме degişme
7. چاتچاق (chaqchaq)
8. хазил hazil

## journalist *n.*
1. журналист jurnalist
2. журналист (zhurnalist)
3. кабарчы (kabarchı)
4. журналист (zhurnalist)
5. gazeteci
6. журналист ∫urnalist
7. مۇخبىر (mukhbir)
8. журналист jurnalist

## journey *n.*
1. cәjaһәt sәyahәt
2. сапар (sapar)
3. сапар (sapar)
4. сәяхәт (säyakhät)
5. yolculuk
6. сыяхат syÿahat
7. سەپەر (säpär)
8. сафар safar

## joy *n.*
1. севинч sevinc
2. қуаныш (quwanısh)
3. кубаныч (kubanıch)
4. шатлык (shatlık)
5. sevinç
6. бегенч begenç
7. خۇشاللىق (khushalliq)
8. шодлик shodlik

## judge *jud. n.*
1. һаким hakim
2. сот (sot)
3. сот (sot)
4. судья, хаким (sud'ya, khakim)
5. yargıç
6. судья sudÿa
7. سوتچى (sotchi)
8. судья sud'ya

## jug *n.*
1. бардаг bardaq
2. құмыра (qumıra)
3. кумура (kumura)
4. чүлмәк (chülmäk)
5. testi
6. күйзе küÿze
7. كوزا (koza)
8. кўза ko'za

---

## July *n.*
1. иjул iyul
2. шiлде (shilde)
3. июль (iyul')
4. июль (iyul')
5. temmuz
6. июль iÿul
7. ئىيۇل (iyul)
8. июль iyul'

## jump *v.*
1. атыл- atıl-
2. секір- (sekir-)
3. секир- (sekir-)
4. сикер- (siker-)
5. sıçra-
6. бөк- bök-
7. سەكرە (säkrä-)
8. сакра- sakra-

## June *n.*
1. иjун iyun
2. маусым (mawsım)
3. июнь (iyun')
4. июнь (iyun')
5. haziran
6. июнь iÿun
7. ئىيۇن (iyun)
8. июнь iyun'

## justice *n.*
1. әдаләт ədalət
2. әдiлет (ädilet)
3. адилдик (adildik)
4. гадаләт (gadalät)
5. adalet
6. адалат adalat
7. ئادالەت (adalät)
8. адолат adolat

## keep *v.*
1. сахла- saxla-
2. сақта- (saqta-)
3. сакта- (sakta-)
4. сакла- (sakla-)
5. tut-
6. сакла- sakla-
7. ساقلا (saqla-)
8. сақла- saqla-

## key *n.*
1. ачар açar
2. кiлт (kilt)
3. килит (kilit)
4. ачкыч (achkıch)
5. anahtar
6. ачар açar
7. ئاچقۇچ (achquch)
8. калит kalit

## kick *v.*
1. тәпиклә- təpiklə-
2. теп- (tep-)
3. теп- (tep-)
4. тип- (tip-)
5. tekmele-
6. деп- dep-
7. تەپ (täp-)
8. теп- tep-

## kidney *phys. n.*
1. бөjрәк böyrək
2. бүйрек (büyrek)
3. бөйрөк (böyrök)
4. бөер (böyer)
5. böbrek
6. бөврек böwrek
7. بۆرەك (börak)
8. буйрак buyrak

## kill *v.*
1. өлдүр- öldür-
2. өлтiр- (öltir-)
3. өлтүр- (öltür-)
4. үтер- (üter-)
5. öldür-
6. өлдүр- öldür-
7. ئۆلتۈر (öltür-)
8. ўлдир- o'ldir-

## kind *adj.*
1. меһрибан mehriban
2. мейiрiмдi (meyirimdi)
3. кайрымдуу (kayrımduu)
4. йомшак күңелле (yomshak küngelle)
5. nazik
6. мәхирли mähirli
7. مىهرىبان (mehriban)
8. мехрибон mehribon

## kind *n.*
1. нөв növ
2. түр (tür)
3. түр (tür)
4. сорт, төр (sort, tör)
5. çeşit
6. хил hil
7. خىل (khil)
8. хил xil

## king *n.*
1. крал kral
2. король (korol')
3. король (korol')
4. король (korol')
5. kral
6. король korol
7. پادىشاھ (padishah)
8. қирол qirol

---

## kiss *v.*
1. өп- öp-
2. сүйіс- (süyis-)
3. өп- (öp-)
4. үп- (üp-)
5. öp-
6. оғша- ogşa-
7. سۆی_ (söy-)
8. ўп- o'p-

## kitchen *n.*
1. мәтбәх mәtbәx
2. ас үй (as üy)
3. ашкана (ashkana)
4. аш ѳе, кухня
   (ash öye, kukhnya)
5. mutfak
6. кухня kuhnÿa
7. ئاشخانا ئۆي (ashkhana öy)
8. ошхона oshxona

## knee *phys. n.*
1. диз diz
2. тізе (tize)
3. тизе (tize)
4. тез (tez)
5. diz
6. дыз dyz
7. تىز (tiz)
8. тизза tizza

## knife *n.*
1. бычаг bıçaq
2. пышақ (pıshaq)
3. бычак (bıchak)
4. пычак (pıchak)
5. bıçak
6. пычак pyçak
7. پىچاق (pichaq)
8. пичоқ pichoq

## knot *n.*
1. дүjүн düyün
2. түйін (tüyin)
3. түйүн (tüyün)
4. жѳй (jöy)
5. düğüm
6. дүвүн düwün
7. تۈگۈن (tügün)
8. түгүн tugun

## know *v.*
1. бил- bil-
2. біл- (bil-)
3. бил- (bil-)
4. бел- (bel-)
5. bil-
6. бил- bil-
7. بىل_ (bil-)
8. бил- bil-

## know (a person) *v.*
1. таны- tanı-
2. таны- (tanı-)
3. тааны- (taanı-)
4. таны- (tanı-)
5. tanı-
6. тана- tana-
7. تونۇ_ (tonu-)
8. тани- tani-

## knowledge *n.*
1. билик bilik
2. білім (bilim)
3. билим (bilim)
4. белем (belem)
5. bilgi
6. билим bilim
7. بىلىم (bilim)
8. билим bilim

## ladder *n.*
1. нәрдиван nәrdivan
2. саты (satı)
3. шаты (shatı)
4. баскыч (baskıch)
5. merdiven
6. мердиван merdiwan
7. شوتا (shota)
8. нарвон narvon

## lady *n.*
1. ханым xanım
2. ханым (khanım)
3. айым (ayım)
4. ханым (khanım)
5. hanım
6. ханым hanym
7. خانم (khanim)
8. хоним xonim

## lake *geo. n.*
1. кѳл göl
2. кѳл (köl)
3. кѳл (köl)
4. күл (kül)
5. göl
6. кѳл köl
7. كۆل (köl)
8. кўл ko'l

## lamb *zool. n.*
1. гузу quzu
2. қозы (qozi)
3. козу (kozu)
4. бәти (bäti)
5. kuzu
6. гузы guzy
7. پاتلان (paqlan)
8. қўзичоқ qo'zichoq

---

1. Azerbaijani  2. Kazakh  3. Kyrgyz  4. Tatar  5. Turkish  6. Turkmen  7. Uighur  8. Uzbek

## lamp *n.*
1. лампа lampa
2. лампа (lampa)
3. лампа (lampa)
4. лампа (lampa)
5. lamba
6. лампа lampa
7. چىراغ (chiragh)
8. чироқ chiroq

## language *n.*
1. дил dil
2. тіл (til)
3. тил (til)
4. тел (tel)
5. dil
6. дил dil
7. تىل (til)
8. тил til

## large *adj.*
1. jekə yekə
2. ірі (iri)
3. ири (iri)
4. зур (zur)
5. büyük
6. улы, гиң uly, giñ
7. زور (zor)
8. катта katta

## last (*for week, year etc.) *adj.*
1. кечән keçən
2. өткен (ötken)
3. өткөн (ötkön)
4. үткән (ütkän)
5. geçen
6. гечен geçen
7. ئۆتكەن (ötkän)
8. ўтган o'tgan

## last (~final) *adj.*
1. ахырынчы axırıncı
2. соңғы (songghı)
3. акыркы (akırkı)
4. соңгы (songgı)
5. son
6. соңкы soñky
7. ئاخىرقى (akhirqi)
8. охирги oxirgi

## late *adv.*
1. кеч gec
2. кеш (kesh)
3. кеч (kech)
4. соң (song)
5. geç
6. гич giç
7. كەچ (käch)
8. кеч kech

## laugh *v.*
1. күл- gül-
2. күл- (kül-)
3. күл- (kül-)
4. көл- (köl-)
5. gül-
6. гүл- gül-
7. كۈل (kül-)
8. кул- kul-

## law *jud. n.*
1. ганун qanun
2. заң (zang)
3. мыйзам (mıyzam)
4. канун (kanun)
5. kanun
6. канун kanun
7. قانۇن (qanun)
8. қонун qonun

## lawyer *jud. n.*
1. вәкил vəkil
2. заңгер (zangger)
3. заңчы (zangchı)
4. адвокат, яклаучы (advokat, yaklauchı)
5. avukat
6. юрист ÿurist
7. ئادۋوكات (advokat)
8. адвокат advokat

## laxative *med. n.*
1. ишләтмә дәрманы işlətmə dərmanı
2. іш өткізетін дәрі (ish ötkizetin däri)
3. ич өткөрүүчү дары (ich ötkörüüchü darı)
4. эч йомшарткыч (ech yomshartkıch)
5. müshil
6. ичиңи сүрйән дерман içiñi sürÿän derman
7. سۈرگە (sürgä)
8. сурги surgi

## laziness *n.*
1. тәнбәллик tənbəllik
2. жалқаулық (zhalqawlıq)
3. жалкоолук (jalkooluk)
4. ялкаулык (yalkaulık)
5. tembellik
6. ялталык ÿaltalyk
7. ھۇرۇنلۇق (hurunluq)
8. дангасалик dangasalik

## lazy *adj.*
1. тәнбәл tənbəl
2. жалқау (zhalqaw)
3. жалкоо (jalkoo)
4. ялкау (yalkau)
5. tembel
6. ялта ÿalta
7. ھۇرۇن (hurun)
8. дангаса dangasa

---

1. Azerbaijani  2. Kazakh  3. Kyrgyz  4. Tatar  5. Turkish  6. Turkmen  7. Uighur  8. Uzbek

## lead *geol. n.*
1. гурғушун qurğuşun
2. қорғасын (qorghasın)
3. коргошун (korgoshun)
4. кургаш(ын) (kurgash[ın])
5. kurşun
6. гуршун gurşun
7. توغوشون (qoghushun)
8. қўрғошин qo'rg'oshin

## leaf *bot. n.*
1. japnaг yarpaq
2. жапырақ (zhapıraq)
3. жалбырак (jalbırak)
4. яфрак (yafrak)
5. yaprak
6. япрак ÿaprak
7. يوپورماق (yopurmaq)
8. барг barg

## learn *v.*
1. өjрəн- öyrən-
2. үйрен- (üyren-)
3. үйрөн- (üyrön-)
4. өйрəн- (öyrän-)
5. öğren-
6. өврен- öwren-
7. ئوگەن- (ögän-)
8. ўрган- o'rgan-

## leather *n.*
1. дəри dəri
2. тepi (teri)
3. тери (teri)
4. тире (tire)
5. deri
6. гайыш gaÿyş
7. كۆن (kön)
8. тери teri

## leave *v.*
1. тəрк ет- tərk et-
2. кет- (ket-)
3. кет- (ket-)
4. ташла- (tashla-)
5. terk et-
6. галдыр- galdyr-
7. كەت- (kät-)
8. (ташлаб) кет-
   [tashlab] ket-

## lecture *n.*
1. мүһазирə mühazirə
2. лекция (lektsiya)
3. лекция (lektsiya)
4. лекция (lektsiya)
5. konferans
6. лекция lektsiÿa
7. لېكسىيە (leksiyä)
8. лекция lektsiya

## left *n.*
1. сол sol
2. сол (sol)
3. сол (sol)
4. сул (sul)
5. sol
6. чеп çep
7. سول (sol)
8. чап chap

## leg *phys. n.*
1. гыч qıç
2. аяқ (ayaq)
3. бут (but)
4. аяк (ayak)
5. bacak
6. аяк aÿak
7. پۇت (put)
8. оёқ oyoq

## legend *lit. n.*
1. əфсанə əfsanə
2. аңыз (angız)
3. уламыш (ulamısh)
4. риваять (rivayat')
5. efsane
6. легенда legenda
7. رىۋايەت (rivayät)
8. афсона afsona

## lemon *bot. n.*
1. лимон limon
2. лимон (limon)
3. лимон (limon)
4. лимон (limon)
5. limon
6. лимон limon
7. لىمون (limon)
8. лимон limon

## length *n.*
1. узунлуг uzunluq
2. ұзындық (uzındıq)
3. узундук (uzunduk)
4. озынлык (ozınlık)
5. uzunluk
6. узынлык uzynlyk
7. ئۇزۇنلۇق (uzunluq)
8. узунлик uzunlik

## lentil *bot. n.*
1. мəрчи mərci
2. жасымык (zhasımıq)
3. жасымык (jasımık)
4. ясмык (yasmık)
5. mercimek
6. мержимек merjimek
7. يەسىموق (yesimuq)
8. ясмик yasmiq

---

**lesson** *n.*
1. дәрс dərs
2. сабақ (sabaq)
3. сабак (sabak)
4. дәрес (däres)
5. ders
6. сапак sapak
7. دەرس (därs)
8. дарс dars

**letter** (*of an alphabet) *n.*
1. һәрф hərf
2. әріп (ärip)
3. арип (arip)
4. хәреф (khäref)
5. harf
6. харп harp
7. ھەرپ (härp)
8. ҳарф harf

**letter** (~mail) *n.*
1. мәктуб məktub
2. хат (khat)
3. кат (kat)
4. хат (khat)
5. mektup
6. хат hat
7. خەت (khät)
8. хат xat

**lettuce** *bot. n.*
1. kahы kahı
2. салат (salat)
3. салат (salat)
4. салат (salat)
5. marul
6. салат salat
7. بىر خىل كۆكتات (bir khil köktat)
8. салат salat

**level** *n.*
1. сәвијјә səviyyə
2. деңгей (denggey)
3. деңгээл (denggeel)
4. дәрәҗә (däräjä)
5. seviye
6. дереже dereje
7. سەۋىيە (säviyä)
8. савия saviya

**library** *n.*
1. китабхана kitabxana
2. кітапхана (kitapkhana)
3. китепкана (kitepkana)
4. китапханә (kitapkhanä)
5. kütüphane
6. китапхана kitaphana
7. كۈتۈپخانا (kütüpkhana)
8. кутубхона kutubxona

**lid** *n.*
1. гапаг qapaq
2. қақпақ (qaqpaq)
3. капкак (kapkak)
4. капкач (kapkach)
5. kapak
6. гапак gapak
7. قاپقاق (qapqaq)
8. қопқоқ qopqoq

**lie** *n.*
1. јалан yalan
2. жалған (zhalghan)
3. жалган (jalgan)
4. ялган (yalgan)
5. yalan
6. ялан ÿalan
7. يالغان گەپ (yalghan gäp)
8. ёлғон yolg'on

**lie** (=tell lie) *v.*
1. јалан данышyalan danış-
2. алда- (alda-)
3. алда- (alda-)
4. ялган сөйлә- (yalgan söylä-)
5. yalan söyle-
6. алда- alda-
7. يالغان سۆزلە- (yalghan sözlä-)
8. алда- alda-

**lie** (down) *v.*
1. узан- uzan-
2. жат- (zhat-)
3. жат- (jat-)
4. ят- (yat-)
5. yat-
6. ят- ÿat-
7. ياتـ- (yat-)
8. ёт- yot-

**life** *n.*
1. һәјат həyat
2. өмір (ömir)
3. өмүр (ömür)
4. тормыш (tormısh)
5. hayat
6. дурмуш durmuş
7. ھايات (hayat)
8. ҳаёт hayot

**lift** *v.*
1. галдыр- qaldır-
2. көтер- (köter-)
3. көтөр- (kötör-)
4. күтәр- (kütär-)
5. kaldır-
6. гөтер- göter-
7. كۆتۈر- (kötür-)
8. кўтар- ko'tar-

## light (x heavy) adj.
1. јүнкүл yüngül
2. жеңіл (zhengil)
3. жеңил (jengil)
4. җиңел (jingel)
5. hafif
6. еңил ÿeñil
7. ينيق (yeniq)
8. енгил yengil

## light (~illumination) n.
1. ишыг işıq
2. жарық (zharıq)
3. жарык (jarık)
4. яктылык (yaktılık)
5. ışık
6. ышык yşyk
7. يورۇقلۇق (yoruqluq)
8. ёруғлик yorug'lik

## lightning n.
1. шимшәк şimşәk
2. найзағай (nayzaghay)
3. чагылган (chagılgan)
4. яшен (yashen)
5. şimşek
6. йылдырым ÿyldyrym
7. چاقماق (chaqmaq)
8. чақмоқ chaqmoq

## like v.
1. хошла- xoşla-
2. ұнат- (unat-)
3. жактыр- (jaktır-)
4. ярат- (yarat-)
5. sev-
6. сөй- söÿ-
7. ياخشى كۆر- (yakhshi kör-)
8. ёқтир- yoqtir-

## like prep.
1. кими kimi
2. сияқты (siyaqtı)
3. сыяктуу (sıyaktuu)
4. охшаш (okhshash)
5. gibi
6. ялы ÿaly
7. ئوخشاش (okhshash)
8. каби kabi

## line (*thin mark) n.
1. хәтт xәtt
2. сызық (sızıq)
3. сызык (sızık)
4. сызык (sızık)
5. çizgi
6. чызык çyzyk
7. سزىق (siziq)
8. чизик chiziq

## linguist n.
1. дилчи dilçi
2. лингвист (lingvist)
3. лингвист (lingvist)
4. телче (telche)
5. dilci
6. дилчи dilçi
7. تىلشۇناس (tilshunas)
8. тилшунос tilshunos

## linguistics n.
1. дилшүнаслыг dilşünaslıq
2. тіл білімі (til bilimi)
3. тил илими (til ilimi)
4. тел белеме (tel beleme)
5. dilbilim
6. лингвистика lingwistika
7. تىلشۇناسلىق (tilshunasliq)
8. тилшунослик tilshunoslik

## lion zool. n.
1. шир şir
2. арыстан (arıstan)
3. арстан (arstan)
4. арыслан (arıslan)
5. aslan
6. ёлбарс ÿolbars
7. شىر (shir)
8. шер sher

## lip phys. n.
1. додаг dodaq
2. ерін (yerin)
3. эрин (erin)
4. ирен (iren)
5. dudak
6. додак dodak
7. كالپۇك (kalpuk)
8. лаб lab

## liquid phy. n.
1. maje maye
2. сұйықтық (suyıqtıq)
3. суюк (suyuk)
4. сыеклык (sıyeklık)
5. sıvı
6. сувук suwuk
7. سۇيۇقلۇق (suyuqluq)
8. суюклик suyuqlik

## listen v.
1. динлә- dinlә-
2. тыңда- (tıngda-)
3. тыңда- (tıngda-)
4. тыңла- (tıngla-)
5. dinle-
6. диңле- diñle-
7. ئاڭلا- (angla-)
8. эшит- eshit-

### literary *adj.*
1. әдәби әdәbi
2. әдеби (ädebiy)
3. адабий (adabiy)
4. әдәби (ädäbi)
5. edebi
6. әдеби edebi
7. ئەدەبىي (ädäbiy)
8. адабий adabiy

### literary work *n.*
1. әдәби әсәр әdәbi әsәr
2. әдеби жұмыс (ädebiy zhumıs)
3. адабий эмгек (adabiy emgek)
4. әдәби әсәр (ädäbi äsär)
5. edebi eser
6. әдеби әсер edebi eser
7. ئەدەبىي ئەسەر (ädäbiy äsär)
8. адабий асар adabiy asar

### literate *adj.*
1. савадлы savadlı
2. сауатты (sawattı)
3. сабаттуу (sabattuu)
4. мәгълүматлы (mäg'lümatlı)
5. okur yazar
6. соватлы sowatly
7. ساۋاتلىق (savatliq)
8. саводли savodli

### literature *n.*
1. әдәбијјат әdәbiyyat
2. әдебиет (ädebiyet)
3. адабият (adabiyat)
4. әдәбият (ädäbiyat)
5. edebiyat
6. әдебият edebiyat
7. ئەدەبىيات (ädäbiyat)
8. адабиёт adabiyot

### little *adv.*
1. бир аз bir az
2. біраз (biraz)
3. бир аз (bir az)
4. бераз (beraz)
5. biraz
6. азажық azajyk
7. بىر ئاز (bir az)
8. бир оз bir oz

### little (x big) *adj.*
1. балача balaca
2. кішкентай (kishkentay)
3. кичинекей (kichinekey)
4. кечкенә (kechkenä)
5. küçük
6. кичи kiçi
7. كىچىك (kichik)
8. кичик kichik

### live *v.*
1. jаша- yaşa-
2. түр- (tur-)
3. жаша- (jasha-)
4. яшә- (yashä-)
5. yaşa-
6. яша- ÿaşa-
7. ياشا_ (yasha-)
8. яша- yasha-

### liver *phys. n.*
1. гарачијәр qaraciyәr
2. бауыр (bawır)
3. боор (boor)
4. бавыр (bavır)
5. karaciğer
6. бағыр bagyr
7. جىگەر (jigär)
8. жигар jigar

### loan *econ. n.*
1. борч borc
2. қарыз (qarız)
3. карыз (karız)
4. бурыч (burıch)
5. borç
6. карз karz
7. قەرز (qärz)
8. қарз, заём qarz, zayom

### lock *n.*
1. килид kilid
2. құлып (qulıp)
3. кулпу (kulpu)
4. йозак (yozak)
5. kilit
6. гулп gulp
7. قۇلۇپ (qulup)
8. қулф qulf

### long *adj.*
1. узун uzun
2. ұзын (uzın)
3. узун (uzun)
4. озын (ozın)
5. uzun
6. узын uzyn
7. ئۇزۇن (uzun)
8. узун uzun

### look *v.*
1. бах- bax-
2. қара- (qara-)
3. кара- (kara-)
4. кара- (kara-)
5. bak-
6. бак- bak-
7. قارا_ (qara-)
8. қара- qara-

---

1. Azerbaijani   2. Kazakh   3. Kyrgyz   4. Tatar   5. Turkish   6. Turkmen   7. Uighur   8. Uzbek

## look for  *v.*
1. ахтар- axtar-
2. ізде- (izde-)
3. изде- (izde-)
4. ээлə- (ezlä-)
5. ara-
6. гөзлə- gözle-
7. ‫ئىزده‬ _ (izdä-)
8. қидир- qidir-

## loose (x tight)  *adj.*
1. бош, кен boş, gen
2. бос, кең (bos, keng)
3. бош, кең (bosh, keng)
4. буш, кин (bush, king)
5. gevşek, bol
6. говшак, гиң gowşak, giñ
7. ‫ كەڭ ‫، ‫بوش‬ (bosh, käng)
8. бўш, кенг bo'sh, keng

## lose  *vt.*
1. итир- itir-
2. жоғалт- (zhoghalt-)
3. жогот- (jogot-)
4. югалт- (yugalt-)
5. kaybet-
6. йитир- ÿitir-
7. ‫يوقات‬ (yoqat-)
8. йўқот- yo'qot-

## loss  *econ. n.*
1. зиjан ziyan
2. зиян (ziyan)
3. зыян (zıyan)
4. зыян (zıyan)
5. ziyan
6. йитги ÿitgi
7. ‫زيان‬ (ziyan)
8. зиён ziyon

## loud  *adj.*
1. бəрк bərk
2. қатты (qattı)
3. катуу (katuu)
4. каты (katı)
5. yüksek (ses)
6. гаты [cec] gaty [ses]
7. ‫قاتتىق‬ (qattiq)
8. баланд [овоз]
baland [ovoz]

## louse  *zool. n.*
1. бит bit
2. бит (biyt)
3. бит (bit)
4. бет (bet)
5. bit
6. бит bit
7. ‫پىت‬ (pit)
8. бит bit

## love  *v.*
1. сев- sev-
2. сүй- (süy-)
3. сүй- (süy-)
4. ярат- (yarat-)
5. sev-
6. сөй- söy-
7. ‫سۆي‬ _ (söy-)
8. сев- sev-

## love  *n.*
1. мəhəббəт məhəbbət
2. махаббат (makhabbat)
3. махаббат (makhabbat)
4. мəхəббəт (mähäbbät)
5. sevgi, aşk
6. сөйги söÿgi
7. ‫مۇھەببەت‬ (muhäbbät)
8. мухаббат muhabbat

## low  *adj.*
1. алчаг alçaq
2. төмен (tömen)
3. төмөн (tömön)
4. түбəн (tübän)
5. alçak
6. пес pes
7. ‫پەس‬ (päs)
8. паст past

## luck  *n.*
1. шанс şans
2. сəттілік (sättilik)
3. саттуу (sattuu)
4. уңыш (ungısh)
5. şans
6. багт bagt
7. ‫ئامەت‬ (amät)
8. омад omad

## lukewarm  *adj.*
1. илыг ılıq
2. жылы (zhılı)
3. жылуу (jıluu)
4. жылы (jılı)
5. ılık
6. йылы ÿyly
7. ‫يىللىق‬ (yilliq)
8. илиқ iliq

## lunch  *n.*
1. икинчи чəhəp jeмəjи
ikinci səhər yeməyi
2. түскі ас (tüski as)
3. түшкү тамак
(tüshkü tamak)
4. төшке аш (töshke ash)
5. öğle yemeği
6. гүнорта нахары
günorta nahary
7. ‫تاماق‬ ‫چۈشلۈك‬ 7.
(chüshlük tamaq)
8. тушлик tushlik

---

1. Azerbaijani   2. Kazakh   3. Kyrgyz   4. Tatar   5. Turkish   6. Turkmen   7. Uighur   8. Uzbek

**lung** *phys. n.*
1. ағчиjəр ağciyər
2. өкпе (ökpe)
3. өпкө (öpkö)
4. үпкә (üpkä)
5. akciğer
6. өйкен öyken
7. ئۆپكە (öpkä)
8. ÿпка o'pka

**machine** *n.*
1. машын maşın
2. машине (mashine)
3. машина (mashina)
4. машина (mashina)
5. makina
6. машын maşyn
7. ماشىنا (mashina)
8. машина mashina

**machine gun** *mil. n.*
1. пулемjот pulemyot
2. пулемет (pulemet)
3. пулемет (pulemet)
4. автомат (avtomat)
5. makinalı tüfek
6. пулемөт pulemÿot
7. پىلىموت (pilimot)
8. автомат avtomat

**magazine** *n.*
1. журнал jurnal
2. журнал (zhurnal)
3. журнал (jurnal)
4. журнал (zhurnal)
5. dergi
6. журнал ʃurnal
7. ژۇرنال (zhurnal)
8. журнал jurnal

**magic** *n.*
1. cehp sehr
2. сиқыр (siyqır)
3. сыйкырдуу (sıykırduu)
4. сихер (sikher)
5. sihir
6. җады jady
7. سېھر (sehir)
8. cexp sehr

**mailbox** *n.*
1. почт гутусу poçt qutusu
2. пошта жәшігі (poshta zhäshigi)
3. почто жашиги (pochto jashigi)
4. почта ящигы (pochta yashchigı)
5. posta kutusu
6. почта ящиги poçta ÿaşçigi
7. پوچتا ساندۇقى (pochta sanduqi)
8. почта қутиси pochta qutisi

**mailman** *n.*
1. почталjон poçtalyon
2. пошташы (poshtashı)
3. почточу (pochtochu)
4. почтальон, хат ташучы (pochtal'on, khat tashuchı)
5. postacı
6. почтальон poçtalon
7. پوچتىكەش (pochtikäsh)
8. почтачи pochtachi

**main** *adj.*
1. əcac əsas
2. негізгі (negizgi)
3. негизги (negizgi)
4. тəп (töp)
5. ana
6. əсасы esasy

7. ئاساسى (asasiy)
8. асосий asosiy

**majority** *pol. n.*
1. əксəрijjəт əksəriyyət
2. көпшілік (köpshilik)
3. көпчүлүк (köpchülük)
4. купчелек (küpchelek)
5. çoğunluk
6. көпчулик köpçülik
7. كۆپ سانلىق (köp sanliq)
8. кӱпчилик ko'pchilik

**make** *v.*
1. ет-, дүзəлт- et-, düzəlt-
2. жаса- (zhasa-)
3. жаса- (jasa-)
4. яса- (yasa-)
5. yap-
6. эт- et-
7. ياسا_ (yasa-)
8. яса- yasa-

**man** (=male) *n.*
1. киши kişi
2. еркек (yerkek)
3. эркек (erkek)
4. ир (ir)
5. erkek
6. эркек erkek
7. ئەر (är)
8. əркак erkak

**manager** *n.*
1. мүдир müdir
2. меңгеруші (menggeruwshi)
3. башкаруучу (bashkaruuchu)
4. идарə итүче (idarä itüche)
5. yönetici, idareci
6. ёлбашчы, менежер yolbaşçy, menejer
7. باشقۇرغۇچى (bashqurghuchi)
8. бошқарувчи boshqaruvchi

## many *adj.*
1. чох çox
2. көп (köp)
3. көп (köp)
4. күп (küp)
5. çok
6. көп, кән köp, kän
7. كۆپ (köp)
8. күп ko'p

## map *n.*
1. хәритә xəritə
2. карта (karta)
3. карта (karta)
4. карта (karta)
5. harita
6. карта karta
7. خەرتە (khäritä)
8. харита xarita

## March *n.*
1. март mart
2. наурыз (nawrız)
3. март (mart)
4. март (mart)
5. mart
6. март mart
7. مارت (mart)
8. март mart

## market *n.*
1. базар bazar
2. базар (bazar)
3. базар (bazar)
4. базар (bazar)
5. pazar
6. базар bazar
7. بازار (bazar)
8. бозор bozor

## marriage *n.*
1. евләнмә evlənmə
2. үйлену (üylenuw)
3. үйлөнүү (üylönüü)
4. өйләну (öylänü)
5. evlilik
6. өйленме, дурмуша чыкма öylenme, durmuşa çykma
7. نكاھ (nikah)
8. уйланиш, турмушга чикиш uylanish, turmushga chiqish

## marry *vi.*
1. евлән- evlən-
2. үйлен- (üylen-)
3. үйлөн- (üylön-)
4. өйлән- (öylän-)
5. evlen-
6. өйлен-, дурмуша чык- öylen-, durmuşa çyk-
7. توي قىل (toy qil-)
8. үйлан-, турмушга чик- o'ylan-, turmushga chiq-

## masterpiece *art. n.*
1. шаһ әсәр şah əsər
2. даналық туынды (danalıq tuwındı)
3. шедевр (shedevr)
4. гүзәл әсәр (güzäl äsär)
5. şaheser
6. непис иш nepis iş
7. زور ئەسەر (zor äsär)
8. шох acap shoh asar

## match *n.*
1. кибрит kibrit
2. сірінке (siringke)
3. ширеңке (shirengke)
4. шырпы (shırpı)
5. kibrit
6. отлучөп otluçöp
7. سەرەڭگە (säränggä)
8. гугурт gugurt

## match *spor. n.*
1. оjyн oyun
2. матч (match)
3. матч (match)
4. матч (match)
5. maç
6. оюн oyun
7. مۇسابىقە (musabiqä)
8. ўйин o'yin

## material *n.*
1. материал material
2. материал (material)
3. материал (material)
4. материал (material)
5. malzeme
6. материал material
7. ماتېرىيال (materiyal)
8. материал material

## mathematics *n.*
1. риjазиjjат riyaziyyat
2. математика (matematika)
3. математика (matematika)
4. математика (matematika)
5. matematik
6. математика matematika
7. ماتېماتىكا (matematika)
8. математика matematika

## matter *phy. n.*
1. маддә maddə
2. зат (zat)
3. зат (zat)
4. матдә (matdä)
5. madde
6. мадда madda
7. ماددا (madda)
8. модда modda

---

**mattress** *n.*
1. дэшэк döşək
2. төсек (tösek)
3. көрпөчө (körpöchö)
4. матрас (matras)
5. yatak
6. дүшек düşek
7. ماتراس (matras)
8. түшак to'shak

**May** *n.*
1. мај may
2. мамыр (mamır)
3. май (may)
4. май (may)
5. mayıs
6. май maÿ
7. ماي (may)
8. май may

**mayor** *n.*
1. мер mer
2. әкім (äkim)
3. аким (akim)
4. мэр (mer)
5. belediye başkanı
6. мэр mer
7. شەھەر باشلىقى
(shähär bashliqi)
8. хоким hokim

**me** *pron.*
1. мәни məni
2. мені (meni)
3. мени (meni)
4. мине (mine)
5. beni
6. мени meni
7. مېنى (meni)
8. мени meni

**meadow** *n.*
1. отлаг otlaq
2. жайылым (zhayılım)
3. жайыт (jayıt)
4. көтүлек (kötülek)
5. otlak
6. яйла ÿaÿla
7. ئوتلاق (otlaq)
8. яйлов yaylov

**measure** *n.*
1. өлчү ölçü
2. өлшем (ölshem)
3. өлчөм (ölchöm)
4. үлчәм (ülchäm)
5. ölçü
6. өлчег ölçeg
7. ئۆلچەم (ölchäm)
8. үлчов o'lchov

**meat** *cul. n.*
1. әт ət
2. ет (yet)
3. эт (et)
4. ит (it)
5. et
6. әг et
7. گۆش (gösh)
8. гүшт go'sht

**medicine** (*profession)
*n.*
1. тибб tibb
2. медицина (meditsina)
3. медицина (meditsina)
4. медицина (meditsina)
5. tıp
6. медицина meditsina
7. دوختۇرلۇق (dokhturluq)
8. медицина meditsina

**medicine** (=drug) *n.*
1. дәрман dərman
2. дәрі (däri)
3. дары (darı)
4. дару (daru)
5. ilaç
6. дерман derman
7. دورا (dora)
8. дори dori

**medium** *adj.*
1. орта orta
2. орта (orta)
3. орто (orto)
4. урта (urta)
5. orta
6. орта orta
7. ئوتتۇرا (ottura)
8. ўртача o'rtacha

**meet** *v.*
1. гаршылаш- qarşılaş-
2. кездес- (kezdes-)
3. кездеш- (kezdesh-)
4. очраш- (ochrash-)
5. karşılaş-
6. душуш- duşuş-
7. ئۇچراش- (uchrash-)
8. учраш- uchrash-

**meeting** *n.*
1. јығынчаг yığıncaq
2. жиналыс (zhiynalıs)
3. жыйын (jıyın)
4. җыелыш (jıyelısh)
5. toplantı
6. йыгнак ÿygnak
7. يىغىن (yighin)
8. мажлис majlis

---

1. Azerbaijani   2. Kazakh   3. Kyrgyz   4. Tatar   5. Turkish   6. Turkmen   7. Uighur   8. Uzbek

## melon *bot. n.*
1. говун qovun
2. қауын (qawın)
3. коон (koon)
4. кавын (kavın)
5. kavun
6. гавун gawun
7. قوغون (qoghun)
8. қовун qovun

## melt *vi.*
1. әри- әri-
2. epi- (yeri-)
3. эри- (eri-)
4. эре- (ere-)
5. eri-
6. эре- ere-
7. ئبرد_ (eri-)
8. эри- eri-

## member *n.*
1. үзв üzv
2. мүше (müshe)
3. мүчө (müchö)
4. әгъза (äg'za)
5. üye
6. агза agza
7. ئەزا (äza)
8. аъзо a'zo

## memory *n.*
1. hафизә hafizә
2. ec (yes)
3. эс (es)
4. хәтер (khäter)
5. hafıza
6. ят ÿat
7. ئەس (äs)
8. хотира xotira

## mend *v.*
1. тә'мир ет- tә'mir et-
2. жөнде- (zhönde-)
3. жөндө- (jöndö-)
4. төзәт- (tözät-)
5. onar-
6. оңар- oñar-
7. توزه تـ (tüzät-)
8. тузат- tuzat-

## menu *n.*
1. менју menyu
2. меню (menyu)
3. меню (menyu)
4. меню (menyu)
5. yemek listesi
6. меню menÿu
7. تاماق تـزـملكى (tamaq tizimliki)
8. таомнома taomnoma

## messy *adj.*
1. гармагарышыг qarmaqarışıq
2. былық (bılıq)
3. аралашкан (aralashkan)
4. буталчык (butalchık)
5. karmakarışık
6. булашык bulaşyk
7. قالايمـقان (qalaymiqan)
8. ағдар-түнтар ag'dar-to'ntar

## metal *geol. n.*
1. метал metal
2. металл (metall)
3. металл (metall)
4. металл (metall)
5. metal
6. метал metal
7. مبتال (metal)
8. металл metall

## middle *adj.*
1. орта orta
2. орта (orta)
3. орто (orto)
4. урта (urta)
5. orta
6. орта orta
7. ئوتتۇرا (ottura)
8. ÿрта o'rta

## midnight *n.*
1. кечә jарысы gecә yarısı
2. түн ортасы (tün ortası)
3. түн ортосу (tün ortosu)
4. төн уртасы (tön urtası)
5. gece yarısı
6. яры гиҗе ÿary gije
7. تۈن يبرـمى (tün yerimi)
8. ярим тун yarim tun

## milk *cul. n.*
1. сүд süd
2. сүт (süt)
3. сүт (süt)
4. сөт (söt)
5. süt
6. сүйт süÿt
7. سۈت (süt)
8. сут sut

## mill *tech. n.*
1. дәјирман dәyirman
2. дигірмен (diyirmen)
3. тегирмен (tegirmen)
4. тегермән (tegermän)
5. değirmen
6. дегирмен degirmen
7. تۈگمـن (tügmän)
8. тегирмон tegirmon

---

**million** *num.*
1. милјон milyon
2. миллион (million)
3. миллион (million)
4. миллион (million)
5. milyon
6. миллион million
7. مليون (milyon)
8. миллион million

**mind** *phys. n.*
1. ағыл ağıl
2. ақыл (aqıl)
3. акыл (akıl)
4. акыл (akıl)
5. akıl
6. акыл akyl
7. ئەقىل (äqil)
8. ақл aql

**mine** *pron.*
1. мәнимки mənimki
2. менікі (meniki)
3. меники (meniki)
4. минеке (mineke)
5. benimki
6. менинки meniñki
7. مبننگکی (meningki)
8. меники meniki

**minister** *pol. n.*
1. назир nazir
2. министр (ministr)
3. министр (ministr)
4. министр (ministr)
5. bakan
6. министр ministr
7. منستر (ministir)
8. вазир vazir

**minority** *pol. n.*
1. азлыг azlıq
2. азшылық (azshılık)
3. азчылык (azchılık)
4. азчылык (azchılık)
5. azınlık
6. азлык azlyk
7. ئاز سانلىق (az sanliq)
8. озчилик ozchilik

**mint** *bot. n.*
1. нанә nanə
2. жалбыз (zhalbız)
3. жалбыз (jalbız)
4. бөтнек (bötnek)
5. nane
6. нарпыз narpyz
7. يالپۇز (yalpuz)
8. ялпиз yalpiz

**minute** *n.*
1. дәгигә dəqiqə
2. минут (minut)
3. мүнөт (münöt)
4. минут (minut)
5. dakika
6. минут minut
7. مىنۇت (minut)
8. дақиқа daqiqa

**mirror** *n.*
1. күзгу güzgü
2. айна (ayna)
3. күзгү (küzgü)
4. көзге (közge)
5. ayna
6. айна aÿna
7. ئەينەك (äynäk)
8. кўзгу ko'zgu

**mistake** *n.*
1. сәhв səhv
2. қате (qate)
3. ката (kata)
4. хата (khata)
5. hata
6. ялңыш ÿalñyş
7. خاتالىق (khataliq)
8. хато xato

**mix** *vt.*
1. гарышдыр- qarışdır-
2. араластыр- (aralastır-)
3. аралаштыр- (aralashtır-)
4. катыштыр- (katıshtır-)
5. karıştır-
6. гарышдыр- garyşdyr-
7. ئارىلاشتۇر- (arilashtur-)
8. аралаштир- aralashtir-

**moist** *adj.*
1. нәм nəm
2. ылғал (ılghal)
3. суу (suu)
4. юеш (yuesh)
5. nemli
6. өл öl
7. نەم (näm)
8. нам nam

**moment** *n.*
1. ан an
2. момент (moment)
3. момент (moment)
4. момент (moment)
5. an
6. салым salym
7. دەم (däm)
8. он on

1. Azerbaijani  2. Kazakh  3. Kyrgyz  4. Tatar  5. Turkish  6. Turkmen  7. Uighur  8. Uzbek

## Monday  *n.*
1. базар ертәси  bazar ertəsi
2. дүйсенбі (düysenbi)
3. дүйшөмбү (düyshömbü)
4. дүшәмбе (düshämbe)
5. pazartesi
6. душенбе duşenbe
7. دوشه‌نبه (düshänbä)
8. душанба dushanba

## money  *n.*
1. пул  pul
2. ақша (aqsha)
3. акча (akcha)
4. акча (akcha)
5. para
6. пул pul
7. پۇل (pul)
8. пул pul

## monkey  *zool. n.*
1. мејмун meymun
2. маймыл (maymıl)
3. маймыл (maymıl)
4. маймыл (maymıl)
5. maymun
6. маймын maÿmyn
7. مايمۇن (maymun)
8. маймун maymun

## month  *n.*
1. aj ay
2. ай (ay)
3. ай (ay)
4. ай (ay)
5. ay
6. ай aÿ
7. ئاي (ay)
8. ой oy

## monument  *n.*
1. абидә abidə
2. ескерткіш (yeskertkish)
3. эстелик (estelik)
4. һәйкәл (häykäl)
5. anıt
6. ядыгәрлик ÿadygärlik
7. خاتىره مۇنارىسى
(khatirä munarisi)
8. ёдгорлик yodgorlik

## moon  *ast. n.*
1. aj ay
2. ай (ay)
3. ай (ay)
4. ай (ay)
5. ay
6. ай aÿ
7. ئاي (ay)
8. ой oy

## more  *adj.*
1. даһа чох  daha çox
2. көбірек (köbirek)
3. көбүрөөк (köbüröök)
4. артыграк (artıgrak)
5. daha çok
6. көпрәк köpräk
7. كۆپره‌ك (köpräk)
8. күпрок ko'proq

## morning  *n.*
1. сәһәр səhər
2. таңертең (tangyerteng)
3. таң әртең (tang erteng)
4. иртә (irtä)
5. sabah
6. эртир ertir
7. ئه‌تىگه‌ن (ätigän)
8. эрталаб ertalab

## mosque  *rel. n.*
1. мәсчид məscid
2. мешіт (meshit)
3. мечит (mechit)
4. мәчет (mächet)
5. cami
6. метжит metjit
7. مه‌سجىت (mäschit)
8. масжид masjid

## mosquito  *zool. n.*
1. ағчағанад ağcaqanad
2. маса (masa)
3. чиркей (chirkey)
4. черки (cherki)
5. sivrisinek
6. чыбын çybyn
7. پاشا (pasha)
8. чивин chivin

## most  *adj.*
1. ән чох  ən çox
2.ең көп (yeng köp)
3. эң көп (eng köp)
4. иң күп (ing küp)
5. en çok
6. иң көп iň köp
7. ئه‌ڭ كۆپ (äng köp)
8. энг күп eng ko'p

## mother  *n.*
1. ана ana
2. ана (ana)
3. эне (ene)
4. ана, әни (ana, äni)
5. anne
6. әҗе eje
7. ئانا (ana)
8. она ona

---

1. Azerbaijani  2. Kazakh  3. Kyrgyz  4. Tatar  5. Turkish  6. Turkmen  7. Uighur  8. Uzbek

**motorcycle** 96 Dictionary of the Turkic Languages

**motorcycle** *n.*
1. мотосикл motosikl
2. мотоцикл (mototsikl)
3. мотоцикл (mototsikl)
4. мотоцикл (mototsikl)
5. motosiklet
6. мотоцикл mototsikl
7. موتسكلت (motsiklit)
8. мотоцикл mototsikl

**mountain** *geo. n.*
1. дағ dağ
2. тау (taw)
3. тоо (too)
4. тау (tau)
5. dağ
6. даг dag
7. تاغ (tagh)
8. тоғ tog'

**mouse** *zool. n.*
1. сичан siçan
2. тышқан (tıshqan)
3. чычкан (chıchkan)
4. тычкан (tıchkan)
5. sıçan
6. сычан syçan
7. چاشقان (chashqan)
8. сичқон sichqon

**mouth** *phys. n.*
1. ағыз ağız
2. ауыз (awız)
3. ооз (ooz)
4. авыз (avız)
5. ağız
6. агыз agyz
7. ئېغىز (eghiz)
8. оғиз og'iz

**move** *vi.*
1. тәрпән- tərpən-
2. қозғал- (qozghal-)
3. козгол- (kozgol-)
4. хәрәкәтлән- (khäräkätlän-)
5. hareket et-
6. гымылда- gymylda-
7. ھەرىكەتلەن- (härikätlän-)
8. кўч- ko'ch-

**movie** *n.*
1. филм film
2. фильм (fil'm)
3. кино (kino)
4. фильм (fil'm)
5. film
6. фильм film
7. كىنو (kino)
8. фильм fil'm

**much** *adj.*
1. чох çox
2. көп (köp)
3. көп (köp)
4. күп (küp)
5. çok
6. көп köp
7. كۆپ (köp)
8. кўп ko'p

**mud** *n.*
1. палчыг palçıq
2. батпақ (batpaq)
3. баткак (batkak)
4. баткак (batkak)
5. çamur
6. палчык palçyk
7. پاتقاق (patqaq)
8. балчиқ balchiq

**mulberry** *bot. n.*
1. тут tut
2. түт (tut)
3. тыт (tıt)
4. тут (tut)
5. dut
6. тут tut
7. توت (tut)
8. тут tut

**multiplication** *math. n.*
1. вурма vurma
2. көбейту (köbeytuw)
3. көбөйтүү (köböytüü)
4. тапкырлау (tapkırlau)
5. çarpma
6. көпелтмек köpeltmek
7. كۆپەيتىش (köpäytish)
8. кўпайтириш ko'paytirish

**municipality** *n.*
1. бәләдијјә bələdiyyə
2. жергілікті үкімет (zhergilikti ükimet)
3. жергиликтүү өкмөт (jergiliktüü ökmöt)
4. муниципалитет (munitsipalitet)
5. belediye
6. шәхер әдарасы şäher edarasy
7. شەھەرلىك ھۆكۈمەت (shähärlik hökümät)
8. шаҳар ҳокимияти shahar hokimiyati

**muscle** *phys. n.*
1. әзәлә əzələ
2. мускул (muskul)
3. булчуң (bulchung)
4. мускул (muskul)
5. kas
6. мышца myştsa
7. مۇسكۇل (muskul)
8. мускул muskul

---

1. Azerbaijani 2. Kazakh 3. Kyrgyz 4. Tatar 5. Turkish 6. Turkmen 7. Uighur 8. Uzbek

## museum  *n.*
1. музеj muzey
2. музей (muzey)
3. музей (muzey)
4. музей (muzey)
5. müze
6. музей muzeÿ
7. موزېيى (muzey)
8. музей muzey

## mushroom  *bot. n.*
1. көбәләк göbələk
2. қозықарын (qozıqarın)
3. козу карын (kozu karın)
4. гөмбә (gömbä)
5. mantar
6. көмелек kömelek
7. موگۇ (mogu)
8. қўзиқорин qo'ziqorin

## music  *n.*
1. мусиги musiqi
2. музыка (muzıka)
3. музыка (muzıka)
4. музыка (muzıka)
5. müzik
6. саз saz
7. موزىكا (muzika)
8. мусиқа musiqa

## musician  *n.*
1. мусигичи musiqiçi
2. музыкант (muzıkant)
3. музыкант (muzıkant)
4. музыкант, музыка остасы (muzıkant, muzıka ostası)
5. müzisyen
6. сазанда sazanda
7. موزىكانت (muzikant)
8. музиқачи muzikachi

## Muslim  *rel. n.*
1. мүсәлман müsəlman
2. мұсылман (musılman)
3. мусулман (musulman)
4. мөселман (möselman)
5. Müslüman
6. мусулман musulman
7. مۇسۇلمان (musulman)
8. мусулмон musulmon

## mustache  *phys. n.*
1. быг bığ
2. мұрт (murt)
3. мурут (murut)
4. мыек (mıyek)
5. bıyık
6. мурт murt
7. بۇرۇت (burut)
8. мўйлов mo'ylov

## mustard  *cul. n.*
1. хардал xardal
2. қыша (qızha)
3. горчица (gorchitsa)
4. горчица (gorchitsa)
5. hardal
6. горчица gorçitsa
7. تىچا (qicha)
8. хантал xantal

## mute  *n.*
1. лал lal
2. мылқау (mılqaw)
3. дудук (duduk)
4. телсез (telsez)
5. dilsiz
6. лал lal
7. گاچا (gacha)
8. соқов soqov

## mutton  *cul. n.*
1. гоjун әти qoyun əti
2. қой еті (qoy yeti)
3. кой эти (koy eti)
4. сарык ите (sarık ite)
5. koyun eti
6. гоюн эти goÿun eti
7. قوي گۆشى (qoy göshi)
8. қўй гўшти qo'y go'shti

## my  *adj.*
1. мәним mənim
2. менің (mening)
3. менин (menin)
4. минем (minem)
5. benim
6. мениң meniñ
7. مېنىڭ (mening)
8. менинг mening

## myself  *pron.*
1. өзүм özüm
2. өзім (özim)
3. өзүм (özüm)
4. үзем (üzem)
5. kendim
6. өзүм özüm
7. ئۆزۈم (özim)
8. ўзим o'zim

## mythology  *n.*
1. мифолокиjа mifologiya
2. мифология (mifologiya)
3. мифология (mifologiya)
4. мифология (mifologiya)
5. mitoloji
6. мифология mifologiÿa
7. ئەپسانىشۇناسلىق (äpsanishunasliq)
8. мифология mifologiya

---

**nail** *phys. n.*
1. дырнаг dırnaq
2. тырнақ (tırnaq)
3. тырмак (tırmak)
4. тырнак (tırnak)
5. tırnak
6. дырнак dyrnak
7. تـرناق (tirnaq)
8. тирнок tirnoq

**nail** *tech. n.*
1. мых mıx
2. шеге (shege)
3. мык (mık)
4. кадак (kadak)
5. çivi
6. чүй çüÿ
7. مـخ (mikh)
8. мих mix

**name** *n.*
1. ад ad
2. ат (at)
3. ат (at)
4. исем (isem)
5. ad
6. аг at
7. ئات (at)
8. исм ism

**napkin** *n.*
1. салфет salfet
2. салфетка (salfetka)
3. кагаз кол аарчы (kagaz kol aarchı)
4. тастымал (tastımal)
5. peçete
6. салфетка salfetka
7. مايلـق (mayliq)
8. салфетка salfetka

**narrow** *adj.*
1. дар dar
2. тар (tar)
3. тар (tar)
4. тар (tar)
5. dar
6. дар dar
7. تار (tar)
8. тор tor

**nation** *n.*
1. милләт millət
2. ұлт (ult)
3. улут (ulut)
4. милләт (millät)
5. millet
6. миллет millet
7. مـلـلـت (millät)
8. миллат millat

**nationalism** *n.*
1. милләтчилик millətçilik
2. ұлтшылдық (ultshıldıq)
3. улутчулдук (ulutchulduk)
4. милләтчелек (millätchelek)
5. milliyetçilik
6. миллетчилик milletçilik
7. مـلـله تجـلـك (millätchilik)
8. миллатчилик millatchilik

**natural** *adj.*
1. тәбии təbii
2. табиғи (tabiyghiy)
3. табигый (tabigıy)
4. табигый (tabigıy)
5. doğal
6. тебигы tebigy
7. تـ بـئـي (täbi'iy)
8. табиий tabiiy

**nature** *n.*
1. тәбиәт təbiət
2. табиғат (tabiyghat)
3. табият (tabiyat)
4. табигатъ (tabigat')
5. doğa
6. тебигат tebigat
7. تـبـئـت (täbi'ät)
8. табиат tabiat

**near** *adv.*
1. јахын, јахында yaxın, yaxında
2. жақын, жақында (zhaqın, zhaqında)
3. жакын, жакында (jakın, jakında)
4. якын, якында (yakın, yakında)
5. yakın, yakında
6. голай, голайда golaÿ, golaÿda
7. يـبـقـن، يـبـقـنـدا (yeqin, yeqinida)
8. яқин, яқинида yaqin, yaqinida

**near** *prep.*
1. јахынында yaxınında
2. жанында (zhanında)
3. жанында (janında)
4. якында (yakında)
5. yakınında
6. голайында golaÿında
7. يـبـقـنـدا (yeqinida)
8. яқинида yaqinida

**necessary** *adj.*
1. кәрәкли gərəkli
2. қажетті (qazhetti)
3. зарыл (zarıl)
4. кирәкле (kiräkle)
5. gerekli
6. зерур zerur
7. زۆرۈر (zörür)
8. зарур zarur

**necessity** *n.*
1. ehтијач ehtiyac
2. қажеттілік (qazhettilik)
3. кажет (kajet)
4. ихтыяж (ikhtıyaj)
5. ihtiyaç
6. зерурлық zerurlyk
7. ئبهتىياج (ehtiyaj)
8. зарурият zaruriyat

**neck** *phys. n.*
1. бојун boyun
2. мойын (moyın)
3. моюн (moyun)
4. муен (muyen)
5. boyun
6. боюн boÿun
7. بوىۇن (boyun)
8. бўйин bo'yin

**need** *v.*
1. ehтијачы ол- ehtiyacı ol-
2. керек бол- (kerek bol-)
3. керек бол- (kerek bol-)
4. мохтаж бул- (mokhtaj bul-)
5. muhtaç ol-
6. герек бол- gerek bol-
7. كبرهك بول— (keräk bol-)
8. керак бўл- kerak bo'l-

**need** *n.*
1. ehтијач ehtiyac
2. қажеттілік (qazhettilik)
3. кажет (kajet)
4. ихтыяж (ikhtıyaj)
5. ihtiyaç
6. зерурлық zerurlyk
7. ئبهتىياج (ehtiyaj)
8. зарурият zaruriyat

**needle** *n.*
1. ијнә iynə
2. ине (iyne)
3. ийне (iyne)
4. әнә (enä)
5. iğne
6. иңңе iññe
7. يىڭنه (yingnä)
8. игна igna

**neighbor** *n.*
1. гоншу qonşu
2. көрші (körshi)
3. конщу (kongshu)
4. күрше (kürshe)
5. komşu
6. гоңшы goñşy
7. توشنا (qoshna)
8. қўшни qo'shni

**neighborhood** *n.*
1. мәhәллә məhəllə
2. көршілік (körshilik)
3. коншу (kongshu)
4. квартал (kvartal)
5. mahalle
6. микрорайон mikrorayon
7. مەهەللە (mähällä)
8. маҳалла mahalla

**neither ... nor** *conj.*
1. нә ... нә (дә) nə ... nə [də]
2. де ... де (de ... de)
3. же ... же (je ... je)
4. ни ... ни (ni ... ni)
5. ne ... ne [de]
6. не... не(-де) ne... ne [-de]
7. نه...نه (nä ... nä)
8. на ... на na ... na

**nerve** *phys. n.*
1. әсәб əsəb
2. жүйке (zhüyke)
3. нерв (nerv)
4. нерв (nerv)
5. sinir
6. нерв nerw
7. نېرۋا (nerva)
8. асаб asab

**never** *adv.*
1. heч вахт heç vaxt
2. ешқашан (yeshqashan)
3. эч качан (ech kachan)
4. hичвакыт (hichvakıt)
5. asla
6. асыл asyl
7. هبچقاچان (hechqachan)
8. хеч қачон hech qachon

**new** *adj.*
1. јени yeni
2. жаңа (zhanga)
3. жаңы (jangı)
4. яңа (yanga)
5. yeni
6. тәзе täze
7. يېڭى (yengi)
8. янги yangi

**New Year** *n.*
1. тәзә ил təzə il
2. жаңа жыл (zhanga zhıl)
3. Жаңы Жыл (Jangı Jıl)
4. яңа ел (yanga yel)
5. yeni yıl
6. тәзе йыл täze ÿyl
7. يېڭى يىل (yengi yil)
8. янги йил yangi yil

---

**news** *n.*
1. хәбәр xәbәr
2. жаңалық (zhangalıq)
3. жаңылык (jangılık)
4. хәбәр (khäbär)
5. haber
6. хабар habar
7. خەۋەر (khävär)
8. хабар xabar

**newspaper** *n.*
1. гәзет qәzet
2. газет (gazet)
3. гезит (gezit)
4. газета (gazeta)
5. gazete
6. газет gazet
7. گېزىت (gezit)
8. газета gazeta

**next** *adj.*
1. нөвбәти növbәti
2. келесі (kelesi)
3. келерки (kelerki)
4. алдагы (aldagı)
5. gelecek
6. индики indiki
7. كېلەر (kelär)
8. келгуси kelgusi

**nice** *adj.*
1. хош xoş
2. жақсы (zhaqsı)
3. жакшы (jakshı)
4. әйбәт (äybät)
5. hoş
6. оңат oñat
7. ياخشى (yakhshi)
8. ажойиб ajoyib

**night** *n.*
1. кечә gecә
2. түн (tün)
3. түн (tün)
4. төн (tön)
5. gece
6. гиҗе gije
7. تۈن (tün)
8. тун tun

**nine** *num.*
1. доггуз doqquz
2. тоғыз (toghız)
3. тогуз (toguz)
4. тугыз (tugız)
5. dokuz
6. докуз dokuz
7. توققۇز (toqquz)
8. тўққиз to'qqiz

**nineteen** *num.*
1. он доггуз on doqquz
2. он тоғыз (on toghız)
3. он тогуз (on toguz)
4. унтугыз (untugız)
5. on dokuz
6. он докуз on dokuz
7. ئون توققۇز (on toqquz)
8. ўн тўққиз o'n to'qqiz

**ninety** *num.*
1. дохсан doxsan
2. тоқсан (toqsan)
3. токсон (tokson)
4. туксан (tuksan)
5. doksan
6. тогсан togsan
7. توقسان (toqsan)
8. тўқсон to'qson

**no** *adv.*
1. jox, xejp yox, xeyr
2. жоқ (zhoq)
3. жок (jok)
4. юк (yuk)
5. hayır
6. ёк ÿok
7. ياق (yaq)
8. йўқ yo'q

**nobody** *pron.*
1. heч кәс heç kәs
2. еш кім (yesh kim)
3. эч ким (ech kim)
4. hичкем (hichkem)
5. hiç kimse
6. хич ким hiç kim
7. ھېچكىم (hechkim)
8. хеч ким hech kim

**noise** *n.*
1. сәс-күj sәs-küy
2. шу (shuw)
3. ызы-чуу (ızı-chuu)
4. гөрелте (görelte)
5. gürültü
6. вагырды wagyrdy
7. ۋاراڭ-چۇرۇڭ (varang-churung)
8. шовқин shovqin

**noon** *n.*
1. күнорта günorta
2. түс (tüs)
3. түш (tüsh)
4. төш вакыты (tösh vakıtı)
5. öğle
6. гүнортан günortan
7. چۈش (chüsh)
8. туш tush

**north** *n.*
1. шимал şimal
2. солтүстік (soltüstik)
3. түндүк (tündük)
4. төньяк (tön'yak)
5. kuzey
6. демиргазык demirgazyk
7. شمال (shimal)
8. шимол shimol

**nose** *phys. n.*
1. бурун burun
2. мұрын (murın)
3. мурун (murun)
4. борын (borın)
5. burun
6. бурун burun
7. بۇرۇن (burun)
8. бурун burun

**not** *adv.*
1. дејил, јох deyil, yox
2. емес (yemes)
3. эмес (emes)
4. түгел (tügel)
5. değil
6. дәл däl
7. ئەمەس (ämäs)
8. эмас emas

**notebook** *n.*
1. дәфтәр däftər
2. дәптер (däpter)
3. дептер (depter)
4. дәфтәр (däftär)
5. defter
6. депдер depder
7. دەپتەر (däptär)
8. дафтар daftar

**nothing** *n.*
1. һеч-нә heç nə
2. еш нәрсе (yesh närse)
3. эч нерсе (ech nerse)
4. һични (hichni)
5. hiçbir şey
6. хич зат hiç zat
7. هيچنيمه (hechnemä)
8. хеч нарса hech narsa

**noun** *ling. n.*
1. исим isim
2. зат есім (zat yesim)
3. зат атооч (zat atooch)
4. исем (isem)
5. isim
6. ат at
7. ئىسىم (isim)
8. от ot

**novel** *lit. n.*
1. роман roman
2. роман (roman)
3. роман (roman)
4. роман (roman)
5. roman
6. роман roman
7. رومان (roman)
8. роман roman

**November** *n.*
1. нојабр noyabr
2. қараша (qarasha)
3. ноябрь (noyabr')
4. ноябрь (noyabr')
5. kasım
6. ноябрь noÿabr
7. نويابىر (noyabir)
8. ноябрь noyabr'

**now** *adv.*
1. инди indi
2. қазір (qazir)
3. азыр (azır)
4. хәзер (khäzer)
5. şimdi
6. хәзир häzir
7. هازىر (hazir)
8. хозир hozir

**nowhere** *adv.*
1. һеч јердә heç yerdə
2. еш жерде (yesh zherde)
3. эч жерде (ech jerde)
4. һичкайда (hichkayda)
5. hiçbir yerde
6. хич ерде hiç ÿerde
7. هىچيەردە (hechyärdä)
8. хеч каерда hech qayerda

**number** *math. n.*
1. сај say
2. сан (san)
3. сан (san)
4. сан (san)
5. sayı
6. сан san
7. سان (san)
8. сон son

**nurse** *med. n.*
1. тибб бачысы tibb bacısı
2. мед биби (med biybi)
3. медсестра (medsestra)
4. шәфкать туташы
   (shäfkat' tutashı)
5. hastabakıcı
6. медсестра medsestra
7. سبسترا (sestra)
8. хамшира hamshira

---

1. Azerbaijani   2. Kazakh   3. Kyrgyz   4. Tatar   5. Turkish   6. Turkmen   7. Uighur   8. Uzbek

## oak *bot. n.*
1. палыд ағачы palıd ağacı
2. емен (yemen)
3. эмен (emen)
4. имән (imän)
5. meşe ağacı
6. дуб dub
7. دۇب دەرىخى (dub därikhi)
8. эман eman

## obey *v.*
1. итаәт ет- itaət et-
2. бағын- (baghın-)
3. бағын- (bagın-)
4. буйсын- (buysın-)
5. itaat et-
6. боюн бол- boyun bol-
7. بويسۇن (boysun-)
8. бўйсун- bo'ysun-

## object *ling. n.*
1. тамамлыг tamamlıq
2. толықтауыш (tolıqtawısh)
3. толуктооч (toluktooch)
4. тәмамлык (tämamlık)
5. nesne
6. долдургыч doldurgyç
7. تولدۇرغۇچى (toldurghuchi)
8. тўлдирувчи to'ldiruvchi

## obvious *adj.*
1. ачыг-ашкар açıq-aşkar
2. анық (anıq)
3. анык (anık)
4. ачык (achık)
5. besbelli
6. анык anyk
7. ئېنىق (eniq)
8. аник aniq

## occupation *n.*
1. пешә peşə
2. кәсіп (käsip)
3. кесип (kesip)
4. һөнәр (hönär)
5. meslek
6. кәр kär
7. كەسىپ (käsip)
8. касб kasb

## ocean *geo. n.*
1. океан okean
2. мұхит (mukhiyt)
3. океан (okean)
4. океан (okean)
5. okyanus
6. океан okean
7. ئوكيان (okyan)
8. океан okean

## October *n.*
1. октјабр oktyabr
2. қазан (qazan)
3. октябрь (oktyabr')
4. октябрь (oktyabr')
5. ekim
6. октябрь oktÿabr
7. ئۆكتەبىر (öktäbir)
8. октябрь oktyabr'

## offer *v.*
1. тәклиф ет- təklif et-
2. ұсын- (usın-)
3. сунуш- (sunush-)
4. тәкъдим ит- (täk'dim it-)
5. teklif et-
6. хөдүрле- hödürle-
7. تەقدىم قىل (täqdim qil-)
8. таклиф эт- taklif et-

## office *n.*
1. бүро büro
2. офис (ofis)
3. оффис (offis)
4. бюро (byuro)
5. büro
6. иш кабинети iş kabineti
7. ئىشخانا (ishkhana)
8. ишхона ishxona

## officer *n.*
1. забит zabit
2. офицер (ofitser)
3. офицер (ofitser)
4. офицер (ofitser)
5. subay
6. офицер ofitser
7. ئوفىتسېر (ofitser)
8. офицер ofitser

## official *adj.*
1. рәсми rəsmi
2. ресми (resmiy)
3. расмий (rasmiy)
4. рәсми (räsmi)
5. resmî
6. ресми resmi
7. رەسمىي (räsmiy)
8. расмий rasmiy

## official *pol. n.*
1. гуллугчу qulluqçu
2. қызметкер (qızmetker)
3. атайын (atayın)
4. хезмәткәр (khezmätkär)
5. memur
6. ресми адам resmi adam
7. خىزمەتچى (khizmätchi)
8. хизматчи xizmatchi

---

**often** *adv.*
1. тез-тез tez-tez
2. жиі, тез-тез (zhiyi, tez-tez)
3. тез-тез (tez-tez)
4. еш-еш (yesh-yesh)
5. sık sık
6. тиз-тизден tiz-tizden
7. پات‌پات (pat-pat)
8. тез-тез tez-tez

**oil** *cul. n.*
1. jaғ yağ
2. май (may)
3. май (may)
4. май (may)
5. yağ
6. яг ÿag
7. ياغ (yagh)
8. ёғ yog'

**oil** *geol. n.*
1. нефт neft
2. мұнай (munay)
3. нефть (neft')
4. нефть (neft')
5. petrol
6. небит nebit
7. نېفىت (nefit)
8. нефт neft

**OK** *adv.*
1. олду oldu
2. жақсы (zhaqsı)
3. жакшы (jakshı)
4. ярый (yarıy)
5. tamam
6. ягшы ÿagşy
7. خوپ (khop)
8. хўп xo'p

**old** (=aged) *adj.*
1. гоча qoca
2. кәрі (käri)
3. кары (karı)
4. карт (kart)
5. yaşlı
6. гарры garry
7. قبرى (qeri)
8. қари qari

**old** (x new) *adj.*
1. көhнә köhnə
2. ески (yeski)
3. эски (eski)
4. иске (iske)
5. eski
6. көне köne
7. كونا (kona)
8. эски eski

**olive** *bot. n.*
1. зеjтун zeytun
2. зәйтун (zäytun)
3. зейтун (zeytun)
4. зәйтүн (zäytün)
5. zeytin
6. зейтун zeÿtun
7. زه يتۈن (zäytun)
8. зайтун zaytun

**on** *prep.*
1. үстүндә üstündə
2. үстінде (üstinde)
3. үстүндө (üstündö)
4. өстендә (östendä)
5. üstünde
6. үстүнде üstünde
7. ئۈستىده (üstidä)
8. устида ustida

**one** *num.*
1. бир bir
2. бір (bir)
3. бир (bir)
4. бер (ber)
5. bir
6. бир bir
7. بىر (bir)
8. бир bir

**onion** *bot. n.*
1. соған soğan
2. пияз (piyaz)
3. пияз (piyaz)
4. суған (sugan)
5. soğan
6. соган sogan
7. پياز (piyaz)
8. пиёз piyoz

**open** *adj.*
1. ачыг açıq
2. ашық (ashıq)
3. ачык (achık)
4. ачык (achık)
5. açık
6. ачык açyk
7. ئوچۇق (ochuq)
8. очиқ ochiq

**open** *vt.*
1. ач- aç-
2. аш- (ash-)
3. ач- (ach-)
4. ач- (ach-)
5. aç-
6. ач- aç-
7. ئاچ‍ (ach-)
8. оч- och-

---

1. Azerbaijani  2. Kazakh  3. Kyrgyz  4. Tatar  5. Turkish  6. Turkmen  7. Uighur  8. Uzbek

**opera** *mus. n.*
1. опера opera
2. опера (opera)
3. опера (opera)
4. опера (opera)
5. opera
6. опера opera
7. ئوپېرا (opera)
8. опера opera

**operation** *med. n.*
1. әмәлијјат əməliyyat
2. операция (operatsiya)
3. операция (operatsiya)
4. операция (operatsiya)
5. ameliyat
6. операция operatsiýa
7. ئوپېراتسىيه (operatsiyä)
8. операция operatsiya

**opinion** *n.*
1. фикир fikir
2. пікір (pikir)
3. пикир (pikir)
4. фикер (fiker)
5. fikir
6. ой-пикир oý-pikir
7. پىكىر (pikir)
8. фикр fikr

**opposite** *adj.*
1. зидд zidd
2. қарама-қарсы (qarama-qarsı)
3. карама-каршы (karama-karshı)
4. капма-каршы (kapma-karshı)
5. zıt
6. гаршы garşy

7. قارىمۇ قارشى
(qarimu qarshi)
8. қарама-қарши qarama-qarshi

**oppression** *pol. n.*
1. зүлм zülm
2. қанау (qanaw)
3. эзүү (ezüü)
4. золым (zolım)
5. zulüm
6. зулум zulum
7. زۇلۇم (zulum)
8. зулм zulm

**optician** *n.*
1. ejнәкчи eynəkçi
2. оптик (optiyk)
3. оптик (optik)
4. оптик (optik)
5. gözlükçü
6. оптик optik
7. كۆزە يىنەك ساتغۇچى
(közäynäk satghuchi)
8. кўзойнак мутахассиси ko'zoynak mutahassisi

**or** *conj.*
1. ja ya
2. немесе (nemese)
3. же (je)
4. яки (yaki)
5. veya
6. я, я-да ÿa, ÿa-da
7. ياكى (yaki)
8. ёки yoki

**orange** *adj.*
1. нарынчы narıncı
2. қызыл-сары (qızıl-sarı)
3. саргылт (sargılt)
4. кызгылт сары (kızgılt sarı)
5. portakal rengi
6. мәмиши mämişi

7. توق سېرىق (toq seriq)
8. түқ сарик, to'q sariq

**orange** *bot. n.*
1. портағал portağal
2. апельсин (apel'sin)
3. апельсин (apel'sin)
4. апельсин (apel'sin)
5. portakal
6. апельсин apelsin
7. جۈزە (jüzä)
8. апельсин apel'sin

**order** (=command) *v.*
1. әмр ет- əmr et-
2. бұйрық бер- (buyrıq ber-)
3. буйрук бер- (buyruk ber-)
4. боерык бир- (boyerık bir-)
5. emret-
6. буйрук бер- buýruk ber-
7. بۇيرۇ- (buyru-)
8. буюр- buyur-

**order** (=request) *v.*
1. сифариш вер- sifariş ver-
2. тапсыр- (tapsır-)
3. тапшыр- (tapshır-)
4. заказ бир- (zakaz bir-)
5. ısmarla-
6. заказ бер-, буюр- zakaz ber-, buýur-
7. بۇيرۇت- (buyrut-)
8. буюрт- buyurt-

**other** *adj.*
1. башга başqa
2. басқа (basqa)
3. башка (bashka)
4. башка (bashka)
5. diğer
6. бейлеки beýleki
7. باشقا (bashqa)
8. бошқа boshqa

## our *adj.*
1. бизим bizim
2. біздің (bizding)
3. биздин (bizdin)
4. безнең (bezneng)
5. bizim
6. бизиң biziñ
7. بـزنـك (bizning)
8. бизнинг bizning

## ours *pron.*
1. бизимки bizimki
2. біздікі (bizdiki)
3. биздики (bizdiki)
4. безнеке (bezneke)
5. bizimki
6. бизиңки biziñki
7. بـزنـگـی (bizningki)
8. бизники bizniki

## ourselves *pron.*
1. өзумуз özümüz
2. өзіміз (özimiz)
3. өзумуз (özümüz)
4. үзебез (üzebez)
5. kendimiz
6. өзумиз özümiz
7. ئوزـمـز (özimiz)
8. ўзимиз o'zimiz

## outside *adv.*
1. бајырда bayırda
2. сыртында (sırtında)
3. тышкарыда (tıshkarıda)
4. тышта (tıshta)
5. dışarıda
6. дашарда daşarda
7. سـرتـدا (sirtida)
8. ташқарида tashqarida

## oven *n.*
1. духовка duxovka
2. духовка (dukhovka)
3. духовка (dukhovka)
4. духовка (dukhovka)
5. fırın
6. духовка duhowka
7. دوخـوپـکـا (dukhupka)
8. духовка duxovka

## over *prep.*
1. устундә üstündə
2. үстінде (üstinde)
3. устундө (üstündö)
4. өстендә (östendä)
5. üzerinde
6. устунде üstünde
7. ئۈسـتـده (üstidä)
8. устида ustida

## overcoat *clo. n.*
1. палто palto
2. пальто (pal'to)
3. пальто (pal'to)
4. пальто (pal'to)
5. palto
6. пальто palto
7. پـهلـتو (pälto)
8. пальто pal'to

## owl *zool. n.*
1. бајгуш bayquş
2. үкі (üki)
3. үкү (ükü)
4. ябалак (yabalak)
5. baykuş
6. байгуш baÿguş
7. مۇشۇك يـاپـلـاق (müshük yapilaq)
8. бойүгли boyo'g'li

## ox *zool. n.*
1. өкуз öküz
2. өгіз (ögiz)
3. өгуз (ögüz)
4. үгез (ügez)
5. öküz
6. өкуз öküz
7. کـالا (kala)
8. хўкиз ho'kiz

## page *n.*
1. сәһифә səhifə
2. бет (bet)
3. бет (bet)
4. бит (bit)
5. sayfa
6. сахыпа sahypa
7. بـت (bät)
8. сахифа sahifa

## pain *n.*
1. ағры ağrı
2. ауру (awruw)
3. оору (ooru)
4. авырту (avırtu)
5. ağrı
6. агыры agyry
7. ئـاغـرـق (aghriq)
8. оғриқ og'riq

## paint *v.*
1. боја- boya-
2. боя- (boya-)
3. боё- (boyo-)
4. буя- (buya-)
5. boya-
6. боя- boÿa-
7. سـرلـا (sirla-)
8. бўя- bo'ya-

---

1. Azerbaijani  2. Kazakh  3. Kyrgyz  4. Tatar  5. Turkish  6. Turkmen  7. Uighur  8. Uzbek

**painter**
(=house painter) *n.*
1. рәнксаз rəngsaz
2. бояушы (boyawshı)
3. сырдоочуу (sırdoochu)
4. буяучы (buyauchı)
5. boyacı
6. художник hudoʃnik
7. سرچی (sirchi)
8. бўёқчи bo'yoqchi

**painting** *art. n.*
1. шәкил şəkil
2. сурет (suwret)
3. сүрөт (süröt)
4. рәсем (räsem)
5. resim
6. сурат surat
7. ره سم (räsim)
8. расм rasm

**pair** *n.*
1. чүт cüt
2. пар (par)
3. пар (par)
4. пар (par)
5. çift
6. жүбүт jübüt
7. جوپ (jüp)
8. жуфт juft

**pajamas** *clo. n.*
1. пижама pijama
2. пижама (piyzhama)
3. пижама (pijama)
4. пижама (pizhama)
5. pijama
6. пижама piʃama
7. ئۇخلاش كىيىمى (ukhlash kiyimi)
8. пижама pijama

**palace** *n.*
1. capaj saray
2. сарай (saray)
3. сарай (saray)
4. сарай (saray)
5. saray
6. көшк köşk
7. ساراي (saray)
8. сарой saroy

**pan** *cul. n.*
1. тава tava
2. таба (taba)
3. мискей (miskey)
4. таба (taba)
5. tava
6. таба taba
7. تاۋا (tava)
8. това tova

**pants** *clo. n.*
1. шалвар şalvar
2. шалбар (shalbar)
3. шым (shım)
4. чалбар (chalbar)
5. pantolon
6. балак balak
7. شىم (shim)
8. шим shim

**paper** *n.*
1. кағыз kağız
2. қағаз (qaghaz)
3. кагаз (kagaz)
4. кәгазь (kägaz')
5. kâğıt
6. кагыз kagyz
7. قەغەز (qäghäz)
8. қоғоз qog'oz

**parade** *n.*
1. парад parad
2. парад (parad)
3. парад (parad)
4. парад (parad)
5. resmigeçit
6. парад parad
7. پارات (parat)
8. парад parad

**paradise** *rel. n.*
1. чәннәт cənnət
2. бейиш (beyish)
3. бейиш (beyish)
4. җәннәт (jännät)
5. cennet
6. җеннет jennet
7. جننت (jännät)
8. жаннат jannat

**paragraph** *ling. n.*
1. абзас abzas
2. параграф (paragraf)
3. параграф (paragraf)
4. параграф (paragraf)
5. paragraf
6. параграф paragraf
7. ئابزاس (abzas)
8. параграф paragraf

**paralysis** *med. n.*
1. ифлич iflic
2. паралич (paralich)
3. паралич (paralich)
4. паралич (paralich)
5. felç
6. паралич paraliç
7. پال چلك (palächlik)
8. фалаж falaj

**parcel** *n.*
1. пакет paket
2. посылка (posılka)
3. посылка (posılka)
4. посылка (posılka)
5. paket
6. посылка posylka
7. پوسؤلكا (posulka)
8. посилка posilka

**parents** *n.*
1. валидејнләр valideynlәr
2. ата-ана (ata-ana)
3. ата-эне (ata-ene)
4. ата-ана (ata-ana)
5. ana baba
6. ата-эне ata-ene
7. ئاتا_ئانا (ata-ana)
8. ота-она ota-ona

**park** *n.*
1. парк park
2. парк (park)
3. парк (park)
4. ял паркы (yal parkı)
5. park
6. парк park
7. باغچه (baghchä)
8. истирохат боғи istirohat bog'i

**parsley** *bot. n.*
1. чәфәри cәfәri
2. петрушка (petrushka)
3. петрушка (petrushka)
4. петрушка (petrushka)
5. maydanoz
6. петрушка petruşka
7. ئاشكؤكى (ashköki)
8. петрушка petrushka

**part** *n.*
1. һиссә hissә
2. бөлім (bölim)
3. бөлүм (bölüm)
4. өлеш (ölesh)
5. kısım
6. бөлүм bölüm
7. قسم (qisim)
8. кисм qism

**partner** *n.*
1. ортаг ortaq
2. серік (serik)
3. орток (ortok)
4. партнёр, иптәш (partnyor, iptäsh)
5. ortak
6. шәрикдеш şärikdeş
7. شېرىك (sherik)
8. шерик sherik

**party** *n.*
1. зијафәт ziyafәt
2. сауық кеши (sawıq keshi)
3. отуруш (oturush)
4. мәжлес (mäjles)
5. parti
6. отурылышык oturylyşyk
7. ئولتۇرۇش (olturush)
8. ўтириш o'tirish

**party** *pol. n.*
1. партија partiya
2. партия (partiya)
3. партия (partiya)
4. партия (partiya)
5. parti
6. партия partiÿa
7. پارتىيە (partiyä)
8. партия partiya

**pass** *v.*
1. кеч- keç-
2. өт- (öt-)
3. өт- (öt-)
4. ут- (üt-)
5. geç-
6. геч- geç-
7. ئۆت_ (öt-)
8. ўт- o't-

**passenger** *n.*
1. сәрнишин sәrnişin
2. жолаушы (zholawshı)
3. жүргүнчү (jürgünchü)
4. пассажир (passazhir)
5. yolcu
6. ёлагчы ÿolagçy
7. يولۇچى (yoluchi)
8. йўловчи yo'lovchi

**passport** *n.*
1. паспорт pasport
2. паспорт (pasport)
3. паспорт (pasport)
4. паспорт (pasport)
5. pasaport
6. паспорт pasport
7. پاسپورت (pasport)
8. паспорт pasport

**patient** *adj.*
1. сәбирли sәbirli
2. сабырлы (sabırlı)
3. чыдамдуу (chıdamduu)
4. сабырлы (sabırlı)
5. sabırlı
6. сабырлы sabyrly
7. سەۋرچان (sävrchan)
8. сабрли sabrli

## patient *med. n.*
1. хәстә xәstә
2. пациент (patsient)
3. пациент (patsient)
4. пациент (patsient)
5. hasta
6. сыркав syrkaw
7. كِسەل (kesäl)
8. бемор bemor

## pay *v.*
1. өдә- ödә-
2. төле- (töle-)
3. төлө- (tölö-)
4. түлә- (tülä-)
5. öde-
6. төле- töle-
7. تۆلە_ (tölä-)
8. тўла- to'la-

## pea *bot. n.*
1. нохуд noxud
2. бұршақ (burshaq)
3. буурчак (buurchak)
4. борчак (borchak)
5. bezelye
6. гөк нохут gök nohut
7. پۇرچاق (purchaq)
8. нўхат no'xat

## peace *n.*
1. сүлһ sülh
2. бейбітшілік (beybitshilik)
3. тынчтык (tınchtık)
4. тыныңлык (tınıchlık)
5. barış
6. парахатчылык parahatçylyk
7. تىنچلىق (tinchliq)
8. тинчлик tinchlik

## peach *bot. n.*
1. шафталы şaftalı
2. шабдалы (shabdalı)
3. шабдалы (shabdalı)
4. персик, шәфталу (persik, shäftalu)
5. şeftali
6. шетдалы şetdaly
7. شاپتۇل (shaptul)
8. шафтоли shaftoli

## pear *bot. n.*
1. армуд armud
2. алмұрт (almurt)
3. алмурут (almurut)
4. груша, армут (grusha, armut)
5. armut
6. армыт armyt
7. ئامۇت (amut)
8. нок nok

## peasant *n.*
1. кәндли kәndli
2. шаруа (sharuwa)
3. дыйкан (dıykan)
4. игенче (igenche)
5. çiftçi
6. дайхан dayhan
7. دېھقان (dehqan)
8. дехқон dehqon

## pedestrian *n.*
1. пиjада piyada
2. жаяу (zhayaw)
3. жөө (jöö)
4. жәяүле (jäyaüle)
5. yaya
6. пыяда pyÿada
7. پىياده ماڭغۇچى (piyadä mangghuchi)
8. пиёда piyoda

## pen *n.*
1. мүрәккәбли гәләм mürәkkәbli qәlәm
2. қалам (qalam)
3. калем (kalem)
4. ручка (ruchka)
5. mürekkepli kalem
6. ручка ruçka
7. قەلەم (qäläm)
8. ручка ruchka

## pencil *n.*
1. карандаш karandaş
2. қарындаш (qarındash)
3. карандаш (karandash)
4. карандаш, кәләм (karandash, kaläm)
5. kurşun kalem
6. галам galam
7. قەرىنداش (qerindash)
8. қалам qalam

## peninsula *geo. n.*
1. jарымада yarımada
2. түбек (tübek)
3. жарым арал (jarım aral)
4. ярымутрау (yarımutrau)
5. yarımada
6. ярымада ÿarymada
7. يېرىم ئارال (yerim aral)
8. ярим орол yarim orol

## people *n.*
1. халг xalq
2. халық (khalıq)
3. эл (el)
4. халык (khalık)
5. halk
6. халк halk
7. خەلق (khälq)
8. халқ xalq

## pepper *cul. n.*
1. истиот istiot
2. бұрыш (burısh)
3. мурч (murch)
4. борыч (borıch)
5. karabiber
6. бурч burç
7. قارىمۇچ (qarimuch)
8. мурч murch

## perfect *adj.*
1. мүкəммəл mükəmməl
2. жетілген (zhetilgen)
3. жетилген (jetilgen)
4. мөкəммəл (mökämmäl)
5. mükemmel
6. берк berk
7. مۇكەممەل (mukämmäl)
8. мукаммал mukammal

## perfume *n.*
1. əтир ətir
2. əтір (ätir)
3. атыр (atır)
4. ислемай (islemay)
5. parfüm
6. атыр atyr
7. ئەتىر (ätir)
8. атир atir

## perhaps *adv.*
1. бəлкə bəlkə
2. бəлкім (bälkim)
3. балким (balkim)
4. бəлки (bälki)
5. belki
6. белки belki
7. ئىھتىمال (ehtimal)
8. эхтимол ehtimol

## period *ling. n.*
1. нөгтə nöqtə
2. нүкте (nükte)
3. чекит (chekit)
4. нокта (nokta)
5. nokta
6. нокат nokat
7. چىبكىت (chekit)
8. нуқта nuqta

## permit *v.*
1. ичазə вер- icazə ver-
2. рұқсат ет- (ruqsat et-)
3. уруксат ет- (uruksat et-)
4. рөхсəт ит- (rökhsät it-)
5. müsade et-
6. ругсат бер- rugsat ber-
7. رۇخسەت بەر (rukhsät bär-)
8. рухсат бер- ruxsat ber-

## person *n.*
1. шəхс şəxs
2. адам (adam)
3. адам, киши (adam, kishi)
4. шəхес (shäkhes)
5. şahıs
6. адам adam
7. شەخس (shäkhs)
8. шахс shaxs

## pharmacist *n.*
1. əчзачы əczaçı
2. фармацевт (farmatsevt)
3. фармацевт (farmatsevt)
4. аптекачы (aptekachı)
5. eczacı
6. аптекарь aptekar
7. دورىگەر (dorigär)
8. доригар dorigar

## pharmacy *n.*
1. аптек aptek
2. дəріхана (därikhana)
3. дарыкана (darıkana)
4. аптека (apteka)
5. eczane
6. аптека apteka
7. دورىخانا (dorikhana)
8. дорихона dorixona

## phone booth *n.*
1. телефон будкасы telefon budkası
2. телефон автомат (telefon avtomat)
3. телефон автомат (telefon avtomat)
4. телефон буткасы (telefon butkası)
5. telefon kulübesi
6. телефон кабинасы telefon kabinasy
7. تېلېفون بوتكىسى (telefon botkisi)
8. телефон будкаси telefon budkasi

## phone number *n.*
1. телефон нөмрəси telefon nömrəsi
2. телефон нөмірі (telefon nömiri)
3. телефон номуру (telefon nomuru)
4. телефон номеры (telefon nomerı)
5. telefon numarası
6. телефон номери telefon nomeri
7. تېلېفون نومۇرى (telefon nomuri)
8. телефон номери telefon nomeri

---

1. Azerbaijani  2. Kazakh  3. Kyrgyz  4. Tatar  5. Turkish  6. Turkmen  7. Uighur  8. Uzbek

**photo** *n.*
1. фотошәкил fotoşәkil
2. фотография (fotografiya)
3. фотография (fotografiya)
4. фотография (fotografiya)
5. fotoğraf
6. фото foto
7. فوتو (foto)
8. сурат surat

**physics** *n.*
1. физика fizika
2. физика (fizika)
3. физика (fizika)
4. физика (fizika)
5. fizik
6. физика fizika
7. فزیكا (fizika)
8. физика fizika

**picture** *n.*
1. шәкил şәkil
2. сурет (suwret)
3. сүрөт (süröt)
4. рәсем (räsem)
5. resim
6. сурат surat
7. ره سم (räsim)
8. расм rasm

**pig** *zool. n.*
1. донуз donuz
2. шошқа (shoshqa)
3. чочко (chochko)
4. дуңгыз (dunggız)
5. domuz
6. доңуз doñuz
7. چوشقا (choshqa)
8. чўчқа cho'chka

**pigeon** *zool. n.*
1. кәјәрчин göyәrçin
2. көгершін (kögershin)
3. көгүчкөн (kögüchkön)
4. күгәрчен (kügärchen)
5. güvercin
6. кепдери kepderi
7. كپتـر (käptär)
8. каптар kaptar

**pill** *med. n.*
1. һәб һәb
2. таблетка (tabletka)
3. таблетка (tabletka)
4. таблетка (tabletka)
5. hap
6. тогалак дерман togalak derman
7. تابلیتـكا (tabletka)
8. хапдори xapdori

**pillow** *n.*
1. балыш balış
2. жастық (zhastıq)
3. жаздык (jazdık)
4. мендәр (mendär)
5. yastık
6. яссык ÿassyk
7. ياستۇق (yastuq)
8. ёстиқ yostiq

**pillowcase** *n.*
1. балышүзү balışüzü
2. жастық тысы (zhastıq tısı)
3. жаздык кап (jazdık kap)
4. ястык тышлыгы (yastık tıshlıgı)
5. yastık kılıfı
6. яссык дашы ÿassyk daşy
7. ياستۇق قپبى (yastuq qepi)
8. ёстиқ жилди yostiq jildi

**pine** *bot. n.*
1. шам ағачы şam ağacı
2. қарағай (qaraghay)
3. карагай (karagay)
4. нарат (narat)
5. çam ağacı
6. сосна sosna
7. قارىغاي (qarighay)
8. қарағай qarag'ay

**pink** *adj.*
1. чәһрајы çәhrayı
2. қызғылт (qızghılt)
3. кызгылт (kızgılt)
4. алсу (alsu)
5. pembe
6. гүлгүн gülgün
7. هالره ڭ (halräng)
8. пушти pushti

**pistachio** *bot. n.*
1. пүстә püstә
2. пісте (piste)
3. писте (piste)
4. пестә (pestä)
5. şam fıstığı
6. писсе pisse
7. پـستە (pistä)
8. писта pista

**pitcher** *cul. n.*
1. графин qrafin
2. графин (grafin)
3. графин (grafin)
4. графин (grafin)
5. sürahi
6. графин grafin
7. كوزا (koza)
8. графин grafin

---

**place** *n.*
1. jep yer
2. орын (orın)
3. орун (orun)
4. урын (urın)
5. yer
6. ер ÿer
7. جاي (jay)
8. жой joy

**plain** *geo. n.*
1. дүзәнлик düzənlik
2. жазық (zhazıq)
3. түз (tüz)
4. тигезлек (tigezlek)
5. ova
6. дүзлүк düzlük
7. تۈزلەڭلىك (tüzlänglik)
8. текислик tekislik

**plane** see airplane

**planet** *ast. n.*
1. планет planet
2. планета (planeta)
3. планета (planeta)
4. планета (planeta)
5. gezegen
6. планета planeta
7. سەييارە (säyyarä)
8. планета planeta

**plant** *v.*
1. әк- әk-
2. ег- (yeg-)
3. эк- (ek-)
4. утырт- (utırt-)
5. dik-, ek-
6. әк- әk-
7. تىك (tik-)
8. эк- ek-

**plant** *bot. n.*
1. битки bitki
2. өсімдік (ösimdik)
3. өсүмдүк (ösümdük)
4. үсемлек (üsemlek)
5. bitki
6. өсүмлик ösümlik
7. ئۆسۈملۈك (ösümlük)
8. ўсимлик o'simlik

**plate** *cul. n.*
1. бошгаб boşqab
2. табақ (tabaq)
3. тарелка (tarelka)
4. тәлинкә (tälinkä)
5. tabak
6. тарелка tarelka
7. تەخسە (täkhsä)
8. тарелка tarelka

**platform** (*for trains) *n.*
1. перрон perron
2. платформа (platforma)
3. платформа (platforma)
4. платформа (platforma)
5. peron
6. платформа platforma
7. پلاتفورما (platforma)
8. платформа platforma

**play** *lit. n.*
1. пјес pyes
2. пьеса (p'yesa)
3. пьеса (p'esa)
4. пьеса (p'yesa)
5. oyun
6. пьеса piyesa
7. سەھنە ئەسىرى (sähnä äsiri)
8. пьеса p'yesa

**play** (*a game) *v.*
1. ojнa- oyna-
2. ойна- (oyna-)
3. ойно- (oyno-)
4. уйна- (uyna-)
5. oyna-
6. ойна- oÿna-
7. ئوينا (oyna-)
8. ÿйна- o'yna-

**play** (*an instrument) *v.*
1. чал- çal-
2. ойна- (oyna-)
3. черт- (chert-)
4. уйна- (uyna-)
5. çal-
6. чал- çal-
7. چال (chal-)
8. чал- chal-

**playing card** *n.*
1. карт kart
2. карта (karta)
3. карта (karta)
4. карта (karta)
5. iskambil kağıdı
6. карт kart
7. قارتا (qarta)
8. қарта qarta

**playwright** *n.*
1. драматург dramaturg
2. драматург (dramaturg)
3. драматург (dramaturg)
4. драматург (dramaturg)
5. oyun yazarı
6. драматург dramaturg
7. دراما يازغۇچىسى (drama yazghuchisi)
8. драматург dramaturg

## please *adv.*

1. зәһмәт олмаса zəhmət olmasa
2. өтінемін (ötinemin)
3. ыракым этиңиз (ırakım etingiz)
4. рәхим итегез (räkhim itegez)
5. lütfen
6. хайыш эдйәрин haÿyş edyärin
7. مەرھەمەت (märhämät)
8. мархамат marhamat

## pleasure *n.*

1. зөвг zövq
2. раҝат (raqat)
3. ырахат (ırakhat)
4. рәхәт (räkhät)
5. zevk
6. кейп keÿp
7. لەززەت (läzzät)
8. рохат rohat

## plow *ag. n.*

1. котан kotan
2. соҝа (soqa)
3. соко (soko)
4. сабан (saban)
5. saban
6. азал azal
7. سوتا (soqa)
8. омоч omoch

## plum *bot. n.*

1. кавалы gavalı
2. қара өрік (qara örik)
3. кара өрүк (kara örük)
4. слива, кара җимеш (sliva, kara jimesh)
5. erik
6. гаралы garaly

7. ئەينۇلا (äynula)
8. олхӱри olxo'ri

## plunder *v.*

1. гарәт ет- qarət et-
2. тала- (tala-)
3. тала- (tala-)
4. тала- (tala-)
5. yağmala-
6. тала- tala-
7. بۇلاڭچىلىق قىل_ (bulangchiliq qil-)
8. тала- tala-

## pocket *clo. n.*

1. чиб cib
2. қалта (qalta)
3. чөнтөк (chöntök)
4. кесә (kesä)
5. сер
6. җүби jübi
7. يانچۇق (yanchuq)
8. чӱнтак cho'ntak

## poem *lit. n.*

1. ше'р şe'r
2. өлең (öleng)
3. ыр (ır)
4. шигырь (shigır')
5. şiir
6. гошгы goşgy
7. شېئىر (she'ir)
8. шеър she'r

## poet *lit. n.*

1. шаир şair
2. ақын (aqın)
3. акын (akın)
4. шагыйрь (shagıyr')
5. şair
6. шахыр şahyr
7. شائىر (sha'ir)
8. шоир shoir

## poetry *lit. n.*

1. поезија poeziya
2. поэзия (poeziya)
3. поэзия (poeziya)
4. шигърият (shig'riyat)
5. şiir
6. поэзия poeziÿa
7. شېئىر (she'ir)
8. назм nazm

## poison *n.*

1. зәһәр zəhər
2. у (uw)
3. уу (uu)
4. агу (agu)
5. zehir
6. зәхер zäher
7. زەھەر (zähär)
8. захар zahar

## poisonous *adj.*

1. зәһәрли zəhərli
2. улы (uwlı)
3. уулуу (uuluu)
4. агулы (agulı)
5. zehirli
6. зәхерли zäherli
7. زەھەرلىك (zähärlik)
8. захарли zaharli

## policeman *n.*

1. полис polis
2. милиция (militsiya)
3. милиция (militsiya)
4. милиционер (militsioner)
5. polis
6. милиция militsiÿa
7. ساقچى (saqchi)
8. полиция politsiya

---

## polite *adj.*
1. нәзакәтли nəzakətli
2. әдепті (ädepti)
3. сыпайы (sıpayı)
4. әдәпле (ädäple)
5. kibar
6. әдепли edepli
7. ﺋﻪﺩﻩ ﺑﻠﻚ (ädäblik)
8. хушмуомала xushmuomala

## politics *n.*
1. сиjасәт siyasət
2. саясат (sayasat)
3. саясат (sayasat)
4. сәясәт (säyasät)
5. siyaset
6. сыясат syÿasat
7. ﺳﯿﺎﺳﻪﺕ (siyasät)
8. сиёсат siyosat

## pomegranate *bot. n.*
1. нар nar
2. анар (anar)
3. анар (anar)
4. анар (anar)
5. nar
6. нар nar
7. ﺋﺎﻧﺎﺭ (anar)
8. анор anor

## pool *spor. n.*
1. һовуз hovuz
2. бассейн (basseyn)
3. бассейн (basseyn)
4. бассейн (basseyn)
5. havuz
6. ховуз howuz
7. ﺳﯘ ﺋﯚﺯﯛﺵ ﻛﯚﻟﻰ
(su üzüsh köli)
8. бассейн basseyn

## poor *adj.*
1. касыб kasıb
2. кедей (kedey)
3. кедей (kedey)
4. ярлы (yarlı)
5. fakir
6. гарып garyp
7. ﻛﻪ ﻣﺒﻪ ﻏﻪﻝ (kämbäghäl)
8. камбағал kambag'al

## poplar *bot. n.*
1. говаг qovaq
2. терек (terek)
3. терек (terek)
4. тирәк (tiräk)
5. kavak
6. дерек derek
7. ﺗﺒﺮﻩﻙ (teräk)
8. терак terak

## population *n.*
1. әһали əhali
2. халық (khalıq)
3. калктын саны
(kalktın sanı)
4. халык саны (khalık sanı)
5. nüfus
6. илат ilat
7. ﻧﻮﭘﯘﺱ (nopus)
8. аҳоли aholi

## pork *cul. n.*
1. донуз әти donuz əti
2. шошқа еті (shoshqa yeti)
3. чочко эти (chochko eti)
4. чучка ите (chuchka ite)
5. domuz eti
6. доңуз эти doñuz eti
7. ﭼﻮﺷﺘﺎ ﮔﯚﺷﻰ (choshqa göshi)
8. чўчқа гўшти
cho'chqa go'shti

## porter *n.*
1. jүкдашыjан yükdaşıyan
2. тасушы (tasuwshı)
3. ташуучу (tashuuchu)
4. йөкче (yökche)
5. hamal
6. хаммал hammal
7. ﻫﺎﻣﺎﻝ (hammal)
8. ҳаммол hammol

## possibility *n.*
1. еһтимал ehtimal
2. мүмкіндік (mümkindik)
3. мүмкүндүк (mümkündük)
4. мөмкинлек (mömkinlek)
5. imkân
6. мумкинчилик
mümkinçilik
7. ﻣﯚﻣﻜﻨﭽﻠﻚ (mumkinchilik)
8. имконият imkoniyat

## possible *adj.*
1. мүмкүн mümkün
2. мүмкін (mümkin)
3. мүмкүн (mümkün)
4. мөмкин (mömkin)
5. mümkün
6. мүмкин mümkin
7. ﻣﯚﻣﻜﻦ (mumkin)
8. мумкин mumkin

## post office *n.*
1. почт poçt
2. пошта (poshta)
3. почто (pochto)
4. почта (pochta)
5. postane
6. почта poçta
7. ﭘﻮﭼﺘﺨﺎﻧﺎ (pochtikhana)
8. почта pochta

---

**postage** *n.*
1. почт хәрчләри poçt xərcləri
2. пошта шығындары (poshta shıghındarı)
3. почто чыгындары (pochto chıgındarı)
4. почта чыгымы (pochta chıgımı)
5. posta ücreti
6. почта чыкдажысы poçta çykdajysy
7. پوچتا ھەققی (pochta häqqi)
8. жүнатма хақи jo'natma haqi

**postcard** *n.*
1. почт карты poçt kartı
2. ашық хат (ashıq khat)
3. открытка (otkrıtka)
4. открытка (otkrıtka)
5. kartpostal
6. открытка otkrytka
7. ئاتكىرىتكا (atkiritka)
8. откритка otkritka

**postpone** *v.*
1. тә'хирә сал- tə'xirə sal-
2. кейінге қалдыр- (keyinge qaldır-)
3. кийинкиге калтыр- (kiyinkige kaltır-)
4. кичектер- (kichekter-)
5. ertele-
6. гайра гой- gaÿra goÿ-
7. كىچىكتۈر_ (kechiktür-)
8. кечиктир- kechiktir-

**potato** *bot. n.*
1. картоф kartof
2. картоп (kartop)
3. картөшкө (kartöshkö)
4. бәрәңге (bärängge)
5. patates
6. картошка kartoşka
7. ياڭيۇ (yangyu)
8. картошка kartoshka

**pour** *vt.*
1. төк- tök-
2. құй- (quy-)
3. куй- (kuy-)
4. кой- (koy-)
5. dök-
6. гуй- guÿ-
7. قۇي- (quy-)
8. қуй- quy-

**power** *n.*
1. күч güc
2. күш (küsh)
3. күч (küch)
4. көч (köch)
5. güç
6. гүйч güÿç
7. كۈچ (küch)
8. куч-қувват kuch-quvvat

**powerful** *adj.*
1. күчлү güclü
2. күшті (küshti)
3. күчтүү (küchtüü)
4. көчле (köchle)
5. güçlü
6. гүйчли güÿçli
7. كۈچلۈك (küchlük)
8. кучли kuchli

**praise** *v.*
1. тә'рифлә- tə'riflə-
2. мақта- (maqta-)
3. макта- (makta-)
4. макта- (makta-)
5. öv-
6. өв- öw-
7. ماختا_ (makhta-)
8. мақта- maqta-

**pray** *rel. v.*
1. дуа ет- dua et-
2. намаз оқы- (namaz oqı-)
3. намаз оку- (namaz oku-)
4. намаз укы- (namaz ukı-)
5. dua et-
6. дога ока- doga oka-
7. دۇئا قىل_ (du'a qil-)
8. ибодат қил- ibodat qil-

**prayer** *rel. n.*
1. дуа dua
2. бата (bata)
3. сыйынуу (sıyınuu)
4. дога (doga)
5. dua
6. дога doga
7. دۇئا (du'a)
8. дуо duo

**precaution** *n.*
1. еһтийат ehtiyat
2. сақтан (saqtan)
3. сактануу (saktanuu)
4. саклык (saklık)
5. tedbir
6. әтиячлык ätiÿaçlyk
7. تەدبىر (tädbir)
8. тадбир tadbir

---

1. Azerbaijani   2. Kazakh   3. Kyrgyz   4. Tatar   5. Turkish   6. Turkmen   7. Uighur   8. Uzbek

## precipitate
(*rain, snow, etc.) *v.*
1. jaғ- yağ-
2. жау- (zhaw-)
3. жаа- (jaa-)
4. ягу- (yau-)
5. yağ-
6. яг- ÿag-
7. ـياغ (yagh-)
8. ёғ- yog'-

## preface *lit. n.*
1. мүгэддимэ müqəddimə
2. кіріспе (kirispe)
3. кириш сөз (kirish söz)
4. сүз башы (süz bashı)
5. önsöz
6. сөзбашы sözbaşy
7. كـريـش سـۆز (kirish söz)
8. сўз боши so'z boshi

## prefer *v.*
1. үстүн тут- üstün tut-
2. артық көр- (artıq kör-)
3. артык көр- (artık kör-)
4. яхшырак күр- (yakhshırak kür-)
5. tercih et-
6. говы гөр- gowy gör-
7. ئەۋزەل كۆر (ävzäl kör-)
8. афзал кўр- afzal ko'r-

## pregnancy
(*for humans) *n.*
1. һамилэлик hamiləlik
2. жүктілік (zhüktilik)
3. кош бойлук (kosh boyluk)
4. йөклелек (yöklelek)
5. hamilelik
6. гөврелилик göwrelilik
7. هاميلـدارلـىق (hamilidarliq)
8. ҳомиладорлик homiladorlik

## pregnant
(*for humans) *adj.*
1. һамилэ hamilə
2. жүкті (zhükti)
3. бооз (booz)
4. йөкле (yökle)
5. hamile
6. гөврели göwreli
7. هامـلـدار (hamilidar)
8. ҳомиладор homilador

## prepare *v.*
1. һазырла- hazırla-
2. дайында- (dayında-)
3. даярда- (dayarda-)
4. эзерлэ- (äzerlä-)
5. hazırla-
6. тайярла- taÿÿarla-
7. تەييارلا (täyyarla-)
8. тайёрла- tayyorla-

## prescription *med. n.*
1. ресепт resept
2. рецепт (retsept)
3. рецепт (retsept)
4. рецепт (retsept)
5. reçete
6. рецепт retsept
7. رېتسېپ (retsep)
8. рецепт retsept

## present *v.*
1. тэгдим ет- təqdim et-
2. сыйла- (sıyla-)
3. сыйла- (sıyla-)
4. тэкъдим ит- (täk'dim it-)
5. sun-
6. гөркез- görkez-
7. تەقدىم قـلـ (täqdim qil-)
8. ҳавола қил- havola qil-

## present (*time) *n.*
1. индики indiki
2. қазіргі (qazirgi)
3. казыркы (kazırkı)
4. хэзер (khäzer)
5. şimdiki zaman
6. хэзирки häzirki
7. هازىـر (hazir)
8. ҳозир hozir

## president *pol. n.*
1. президент prezident
2. президент (prezident)
3. президент (prezident)
4. президент (prezident)
5. cumhurbaşkanı
6. президент prezident
7. پرېزىـدېنت (prezident)
8. президент prezident

## press (=squeeze) *v.*
1. сых- sıx-
2. бас- (bas-)
3. бас- (bas-)
4. сык- (sık-)
5. sık-
6. сык- syk-
7. سـىـق (siq-)
8. сиқ- siq-

## press (~print media) *n.*
1. мэтбуат mətbuat
2. баспасөз (baspasöz)
3. басма сөз (basma söz)
4. матбугат (matbugat)
5. basın
6. метбугат metbugat
7. مەتبۇئات (mätbu'at)
8. матбуот matbuot

## pretty *adj.*
1. көјчәк göyçək
2. сүйкімді (süykimdi)
3. сүйкүмдүү (süykümdüü)
4. матур (matur)
5. güzel
6. гөзәл gözel
7. چىرايلىق (chirayliq)
8. чиройли chiroyli

## prevent *v.*
1. гаршысыны ал- qarşısını al-
2. сақтан- (saqtan-)
3. сактан- (saktan-)
4. юл куйма- (yul kuyma-)
5. önle-
6. өңүни ал- öňüni al-
7. ئالدىنى ئال (aldini al-)
8. олдини ол- oldini ol-

## price *n.*
1. гијмәт qiymət
2. баға (bagha)
3. баа (baa)
4. бәя (bäya)
5. fiyat
6. баха baha
7. باها (baha)
8. нарх narx

## pride *n.*
1. ифтихар iftixar
2. мақтаныш (maqtanısh)
3. мактаныч (maktanıch)
4. горурлык (gorurlık)
5. gurur
6. гуванч guwanç
7. ئىپتىخار (iptikhar)
8. ифтихор iftixor

## priest *rel. n.*
1. кешиш keşiş
2. поп (pop)
3. поп (pop)
4. рухани (rukhani)
5. papaz
6. руханы ruhany
7. پوپ (pop)
8. руҳоний ruhoniy

## prime minister *pol. n.*
1. баш назир baş nazir
2. премьер-министр (prem'yer-ministr)
3. премьер-министр (prem'er-ministr)
4. хөкүмәт башлыгы (khökümät bashlıgı)
5. başbakan
6. премьер министр premýer ministr
7. باش مىنىستىر (bash ministir)
8. хукумат бошлиги hukumat boshlig'i

## print *vt.*
1. чап ет- çap et-
2. бас- (bas-)
3. бас- (bas-)
4. бас- (bas-)
5. bas-
6. чап әт- çap et-
7. باس (bas-)
8. бос- bos-

## printing press *n.*
1. мәтбәә mətbəə
2. баспахана (baspakhana)
3. басмакана (basmakana)
4. матбугат йорты (matbugat yortı)
5. matbaa
6. чапхана çaphana

7. مەتبەئە (mätbä'ä)
8. матбаа matbaa

## prison *n.*
1. дустагхана dustaqxana
2. түрме (türme)
3. түрмө (türmö)
4. төрмә (törmä)
5. hapishane
6. түрме türme
7. تۈرمە (türmä)
8. қамоқхона qamoqxona

## prize *n.*
1. мүкафат mükafat
2. жүлде (zhülde)
3. байге (bayge)
4. бүләк (büläk)
5. ödül
6. байрак bayrak
7. مۇكاپات (mukapat)
8. соврин sovrin

## probably *adv.*
1. еһтимал ки ehtimal ki
2. мүмкін (mümkin)
3. балким, мүмкүн (balkim, mümkün)
4. ихтимал (ikhtimal)
5. muhtemelen
6. әхтимал ähtimal
7. ئىھتىمال (ehtimal)
8. балки balki

## problem *n.*
1. мәсәлә məsələ
2. проблема (problema)
3. проблема (problema)
4. мәсьәлә (mäs'älä)
5. sorun
6. проблема, меселе problema, mesele
7. مەسىلە (mäsilä)
8. масала masala

---

## produce  *v.*
1. истеһсал ет- istehsal et-
2. өндір- (öndir-)
3. өндүр- (öndür-)
4. эшләп чыгар-
   (eshläp chıgar-)
5. üret-
6. өндүр- öndür-
7. ئىشلەپ چىقار (ishläp chiqar-)
8. ишлаб чиқар-
   ishlab chiqar-

## profit  *econ. n.*
1. газанч qazanc
2. пайда (payda)
3. пайда (payda)
4. төшем (töshem)
5. kâr
6. пейда peÿda
7. پايدا (payda)
8. фойда foyda

## program  *n.*
1. програм proqram
2. программа (programma)
3. программа (programma)
4. программа (programma)
5. program
6. программа programma
7. پروگرامما (programma)
8. дастур dastur

## promise  *v.*
1. сөз вер- söz ver-
2. уәде бер- (wäde ber-)
3. убада бер- (ubada ber-)
4. вәгъдә бир- (väg'dä bir-)
5. söz ver-
6. сөз бер- söz ber-
7. ۋەدە بەر (vädä bär-)
8. ваъда бер- va'da ber-

## pronoun  *ling. n.*
1. әвәзлик әvәzlik
2. есімдік (yesimdik)
3. ат атооч (at atooch)
4. алмашлык (almashlık)
5. zamir
6. чалышма çalyşma
7. ئالماش (almash)
8. олмош olmosh

## proof  *jud. n.*
1. сүбут sübut
2. дәлел (dälel)
3. далил (dalil)
4. дәлил (dälil)
5. delil
6. субутнама subutnama
7. دەلىل (dälil)
8. далил dalil

## propaganda  *n.*
1. тәблигат tәbliğat
2. насихат (nasiykhat)
3. үгүт-насыят
   (ügüt-nasıyat)
4. пропаганда (propaganda)
5. propaganda
6. пропаганда propaganda
7. تەشۋىقات (täshviqat)
8. ташвиқот tashviqot

## prophet  *rel. n.*
1. пејғәмбәр peyğәmbәr
2. пайғамбар (payghambar)
3. пайғамбар (paygambar)
4. пәйгамбәр (päygambär)
5. peygamber
6. пыгамбер pygamber
7. پەيغەمبەر (päyghämbär)
8. пайғамбар payg'ambar

## prose  *lit. n.*
1. нәср nәsr
2. проза (proza)
3. проза (proza)
4. проза (proza)
5. nesir
6. проза proza
7. پروزا (proza)
8. нacp nasr

## protect  *v.*
1. мүдафиә ет- müdafiә et-
2. қорға- (qorgha-)
3. корго- (korgo-)
4. сакла- (sakla-)
5. koru-
6. гора- gora-
7. قوغدا (qoghda-)
8. химоя қил- himoya qil-

## proverb  *n.*
1. аталар сөзү atalar sözü
2. мақал (maqal)
3. макал (makal)
4. мәкаль (mäkal')
5. atasözü
6. накыл nakyl
7. ماقال (maqal)
8. мақол maqol

## province  *n.*
1. вилајәт vilayәt
2. провинция (provintsiya)
3. провинция (provintsiya)
4. өлкә (ölkä)
5. vilayet
6. велаят welaÿat
7. ئۆلكە (ölkä)
8. вилоят viloyat

---

## public phone  *n.*
1. телефон-автомат telefon-avtomat
2. телефон автомат (telefon avtomat)
3. телефон автомат (telefon avtomat)
4. телефон автомат (telefon avtomat)
5. umumî telefon
6. җемгыетчилик телефоны jemgyÿetçilik telefony
7. ئاممىۋى تېلېفون (ammivi telefon)
8. жамоат телефони jamoat telefoni

## publishing house  *n.*
1. нәшријјат nəşriyyat
2. баспа үй (baspa üy)
3. басма (basma)
4. нәшрият (näshriyat)
5. yayınevi
6. неширят neşirÿat
7. نەشرىيات (näshriyat)
8. нашриёт nashriyot

## pull  *v.*
1. дарт- dart-
2. тарт- (tart-)
3. тарт- (tart-)
4. тарт- (tart-)
5. çek-
6. чек- çek-
7. تارتـ (tart-)
8. торт- tort-

## punish  *v.*
1. чәза вер- cəza ver-
2. жазала- (zhazala-)
3. жазала- (jazala-)
4. җәзала- (jäzala-)
5. ceza ver-
6. җеза бер- jeza ber-
7. جازالا- (jazala-)
8. жазола- jazola-

## punishment  *n.*
1. чәза cəza
2. жаза (zhaza)
3. жаза (jaza)
4. җәза (jäza)
5. ceza
6. җеза jeza
7. جازا (jaza)
8. жазо jazo

## pure  *adj.*
1. саф saf
2. таза (taza)
3. таза (taza)
4. саф (saf)
5. saf
6. сап sap
7. ساپ (sap)
8. соф sof

## purple  *adj.*
1. бәнөвшәји bənövşəyi
2. күлгін (külgin)
3. күлгүн (külgün)
4. шәмәхә (shämäkhä)
5. mor
6. беневше benewşe
7. سۆسۈن (sösün)
8. бинафша ранг binafsha rang

## purpose  *n.*
1. мәгсәд məqsəd
2. мақсат (maqsat)
3. максат (maksat)
4. максат (maksat)
5. maksat
6. максат maksat
7. مەقسەت (mäqsät)
8. мақсад maqsad

## purse  *n.*
1. пул кисәси pul kisəsi
2. қапшық (qapshıq)
3. капчык (kapchık)
4. акча янчыгы (akcha yanchıgı)
5. cüzdan
6. гапҗык gapjyk
7. پورتمال (portmal)
8. ҳамён hamyon

## push  *v.*
1. итәлә- itələ-
2. итер- (iter-)
3. итер- (iter-)
4. әтәр- (etär-)
5. ittir-
6. ит- it-
7. ئىتتەرـ (ittär-)
8. итар- itar-

## put  *v.*
1. гој- qoy-
2. қой- (qoy-)
3. кой- (koy-)
4. куй- (kuy-)
5. koy-
6. гой- goÿ-
7. قويـ (qoy-)
8. қўй- qo'y-

**put on** (=wear) *v.*
1. ҝеј- gey-
2. ки- (kiy-)
3. кий- (kiy-)
4. кий- (kiy-)
5. giy-
6. гей- geÿ-
7. كىـ (kiy-)
8. кий- kiy-

**put out** (=extinguish) *v.*
1. сөндүр- söndür-
2. өшір- (öshir-)
3. өчүр- (öchür-)
4. сүндер- (sünder-)
5. söndür-
6. сөндүр- söndür-
7. ـۆچۈرـ (öchür-)
8. ўчир- o'chir-

**quality** *n.*
1. кејфијјәт keyfiyyət
2. сапа (sapa)
3. сапат (sapat)
4. сыйфат (sıyfat)
5. kalite
6. хил hil
7. سۈپەت (süpät)
8. сифат sifat

**quantity** *n.*
1. мигдар miqdar
2. мөлшер (mölsher)
3. сан (san)
4. күләм (küläm)
5. miktar
6. мукдар mukdar
7. مىقدار (miqdar)
8. микдор miqdor

**question** *n.*
1. суал sual
2. сұрақ (suraq)
3. суроо (suroo)
4. сорау (sorau)
5. soru
6. сораг sorag
7. سوئال (so'al)
8. сўрок so'roq

**quick** *adj.*
1. тез tez
2. тез (tez)
3. тез (tez)
4. тиз (tiz)
5. çabuk
6. тиз tiz
7. تېز (tez)
8. тез tez

**quiet** *adj.*
1. сакит sakit
2. тыныш (tınısh)
3. тынч (tinch)
4. тыныч (tınıch)
5. sessiz
6. үмсүм ümsüm
7. تىنچ (tinch)
8. сокин sokin

**quiet: be quiet** *v.*
1. сакит ол- sakit ol-
2. тыныштал- (tınıshtal-)
3. тынчы- (tinchı-)
4. тыныҷлан- (tınıchlan-)
5. sessiz ol-
6. юваш бол- ÿuwaş bol-
7. تىنچىـ (tinchi-)
8. тинчлан- tinchlan-

**quilt** *n.*
1. јорған yorğan
2. көрпе (körpe)
3. көрпө (körpö)
4. юрган (yurgan)
5. yorgan
6. ёрган ÿorgan
7. يوتقان (yotqan)
8. кўрпа ko'rpa

**quince** *bot. n.*
1. һејва heyva
2. айва (ayva)
3. айва (ayva)
4. айва (ayva)
5. ayva
6. бейи beÿi
7. بېھى (behi)
8. беҳи behi

**rabbit** *zool. n.*
1. довшан dovşan
2. қоян (qoyan)
3. коён (koyon)
4. куян (kuyan)
5. tavşan
6. товшан towşan
7. توشقان (toshqan)
8. қуён quyon

**race** *spor. n.*
1. јарыш yarış
2. жарыс (zharıs)
3. жарыш (jarısh)
4. ярыш (yarısh)
5. yarış
6. ярыш ÿaryş
7. مۇسابىقە (musabiqä)
8. мусобақа musobaqa

**radio** *n.*
1. радио radio
2. радио (radio)
3. радио (radio)
4. радио (radio)
5. radyo
6. радио radio
7. رادىئو (radi'o)
8. радио radio

**railroad** *n.*
1. дәмир jолу dəmir yolu
2. темір жол (temir zhol)
3. темир жол (temir jol)
4. тимер юл (timer yul)
5. demiryolu
6. демир ёл demir ÿol
7. تۆمۇريول (tömüryol)
8. темирйўл temiryo'l

**rain** *n.*
1. jағыш yağış
2. жаңбыр (zhangbır)
3. жамгыр (jamgır)
4. яңгыр (yanggır)
5. yağmur
6. ягыш, ягын ÿagyş, ÿagyn
7. يامغۇر (yamghur)
8. ёмғир yomg'ir

**rainbow** *n.*
1. көj гуршағы göy qurşağı
2. кемпірқосақ (kempirqosaq)
3. асан-үсөн (asan-üsön)
4. салават күпере (salavat küpere)
5. gökkuşağı
6. әлемгошар älemgoşar
7. ھەسەن_ھۈسەن (häsän-hüsän)
8. камалак kamalak

**raincoat** *clo. n.*
1. плаш plaş
2. плащ (plashch)
3. плащ (plashch)
4. плащ (plashch)
5. yağmurluk
6. плащ plaşç
7. يامغۇرلۇق (yamghurluq)
8. плаш plash

**raise** (=lift) *v.*
1. галдыр- qaldır-
2. көтер- (köter-)
3. көтөр- (kötör-)
4. күтәр- (kütär-)
5. kaldır-
6. гөтер- göter-
7. كۆتۈر_ (kötür-)
8. күтар- ko'tar-

**raw** *adj.*
1. чиj çiy
2. шикі (shiyki)
3. чийки (chiyki)
4. чи (chi)
5. çiğ
6. чиг çig
7. خام (kham)
8. хом xom

**ray** *phy. n.*
1. шүа şüa
2. сәуле (säwlye)
3. шоола (shoola)
4. нур (nur)
5. ışın
6. шөхле şöhle
7. نۇر (nur)
8. нур nur

**razor** *n.*
1. үлкүч ülgüc
2. ұстара (ustara)
3. устара (ustara)
4. бритва (britva)
5. ustura
6. пәки päki
7. ئۇستۇرا (ustura)
8. устара ustara

**reach** (=arrive at) *v.*
1. чат- çat-
2. жет- (zhet-)
3. жет- (jet-)
4. җит- (jit-)
5. ulaş-
6. ет- ÿet-
7. يەت_ (yät-)
8. ет- yet-

**reach** (~stretch out one's hand) *v.*
1. әл узат- әl uzat-
2. қол соз- (qol soz-)
3. кол сун- (kol sun-)
4. кул суз- (kul suz-)
5. uzan-
6. әл етир- el ÿetir-
7. سوزۇل_ (sozul-)
8. чўзил- cho'zil-

**read** *v.*
1. оху- oxu-
2. оқы- (oqı-)
3. оку- (oku-)
4. укы- (ukı-)
5. oku-
6. ока- oka-
7. ئوقۇ_ (oqu-)
8. ўқи- o'qi-

---

1. Azerbaijani 2. Kazakh 3. Kyrgyz 4. Tatar 5. Turkish 6. Turkmen 7. Uighur 8. Uzbek

## reader *n.*
1. охучу oxucu
2. оқушы (oquwshı)
3. окуучу (okuuchu)
4. укучы (ukuchı)
5. okur
6. окыжы okyjy
7. كتابخان (kitabkhan)
8. ўқувчи o'quvchi

## ready *adj.*
1. hазыр hazır
2. дайын (dayın)
3. даяр (dayar)
4. әзер (äzer)
5. hazır
6. тайяр taÿyar
7. تەييار (täyyar)
8. тайёр tayyor

## real *adj.*
1. hәгиги hәqiqi
2. шын (shın)
3. чын (chın)
4. чын (chın)
5. gerçek
6. хакыкы hakyky
7. راست (rast)
8. хақиқий haqiqiy

## realism *lit. n.*
1. реализм realizm
2. реализм (realizm)
3. реализм (realizm)
4. реализм (realizm)
5. gerçekçilik
6. реализм realizm
7. رېئالىزم (re'alizm)
8. реализм realizm

## reason *n.*
1. сәбәб sәbәb
2. себеп (sebep)
3. себеп (sebep)
4. сәбәп (säbäp)
5. sebep
6. себәп sebäp
7. سەۋەب (säväb)
8. сабаб sabab

## rebellion *n.*
1. үсjан üsyan
2. көтеріліс (köterilis)
3. көтөрүлүш (kötörülüsh)
4. фетнә (fetnä)
5. isyan
6. гозгалаң gozgalañ
7. ئىسيان (isyan)
8. исён isyon

## receipt *n.*
1. гәбз qәbz
2. квитанция (kvitantsiya)
3. квитанция (kvitantsiya)
4. квитанция (kvitantsiya)
5. makbuz
6. квитанция kwitantsiÿa
7. تالون (talon)
8. квитанция kvitantsiya

## recognize *v.*
1. таны- tanı-
2. таны- (tanı-)
3. тааны- (taanı-)
4. таны- (tanı-)
5. tanı-
6. тана- tana-
7. تونۇ (tonu-)
8. тани- tani-

## recommend *v.*
1. мәсләhәт көр-
   mәsləhәt gör-
2. үсын- (usın-)
3. сунуш кыл- (sunush kıl-)
4. тәвсия ит- (tävsiya it-)
5. tavsiye et-
6. хөдүрле- hödürle-
7. تونۇشتۇر (tonushtur-)
8. тавсия қил- tavsiya qil-

## record *mus. n.*
1. пластинка plastinka
2. пластинка (plastinka)
3. пластинка (plastinka)
4. пластинка (plastinka)
5. plak
6. пластинка plastinka
7. پاتېفون تەخسىسى
   (patefon täkhsisi)
8. пластинка plastinka

## red *adj.*
1. гырмызы qırmızı
2. қызыл (qizil)
3. кызыл (kızıl)
4. кызыл (kızıl)
5. kırmızı
6. гызыл gyzyl
7. قىزىل (qizil)
8. қизил qizil

## refrigerator *n.*
1. соjудучу soyuducu
2. тоңазытқыш (tongazıtqısh)
3. муздаткыч (muzdatkıch)
4. суыткыч (suıtkıch)
5. buzdolabı
6. холодильник holodilnik
7. مۇزلاتقۇ (muzlatqu)
8. музлаттич muzlatgich

---

1. Azerbaijani  2. Kazakh  3. Kyrgyz  4. Tatar  5. Turkish  6. Turkmen  7. Uighur  8. Uzbek

## registration  *n.*
1. гејдијјат qeydiyyat
2. тіркеу (tirkew)
3. каттоо (kattoo)
4. регистрация (registratsiya)
5. kayıt
6. регистрирлеме registrirleme
7. تىزىملاشتۇرۇش (tizimlashturush)
8. қайд қилиш qayd qilish

## regret  *n.*
1. пешманлыг peşmanlıq
2. өкініш (ökinish)
3. өкүнүч (ökünüch)
4. үкенеч (ükenech)
5. pişmanlık
6. өкүнме ökünme
7. ئۆكۈنچ (ökünch)
8. ўкиниш o'kinish

## relative  *n.*
1. roһум qohum
2. туысқан (tuwısqan)
3. тууган (tuugan)
4. туган (tugan)
5. akraba
6. гарындаш garyndaş
7. تۇغقان (tughqan)
8. қариндош qarindosh

## release (=let go)  *v.*
1. бурах- burax-
2. босат- (bosat-)
3. бошот- (boshot-)
4. бушат- (bushat-)
5. bırak-
6. гойбер- goÿber-
7. بوشات (boshat-)
8. бўшат- bo'shat-

## religion  *n.*
1. дин din
2. дін (din)
3. дин (din)
4. дин (din)
5. din
6. дин din
7. دىن (din)
8. дин din

## religious  *adj.*
1. дини dini
2. діни (diniy)
3. диний (diniy)
4. дини (dini)
5. dinî
6. дини dini
7. دىنى (diniy)
8. диний diniy

## religious holiday  *n.*
1. дини бајрам dini bayram
2. діни мейрам (diniy meyram)
3. диний майрам (diniy mayram)
4. дини бәйрәм (dini bäyräm)
5. dinî bayram
6. дини байрам dini baÿram
7. ھېيت (heyt)
8. диний байрам diniy bayram

## rely  *v.*
1. күвән- güvən-
2. сүйен- (süyen-)
3. сүйөн- (süyön-)
4. ышан- (ıshan-)
5. güven-
6. бил багла- bil bagla-
7. ئىشەن (ishän-)
8. ишон- ishon-

## remain  *v.*
1. гал- qal-
2. қал- (qal-)
3. кал- (kal-)
4. кал- (kal-)
5. kal-
6. гал- gal-
7. قال (qal-)
8. қол- qol-

## remember  *v.*
1. јада сал- yada sal-
2. еске түсір- (yeske tüsir-)
3. эске түшүр- (eske tüshür-)
4. хәтерлә- (khäterlä-)
5. hatırla-
6. ятла- ÿatla-
7. ئەسلە (äslä-)
8. эсла- esla-

## remind  *v.*
1. јадына сал- yadına sal-
2. еске түсірт- (yeske tüsirt-)
3. эске түшүрт- (eske tüshürt-)
4. искә төшер- (iskä tösher-)
5. hatırlat-
6. яда сал- ÿada sal-
7. ئەسلەت (äslät-)
8. эсга сол- esga sol-

## rent  *n.*
1. ичарә icarə
2. жал (zhal)
3. жалдоо (jaldoo)
4. аренда (arenda)
5. kira
6. кирей kireÿ
7. ئىجارە (ijarä)
8. ижара хақи ijara haqi

---

1. Azerbaijani  2. Kazakh  3. Kyrgyz  4. Tatar  5. Turkish  6. Turkmen  7. Uighur  8. Uzbek

## repair    *v.*

1. тә'мир ет- tə'mir et-
2. жөнде- (zhönde-)
3. оңдо- (ongdo-)
4. төзәт- (tözät-)
5. onar-
6. оңар- oñar-
7. تۈزه‌ت ‍ (tüzät-)
8. тузат- tuzat-

## repeat    *v.*

1. тәкрар ет- təkrar et-
2. қайтала- (qaytala-)
3. кайтала- (kaytala-)
4. тәкрар ит- (täkrar it-)
5. tekrar et-
6. гайтала- gaÿtala-
7. تكرارلا‍ (täkrarla-)
8. такрорла- takrorla-

## reply    *v.*

1. чаваб вер- cavab ver-
2. жауап бер- (zhawap ber-)
3. жооп бер- (joop ber-)
4. җавап бир- (javap bir-)
5. cevap ver-
6. жогап бер- jogap ber-
7. جاۋاب بەر‍ (javab bär-)
8. жавоб бер- javob ber-

## reply    *n.*

1. чаваб cavab
2. жауап (zhawap)
3. жооп (joop)
4. җавап (javap)
5. cevap
6. жогап jogap
7. جاۋاب (javab)
8. жавоб javob

## represent    *v.*

1. тәмсил ет- təmsil et-
2. дәлелде- (dälelde-)
3. далилде- (dalilde-)
4. вәкиле бул- (väkile bul-)
5. temsil et-
6. векиллик әт- wekillik et-
7. ۋەكىللىك قىل‍ (väkillik qil-)
8. вакил бўл- vakil bo'l-

## republic    *n.*

1. республика respublika
2. республика (respublika)
3. республика (respublika)
4. республика (respublika)
5. cumhuriyet
6. республика respublika
7. جۇمھۇرىيەت (jumhuriyät)
8. республика respublika

## request    *v.*

1. хаһиш ет- xahiş et-
2. өтін- (ötin-)
3. сура- (sura-)
4. сора- (sora-)
5. rica et-
6. хайыш әт- haÿş et-
7. ئىلتىماس قىل‍ (iltimas qil-)
8. илтимос қил- iltimos qil-

## rescue    *v.*

1. хилас ет- xilas et-
2. қутқар- (qutqar-)
3. куткар- (kutkar-)
4. коткар- (kotkar-)
5. kurtar-
6. халас әт- halas et-
7. قۇتقۇز‍ (qutquz-)
8. қутқар- qutqar-

## research    *n.*

1. тәдгигат tədqiqat
2. зерттеу (zerttew)
3. изилдөө (izildöö)
4. фәнни хезмәт
   (fänni khezmät)
5. araştırma
6. ылмы иш ylmy iş
7. تەتقىقات (tätqiqat)
8. тадқиқот tadqiqot

## resemble    *v.*

1. охша- oxşa-
2. ұқса- (uqsa-)
3. окшо- (oksho-)
4. охша- (okhsha-)
5. benze-
6. мензе- meñze-
7. ئوخشا‍ (okhsha-)
8. ўхша- o'xsha-

## reservation    *n.*

1. габагчадан сифариш
   едилмиш jep qabaqcadan
   sifariş edilmiş yer
2. орын сақтау (orın saqtaw)
3. резервация (reservatsiya)
4. резервта сақлау
   (rezervta saklau)
5. yer ayırtma
6. резервация rezerwatsiÿa
7. ساقلاپ قويۇش
   (saqlap qoyush)
8. жойни олдиндан банд
   қилиш
   joyni oldindan band qilish

## respect    *v.*

1. һөрмәт ет- hörmət et-
2. құрметте- (qurmette-)
3. урматта- (urmatta-)
4. хөрмәтлә- (khörmätlä-)
5. hürmet et-
6. сыла- syla-
7. ھۆرمەتلە‍ (hürmätlä-)
8. хурматла- hurmatla-

**respect** *n.*
1. һөрмәт hörmət
2. құрмет (qurmet)
3. урмат (urmat)
4. хөрмәт (khörmät)
5. saygı
6. хормат hormat
7. هؤرمت (hürmät)
8. ҳурмат hurmat

**rest** *n.*
1. истираһәт istirahət
2. демалыс (demalıs)
3. дем алыш (dem alısh)
4. ял (yal)
5. dinlenme
6. дынч алма dynç alma
7. دەم ئبلش (däm elish)
8. дам олиш dam olish

**restaurant** *n.*
1. ресторан restoran
2. ресторан (restoran)
3. ресторан (restoran)
4. ресторан (restoran)
5. lokanta
6. ресторан restoran
7. رېستوران (restoran)
8. ресторан restoran

**restrict** *v.*
1. мәһдудлашдыр-
məhdudlaşdır-
2. шек кой- (shek qoy-)
3. чек кой- (chek koy-)
4. чиклә- (chiklä-)
5. kısıtla-
6. чәкләндир- çäklendir-
7. چەكلە (chäklä-)
8. чекла- chekla-

**result** *n.*
1. нәтичә nəticə
2. нәтиже (nätiyzhe)
3. натыйжа (natıyja)
4. нәтижә (nätijä)
5. sonuç
6. нетиже netije
7. نەتیجە (nätijä)
8. натижа natija

**retire** *vi.*
1. исте'фаja чых-
iste'faya çıx-
2. отставкаға шык-
(otstavkagha shıq-)
3. отставкага чык-
(otstavkaga chık-)
4. отставкага чык-
(otstavkaga chık-)
5. emekliye ayrıl-
6. пенсия чык- pensiýa çyk-
7. پېنسییگ چىقـ
(pensiyigä chiq-)
8. пенсияга чик-
pensiyaga chiq-

**return** *vi.*
1. гаjыт- qayıt-
2. қайт- (qayt-)
3. кайт- (kayt-)
4. кайт- (kayt-)
5. geri dön-
6. гайт- gaýt-
7. قایتـ (qayt-)
8. қайт- qayt-

**revenge** *n.*
1. интигам intiqam
2. өш (ösh)
3. өч алуу (öch aluu)
4. үч (üch)
5. öç
6. ар ar

7. ئنتىقام (intiqam)
8. қасос qasos

**revolution** *pol. n.*
1. инғилаб inqilab
2. төңкеріс (töngkeris)
3. төңкөрүш (töngkörüsh)
4. инкыйлап (inkıylap)
5. devrim
6. революция rewolýutsiýa
7. ئنقىلاب (inqilab)
8. инқилоб inqilob

**rice** *bot. n.*
1. дүjү düyü
2. күріш (kürish)
3. күрүч (kürüch)
4. дөге (döge)
5. pirinç
6. түви tüwi
7. گۈرۈچ (gürüch)
8. гурунч gurunch

**rice** *cul. n.*
1. плов plov
2. палау (palaw)
3. палоо (paloo)
4. пылау (pılau)
5. pilav
6. палав palaw
7. پولۇ (polu)
8. ош osh

**rich** *adj.*
1. варлы varlı
2. бай (bay)
3. бай (bay)
4. бай (bay)
5. zengin
6. бай baÿ
7. باي (bay)
8. бой boy

---

**ride** *v.*
1. мин-, сүр- min-, sür-
2. мініп жүр- (minip zhür-)
3. мин- (min-)
4. мен- (men-)
5. bin-
6. мүн- mün-
7. ‎منـ‎ (min-)
8. мин- min-

**rifle** *mil. n.*
1. түфәнк tüfəng
2. мылтық (mıltıq)
3. мылтык (mıltık)
4. мылтык (mıltık)
5. tüfek
6. түпең tüpeň
7. ‎ملتـق‎ (miltiq)
8. милтиқ miltiq

**right** (*direction) *n.*
1. сағ sağ
2. оң (ong)
3. оң (ong)
4. уң (ung)
5. sağ
6. саг sag
7. ‎ئوڭ‎ (ong)
8. ўнг o'ng

**ripe** *adj.*
1. јетишмиш yetişmiş
2. піскен (pisken)
3. бышкан (bıshkan)
4. пешкән (peshkän)
5. olgun
6. бишен bişen
7. ‎پـشـشـق‎ (pishshiq)
8. пишган pishgan

**river** *geo. n.*
1. чај çay
2. өзен (özen)
3. дарыя (darıya)
4. елга (yelga)
5. nehir
6. деря derÿa
7. ‎دەريا‎ (därya)
8. дарё daryo

**road** *n.*
1. јол yol
2. жол (zhol)
3. жол (jol)
4. юл (yul)
5. yol
6. ёл ÿol
7. ‎يول‎ (yol)
8. йўл yo'l

**roast** *v.*
1. гызарт- qızart-
2. қуыр- (quwır-)
3. куур- (kuur-)
4. кыздыр- (kızdır-)
5. kızart-
6. говур- gowur-
7. ‎كاۋاپ قـلـ‎ (kavap qil-)
8. қовур- qovur-

**rock** *geol. n.*
1. гаја qaya
2. жартас (zhartas)
3. аска (aska)
4. кыя (kıya)
5. kaya
6. даш daş
7. ‎تاش‎ (tash)
8. қоя qoya

**roll** *vt.*
1. дијирлә- diyirlə-
2. домала- (domala-)
3. томоло- (tomolo-)
4. тәгәрәт- (tägärät-)
5. yuvarla-
6. тигирле- tigirle-
7. ‎دومـلا تـ‎ (domilat-)
8. думалат- dumalat-

**roof** *n.*
1. дам dam
2. төбе (töbe)
3. чатыр (chatır)
4. түбә (tübä)
5. çatı
6. тамың усти tamyñ üsti
7. ‎ئۆگزە‎ (ögzä)
8. том tom

**room** *n.*
1. отаг otaq
2. бөлме (bölme)
3. бөлмө (bölmö)
4. бүлмә (bülmä)
5. oda
6. отаг otag
7. ‎ئۆي‎ (öy)
8. хона xona

**rooster** *zool. n.*
1. хоруз xoruz
2. қораз (qoraz)
3. короз (koroz)
4. әтәч (ätäch)
5. horoz
6. хораз horaz
7. ‎خوراز‎ (khoraz)
8. хўроз xo'roz

---

1. Azerbaijani  2. Kazakh  3. Kyrgyz  4. Tatar  5. Turkish  6. Turkmen  7. Uighur  8. Uzbek

**root** *bot. n.*
1. көк kök
2. тамыр (tamır)
3. тамыр (tamır)
4. тамыр (tamır)
5. kök
6. көк kök
7. يلتىز (yiltiz)
8. илдиз ildiz

**rose** *bot. n.*
1. гызылгүл qızılgül
2. роза (roza)
3. роза (roza)
4. роза, гөлчәчәк (roza, gölchächäk)
5. gül
6. бәгүл bägül
7. ئە تىرگۈل (ätirgül)
8. атиргул atirgul

**rot** *v.*
1. чүрү- çürü-
2. шір- (shir-)
3. чири- (chiri-)
4. чер- (cher-)
5. çürü-
6. чүйре- çüyre-
7. چىرى (chiri-)
8. чири- chiri-

**round** *adj.*
1. дәјирми dəyirmi
2. дөнгелек (dönggelek)
3. дөңгөлөк (dönggölök)
4. түгәрәк (tügäräk)
5. yuvarlak
6. тегелек tegelek
7. دۇگىلەك (dügiläk)
8. думалоқ dumaloq

**row** *n.*
1. сыра sıra
2. қатар (qatar)
3. катар (katar)
4. рәт (rät)
5. sıra
6. хатар hatar
7. قاتار (qatar)
8. қатор qator

**rub** *v.*
1. сүрт- sürt-
2. уқала- (uqala-)
3. уйкала- (uykala-)
4. ышк- (ıshk-)
5. ov-
6. сүрт- sürt-
7. سۈر (sür-)
8. ишқала- ishqala-

**rude** *adj.*
1. кобуд kobud
2. өрескел (öreskel)
3. копол (kopol)
4. тупас (tupas)
5. kaba
6. гөдек gödek
7. قوپال (qopal)
8. қўпол qo'pol

**rug** *n.*
1. халча xalça
2. қалы (qalı)
3. түктүү килем (tüktüü kilem)
4. хәтфә келәм (khätfä keläm)
5. halı
6. халыча halyça
7. كىچىك گىلەم (kichik giläm)
8. гиламча gilamcha

**ruler** (~a straightedge) *n.*
1. хәткәш xətkeş
2. сызғыш (sızghısh)
3. сызгыч (sızgıch)
4. сызгыч (sızgıch)
5. cetvel
6. линейка lineÿka
7. سىزغۇچ (sizghuch)
8. чизғич chizg'ich

**run** *v.*
1. гач- qaç-
2. жүгір- (zhügir-)
3. жүгүр- (jügür-)
4. йөгер- (yöger-)
5. koş-
6. ылга- ylga-
7. يۇگۈر (yügür-)
8. югур- yugur-

**run away** *v.*
1. гач- qaç-
2. қаш- (qash-)
3. кач- (kach-)
4. кач- (kach-)
5. kaç-
6. гач- gaç-
7. قاچ (qach-)
8. қочиб кет- qochib ket-

**sacrifice** *rel. n.*
1. гурбан qurban
2. құрбан (qurban)
3. курмандык (kurmandık)
4. корбан (korban)
5. kurban
6. гурбан gurban
7. قۇربان (qurban)
8. қурбон qurbon

## sad *adj.*

1. кәдәрли kədərli
2. көңілсіз (köngilsiz)
3. кайгылуу (kaygıluu)
4. моңлы (monglı)
5. üzgün
6. гынанчлы gynançly
7. قايغۇلۇق (qayghuluq)
8. ғамгин g'amg'in

## safe *adj.*

1. тәһлүкәсиз təhlükəsiz
2. қауіпсіз (qawipsiz)
3. коопсуз (koopsuz)
4. хәвефсез (khävefsez)
5. emin
6. ховпсуз howpsuz
7. بىخەتەر (bikhätär)
8. хавфсиз xavfsiz

## sailboat *n.*

1. јелкәнли кәми
   yelkənli gəmi
2. жел қайық (zhel kayık)
3. жел кайык (jel kayık)
4. җилкәнле көймә
   (jilkänle köymä)
5. yelkenli gemi
6. елкенли гәми
   ÿelkenli gämi
7. يەلكەنلىك كېمە
   (yälkänlik kemä)
8. елканли кема
   yelkanli kema

## salad *cul. n.*

1. салат salat
2. салат (salat)
3. салат (salat)
4. салат (salat)
5. salata
6. салат salat

7. سالاد (salad)
8. салат salat

## salary *n.*

1. мааш maaş
2. жалақы (zhalaqı)
3. маяна (mayana)
4. эш хакы (esh khakı)
5. maaş
6. айлык aÿlyk
7. مائاش (ma'ash)
8. маош maosh

## sale (=act of selling) *n.*

1. сатыш satış
2. сату (satuw)
3. сатуу (satuu)
4. сату (satu)
5. satış
6. сатув satuw
7. سېتىش (setish)
8. сотиш sotish

## sale (=discount) *n.*

1. учузлашдырма
   ucuzlaşdırma
2. арзандату (arzandatuw)
3. арзандатуу (arzandatuu)
4. төшерү (tösherü)
5. indirim
6. арзанладып сатыш
   arzanladyp satyş
7. باھاسىنى چۈشۈرۈش
   (bahasini chüshürüsh)
8. арзонлаштириш
   arzonlashtirish

## salesperson *n.*

1. сатычы satıcı
2. сатушы (satuwshı)
3. сатуучу (satuuchu)
4. сатучы (satuchı)
5. satıcı
6. сатыҗы satyjy

7. ساتقۇچى (satquchi)
8. сотувчи sotuvchi

## salt *cul. n.*

1. дуз duz
2. тұз (tuz)
3. туз (tuz)
4. тоз (toz)
5. tuz
6. дуз duz
7. توز (tuz)
8. туз tuz

## same *adj.*

1. ејни eyni
2. дәл (däl)
3. окшош (okshosh)
4. бер төрле (ber törle)
5. aynı
6. о-да шейле o-da şeÿle
7. پەرقسىز (pärqsiz)
8. айни ayni

## sand *geol. n.*

1. гум qum
2. құм (qum)
3. кум (kum)
4. ком (kom)
5. kum
6. чәге çäge
7. قۇم (qum)
8. қум qum

## sandwich *cul. n.*

1. бутерброд buterbrod
2. бутерброд (buterbrod)
3. бутерброд (buterbrod)
4. бутерброд (buterbrod)
5. sandviç
6. бутерброд buterbrod
7. گۆشنان (göshnan)
8. бутерброд buterbrod

**Satan** *rel. n.*
1. шеjтан şeytan
2. шайтан (shaytan)
3. шайтан (shaytan)
4. шайтан (shaytan)
5. şeytan
6. шейтан şeÿtan
7. شەيتان (shäytan)
8. шайтон shayton

**Saturday** *n.*
1. шәнбә şənbə
2. сенбі (senbi)
3. ишемби (ishembi)
4. шимбә (shimbä)
5. cumartesi
6. шенбе şenbe
7. شنبه (shänbä)
8. шанба shanba

**saucepan** *cul. n.*
1. газанча qazança
2. кастрюль (kastryul')
3. каструля (kastrulya)
4. кастрюль (kastryul')
5. tencere
6. газан gazan
7. قازان (qazan)
8. қозонча qozoncha

**saucer** *cul. n.*
1. нәлбәки nəlbəki
2. табақша (tabaqsha)
3. кичине табак (kichine tabak)
4. чәй тәлинкәсе (chäy tälinkäse)
5. fincan tabağı
6. табаҗык tabajyk
7. تەخسە (täkhsä)
8. тақсимча taqsimcha

**sausage** *cul. n.*
1. колбаса kolbasa
2. колбаса (kolbasa)
3. колбаса (kolbasa)
4. колбаса (kolbasa)
5. sosis
6. сосиска sosiska
7. كولباسا (kolbasa)
8. колбаса kolbasa

**saw** *tech. n.*
1. мишар mişar
2. ара (ara)
3. араа (araa)
4. пычкы (pıchkı)
5. testere
6. бычгы byçgy
7. ھەرە (härä)
8. арра arra

**say** *v.*
1. де- de-
2. айт- (ayt-)
3. айт- (ayt-)
4. әйт- (äyt-)
5. de-
6. дий- diÿ-
7. دە- (dä-)
8. де- de-

**scale** (*for weighing) *n.*
1. тәрәзи tərəzi
2. таразы (tarazı)
3. тараза (taraza)
4. улчәу (ülchäü)
5. terazi
6. терези terezi
7. تارازا (taraza)
8. тарози tarozi

**scarf** *clo. n.*
1. шәрф şərf
2. шарф (sharf)
3. моюн орогуч (moyun oroguch)
4. шарф (sharf)
5. eşarp
6. шарф şarf
7. شارپا (sharpa)
8. шарф sharf

**scatter** *vt.*
1. дағыт- dağıt-
2. шаш- (shash-)
3. чачырат- (chachırat-)
4. чәч- (chäch-)
5. saç-
6. даргат- dargat-
7. چاچ- (chach-)
8. соч- soch-

**school** *n.*
1. мәктәб məktəb
2. мектеп (mektep)
3. мектеп (mektep)
4. мәктәп (mäktäp)
5. okul
6. мекдеп mekdep
7. مەكتەپ (mäktäp)
8. мактаб maktab

**scientist** *n.*
1. алим alim
2. ғалым (ghalım)
3. илим (ilim)
4. галим (galim)
5. bilim adamı
6. алым alym
7. ئالىم (alim)
8. олим olim

## scissors *n.*
1. гајчы qayçı
2. қайшы (qayshı)
3. кайчы (kaychı)
4. кайчы (kaychı)
5. makas
6. гайчы gaÿçy
7. قايچا (qaycha)
8. қайчи qaychi

## scrape *v.*
1. газы- qazı-
2. қыр- (qır-)
3. кир- (kir-)
4. кыр- (kır-)
5. kazı-
6. газа- gaza-
7. قىر (qir-)
8. қир- qir-

## scream *v.*
1. чыгыр- çığır-
2. шыңгыр- (shıngghır-)
3. кыйкыр- (kıykır-)
4. кычкыр- (kıchkır-)
5. bağır-
6. чыгыр- çygyr-
7. چىرقىرا (chirqira-)
8. қичқир- qichqir-

## screen (*TV, etc.) *n.*
1. екран ekran
2. экран (ekran)
3. экран (ekran)
4. экран (ekran)
5. ekran
6. экран ekran
7. ئېكران (ekran)
8. экран ekran

## screw *tech. n.*
1. винт vint
2. бурандалы шеге (burandalı shege)
3. мык (mık)
4. шөреп, винт (shörep, vint)
5. vida
6. нурбат nurbat
7. بۇرما مىخ (burma mikh)
8. бурама мих burama mix

## screwdriver *tech. n.*
1. винтачан vintaçan
2. бурагыш (buraghısh)
3. бурагыч (buragıch)
4. шөреп боргыч, отвёртка (shörep borgıch, otvyortka)
5. tornavida
6. отвёртка otwÿortka
7. ئەتۆرركا (ätvirkä)
8. отвертка otvertka

## sculpture *art. n.*
1. һејкәлтәрашлыг heykәltәraşlıq
2. скульптура (skul'ptura)
3. скульптура (skulptura)
4. скульптура (skul'ptura)
5. heykeltıraşlık
6. хейкел heÿkel
7. ھەيكەلتىراشلىق (häykältirashliq)
8. ҳайкалтарошлик haykaltaroshlik

## sea *geo. n.*
1. дәниз dәniz
2. теңіз (tengiz)
3. деңиз (dengiz)
4. дингез (dinggez)
5. deniz
6. деңиз deñiz
7. دېڭىز (dengiz)
8. денгиз dengiz

## search *v.*
1. ахтар- axtar-
2. ізде- (izde-)
3. изде- (izde-)
4. эзлә- (ezlä-)
5. ara-
6. агтар- agtar-
7. ئىزدە (izdä-)
8. қидир- qidir-

## season *n.*
1. фәсил fәsil
2. мезгіл (mezgil)
3. мезгил (mezgil)
4. фасыл (fasıl)
5. mevsim
6. пасыл pasyl
7. پەسىل (päsil)
8. фасл fasl

## seat *n.*
1. jep yer
2. орын (orın)
3. орун (orun)
4. урын (urın)
5. yer
6. ер ÿer
7. ئورۇن (orun)
8. ўрин o'rin

## second (*time) *n.*
1. санијә saniyә
2. секунд (sekund)
3. секунда (sekunda)
4. секунд (sekund)
5. saniye
6. секунд sekund
7. سېكۇنت (sekunt)
8. секунд sekund

---

## secret *adj.*
1. кизли gizli
2. жасырын (zhasırın)
3. жашырын (jashırın)
4. серле (serle)
5. gizli
6. гизлин gizlin
7. مەخپى (mäkhpiy)
8. яширин yashirin

## secretary *n.*
1. катиб(ə) katib[ə]
2. секретарь (sekretar')
3. секретарь (sekretar')
4. секретарь (sekretar')
5. sekreter
6. секретарь sekretar
7. كاتىپ (katip)
8. котиб kotib

## sect *rel. n.*
1. мәзһәб məzhəb
2. секта (sekta)
3. диний секта (diniy sekta)
4. мәзһәп (mäzhäp)
5. mezhep
6. секта, мезхеп
   sekta, mezhep
7. مەزھەپ (mäzhäp)
8. мазхаб mazhab

## section *n.*
1. бөлмә bölmə
2. секция (sektsiya)
3. секция (sektsiya)
4. секция (sektsiya)
5. bölüm
6. бөлүм bölüm
7. قىسىم (qisim)
8. бүлим bo'lim

## see *v.*
1. көр- gör-
2. көр- (kör-)
3. көр- (kör-)
4. күр- (kür-)
5. gör-
6. гөр- gör-
7. كۆر (kör-)
8. кўр- ko'r-

## seed *ag. n.*
1. тохум toxum
2. ұрық (urıq)
3. урук (uruk)
4. орлык (orlık)
5. tohum
6. тохум tohum
7. ئۇرۇق (uruq)
8. уруғ urug'

## seek (=look for) *v.*
1. ахтар- axtar-
2. ізде- (izde-)
3. изде-, тинт- (izde-, tint-)
4. эзлә- (ezlä-)
5. ara-
6. гөзле- gözle-
7. ئىزدە (izdä-)
8. қидир- qidir-

## seldom *adv.*
1. надир һалларда
   nadir hallarda
2. анда-санда (anda-sanda)
3. сейрек (seyrek)
4. сирәк (siräk)
5. nadiren
6. сейрек seÿrek
7. ناھايىتى ئاز (nahayiti az)
8. аҳён-аҳён ahyon-ahyon

## select *v.*
1. сеч- seç-
2. таңда- (tangda-)
3. таңда- (tanda-)
4. сайла- (sayla-)
5. seç-
6. сайла- saÿla-
7. تاللا (talla-)
8. танла- tanla-

## sell *v.*
1. сат- sat-
2. сат- (sat-)
3. сат- (sat-)
4. сат- (sat-)
5. sat-
6. сат- sat-
7. ساتـ (sat-)
8. сот- sot-

## seller *n.*
1. сатычы satıcı
2. сатушы (satuwshı)
3. сатуучу (satuuchu)
4. сатучы (satuchı)
5. satıcı
6. сатыжы satyjy
7. ساتقۇچى (satquchi)
8. сотувчи sotuvchi

## send *v.*
1. көндәр- göndər-
2. жібер- (zhiber-)
3. жибер- (jiber-)
4. җибәр- (jibär-)
5. gönder-
6. ибер- iber-
7. ئەۋەت (ävät-)
8. жўнат- jo'nat-

---

## sentence *ling. n.*
1. чумлә cümlə
2. сөйлем (söylem)
3. сүйлөм (süylöm)
4. җөмлә (jömlä)
5. cümle
6. сөзлем sözlem
7. جۇملە (jümlä)
8. гап gap

## separate *adj.*
1. ајры ayrı
2. бөлек (bölek)
3. бөлөк (bölök)
4. аерым (ayerım)
5. ayrı
6. айра aÿra
7. ئايرىم (ayrim)
8. алоҳида alohida

## separate *vt.*
1. ајыр- ayır-
2. бөл- (böl-)
3. бөл- (böl-)
4. аер- (ayer-)
5. ayır-
6. айыр- aÿyr-
7. ئايرى‍ (ayri-)
8. ажрат- ajrat-

## separated:
## be separated *v.*
1. ајрыл- ayrıl-
2. бөлін- (bölin-)
3. бөлүн- (bölün-)
4. аерыл- (ayerıl-)
5. ayrıl-
6. айрыл- aÿryl-
7. ئاجرال‍ (ajral-)
8. ажрал- ajral-

## September *n.*
1. сентјабр sentyabr
2. қыркүйек (qırküyek)
3. сентябрь (sentyabr')
4. сентябрь (sentyabr')
5. eylül
6. сентябрь sentÿabr
7. سبنته بر (sentäbr)
8. сентябрь sentyabr'

## serious *adj.*
1. чидди ciddi
2. салмақты (salmaqtı)
3. салмактуу (salmaktuu)
4. җитди (jitdi)
5. ciddi
6. аграс agras
7. جددى‍ (jiddiy)
8. жиддий jiddiy

## servant *n.*
1. хидмәтчи xidmətçi
2. қызметші (qızmetshi)
3. кызматкер (kızmatker)
4. хезмәтче (khezmätche)
5. hizmetçi
6. хызматкәр hyzmatkär
7. خزمه تچى (khizmätchi)
8. хизматкор xizmatkor

## seven *num.*
1. једди yeddi
2. жеті (zheti)
3. жети (jeti)
4. җиде (jide)
5. yedi
6. еди ÿedi
7. يه تته (yättä)
8. етти yetti

## seventeen *num.*
1. он једди on yeddi
2. он жеті (on zheti)
3. он жети (on jeti)
4. унҗиде (unjide)
5. on yedi
6. он еди on ÿedi
7. ئون يه تته (on yättä)
8. ўн етти o'n yetti

## seventy *num.*
1. јетмиш yetmiş
2. жетпіс (zhetpis)
3. жетимиш (jetimish)
4. җитмеш (jitmesh)
5. yetmiş
6. етмиш ÿetmiş
7. يه تمش (yätmish)
8. етмиш yetmish

## several *adj.*
1. бир нечә bir neçə
2. бірнеше (birneshe)
3. бир нече (bir neche)
4. берничә (bernichä)
5. birkaç
6. бирнәче birnäçe
7. بىر نه چچه (birnächchä)
8. бир неча bir necha

## sew *v.*
1. тик- tik-
2. тіг- (tig-)
3. тик- (tik-)
4. тек- (tek-)
5. dik-
6. тик- tik-
7. تىك‍ (tik-)
8. тик- tik-

---

## shade *n.*
1. көлкә kölgə
2. көленке (kölengke)
3. көлөкө (kölökö)
4. күләгә (külägä)
5. gölge
6. көлеге kölege
7. سايه (sayä)
8. соя soya

## shadow *n.*
1. көлкә kölgə
2. көленке (kölengke)
3. көлөкө (kölökö)
4. күләгә (külägä)
5. gölge
6. көлеге kölege
7. سايه (sayä)
8. соя soya

## shake *vt.*
1. титрәт-, тәрпәт-
   titrət-, tərpət-
2. сілк- (silk-)
3. чайка- (chayka-)
4. селкет- (selket-)
5. salla-
6. силк- silk-
7. لىڭشىت_ (lingshit-)
8. силкит- silkit-

## shallow *adj.*
1. дајаз dayaz
2. таяз (tayaz)
3. тайыз (tayız)
4. сай (say)
5. sığ
6. сай saÿ
7. تېيىز (teyiz)
8. саёз sayoz

## shape *n.*
1. шәкил şəkil
2. форма (forma)
3. форма (forma)
4. форма (forma)
5. şekil
6. гөрнүш görnüş
7. شەكىل (shäkil)
8. шакл shakl

## sharp *adj.*
1. ити iti
2. өткір (ötkir)
3. өткүр (ötkür)
4. үткен (ütken)
5. keskin
6. йити ÿiti
7. ئىتتىك (ittik)
8. ўткир o'tkir

## she *pron.*
1. o o
2. ол (ol)
3. ал (al)
4. ул (ul)
5. o
6. ол, о ol, o
7. ئۇ (u)
8. y u

## sheep *zool n.*
1. гојун qoyun
2. қой (qoy)
3. кой (koy)
4. сарык (sarık)
5. koyun
6. гоюн goÿun
7. قوي (qoy)
8. қўй qo'y

## sheet (=a bed cover) *n.*
1. чаршаб çarşab
2. жайма (zhayma)
3. шейшеп (sheyshep)
4. простыня, түшәк
   жәймәсе
   (prostınya, tüshäk jäymäse)
5. çarşaf
6. простын prostyn
7. كىرلىك (kirlik)
8. чойшаб choyshab

## shelf *n.*
1. рәф rəf
2. сөре (söre)
3. текче (tekche)
4. киштә (kishtä)
5. raf
6. текҗе tekje
7. جازا (jaza)
8. токча tokcha

## shine *vi.*
1. парла- parla-
2. жарқыра- (zharqıra-)
3. жаркылда- (jarkılda-)
4. ялтыра- (yaltıra-)
5. parla-
6. ялдыра- ÿaldyra-
7. يورۇ_ (yoru-)
8. ялтира- yaltira-

## ship *n.*
1. кәми gəmi
2. кеме (keme)
3. кеме (keme)
4. корабль (korabl')
5. gemi
6. гәми gämi
7. پاراخوت (parakhot)
8. кема kema

---

**shirt** *clo. n.*
1. көјнәк köynək
2. көйлек (köylek)
3. көйнөк (köynök)
4. күлмәк (külmäk)
5. gömlek
6. көйнек köynek
7. کۆگلك (köngläk)
8. кўйлак ko'ylak

**shoe** *clo. n.*
1. ајаггабы ayaqqabı
2. аяқ киім (ayaq kiyim)
3. бут кийим (but kiyim)
4. аяк киеме (ayak kiyeme)
5. ayakkabı
6. аяhгап aÿakgap
7. ئاياغ (ayagh)
8. туфли tufli

**shoemaker** *n.*
1. чәкмәчи çәkmәçi
2. етікші (yetikshi)
3. өтүкчү (ötükchü)
4. итекче (itekche)
5. ayakkabıcı
6. әдикчи ädikçi
7. موزدوز (mozduz)
8. этикдўз etikdo'z

**shop** *v.*
1. базарлыг ет- bazarlıq et-
2. сатып ал- (satıp al-)
3. сатып ал- (satıp al-)
4. сатып ал- (satıp al-)
5. alışveriş et-
6. зат ал- zat al-
7. سېتىۋالـ (setival-)
8. харид қил- xarid qil-

**shop** *n.*
1. дүкан dükan
2. дүкен (düken)
3. дүкөн (dükön)
4. кибет (kibet)
5. dükkân
6. дүкан dükan
7. دۇكان (dukan)
8. дўкон do'kon

**short** *adj.*
1. гыса qısa
2. қысқа (qısqa)
3. кыска (kıska)
4. кыска (kıska)
5. kısa
6. гысга gysga
7. قىسقا (qisqa)
8. қисқа qisqa

**shorts** *clo. n.*
1. шорт şort
2. шорт (short)
3. шорт (short)
4. шорт (short)
5. şort
6. шорт şort
7. كالتە شىم (kaltä shim)
8. шорт short

**shot** *med. n.*
1. пејвәнд peyvәnd
2. егу (yeguw)
3. сайу (sayu)
4. прививка (privivka)
5. aşı
6. вакцина waktsina
7. ئوكۇل (okul)
8. эмлаш emlash

**shoulder** *phys. n.*
1. чијин çiyin
2. иық (iyıq)
3. ийин (iyin)
4. иңбаш (ingbash)
5. omuz
6. эгин egin
7. مۆرە (mürä)
8. елка yelka

**shout** *v.*
1. чығыр- çığır-
2. айқайла- (ayqayla-)
3. кыйкыр- (kıykır-)
4. кычкыр- (kıchkır-)
5. bağır-
6. гыгыр- gygyr-
7. قىچقارـ (qichqar-)
8. бақир- baqir-

**shovel** *tech. n.*
1. күрәк kürәk
2. күрек (kürek)
3. күрөк (kürök)
4. көрәк (köräk)
5. kürek
6. күрек kürek
7. كۆرەك (küräk)
8. курак kurak

**show** *v.*
1. көстәр- göstәr-
2. көрсет- (körset-)
3. көрсөт- (körsöt-)
4. күрсәт- (kürsät-)
5. göster-
6. гөркез- görkez-
7. كۆرسەتـ (körsät-)
8. кўрсат- ko'rsat-

---

1. Azerbaijani  2. Kazakh  3. Kyrgyz  4. Tatar  5. Turkish  6. Turkmen  7. Uighur  8. Uzbek

## shower *n.*
1. душ duş
2. душ (dush)
3. душ (dush)
4. душ (dush)
5. duş
6. душ duş
7. دۇش (dush)
8. душ dush

## shut *v.*
1. бағла- bağla-
2. жап- (zhap-)
3. жап- (jap-)
4. яп- (yap-)
5. kapa-
6. яп- ýap-
7. ياپ_ (yap-)
8. ёп- yop-

## shy *adj.*
1. утанчағ utancaq
2. ұялшақ (uyalshaq)
3. уялчаак (uyalchaak)
4. оялчан (oyalchan)
5. utangaç
6. утанҗаң utanjañ
7. ئۇ ياتچان (uyatchan)
8. уятчан uyatchan

## sick *adj.*
1. хәстә xəstə
2. аұру (awruw)
3. ооруу (ooruu)
4. авыру (avıru)
5. hasta
6. сыркав syrkaw
7. كېسەل (kesäl)
8. касал kasal

## sickle *ag. n.*
1. орағ oraq
2. орақ (oraq)
3. орок (orok)
4. урак (urak)
5. orak
6. орак orak
7. ئورغاق (orghaq)
8. ўроқ o'roq

## side *n.*
1. тәрәф tərəf
2. жақ (zhaq)
3. жак (jak)
4. як (yak)
5. yan
6. гапдал gapdal
7. تەرەپ (täräp)
8. тараф taraf

## sidewalk *n.*
1. сәки səki
2. тротуар (trotuar)
3. тротуар (trotuar)
4. тротуар (trotuar)
5. kaldırım
6. тротуар trotuar
7. پىيادىلەر يولى (piyadilär yoli)
8. йўлка yo'lka

## siege *mil. n.*
1. мүһасирә mühasirə
2. қоршау (qorshaw)
3. курчоо (kurchoo)
4. камау (kamau)
5. kuşatma
6. габав gabaw
7. مۇھاسىرە (muhasirä)
8. қамал qamal

## sign *v.*
1. имзала- imzala-
2. қол қой- (qol qoy-)
3. кол кой- (kol koy-)
4. имза куй- (imza kuy-)
5. imzala-
6. гол чек- gol çek-
7. قول قوى_ (qol qoy-)
8. қўл қўй- qo'l qo'y-

## signature *n.*
1. имза imza
2. қолтаңба (qoltangba)
3. кол тамга (kol tamga)
4. имза (imza)
5. imza
6. гол gol
7. ئىمزا (imza)
8. имзо imzo

## silence *n.*
1. сакитлик sakitlik
2. тыныштық (tınıshtıq)
3. тынчтык (tınchtık)
4. тынлык (tınlık)
5. sessizlik
6. үмсүмлик ümsümlik
7. جىمجىتلىق (jimjitliq)
8. сукунат sukunat

## silk *n.*
1. ипәк ipək
2. жібек (zhibek)
3. жибек (jibek)
4. ефәк (yefäk)
5. ipek
6. йүпек ÿüpek
7. يىپەك (yipäk)
8. ипак ipak

## silver *geol. n.*
1. күмүш gümüş
2. күміс (kümis)
3. күмүш (kümüsh)
4. көмеш (kömesh)
5. gümüş
6. күмүш kümüş
7. كـﯜمﯜش (kümüsh)
8. кумуш kumush

## similar *adj.*
1. охшар oxşar
2. ұқсас (uqsas)
3. окшош (okshosh)
4. охшаш (okhshash)
5. benzer
6. меңзеш meñzeş
7. ئوخشاش (okhshash)
8. ўхшаш o'xshash

## simple (~ordinary) *adj.*
1. садә sadə
2. қарапайым (qarapayım)
3. жөнөкөй (jönököy)
4. гади (gadi)
5. basit
6. йөнекей yönekeÿ
7. ئاددىـﯼ (addiy)
8. оддий oddiy

## since *prep.*
1. бәри bəri
2. бері (beri)
3. бери (beri)
4. бирле (birle)
5. beri
6. бәри bäri
7. بېرى (beri)
8. бери beri

## sing *v.*
1. маhны оху- mahnı oxu-
2. өлең айт- (öleng ayt-)
3. ырда- (ırda-)
4. жырла- (jırla-)
5. şarkı söyle-
6. айдым айт- aÿdym aÿt-
7. ناخشا ئوقۇ (nakhsha oqu-)
8. ашула айт- ashula ayt-

## singer *n.*
1. мүғәнни müğənni
2. әнші (änshi)
3. ырчы (ırchı)
4. жырчы (jırchı)
5. şarkıcı
6. айдымчы aÿdymçy
7. ناخشىچى (nakhshichi)
8. қўшиқчи qo'shiqchi

## sink *n.*
1. чанаг çanaq
2. қол жуғыш (qol zhuwghısh)
3. кол жуугуч (kol juuguch)
4. юынгыч (yuıngıch)
5. lavabo
6. раковина rakowina
7. ئومۇۋالنىك (omuvalnik)
8. чаноқ chanoq

## sink *vi.*
1. бат- bat-
2. бат- (bat-)
3. бат- (bat-)
4. бат- (bat-)
5. bat-
6. бат- bat-
7. چۆك (chök-)
8. чўк- cho'k-

## sister *n.*
1. бачы bacı
2. апа, сіңлі (apa, singli)
3. эже, синди (eje, singdi)
4. апа, сеңел (apa, sengel)
5. kızkardeş, abla
6. уя, аял доган, әҗеке uÿa, aÿal dogan, ejeke
7. ئاچا، سـﯔگـﯩـﻞ (acha, singil)
8. опа, сингил opa, singil

## sit *v.*
1. отур- otur-
2. отыр- (otır-)
3. отур- (otur-)
4. утыр- (utır-)
5. otur-
6. отур- otur-
7. ئولتۇر (oltur-)
8. ўтир- o'tir-

## situated: be situated *v.*
1. јерләш- yerləş-
2. орналас- (ornalas-)
3. орнош- (ornosh-)
4. урнаш- (urnash-)
5. yerleş-
6. ерлеш- ÿerleş-
7. جايلاشـ (jaylash-)
8. жойлаш- joylash-

## situation *n.*
1. вәзијјәт vəziyyət
2. жағдай (zhaghday)
3. жагдай (jagday)
4. хәл (khäl)
5. durum
6. ягдай ÿagdaÿ
7. ۋەزىيەت (väziyät)
8. вазият vaziyat

## six *num.*
1. алты altı
2. алты (altı)
3. алты (altı)
4. алты (altı)
5. altı
6. алты alty
7. ئالتە (altä)
8. олти olti

## sixteen *num.*
1. он алты on altı
2. он алты (on altı)
3. он алты (on altı)
4. уналты (unaltı)
5. on altı
6. он алты on alty
7. ئون ئالتە (on altä)
8. ўн олти o'n olti

## sixty *num.*
1. алтмыш altmış
2. алпыс (alpıs)
3. алтымыш (altımısh)
4. алтмыш (altmısh)
5. altmış
6. алтмыш altmyş
7. ئاتمىش (atmish)
8. олтмиш oltmish

## size *n.*
1. өлчү ölçü
2. размер (razmer)
3. размер (razmer)
4. үлчәм (ülchäm)
5. ölçü
6. өлчег ölçeg
7. ئۆلچەم (ölchäm)
8. размер razmer

## skeleton *phys. n.*
1. скелет skelet
2. қаңқа (qangqa)
3. скелет (skelet)
4. скелет (skelet)
5. iskelet
6. скелет skelet
7. ئۇستىخان (ustikhan)
8. скелет skelet

## skiing *spor. n.*
1. ајаг хизәји идманы ayaq xizәyi idmanı
2. шаңғы (shangghı)
3. лыжа (lıja)
4. чаңгы спорты (changgı sportı)
5. kayak
6. лыжа lyʃa
7. چاڭغا تەيىلىش (changgha teyilish)
8. чанги спорти chang'i sporti

## skill *n.*
1. бачарыг bacarıq
2. шеберлік (sheberlik)
3. чеберлик (cheberlik)
4. һөнәр (hönär)
5. hüner
6. хүнәр hünär
7. ماھارەت (maharät)
8. моҳирлик mohirlik

## skin *phys. n.*
1. дәри dәri
2. тері (teri)
3. тери (teri)
4. тире (tire)
5. deri
6. дери deri
7. تېرە (terä)
8. тери teri

## skirt *clo. n.*
1. јубка yubka
2. юбка (yubka)
3. юбка (yubka)
4. итәк, юбка (itäk, yubka)
5. etek
6. юбка ÿubka
7. يوپكا (yopka)
8. юбка yubka

## sky *n.*
1. көј göy
2. аспан (aspan)
3. көк (kök)
4. күк (kük)
5. gökyüzü
6. асман asman
7. ئاسمان (asman)
8. осмон osmon

## sled *n.*
1. хизәк xizәk
2. шана (shana)
3. чана (chana)
4. чана (chana)
5. kızak
6. сани sani
7. چانا (chana)
8. чана chana

## sleep *n.*
1. јуху yuxu
2. ұйқы (uyqı)
3. уйку (uyku)
4. йокы (yokı)
5. uyku
6. укы uky
7. ئۇيقۇ (uyqu)
8. уйқу uyqu

## sleep v.
1. јат- yat-
2. ұйықта- (uyıqta-)
3. укта- (ukta-)
4. йокла- (yokla-)
5. uyu-
6. укла- ukla-
7. ئۇخلا- (ukhla-)
8. ухла- uxla-

## slide vi.
1. сүрүш- sürüş-
2. жылжы- (zhılzhı-)
3. жылып өт- (jılıp öt-)
4. шу- (shu-)
5. kay-
6. тып- typ-
7. تېيىل- (teyil-)
8. сирған- sirg'an-

## slim adj.
1. инчә incə
2. жіңішке (zhingishke)
3. ичке (ichke)
4. арык (arık)
5. ince
6. аррык arryk
7. ئورۇق (oruq)
8. ориқ oriq

## slip v.
1. сүрүш- sürüş-
2. тай- (tay-)
3. тай- (tay-)
4. тай- (tay-)
5. kay-
6. сүрч- sürç-
7. تېيىل- (teyil-)
8. тойиб кет- toyib ket-

## slipper clo. n.
1. ев ајаггабысы ev ayaqqabısı
2. тапошке (taposhke)
3. тапичке (tapichke)
4. чабата (chabata)
5. terlik
6. шыпбык şypbyk
7. كەش (käsh)
8. шиппак shippak

## slippery adj.
1. сүрүшкән sürüşkən
2. тайғақ (tayghaq)
3. тайгак (taygak)
4. тайғалақ (taygalak)
5. kaygan
6. тыпанчак typançak
7. تېيىلغاق (teyilghaq)
8. сирпанчиқ sirpanchiq

## slow adj.
1. јаваш yavaş
2. ақырын (aqırın)
3. акырын (akırın)
4. акрын (akrın)
5. yavaş
6. юваш ÿuwaş
7. ئاستا (asta)
8. секин sekin

## small adj.
1. балача balaca
2. кіші (kishi)
3. кичине (kichine)
4. кечкенә (kechkenä)
5. küçük
6. кичи kiçi
7. كىچىك (kichik)
8. кичик kichik

## smell n.
1. гоху qoxu
2. ийс (iyis)
3. жыт (jıt)
4. ис (is)
5. koku
6. ыс ys
7. پۇراق (puraq)
8. хид hid

## smell vi.
1. гоху- qoxu-
2. ийс шыгар- (iyis shıghar-)
3. жыт- (jıt-)
4. ис чык- (is chık-)
5. kok-
6. ыс бер- ys ber-
7. پۇرا- (pura-)
8. хид тарат- hid tarat-

## smell vt.
1. ийлә- iylə-
2. ийске- (iyiske-)
3. жытта- (jıtta-)
4. иснә- (isnä-)
5. kokla-
6. ысга- ysga-
7. پۇرا- (pura-)
8. хидла- hidla-

## smile v.
1. күлүмсә- gülümsə-
2. күлімсіре- (külimsire-)
3. жымый- (jımıy-)
4. көл- (köl-)
5. gülümse-
6. йылгыр- ÿylgyr-
7. كۈلۈمسىرە- (külümsirä-)
8. жилмай- jilmay-

---

1. Azerbaijani  2. Kazakh  3. Kyrgyz  4. Tatar  5. Turkish  6. Turkmen  7. Uighur  8. Uzbek

**smoke** (*cigarette) *v.*
1. сигарет чэк- siqaret çək-
2. темекі шег- (temeki sheg-)
3. тамеки тарт- (tameki tart-)
4. тәмәке тарт- (tämäke tart-)
5. sigara iç-
6. чилим чек- çilim çek-
7. تاماكا چەك‍ (tamaka chäk-)
8. чек- chek-

**snake** *zool. n.*
1. илан ilan
2. жылан (zhılan)
3. жылан (jılan)
4. елан (yelan)
5. yılan
6. йылан ÿylan
7. يىلان (yilan)
8. илон ilon

**snow** *n.*
1. гар qar
2. қар (qar)
3. кар (kar)
4. кар (kar)
5. kar
6. гар gar
7. قار (qar)
8. қор qor

**soap** *n.*
1. сабун sabun
2. сабын (sabın)
3. самын (samın)
4. сабын (sabın)
5. sabun
6. сабын sabyn
7. سوپۇن (sopun)
8. совун sovun

**soccer** *spor. n.*
1. футбол futbol
2. футбол (futbol)
3. футбол (futbol)
4. футбол (futbol)
5. futbol
6. футбол futbol
7. پۇتبول (putbol)
8. футбол futbol

**society** *n.*
1. чәмијјәт cəmiyyət
2. коғам (qogham)
3. коом (koom)
4. җәмгыять (jämgıyat')
5. toplum
6. җемгыет jemgyÿet
7. جەمئىيەت (jäm'iyät)
8. жамият jamiyat

**sock** *clo. n.*
1. чораб corab
2. ұйық (uyıq)
3. байпак (baypak)
4. оекбаш (oyekbash)
5. çorap
6. җорап jorap
7. پايپاق (paypaq)
8. пайпоқ paypoq

**soft** *adj.*
1. јумшаг yumşaq
2. жұмсақ (zhumsaq)
3. жумшак (jumshak)
4. йомшак (yomshak)
5. yumuşak
6. юмшак ÿumşak
7. يۇمشاق (yumshaq)
8. юмшоқ yumshoq

**soil** *ag. n.*
1. торпаг torpaq
2. топырак (topiraq)
3. топурак (topurak)
4. туфрак (tufrak)
5. toprak
6. топрак toprak
7. توپا (topa)
8. тупроқ tuproq

**soldier** *mil. n.*
1. әскәр əsgər
2. әскер (äsker)
3. аскер (asker)
4. солдат (soldat)
5. asker
6. эсгер esger
7. ئەسكەر (äskär)
8. аскар askar

**solve** *v.*
1. һәлл ет- həll et-
2. шеш- (shesh-)
3. чеч- (chech-)
4. хәл ит- (khäl it-)
5. çöz-
6. чөз- çöz-
7. ھەل قىل‍ (häl qil-)
8. ҳал қил- hal qil-

**some** *adj.*
1. бир аз, бә'зи bir az, bə'zi
2. біраз, кейбір
   (biraz, keybir)
3. бир аз, кее бир
   (bir az, kee bir)
4. бернича, бәгъзе
   (bernichä, bäg'ze)
5. biraz, bazı
6. бираз, кәбир biraz, käbir
7. بىر ئاز، بەزى (bir az, bäzi)
8. бир неча, баъзи
   bir necha, ba'zi

## sometimes *adv.*
1. бә'зән bə'zən
2. кейде (keyde)
3. кээде (keede)
4. кайчакта (kaychakta)
5. bazen
6. кәвагт käwagt
7. بزیده (bäzidä)
8. баъзан ba'zan

## son *n.*
1. оғул oğul
2. ұл (ul)
3. уул (uul)
4. ул (ul)
5. oğul
6. огул ogul
7. ئوغۇل (oghul)
8. ўғил o'g'il

## song *n.*
1. маһны mahnı
2. өлең, ән (öleng, än)
3. ыр (ır)
4. жыр (jır)
5. şarkı
6. айдым aÿdym
7. ناخشا (nakhsha)
8. қўшиқ qo'shiq

## soon *adv.*
1. тезликлә tezliklə
2. жақында (zhaqında)
3. жакында (jakında)
4. озакламый (ozaklamıy)
5. yakında
6. якында ÿakynda
7. پات ئارىدا (pat arida)
8. тез орада tez orada

## sorry *adj.*
1. кәдәрли kədərli
2. ренжіген (renzhigen)
3. кайғылуу (kaygıluu)
4. кайгылы (kaygılı)
5. üzgün
6. гынанчлы gynançly
7. رەنجىگەن (ränjigän)
8. қайғули qayg'uli

## sound *phy. n.*
1. сәс səs
2. дыбыс (dıbıs)
3. дабыш (dabısh)
4. тавыш (tavısh)
5. ses
6. сес ses
7. تاۋۇش (tavush)
8. товуш tovush

## soup *cul. n.*
1. шорба şorba
2. сорпа (sorpa)
3. шорпо (shorpo)
4. шулпа (shulpa)
5. çorba
6. чорба çorba
7. شوربا (shorpa)
8. шўрва sho'rva

## sour *adj.*
1. турш turş
2. қышқыл (qıshqıl)
3. кычкыл (kıchkıl)
4. әчи (ächi)
5. ekşi
6. туршы turşy
7. چۈچۈك (chüchük)
8. нордон nordon

## south *n.*
1. чәнуб cənub
2. оңтүстік (ongtüstik)
3. түштүк (tüshtük)
4. көньяк (kön'yak)
5. güney
6. гүнорта günorta
7. جەنۇب (jänub)
8. жануб janub

## sow *v.*
1. әк- ək-
2. ек- (yek-)
3. эк- (ek-)
4. утырт- (utırt-)
5. tohum ek-
6. эк- ek-
7. تەرى (teri-)
8. эк- ek-

## space *ast. n.*
1. космос kosmos
2. ғарыш (gharısh)
3. космос (kosmos)
4. космос (kosmos)
5. uzay
6. космос kosmos
7. ئالەم بوشلۇقى (aläm boshluqi)
8. фазо fazo

## spacious *adj.*
1. кениш geniş
2. кең (keng)
3. кең (keng)
4. кин (king)
5. geniş
6. гиң giñ
7. كەڭ (käng)
8. кенг keng

---

**spade** *ag. n.*
1. күрәк kürək
2. күрек (kürek)
3. күрөк (kürök)
4. көрәк (köräk)
5. bel
6. пил pil
7. گۆرجەك (gürjäk)
8. белкурак belkurak

**sparrow** *zool. n.*
1. сәрчә sərçə
2. торғай (torghay)
3. торгой (torgoy)
4. чыпчык (chıpchık)
5. serçe
6. серче serçe
7. قۇشقاچ (qushqach)
8. чумчук chumchuq

**speak** *v.*
1. даныш- danış-
2. сөйле- (söyle-)
3. сүйле- (süylö-)
4. сөйләш- (söyläsh-)
5. konuş-
6. гепле- geple-
7. سۆزلە- (sözlä-)
8. гапир- gapir-

**spear** *mil. n.*
1. мизраг mizraq
2. найза (nayza)
3. найза (nayza)
4. сөнге (söngge)
5. mızrak
6. найза naўza
7. نەيزە (näyzä)
8. найза nayza

**speech** *n.*
1. данышыг, нитг danışıq, nitq
2. сөз (söz)
3. сөз (söz)
4. сөйләшү (söyläshü)
5. konuşma
6. геплеме gepleme
7. نۇتۇق (nutuq)
8. нутқ nutq

**speed** *n.*
1. сүр'әт sür'ət
2. жылдамдық (zhıldamdıq)
3. ылдамдык (ıldamdık)
4. тизлек (tizlek)
5. hız
6. тизлик tizlik
7. تېزلىك (tezlik)
8. тезлик tezlik

**speedy** *adj.*
1. чәлд cəld
2. жылдам (zhıldam)
3. тез (tez)
4. тиз (tiz)
5. hızlı
6. чалт çalt
7. تېز (tez)
8. тез tez

**spell** *rel. n.*
1. сеһр sehr
2. сиқыр (siyqır)
3. сыйкыр (sıykır)
4. тылсым (tılsım)
5. büyü
6. өвсүн öwsün
7. ئەپسۇن (äpsun)
8. афсун afsun

**spend** (*money) *v.*
1. хәрчлә- xərclə-
2. жұмса- (zhumsa-)
3. сарпта- (sarpta-)
4. сарыф ит- (sarıf it-)
5. harca-
6. харчла- harçla-
7. خەرجلە- (khäjlä-)
8. сарфла- sarfla-

**spider** *zool. n.*
1. һөрүмчәк hörümçək
2. өрмекши (örmekshi)
3. жөргөмүш (jörgömüsh)
4. урмәкүч (ürmäküch)
5. örümcek
6. мөй möy
7. ئۆمۈچۈك (ömüchük)
8. ўргимчак o'rgimchak

**spinach** *bot. n.*
1. испанаг ispanaq
2. шпинат (shpiynat)
3. шпинат (shpinat)
4. шпинат (shpinat)
5. ıspanak
6. ысманак ysmanak
7. پالەك (paläk)
8. исмалоқ ismaloq

**spine** *phys. n.*
1. онурға onurğa
2. омыртка (omırtqa)
3. омуртка (omurtka)
4. умыртка баганасы (umırtka baganası)
5. omurga
6. оңурга oňurga
7. ئومۇرتقا (omurtqa)
8. умуртқа umurtqa

## spirit *rel. n.*
1. pyħ ruh
2. рух (rukh)
3. рух (rukh)
4. рух (rukh)
5. ruh
6. рух ruh
7. روه (roh)
8. рух ruh

## spit *v.*
1. түпүр- tüpür-
2. түкір- (tükir-)
3. түкүр- (tükür-)
4. төкер- (töker-)
5. tükür-
6. түйкүр- tüÿkür-
7. توكُر_ (tükür-)
8. тупур- tupur-

## split *vt.*
1. jаp- yar-
2. жар- (zhar-)
3. жар- (jar-)
4. яр- (yar-)
5. yar-
6. яр- ÿar-
7. يار_ (yar-)
8. ёр- yor-

## spoon *cul. n.*
1. гашыг qaşıq
2. қасық (qasıq)
3. кашык (kashık)
4. кашык (kashık)
5. kaşık
6. чемче çemçe
7. توشوق (qoshuq)
8. қошиқ qoshiq

## sport *n.*
1. идман idman
2. спорт (sport)
3. спорт (sport)
4. спорт (sport)
5. spor
6. спорт sport
7. تەنهەرىكەت (tänhärikät)
8. спорт sport

## spread *vt.*
1. jаj- yay-
2. жай- (zhay-)
3. жай- (jay-)
4. тарат- (tarat-)
5. yay-
6. яйрат- ÿaÿrat-
7. يايـ_ (yay-)
8. ёй- yoy-

## spring *tech. n.*
1. jаj yay
2. серіппе (serippe)
3. серпилме зым (serpilme zım)
4. пружина (pruzhina)
5. yay
6. пружин pruʃin
7. پۇرژىنا (purzhina)
8. пружина prujina

## spring (*season) *n.*
1. jаз yaz
2. көктем (köktem)
3. жаз (jaz)
4. яз (yaz)
5. ilkbahar
6. яз, бахар ÿaz, bahar
7. ئەتياز (ätiyaz)
8. баҳор bahor

## square *geo. n.*
1. квадрат kvadrat
2. шаршы (sharshı)
3. чарчы (charchı)
4. квадрат (kvadrat)
5. kare
6. квадрат kwadrat
7. چاسا (chasa)
8. квадрат kvadrat

## square (=plaza) *n.*
1. мејдан meydan
2. алаң (alang)
3. аянт (ayant)
4. мәйдан (mäydan)
5. meydan
6. мейдан meÿdan
7. مەيدان (mäydan)
8. майдон maydon

## squirrel *zool. n.*
1. дәлә dələ
2. тиін (tiyin)
3. тыйын чычкан (tıyın chıchkan)
4. тиен (tiyen)
5. sincap
6. белка belka
7. تىيىن (tiyin)
8. олмахон olmaxon

## stage *art. n.*
1. сәһнә səhnə
2. сахна (sakhna)
3. сахна (sakhna)
4. сәхнә (säkhnä)
5. sahne
6. сахна sahna
7. سەھنە (sähnä)
8. саҳна sahna

---

1. Azerbaijani  2. Kazakh  3. Kyrgyz  4. Tatar  5. Turkish  6. Turkmen  7. Uighur  8. Uzbek

**stairs** *n.*
1. пиллəкəн pillǝkǝn
2. саты (satı)
3. шаты (shatı)
4. баскыч (baskıch)
5. merdiven
6. мердиван merdiwan
7. پەلەمپەی (pälämpäy)
8. зинапоя zinapoya

**stamp** (*postal) *n.*
1. марка marka
2. марка (marka)
3. марка (marka)
4. марка (marka)
5. pul
6. марка marka
7. ماركا (marka)
8. марка marka

**stand** *v.*
1. дур- dur-
2. тұр- (tur-)
3. тур- (tur-)
4. тор- (tor-)
5. ayakta dur-
6. туруп дур- turup dur-
7. تۇر (tur-)
8. тур- tur-

**star** *ast. n.*
1. улдуз ulduz
2. жұлдыз (zhuldız)
3. жылдыз (jıldız)
4. йолдыз (yoldız)
5. yıldız
6. йылдыз ÿyldyz
7. يۇلتۇز (yultuz)
8. юлдуз yulduz

**start** *vi.*
1. башла- başla-
2. баста- (basta-)
3. башта- (bashta-)
4. башла- (bashla-)
5. başla-
6. башла- başla-
7. باشلا (bashla-)
8. бошла- boshla-

**state** *pol. n.*
1. дөвлəт dövlǝt
2. мемлекет (memleket)
3. мамлекет (mamleket)
4. дәүлəт (däülät)
5. devlet
6. дөвлет döwlet
7. دۆلەت (dölät)
8. давлат davlat

**station** (*train) *n.*
1. вағзал vağzal
2. станция (stantsiya)
3. станция (stantsiya)
4. станция (stantsiya)
5. istasyon
6. станция stantsiÿa
7. ئىستانسا (istansa)
8. станция stantsiya

**statue** *art. n.*
1. һејкəл heykǝl
2. мүсін (müsin)
3. айкел (aykel)
4. сын (sın)
5. heykel
6. хейкел heÿkel
7. ھەيكەل (häykäl)
8. хайкал haykal

**stay** *v.*
1. гал- qal-
2. қал- (qal-)
3. кал- (kal-)
4. кал- (kal-)
5. kal-
6. гал- gal-
7. قال (qal-)
8. қол- qol-

**steal** *v.*
1. оғурла- oğurla-
2. ұрла- (urla-)
3. уурда- (uurda-)
4. урла- (urla-)
5. çal-
6. огурла- ogurla-
7. ئوغرىلا (oghrila-)
8. ўғирла- o'g'irla-

**steel** *geol. n.*
1. полад polad
2. болат (bolat)
3. болот (bolot)
4. корыч (korıch)
5. çelik
6. полат polat
7. پولات (polat)
8. пўлат po'lat

**step** *n.*
1. аддым addım
2. қадам (qadam)
3. кадам (kadam)
4. адым (adım)
5. adım
6. əдим ädim
7. قەدەم (qädäm)
8. қадам qadam

---

1. Azerbaijani  2. Kazakh  3. Kyrgyz  4. Tatar  5. Turkish  6. Turkmen  7. Uighur  8. Uzbek

**stick** *(=adhere)* *vi.*
1. japыш- yapış-
2. жабыс- (zhabıs-)
3. жабыш- (jabısh-)
4. ябыш- (yabısh-)
5. yapış-
6. елмеш- ÿelmeş-
7. ـچاپلاش (chaplash-)
8. ёпиш- yopish-

**still** *adv.*
1. həлə hələ
2. әлі (äli)
3. али (ali)
4. әлегәчә (älegächä)
5. hâlâ
6. хениз heniz
7. تبخى (tekhi)
8. хали хам hali ham

**stocking** *clo. n.*
1. чораб corab
2. шұлық (shulıq)
3. байпак (baypak)
4. оек (oyek)
5. çorap
6. жорап jorap
7. پايپاق (paypaq)
8. пайпоқ paypoq

**stomach** *phys. n.*
1. мә'дә mə'də
2. асқазан (asqazan)
3. ашказан (ashkazan)
4. ашказан (ashkazan)
5. mide
6. ашгазан aşgazan
7. ئاشقازان (ashqazan)
8. ошқозон oshqozon

**stone** *n.*
1. даш daş
2. тас (tas)
3. таш (tash)
4. таш (tash)
5. taş
6. даш daş
7. تاش (tash)
8. тош tosh

**stool** *n.*
1. кәтил kətil
2. орындық (orındıq)
3. олтургуч (olturguch)
4. урындык (urındık)
5. tabure
6. табуретка taburetka
7. ئورۇندۇق (orunduq)
8. курси kursi

**stop** *vi.*
1. дајан- dayan-
2. тоқта- (toqta-)
3. токто- (tokto-)
4. тукта- (tukta-)
5. dur-
6. дур- dur-
7. ـتوختا (tokhta-)
8. тўхта- to'xta-

**stop** *vt.*
1. дајандыр- dayandır-
2. тоқтат- (toqtat-)
3. токтот- (toktot-)
4. туктат- (tuktat-)
5. durdur-
6. дуруз- duruz-
7. ـتوختات (tokhtat-)
8. тўхтат- to'xtat-

**stop** *(*for vehicles) n.*
1. дајаначаг dayanacaq
2. аялдама (ayaldama)
3. аялдама (ayaldama)
4. туктальш (tuktalısh)
5. durak
6. дуралга duralga
7. ببكـت (bekät)
8. бекат bekat

**store** *n.*
1. мағаза mağaza
2. дүкен (düken)
3. дүкөн (dükön)
4. кибет, магазин
   (kibet, magazin)
5. mağaza
6. магазин magazin
7. ماگـزين (magizin)
8. дўкон do'kon

**storey** *n.*
1. мәртәбә mərtəbə
2. қабат (qabat)
3. кабат (kabat)
4. кат (kat)
5. kat
6. этаж etaʃ
7. قـۆەت (qävät)
8. қават qavat

**stork** *zool. n.*
1. лејләк leylək
2. көкқұтан (kökqutan)
3. көк кытан (kök kıtan)
4. ләкләк (läkläk)
5. leylek
6. леглек leglek
7. لـيلـك (läyläk)
8. лайлак laylak

---

1. Azerbaijani  2. Kazakh  3. Kyrgyz  4. Tatar  5. Turkish  6. Turkmen  7. Uighur  8. Uzbek

## storm *n.*
1. фыртына fırtına
2. боран (boran)
3. бороон (boroon)
4. буран (buran)
5. fırtına
6. тупан tupan
7. بوران (boran)
8. бўрон bo'ron

## story *lit. n.*
1. һекаjə hekayə
2. әңгіме (änggime)
3. аңгеме (anggeme)
4. хикәя (khikäya)
5. hikâye
6. хекая hekaÿa
7. هبكايه (hekayä)
8. ҳикоя hikoya

## stove *n.*
1. соба soba
2. пеш (pesh)
3. меш (mesh)
4. мич (mich)
5. soba
6. печь peç
7. مەش (mäsh)
8. печка pechka

## straight *adj.*
1. дүз düz
2. тура (tuwra)
3. туура (tuura)
4. туры (turı)
5. düz
6. гөни göni
7. توز (tüz)
8. тўгри to'g'ri

## strainer *cul. n.*
1. сүзкәч süzgəc
2. сүзгіш (süzgish)
3. сүзгүч (süzgüch)
4. кыл иләк (kıl iläk)
5. süzgeç
6. сүзгүч süzgüç
7. سۈزگۈچ (süzgüch)
8. сузгич suzgich

## strange *adj.*
1. гəрибə qəribə
2. бір түрлі (bir türli)
3. бир түрлүү (bir türlüü)
4. гажәп (gajäp)
5. acayip
6. ген geñ
7. غەلىتە (ghälitä)
8. ғалати g'alati

## straw *ag. n.*
1. саман saman
2. сабан (saban)
3. саман (saman)
4. салам (salam)
5. saman
6. саман saman
7. سامان (saman)
8. сомон somon

## strawberry *bot. n.*
1. чиjəлəк çiyələk
2. күлпынай (kulpınay)
3. кулпунай (kulpunay)
4. җир җиләге (jir jiläge)
5. çilek
6. землияника zemliÿanika
7. بۆلجۈرگەن (böljürgän)
8. қулупнай qulupnay

## street *n.*
1. күчә küçə
2. көше (köshe)
3. көчө (köchö)
4. урам (uram)
5. sokak
6. көче köçe
7. كوچا (kocha)
8. кўча ko'cha

## strength *n.*
1. күч güc
2. күш (küsh)
3. күч (küch)
4. көч (köch)
5. güç
6. гүйч güÿç
7. كۈچ (küch)
8. куч kuch

## strike *pol. n.*
1. тә'тил tə'til
2. ереуіл (yerewil)
3. иш таштоо (ish tashtoo)
4. эш ташлау (esh tashlau)
5. grev
6. иш ташлайыш iş taşlaÿış
7. ئىش تاشلاش (ish tashlash)
8. ишташлаш ishtashlash

## stroke (=caress) *v.*
1. сығалла- sığalla-
2. сипа- (siypa-)
3. сыйпала- (sıypala-)
4. сыпыр- (sıpır-)
5. okşa-
6. сыпала- sypala-
7. ـسـلا (sila-)
8. сила- sila-

## stroll *v.*
1. кәзин- gəzin-
2. серуенде- (seruwende-)
3. серүүндө- (serüündö-)
4. йөр- (yör-)
5. gezin-
6. гезмеле- gezmele-
7. ﻧﺎﻳﻼﻥ (aylan-)
8. сайр қил- sayr qil-

## strong *adj.*
1. күчлү güclü
2. күшті (küshti)
3. күчтүү (küchtüü)
4. көчле (köchle)
5. güçlü
6. гүйчли güÿçli
7. كۇچلۇك (küchlük)
8. кучли kuchli

## student *n.*
1. тәләбә tələbə
2. студент (student)
3. студент (student)
4. студент (student)
5. öğrenci
6. студент student
7. ﺋﻮﻗﯘﻏﯘﭼﻰ (oqughuchi)
8. ўқувчи o'quvchi

## study *v.*
1. оху-, өјрән- oxu-, öyrən-
2. оқы- (oqı-)
3. оку изилде- (oku izilde-)
4. өйрән- (öyrän-)
5. çalış-
6. өврен- öwren-
7. ﺋﯚﮔﻪﻥ (ögän-)
8. ўрган- o'rgan-

## stupid *adj.*
1. ағылсыз ağılsız
2. ақымақ (aqımaq)
3. акмак (akmak)
4. аңгыра (anggıra)
5. aptal
6. самсық samsyk
7. ﺩﯙﺕ (döt)
8. аҳмоқ ahmoq

## subject *ling. n.*
1. мүбтәда mübtəda
2. бастауыш (bastawısh)
3. ээ (ee)
4. субъект (sub'yekt)
5. özne
6. әе eÿe
7. ﺋﯩﮕﺎ (igä)
8. эга ega

## subject (~theme) *lit. n.*
1. мөвзу mövzu
2. тақырып (taqırıp)
3. тема (tema)
4. тема (tema)
5. konu
6. тема tema
7. ﻣﺎﯞﺯﯗ (mavzu)
8. мавзу mavzu

## submarine *mil. n.*
1. суалты кәми sualtı gəmi
2. сүңгүір қайық
(süngguwir qayıq)
3. суу астында сүзүүчү
кеме
(suu astında süzüüchü keme)
4. су асты көймәсе
(su astı köymäse)
5. denizaltı
6. сувасты suwasty

7. ﺳﯘ ﺋﺎﺳﺘﻰ ﻛﯧﻤﯩﺴﻰ
(su asti kemisi)
8. сув ости кемаси
suv osti kemasi

## subtraction *math. n.*
1. чыхма çıxma
2. алу (aluw)
3. алуу (aluu)
4. алу (alu)
5. çıkarma
6. айырмак aÿyrmak
7. ﺋﯧﻠﯩﺶ (elish)
8. айириш ayirish

## suburb *n.*
1. шәһәрәтрафы şəhərətrafı
2. қаланың шеті
(qalanıng sheti)
3. шаардын чети
(shaardın cheti)
4. бистә (bistä)
5. banliyö
6. шәхер әтеги şäher etegi
7. ﺷﻪﮬﻪﺭ ﺋﻪﺗﺮﺍﭘﻰ
(shähär ätrapi)
8. шаҳар атрофи shahar atrofi

## subway *n.*
1. метро metro
2. метро (metro)
3. метро (metro)
4. метро (metro)
5. metro
6. метро metro
7. ﻣﯧﺘﺮﻭ (metro)
8. метро metro

---

1. Azerbaijani   2. Kazakh   3. Kyrgyz   4. Tatar   5. Turkish   6. Turkmen   7. Uighur   8. Uzbek

## succeed v.
1. бачар- bacar-
2. табысқа жет-
   (tabısqa zhet-)
3. табышка жет-
   (tabıshka jet-)
4. уңышка иреш-
   (ungıshka iresh-)
5. başar-
6. устунлик газан-
   üstünlik gazan-
7. مۇۋەپپەقىيەت قازانـ
   (muväppäqiyät qazan-)
8. муваффақият қозон-
   muvaffaqiyat qozon-

## success n.
1. мувәффәгијјәт
   müvəffəqiyyət
2. табыс (tabıs)
3. ийгилик (iygilik)
4. уңыш (ungısh)
5. başarı
6. устунлик üstünlik
7. مۇۋەپپەقىيەت
   (muväppäqiyät)
8. муваффақият muvaffaqiyat

## such adv.
1. белә, елә belə, elə
2. осындай (osınday)
3. ошондой (oshondoy)
4. мондый, андый
   (mondıy, andıy)
5. şöyle, böyle
6. шейле, бейле şeýle, beýle
7. بۇنداق، شۇنداق
   (bundaq, shundaq)
8. бундай, шундай
   bunday, shunday

## suck v.
1. әм- əm-
2. ем- (yem-)
3. эм- (em-)
4. им- (im-)
5. em-
6. әм- em-
7. ئە مـ (äm-)
8. сур- so'r-

## sudden adj.
1. ани ani
2. күтпеген (kütpegen)
3. күтпөгөн жерден
   (kütpögön jerden)
4. көтелмәгән (kötelmägän)
5. ani
6. бирден birden
7. تاساد يپـى (tasadipiy)
8. тусатдан to'satdan

## sufficient adj.
1. кафи kafi
2. жеткілікті (zhetkilikti)
3. жетишээрлик
   (jetisheerlik)
4. житәрлек (jitärlek)
5. kâfi
6. етерлик[ли] ýeterlik[li]
7. يىتەرلىك (yetärlik)
8. етарли yetarli

## suffix ling. n.
1. шәкилчи şəkilçi
2. суффикс (suffiks)
3. мүчө (müchö)
4. кушымча (kushımcha)
5. sonek
6. гошулма goşulma
7. قوشۇمچە (qoshumchä)
8. қушимча qo'shimcha

## sugar cul. n.
1. гәнд qənd
2. қант (qant)
3. кант (kant)
4. шикәр (shikär)
5. şeker
6. шекер, гант şeker, gant
7. قەنت (qänt)
8. қанд qand

## suggestion n.
1. тәклиф təklif
2. усыныс (usınıs)
3. өтүнүч (ötünüch)
4. тәкъдим (täk'dim)
5. öneri
6. теклип teklip
7. پىكىر (pikir)
8. таклиф taklif

## suit clo. n.
1. костјум kostyum
2. костюм (kostyum)
3. костюм (kostyum)
4. костюм (kostyum)
5. takım elbise
6. костюм kostyum
7. كاستۇم (kastum)
8. костюм kostyum

## suit (=be fitting) v.
1. ујғун кәл-, japaш-
   uyğun gəl-, yaraş-
2. жарас- (zharas-)
3. жараш- (jarash-)
4. туры кил- (turı kil-)
5. uygun ol-
6. гелиш- geliş-
7. ياراشـ (yarash-)
8. мос кел- mos kel-

---

1. Azerbaijani  2. Kazakh  3. Kyrgyz  4. Tatar  5. Turkish  6. Turkmen  7. Uighur  8. Uzbek

## suitcase *n.*
1. чамадан çamadan
2. чемодан (chemodan)
3. чемодан (chemodan)
4. чемодан (chemodan)
5. bavul
6. чемедан çemedan
7. چامادان (chamadan)
8. чамадон chamadon

## summer *n.*
1. jaj yay
2. жаз (zhaz)
3. жай (jay)
4. жәй (jäy)
5. yaz
6. томус tomus
7. ياز (yaz)
8. ёз yoz

## summon *v.*
1. чағыр- çağır-
2. шақыр- (shaqır-)
3. чакыр- (chakır-)
4. чакыр- (chakır-)
5. çağır-
6. чагыр- çagyr-
7. چاقىر (chaqir-)
8. чақир- chaqir-

## sun *n.*
1. күнәш günəş
2. күн (kün)
3. күн (kün)
4. кояш (koyash)
5. güneş
6. гүн gün
7. كۈن (kün)
8. қуёш quyosh

## Sunday *n.*
1. базар bazar
2. жексенбі (zheksenbi)
3. жекшемби (jekshembi)
4. якшәмбе (yakshämbe)
5. pazar
6. екшенбе yekşenbe
7. يەكشەنبە (yäkshänbä)
8. якшанба yakshanba

## sunflower *bot. n.*
1. күнәбахан günəbaxan
2. күнбағыс (künbaghıs)
3. күн карама (kün karama)
4. көнбагыш (könbagısh)
5. ayçiçeği
6. гүнебакар günebakar
7. ئاپتاپپەرەس (aptappäräs)
8. кунгабоқар kungaboqar

## sunrise *n.*
1. күнәшин доғмасы günəşin doğması
2. күн шығу (kün shıghuw)
3. күн чыгыш (kün chıgısh)
4. кояш чыгу (koyash chıgu)
5. gün doğuşu
6. гүнүң догмагы günüñ dogmagy
7. كۈنچىقىش (künchiqish)
8. қуёш чиқиши quyosh chiqishi

## sunset *n.*
1. күнәшин батмасы günəşin batması
2. күн бату (kün batuw)
3. күн батыш (kün batısh)
4. кояш бату (koyash batu)
5. günbatımı
6. гүнүң яшмагы günüñ ÿaşmagy

## 
7. كۈنپىتىش (künpetish)
8. қуёш ботиши quyosh botishi

## surgery *med. n.*
1. чәррәһлыг cərrahlıq
2. хирургия (khirurgiya)
3. хирургия (khirurgiya)
4. хирургия (khirurgiya)
5. cerrahlık
6. хирургия hirurgiÿa
7. ئوپېراتسىيە (operatsiyä)
8. жаррохлик jarrohlik

## surname *n.*
1. фамилиja familiya
2. фамилия (familiya)
3. фамилия (familiya)
4. фамилия (familiya)
5. soyadı
6. фамилия familiÿa
7. فامىلە (familä)
8. фамилия familiya

## surpass *v.*
1. үстүн ол- üstün ol-
2. асып кет- (asıp ket-)
3. озуп кет- (ozup ket-)
4. жин- (jing-)
5. geç-
6. үстүн чык- üstün çyk-
7. ئېشىپ كەت (eship ket-)
8. устун кел- ustun kel-

## surrender *mil. n.*
1. тәслим олма təslim olma
2. берілу (beriluw)
3. багынуу (bagınuu)
4. бирелү (birelü)
5. teslim olma
6. боюн әгме boÿun egme
7. تەسلىم بولۇش (täslim bolush)
8. таслим бүлиш taslim bo'lish

---

**surround** *v.*
1. əhatə ет- əhatə et-
2. қорша- (qorsha-)
3. курча- (kurcha-)
4. уратып ал- (uratıp al-)
5. kuşat-
6. гурша- gurşa-
7. تورشا ـ (qorsha-)
8. қурша- qursha-

**swallow** *zool. n.*
1. гарангуш qaranquş
2. қарлығаш (qarlıghash)
3. карлыгач (karlıgach)
4. карлыгач (karlıgach)
5. kırlangıç
6. гарлавач garlawaç
7. قارلىغاچ (qarlighach)
8. қалдирғоч qaldirg'och

**swamp** *geo. n.*
1. батаглыг bataqlıq
2. батпақ (batpaq)
3. саз (saz)
4. саз(лық) (saz[lık])
5. bataklık
6. батга batga
7. سازلىق (sazliq)
8. ботқоқ botqoq

**swan** *zool. n.*
1. гу гушу qu quşu
2. аққу (aqquw)
3. ак куу (ak kuu)
4. аккош (akkosh)
5. kuğu
6. гув guw
7. ئاق قۇ (aq qu)
8. оққуш oqqush

**swear** (=take an oath) *v.*
1. анд ич- and iç-
2. ант бер- (ant ber-)
3. ант бер- (ant ber-)
4. ант ит- (ant it-)
5. yemin et-
6. ант ич- ant iç-
7. قەسەم قىلـ (qäsäm qil-)
8. қасам ич- qasam ich-

**sweat** *v.*
1. тәрлә- tərlə-
2. терле- (terle-)
3. терде- (terde-)
4. тирлә- (tirlä-)
5. terle-
6. дерле- derle-
7. تەرلە (tärlä-)
8. терла- terla-

**sweater** *clo. n.*
1. свитер sviter
2. свитер (sviter)
3. свитер (sviter)
4. свитер (sviter)
5. kazak
6. свитер switer
7. پوپايكا (popayka)
8. свитер sviter

**sweep** *v.*
1. сүпүр- süpür-
2. сыпыр- (sıpır-)
3. шыпыр- (shıpır-)
4. себер- (seber-)
5. süpür-
6. сүпүр- süpür-
7. سۈپۈرـ (süpür-)
8. супур- supur-

**sweet** *adj.*
1. ширин şirin
2. тәтті (tätti)
3. таттуу (tattuu)
4. татлы (tatlı)
5. tatlı
6. сүйҗи süýji
7. تاتلىق (tatliq)
8. ширин shirin

**swell** *v.*
1. шиш- şiş-
2. ic- (is-)
3. шиши- (shishi-)
4. шеш- (shesh-)
5. şiş-
6. чиш- çiş-
7. ئىششىـ (ishshi-)
8. шиш- shish-

**swelling** *n.*
1. шиш şiş
2. icik (isik)
3. шишик (shishik)
4. шеш (shesh)
5. şiş
6. чиш çiş
7. ئىششىق (ishshiq)
8. шиш shish

**swim** *v.*
1. үз- üz-
2. жүз- (zhüz-)
3. сүз- (süz-)
4. йөз- (yöz-)
5. yüz-
6. йүз- ýüz-
7. سۇ ئۈزـ (su üz-)
8. сүз- suz-

---

1. Azerbaijani  2. Kazakh  3. Kyrgyz  4. Tatar  5. Turkish  6. Turkmen  7. Uighur  8. Uzbek

## swimming *spor. n.*
1. үзкүчүлүк üzgüçülük
2. жүзу (zhüzuw)
3. сүзүү (süzüü)
4. йөзу (yözü)
5. yüzme
6. йүзме ÿüzme
7. ئۈزۈش (üzüsh)
8. сузиш suzish

## sword *mil. n.*
1. гылынч qılınc
2. қылыш (qılısh)
3. кылыч (kılıch)
4. кылыч (kılıch)
5. kılıç
6. гылыч gylyç
7. قىلىچ (qilich)
8. қилич qilich

## symbol *n.*
1. символ simvol
2. символ (simvol)
3. символ (simvol)
4. символ (simvol)
5. sembol
6. символ simwol
7. سىمۋول (simvol)
8. аломат alomat

## table *n.*
1. маса masa
2. стол (stol)
3. үстәл (üstöl)
4. өстәл (östäl)
5. masa
6. стол stol
7. جوزا (joza)
8. стол stol

## tablecloth *n.*
1. сүфрә süfrə
2. дастарқан (dastarqan)
3. дасторкон (dastorkon)
4. ашъяулык (ash'yaulık)
5. masa örtüsü
6. сачақ saçak
7. داستىخان (dastikhan)
8. дастурхон dasturxon

## tail *zool. n.*
1. гујруг quyruq
2. құйрық (quyrıq)
3. куйрук (kuyruk)
4. койрык (koyrık)
5. kuyruk
6. гуйрук guÿruk
7. قۇيرۇق (quyruq)
8. дум dum

## tailor *n.*
1. дәрзи dərzi
2. тігінші (tiginshi)
3. тикмечи (tikmechi)
4. тегүче (tegüche)
5. terzi
6. тикинчи tikinçi
7. سەيپۇڭ (säypung)
8. тикувчи tikuvchi

## take *v.*
1. көтүр- götür-
2. ал- (al-)
3. ал- (al-)
4. ал- (al-)
5. al-
6. ал- al-
7. ئال (al-)
8. ол- ol-

## talk *v.*
1. даныш- danış-
2. әңгімелес- (änggimeles-)
3. аңгемелеш- (anggemelesh-)
4. сөйләш- (söyläsh-)
5. konuş-
6. гепле- geple-
7. سۆزلە (sözlä-)
8. гаплаш- gaplash-

## tall (*person) *adj.*
1. һүндүр бојлу
   hündür boylu
2. ұзын бойлы (uzın boylı)
3. бою узун (boyu uzun)
4. озын буйлы (ozın buylı)
5. uzun boylu
6. узын uzyn
7. بويى ئېگىز (boyi egiz)
8. новча novcha

## tall (=high) *adj.*
1. уча uca
2. бійік (biyik)
3. бийик (biyik)
4. биек (biyek)
5. yüksek
6. бейик beÿik
7. ئېگىز (egiz)
8. баланд baland

## tape recorder *mus. n.*
1. магнитофон maqnitofon
2. магнитофон (magnitofon)
3. магнитофон (magnitofon)
4. магнитофон (magnitofon)
5. teyp
6. магнитофон magnitofon
7. ئۈنئالغۇ (ün'alghu)
8. магнитофон magnitofon

---

**taste** *v.*
1. дад- dad-
2. дәмін көр- (dämin kör-)
3. даам тат- (daam tat-)
4. тат- (tat-)
5. tat-
6. дат- dat-
7. تەتى_ (teti-)
8. татиб кўр- tatib ko'r-

**tasty** *adj.*
1. ләззәтли ləzzətli
2. дәмді (dämdi)
3. даамдуу (daamduu)
4. татлы (tatlı)
5. lezzetli
6. тагамлы tagamly
7. تە ملك (tämlik)
8. мазали mazali

**tax** *n.*
1. верки vergi
2. салық (salıq)
3. салык (salık)
4. салым (salım)
5. vergi
6. салгыт salgyt
7. باج (baj)
8. солиқ soliq

**taxi** *n.*
1. такси taksi
2. такси (taksi)
3. такси (taksi)
4. такси (taksi)
5. taksi
6. такси taksi
7. كىرا ماشىنىسى
     (kira mashinisi)
8. такси taksi

**tea** *n.*
1. чај çay
2. шай (shay)
3. чай (chay)
4. чәй (chäy)
5. çay
6. чай чаÿ
7. چاي (chay)
8. чой choy

**teach** *v.*
1. әјрәт- öyrət-
2. оқыт- (oqıt-)
3. окут- (okut-)
4. укыт- (ukıt-)
5. öğret-
6. өврет- öwret-
7. ئوقۇتـ (oqut-)
8. ўргат- o'rgat-

**teacher** *n.*
1. мүәллим müəllim
2. мұғалім (mughalim)
3. мугалим (mugalim)
4. укытучы (ukıtuchı)
5. öğretmen
6. мугаллым mugallym
7. ئوقۇتغۇچى (oqutquchi)
8. ўқитувчи o'qituvchi

**teapot** *cul. n.*
1. чајдан çaydan
2. шәйнек (shäynek)
3. чайнек (chaynek)
4. чәйнек (chäynek)
5. çaydanlık
6. чайник çaÿnik
7. چە ينەك (chäynäk)
8. чойнак choynak

**tear** *v.*
1. чыр- cır-
2. жырт- (zhırt-)
3. жырт- (jırt-)
4. ерт- (yert-)
5. yırt-
6. йырт- ÿyrt-
7. يىرتـ (yirt-)
8. йирт- yirt-

**telegram** *n.*
1. телеграм teleqram
2. телеграмма (telegramma)
3. телеграмма (telegramma)
4. телеграмма (telegramma)
5. telgraf
6. телеграмма telegramma
7. تېلېگرامما (telegramma)
8. телеграмма telegramma

**telephone** *n.*
1. телефон telefon
2. телефон (telefon)
3. телефон (telefon)
4. телефон (telefon)
5. telefon
6. телефон telefon
7. تېلېفون (telefon)
8. телефон telefon

**television** *n.*
1. телевизор televizor
2. телевизор (televizor)
3. телевизор (televizor)
4. телевизор (televizor)
5. televizyon
6. телевизор telewizor
7. تېلېۋىزور (televizor)
8. телевизор televizor

---

## tell *v.*
1. де-, сөјлә- de-, söylə-
2. айт- (ayt-)
3. айт- (ayt-)
4. әйт- (äyt-)
5. söyle-
6. айт- aÿt-
7. ‫ئبيت_‬ (eyt-)
8. айт- ayt-

## temperature *n.*
1. истилик istilik
2. температура (temperatura)
3. температура (temperatura)
4. температура (temperatura)
5. sıcaklık
6. температура temperatura
7. ‫تيمپبراتۇرا‬ (temperatura)
8. ҳарорат harorat

## temple *rel. n.*
1. мә'бәд mə'bəd
2. гибадатхана (ghiybadatkhana)
3. ибадаткана (ibadatkana)
4. гыйбадәтханә (gıybadätkhanä)
5. tapınak
6. ыбадатхана ybadathana
7. ‫ئباده تخانا‬ (ibadätkhana)
8. ибодатхона ibodatxona

## ten *num.*
1. он on
2. он (on)
3. он (on)
4. ун (un)
5. on
6. он on
7. ‫ئون‬ (on)
8. ўн o'n

## test *v.*
1. имтаһан ет- imtahan et-
2. сына- (sına-)
3. сына- (sına-)
4. тикшер- (tiksher-)
5. sına-
6. сына- syna-
7. ‫سىنا_‬ (sina-)
8. сина- sina-

## textile *n.*
1. тохучулуг toxuculuq
2. тоқыма (toqıma)
3. кездеме (kezdeme)
4. тукыма (tukıma)
5. dokuma
6. докма dokma
7. ‫گزمال‬ (gäzmal)
8. газмол gazmol

## thank *v.*
1. тәшәккүр ет- təşəkkür et-
2. рахмет айт- (rakhmet ayt-)
3. ыракмат айт- (ırakmat ayt-)
4. шөкер кыл- (shöker kıl-)
5. teşekkür et-
6. саг бол айт- sag bol aÿt-
7. ‫ره همەت ئبيت_‬ (rähmät eyt-)
8. миннатдорчилик билдир- minnatdorchilik bildir-

## that *pron.*
1. о o
2. сол (sol)
3. тиги (tigi)
4. шул (shul)
5. o
6. ол, о ol, o
7. ‫ئۇ‬ (u)
8. у u

## that *conj.*
1. ки ki
2. екен (yeken)
3. тиги (tigi)
4. ки (ki)
5. ki
6. -ан, -эн, -ян, -йән -an, -en, -ÿan, -ÿän
7. ‫دەپ‬ (däp)
8. ки ki

## theater *art. n.*
1. театр teatr
2. театр (teatr)
3. театр (teatr)
4. театр (teatr)
5. tiyatro
6. театр teatr
7. ‫تىياتىرخانا‬ (tiyatirkhana)
8. театр teatr

## their *adj.*
1. онларын onların
2. олардың (olardıng)
3. алардын (alardın)
4. аларның (alarnıng)
5. onların
6. оларың olaryñ
7. ‫ئۇلارنىڭ‬ (ularning)
8. уларнинг ularning

## them *pron.*
1. онлары onları
2. олlarды (olardı)
3. аларды (alardı)
4. аларны (alarnı)
5. onları
6. олары olary
7. ‫ئۇلارنى‬ (ularni)
8. уларни ularni

---

## then (=after that) *adv.*
1. ондан сонра ondan sonra
2. сонан кейін (sonan keyin)
3. андан соң (andan song)
4. аннан соң (annan song)
5. ondan sonra
6. соңра soñra
7. ئاندىن كېيىن (andin keyin)
8. кейин keyin

## then (=at that time) *adv.*
1. о заман o zaman
2. сол уақытта (sol waqıtta)
3. анан (anan)
4. ул вакытта (ul vakıtta)
5. o zaman
6. онда onda
7. شۇ چاغدا (shu chaghda)
8. у вақтда u vaqtda

## theory *n.*
1. нәзәријјә nəzəriyyə
2. теория (teoriya)
3. теория (teoriya)
4. теория (teoriya)
5. kuram
6. теория teoriýa
7. نەزەرىيە (näzäriyä)
8. назария nazariya

## there *adv.*
1. орада, ораја orada, oraya
2. сонда, анда (sonda, anda)
3. тиги жерде (tigi jerde)
4. анда, ары (anda, arı)
5. orada, oraya
6. ол ерде, ол ере
   ol ÿerde, ol ÿere
7. ئۇ يەردە، ئۇ يەرگە
   (u yärdä, u yärgä)
8. у ерда, у ерга
   u yerda, u yerga

## therefore *adv.*
1. онун үчүн onun üçün
2. сондықтан (sondıqtan)
3. ошондуктан
   (oshonduktan)
4. шунлыктан (shunlıktan)
5. bundan dolayı
6. шонуң үчин şonuñ üçin
7. شۇنىڭ ئۈچۈن
   (shuning üchün)
8. шунинг учун
   shuning uchun

## thermometer *n.*
1. термометр termometr
2. термометр (termometr)
3. термометр (termometr)
4. термометр (termometr)
5. termometre
6. термометр termometr
7. تېرمومېتر (termometr)
8. термометр termometr

## these *pron.*
1. бунлар bunlar
2. бұлар (bular)
3. булар (bular)
4. болар (bolar)
5. bunlar
6. булар bular
7. بۇلار (bular)
8. булар bular

## they *pron.*
1. онлар onlar
2. олар (olar)
3. алар (alar)
4. алар (alar)
5. onlar
6. олар olar
7. ئۇلار (ular)
8. улар ular

## thick (=dense) *adj.*
1. сых sıx
2. қалың (qalıng)
3. калың (kalıng)
4. тыгыз (tıgız)
5. sık
6. гүр gür
7. قويۇق (qoyuq)
8. зич zich

## thick (x thin) *adj.*
1. галын qalın
2. жуан (zhuwan)
3. жоон (joon)
4. калын (kalın)
5. kalın
6. ёгын ÿogyn
7. قېلىن (qelin)
8. қалин qalin

## thief *n.*
1. оғру oğru
2. ұры (urı)
3. ууру (uuru)
4. карак (karak)
5. hırsız
6. огры ogry
7. ئوغرى (oghri)
8. ўғри o'g'ri

## thigh *phys. n.*
1. буд bud
2. сан (san)
3. сан (san)
4. бот (bot)
5. but
6. бут but
7. يوتا (yota)
8. сон son

---

**thin** *adj.*
1. инчэ incə
2. жұқа (zhuqa)
3. жука (juka)
4. юка (yuka)
5. ince
6. инче inçe
7. ئىنچىكە (inchikä)
8. юпқа yupqa

**thing** *n.*
1. шеj şey
2. зат (zat)
3. зат (zat)
4. нэрсэ (närsä)
5. şey
6. зат zat
7. نەرسە (närsä)
8. нарса narsa

**think** (=ponder) *v.*
1. дүшүн- düşün-
2. ойла- (oyla-)
3. ойло- (oylo-)
4. уйла- (uyla-)
5. düşün-
6. ойлан- oÿlan-
7. ئويلا_ (oyla-)
8. ўйла- o'yla-

**thirsty** *adj.*
1. сусуз susuz
2. шөлдеген (shöldegen)
3. чаңкаган (changkagan)
4. эчэсе килгэн
(echäse kilgän)
5. susamış
6. сувсан suwsan
7. ئۇسسۇز (ussuz)
8. ташна tashna

**thirteen** *num.*
1. он үч on üç
2. он ұш (on üsh)
3. он үч (on üch)
4. унөч (unöch)
5. on üç
6. он үч on üç
7. ئون ئۈچ (on üch)
8. ўн уч o'n uch

**thirty** *num.*
1. отуз otuz
2. отыз (otız)
3. отуз (otuz)
4. утыз (utız)
5. otuz
6. отуз otuz
7. ئوتتۇز (ottuz)
8. ўттиз o'ttiz

**this** *pron.*
1. бу bu
2. бұл (bul)
3. бул (bul)
4. бу (bu)
5. bu
6. бу bu
7. بۇ (bu)
8. бу bu

**those** *pron.*
1. онлар onlar
2. олар (olar)
3. алар (alar)
4. шулар (shular)
5. onlar
6. олар olar
7. ئۇلار (ular)
8. улар ular

**thought** *n.*
1. дүшүнчэ düşüncə
2. ой (oy)
3. ой (oy)
4. уй (uy)
5. düşünce
6. пикир pikir
7. ئوي (oy)
8. фикр fikr

**thousand** *num.*
1. мин min
2. мың (mıng)
3. мин (ming)
4. мең (meng)
5. bin
6. мүң müñ
7. مىڭ (ming)
8. минг ming

**three** *num.*
1. үч üç
2. үш (üsh)
3. үч (üch)
4. өч (öch)
5. üç
6. үч üç
7. ئۈچ (üch)
8. уч uch

**throat** *phys. n.*
1. богаз boğaz
2. тамақ (tamaq)
3. тамак (tamak)
4. тамак (tamak)
5. boğaz
6. богаз bogaz
7. گال (gal)
8. томоқ tomoq

---

1. Azerbaijani   2. Kazakh   3. Kyrgyz   4. Tatar   5. Turkish   6. Turkmen   7. Uighur   8. Uzbek

# throw v.
1. тулла- tulla-
2. лақтыр- (laqtır-)
3. ыргыт- (ırgıt-)
4. ташла- (tashla-)
5. at-
6. окла- okla-
7. _ت‌ا‌ك (at-)
8. ташла- tashla-

# thunder n.
1. кɵј ҟурултусу
göy gurultusu
2. күн күркiрey
(kün kürkirew)
3. күн күркүрɵɵ
(kün kürküröö)
4. күкрɘʏ (kükräü)
5. gök gürlemesi
6. гɵк гүррүлдиси
gök gürrüldisi
7. گۈلدۈرماما (güldürmama)
8. момақалдироқ
momaqaldiroq

# Thursday n.
1. чʏмɘ ахшамы
cümə axşamı
2. бейсенбi (beysenbi)
3. бейшемби (beyshembi)
4. пɘнҗешɘмбе
(pänjeshämbe)
5. perşembe
6. пеншенбе penşenbe
7. پ‌يش‌نبه (päyshänbä)
8. пайшанба payshanba

# ticket n.
1. билет bilet
2. билет (bilet)
3. билет (bilet)
4. билет (bilet)
5. bilet
6. билет bilet

7. بيل‌ت (belät)
8. билет bilet

# tie clo. n.
1. галстук qalstuk
2. галстук (galstuk)
3. галстук (galstuk)
4. галстук (galstuk)
5. kravat
6. галстук galstuk
7. گال‌ستۇك (galstuk)
8. галстук galstuk

# tie (=fasten) v.
1. багла- bağla-
2. байла- (bayla-)
3. байла- (bayla-)
4. бɘйлɘ- (bäylä-)
5. bağla-
6. даң- dañ-
7. ب‌اغل‌ا (baghla-)
8. богла- bog'la-

# tiger zool. n.
1. пɘлɘнк pələng
2. жолбарыс (zholbarıs)
3. жолборс (jolbors)
4. юлбарыс (yulbarıs)
5. kaplan
6. гаплаң gaplañ
7. يولواس (yolvas)
8. йʏлбарс yo'lbars

# tight adj.
1. дар dar
2. тар (tar)
3. тар (tar)
4. тар (tar)
5. sıkı
6. дар dar
7. چ‌ملك (ching)
8. тор tor

# time n.
1. вахт vaxt
2. уақыт (waqıt)
3. убакыт (ubakıt)
4. вакыт (vakıt)
5. zaman
6. вагт wagt
7. واقت (vaqit)
8. вақт vaqt

# tip (*money) n.
1. чајпулу çaypulu
2. шай пʏл (shay pul)
3. чай пулу (chay pulu)
4. чɘйлек (chäylek)
5. bahşiş
6. чай пулы çaÿ puly
7. چاي پۈلي (chay puli)
8. чойчақа choychaqa

# tire n.
1. шин şin
2. шин (shiyn)
3. дɵңгɵлɘк (dönggölök)
4. шина (shina)
5. lastik
6. шин şin
7. چ‌اق (chaq)
8. шина shina

# tired adj.
1. јорғун yorğun
2. шаршаған (sharshaghan)
3. чарчаган (charchagan)
4. арыган (arıgan)
5. yorgun
6. ядав ÿadaw
7. هارغ‌ين (harghin)
8. хорғин horg'in

---

1. Azerbaijani  2. Kazakh  3. Kyrgyz  4. Tatar  5. Turkish  6. Turkmen  7. Uighur  8. Uzbek

**title** *lit. n.*
1. сәрлөвһә sərlövhə
2. ат (at)
3. ат (at)
4. исем (isem)
5. başlık
6. аг at
7. سەرلەۋھە (särlävhä)
8. сарлавха sarlavha

**to** *prep.*
1. -a, -ə, -ja, -jə -a, -ə, -ya, -yə
2. -га, -ге, -қа, -ке
(-gha, -ge, -qa, -ke)
3. -га, -ге, -го, -гө, -ка, -ке,
-ко, -кө (-ga, -ge, -go, -gö,
-ka, -ke, -ko, -kö)
4. -га, -гә, -ка, -кә
(-ga, -gä, -ka, -kä)
5. -a, -e, -ya, -ye
6. -a, -ə -a, -e
7. ـگە، ـقا، ـکە، ـقە ، ـکا
ـغا، (-gha, -gä, -qa, -kä,
-qä, -ka)
8. -га -ga

**tobacco** *n.*
1. түтүн tütün
2. темекі (temeki)
3. тамеки (tameki)
4. тәмәке (tämäke)
5. tütün
6. теммәки temmäki
7. تاماكا (tamaka)
8. тамаки tamaki

**today** *n.*
1. бу күн bu gün
2. бүгін (bügin)
3. бүгүн (bügün)
4. бүген (bügen)
5. bugün
6. бу гүн bu gün

7. بۈگۈن (bügün)
8. бугун bugun

**together** *adv.*
1. бирликдә birlikdə
2. бірге (birge)
3. бирге (birge)
4. бергә (bergä)
5. birlikte
6. биле bile
7. بىرگە (birgä)
8. бирга birga

**toilet** *n.*
1. туалет tualet
2. әжетхана (äzhetkhana)
3. даараткана (daaratkana)
4. әжәтханә (äjätkhanä)
5. tuvalet
6. хажатхана hajathana
7. ھاجەتخانا (hajätkhana)
8. хожатхона hojatxona

**tomato** *bot. n.*
1. помидор pomidor
2. помидор (pomidor)
3. помидор (pomidor)
4. помидор (pomidor)
5. domates
6. помидор pomidor
7. پەمىدۇر (pämidur)
8. помидор pomidor

**tomorrow** *n.*
1. сабаһ sabah
2. ертең (yerteng)
3. эртең (erteng)
4. иртәгә (irtägä)
5. yarın
6. эртир ertir
7. ئەتە (ätä)
8. эртага ertaga

**tongue** *phys. n.*
1. дил dil
2. тіл (til)
3. тил (til)
4. тел (tel)
5. dil
6. дил dil
7. تىل (til)
8. тил til

**too** *adv.*
1. да, дә da, də
2. тағы да (taghı da)
3. да (da)
4. да, дә (da, dä)
5. da, de
6. да, де, хем da, de, hem
7. ـمۇ (-mu)
8. хам ham

**tool** *n.*
1. аләт alət
2. аспап (aspap)
3. аспап (aspap)
4. корал (koral)
5. alet
6. гурал gural
7. ئەسۋاب (äsvab)
8. асбоб asbob

**tooth** *phys. n.*
1. диш diş
2. тіс (tis)
3. тиш (tish)
4. теш (tesh)
5. diş
6. диш diş
7. چىش (chish)
8. тиш tish

---

## toothache  *n.*
1. диш ағрысы diş ağrısı
2. тіс ауруы (tis awruwı)
3. тиш оору (tish ooru)
4. теш авыруы (tesh avıruı)
5. diş ağrısı
6. диш агыры diş agyry
7. چىش ئاغرىقى (chish aghriqi)
8. тиш оғриғи tish og'rig'i

## toothbrush  *n.*
1. диш фырчасы diş fırçası
2. тіс шөткесі (tis shötkesi)
3. тиш щётка (tish shchyotka)
4. теш щёткасы (tesh shchyotkası)
5. diş fırçası
6. диш чотгасы diş çotgasy
7. چىش چوتكىسى (chish chotkisi)
8. тиш чўткаси tish cho'tkasi

## toothpaste  *n.*
1. диш пастасы diş pastası
2. тіс пастасы (tis pastası)
3. тиш паста (tish pasta)
4. теш чистарту пастасы (tesh chistartu pastası)
5. diş macunu
6. диш пастасы diş pastasy
7. چىش پاستىسى (chish pastisi)
8. тиш пастаси tish pastasi

## tortoise  *zool. n.*
1. тысбаға tısbağa
2. тасбақа (tasbaqa)
3. ташбака (tashbaka)
4. ташбака (tashbaka)
5. kaplumbağa
6. пышбага pyşbaga

7. تاشپاقا (tashpaqa)
8. тошбақа toshbaqa

## touch  *v.*
1. тохун-, дәј- toxun-, dəy-
2. ти- (tiy-)
3. тий- (tiy-)
4. ти- (ti-)
5. dokun-
6. дег- deg-
7. تەگ (täg-)
8. тег- teg-

## tourism  *n.*
1. туризм turizm
2. туризм (turizm)
3. туризм (turizm)
4. сәяхәт (säyakhät)
5. turizm
6. туризм turizm
7. سايامە تچىلىك (sayahätchilik)
8. саёхат sayohat

## tourist  *n.*
1. турист turist
2. турист (turist)
3. турист (turist)
4. сәяхәтче (säyakhätche)
5. turist
6. турист turist
7. سايامە تچى (sayahätchi)
8. сайёх sayyoh

## towards  *prep.*
1. доғру doğru
2. қарай (qaray)
3. карай (karay)
4. таба (taba)
5. doğru
6. тарапа tarapa
7. تەرەپكە (täräpkä)
8. томонга tomonga

## towel  *n.*
1. дәсмал dəsmal
2. сүлгі (sülgi)
3. сүлгү (sülgü)
4. сөлге (sölge)
5. havlu
6. полотенце polotentse
7. لۆڭگە (lönggä)
8. сочиқ sochiq

## tower  *n.*
1. гүллә qüllə
2. мұнара (munara)
3. мунара (munara)
4. манара (manara)
5. kule
6. минара minara
7. مۇنار (munar)
8. минора minora

## town  *n.*
1. рәсәбә qəsəbə
2. қала (qala)
3. шаар (shaar)
4. шәһәр (shähär)
5. kasaba
6. шәхер şäher
7. شەمەرچە (shähärchä)
8. шахарча shaharcha

## toy  *n.*
1. ojынчағ oyuncaq
2. ойыншық (oyınshıq)
3. оюнчук (oyunchuk)
4. уенчык (uyenchık)
5. oyuncak
6. ойнавач oÿnawaç
7. ئويۇنچۇق (oyunchuq)
8. ўйинчоқ o'yinchoq

---

## trace *n.*
1. из iz
2. iз (iz)
3. из (iz)
4. эз (ez)
5. iz
6. ыз yz
7. ئىز (iz)
8. из iz

## traffic *n.*
1. күчə һərəкəти
   küçə hərəkəti
2. транспорт ағымы
   (transport aghımı)
3. транспорт (transport)
4. урам хərəкəте
   (uram khäräkäte)
5. trafik
6. херекет hereket
7. قاتناش (qatnash)
8. йўл харакати yo'l harakati

## traffic light *n.*
1. светофор svetofor
2. светофор (svetofor)
3. светофор (svetofor)
4. светофор (svetofor)
5. trafik ışığı
6. светофор swetofor
7. قاتناش چىرىقى
   (qatnash chiriqi)
8. светофор svetofor

## train *n.*
1. гатар qatar
2. поезд (poyezd)
3. поезд (poezd)
4. поезд (poyezd)
5. tren
6. отлы otly
7. پويىز (poyiz)
8. поезд poyezd

## tram *n.*
1. трамваj tramvay
2. трамвай (tramvay)
3. трамвай (tramvay)
4. трамвай (tramvay)
5. tramvay
6. трамвай tramwaÿ
7. ترامۋاي (tramvay)
8. трамвай tramvay

## translate *v.*
1. тəрчүмə ет- tərcümə et-
2. аудар- (awdar-)
3. котор- (kotor-)
4. тəрҗемə ит- (tärjemä it-)
5. tercüme et-
6. терҗиме əт- terjime et-
7. ترجمه قىل (tärjimä qil-)
8. таржима қил- tarjima qil-

## translation *n.*
1. тəрчүмə tərcümə
2. аударма (awdarma)
3. котормо (kotormo)
4. тəрҗемə (tärjemä)
5. tercüme
6. терҗиме terjime
7. ترجمه (tärjimä)
8. таржима tarjima

## trash *n.*
1. зибил zibil
2. қоқыс (qoqıs)
3. таштанды (tashtandı)
4. чүп-чар (chüp-char)
5. çöp
6. зибил zibil
7. ئەخلەت (äkhlät)
8. ахлат axlat

## travel *n.*
1. cəjahət səyahət
2. саяхат (sayakhat)
3. саякат (sayakat)
4. сəяхəт (säyakhät)
5. seyahat
6. сыяхат syÿahat
7. سايا هەت (sayahät)
8. саёхат sayohat

## treasure *n.*
1. хəзинə xəzinə
2. қазына (qazına)
3. казына (kazına)
4. хəзинə (khäzinä)
5. hazine
6. хазына hazyna
7. بايلىق (bayliq)
8. хазина xazina

## tree *bot. n.*
1. ағач ağac
2. ағаш (aghash)
3. жыгач (jıgach)
4. агач (agach)
5. ağaç
6. агач agaç
7. دەرەخ (däräkh)
8. дарахт daraxt

## tremble *v.*
1. титрə- titrə-
2. дiрiлде- (dirilde-)
3. дирилде- (dirilde-)
4. калтыра- (kaltıra-)
5. titre-
6. титре- titre-
7. تىترە (titrä-)
8. қалтира- qaltira-

---

1. Azerbaijani  2. Kazakh  3. Kyrgyz  4. Tatar  5. Turkish  6. Turkmen  7. Uighur  8. Uzbek

**triangle** *geo. n.*
1. үчбүчаг üçbucaq
2. үшбұрыш (üshburısh)
3. үч бурчтук (üch burchtuk)
4. өчпочмак (öchpochmak)
5. üçgen
6. үчбурчлук üçburçluk
7. ئۇچ بۇلۇڭ (üch bulung)
8. учбурчак uchburchak

**truck** *n.*
1. jүк машыны yük maşını
2. жүк тасыйтын машина (zhük tasıytın mashina)
3. жүк ташуучу машине (jük tashuuchu mashine)
4. йөк машинасы (yök mashinası)
5. kamyon
6. йүк машыны ÿük maşyny
7. يۈك ماشىنسى (yük mashinisi)
8. юк машинаси yuk mashinasi

**true** *adj.*
1. həгиги həqiqi
2. шын (shın)
3. чын (chın)
4. хакыйкый (khakıykıy)
5. hakiki
6. хакыкы hakyky
7. ھەقىقى (häqiqiy)
8. ҳақиқий haqiqiy

**truth** *n.*
1. həгигəт həqiqət
2. шындық (shındıq)
3. чындык (chındık)
4. хакыйкать (khakıykat')
5. hakikat
6. хакыкат hakykat

7. ھەقىقەت (häqiqät)
8. ҳақиқат haqiqat

**try** (=endevour) *v.*
1. чалыш- çalış-
2. тырыс- (tırıs-)
3. тырыш- (tırısh-)
4. тырыш- (tırısh-)
5. çalış-
6. чалыш- çalyş-
7. تىرىش (tirish-)
8. ҳаракат қил- harakat qil-

**Tuesday** *n.*
1. чəршəнбə ахшамы çərşənbə axşamı
2. сейсенбі (seysenbi)
3. шейшембú (sheyshembi)
4. сишəмбе (sishämbe)
5. salı
6. сишенбе sişenbe
7. سەيشەنبە (säyshänbä)
8. сешанба seshanba

**tuition** (*fee) *n.*
1. тəһсил һаггы təhsil haqqı
2. оқу ақысы (oquw aqısı)
3. окуу акысы (okuu akısı)
4. укыту акчасы (ukıtu akchası)
5. okul parası
6. окув төлеги okuw tölegi
7. ئوقۇش بەدەلى (oqush bädäli)
8. ўқиш учун түланган пул o'qish uchun to'langan pul

**tulip** *bot. n.*
1. лалə lalə
2. қызғалдақ (qızghaldaq)
3. кызгалдак (kızgaldak)
4. лалə (lalä)
5. lâle
6. лəле läle

7. لاۍ (lalä)
8. лола lola

**tune** *mus. n.*
1. мелодиja melodiya
2. күй (küy)
3. обон (obon)
4. көй (köy)
5. nağme
6. хең heñ
7. كۈي (küy)
8. оҳанг ohang

**turkey** *zool. n.*
1. һинд тоjуғу hind toyuğu
2. күрке тауық (kürke tawıq)
3. күрп (kürp)
4. күркə (kürkä)
5. hindi
6. индюк indÿuk
7. كۈركە (kürkä)
8. курка kurka

**turn** *vi.*
1. дөн- dön-
2. бұрыл- (burıl-)
3. бурул- (burul-)
4. борыл- (borıl-)
5. dön-
6. айлан- aÿlan-
7. بۇرۇل (burul-)
8. бурил- buril-

**twelve** *num.*
1. он ики on iki
2. он екі (on yeki)
3. он əки (on eki)
4. унике (unike)
5. on iki
6. он ики on iki
7. ئون ئىككى (on ikki)
8. ўн икки o'n ikki

---

**twenty** *num.*
1. ијирми iyirmi
2. жиырма (zhiyırma)
3. жыйырма (jıyırma)
4. егерме (yegerme)
5. yirmi
6. йигрими ÿigrimi
7. ينگرمه (yigirmä)
8. йигирма yigirma

**twin** *n.*
1. экиз әkiz
2. егіз (yegiz)
3. эгиз (egiz)
4. игезәклэр (igezäklär)
5. ikiz
6. экиз ekiz
7. توشكبزەك (qoshkezäk)
8. эгизак egizak

**twist** *vt.*
1. бур- bur-
2. бұра- (bura-)
3. бура- (bura-)
4. бор- (bor-)
5. bük-
6. товла- towla-
7. بۇرا (bura-)
8. бура- bura-

**two** *num.*
1. ики iki
2. екі (yeki)
3. эки (eki)
4. ике (ike)
5. iki
6. ики iki
7. ئىككى (ikki)
8. икки ikki

**typewriter** *n.*
1. јазы макинасы
yazı makinası

2. машинка (mashinka)
3. машинка (mashinka)
4. язу машинкасы
(yazu mashinkası)
5. daktilo
6. машынка maşynka
7. خەت بېسىش ماشىنىسى (khät besish mashinisi)
8. машинка mashinka

**ugly** *adj.*
1. чиркин çirkin
2. көріксіз (köriksiz)
3. түрү сүук (türü suuk)
4. ямьсез (yam'sez)
5. çirkin
6. гелшиксиз gelşiksiz
7. سەت (sät)
8. хунук xunuk

**umbrella** *n.*
1. чәтир çətir
2. қол шатыр (qol shatır)
3. кол чатыр (kol chatır)
4. зонтик (zontik)
5. şemsiye
6. саяван saÿawan
7. كۈنلۈك (künlük)
8. соябон soyabon

**uncle** *n.*
1. дајы, әми dayı, əmi
2. нағашы аға, аға
(naghashı agha, agha)
3. таяке, байке
(tayake, bayke)
4. ага, абый (aga, abıy)
5. dayı, amca
6. дайы, ага daÿy, aga
7. تاغا (tagha)
8. тоға, амаки
tog'a, amaki

**under** *prep.*
1. алтында altında
2. астында (astında)
3. астында (astında)
4. астында (astında)
5. altında
6. ашагында aşagynda
7. تېگىدە (tegidä)
8. тагида tagida

**underneath** *adv.*
1. алтда, алтында
altda, altında
2. астында, төменде
(astında, tömende)
3. астында (astında)
4. астында (astında)
5. altta, altında
6. ашакда, ашагында
aşakda, aşagynda
7. ئاستىدا، تېگىدە
(astida, tegidä)
8. тагида tagida

**understand** *v.*
1. баша дүш- başa düş-
2. түсін- (tüsin-)
3. түшүн- (tüshün-)
4. аңла- (angla-)
5. anla-
6. дүшүн- düşün-
7. چۈشەن (chüshän-)
8. тушун- tushun-

**unhappy** *adj.*
1. бэдбэхт bədbəxt
2. бақытсыз (baqıtsız)
3. бактысыз (baktısız)
4. бэхетсез (bäkhetsez)
5. mutsuz
6. багтсыз bagtsyz
7. بەختسىز (bäkhtsiz)
8. бахтсиз baxtsiz

**union** *pol. n.*
1. иттифаг ittifaq
2. одақ (odaq)
3. союз (soyuz)
4. союз (soyuz)
5. sendika
6. профсоюз profsoÿuz
7. ئۇيۇشما (uyushma)
8. уюшма uyushma

**university** *n.*
1. университет universitet
2. университет (universitet)
3. университет (universitet)
4. университет (universitet)
5. üniversite
6. университет uniwersitet
7. ئۇنىۋېرسىتېت (universitet)
8. университет universitet

**until** *prep.*
1. гәдәр qədər
2. дейін (deyin)
3. чейин (cheyin)
4. кадәр (kadär)
5. kadar
6. ченли çenli
7. ـقىچە ، ـگىچە ، ـكىچە ، ـغىچە (-ghichä, -qichä, -gichä, -kichä)
8. -гача -gacha

**urinate** *v.*
1. ишә- işə-
2. сій- (siy-)
3. сий- (siy-)
4. си- (si-)
5. işe-
6. сий- siÿ-
7. ـسىي (siy-)
8. сий- siy-

**us** *pron.*
1. бизи bizi
2. бізді (bizdi)
3. бизди (bizdi)
4. безне (bezne)
5. bizi
6. бизи bizi
7. بىزنى (bizni)
8. бизни bizni

**use** *v.*
1. ишләт- işlət-
2. қолдан- (qoldan-)
3. колдон- (koldon-)
4. куллан- (kullan-)
5. kullan-
6. улан- ulan-
7. ئىشلەت- (ishlät-)
8. ишлат- ishlat-

**used: be used to** *v.*
1. адәт ет- adət et-
2. үйреніп кет- (üyrenip ket-)
3. үйрөн- (üyrön-)
4. гадәтлән- (gadätlän-)
5. alış-
6. эндик эт- endik et-
7. ئادەتلەن- (adätlän-)
8. одатлан- odatlan-

**useful** *adj.*
1. файдалы faydalı
2. пайдалы (paydalı)
3. пайдалуу (paydaluu)
4. файдалы (faydalı)
5. faydalı
6. пейдалы peÿdaly
7. پايدىلىق (paydiliq)
8. фойдали foydali

**vacation** *n.*
1. тә'тил tə'til
2. демалыс (demalıs)
3. дем алыш (dem alısh)
4. ял (yal)
5. tatil
6. каникул kanikul
7. دەم ئېلىش (däm elish)
8. таътил ta'til

**valley** *geo. n.*
1. вади vadi
2. алқап (alqap)
3. өрөөн (öröön)
4. үзән (üzän)
5. vadi
6. дере dere
7. ۋادى (vadi)
8. водий vodiy

**valuable** *adj.*
1. гијмәтли qiymətli
2. бағалы (baghalı)
3. баалуу (baaluu)
4. кыйммәтле (kıymmätle)
5. kıymetli
6. гымматлы gymmatly
7. قىممەتلىك (qimmätlik)
8. қимматли qimmatli

**value** *n.*
1. гијмәт qiymət
2. қун (qun)
3. нарк (nark)
4. кыйммәт (kıymmät)
5. kıymet
6. баха baha
7. قەدىر (qädir)
8. қиймат qiymat

## veal *cul. n.*
1. дана әти dana әti
2. бҰзау еті (buzaw yeti)
3. музоо эти (muzoo eti)
4. бозау ите (bozau ite)
5. dana eti
6. гөле эти göle eti
7. موزاي گۆشى (mozay göshi)
8. бузоқ гўшти buzoq go'shti

## vegetable *bot. n.*
1. тәрәвәз tәrәvәz
2. көкөніс (kökönis)
3. жашылча (jashılcha)
4. яшелчә (yashelchä)
5. sebze
6. гөк өнүм gök önüm
7. كۆزكتات (köktat)
8. сабзавот sabzavot

## verb *ling. n.*
1. фе'л fe'l
2. етістік (yetistik)
3. этиш (etish)
4. фигыль (figıl')
5. fiil
6. ишлик işlik
7. پېئىل (pe'il)
8. феъл fe'l

## verdict *jud. n.*
1. һөкм hökm
2. үкім (ükim)
3. өкүм (öküm)
4. хөкем (khökem)
5. hüküm
6. хөкүм höküm
7. ھۆكۈم (höküm)
8. хукм hukm

## very *adv.*
1. чох çox
2. өте (öte)
3. өтө (ötö)
4. бик (bik)
5. çok
6. өрән örän
7. ناھايتى (nahayiti)
8. жуда juda

## victory *mil. n.*
1. гәләбә qәlәbә
2. жеңіс (zhengis)
3. жеңиш (jengish)
4. җиңеш (jingesh)
5. zafer
6. еңиш ÿeñiş
7. غەلبە (ghälibä)
8. ғалаба g'alaba

## video *n.*
1. видео video
2. видео (video)
3. видео (video)
4. видео (video)
5. video
6. видео wideo
7. رەسىملىك لېنتا (räsimlik lenta)
8. видео video

## village *n.*
1. кәнд kәnd
2. ауыл (awıl)
3. айыл (ayıl)
4. авыл (avıl)
5. köy
6. оба oba
7. يېزا (yeza)
8. қишлоқ qishloq

## vinegar *cul. n.*
1. сиркә sirkә
2. сірке суы (sirke suwı)
3. уксус (uksus)
4. серкә (serkä)
5. sirke
6. сирке sirke
7. ئاچچىقسۇ (achchiqsu)
8. сирка sirka

## visit *v.*
1. гонаг кет- qonaq get-
2. бар-, кел- (bar-, kel-)
3. бар-, кел- (bar-, kel-)
4. зиярәт кыл- (ziyärät kıl-)
5. ziyaret et-
6. гөрмәге бар- görmäge bar-
7. زىيارەت قىل (ziyärät qil-)
8. ташриф буюр- tashrif buyur-

## visit *n.*
1. зиjарәт ziyarәt
2. бару, келу (baruw, keluw)
3. баруу, келүү (baruu, kelüü)
4. визит (vizit)
5. ziyaret
6. визит wizit
7. زىيارەت (ziyarät)
8. зиёрат ziyorat

## voice *n.*
1. сәс sәs
2. дауыс (dawıs)
3. добуш (dobush)
4. тавыш (tavısh)
5. ses
6. сәс ses
7. ئاۋاز (avaz)
8. овоз ovoz

**vomit** *v.*
1. гус- qus-
2. құс- (qus-)
3. кус- (kus-)
4. кос- (kos-)
5. kus-
6. гус- gus-
7. قوس (qus-)
8. қус- qus-

**vote** *pol. v.*
1. сәс вер- səs ver-
2. дауыс бер- (dawıs ber-)
3. добуш бер- (dobush ber-)
4. тавыш бир- (tavısh bir-)
5. oy ver-
6. сес бер- ses ber-
7. ئاۋاز بەر (avaz bär-)
8. овоз бер- ovoz ber-

**vote** *pol. n.*
1. сәс səs
2. дауыс (dawıs)
3. добуш (dobush)
4. тавыш (tavısh)
5. oy
6. сес ses
7. ئاۋاز (avaz)
8. овоз ovoz

**vowel** *ling. n.*
1. саит sait
2. дауысты (dawıstı)
3. үндүү (ündüü)
4. сузык (suzık)
5. ünlü
6. чекимли çekimli
7. سوزۇق تاۋۇش (sozuq tavush)
8. унли unli

**wage** *n.*
1. әмәк һаггы əmək haqqı
2. еңбек ақы (yengbek aqı)
3. әмгек акы (emgek akı)
4. эш хакы (esh khakı)
5. ücret
6. айлық aÿlyk
7. ئىش ھەققى (ish häqqi)
8. иш хақи ish haqi

**wait** *v.*
1. көзлә- gözlə-
2. күт- (küt-)
3. күт- (küt-)
4. көт- (köt-)
5. bekle-
6. гараш- garaş-
7. كۈت (küt-)
8. кут- kut-

**waiter** *n.*
1. офисиант ofisiant
2. даяшы (dayashı)
3. официант (ofitsiant)
4. официант (ofitsiant)
5. garson
6. официант ofitsiant
7. كۈتكۈچى (kütküchi)
8. официант ofitsiant

**wake** *vi.*
1. ojan- oyan-
2. оян- (oyan-)
3. ойгон- (oygon-)
4. уян- (uyan-)
5. uyan-
6. оян- oÿan-
7. ئويغان (oyghan-)
8. уйгон- uyg'on-

**wake** *vt.*
1. ojat- oyat-
2. оят- (oyat-)
3. ойгот- (oygot-)
4. уят- (uyat-)
5. uyandır-
6. ояр-, оят- oÿar-, oÿat-
7. ئويغات (oyghat-)
8. уйгот- uyg'ot-

**walk** *v.*
1. јери- yeri-
2. жүр- (zhür-)
3. жүр- (jür-)
4. йөр- (yör-)
5. yürü-
6. йөре- ÿöre-
7. ماڭ (mang-)
8. юр- yur-

**wall** *n.*
1. дивар divar
2. қабырға (qabırgha)
3. дубал (dubal)
4. стена (stena)
5. duvar
6. дивар diwar
7. تام (tam)
8. девор devor

**wallet** *n.*
1. пул кисәси pul kisəsi
2. қапшық (qapshıq)
3. капчык (kapchık)
4. капчык (kapchık)
5. para cüzdanı
6. гапжык gapjyk
7. پورتمان (portman)
8. хамён hamyon

---

**walnut** *bot. n.*
1. гоз qoz
2. жаңғақ (zhangghaq)
3. жаңгак (janggak)
4. чикләвек (chiklävek)
5. ceviz
6. хоз hoz
7. ياگۇات (yangaq)
8. ёнғоқ yong'oq

**want** *v.*
1. истә- istə-
2. қала- (qala-)
3. каала- (kaala-)
4. телә- (telä-)
5. iste-
6. исле- isle-
7. خالا_ (khala-)
8. хоҳла- xohla-

**war** *n.*
1. мүһарибә müharibə
2. соғыс (soghıs)
3. согуш (sogush)
4. сугьш (sugish)
5. savaş
6. уруш uruş
7. ئۇرۇش (urush)
8. уруш urush

**warm** *adj.*
1. илыг ilıq
2. жылы (zhılı)
3. жылуу (jıluu)
4. җылы (jılı)
5. ılık
6. йылы ÿyly
7. يىللىق (yilliq)
8. илиқ iliq

**wash** *v.*
1. jy- yu-
2. жу- (zhuw-)
3. жуу- (juu-)
4. ю- (yu-)
5. yıka-
6. юв- ÿuw-
7. يۇ_ (yu-)
8. юв- yuv-

**watch** *n.*
1. чиб сааты cib saati
2. қол сағат (qol saghat)
3. кол саат (kol saat)
4. кул сәгате (kul sägate)
5. kol saati
6. сағат sagat
7. قول سائىتى (qol sa'iti)
8. қўл соати qo'l soati

**watchmaker** *n.*
1. саатсаз saatsaz
2. сағат жөндеуші
   (saghat zhöndewshi)
3. саат ондоочу
   (saat ongdoochu)
4. сәгать остасы
   (sägat' ostası)
5. saatçi
6. сагатчы sagatçy
7. ساەت تچى (saätchi)
8. соатсоз soatsoz

**water** *n.*
1. су su
2. су (suw)
3. сyy (suu)
4. су (su)
5. su
6. сув suw
7. سۇ (su)
8. сув suv

**watermelon** *bot. n.*
1. гарпыз qarpız
2. қарбыз (qarbız)
3. дарбыз (darbız)
4. карбыз (karbız)
5. karpuz
6. гарпыз garpyz
7. تاۋۇز (tavuz)
8. тарвуз tarvuz

**wave** *n.*
1. далға dalğa
2. толқын (tolqın)
3. толкун (tolkun)
4. дулкын (dulkın)
5. dalga
6. толкун tolkun
7. دولقۇن (dolqun)
8. тўлқин to'lqin

**way** (*direction) *n.*
1. чәһәт cəhət
2. жақ (zhaq)
3. жак (jak)
4. як (yak)
5. yön
6. угур ugur
7. تەرەپ (tärәp)
8. томон tomon

**way** (=road/path) *n.*
1. joл yol
2. жол (zhol)
3. жол (jol)
4. юл (yul)
5. yol
6. ёл ÿol
7. يول (yol)
8. йўл yo'l

---

1. Azerbaijani  2. Kazakh  3. Kyrgyz  4. Tatar  5. Turkish  6. Turkmen  7. Uighur  8. Uzbek

**we** *pron.*
1. биз biz
2. біз (biz)
3. биз (biz)
4. без (bez)
5. biz
6. биз biz
7. بـِز (biz)
8. биз biz

**weak** *adj.*
1. зәиф zəif
2. әлсіз (älsiz)
3. күчсүз (küchsüz)
4. көчсез (köchsez)
5. zayıf
6. кувватсыз kuwwatsyz
7. ئاجىز (ajiz)
8. кучсиз kuchsiz

**wealth** *n.*
1. вар-дөвләт var-dövlət
2. байлық (baylıq)
3. байлык (baylık)
4. байлык (baylık)
5. zenginlik
6. байлык baÿlyk
7. بايلىق (bayliq)
8. бойлик boylik

**weapon** *mil. n.*
1. силаһ silah
2. қару (qaruw)
3. курал (kural)
4. корал (koral)
5. silah
6. ярағ ÿarag
7. قورال (qoral)
8. қурол qurol

**wear** (=put on) *vt.*
1. кеј- gey-
2. ки- (kiy-)
3. кий- (kiy-)
4. кий- (kiy-)
5. giy-
6. гей- geÿ-
7. كـِيـ (kiy-)
8. кий- kiy-

**weather** *n.*
1. һава hava
2. ауа райы (awa rayı)
3. аба-ырайы (aba-ırayı)
4. һава (hava)
5. hava
6. хова howa
7. ھاۋا (hava)
8. об-хаво ob-havo

**weather report** *n.*
1. һава мә'луматы
   hava mə'lumatı
2. ауа райы мәліметі
   (awa rayı mälimeti)
3. аба-ырай маалыматы
   (aba-ıray maalımatı)
4. һава торышы турында
   прогноз (hava torıshı
   turında prognoz)
5. hava raporu
6. хова маглуматы
   howa maglumaty
7. ھاۋادىن مەلۇمات
   (havadin mälumat)
8. об-хаво маълумоти
   ob-havo ma'lumoti

**Wednesday** *n.*
1. чәршәнбә çərşənbə
2. сәрсенбі (särsenbi)
3. шаршемби (sharshembi)
4. чәршәмбе (chärshämbe)
5. çarşamba
6. чаршенбе çarşenbe

7. چارشەنبە (charshänbä)
8. чоршанба chorshanba

**week** *n.*
1. һәфтә həftə
2. апта (apta)
3. жума (juma)
4. атна (atna)
5. hafta
6. хепде hepde
7. ھەپتە (häptä)
8. хафта hafta

**weep** *v.*
1. ағла- ağla-
2. жыла- (zhıla-)
3. ыйла- (ıyla-)
4. ела- (yela-)
5. ağla-
6. агла- agla-
7. يـِغلا (yighla-)
8. йигла- yig'la-

**welcome** *interj.*
1. хош кәлмишсин(из)
   xoş gəlmişsin[iz]
2. қош келдіңіз
   (qosh keldingiz)
3. кош келипсиз
   (kosh kelipsiz)
4. хуш килдегез
   (khush kildegez)
5. hoş geldin[iz]
6. хош гелдиң[из]
   hoş geldiñ[iz]
7. خۇش كەپسىز (khush käpsiz)
8. хуш келибсиз
   xush kelibsiz

**well** *adv.*
1. jaxшы yaxşı
2. жақсы (zhaqsı)
3. жакшы (jakshı)
4. яхшы (yakhshı)
5. iyi
6. говы gowy
7. ياخشى (yakhshi)
8. яхши yaxshi

**west** *n.*
1. гәрб qərb
2. батыс (batıs)
3. батыш (batısh)
4. көнбатыш (könbatısh)
5. batı
6. гүнбатар günbatar
7. غرب (ghärb)
8. ғарб g'arb

**wet** *adj.*
1. jaш yaş
2. сулы (suwlı)
3. суулу (suulu)
4. юеш (yuyesh)
5. ıslak
6. өл öl
7. هۆل (höl)
8. нам nam

**what** *pron.*
1. нә nə
2. не (ne)
3. эмне (emne)
4. нәрсә (närsä)
5. ne
6. нәме näme
7. نېمه (nemä)
8. нима nima

**wheat** *bot. n.*
1. буғда buğda
2. бидай (biyday)
3. буудай (buuday)
4. бодай (boday)
5. buğday
6. бугдай bugdaÿ
7. بۇغداي (bughday)
8. буғдой bug'doy

**wheel** *n.*
1. тәкәр təkər
2. дөнгелек (dönggelek)
3. дөнгөлөк (dönggölök)
4. тәгәрмәч (tägärmäch)
5. tekerlek
6. тигир tigir
7. چاق (chaq)
8. ғилдирак g'ildirak

**when** *adv.*
1. нә вахт nə vaxt
2. қашан (qashan)
3. качан (kachan)
4. кайчан (kaychan)
5. ne zaman
6. хачан haçan
7. قاچان (qachan)
8. қачон qachon

**where** *adv.*
1. һарада, һараја
   harada, haraya
2. қай жерде, қай жерге
   (qay zherde, qay zherge)
3. кайда, кай жерге
   (kayda, kay jerge)
4. кайда, кая (kayda, kaya)
5. nerede, nereye
6. ниреде, нире nirede, nire
7. تەيەردە، تەيەرگ
   (qäyärdä, qäyärgä)
8. қаерда, қаерга
   qayerda, qayerga

**which** *pron.*
1. һансы hansı
2. қайсы (qaysı)
3. кайсы (kaysı)
4. кайсы (kaysı)
5. hangi
6. хайсы haÿsy
7. قايسى (qaysi)
8. қайси qaysi

**white** *adj.*
1. ағ ağ
2. ақ (aq)
3. ак (ak)
4. ак (ak)
5. beyaz
6. ак ak
7. ئاق (aq)
8. оқ oq

**who** *pron.*
1. ким kim
2. кім (kim)
3. ким (kim)
4. кем (kem)
5. kim
6. ким kim
7. كىم (kim)
8. ким kim

**whole** *adj.*
1. бүтүн, бүтөв
   bütün, bütöv
2. бүтін (bütin)
3. бүтүн (bütün)
4. бөтен (böten)
5. bütün
6. тутуш tutuş
7. بۇتۇن (pütün)
8. бутун butun

---

## wholesale *econ. n.*

1. топдан сатыш
topdan satış
2. көтерме сауда
(köterme sawda)
3. оптому менен сатуу
(optomu menen satuu)
4. күмәртәләп (сату)
(kümärtäläp [satu])
5. toptan satış
6. ломай совда lomaý sowda
7. ئۇلگۈجە سېتىش
(ülgüjä setish)
8. кӱтара (савдо)
ko'tara (savdo)

## why *adv.*

1. нә үчүн nə üçün
2. неге (nege)
3. эмне үчүн (emne üchün)
4. нигә (nigä)
5. niçin
6. нәме үчин näme üçin
7. نېمە ئۈچۈن (nemä üchün)
8. нима учун nima uchun

## wide *adj.*

1. кениш geniş
2. кең (keng)
3. кең (keng)
4. киң (king)
5. geniş
6. гиң giñ
7. كەڭ (käng)
8. кенг keng

## wife *n.*

1. арвад arvad
2. әйел (äyel)
3. аял (ayal)
4. хатын (khatın)
5. karı
6. аял aýal

7. ئايال (ayal)
8. хотин xotin

## wild *adj.*

1. вәһши vəhşi
2. жабайы (zhabayı)
3. жапайы (japayı)
4. кыргый (kırgıy)
5. vahşi
6. ябаны ýabany
7. ياۋايى (yavayi)
8. ёввойи yovvoyi

## willow *bot. n.*

1. сөјүд söyüd
2. тал (tal)
3. тал (tal)
4. тал (tal)
5. söğüt
6. сөвүт, тал söwüt, tal
7. سۆگەت (sögät)
8. тол tol

## win (=be victorious) *v.*

1. галиб кәл- qalib gəl-
2. жең- (zheng-)
3. жең- (jeng-)
4. җиң- (jing-)
5. kazan-
6. ең- ýeñ-
7. يەڭـ (yäng-)
8. ғалаба қил- g'alaba qil-

## wind *n.*

1. күләк külək
2. жел (zhel)
3. жел (jel)
4. җил (jil)
5. rüzgâr
6. ел ýel
7. شامال (shamal)
8. шамол shamol

## window *n.*

1. пәнчәрә pəncərə
2. терезе (tereze)
3. терезе (tereze)
4. тәрәзә (täräzä)
5. pencere
6. әпишге äpişge
7. دەرىزە (derizä)
8. дераза deraza

## wine *cul. n.*

1. шәраб şərab
2. шарап (sharap)
3. шарап (sharap)
4. шәраб (shärab)
5. şarap
6. чакыр çakyr
7. ئۈزۈم ھارىقى (üzüm hariqi)
8. вино vino

## wing *zool. n.*

1. ганад qanad
2. қанат (qanat)
3. канат (kanat)
4. канат (kanat)
5. kanat
6. ганат ganat
7. قانات (qanat)
8. қанот qanot

## winter *n.*

1. гъш qış
2. қыс (qıs)
3. кыш (kısh)
4. кыш (kısh)
5. kış
6. гъш gyş
7. قىش (qish)
8. қиш qish

## wire (~cable) *n.*
1. тел, сим  tel, sim
2. сым (sım)
3. зым (zım)
4. тимер чыбык (timer chıbık)
5. tel
6. сим  sim
7. سم (sim)
8. сим  sim

## wish *v.*
1. арзула-  arzula-
2. тіле-  (tile-)
3. тиле-  (tile-)
4. телә-  (telä-)
5. dile-
6. арзув әт-  arzuw et-
7. تلـ (tilä-)
8. тила-  tila-

## wish *n.*
1. арзу  arzu
2. тілек  (tilek)
3. тилек  (tilek)
4. телэк  (teläk)
5. dilek
6. дилег  dileg
7. ئارزۇ (arzu)
8. орзу  orzu

## with *prep.*
1. илә  ilə
2. бірге  (birge)
3. менен  (menen)
4. белән  (belän)
5. ile
6. билен  bilen
7. بلـن (bilän)
8. билан  bilan

## witness *n.*
1. шаһид  şahid
2. кує (kuwä)
3. күбө (kübö)
4. шаһит (shahit)
5. şahit
6. шаят  şaÿat
7. گۇۋاھچى (guvahchi)
8. гувоҳ  guvoh

## wolf *zool. n.*
1. гурд  qurd
2. қасқыр (qasqır)
3. карышкыр (karıshkır)
4. бүре (büre)
5. kurt
6. мөҗек  möjek
7. بۆرە (börä)
8. бўри  bo'ri

## woman *n.*
1. гадын  qadın
2. әйел (äyel)
3. аял (ayal)
4. хатын (khatın)
5. kadın
6. аял  aÿal
7. خوتون (khotun)
8. аёл  ayol

## wood (=a forest) *n.*
1. мешә  meşə
2. тоғай (toghay)
3. токойчо (tokoycho)
4. урман (urman)
5. koru
6. токай  tokaÿ
7. دەرە خلك (däräkhlik)
8. ўрмон  o'rmon

## wood (=lumber) *n.*
1. тахта  taxta
2. ағаш (aghash)
3. тактай (taktay)
4. агач (agach)
5. tahta
6. агач  agaç
7. ياغاچ (yaghach)
8. ёғоч  yog'och

## wool *n.*
1. јүн  yun
2. жүн (zhün)
3. жүн (jün)
4. йон (yon)
5. yün
6. йүң  yüñ
7. يۇڭ (yung)
8. жун  jun

## word *ling. n.*
1. сөз  söz
2. сөз (söz)
3. сөз (söz)
4. сүз (süz)
5. kelime
6. сөз  söz
7. سۆز (söz)
8. сўз  so'z

## work *v.*
1. ишлә-  işlə-
2. жұмыс істе- (zhumıs iste-)
3. иште- (ishte-)
4. эшлә- (eshlä-)
5. çalış-
6. ишле-  işle-
7. ئىشلـ (ishlä-)
8. ишла-  ishla-

## worker *n.*
1. фәһлә, ишчи fəhlə, işçi
2. жұмысшы (zhumısshı)
3. жумушчу (jumushchu)
4. эшче (eshche)
5. işçi
6. ишгәр işgär
7. ئىشچى (ishchi)
8. ишчи ishchi

## world *n.*
1. дүнja dünya
2. дүние (düniye)
3. дүйнө (düynö)
4. дөнья (dön'ya)
5. dünya
6. дүнйә dünyä
7. دونيا (dunya)
8. дунё dunyo

## worm *zool. n.*
1. гурд qurd
2. құрт (qurt)
3. курт (kurt)
4. корт (kort)
5. kurt
6. гурчук gurçuk
7. قۇرت (qurt)
8. құрт qurt

## worry *v.*
1. нараһат ол- narahat ol-
2. абыржы- (abırzhı-)
3. кайгылан- (kaygılan-)
4. борчыл- (borchıl-)
5. kaygılan-
6. ынжалыксызлан-
   ynjalyksyzlan-
7. غەم قىل_ (ghäm qil-)
8. ташвишлан- tashvishlan-

## worship *rel. n.*
1. ибадәт ibadət
2. табыну (tabınuw)
3. табынуу (tabınuu)
4. гыйбадәт (gıybadät)
5. ibadet
6. ыбадат ybadat
7. ئىبادەت (ibadät)
8. ибодат ibodat

## wound *n.*
1. japa yara
2. жара (zhara)
3. жара (jara)
4. яра (yara)
5. yara
6. яра ÿara
7. جاراھەت (jarahät)
8. яра yara

## wrap *v.*
1. сары- sarı-
2. ора- (ora-)
3. оро- (oro-)
4. ура- (ura-)
5. sar-
6. дола- dola-
7. ئورا_ (ora-)
8. ÿра- o'ra-

## wrench *tech. n.*
1. гаjка qayka
2. кілт (kilt)
3. ачкыч (achkıch)
4. гайка ачкычы
   (gayka achkıchı)
5. ingiliz anahtarı
6. гайка ачары gaÿka açary
7. كۇلۇچ (kuluch)
8. гайка калити gayka kaliti

## wrestling *spor. n.*
1. күләш güləş
2. күрес (küres)
3. күрөш (kürösh)
4. көрәш (köräsh)
5. güreş
6. гөреш göreş
7. چەلىش (chelish)
8. кураш kurash

## wrist *phys. n.*
1. биләк bilək
2. білек (bilek)
3. билек (bilek)
4. беләзек сөяге
   (beläzek söyage)
5. bilek
6. гошар goşar
7. بېغىش (beghish)
8. билак bilak

## write *v.*
1. jаз- yaz-
2. жаз- (zhaz-)
3. жаз- (jaz-)
4. яз- (yaz-)
5. yaz-
6. яз- ÿaz-
7. ياز_ (yaz-)
8. ёз- yoz-

## writer *lit. n.*
1. jазычы yazıçı
2. жазушы (zhazuwshı)
3. жазуучу (jazuuchu)
4. язучы (yazuchı)
5. yazar
6. языҗы ÿazyjy
7. يازغۇچى (yazghuchi)
8. ёзувчи yozuvchi

**writing** *n.*
1. jaзы yazı
2. жазу (zhazuw)
3. жазуу (jazuu)
4. язу (yazu)
5. yazı
6. язув ÿazuw
7. يبزق (yeziq)
8. ёзув yozuv

**wrong** *adj.*
1. jaнлыш yanlış
2. қате (qate)
3. ката (kata)
4. ялгыш (yalgısh)
5. yanlış
6. ялңыш ÿalñyş
7. خاتا (khata)
8. нотўғри noto'g'ri

**yawn** *v.*
1. эснә- əsnə-
2. есіне- (yesine-)
3. эсте- (este-)
4. иснә- (isnä-)
5. esne-
6. палла- palla-
7. ئەسنە (äsnä-)
8. эсна- esna-

**year** *n.*
1. ил il
2. жыл (zhıl)
3. жыл (jıl)
4. ел (yel)
5. yıl
6. йыл ÿyl
7. يل (yil)
8. йил yil

**yellow** *adj.*
1. сары sarı
2. сары (sarı)
3. сары (sarı)
4. сары (sarı)
5. sarı
6. сары sary
7. سيرق (seriq)
8. сариқ sariq

**yes** *adv.*
1. бәли, һә bəli, hə
2. иә (iyä)
3. ооба (ooba)
4. әйе (äye)
5. evet
6. хава hawa
7. ھەئە (hä'ä)
8. ха ha

**yesterday** *n.*
1. дүнән dünən
2. кеше (keshe)
3. кечээ (kechee)
4. кичә (kichä)
5. dün
6. дүйн düÿn
7. تونۇگۇن (tünügün)
8. кеча kecha

**yet** *adv.*
1. һәлә hələ
2. әли (äli)
3. али (ali)
4. әле (äle)
5. henüz
6. әнтек entek
7. تېخى (tekhi)
8. хали hali

**yogurt** *cul. n.*
1. гатыг qatıq
2. айран (ayran)
3. айран (ayran)
4. йогырт (yogırt)
5. yoğurt
6. гатык gatyk
7. قتـتـق (qetiq)
8. қатиқ qatiq

**you** (*plural) *pron.*
1. сиз siz
2. сіздер (sizder)
3. силер, сиздер (siler, sizder)
4. сез (sez)
5. siz
6. сиз siz
7. سـلەر (silär)
8. сиз siz

**you** (*singular) *pron.*
1. сән, сиз sən, siz
2. сен, сіз (sen, siz)
3. сен, сиз (sen, siz)
4. син, сез (sin, sez)
5. sen, siz
6. сен, сиз sen, siz
7. سـز، سـەن (sän, siz)
8. сен, сиз sen, siz

**young** *adj.*
1. чаван cavan
2. жас (zhas)
3. жаш (jash)
4. яшь (yash')
5. genç
6. яш ÿaş
7. ياش (yash)
8. ёш yosh

---

## your *adj.*
1. сәнин, сизин sənin, sizin
2. сенің, сіздің
   (sening, sizding)
3. сенин, силердин
   (senin, silerdin)
4. синең, сезнең
   (sineng, sezneng)
5. senin, sizin
6. сениң, сизиң seniñ, siziñ
7. سبنك، سزنك
   (sening, sizning)
8. сенинг, сизнинг
   sening, sizning

## yours *pron.*
1. сәнинки, сизинки
   səninki, sizinki
2. сеникі, сіздікі
   (seniki, sizdiki)
3. сеники, сиздики
   (seniki, sizdiki)
4. синеке, сезнеке
   (sineke, sezneke)
5. seninki, sizinki
6. сениңки, сизиңки
   seniñki, siziñki
7. سبنگکی، سزنگکی
   (seningki, sizningki)
8. сеники, сизники
   seniki, sizniki

## yourself *pron.*
1. өзүн özün
2. өзің (özing)
3. өзүң (özüng)
4. үзең (üzeng)
5. kendin
6. өзүң özüñ
7. ئوزلسرى، ئوززۇڭ
   (özüng, özliri)
8. ўзинг o'zing

## yourselves *pron.*
1. өзүнүз özünüz
2. өзіңіз (özingiz)
3. өзүңүз (özüngüz)
4. үзегез (üzegez)
5. kendiniz
6. өзүңиз özüñiz
7. ئوزنگز (özingiz)
8. ўзингиз o'zingiz

## youth *n.*
1. кәнчлик gənclik
2. жастық (zhastıq)
3. жаштык (jashtık)
4. яшьлек (yash'lek)
5. gençlik
6. яшлык ýaşlyk
7. ياشلىق (yashliq)
8. ёшлик yoshlik

## zero *num.*
1. сыфыр sıfır
2. нәл (nöl)
3. нәл (nöl)
4. ноль (nol')
5. sıfır
6. ноль nol
7. نۆل (nöl)
8. ноль nol'

## zoo *n.*
1. зоопарк zoopark
2. зоопарк (zoopark)
3. зоопарк (zoopark)
4. зоопарк (zoopark)
5. hayvanat bahçesi
6. зоопарк zoopark
7. هايۋانات باغچىسى
   (hayvanat baghchisi)
8. хайвонот боғи
   hayvonot bog'i

# AZERBAIJANI - ENGLISH INDEX

| | | |
|---|---|---|
| -a, -ə | -a, -ə | to |
| abidə | абидə | monument |
| abzas | абзас | paragraph |
| ac | ач | hungry |
| acı | ачы | bitter |
| acıqlı | ачыглы | angry |
| aclıq | ачлыг | famine, hunger |
| aç- | ач- | open |
| açar | ачар | key |
| açıq | ачыг | open |
| açıq-aşkar | ачыг-ашкар | obvious |
| ad | ад | name |
| ad günü | ад күнү | birthday |
| ada | ада | island |
| addım | аддым | step |
| adət | адəт | custom, habit |
| adət et- | адəт ет- | used: be used to |
| adyal | адјал | blanket |
| ağ | аг | white |
| ağac | агач | tree |
| ağcaqanad | агчаганад | mosquito |
| ağciyər | агчијəр | lung |
| ağıl | агыл | mind |
| ağıllı | агыллы | clever, intelligent |
| ağılsız | агылсыз | stupid |
| ağır | агыр | heavy |
| ağız | агыз | mouth |
| ağla- | агла- | cry, weep |
| ağrı | агры | pain |
| ahəng | аhəнк | harmony |
| ax- | ах- | flow |
| axırıncı | ахырынчы | last |
| axşam | ахшам | evening |
| axtar- | ахтар- | look for, search, seek |
| ailə | аилə | family |
| alçaq | алчаг | low |
| alət | алəт | tool |
| alıcı | алычы | buyer |
| alın | алын | forehead |
| alim | алим | scientist |
| alma | алма | apple |
| alov | алов | flame |
| altda | алтда | underneath |
| altı | алты | six |
| altında | алтында | under, underneath |
| altmış | алтмыш | sixty |
| amma | амма | but |
| an | ан | moment |
| ana | ана | mother |
| anarxiya | анархија | anarchy |
| and iç- | анд ич- | swear |
| ani | ани | sudden |
| antenna | антенна | antenna |
| aprel | апрел | April |
| aptek | аптек | pharmacy |
| araba | араба | cart |
| arasında | арасында | between |
| arxa | арха | back |
| arxada | архада | behind |
| arı | ары | bee |
| armud | армуд | pear |
| arpa | арпа | barley |
| art- | арт- | increase |
| artilleriya | артиллерија | artillery |
| arvad | арвад | wife |
| arzu | арзу | desire, wish |
| arzula- | арзула- | wish |
| as- | ас- | hang |
| asan | асан | easy |
| asqı | асгы | hanger |
| aşağı | ашагы | down |
| aşağıda | ашагыда | below |
| aşpaz | ашпаз | cook |
| at | ат | horse |
| ata | ата | father |
| atalar sözü | аталар сөзү | proverb |
| atıl- | атыл- | jump |
| avadanlıq | аваданлыг | equipment |
| avqust | август | August |
| avtobus | автобус | bus |
| avtomobil | автомобил | automobile |
| ay | ај | month, moon |
| ayaq | ајаг | foot |
| ayaq xizəyi idmanı | ајаг хизəји идманы | skiing |
| ayaqqabı | ајаггабы | shoe |
| ayı | ајы | bear |
| ayır- | ајыр- | separate |
| aypara | ајпара | crescent |
| ayrı | ајры | separate |
| ayrıl- | ајрыл- | separated: be separated |
| az | аз | few |

| azad | азад | free |
| azadlıq | азадлыг | freedom |
| azal- | азал- | decrease |
| azlıq | азлыг | minority |
| | | |
| baba | баба | grandfather |
| baca | бача | chimney |
| bacar- | бачар- | succeed |
| bacarıq | бачарыг | skill |
| bacı | бачы | sister |
| badam | бадам | almond |
| badımcan | бадымчан | eggplant |
| bağ | баг | garden |
| bağban | багбан | gardener |
| bağırsaq | багырсаг | intestine |
| bağışla- | багышла- | forgive |
| bağla- | багла- | close, fasten, shut, tie |
| bağlı | баглы | closed |
| baha | баха | expensive |
| bax- | бах- | look |
| bal | бал | honey |
| bal ayı | бал айы | honeymoon |
| balaca | балача | little, small |
| balet | балет | ballet |
| balıq | балыг | fish |
| balıqçı | балыгчы | fisherman |
| balış | балыш | pillow |
| balışüzü | балышузу | pillowcase |
| balkon | балкон | balcony |
| balta | балта | axe |
| banan | банан | banana |
| bank | банк | bank |
| banka | банка | jar |
| bardaq | бардаг | jug |
| barmaq | бармаг | finger |
| barometr | барометр | barometer |
| basdır- | басдыр- | bury |
| basketbol | баскетбол | basketball |
| baş | баш | head |
| baş ağrısı | баш агрысы | headache |
| baş nazir | баш назир | prime minister |
| baş vur- | баш вур- | dive |
| başa düş- | баша душ- | understand |
| başqa | башга | another, besides, other |
| başla- | башла- | begin, start |
| bat- | бат- | sink |
| bataqlıq | батаглыг | swamp |
| bayırda | бајырда | outside |
| bayquş | бајгуш | owl |
| bayram | бајрам | holiday |
| bayram et- | бајрам ет- | celebrate |
| bayram etmə | бајрам етмə | celebration |
| bayraq | бајраг | flag |
| bazar | базар | market, Sunday |
| bazar ertəsi | базар ертəси | Monday |
| bazarlıq et- | базарлыг ет- | shop |
| belə | белə | such |
| benzin | бензин | gasoline |
| beş | беш | five |
| beyin | бејин | brain |
| beynəlxalq | бејнəлхалг | international |
| bədbəxt | бəдбəхт | unhappy |
| bədən | бəдəн | body |
| bəhanə | бəханə | excuse |
| bələdiyyə | бəлəдијјə | municipality |
| bəli | бəли | yes |
| bəlkə | бəлкə | perhaps |
| bənd | бəнд | dam |
| bənövşəyi | бəнөвшəји | purple |
| bərabər | бəрабəр | equal |
| bərbər | бəрбəр | hairdresser |
| bəri | бəри | since |
| bərk | бəрк | hard, loud |
| bəstəkar | бəстəкар | composer |
| bəy | бəј | bridegroom |
| be'zən | бə'зəн | sometimes |
| be'zi | бə'зи | some |
| bıçaq | бычаг | knife |
| bığ | быг | mustache |
| bibi | биби | aunt |
| biçin | бичин | harvest |
| bil- | бил- | know |
| bilet | билет | ticket |
| bilik | билик | knowledge |
| bilək | билəк | wrist |
| bina | бина | building |
| bint | бинт | bandage |
| bir | бир | one |
| bir az | бир аз | little, some |
| birə | бирə | flea |
| bir neçə | бир нечə | several |
| birlikdə | бирликдə | together |
| biş- | биш- | cook |

| bişir- | биишр- | cook |
|---|---|---|
| bit | бит | louse |
| bitki | битки | herb, plant |
| biz | биз | we |
| bizi | бизи | us |
| bizim | бизим | our |
| bizimki | бизимки | ours |
| biznesmen | бизнесмен | businessman |
| blank | бланк | form |
| bluz | блуз | blouse |
| bomba | бомба | bomb |
| borc | борч | debt, loan |
| borc al- | борч ал- | borrow |
| boğaz | боғаз | throat |
| boğul- | боғул- | drown |
| boş | бош | empty |
| boşalt- | бошалт- | empty, loose |
| boşan- | бошан- | divorce |
| boşanma | бошанма | divorce |
| boşqab | бошгаб | dish, plate |
| boya- | боја- | dye, paint |
| boyun | бојун | neck |
| boz | боз | grey |
| böcək | бөчәк | insect |
| böl- | бөл- | divide |
| bölmə | бөлмә | division, section |
| böyrək | бөјрәк | kidney |
| böyü- | бөјү- | grow |
| böyük | бөјүк | big, great |
| böyümə | бөјүмә | growth |
| bu | бу | this |
| bu gün | бу күн | today |
| bucaq | бучаг | angle |
| bud | буд | thigh |
| budaq | будаг | branch |
| buğa | буға | bull |
| buğda | буғда | wheat |
| bulud | булуд | cloud |
| bunlar | бунлар | these |
| bur- | бур- | twist |
| burada | бурада | here |
| burax- | бурах- | release |
| buraya | бураја | here |
| burğu | бурғу | drill |
| burun | бурун | nose |
| buterbrod | бутерброд | sandwich |
| buynuz | бујнуз | horn |
| buz | буз | ice |

| büdcə | будчә | budget |
|---|---|---|
| büro | буро | office |
| bütöv | бүтөв | whole |
| bütün | бүтүн | all, whole |
| canlı | чанлы | alive |
| cavab | чаваб | answer, reply |
| cavab ver- | чаваб вер- | answer, reply |
| cavan | чаван | young |
| cazibə | чазибә | attraction |
| cəbr | чәбр | algebra |
| cəfəri | чәфәри | parsley |
| cəhənnəm | чәһәннәм | hell |
| cəhət | чәһәт | way |
| cəld | чәлд | fast, speedy |
| cəmiyyət | чәмијјәт | society |
| cənab | чәнаб | gentleman |
| cənnət | чәннәт | paradise |
| cənub | чәнуб | south |
| cərrahlıq | чәррањлыг | surgery |
| cəsarət | чәсарәт | courage |
| cəsur | чәсур | brave, courageous |
| cəza | чәза | punishment |
| cəza ver- | чәза вер- | punish |
| cır- | чыр- | tear |
| cib | чиб | pocket |
| cib saati | чиб сааты | watch |
| ciddi | чидди | serious |
| cinayət | чинајәт | crime |
| cinayətkar | чинајәткар | criminal |
| coğrafiya | чоғрафија | geography |
| corab | чораб | sock, stocking |
| cümə | чүмә | Friday |
| cümə axşamı | чүмә ахшамы | Thursday |
| cümlə | чүмлә | sentence |
| cüt | чүт | pair |
| çağır- | чағыр- | call, summon |
| çal- | чал- | play |
| çalğı aləti | чалғы ләти | instrument |
| çalış- | чалыш- | try |
| çalışqan | чалышган | diligent |
| çamadan | чамадан | suitcase |
| çanaq | чанаг | sink |
| çanta | чанта | bag |
| çap et- | чап ет- | print |

| çarşab | чаршаб | sheet |
|---|---|---|
| çat- | чат- | arrive, reach |
| çay | чај | river, tea |
| çaydan | чајдан | teapot |
| çaypulu | чајпулу | tip |
| çek | чек | check |
| çeynə- | чејнә- | chew |
| çəhrayı | чәһрајы | pink |
| çəkic | чәкич | hammer |
| [uzunboğaz] çəkmə | (узунбоғаз) чәкмә | boot |
| çəkməçi | чәкмәчи | shoemaker |
| çəmən | чәмән | grass |
| çənə | чәнә | chin |
| çəngəl | чәнкәл | fork |
| çəpər | чәпәр | fence |
| çərçivə | чәрчивә | frame |
| çərşənbə | чәршәнбә | Wednesday |
| çərşənbə axşamı | чәршәнбә ахшамы | Tuesday |
| çətin | чәтин | difficult, hard |
| çətir | чәтир | umbrella |
| çəyirtkə | чәјирткә | grasshopper |
| çıx- | чых- | exit |
| çıxış | чыхыш | exit |
| çıxma | чыхма | subtraction |
| çığır- | чығыр- | scream, shout |
| çılğın | чылғын | crazy |
| çılpaq | чылпаг | bare |
| çimərlik | чимәрлик | beach |
| çirk[li] | чирк(ли) | dirty |
| çirkin | чиркин | ugly |
| çiy | чиј | raw |
| çiyələk | чијәләк | strawberry |
| çiyin | чијин | shoulder |
| çox | чох | many, much, very |
| çox böyük | чох бөјүк | huge |
| çöllük | чөллүк | desert |
| çörək | чөрәк | bread |
| çörəkçi | чөрәкчи | baker |
| çörəkxana | чөрәкхана | bakery |
| çünki | чүнки | because |
| çürü- | чүрү- | rot |
| -da, -də | -да, -дә | at, in |
| da, də | да, дә | also, too |
| dad- | дад- | taste |
| dağ | дағ | mountain |

| dağıt- | дағыт- | destroy, scatter |
|---|---|---|
| daha çox | даһа чох | more |
| daha yaxşı | даһа јахшы | better |
| dairə | даирә | circle |
| dalğa | далға | wave |
| dam | дам | roof |
| damcı | дамчы | drop |
| -dan, -dən | -дан, -дән | from |
| dan | дан | dawn |
| dana əti | дана әти | veal |
| danış- | даныш- | speak, talk |
| danışıq | данышыг | speech |
| dar | дар | narrow, tight |
| dara- | дара- | comb |
| daraq | дараг | comb |
| darıx- | дарых- | bored: be bored |
| darıxdırıcı | дарыхдырычы | boring |
| dart- | дарт- | pull |
| darvaza | дарваза | gate |
| dastan | дастан | epic |
| daş | даш | stone |
| daşı- | дашы- | carry |
| davam et- | давам ет- | continue |
| davran- | давран- | behave |
| davranış | давраныш | behavior |
| dayan- | дајан- | stop |
| dayanacaq | дајаначаг | stop |
| dayandır- | дајандыр- | stop |
| dayaz | дајаз | shallow |
| dayı | дајы | uncle |
| de- | де- | say, tell |
| dekabr | декабр | December |
| demokratiya | демократија | democracy |
| demək olar ki | демәк олар ки | almost |
| deyil | дејил | not |
| dəftər | дәфтәр | notebook |
| dələ | дәлә | squirrel |
| dəlik | дәлик | hole |
| dəlilik | дәлилик | insanity |
| dəllək | дәлләк | hairdresser |
| dəmir | дәмир | iron |
| dəmir pul | дәмир пул | coin |
| dəmir yolu | дәмир јолу | railroad |
| dən | дән | grain |
| dəniz | дәниз | sea |
| dəqiqə | дәгигә | minute |
| dərəcə | дәрәчә | degree |

| | | |
|---|---|---|
| dərhal | дәрһал | immediately |
| dəri | дәри | leather, skin |
| dərin | дәрин | deep |
| dərinlik | дәринлик | depth |
| dərman | дәрман | drug, medicine |
| dərs | дәрс | lesson |
| dərzi | дәрзи | tailor |
| dəsmal | дәсмал | handkerchief, towel |
| dəstək | дәстәк | handle |
| dəvə | дәвә | camel |
| də'vət | дә'вәт | invitation |
| də'vət et- | дә'вәт ет- | invite |
| dəy- | дәј- | touch |
| dəyirman | дәјирман | mill |
| dəyirmi | дәјирми | round |
| dəyişdir- | дәјишдир- | change |
| dırman- | дырман- | climb |
| dırnaq | дырнаг | nail |
| diqqət | диггәт | attention |
| diqqətli | диггәтли | careful |
| dil | дил | language, tongue |
| dilçi | дилчи | linguist |
| dilşünaslıq | дилшүнаслыг | linguistics |
| dimdik | димдик | beak |
| din | дин | religion |
| dini | дини | religious |
| dini bayram | дини бајрам | religious holiday |
| dinlə- | динлә- | listen |
| diplom | диплом | diploma |
| dirsək | дирсәк | elbow |
| diş | диш | tooth |
| diş ağrısı | диш ағрысы | toothache |
| diş fırçası | диш фырчасы | toothbrush |
| diş həkimi | диш һәкими | dentist |
| diş pastası | диш пастасы | toothpaste |
| dişlə- | дишлә- | bite |
| div | див | giant |
| divar | дивар | wall |
| divar saatı | дивар сааты | clock |
| diyirlə- | дијирлә- | roll |
| diz | диз | knee |
| dodaq | додаг | lip |
| doğru | доғру | towards |
| doğul- | доғул- | born: be born |
| doğum | доғум | birth |
| doxsan | дохсан | ninety |
| doqquz | доггуз | nine |
| dolab | долаб | cupboard |
| doldur- | долдур- | fill |
| dolu | долу | full, hail |
| don- | дон- | freeze |
| dondurma | дондурма | ice cream |
| donuz | донуз | pig |
| donuz əti | донуз әти | pork |
| dost | дост | friend |
| dostluq | достлуг | friendship |
| dovşan | довшан | rabbit |
| dön- | дөн- | turn |
| dörd | дөрд | four |
| döş | дөш | breast |
| döşək | дөшәк | mattress |
| döşəmə | дөшәмә | floor |
| dövlət | дөвләт | state |
| dövr | дөвр | era |
| döyüş- | дөјүш- | fight |
| dram əsəri | драм әсәри | drama |
| dramaturg | драматург | playwright |
| dua | дуа | prayer |
| dua et- | дуа ет- | pray |
| duxovka | духовка | oven |
| duman | думан | fog |
| dur- | дур- | stand |
| dustaqxana | дустагхана | prison |
| duş | душ | shower |
| duyğu | дујғу | feeling |
| duz | дуз | salt |
| düjün | дүжүн | dozen |
| dükan | дүкан | shop |
| dünən | дүнән | yesterday |
| dünya | дүнја | world |
| dürüst | дүрүст | honest |
| düş- | дүш- | fall, get off |
| düşmən | дүшмән | enemy |
| düşmənçilik | дүшмәнчилик | enmity |
| düşün- | дүшүн- | think |
| düşüncə | дүшүнчә | thought |
| düymə | дүјмә | button |
| düyü | дүјү | rice |
| düyün | дүјүн | knot |
| düz | дүз | correct, straight |
| düzəlt- | дүзәлт- | correct, make |
| düzənlik | дүзәнлик | plain |
| ehtimal | еһтимал | possibility |

| | | |
|---|---|---|
| ehtimal ki | еһтимал ки | probably |
| ehtiyac | еһтијач | necessity, need |
| ehtiyacı ol- | еһтијачы ол- | need |
| ehtiyat | еһтијат | precaution |
| ekran | екран | screen |
| elektrik | електрик | electricity |
| elə | елә | such |
| erkən | еркән | early |
| eşit- | ешит- | hear |
| eşşək | ешшәк | donkey |
| et- | ет- | make, do |
| e'tiqad | е'тигад | faith |
| e'timad | е'тимад | confidence |
| ev | ев | home, house |
| ev | ев | slipper |
|  ayaqqabısı |  ајаггабысы | |
| ev sahibi | ев саһиби | host |
| evlən- | евлән- | marry |
| evlənmə | евләнмә | marriage |
| eynəkçi | ејнәкчи | optician |
| eyni | ејни | same |
| | | |
| əbədiyyət | әбәдијјәт | eternity |
| əczaçı | әчзачы | pharmacist |
| ədalət | әдаләт | justice |
| ədəbi | әдәби | literary |
| ədəbi əsər | әдәби әсәр | literary work |
| ədəbiyyat | әдәбијјат | literature |
| əfsanə | әфсанә | legend |
| əgər | әкәр | if |
| əhali | әһали | population |
| əhatə et- | әһатә ет- | surround |
| ək- | әк- | plant, sow |
| əkiz | әкиз | twin |
| əksəriyyət | әксәријјәт | majority |
| əl | әл | hand |
| əl çal- | әл чал- | clap |
| əl çantası | әл чантасы | handbag |
| əl uzat- | әл узат- | reach |
| əlaqə | әлагә | communication |
| əlavə et- | әлавә ет- | add |
| əlbəttə | әлбәттә | course: of course |
| əlcək | әлчәк | glove |
| əliaçıq | әлиачыг | generous |
| əlifba | әлифба | alphabet |
| əlli | әлли | fifty |
| əlverişli | әлверишли | convenient |
| əm- | әм- | suck |

| | | |
|---|---|---|
| əmək haqqı | әмәк һаггы | wage |
| əməliyyat | әмәлијјат | operation |
| əmi | әми | uncle |
| əmr et- | әмр ет- | command, order |
| ən çox | ән чох | most |
| ən yaxşı | ән јахшы | best |
| əncir | әнчир | fig |
| ər | әр | husband |
| əri- | әри- | melt |
| ərik | әрик | apricot |
| əsas | әсас | main |
| əsəb | әсәб | nerve |
| əsgər | әскәр | soldier |
| əsnə- | әснә- | yawn |
| əsr | әср | century |
| ət | әт | meat |
| ət dükanı | әт дүканы | butcher shop |
| ətir | әтир | perfume |
| əvvəl | әввәл | before |
| əvəzlik | әвәзлик | pronoun |
| əy- | әј- | bend |
| əyə | әјә | file |
| əyləncə | әјләнчә | entertainment |
| əz- | әз- | crush |
| əzələ | әзәлә | muscle |
| | | |
| fabrik | фабрик | factory |
| faiz | фаиз | interest |
| familiya | фамилија | surname |
| fayda | фајда | benefit |
| faydalı | фајдалы | useful |
| fe'l | фе'л | verb |
| festival | фестивал | festival |
| fevral | феврал | February |
| fəhlə | фәһлә | worker |
| fərq | фәрг | difference |
| fərqli | фәргли | different |
| fəsil | фәсил | season |
| fındıq | фындыг | hazelnut |
| fırça | фырча | brush |
| fırtına | фыртына | storm |
| fikir | фикир | idea, opinion |
| fil | фил | elephant |
| film | филм | movie |
| fincan | финчан | cup |
| firma | фирма | firm |
| fizika | физика | physics |
| folklor | фолклор | folklore |

| | | |
|---|---|---|
| fontan | фонтан | fountain |
| fotoaparat | фотоапарат | camera |
| fotoşəkil | фотошəкил | photo |
| futbol | футбол | soccer |
| gavalı | кавалы | plum |
| gec | кеч | late |
| gecə | кечə | night |
| gecə yarısı | кечə јарысы | midnight |
| gen | кен | loose |
| geniş | кениш | broad, spacious, wide |
| geologiya | кеолокија | geology |
| get- | кет- | go |
| gey- | кеј- | put on, wear |
| gəl- | кəл- | come |
| gələcək | кəлəчəк | future |
| gəlin | кəлин | bride |
| gəlir | кəлир | income |
| gəliş | кəлиш | arrival |
| gəmi | кəми | ship |
| gənclik | кəнчлик | youth |
| gərəkli | кəрəкли | necessary |
| gətir- | кəтир- | bring |
| gəzin- | кəзин- | stroll |
| gil | кил | clay |
| gilas | килас | cherry |
| gir- | кир- | enter |
| giriş | кириш | entrance |
| gizlət- | кизлəт- | hide |
| gizli | кизли | secret |
| göbələk | көбəлəк | mushroom |
| göl | көл | lake |
| gömrük | көмрүк | customs |
| göndər- | көндəр- | send |
| gör- | көр- | see |
| görün- | көрүн- | appear |
| göstər- | көстəр- | show |
| götür- | көтүр- | take |
| göy | көј | blue, sky |
| göy qurşağı | көј гуршағы | rainbow |
| göy gurultusu | көј курултусу | thunder |
| göyçək | көјчəк | pretty |
| göyərçin | көјəрчин | pigeon |
| göz | көз | eye |
| gözəl | көзəл | beautiful, fine |
| gözəllik | көзəллик | beauty |
| gözlə- | көзлə- | wait |
| gözlük | көзлүк | glasses |
| gübrə | күбрə | fertilizer |
| güc | күч | force, power, strength |
| güclü | күчлү | powerful, strong |
| gül | күл | flower |
| gül- | күл- | laugh |
| güləş | күлəш | wrestling |
| gülümsə- | күлүмсə- | smile |
| gümüş | күмүш | silver |
| gün | күн | day |
| günahkar | күнаһкар | guilty |
| günahsız | күнаһсыз | innocent |
| günahsızlıq | күнаһсызлығ | innocence |
| gündüz | күндүз | daytime |
| günəbaxan | күнəбахан | sunflower |
| günəş | күнəш | sun |
| günəşin batması | күнəшин батмасы | sunset |
| günəşin doğması | күнəшин доғмасы | sunrise |
| günorta | күнорта | noon |
| günortadan sonra | күнортадан сонра | afternoon |
| güvən- | күвəн- | rely |
| güzgü | күзкү | mirror |
| güzəşt | күзəшт | discount |
| hadisə | һадисə | event |
| hafizə | һафизə | memory |
| hakim | һаким | judge |
| haqqında | һаггында | about |
| hal | һал | condition |
| hamı | һамы | all |
| hamilə | һамилə | pregnant |
| hamiləlik | һамилəлик | pregnancy |
| hansı | һансы | which |
| harada | һарада | where |
| haraya | һараја | where |
| hava | һава | air, weather |
| hava mə'lumatı | һава мə'луматы | weather report |
| hava poçtu | һава почту | airmail |
| hava yolu | һава јолу | airline |
| hazır | һазыр | ready |
| hazırla- | һазырла- | prepare |
| heç kəs | һеч кəс | nobody |
| heç nə | һеч-нə | nothing |
| heç vaxt | һеч вахт | never |

| | | |
|---|---|---|
| heç yerdə | һеч јердə | nowhere |
| hekayə | һекајə | story |
| hesab | һесаб | account, bill |
| hesabla- | һесабла- | calculate |
| heykəl | һејкəл | statue |
| heykəltəraşlıq | һејкəлтəрашлыг | sculpture |
| heyran ol- | һејран ол- | admire |
| heyva | һејва | quince |
| heyvan | һејван | animal |
| hə | һə | yes |
| həb | һəб | pill |
| həbsxana | һəбсхана | jail |
| həddi - bülüğa çatmış | һəдди - бүлуға чатмыш | adult |
| həftə | һəфтə | week |
| həkim | һəким | doctor |
| həqiqət | һəгигəт | truth |
| həqiqi | һəгиги | real, true |
| hələ | һəлə | still, yet |
| həll et- | һəлл ет- | solve |
| həm ... həm də | һəм ... һəм дə | both ... and |
| həmişə | һəмишə | always |
| həndəsə | һəндəсə | geometry |
| hər | һəр | every |
| hər hansı | һəр һансы | any |
| hər hansı bir şey | һəр һансы бир шеj | anything |
| hər kəs | һəр кəс | anybody, everybody |
| hər şey | һəр шеj | everything |
| hər yerdə | һəр јердə | everywhere |
| hərarət | һəрарəт | heat |
| hərf | һəрф | letter |
| həsəd | һəсəд | envy |
| hətta | һəтта | even |
| həyat | һəјат | life |
| həyəcan | һəjəчан | excitement |
| həyət | һəjəт | courtyard |
| hind toyuğu | һинд тојуғу | turkey |
| hiss et- | һисс ет- | feel |
| hissə | һиссə | part |
| hovuz | һовуз | pool |
| hökm | һөкм | verdict |
| hökumət | һөкумəт | government |
| hörmət | һөрмəт | respect |
| hörmət et- | һөрмəт ет- | respect |
| hörümçək | һөрумчəк | spider |
| huşunu itir- | һушуну итир- | faint |
| hücum | һүчум | attack |
| hücum et- | һүчум ет- | attack |
| hündür boylu | һүндүр бојлу | tall |
| xahiş et- | хаһиш ет- | request |
| xala | хала | aunt |
| xalça | халча | rug |
| xalı | халы | carpet |
| xalq | халг | people |
| xanım | ханым | lady |
| xardal | хардал | mustard |
| xarici | харичи | foreigner |
| xeyr | хејр | no |
| xəbər | хəбəр | news |
| xəbər ver- | хəбəр вер- | inform |
| xəncər | хəнчəр | dagger |
| xərc | хəрч | expense |
| xərclə- | хəрчлə- | spend |
| xərçəng | хəрчəнк | cancer |
| xəritə | хəритə | map |
| xəstə | хəстə | ill, patient, sick |
| xəstəxana | хəстəхана | hospital |
| xəstəlik | хəстəлик | illness |
| xəta | хəта | fault |
| xətkeş | хəткəш | ruler |
| xətt | хəтт | line |
| xəz | хəз | fur |
| xəzinə | хəзинə | treasure |
| xırda pul | хырда пул | change |
| xidmətçi | хидмəтчи | servant |
| xilas et- | хилас ет- | rescue |
| xiyaban | хијабан | avenue |
| xiyar | хијар | cucumber |
| xizək | хизəк | sled |
| xoruz | хоруз | rooster |
| xoş | хош | nice |
| xoş gəlmişsin[iz] | хош кəлмишсин(из) | welcome |
| xoşbəxt | хошбəхт | happy |
| xoşla- | хошла- | like |
| xristian | христиан | Christian |
| xudahafiz | худаһафиз | bye-bye |
| xurma | хурма | date |
| xüsusilə | хүсусилə | especially |
| ibadət | ибадəт | worship |
| icarə | ичарə | rent |

| | | |
|---|---|---|
| icazə ver- | ичазə вер- | permit |
| iç- | ич- | drink |
| içəridə | ичəридə | inside |
| içki | ички | beverage, drink |
| idman | идман | sport |
| ifadə | ифадə | idiom |
| iflic | ифлич | paralysis |
| iftixar | ифтихар | pride |
| iki | ики | two |
| ikinci səhər yeməyi | икинчи сəhəр jеməjи | lunch |
| iqlim | иглим | climate |
| iqtisadiyyat | игтисадиjjат | economics |
| il | ил | year |
| ilan | илан | snake |
| ildönümü | илдөнүмү | anniversary |
| ilə | илə | by, with |
| ılıq | ылыг | lukewarm, warm |
| imkansız | имкансыз | impossible |
| imtahan | имтаhан | examination |
| imtahan et- | имтаhан ет- | test |
| imza | имза | signature |
| imzala- | имзала- | sign |
| inam | инам | belief |
| inan- | инан- | believe |
| incə | инчə | fine, slim, thin |
| incəsənət | инчəсəнəт | art |
| indi | инди | now |
| indiki | индики | present |
| inək | инəк | cow |
| infeksiya | инфексиjа | infection |
| inflyasiya | инфлjасиjа | inflation |
| inkar et- | инкар ет- | deny |
| inkişaf | инкишаф | development |
| inqilab | ингилаб | revolution |
| insan | инсан | human being |
| intiqam | интигам | revenge |
| ipək | ипəк | silk |
| irəli | ирəли | forward |
| ishal | исhал | diarrhea |
| isim | исим | noun |
| ispanaq | испанаг | spinach |
| iste'faya çıx- | исте'фаjа чых- | retire |
| istehlakçı | истеhлакчы | consumer |
| istehsal et- | истеhсал ет- | produce |
| istə- | истə- | want |
| isti | исти | hot |
| istilik | истилик | temperature |

| | | |
|---|---|---|
| istiqamət | истигамəт | direction |
| istiot | истиот | pepper |
| istirahət | истираhəт | rest |
| iş | иш | job |
| işçi | ишчи | worker |
| işə- | ишə- | urinate |
| işıq | ишыг | light |
| işlə- | ишлə- | work |
| işlət- | ишлəт- | use |
| işlətmə dərmanı | ишлəтмə дəрманы | laxative |
| it | иг | dog |
| itaət et- | итаəт ет- | obey |
| itələ- | итəлə- | push |
| iti | ити | sharp |
| itir- | итир- | lose |
| ittifaq | иттифаг | union |
| iyirmi | иjирми | twenty |
| iylə- | иjлə- | smell |
| iynə | иjнə | needle |
| iyul | иjул | July |
| iyun | иjун | June |
| iz | из | trace |
| izah et- | изаh ет- | explain |
| izahat | изаhат | explanation |
| izdiham | издиhам | crowd |
| izlə- | излə- | chase, follow |
| | | |
| jaket | жакет | jacket |
| jurnal | журнал | magazine |
| jurnalist | журналист | journalist |
| | | |
| kabus | кабус | ghost |
| kafe | кафе | café |
| kafi | кафи | sufficient |
| kağız | кағыз | paper |
| kahı | каhы | lettuce |
| kanal | канал | canal, channel |
| kapital qoyuluşu | капитал гоjулушу | investment |
| kapitan | капитан | captain |
| kar | кар | deaf |
| karandaş | карандаш | pencil |
| karikatura | карикатура | cartoon |
| karlıq | карлыг | deafness |
| kart | карт | playing card |
| kartof | картоф | potato |
| kasa | каса | bowl |
| kaset | касет | cassette |

| | | |
|---|---|---|
| kasıb | касыб | poor |
| kassir | кассир | cashier |
| katib[ə] | катиб(ə) | secretary |
| keç- | кеч- | pass |
| keçi | кечи | goat |
| keçəl | кечəл | bald |
| keçən | кечəн | last |
| keşiş | кешиш | priest |
| keyfiyyət | кеjфиjjəт | quality |
| kədərli | кəдəрли | sad, sorry |
| kələm | кəлəм | cabbage |
| kəmər | кəмəр | belt |
| kənar | кəнар | edge |
| kənd | кəнд | countryside, village |
| kənd təsərrüfatı | кəнд тəсəрруфаты | agriculture |
| kəndli | кəндли | peasant |
| kəpənək | кəпəнəк | butterfly |
| kərə yağı | кəрə jағы | butter |
| kərəviz | кəрəвиз | celery |
| kərpic | кəрпич | brick |
| kəs- | кəс- | cut |
| kəsir | кəсир | fraction |
| kəşf et- | кəшф ет- | discover |
| kətil | кəтил | stool |
| ki | ки | that |
| kibrit | кибрит | match |
| kifayət qədər | кифаjəт гəдəр | enough |
| kilid | килид | lock |
| kilsə | килсə | church |
| kim | ким | who |
| kimi | кими | like |
| kimsə | кимсə | anybody |
| kinoteatr | кинотеатр | cinema |
| kiprik | киприк | eyelash |
| kişi | киши | man |
| kitab | китаб | book |
| kitab mağazası | китаб мағазасы | bookshop |
| kitab satan | китаб сатан | bookseller |
| kitab şkafı | китаб шкафы | bookcase |
| kitabxana | китабхана | library |
| klinika | клиника | clinic |
| klub | клуб | club |
| kobud | кобуд | rude |
| kolbasa | колбаса | sausage |
| komediya | комедиjа | comedy |

| | | |
|---|---|---|
| kompüter | компүтер | computer |
| konfet | конфет | candy |
| konkret | конкрет | concrete |
| konsert | консерт | concert |
| kor | кор | blind |
| korluq | корлуг | blindness |
| korrupsiya | коррупсиjа | corruption |
| kosmos | космос | space |
| kostyum | костjум | suit |
| kotan | котан | plow |
| köhnə | көhнə | old |
| kök | көк | fat, root |
| kölgə | көлкə | shade, shadow |
| kömək | көмəк | assistance, help |
| kömək et- | көмəк ет- | assist, help |
| kömür | көмүр | coal |
| körfəz | көрфəз | bay |
| körpə | көрпə | baby |
| körpü | көрпү | bridge |
| köynək | көjнəк | shirt |
| kral | крал | king |
| kran | кран | faucet |
| kredit | кредит | credit |
| kreslo | кресло | armchair |
| küçə | күчə | street |
| küçə hərəkəti | күчə həрəкəти | traffic |
| küknar | күкнар | fir |
| kül | күл | ash |
| külək | күлəк | wind |
| künc | күнч | corner |
| kürək | күрəк | shovel, spade |
| kvadrat | квадрат | square |
| | | |
| qabaqcadan sifariş edilmiş yer | габагчадан сифариш едилмиш jер | reservation |
| qabıq | габыг | bark |
| qabyuyan maşın | габjуjан машын | dishwasher |
| qaç- | гач- | escape, run, run away, flee |
| qadağan et- | гадаған ет- | forbid |
| qadın | гадын | woman |
| qal- | гал- | remain, stay |
| qaldır- | галдыр- | lift, raise |
| qalx- | галх- | get up |
| qalın | галын | thick |
| qalib gəl- | галиб кəл- | win |

| | | |
|---|---|---|
| qalstuk | галстук | tie |
| qan | ган | blood |
| qan təzyiqi | ган тәзјиги | blood pressure |
| qana- | гана- | bleed |
| qanad | ганад | wing |
| qanun | ганун | law |
| qapaq | гапаг | lid |
| qapı | гапы | door |
| qar | гар | snow |
| qara | гара | black |
| qaraciyər | гарачијәр | liver |
| qaraj | гараж | garage |
| qaranquş | гарангуш | swallow |
| qaranlıq | гаранлыг | dark, darkness |
| qardaş | гардаш | brother |
| qarət et- | гарәт ет- | plunder |
| qarğa | гарға | crow |
| qarğıdalı | гарғыдалы | corn |
| qarın | гарын | belly |
| qarışdır- | гарышдыр- | mix |
| qarışqa | гарышга | ant |
| qarmaqarışıq | гармагарышыг | messy |
| qarpız | гарпыз | watermelon |
| qarşı | гаршы | against |
| qarşılaş- | гаршылаш- | meet |
| qarşısını al- | гаршысыны ал- | prevent |
| qartal | гартал | eagle |
| qaş | гаш | eyebrow |
| qaşıq | гашыг | spoon |
| qatar | гатар | train |
| qatıq | гатыг | yogurt |
| qatla- | гатла- | fold |
| qaya | гаја | rock |
| qayçı | гајчы | scissors |
| qayıq | гајыг | boat |
| qayıt- | гајыт- | return |
| qayka | гајка | wrench |
| qaymaq | гајмаг | cream |
| qayna- | гајна- | boil |
| qaysı | гајсы | apricot |
| qaz | газ | gas, goose |
| qazanc | газанч | profit |
| qazança | газанча | saucepan |
| qazı- | газы- | dig, scrape |
| qeydiyyat | гејдијјат | registration |
| qəbiristan | гәбиристан | cemetery |
| qəbizlik | гәбизлик | constipation |
| qəbul et- | гәбул ет- | accept |
| qəbz | гәбз | receipt |
| qədər | гәдәр | until |
| qəhvə | гәhвә | coffee |
| qəhvəyi | гәhвәји | brown |
| qələbə | гәләбә | victory |
| qənd | гәнд | sugar |
| qərar | гәрар | decision |
| qərara gəl- | гәрара кәл- | decide |
| qərb | гәрб | west |
| qəribə | гәрибә | strange |
| qərənfil | гәрәнфил | carnation |
| qəsəbə | гәсәбә | town |
| qəssab | гәссаб | butcher |
| qəşəng | гәшәнк | handsome |
| qəza | гәза | accident |
| qəzet | гәзет | newspaper |
| qəzəb | гәзәб | anger |
| qıç | гыч | leg |
| qılınc | гылынч | sword |
| qırx | гырх | forty |
| qırıq | гырыг | broken |
| qırmızı | гырмызы | red |
| qısa | гыса | short |
| qısqanc | гысганч | jealous |
| qış | гыш | winter |
| qız | гыз | daughter, girl |
| qızart- | гызарт- | roast |
| qızçiçəyi | гызчичәји | daisy |
| qızdırma | гыздырма | fever |
| qızıl | гызыл | gold |
| qızılgül | гызылкул | rose |
| qibtə et- | гибтә ет- | envy |
| qida | гида | food |
| qiymət | гијмәт | cost, price, value |
| qiymətli | гијмәтли | valuable |
| qoca | гоча | old |
| qohum | гоhум | relative |
| qoxu | гоху | smell |
| qoxu- | гоху- | smell |
| qol | гол | arm |
| qonaq | гонаг | guest |
| qonaq get- | гонаг кет- | visit |
| qonaqsevərlik | гонагсевәрлик | hospitality |
| qonşu | гоншу | neighbor |
| qorx- | горх- | afraid: be afraid |
| qorxaq | горхаг | coward |

| | | |
|---|---|---|
| qorxaqlıq | горхаглыг | cowardice |
| qorxu | горху | fear |
| qovaq | говаг | poplar |
| qovun | говун | melon |
| qoy- | гоj- | put |
| qoyun | гоjун | sheep |
| qoyun əti | гоjун әти | mutton |
| qoz | гоз | walnut |
| qrafin | графин | pitcher |
| qrip | грип | flu |
| qu quşu | гу гушу | swan |
| qucaqla- | гучагла- | embrace |
| qulaq | гулаг | ear |
| qulluqçu | гуллугчу | official |
| qum | гум | sand |
| quraqlıq | гураглыг | drought |
| qurbağa | гурбаға | frog |
| qurban | гурбан | sacrifice |
| qurd | гурд | wolf, worm |
| qurğuşun | гургушун | lead |
| qurtar- | гуртар- | finish |
| quru | гуру | dry |
| quru- | гуру- | dry |
| qus- | гус- | vomit |
| quş | гуш | bird |
| quş tükü | гуш түкү | feather |
| qutu | гуту | box |
| quyruq | гуjруг | tail |
| quzu | гузу | lamb |
| qüllə | гүллә | tower |
| | | |
| lal | лал | mute |
| lalə | лалә | tulip |
| lampa | лампа | lamp |
| lent | лент | film |
| leylək | леjләк | stork |
| ləzzətli | ләззәтли | delicious, tasty |
| lift | лифт | elevator |
| liman | лиман | harbor |
| limon | лимон | lemon |
| lobya | лобjа | bean |
| lüğət | лүғәт | dictionary |
| | | |
| maaş | мааш | salary |
| maddə | маддә | matter |
| mağaza | мағаза | store |
| mahnı | маһны | song |
| mahnı oxu- | маһны оху- | sing |

| | | |
|---|---|---|
| maqnitofon | магнитофон | tape recorder |
| mal | мал | goods |
| mal əti | мал әти | beef |
| mal-qara | мал-гара | cattle |
| maral | марал | deer |
| maraq | мараг | interest |
| maraqlı | мараглы | interesting |
| marka | марка | stamp |
| mart | март | March |
| masa | маса | table |
| maşın | машын | car, machine |
| material | материал | material |
| may | маj | May |
| maye | маjе | liquid |
| mebel | мебел | furniture |
| məğlub et- | мәғлуб ет- | defeat |
| məğlubiyyət | мәғлубијјәт | defeat |
| mehmanxana | меһманхана | hotel |
| mehriban | меһрибан | kind |
| melodiya | мелодиjа | tune |
| me'mar | ме'мар | architect |
| menyu | менjу | menu |
| mer | мер | mayor |
| meşə | мешә | forest, wood |
| metal | метал | metal |
| metro | метро | subway |
| meydan | меjдан | square |
| meymun | меjмун | monkey |
| meyvə | меjвә | fruit |
| meyvə şirəsi | меjвә ширәси | fruit juice |
| mə'bəd | мә'бәд | temple |
| mə'də | мә'дә | stomach |
| mədəniyyət | мәдәнијјәт | culture |
| məhdudlaşdır- | мәһдудлашдыр- | restrict |
| məhəbbət | мәһәббәт | love |
| məhəllə | мәһәллә | neighborhood |
| məhkəmə | мәһкәмә | court |
| məhsul | мәһсул | crop |
| məktəb | мәктәб | school |
| məktəb bitirmə | мәктәб битирмә | graduation |
| məktub | мәктуб | letter |
| məqalə | мәгалә | article |
| məqsəd | мәгсәд | purpose |
| mələk | мәләк | angel |
| mə'lumat | мә'лумат | data, information |
| mən | мән | I |
| məni | мәни | me |

| mənim | мәним | my |
|---|---|---|
| mənimki | мәнимки | mine |
| mənzil | мәнзил | apartment |
| mərci | мәрчи | lentil |
| mərkəz | мәркәз | center |
| mərtəbə | мәртәбә | storey |
| məsafə | мәсафә | distance |
| məscid | мәсчид | mosque |
| məsələ | мәсәлә | problem |
| məsləhət | мәсләһәт | advice |
| məsləhət gör- | мәсләһәт көр- | recommend |
| məst | мәст | drunk |
| məşğul | мәшғул | busy |
| məşhur | мәшһур | famous |
| mətbəə | мәтбәә | printing press |
| mətbəx | мәтбәх | kitchen |
| mətbuat | мәтбуат | press |
| məzhəb | мәзһәб | sect |
| mıx | мых | nail |
| mifologiya | мифолокија | mythology |
| miqdar | мигдар | amount, quantity |
| milçək | милчәк | fly |
| millət | милләт | nation |
| millətçilik | милләтчилик | nationalism |
| milyard | милјард | billion |
| milyon | милјон | million |
| min | мин | thousand |
| min- | мин- | get on, ride |
| minnətdarlıq | миннәтдарлыг | gratitude |
| mis | мис | copper |
| mişar | мишар | saw |
| mizraq | мизраг | spear |
| moda | мода | fashion |
| motor | мотор | engine |
| motosikl | мотосикл | motorcycle |
| mövzu | мөвзу | subject |
| muxtariyyət | мухтаријјәт | autonomy |
| musiqi | мусиги | music |
| musiqi əsəri | мусиги әсәри | composition |
| musiqiçi | мусигичи | musician |
| muzey | музеј | museum |
| müalicə | мүаличә | cure |
| müalicə et- | мүаличә ет- | cure |
| mübahisə | мүбаһисә | argument |
| mübahisə et- | мүбаһисә ет- | argue |
| mübtəda | мүбтәда | subject |
| mücərrəd | мүчәррәд | abstract |

| müdafiə | мүдафиә | defense |
|---|---|---|
| müdafiə et- | мүдафиә ет- | defend, protect |
| müdir | мүдир | manager |
| müəllim | мүәллим | teacher |
| müğənni | мүғәнни | singer |
| müharibə | мүһарибә | battle, war |
| mühasirə | мүһасирә | siege |
| mühazirə | мүһазирә | lecture |
| mühəndis | мүһәндис | engineer |
| mühüm | мүһүм | important |
| mükafat | мүкафат | prize |
| mükəmməl | мүкәммәл | perfect |
| müqavilə | мүгавилә | agreement |
| müqayisə | мүгајисә | comparison |
| müqəddimə | мүгәддимә | preface |
| mülayim | мүлајим | gentle |
| mümkün | мүмкүн | possible |
| müraciət et- | мүрачиәт ет- | apply |
| mürəbbə | мүрәббә | jam |
| mürəkkəb | мүрәккәб | ink |
| mürəkkəbli qələm | мүрәккәбли гәләм | pen |
| müsəlman | мүсәлман | Muslim |
| müstəqillik | мүстәгиллик | independence |
| müştəri | мүштәри | customer |
| müvəffəqiyyət | мүвәффәгијјәт | success |
| müzakirə | мүзакирә | discussion |
| nadir hallarda | надир һалларда | seldom |
| nağıl | нағыл | folktale |
| nahar | наһар | dinner |
| nanə | нанә | mint |
| nar | нар | pomegranate |
| narahat et- | нараһат ет- | bother, disturb |
| narahat ol- | нараһат ол- | worry |
| narıncı | нарынчы | orange |
| nazir | назир | minister |
| necə | нечә | how |
| neçəyə | нечәјә | how much |
| neft | нефт | oil |
| nə | нә | what |
| nə ... nə [də] | нә ... нә (дә) | neither ... nor |
| nə qədər | нә гәдәр | how much |
| nə üçün | нә үчүн | why |
| nə vaxt | нә вахт | when |
| nəfəs | нәфәс | breath |
| nəqd pul | нәгд пул | cash |
| nəlbəki | нәлбәки | saucer |

| | | |
|---|---|---|
| nəm | нəм | damp, moist |
| nənə | нəнə | grandmother |
| nərdivan | нəрдиван | ladder |
| nəsr | нəср | prose |
| nəşriyyat | нəшрийjат | publishing house |
| nəticə | нəтичə | result |
| nəvə | нəвə | grandchild |
| nəzakətli | нəзакəтли | polite |
| nəzəriyyə | нəзəрийjə | theory |
| nifrət | нифрəт | disgust |
| nifrət et- | нифрəт ет- | hate |
| nitq | нитг | speech |
| niyyət | нийjəт | intention |
| noxud | нохуд | pea |
| noyabr | нojaбр | November |
| nöqtə | нөгтə | period |
| növ | нөв | kind |
| növbəti | нөвбəти | next |
| nümayiş | нүмajиш | demonstration |
| nümunə | нүмунə | example |
| | | |
| o | о | he, it, she, that |
| o zaman | о заман | then |
| od | од | fire |
| ofisiant | офисиант | waiter |
| oğlan | оғлан | boy |
| oğru | оғру | burglar, thief |
| oğul | оғул | son |
| oğurla- | оғурла- | steal |
| ox | ох | arrow |
| oxşa- | охша- | resemble |
| oxşar | охшар | alike, similar |
| oxu- | оху- | study, read |
| oxucu | охучу | reader |
| okean | океан | ocean |
| oktyabr | октjaбр | October |
| ol- | ол- | be, become, happen |
| oldu | олду | OK |
| on | он | ten |
| on altı | он алты | sixteen |
| on beş | он беш | fifteen |
| on bir | он бир | eleven |
| on doqquz | он доггуз | nineteen |
| on dörd | он дөрд | fourteen |
| on iki | он ики | twelve |
| on səkkiz | он сəккиз | eighteen |
| on üç | он үч | thirteen |

| | | |
|---|---|---|
| on yeddi | он jедди | seventeen |
| ondan sonra | ондан сонра | then |
| onlar | онлар | they, those |
| onları | онлары | them |
| onların | онларын | their |
| onu | ону | her, him |
| onun | онун | her, his, its |
| onun üçün | онун үчүн | therefore |
| onunku | онунку | hers, his, its |
| onurğa | онурға | spine |
| opera | опера | opera |
| orada | орада | there |
| oraq | ораг | sickle |
| oraya | ораja | there |
| ordu | орду | army |
| orta | орта | medium, middle |
| ortaq | ортаг | partner |
| oruc | оруч | fast |
| ot | от | grass, herb |
| otaq | отаг | room |
| otlaq | отлаг | meadow |
| otur- | отур- | sit |
| otuz | отуз | thirty |
| ov | ов | game |
| ovla- | овла- | hunt |
| oyan- | оjaн- | awake, wake |
| oyat- | оjaт- | awake, wake |
| oyna- | оjнa- | play |
| oyun | оjун | game, match |
| oyuncaq | оjунчаг | toy |
| | | |
| ödə- | өдə- | pay |
| öküz | өкүз | ox |
| öl- | өл- | die |
| ölçü | өлчү | measure, size |
| öldür- | өлдүр- | kill |
| ölü | өлү | dead |
| ölüm | өлүм | death |
| öncə | өнчə | ago |
| önündə | өнүндə | front: in front of |
| öp- | өп- | kiss |
| ördək | өрдəк | duck |
| ört- | өрт- | cover |
| öskürək | өскүрəк | cough |
| öyrən- | өjрəн- | learn, study |
| öyrət- | өjрəт- | teach |
| öyün- | өjүн- | boast |

| | | |
|---|---|---|
| özü | өзү | herself, himself, itself |
| özüm | өзүм | myself |
| özümüz | өзүмүз | ourselves |
| özün | өзүн | yourself |
| özünüz | өзүнүз | yourselves |
| | | |
| paxla | пахла | bean |
| paket | пакет | parcel |
| palçıq | палчыг | mud |
| palıd ağacı | палыд ағачы | oak |
| paltar | палтар | clothes, dress |
| palto | палто | overcoat |
| pambıq | памбыг | cotton |
| papaq | папаг | hat |
| parad | парад | parade |
| park | парк | park |
| parla- | парла- | shine |
| parlaq | парлаг | bright |
| parta | парта | desk |
| partiya | партија | party |
| pasport | паспорт | passport |
| payız | пајыз | autumn |
| payla- | пајла- | distribute |
| paytaxt | пајтахт | capital |
| peçenye | печенје | cookie |
| pendir | пендир | cheese |
| perron | перрон | platform |
| peşə | пешə | occupation |
| peşmanlıq | пешманлыг | regret |
| peyğəmbər | пејғəмбəр | prophet |
| peyvənd | пејвəнд | shot |
| pələng | пелəнк | tiger |
| pəncərə | пəнчəрə | window |
| pərdə | пəрдə | curtain |
| pijama | пижама | pajamas |
| pilləkən | пилləкəн | stairs |
| pirojna | пирожна | cake |
| pis | пис | bad |
| pişik | пишик | cat |
| pivə | пивə | beer |
| piyada | пијада | pedestrian |
| piyada keçidi | пијада кечиди | crosswalk |
| planet | планет | planet |
| plastinka | пластинка | record |
| plaş | плаш | raincoat |
| plov | плов | rice |
| poçt | почт | post office |
| poçt xərcləri | почт хəрчлəри | postage |
| poçt kartı | почт карты | postcard |
| poçt qutusu | почт гутусу | mailbox |
| poçtalyon | почталјон | mailman |
| poeziya | поезија | poetry |
| polad | полад | steel |
| polis | полис | policeman |
| pomidor | помидор | tomato |
| portağal | портағал | orange |
| pozan | позан | eraser |
| prezident | президент | president |
| proqram | програм | program |
| pul | пул | currency, money |
| pul kisəsi | пул кисəси | purse, wallet |
| pulemyot | пулемјот | machine gun |
| pulsuz | пулсуз | free |
| püstə | пустə | pistachio |
| pyes | пјес | play |
| | | |
| radio | радио | radio |
| rahat | раһат | comfortable |
| razı ol- | разы ол- | agree |
| realizm | реализм | realism |
| reklam | реклам | advertisement |
| resept | ресепт | prescription |
| respublika | республика | republic |
| restoran | ресторан | restaurant |
| rəf | рəф | shelf |
| rəqabət | рəгабəт | competition |
| rəqqas[ə] | рəггас(ə) | dancer |
| rəqs et- | рəгс ет- | dance |
| rəng | рəнк | color |
| rəngsaz | рəнксаз | painter |
| rəsmi | рəсми | official |
| rəssam | рəссам | artist |
| riyaziyyat |ријазијјат | mathematics |
| roman | роман | novel |
| romb | ромб | diamond |
| ruh | руһ | spirit |
| | | |
| saat | саат | hour |
| saatsaz | саатсаз | watchmaker |
| sabah | сабаһ | tomorrow |
| sabun | сабун | soap |
| saç | сач | hair |
| sadə | садə | simple |

| saf | саф | pure |
|-----|-----|------|
| sağ | сағ | right |
| sağlam | сағлам | healthy |
| sağlamlıq | сағламлыг | health |
| sahil | саһил | coast |
| saxla- | сахла- | keep |
| saxta | сахта | false |
| sait | саит | vowel |
| sakit | сакит | calm, quiet |
| sakit ol- | сакит ол- | quiet: be quiet |
| sakitlik | сакитлик | silence |
| saqqal | саггал | beard |
| salam | салам | hello |
| salamlaş- | саламлаш- | greet |
| salat | салат | salad |
| salfet | салфет | napkin |
| saman | саман | straw |
| samit | самит | consonant |
| saniyə | санијə | second |
| sanki | санки | as if |
| saray | сарај | palace |
| sarı | сары | yellow |
| sarı- | сары- | wrap |
| sarımsaq | сарымсаг | garlic |
| sat- | сат- | sell |
| satıcı | сатычы | salesperson, seller |
| satın al- | сатын ал- | buy |
| satış | сатыш | sale |
| savadlı | савадлы | literate |
| say | сај | number |
| say- | сај- | count |
| seç- | сеч- | choose, elect, select |
| seçki | сечки | election |
| sehr | сеһр | magic, spell |
| sel | сел | flood |
| sement | семент | cement |
| sentyabr | сентјабр | September |
| senzura | сензура | censorship |
| sev- | сев- | love |
| sevimli | севимли | dear |
| sevinc | севинч | joy |
| səbəb | сəбəб | cause, reason |
| səbət | сəбəт | basket |
| səbirli | сəбирли | patient |
| səfir | сəфир | ambassador |
| səhər | сəһəр | morning |
| səhər yeməyi | сəһəр јемəји | breakfast |
| səhifə | сəһифə | page |
| səhnə | сəһнə | stage |
| səhv | сəһв | mistake |
| səki | сəки | sidewalk |
| səkkiz | сəккиз | eight |
| səksən | сəксəн | eighty |
| sən | сəн | you |
| sənin | сəнин | your |
| səninki | сəнинки | yours |
| sərçə | сəрчə | sparrow |
| sərgi | сəрки | exhibition |
| sərhəd | сəрһəд | border |
| sərin | сəрин | cool |
| sərlövhə | сəрлөвһə | title |
| sərnişin | сəрнишин | passenger |
| səs | сəс | sound, voice, vote |
| səs ver- | сəс вер- | vote |
| səs-küy | сəс-күј | noise |
| səviyyə | сəвијјə | level |
| səyahət | сəјаһəт | journey, travel |
| sıfır | сыфыр | zero |
| sığalla- | сығалла- | stroke |
| sığorta | сығорта | insurance |
| sıx | сых | thick |
| sıx- | сых- | press |
| sındır- | сындыр- | break |
| sıra | сыра | row |
| siçan | сичан | mouse |
| sifariş ver- | сифариш вер- | order |
| sifət | сифəт | adjective |
| sil- | сил- | erase |
| silah | силаһ | gun, weapon |
| sim | сим | wire |
| simvol | символ | symbol |
| sinə | синə | chest |
| sinif | синиф | classroom |
| siqaret | сигарет | cigarette |
| siqaret çək- | сигарет чəк- | smoke |
| sirk | сирк | circus |
| sirkə | сиркə | vinegar |
| siyasət | сијасəт | politics |
| siz | сиз | you |
| sizin | сизин | your |
| sizinki | сизинки | yours |
| skelet | скелет | skeleton |

| soba | соба | stove |
|---|---|---|
| soğan | соған | onion |
| sol | сол | left |
| son | сон | end |
| sonra | сонра | after |
| soruş- | соруш- | ask |
| soyuducu | сојудучу | refrigerator |
| soyuq | сојуг | cold |
| soyuqdəymə | сојугдәјмә | cold |
| söndür- | сөндүр- | extinguish, put out |
| söylə- | сөјлә- | tell |
| söyüd | сөјүд | willow |
| söz | сөз | word |
| söz ver- | сөз вер- | promise |
| stəkan | стәкан | glass |
| stul | стул | chair |
| su | су | water |
| sual | суал | question |
| sualtı gəmi | суалты кәми | submarine |
| susuz | сусуз | thirsty |
| sübut | сүбут | proof |
| süd | сүд | milk |
| süfrə | сүфрә | tablecloth |
| sülh | сүлһ | peace |
| sümük | сүмүк | bone |
| sün'i | сүн'и | artificial |
| süpür- | сүпүр- | sweep |
| süpürgə | сүпүркә | broom |
| sür- | сүр- | drive, ride |
| sür'ət | сүр'әт | speed |
| sürt- | сүрт- | rub |
| sürü | сүрү | herd |
| sürücü | сүрүчү | driver |
| sürüş- | сүрүш- | slide, slip |
| sürüşkən | сүрүшкән | slippery |
| süzgəc | сүзкәч | strainer |
| svetofor | светофор | traffic light |
| sviter | свитер | sweater |
| şabalıd | шабалыд | chestnut |
| şad | шад | glad |
| şaftalı | шафталы | peach |
| şah əsər | шаһ әсәр | masterpiece |
| şahid | шаһид | witness |
| şahmat | шаһмат | chess |
| şaxta | шахта | frost |
| şair | шаир | poet |
| şalvar | шалвар | pants |
| şam | шам | candle |
| şam ağacı | шам аѓачы | pine |
| şans | шанс | luck |
| şe'r | ше'р | poem |
| şey | шеј | thing |
| şeytan | шејтан | demon, Satan |
| şəhər | шәһәр | city |
| şəhərətrafı | шәһәрәтрафы | suburb |
| şəxs | шәхс | person |
| şəkil | шәкил | drawing, painting, picture, shape |
| şəkilçi | шәкилчи | suffix |
| şənbə | шәнбә | Saturday |
| şərab | шәраб | wine |
| şərəf | шәрәф | honor |
| şərf | шәрф | scarf |
| şərq | шәрг | east |
| şərt | шәрт | condition |
| şikayət | шикајәт | complaint |
| şikayət et- | шикајәт ет- | complain |
| şimal | шимал | north |
| şimşək | шимшәк | lightning |
| şin | шин | tire |
| şir | шир | lion |
| şirin | ширин | sweet |
| şirkət | ширкәт | company |
| şirniyyat | ширнијјат | dessert |
| şiş | шиш | swelling |
| şiş- | шиш- | swell |
| şorba | шорба | soup |
| şort | шорт | shorts |
| şö'bə | шө'бә | department |
| şüa | шүа | ray |
| şübhə | шүбһә | doubt |
| şüşə | шүшә | bottle, glass |
| taxta | тахта | wood |
| taksi | такси | cab, taxi |
| tale | тале | fate |
| tam | там | complete |
| tamamlıq | тамамлыг | object |
| tanı- | таны- | know, recognize |
| tanış et- | таныш ет- | introduce |
| tanrı | танры | God |
| tap- | тап- | find |
| tarix | тарих | date, history |

| | | |
|---|---|---|
| tarixçi | тарихчи | historian |
| tarla | тарла | field |
| tava | тава | pan |
| tavan | таван | ceiling |
| teatr | театр | theater |
| tel | тел | wire |
| telefon | телефон | telephone |
| telefon-avtomat | телефон-автомат | public phone |
| telefon budkası | телефон будкасы | phone booth |
| telefon nömrəsi | телефон нөмрəси | phone number |
| teleqram | телеграм | telegram |
| televizor | телевизор | television |
| termometr | термометр | thermometer |
| tərpət- | тəрпəт- | shake |
| tez | тез | quick |
| tez-tez | тез-тез | often |
| tezliklə | тезликлə | soon |
| təbiət | тəбиəт | nature |
| təbii | тəбии | natural |
| təbliğat | тəблиғат | propaganda |
| təbrik | тəбрик | congratulation |
| təbrik et- | тəбрик ет- | congratulate |
| tə'cili yardım maşını | тə'чили jардым машыны | ambulance |
| təcrübə | тəчрүбə | experience |
| tədqiqat | тəдгигат | investigation, research |
| tədricən | тəдричəн | gradually |
| təhlükə | тəhлүкə | danger |
| təhlükəli | тəhлүкəли | dangerous |
| təhlükəsiz | тəhлүкəсиз | safe |
| təhsil | тəhсил | education |
| təhsil haqqı | тəhсил hаггы | tuition |
| tə'xirə sal- | тə'хирə сал- | postpone |
| təxminən | тəхминəн | about |
| təkər | тəкəр | wheel |
| təklif | тəклиф | suggestion |
| təklif et- | тəклиф ет- | offer |
| təkrar et- | тəкрар ет- | repeat |
| təqdim et- | тəгдим ет- | present |
| təqvim | тəгвим | calendar |
| tələbə | тəлəбə | student |
| tələs- | тəлəс- | hurry |
| tələsiklik | тəлəсиклик | haste |
| tə'mir et- | тə'мир ет- | mend, repair |
| təmiz | тəмиз | clean |
| təmizlə- | тəмизлə- | clean |
| təmsil et- | тəмсил ет- | represent |
| tənbəl | тəнбəл | lazy |
| tənbəllik | тəнбəллик | laziness |
| təntənə | тəнтəнə | ceremony |
| təpiklə- | тəпиклə- | kick |
| təpə | тəпə | hill |
| tərcümə | тəрчүмə | translation |
| tərcümə et- | тəрчүмə ет- | translate |
| tərəf | тəрəф | side |
| tərəfindən | тəрəфиндəн | by |
| tərəvəz | тəрəвəз | vegetable |
| tərəzi | тəрəзи | scale |
| tə'riflə- | тə'рифлə- | praise |
| tərk et- | тəрк ет- | leave |
| tərlə- | тəрлə- | sweat |
| tərpən- | тəрпəн- | move |
| təsdiq etmə | тəсдиг етмə | approval |
| təsərrüfat | тəсəрруфат | farm |
| tə'sir | тə'сир | effect, influence |
| təslim olma | тəслим олма | surrender |
| təsvir | тəсвир | description |
| təsvir et- | тəсвир ет- | describe |
| təşəbbüs | тəшəббүс | attempt |
| təşəkkür et- | тəшəккүр ет- | thank |
| tə'til | тə'тил | holiday, strike, vacation |
| tə'yin | тə'jин | appointment |
| tə'yin olunmuş görüş | тə'jин олунмуш көрүш | appointment |
| təyyarə | тəjjарə | airplane, plane |
| təyyarə limanı | тəjjарə лиманы | airport |
| təzə | тəзə | fresh |
| təzə il | тəзə ил | New Year |
| tısbağa | тысбаға | tortoise |
| tibb | тибб | medicine |
| tibb bacısı | тибб бачысы | nurse |
| ticarət | тичарəт | business |
| tik- | тик- | build, sew |
| timsah | тимсаh | crocodile |
| tiraj | тираж | circulation |
| titrə- | титрə- | tremble |
| titrət- | титрəт- | shake |
| toxuculuq | тохучулуг | textile |
| toxum | тохум | grain, seed |
| toxun- | тохун- | touch |

| | | |
|---|---|---|
| top | топ | ball, cannon, gun |
| topdan satış | топдан сатыш | wholesale |
| topla- | топла- | collect |
| toplama | топлама | addition |
| toranlıq | торанлыг | dusk |
| torpaq | торпаг | earth, soil |
| toyuq | тојуг | hen |
| toyuq əti | тојуг эти | chicken |
| toz | тоз | dust |
| tök- | тѳк- | pour |
| tramvay | трамвај | tram |
| tualet | туалет | toilet |
| tulla- | тулла- | throw |
| turist | турист | tourist |
| turizm | туризм | tourism |
| turş | турш | sour |
| tut | тут | mulberry |
| tut- | тут- | hold |
| tüfəng | түфэнк | rifle |
| tülkü | түлку | fox |
| tüpür- | түпүр- | spit |
| tütün | түтүн | tobacco |
| | | |
| uca | уча | high, tall |
| ucuz | учуз | cheap |
| ucuzlaşdırma | учузлашдырма | sale |
| uç- | уч- | fly |
| uçuş | учуш | flight |
| ulduz | улдуз | star |
| un | ун | flour |
| univermaq | универмаг | department store |
| universitet | университет | university |
| unut- | унут- | forget |
| uşaq | ушаг | child |
| utan- | утан- | ashamed: be ashamed |
| utancaq | утанчаг | shy |
| uyğun gəl- | ујғун кэл- | suit |
| uzaq | узаг | far |
| uzan- | узан- | lie |
| uzun | узун | long |
| [uzunboğaz] çəkmə | (узунбоғаз) чэкмэ | boot |
| uzunluq | узунлуг | length |
| | | |
| üç | үч | three |
| üçbucaq | үчбучаг | triangle |
| üçün | үчүн | for |

| | | |
|---|---|---|
| üfüq | үфүг | horizon |
| ülgüc | үлкүч | razor |
| ümid | үмид | hope |
| ümid et- | үмид ет- | hope |
| ümumi | үмуми | general |
| ünvan | үнван | address |
| ürək | үрэк | heart |
| üstün ol- | үстүн ол- | surpass |
| üstün tut- | үстүн тут- | prefer |
| üstündə | үстүндэ | above, on, over |
| üsyan | үсјан | rebellion |
| ütü | үтү | iron |
| üyüt- | үјүт- | grind |
| üz | үз | face |
| üz- | үз- | swim |
| üzgüçülük | үзкүчүлүк | swimming |
| üzr | үзр | apology |
| üzr istə- | үзр истэ- | apologize |
| üzüm | үзүм | grape |
| üzv | үзв | member |
| | | |
| vadi | вади | valley |
| vağzal | вағзал | station |
| vaxt | вахт | time |
| valideynlər | валидејнлэр | parents |
| vanna otağı | ванна отағы | bathroom |
| var-dövlət | вар-дѳвлэт | wealth |
| varlı | варлы | rich |
| varlıq | варлыг | existence |
| vedrə | ведрэ | bucket |
| velosiped | велосипед | bicycle |
| ver- | вер- | give |
| vergi | верки | tax |
| vergül | веркүл | comma |
| vertolyot | вертолјот | helicopter |
| və | вэ | and |
| vəhşi | вэһши | wild |
| vəkil | вэкил | lawyer |
| vətəndaş | вэтэндаш | citizen |
| vəzifə | вэзифэ | assignment, duty |
| vəziyyət | вэзијјэт | situation |
| vicdan | вичдан | conscience |
| video | видео | video |
| vilayət | вилајэт | province |
| vint | винт | screw |
| vintaçan | винтачан | screwdriver |
| vur- | вур- | hit |
| vurma | вурма | multiplication |

| | | |
|---|---|---|
| -ya, -yə | -ja, -jə | to |
| ya | ja | or |
| ya ... ya [da] | ja ... ja (да) | either ... or |
| yada sal- | jада сал- | remember |
| yadına sal- | jадына сал- | remind |
| yağ | jағ | fat, oil |
| yağ- | jағ- | precipitate |
| yağış | jағыш | rain |
| yaxa | jаха | collar |
| yaxala- | jахала- | catch |
| yaxın | jахын | near |
| yaxında | jахында | near |
| yaxınında | jахынында | near |
| yaxınlaş- | jахынлаш- | approach |
| yaxşı | jахшы | good, well |
| yalan | jалан | lie |
| yalan danış- | jалан даныш- | lie |
| yalqız | jалғыз | alone |
| yan- | jан- | burn |
| yanaq | jанаг | cheek |
| yanğın | jанғын | fire |
| yandır- | jандыр- | burn |
| yanında | jанында | beside |
| yanlış | jанлыш | wrong |
| yanvar | jанвар | January |
| yapış- | jапыш- | stick |
| yapışqan | jапышган | glue |
| yar- | jар- | split |
| yara | jара | wound |
| yaraş- | jараш- | suit |
| yarım | jарым | half |
| yarımada | jарымада | peninsula |
| yarış | jарыш | race |
| yarpaq | jарпаг | leaf |
| yastıq | jастыг | cushion |
| yaş | jаш | age, wet |
| yaşa- | jаша- | live |
| yaşıl | jашыл | green |
| yat- | jат- | sleep |
| yataq | jатаг | bed |
| yataq otağı | jатаг отағы | bedroom |
| yavaş | jаваш | slow |
| yay | jаj | bow, spring, summer |
| yay- | jаj- | spread |
| yaz | jаз | spring |
| yaz- | jаз- | write |
| yazı | jазы | writing |
| yazı makinası | jазы макинасы | typewriter |
| yazıçı | jазычы | author, writer |
| ye- | jе- | eat |
| yeddi | jедди | seven |
| yekə | jекə | large |
| yelkənli gəmi | jелкəнли кəми | sailboat |
| yemək | jемəк | dish |
| yemək otağı | jемəк отағы | dining room |
| yeni | jени | new |
| yenidən | jенидəн | again |
| yer | jер | earth, place, seat |
| yeri- | jери- | walk |
| yerkökü | jеркөкү | carrot |
| yerləş- | jерлəш- | situated: be situated |
| yetiş- | jетиш- | arrive |
| yetişdirmə | jетишдирмə | cultivation |
| yetişmiş | jетишмиш | ripe |
| yetmiş | jетмиш | seventy |
| yəhudi | jəһуди | Jew |
| yığıncaq | jығынчаг | meeting |
| yıxıl- | jыхыл- | fall |
| yox | jох | no, not |
| yox ol- | jох ол- | disappear |
| yol | jол | road, way |
| yol pulu | jол пулу | fare |
| yola düş- | jола дүш- | depart |
| yola düşmə | jола дүшмə | departure |
| yorğan | jорған | quilt |
| yorğun | jорғун | tired |
| yu- | jу- | wash |
| yubanma | jубанма | delay |
| yubka | jубка | skirt |
| yuxarıda | jухарыда | above |
| yuxu | jуху | dream, sleep |
| yumşaq | jумшаг | soft |
| yumurta | jумурта | egg |
| yun | jун | wool |
| yük | jүк | baggage, cargo |
| yük maşını | jүк машыны | truck |
| yükdaşıyan | jүкдашыjан | porter |
| yüksəklik | jүксəклик | height |
| yüngül | jүнкүл | light |
| yüz | jүз | hundred |

| | | |
|---|---|---|
| zabit | забит | officer |
| zalım | залым | cruel |
| zarafat | зарафат | joke |
| zeytun | зеjтун | olive |
| zəhər | зəhəр | poison |
| zəhərli | зəhəрли | poisonous |
| zəhmət | зəhмəт | please |
| olmasa | олмаса | |
| zəif | зəиф | weak |
| zəlzələ | зəлзəлə | earthquake |
| zəng | зəнк | bell |
| zənn et- | зəнн ет- | guess |
| zərər | зəрəр | harm |

| | | |
|---|---|---|
| zərərli | зəрəрли | harmful |
| zərf | зəрф | adverb, envelope |
| zərgər | зəркəр | jeweler |
| zibil | зибил | trash |
| zidd | зидд | opposite |
| ziyafət | зиjафəт | banquet, party |
| ziyalı | зиjалы | intellectual |
| ziyan | зиjан | damage, loss |
| ziyarət | зиjарəт | visit |
| zoopark | зоопарк | zoo |
| zövq | зөвг | pleasure |
| zövq al- | зөвг ал- | enjoy |
| zülm | зүлм | oppression |

# KAZAKH - ENGLISH INDEX

| | | |
|---|---|---|
| абай | (abay) | careful |
| абстракт | (abstrakt) | abstract |
| абыржы- | (abırzhı-) | worry |
| авария | (avariya) | accident |
| авиапочта | (aviapochta) | airmail |
| автобус | (avtobus) | bus |
| автомобиль | (avtomobil') | automobile |
| автономия | (avtonomiya) | autonomy |
| автор | (avtor) | author |
| аг- | (agh-) | flow |
| аға | (ini) | brother, uncle |
| ағаш | (aghash) | tree, wood |
| адал | (adal) | honest |
| адам | (adam) | human being, person |
| адрес | (adres) | address |
| ажырас- | (azhıras-) | divorce |
| ажырасу | (azhırasuw) | divorce |
| аз | (az) | few |
| азай- | (azay-) | decrease |
| азамат | (azamat) | citizen |
| азат | (azat) | free |
| азаттық | (azattıq) | freedom |
| азшылық | (azshılık) | minority |
| азық-түлік | (azıq-tülik) | food |
| ай | (ay) | month, moon |
| айва | (ayva) | quince |
| айда- | (ayda-) | drive |
| айқайла- | (ayqayla-) | shout |
| айна | (ayna) | mirror |
| айран | (ayran) | yogurt |
| айт- | (ayt-) | inform, say, tell |
| айуан | (aywan) | animal |
| айыпсыз | (ayıpsız) | innocent |
| айыпты | (ayıptı) | guilty |
| айырма | (ayırma) | difference |
| ақ | (aq) | white |
| аққу | (aqquw) | swan |
| ақпан | (aqpan) | February |
| ақша | (aqsha) | currency, money |
| ақыл | (aqıl) | mind |
| ақыл-кеңес | (aqıl-kenges) | advice |
| ақылды | (aqıldı) | clever |
| ақымақ | (aqımaq) | stupid |
| ақын | (aqın) | poet |
| ақырын | (aqırın) | slow |
| ал- | (al-) | take |
| алаң | (alang) | square |
| алгебра | (algebra) | algebra |
| алға | (algha) | forward |
| алғыс | (alghıs) | gratitude |
| алда- | (alda-) | lie |
| алдында | (aldında) | front: in front of |
| алқап | (alqap) | valley |
| алма | (alma) | apple |
| алмұрт | (almurt) | pear |
| алпыс | (alpıs) | sixty |
| алты | (altı) | six |
| алтын | (altın) | gold |
| алу | (aluw) | subtraction |
| алфавит | (alfavit) | alphabet |
| алыс | (alıs) | far |
| амандас- | (amandas-) | greet |
| ана | (ana) | mother |
| анар | (anar) | pomegranate |
| анархия | (anarkhiya) | anarchy |
| анда | (anda) | there |
| анда-санда | (anda-sanda) | seldom |
| ант бер- | (ant ber-) | swear |
| антенна | (antenna) | antenna |
| анық | (anıq) | obvious |
| аң | (ang) | game |
| аң аула- | (ang awla-) | hunt |
| аңыз | (angız) | legend |
| апа | (apa) | aunt, sister |
| апельсин | (apel'sin) | orange |
| апта | (apta) | week |
| ар | (ar) | conscience |
| ара | (ara) | bee, saw |
| ара қашықтық | (ara qashıqtıq) | distance |
| арал | (aral) | island |
| араластыр- | (aralastır-) | mix |
| арасында | (arasında) | between |
| арба | (arba) | cart |
| арзан | (arzan) | cheap |
| арзандату | (arzandatuw) | discount, sale |
| арқа | (arqa) | back |
| арқылы | (arqılı) | by |
| армия | (armiya) | army |
| арпа | (arpa) | barley |
| артиллерия | (artilleriya) | artillery |
| артта | (artta) | behind |
| артық көр- | (artıq kör-) | prefer |
| арыз | (arız) | complaint |
| арыздан- | (arızdan-) | complain |
| арыстан | (arıstan) | lion |
| ас үй | (as üy) | kitchen |

| | | |
|---|---|---|
| ас ішетін бөлме | (as ishetin bölme) | dining room |
| асқазан | (asqazan) | stomach |
| аспаз | (aspaz) | cook |
| аспан | (aspan) | sky |
| аспап | (aspap) | instrument, tool |
| астана | (astana) | capital |
| астында | (astında) | under, underneath |
| асығыстық | (asıghıstıq) | haste |
| асық- | (asıq-) | hurry |
| асып кет- | (asıp ket-) | surpass |
| ат | (at) | horse, name, title |
| ата | (ata) | grandfather |
| ата-ана | (ata-ana) | parents |
| атақты | (ataqtı) | famous |
| ауа | (awa) | air |
| ауа жолы | (awa zholı) | airline |
| ауа райы | (awa rayı) | climate, weather |
| ауа райы мәліметі | (awa rayı mälimeti) | weather report |
| аудар- | (awdar-) | translate |
| аударма | (awdarma) | translation |
| аула | (awla) | courtyard |
| ауру | (awruw) | ill, illness, pain, sick |
| аурухана | (awruwkhana) | hospital |
| ауыз | (awız) | mouth |
| ауыл | (awıl) | countryside, village |
| ауыл шар- уашылық | (awıl sharwashılıq) | agriculture |
| ауыр | (awır) | heavy |
| аш | (ash) | hungry |
| аш- | (ash-) | discover, open |
| ашаршылық | (asharshılıq) | famine |
| аштық | (ashtıq) | hunger |
| ашу | (ashuw) | anger |
| ашулы | (ashuwlı) | angry |
| ашық | (ashıq) | open |
| ашық хат | (ashıq khat) | postcard |
| ащы | (ashchı) | bitter |
| аэропорт | (aeroport) | airport |
| аяз | (ayaz) | frost |
| аяқ | (ayaq) | foot, leg |
| аяқ киім | (ayaq kiyim) | shoe |
| аялдама | (ayaldama) | stop |
| аю | (ayu) | bear |

| | | |
|---|---|---|
| әдеби | (ädebiy) | literary |
| әдеби жұмыс | (ädebiy zhumıs) | literary work |
| әдебиет | (ädebiyet) | literature |
| әдемі | (ädemi) | beautiful, handsome |
| әдепті | (ädepti) | polite |
| әдет | (ädet) | habit |
| әдет-ғұрып | (ädet-ghurıp) | custom |
| әділет | (ädilet) | justice |
| әже | (äzhe) | grandmother |
| әжетхана | (äzhetkhana) | toilet |
| әзіл | (äzil) | joke |
| әйел | (äyel) | wife, woman |
| әке | (äke) | father |
| әкел- | (äkel-) | bring |
| әкім | (äkim) | mayor |
| әлсіз | (älsiz) | weak |
| әлі | (äli) | still, yet |
| ән | (än) | song |
| әнші | (änshi) | singer |
| әңгіме | (änggime) | story |
| әңгімелес- | (änggimeles-) | talk |
| әр | (är) | any, every |
| әр бір | (är bir) | any |
| әр кім | (är kim) | any, anybody, everybody |
| әрекет | (äreket) | attempt |
| әрине | (äriyne) | course: of course |
| әрқашан | (ärqashan) | always |
| әріп | (ärip) | letter |
| әсер | (äser) | effect, influence |
| әскер | (äsker) | soldier |
| әтір | (ätir) | perfume |
| б아ға | (bagha) | cost, price |
| бағалы | (baghalı) | valuable |
| бағбан | (baghban) | gardener |
| бағын- | (baghın-) | obey |
| бағыт | (baghıt) | direction |
| базар | (bazar) | market |
| бай | (bay) | rich |
| байла- | (bayla-) | tie |
| байланыс | (baylanıs) | communication |
| байлық | (baylıq) | wealth |
| баклажан | (baklazhan) | eggplant |
| бақша | (baqsha) | garden |

| | | |
|---|---|---|
| бақытсыз | (baqıtsız) | unhappy |
| бақытты | (baqıttı) | happy |
| бал | (bal) | honey |
| бал ай | (bal ay) | honeymoon |
| бала | (bala) | child |
| балға | (balgha) | hammer |
| балет | (balet) | ballet |
| балкон | (balkon) | balcony |
| балмұздақ | (balmuzdaq) | ice cream |
| балта | (balta) | axe |
| балшық | (balshıq) | clay |
| балық | (balıq) | fish |
| балықшы | (balıqshı) | fisherman |
| банан | (banan) | banana |
| банк | (bank) | bank |
| банка | (banka) | jar |
| банкет | (banket) | banquet |
| бар- | (bar-) | go, visit |
| барлық | (barlıq) | existence |
| барлық жерде | (barlıq zherde) | everywhere |
| барометр | (barometr) | barometer |
| бару | (baruw) | visit |
| бас | (bas) | head |
| бас ауруы | (bas awruwı) | headache |
| бас- | (bas-) | press, print |
| баскетбол | (basketbol) | basketball |
| басқа | (basqa) | another, besides, different, other |
| баспа үй | (baspa üy) | publishing house |
| баспасөз | (baspasöz) | press |
| баспахана | (baspakhana) | printing press |
| бассейн | (basseyn) | pool |
| баста- | (basta-) | begin, start |
| бастауыш | (bastawısh) | subject |
| бат- | (bat-) | drown, sink |
| бата | (bata) | prayer |
| батпақ | (batpaq) | mud, swamp |
| батыл | (batıl) | brave, courageous |
| батылдық | (batıldıq) | courage |
| батыс | (batıs) | west |
| бауыр | (bawır) | liver |
| бәлкім | (bälkim) | perhaps |
| бәрі | (bäri) | all, all |
| бейбітшілік | (beybitshilik) | peace |
| бейсенбі | (beysenbi) | Thursday |
| бейіш | (beyish) | paradise |
| бекіт- | (bekit-) | fasten |
| белбеу | (belbew) | belt |
| бензин | (benzin) | gasoline |
| бер- | (ber-) | give |
| бәрі | (beri) | everything, since |
| берілу | (beriluw) | surrender |
| бес | (bes) | five |
| бет | (bet) | cheek, face, page |
| бидай | (biyday) | wheat |
| бинт | (bint) | bandage |
| биле- | (biyle-) | dance |
| билет | (bilet) | ticket |
| бит | (biyt) | louse |
| биші | (biyshi) | dancer |
| биік | (biyik) | high, tall |
| биіктік | (biyiktik) | height |
| бланк | (blank) | form |
| блузка | (bluwzka) | blouse |
| бол- | (bol-) | be, become |
| болат | (bolat) | steel |
| болашақ | (bolashaq) | future |
| болжа- | (bolzha-) | guess |
| болып қал- | (bolıp qal-) | happen |
| бомбы | (bombı) | bomb |
| боран | (boran) | storm |
| бос | (bos) | empty, loose |
| бос емес | (bos yemes) | busy |
| босат- | (bosat-) | empty, release |
| боя- | (boya-) | dye, paint |
| бояушы | (boyawshı) | painter |
| бөбек | (böbek) | baby |
| бөгет | (böget) | dam |
| бөл- | (böl-) | distribute, divide, separate |
| бөлек | (bölek) | separate |
| бөлме | (bölme) | room |
| бөлу | (böluw) | division |
| бөлшек | (bölshek) | fraction |
| бөлім | (bölim) | department, part |
| бөлін- | (bölin-) | separated: be separated |
| бутерброд | (buterbrod) | sandwich |
| бұғы | (bughı) | deer |
| бұз- | (buz-) | destroy, disturb |
| бұзау еті | (buzaw yeti) | veal |

| | | |
|---|---|---|
| бұйрық бер- | (buyrıq ber-) | command, order |
| бұйым | (buyım) | goods |
| бұқа | (buqa) | bull |
| бұл | (bul) | this |
| бұлар | (bular) | these |
| бұлт | (bult) | cloud |
| бұра- | (bura-) | twist |
| бұрағыш | (buraghısh) | screwdriver |
| бұрандалы шеге | (burandalı shege) | screw |
| бұрғы | (burghı) | drill |
| бұршақ | (burshaq) | bean, hail, pea |
| бұрыл- | (burıl-) | turn |
| бұрын | (burın) | ago, before |
| бұрыш | (burısh) | angle, corner, pepper |
| бұтақ | (butaq) | branch |
| бүг- | (büg-) | bend |
| бүгін | (bügin) | today |
| бүйрек | (büyrek) | kidney |
| бүрге | (bürge) | flea |
| бүркіт | (bürkit) | eagle |
| бүтін | (bütin) | whole |
| былық | (bılıq) | messy |
| біз | (biz) | we |
| бізді | (bizdi) | us |
| біздікі | (bizdiki) | ours |
| біздің | (bizding) | our |
| біл- | (bil-) | know |
| білек | (bilek) | wrist |
| білім | (bilim) | education, knowledge |
| бір | (bir) | one |
| бір нәрсе | (bir närse) | anything |
| бір түрлі | (bir türli) | strange |
| біраз | (biraz) | little, some |
| бірақ | (biraq) | but |
| бірге | (birge) | together, with |
| біреу | (birew) | anybody |
| бірнеше | (birneshe) | several |
| біртіндеп | (birtindep) | gradually |
| бітір- | (bitir-) | finish |
| бітіру | (bitiruw) | graduation |
| бюджет | (byudzhet) | budget |
| ванна бөлмесі | (vanna bölmesi) | bathroom |
| велосипед | (velosiped) | bicycle |
| вертолёт | (vertolyot) | helicopter |
| видео | (video) | video |
| гавань | (gavan') | harbor |
| газ | (gaz) | gas |
| газет | (gazet) | newspaper |
| галстук | (galstuk) | tie |
| гараж | (garazh) | garage |
| гармония | (garmoniya) | harmony |
| география | (geografiya) | geography |
| геология | (geologiya) | geology |
| геометрия | (geometriya) | geometry |
| градус | (gradus) | degree |
| графин | (grafin) | pitcher |
| грипп | (gripp) | flu |
| гүл | (gül) | flower |
| -ға, -ге | (-gha, -ge) | to |
| ғалым | (ghalım) | scientist |
| ғарыш | (gharısh) | space |
| ғасыр | (ghasır) | century |
| ғибадатхана | (ghiybadatkhana) | temple |
| -да, -де | (-da, -de) | at, in |
| да ... да | (da ... da) | both ... and |
| дайын | (dayın) | ready |
| дайында- | (dayında-) | prepare |
| даму | (damuw) | development |
| -дан, -ден | (-dan, -den) | from |
| даналық туынды | (danalıq tuwındı) | masterpiece |
| дастарқан | (dastarqan) | tablecloth |
| дауыс | (dawıs) | voice, vote |
| дауыс бер- | (dawıs ber-) | vote |
| дауыссыз | (dawıssız) | consonant |
| дауысты | (dawıstı) | vowel |
| даяшы | (dayashı) | waiter |
| дәл | (däl) | same |
| дәлел | (dälel) | proof |
| дәлелде- | (dälelde-) | represent |
| дәмді | (dämdi) | delicious, tasty |
| дәмін көр- | (dämin kör-) | taste |
| дән | (dän) | grain |
| дәптер | (däpter) | notebook |
| дәрі | (däri) | drug, medicine |
| дәрігер | (däriger) | doctor |
| дәріхана | (därikhana) | pharmacy |
| дәу | (däw) | giant |
| дәуір | (däwir) | era |
| де ... де | (de ... de) | neither ... nor |
| дейін | (deyin) | until |

| | | |
|---|---|---|
| дем | (dem) | breath |
| демалыс | (demalıs) | holiday, rest, vacation |
| демократия | (demokratiya) | democracy |
| демон | (demon) | demon |
| демонстрация | (demonstratsiya) | demonstration |
| дене | (dene) | body |
| денсаулық | (densawlıq) | health |
| деңгей | (denggey) | level |
| дереу | (derew) | immediately |
| дерлік | (dyerlik) | almost |
| диплом | (diplom) | diploma |
| диірмен | (diyirmen) | mill |
| домала- | (domala-) | roll |
| доп | (dop) | ball |
| дос | (dos) | friend |
| достық | (dostıq) | friendship |
| дөңгелек | (dönggelek) | round, wheel |
| драма | (drama) | drama |
| драматург | (dramaturg) | playwright |
| духовка | (dukhovka) | oven |
| душ | (dush) | shower |
| дұшпандық | (dushpandıq) | enmity |
| дүйсенбі | (düysenbi) | Monday |
| дүкен | (düken) | shop, store |
| дүние | (düniye) | world |
| дыбыс | (dıbıs) | sound |
| дымқыл | (dımqıl) | damp |
| дін | (din) | religion |
| діни | (diniy) | religious |
| діни мейрам | (diniy meyram) | religious holiday |
| дірілде- | (dirilde-) | tremble |
| дюжина | (dyuzhiyna) | dozen |
| | | |
| еврей | (yevrey) | Jew |
| ег- | (yeg-) | plant |
| егер | (yeger) | if |
| егеу | (yegew) | file |
| егу | (yeguw) | shot |
| егіз | (yegiz) | twin |
| егін | (yegin) | crop |
| егін даласы | (yegin dalası) | field |
| егін ору | (yegin oruw) | harvest |
| еден | (yeden) | floor |
| ез- | (yez-) | crush |
| ек- | (yek-) | sow |
| екен | (yeken) | that |
| екі | (yeki) | two |
| елу | (yeluw) | fifty |

| | | |
|---|---|---|
| елші | (yelshi) | ambassador |
| ем | (yem) | cure |
| ем- | (yem-) | suck |
| ем шөп | (yem shöp) | herb |
| емде- | (yemde-) | cure |
| емен | (yemen) | oak |
| емес | (yemes) | not |
| емтихан | (yemtiykhan) | examination |
| емхана | (yemkhana) | clinic |
| емшек | (yemshek) | breast |
| ең жақсы | (yeng zhaqsı) | best |
| ең көп | (yeng köp) | most |
| еңбек ақы | (yengbek aqı) | wage |
| ер- | (yer-) | follow |
| ер жеткен | (yer zhetken) | adult |
| ерекше | (yerekshe) | especially |
| ереуіл | (yerewil) | strike |
| еркек | (yerkek) | man |
| ерте | (yerte) | early |
| ертек | (yertek) | folktale |
| ертең | (yerteng) | tomorrow |
| ері- | (yeri-) | melt |
| ерін | (yerin) | lip |
| ес | (yes) | memory |
| есек | (yesek) | donkey |
| есеп | (yesep) | account, bill |
| есепте- | (yesepte-) | calculate |
| еске түсір- | (yeske tüsir-) | remember |
| еске түсірт- | (yeske tüsirt-) | remind |
| ескерткіш | (yeskertkish) | monument |
| ескі | (yeski) | old |
| есік | (yesik) | door |
| есімдік | (yesimdik) | pronoun |
| есіне- | (yesine-) | yawn |
| есіт- | (yesit-) | hear |
| ет | (yet) | meat |
| ет дүкені | (yet dükeni) | butcher shop |
| етік | (yetik) | boot |
| етікші | (yetikshi) | shoemaker |
| етістік | (yetistik) | verb |
| еш жерде | (yesh zherde) | nowhere |
| еш кім | (yesh kim) | nobody |
| еш нәрсе | (yesh närse) | nothing |
| ешкі | (yeshki) | goat |
| ешқашан | (yeshqashan) | never |
| | | |
| жаб- | (zhab-) | close, cover |
| жабайы | (zhabayı) | wild |
| жабық | (zhabıq) | closed |
| жабыс- | (zhabıs-) | stick |

| жағ- | (zhagh-) | burn |
|------|----------|------|
| жаға | (zhagha) | coast, collar |
| жағдай | (zhaghday) | condition, situation |
| жаз | (zhaz) | summer |
| жаз- | (zhaz-) | write |
| жаза | (zhaza) | punishment |
| жазала- | (zhazala-) | punish |
| жазу | (zhazuw) | writing |
| жазушы | (zhazuwshı) | writer |
| жазық | (zhazıq) | plain |
| жай- | (zhay-) | spread |
| жайма | (zhayma) | sheet |
| жайылым | (zhayılım) | meadow |
| жақ | (zhaq) | side, way |
| жақсы | (zhaqsı) | fine, good, nice, OK, well |
| жақсырақ | (zhaqsıraq) | better |
| жақтау | (zhaqtaw) | frame |
| жақын | (zhaqın) | near |
| жақында | (zhaqında) | near, soon |
| жақында- | (zhaqında-) | approach |
| жал | (zhal) | rent |
| жалақы | (zhalaqı) | salary |
| жалаңаш | (zhalangash) | bare |
| жалау | (zhalaw) | flag |
| жалбыз | (zhalbız) | mint |
| жалған | (zhalghan) | false, lie |
| жалғыз | (zhalghız) | alone |
| жалқау | (zhalqaw) | lazy |
| жалқаулық | (zhalqawlıq) | laziness |
| жалпы | (zhalpı) | general |
| жалын | (zhalın) | flame |
| жаман | (zhaman) | bad |
| жан- | (zhan-) | burn |
| жанында | (zhanında) | beside, near |
| жаңа | (zhanga) | fresh, new |
| жаңа жыл | (zhanga zhıl) | New Year |
| жаңалық | (zhangalıq) | news |
| жаңбыр | (zhangbır) | rain |
| жаңғақ | (zhangghaq) | walnut |
| жап- | (zhap-) | shut |
| жапырақ | (zhapıraq) | leaf |
| жар- | (zhar-) | split |
| жара | (zhara) | wound |
| жарас- | (zharas-) | suit |
| жарқыра- | (zharqıra-) | shine |
| жартас | (zhartas) | rock |
| жарты | (zhartı) | half |
| жарты ай | (zhartı ay) | crescent |

| жарық | (zharıq) | bright, light |
|------|----------|------|
| жарыс | (zharıs) | competition, race |
| жас | (zhas) | age, young |
| жаса- | (zhasa-) | make |
| жасанды | (zhasandı) | artificial |
| жастық | (zhastıq) | cushion, pillow, youth |
| жастық тысы | (zhastıq tısı) | pillowcase |
| жасыл | (zhasıl) | green |
| жасымық | (zhasımıq) | lentil |
| жасыр- | (zhasır-) | hide |
| жасырын | (zhasırın) | secret |
| жат- | (zhat-) | lie (down) |
| жау | (zhaw) | enemy |
| жау- | (zhaw-) | precipitate |
| жауап | (zhawap) | answer, reply |
| жауап бер- | (zhawap ber-) | answer, reply |
| жаяу | (zhayaw) | pedestrian |
| жәкет | (zhäket) | jacket |
| және | (zhäne) | and |
| жәрдемдес- | (zhärdemdes-) | assist |
| жәшік | (zhäshik) | box |
| же- | (zhe-) | eat |
| жебе | (zhebe) | arrow |
| жедел жәрдем | (zhedel zhärdem) | ambulance |
| жек көр- | (zhek kör-) | hate |
| жексенбі | (zheksenbi) | Sunday |
| жел | (zhel) | wind |
| жел қайық | (zhel kayık) | sailboat |
| желтоқсан | (zheltoqsan) | December |
| желім | (zhelim) | glue |
| жеміс | (zhemis) | fruit |
| жең- | (zheng-) | defeat, win |
| жеңіл | (zhengil) | light |
| жеңіліс | (zhengilis) | defeat |
| жеңіс | (zhengis) | victory |
| жер | (zher) | earth |
| жер сілкініс | (zher silkinis) | earthquake |
| жергілікті үкімет | (zhergilikti ükimet) | municipality |
| жет- | (zhet-) | arrive, reach |
| жеткілікті | (zhetkilikti) | enough, sufficient |
| жетпіс | (zhetpis) | seventy |
| жеті | (zheti) | seven |
| жетілген | (zhetilgen) | perfect |
| жина- | (zhiyna-) | collect |

| | | |
|---|---|---|
| жиналыс | (zhiynalıs) | meeting |
| жиырма | (zhiyırma) | twenty |
| жиі | (zhiyi) | often |
| жиіркену | (zhiyirkenuw) | disgust |
| жоғал- | (zhoghal-) | disappear |
| жоғалт- | (zhoghalt-) | lose |
| жоғарыда | (zhogharıda) | above |
| жоқ | (zhoq) | no |
| жол | (zhol) | road, way |
| жол ақы | (zhol aqı) | fare |
| жолаушы | (zholawshı) | passenger |
| жолбарыс | (zholbarıs) | tiger |
| жолдың қиылысы | (zholdıng qiyılısı) | crosswalk |
| жомарт | (zhomart) | generous |
| жөнде- | (zhönde-) | mend, repair |
| жөтел | (zhötel) | cough |
| жу- | (zhuw-) | wash |
| жуан | (zhuwan) | thick |
| журнал | (zhurnal) | magazine |
| журналист | (zhurnalist) | journalist |
| жұқа | (zhuqa) | fine, thin |
| жұлдыз | (zhuldız) | star |
| жұма | (zhuma) | Friday |
| жұмса- | (zhumsa-) | spend |
| жұмсақ | (zhumsaq) | soft |
| жұмыртқа | (zhumırtqa) | egg |
| жұмыс | (zhumıs) | job |
| жұмыс істе- | (zhumıs iste-) | work |
| жұмысшы | (zhumısshı) | worker |
| жүгері | (zhügeri) | corn |
| жүгір- | (zhügir-) | run |
| жүз | (zhüz) | hundred |
| жүз- | (zhüz-) | swim |
| жүзу | (zhüzuw) | swimming |
| жүзім | (zhüzim) | grape |
| жүйке | (zhüyke) | nerve |
| жүк | (zhük) | baggage, cargo |
| жүк тасыйтын машина | (zhük tasıytın mashina) | truck |
| жүкті | (zhükti) | pregnant |
| жүктілік | (zhüktilik) | pregnancy |
| жүлде | (zhülde) | prize |
| жүн | (zhün) | wool |
| жүр- | (zhür-) | walk |
| жүрек | (zhürek) | heart |
| жыл | (zhıl) | year |
| жыла- | (zhıla-) | cry, weep |
| жылан | (zhılan) | snake |

| | | |
|---|---|---|
| жылдам | (zhıldam) | fast, speedy |
| жылдамдық | (zhıldamdıq) | speed |
| жылдық мереке | (zhıldıq mereke) | anniversary |
| жылжы- | (zhılzhı-) | slide |
| жылы | (zhılı) | lukewarm, warm |
| жын | (zhın) | ghost |
| жынды | (zhındı) | crazy |
| жындылық | (zhındılıq) | insanity |
| жырт- | (zhırt-) | tear |
| жібек | (zhibek) | silk |
| жібер- | (zhiber-) | send |
| жіңішке | (zhingishke) | slim |
| | | |
| залал | (zalal) | harm |
| заң | (zang) | law |
| заңгер | (zangger) | lawyer |
| зат | (zat) | matter, thing |
| зат есім | (zat yesim) | noun |
| зәйтүн | (zäytun) | olive |
| зеңбірек | (zengbirek) | cannon |
| зергер | (zerger) | jeweler |
| зерек | (zerek) | intelligent |
| зерттеу | (zerttew) | research |
| зеріг- | (zerig-) | bored: be bored |
| зеріктіретін | (zeriktiretin) | boring |
| зират | (ziyrat) | cemetery |
| зиялы | (ziyalı) | intellectual |
| зиян | (ziyan) | damage, loss |
| зиянды | (ziyandı) | harmful |
| зоопарк | (zoopark) | zoo |
| | | |
| идиома | (idioma) | idiom |
| иә | (iyä) | yes |
| иек | (iyek) | chin |
| ине | (iyne) | needle |
| инженер | (inzhener) | engineer |
| инфекция | (infektsiya) | infection |
| инфляция | (inflyatsiya) | inflation |
| информация | (informatsiya) | information |
| ит | (iyt) | dog |
| итер- | (iter-) | push |
| иық | (iyıq) | shoulder |
| иіс | (iyis) | smell |
| иіс шығар- | (iyis shıghar-) | smell |
| иіске- | (iyiske-) | smell |
| | | |
| календарь | (kalendar') | calendar |
| канал | (kanal) | canal, channel |

| | | |
|---|---|---|
| капитан | (kapitan) | captain |
| капуста | (kapusta) | cabbage |
| карикатура | (karikatura) | cartoon |
| карта | (karta) | map, playing card |
| картоп | (kartop) | potato |
| кассет | (kasset) | cassette |
| кассир | (kassir) | cashier |
| кастрюль | (kastryul') | saucepan |
| кафе | (kafe) | café |
| каштан | (kashtan) | chestnut |
| кәмпит | (kämpit) | candy |
| кәрзінкә | (kärzinkä) | basket |
| кәрі | (käri) | old |
| кәсіп | (käsip) | occupation |
| квитанция | (kvitantsiya) | receipt |
| кедей | (kedey) | poor |
| кездес- | (kezdes-) | meet |
| кездесу | (kezdesuw) | appointment |
| кейбір | (keybir) | some |
| кейде | (keyde) | sometimes |
| кейінге қалдыр- | (keyinge qaldır-) | postpone |
| кейінге қалу | (keyinge qaluw) | delay |
| кел- | (kel-) | arrive, come, visit |
| келесі | (kelesi) | next |
| келу | (keluw) | arrival, visit |
| келіс- | (kelis-) | agree |
| келісім | (kelisim) | agreement |
| кеме | (keme) | ship |
| кемпірқосақ | (kempirqosaq) | rainbow |
| кең | (keng) | loose, broad, spacious, wide |
| керек бол- | (kerek bol-) | need |
| керең | (kereng) | deaf |
| кереңдік | (kerengdik) | deafness |
| кереует | (kerewet) | bed |
| кес- | (kes-) | cut |
| кесе | (kese) | bowl |
| кет- | (ket-) | depart, leave |
| кету | (ketuw) | departure |
| кеш | (kesh) | evening, late |
| кеше | (keshe) | yesterday |
| кешкі ас | (keshki as) | dinner |
| кешір- | (keshir-) | forgive |
| кешірім | (keshirim) | apology |
| кешірім сұра- | (keshirim sura-) | apologize |

| | | |
|---|---|---|
| ки- | (kiy-) | put on, wear |
| кино | (kino) | cinema |
| киім | (kiyim) | clothes |
| класс | (klass) | classroom |
| клуб | (klub) | club |
| колбаса | (kolbasa) | sausage |
| комедия | (komediya) | comedy |
| компания | (kompaniya) | company, firm |
| композитор | (kompozitor) | composer |
| компьютер | (komp'yuter) | computer |
| конверт | (konvert) | envelope |
| концерт | (kontsert) | concert |
| король | (korol') | king |
| коррупция | (korruptsiya) | corruption |
| костюм | (kostyum) | suit |
| кофе | (kofe) | coffee |
| көбелек | (köbelek) | butterfly |
| көбей- | (köbey-) | increase |
| көбейту | (köbeytuw) | multiplication |
| көбірек | (köbirek) | more |
| көгершін | (kögershin) | pigeon |
| көз | (köz) | eye |
| көзілдірік | (közildirik) | glasses |
| көйлек | (köylek) | dress, shirt |
| көк | (kök) | blue |
| көк жиек | (kök zhiyek) | horizon |
| көкек | (kökek) | April |
| көкқұтан | (kökqutan) | stork |
| көкөніс | (kökönis) | vegetable |
| көктем | (köktem) | spring |
| көкірек | (kökirek) | chest |
| көл | (köl) | lake |
| көлеңке | (kölengke) | shade, shadow |
| көм- | (köm-) | bury |
| көмек | (kömek) | assistance, help |
| көмектес- | (kömektes-) | help |
| көмір | (kömir) | coal |
| көңілсіз | (köngilsiz) | sad |
| көп | (köp) | many, much |
| көп халық | (köp khalıq) | crowd |
| көпшілік | (köpshilik) | majority |
| көпір | (köpir) | bridge |
| көр- | (kör-) | see |
| көре алма- | (köre alma-) | envy |
| көрме | (körme) | exhibition |
| көрпе | (körpe) | quilt |
| көрсет- | (körset-) | show |
| көрші | (körshi) | neighbor |
| көршілік | (körshilik) | neighborhood |
| көріксіз | (köriksiz) | ugly |

| | | |
|---|---|---|
| көрін- | (körin-) | appear |
| көтер- | (köter-) | lift, raise |
| көтеріліс | (köterilis) | rebellion |
| көтерме сауда | (köterme sawda) | wholesale |
| көше | (köshe) | street |
| кран | (kran) | faucet |
| кредит | (kredit) | credit |
| кресло | (kreslo) | armchair |
| крокодил | (krokodil) | crocodile |
| куә | (kuwä) | witness |
| култивация | (kultivatsiya) | cultivation |
| күлпынай | (kulpınay) | strawberry |
| күз | (küz) | autumn |
| күй | (küy) | tune |
| күйеу | (küyew) | bridegroom, husband |
| күл | (kül) | ash |
| күл- | (kül-) | laugh |
| күлгін | (külgin) | purple |
| күлімсіре- | (külimsire-) | smile |
| күмән | (kümän) | doubt |
| күміс | (kümis) | silver |
| күн | (kün) | day, sun |
| күн бату | (kün batuw) | sunset |
| күн күркіреу | (kün kürkirew) | thunder |
| күн шығу | (kün shıghuw) | sunrise |
| күнәсіздік | (künäsizdik) | innocence |
| күнбағыс | (künbaghıs) | sunflower |
| күндіз | (kündiz) | daytime |
| күрек | (kürek) | shovel, spade |
| күрес | (küres) | wrestling |
| күрес- | (küres-) | fight |
| күрке тауық | (kürke tawıq) | turkey |
| күріш | (kürish) | rice |
| күт- | (küt-) | wait |
| күтпеген | (kütpegen) | sudden |
| күш | (küsh) | force, power, strength |
| күшті | (küshti) | powerful, strong |
| кілем | (kilem) | carpet |
| кілт | (kilt) | key, wrench |
| кім | (kim) | who |
| кір- | (kir-) | enter |
| кірпік | (kirpik) | eyelash |
| кірпіш | (kirpish) | brick |
| кіру | (kiruw) | entrance |
| кіріс | (kiris) | income |
| кіріспе | (kirispe) | preface |
| кітап | (kitap) | book |
| кітап дүкені | (kitap dükeni) | bookshop |
| кітап сатушы | (kitap satuwshı) | bookseller |
| кітап шкафы | (kitap shkafı) | bookcase |
| кітапхана | (kitapkhana) | library |
| кіші | (kishi) | small |
| кішкентай | (kishkentay) | little |
| -қа, -ке | (-qa, -ke) | to |
| қабат | (qabat) | storey |
| қабық | (qabıq) | bark |
| қабылда- | (qabılda-) | accept |
| қабырға | (qabırgha) | wall |
| қағаз | (qaghaz) | paper |
| қадам | (qadam) | step |
| қажетті | (qazhetti) | necessary |
| қажеттілік | (qazhettilik) | necessity, need |
| қаз | (qaz) | goose |
| қаз- | (qaz-) | dig |
| қазан | (qazan) | October |
| қазына | (qazına) | treasure |
| қазір | (qazir) | now |
| қазіргі | (qazirgi) | present |
| қай жерде | (qay zherde) | where |
| қай жерге | (qay zherge) | where |
| қаймақ | (qaymaq) | cream |
| қайна- | (qayna-) | boil |
| қайнатпа | (qaynatpa) | jam |
| қайсы | (qaysı) | which |
| қайт- | (qayt-) | return |
| қайтадан | (qaytadan) | again |
| қайтала- | (qaytala-) | repeat |
| қайшы | (qayshı) | scissors |
| қайық | (qayıq) | boat |
| қақпа | (qaqpa) | gate |
| қақпақ | (qaqpaq) | lid |
| қал- | (qal-) | remain, stay |
| қала | (qala) | city, town |
| қала- | (qala-) | want |
| қалай | (qalay) | how |
| қалам | (qalam) | pen |
| қалампыр | (qalampır) | carnation |
| қаланың шеті | (qalanıng sheti) | suburb |
| қалау | (qalaw) | desire |
| қалпақ | (qalpaq) | hat |

| қалта | (qalta) | pocket |
|---|---|---|
| қалы | (qalı) | rug |
| қалың | (qalıng) | thick |
| қалыңдық | (qalıngdıq) | bride |
| қан | (qan) | blood |
| қан қысымы | (qan qısımı) | blood pressure |
| қана- | (qana-) | bleed |
| қанат | (qanat) | wing |
| қанау | (qanaw) | oppression |
| қанжар | (qanzhar) | dagger |
| қант | (qant) | sugar |
| қанша | (qansha) | how much |
| қаңқа | (qangqa) | skeleton |
| қаңтар | (qangtar) | January |
| қапшық | (qapshıq) | purse, wallet |
| қар | (qar) | snow |
| қара | (qara) | black |
| қара мал | (qara mal) | cattle |
| қара өрік | (qara örik) | plum |
| қара- | (qara-) | look |
| қарағай | (qaraghay) | pine |
| қарай | (qaray) | towards |
| қарама-қарсы | (qarama-qarsı) | opposite |
| қараңғы | (qarangghı) | dark |
| қараңғылық | (qarangghılıq) | darkness |
| қарапайым | (qarapayım) | simple |
| қараша | (qarasha) | November |
| қарбыз | (qarbız) | watermelon |
| қарға | (qargha) | crow |
| қаржыландыру | (qarzhılandıruw) | investment |
| қарлығаш | (qarlıghash) | swallow |
| қарсы | (qarsı) | against |
| қару | (qaruw) | gun |
| қарыз | (qarız) | debt, loan |
| қарыз ал- | (qarız al-) | borrow |
| қарын | (qarın) | belly |
| қарындаш | (qarındash) | pencil |
| қас | (qas) | eyebrow |
| қасапшы | (qasapshı) | butcher |
| қасқыр | (qasqır) | wolf |
| қасық | (qasıq) | spoon |
| қатал | (qatal) | cruel |
| қатар | (qatar) | row |
| қате | (qate) | fault, mistake, wrong |
| қатта- | (qatta-) | fold |
| қатты | (qattı) | hard, loud |
| қауын | (qawın) | melon |

| қауіп | (qawip) | danger |
|---|---|---|
| қауіпсіз | (qawipsiz) | safe |
| қауіпті | (qawipti) | dangerous |
| қаш- | (qash-) | escape, flee, run away |
| қашан | (qashan) | when |
| қиын | (qiyın) | difficult, hard |
| қияр | (qiyar) | cucumber |
| қоғам | (qogham) | society |
| қожайын | (qozhayın) | host |
| қозғал- | (qozghal-) | move |
| қозу | (qozuw) | excitement |
| қозы | (qozı) | lamb |
| қозықарын | (qozıqarın) | mushroom |
| қой | (qoy) | sheep |
| қой еті | (qoy yeti) | mutton |
| қой- | (qoy-) | put |
| қоқыс | (qoqıs) | trash |
| қол | (qol) | arm, hand |
| қол жуғыш | (qol zhuwghısh) | sink |
| қол қой- | (qol qoy-) | sign |
| қол орамал | (qol oramal) | handkerchief |
| қол сағат | (qol saghat) | watch |
| қол соз- | (qol soz-) | reach |
| қол сөмке | (qol sömke) | handbag |
| қол шатыр | (qol shatır) | umbrella |
| қолайлы | (qolaylı) | convenient |
| қолғап | (qolghap) | glove |
| қолдан- | (qoldan-) | use |
| қолтаңба | (qoltangba) | signature |
| қонақ | (qonaq) | guest |
| қонақ үйі | (qonaq üyi) | hotel |
| қоңыр | (qongır) | brown |
| қоңырау | (qongıraw) | bell |
| қораз | (qoraz) | rooster |
| қорға- | (qorgha-) | defend, protect |
| қорғасын | (qorghasın) | lead |
| қорғау | (qorghaw) | defense |
| қорқ- | (qorq-) | afraid: be afraid |
| қорқақ | (qorqaq) | coward |
| қорқақтық | (qorqaqtıq) | cowardice |
| қорқыныш | (qorqınısh) | fear |
| қорша- | (qorsha-) | surround |
| қоршау | (qorshaw) | siege |
| қос- | (qos-) | add |
| қосу | (qosuw) | addition |
| қош болыңыз | (qosh bolıngız) | bye-bye |

| Kazakh | Transcription | English |
|--------|---------------|---------|
| қош келдіңіз | (qosh keldingiz) | welcome |
| қоян | (qoyan) | rabbit |
| қуаныш | (quwanısh) | joy |
| қуыр- | (quwır-) | roast |
| құдай | (quday) | God |
| құй- | (quy-) | pour |
| құйрық | (quyrıq) | tail |
| құла- | (qula-) | fall |
| құлақ | (qulaq) | ear |
| құлып | (qulıp) | lock |
| құм | (qum) | sand |
| құмыра | (qumıra) | jug |
| құмырсқа | (qumırsqa) | ant |
| құн | (qun) | value |
| құр- | (qur-) | build |
| құрал | (qural) | equipment |
| құрбақа | (qurbaqa) | frog |
| құрбан | (qurban) | sacrifice |
| құрға- | (qurgha-) | dry |
| құрғақ | (qurghaq) | dry |
| құрғақшылық | (qurghaqshılıq) | drought |
| құрма | (qurma) | date |
| құрмет | (qurmet) | respect |
| құрметте- | (qurmette-) | respect |
| құрт | (qurt) | worm |
| құрт-құмырсқа | (qurt-qumırsqa) | insect |
| құрылыс | (qurılıs) | building |
| құс | (qus) | bird |
| құс жүні | (qus zhüni) | feather |
| құс- | (qus-) | vomit |
| құтқар- | (qutqar-) | rescue |
| құттықта- | (quttıqta-) | congratulate |
| құттықтау | (quttıqtaw) | congratulation |
| құшақта- | (qushaqta-) | embrace |
| қыз | (qız) | daughter |
| қыз бала | (qız bala) | girl |
| қызғалдақ | (qızghaldaq) | tulip |
| қызғаншақ | (qızghanshaq) | jealous |
| қызғылт | (qızghılt) | pink |
| қызметкер | (qızmetker) | official |
| қызметші | (qızmetshi) | servant |
| қызу | (qızuw) | fever |
| қызығу | (qızığhuw) | interest |
| қызық | (qızıq) | interesting |
| қызыл | (qızıl) | red |
| қызыл-сары | (qızıl-sarı) | orange |
| қыл- | (qıl-) | do |
| қылмыс | (qılmıs) | crime |
| қылмыскер | (qılmısker) | criminal |
| қылыш | (qılısh) | sword |
| қымбат | (qımbat) | expensive |
| қымбатты | (qımbattı) | dear |
| қыр- | (qır-) | scrape |
| қыркүйек | (qırküyek) | September |
| қырық | (qırıq) | forty |
| қыс | (qıs) | winter |
| қысқа | (qısqa) | short |
| қыша | (qısha) | mustard |
| қышқыл | (qishqıl) | sour |
| лампа | (lampa) | lamp |
| лақтыр- | (laqtır-) | throw |
| лас | (las) | dirty |
| лекция | (lektsiya) | lecture |
| лимон | (limon) | lemon |
| лингвист | (lingwist) | linguist |
| лифт | (lift) | elevator |
| магнитофон | (magnitofon) | tape recorder |
| мазала- | (mazala-) | bother |
| май | (may) | fat, oil |
| майда ақша | (mayda aqsha) | change |
| маймыл | (maymıl) | monkey |
| мақал | (maqal) | proverb |
| мақала | (maqala) | article |
| мақсат | (maqsat) | purpose |
| мақта | (maqta) | cotton |
| мақта- | (maqta-) | praise |
| мақтан- | (maqtan-) | boast |
| мақтаныш | (maqtanısh) | pride |
| мақұлдау | (maquldaw) | approval |
| мамыр | (mamır) | May |
| маңдай | (mangday) | forehead |
| маңызды | (mangızdı) | important |
| марка | (marka) | stamp |
| мас | (mas) | drunk |
| маса | (masa) | mosquito |
| математика | (matematika) | mathematics |
| материал | (material) | material |
| матч | (match) | match |
| маусым | (mawsım) | June |
| махаббат | (makhabbat) | love |
| машина | (mashina) | car |
| машине | (mashine) | machine |
| машинка | (mashinka) | typewriter |
| мәдениет | (mädeniyet) | culture |
| мәлімет | (mälimet) | data |

| | | |
|---|---|---|
| мәңгілік | (mänggilik) | eternity |
| мебель | (mebel') | furniture |
| мед бибі | (med biybi) | nurse |
| медицина | (meditsina) | medicine |
| мезгіл | (mezgil) | season |
| меймандостық | (meymandostıq) | hospitality |
| мейрам | (meyram) | ceremony, holiday |
| мейрамдау | (meyramdaw) | celebration |
| мейірімді | (meyirimdi) | kind |
| мектеп | (mektep) | school |
| мемлекет | (memleket) | state |
| мен | (men) | by, I |
| мені | (meni) | me |
| менікі | (meniki) | mine |
| менің | (mening) | my |
| меню | (menyu) | menu |
| меңгеруші | (menggeruwshi) | manager |
| мереке | (mereke) | festival |
| мерекеле- | (merekele-) | celebrate |
| металл | (metall) | metal |
| метро | (metro) | subway |
| мешіт | (meshit) | mosque |
| ми | (miy) | brain |
| милиция | (militsiya) | policeman |
| миллиард | (milliard) | billion |
| миллион | (million) | million |
| миндаль | (mindal') | almond |
| министр | (ministr) | minister |
| минут | (minut) | minute |
| мифология | (mifologiya) | mythology |
| мода | (moda) | fashion |
| мойын | (moyın) | neck |
| мойындама- | (moyındama-) | deny |
| момент | (moment) | moment |
| мотор | (motor) | engine |
| мотоцикл | (mototsikl) | motorcycle |
| мөлшер | (mölsher) | quantity |
| мускул | (muskul) | muscle |
| музей | (muzey) | museum |
| музыка | (muzıka) | music |
| музыкант | (muzıkant) | musician |
| мұғалім | (mughalim) | teacher |
| мұз | (muz) | ice |
| мұнай | (munay) | oil |
| мұнара | (munara) | tower |
| мұнда | (munda) | here |
| мұржа | (murzha) | chimney |
| мұрт | (murt) | mustache |
| мұрын | (murın) | nose |

| | | |
|---|---|---|
| мұсылман | (musılman) | Muslim |
| мұхит | (mukhiyt) | ocean |
| мүйіз | (müyiz) | horn |
| мүмкін | (mümkin) | possible, probably |
| мүмкін емес | (mümkin yemes) | impossible |
| мүмкіндік | (mümkindik) | possibility |
| мүсін | (müsin) | statue |
| мүше | (müshe) | member |
| мылқау | (mılqaw) | mute |
| мылтық | (mıltıq) | rifle |
| мың | (mıng) | thousand |
| мырза | (mırza) | gentleman |
| мыс | (mıs) | copper |
| мысал | (mısal) | example |
| мысық | (mısıq) | cat |
| мін- | (min-) | get on |
| міндет | (mindet) | duty |
| мініп жүр- | (minip zhür-) | ride |
| нағашы аға | (naghashı agha) | uncle |
| назар | (nazar) | attention |
| найза | (nayza) | spear |
| найзағай | (nayzaghay) | lightning |
| нақты | (naqtı) | concrete |
| нақты ақша | (naqtı aqsha) | cash |
| намаз оқы- | (namaz oqı-) | pray |
| намыс | (namıs) | honor |
| -нан, -нен | (-nan, -nen) | from |
| нан | (nan) | bread |
| насихат | (nasiykhat) | propaganda |
| наубайхана | (nawbaykhana) | bakery |
| наубайшы | (nawbayshı) | baker |
| наурыз | (nawrız) | March |
| нәтиже | (nätiyzhe) | result |
| нәзік | (näzik) | gentle |
| не | (ne) | what |
| не ... не | (ne ... ne) | either ... or |
| неге | (nege) | why |
| негізгі | (negizgi) | main |
| немере | (nemere) | grandchild |
| немесе | (nemese) | or |
| ниет | (niyet) | intention |
| нөл | (nöl) | zero |
| нүкте | (nükte) | period |
| одақ | (odaq) | union |
| одеял | (odeyal) | blanket |

| | | |
|---|---|---|
| ой | (oy) | idea, thought |
| ойла- | (oyla-) | think |
| ойна- | (oyna-) | play |
| ойын | (oyın) | game |
| ойын-сауық | (oyın-sawıq) | entertainment |
| ойыншық | (oyınshıq) | toy |
| оқиға | (oqiygha) | event |
| оқу ақысы | (oquw aqısı) | tuition |
| оқушы | (oquwshı) | reader |
| оқы- | (oqı-) | read, study |
| оқыт- | (oqıt-) | teach |
| ол | (ol) | he, it, she |
| олар | (olar) | they, those |
| оларды | (olardı) | them |
| олардың | (olardıng) | their |
| омыртқа | (omırtqa) | spine |
| он | (on) | ten |
| он алты | (on altı) | sixteen |
| он бес | (on bes) | fifteen |
| он бір | (on bir) | eleven |
| он екі | (on yeki) | twelve |
| он жеті | (on zheti) | seventeen |
| он сегіз | (on segiz) | eighteen |
| он тоғыз | (on toghız) | nineteen |
| он төрт | (on tört) | fourteen |
| он үш | (on üsh) | thirteen |
| оны | (onı) | her, him |
| оның | (onıng) | her, his, its |
| онікі | (oniki) | its |
| онікі | (oniki) | hers, his |
| оң | (ong) | right |
| оңай | (ongay) | easy |
| оңтүстік | (ongtüstik) | south |
| опера | (opera) | opera |
| операция | (operatsiya) | operation |
| оптик | (optiyk) | optician |
| ора- | (ora-) | wrap |
| ораза | (oraza) | fast |
| орақ | (oraq) | sickle |
| орман | (orman) | forest |
| орман жаңғақ | (orman zhangghaq) | hazelnut |
| орналас- | (ornalas-) | situated: be situated |
| орта | (orta) | medium, middle |
| орталық | (ortalıq) | center |
| орын | (orın) | place, seat |
| орын сақтау | (orın saqtaw) | reservation |
| орындық | (orındıq) | chair, stool |
| осында | (osında) | here |
| осындай | (osınday) | such |
| от | (ot) | fire |
| отар | (otar) | herd |
| отставкаға шық- | (otstavkagha shıq-) | retire |
| отыз | (otız) | thirty |
| отыр- | (otır-) | sit |
| офис | (ofis) | office |
| офицер | (ofitser) | officer |
| оян- | (oyan-) | awake, wake |
| оят- | (oyat-) | awake, wake |
| | | |
| өгіз | (ögiz) | ox |
| өзгерт- | (özgert-) | change |
| өзен | (özen) | river |
| өзі | (özi) | herself, himself, itself |
| өзім | (özim) | myself |
| өзіміз | (özimiz) | ourselves |
| өзін ұста- | (özin usta-) | behave |
| өзің | (özing) | yourself |
| өзіңіз | (özingiz) | yourselves |
| өкпе | (ökpe) | lung |
| өкініш | (ökinish) | regret |
| өл- | (öl-) | die |
| өлең | (öleng) | poem, song |
| өлең айт- | (öleng ayt-) | sing |
| өлтір- | (öltir-) | kill |
| өлшем | (ölshem) | measure |
| өлік | (ölik) | dead |
| өлім | (ölim) | death |
| өмір | (ömir) | life |
| өндір- | (öndir-) | produce |
| өнер | (öner) | art |
| өрескел | (öreskel) | rude |
| өрмекші | (örmekshi) | spider |
| өрмеле- | (örmele-) | climb |
| өрт | (ört) | fire |
| өрік | (örik) | apricot |
| өс- | (ös-) | grow |
| өсу | (ösuw) | growth |
| өсімдік | (ösimdik) | plant |
| өт- | (öt-) | pass |
| өте | (öte) | very |
| өткен | (ötken) | last |
| өткір | (ötkir) | sharp |
| өтін- | (ötin-) | apply, request |
| өтінемін | (ötinemin) | please |

| | | |
|---|---|---|
| өш | (ösh) | revenge |
| өшір- | (öshir-) | erase, extinguish, put out |
| өшіргіш | (öshirgish) | eraser |
| пайғамбар | (payghambar) | prophet |
| пайда | (payda) | benefit, interest, profit |
| пайдалы | (paydalı) | useful |
| палау | (palaw) | rice |
| пальто | (pal'to) | overcoat |
| пар | (par) | pair |
| параграф | (paragraf) | paragraph |
| парад | (parad) | parade |
| паралич | (paralich) | paralysis |
| парк | (park) | park |
| парта | (parta) | desk |
| партия | (partiya) | party |
| паспорт | (pasport) | passport |
| пациент | (patsient) | patient |
| пәтер | (päter) | apartment |
| перде | (perde) | curtain |
| періште | (perishte) | angel |
| петрушка | (petrushka) | parsley |
| печенье | (pechen'ye) | cookie |
| пеш | (pesh) | stove |
| пижама | (piyzhama) | pajamas |
| пияз | (piyaz) | onion |
| планета | (planeta) | planet |
| пластинка | (plastinka) | record |
| платформа | (platforma) | platform |
| плащ | (plashch) | raincoat |
| плёнка | (plyonka) | film |
| пляж | (plyazh) | beach |
| поезд | (poyezd) | train |
| помидор | (pomidor) | tomato |
| поп | (pop) | priest |
| посылка | (posılka) | parcel |
| пошта | (poshta) | post office |
| пошта жәшігі | (poshta zhäshigi) | mailbox |
| пошта шығындары | (poshta shıghındarı) | postage |
| пошташы | (poshtashı) | mailman |
| поэзия | (poeziya) | poetry |
| президент | (prezident) | president |
| премьер-министр | (prem'yer-ministr) | prime minister |
| проблема | (problema) | problem |

| | | |
|---|---|---|
| провинция | (provintsiya) | province |
| программа | (programma) | program |
| проза | (proza) | prose |
| проспект | (prospekt) | avenue |
| пулемет | (pulemet) | machine gun |
| пышақ | (pıshaq) | knife |
| пікір | (pikir) | opinion |
| піл | (pil) | elephant |
| піс- | (pis-) | cook |
| піскен | (pisken) | ripe |
| пісте | (piste) | pistachio |
| пісір- | (pisir-) | cook |
| пьеса | (p'yesa) | play |
| радио | (radio) | radio |
| размер | (razmer) | size |
| рак | (rak) | cancer |
| рақат | (raqat) | pleasure |
| рақаттан- | (raqattan-) | enjoy |
| рахмет айт- | (rakhmet ayt-) | thank |
| реализм | (realizm) | realism |
| рейс | (reys) | flight |
| ренжіген | (renzhigen) | sorry |
| ресми | (resmiy) | official |
| республика | (respublika) | republic |
| ресторан | (restoran) | restaurant |
| рецепт | (retsept) | prescription |
| риза | (riyza) | glad |
| роза | (roza) | rose |
| роман | (roman) | novel |
| ромашка | (romashka) | daisy |
| ромбы | (rombı) | diamond |
| рух | (rukh) | spirit |
| рұқсат ет- | (ruqsat et-) | permit |
| сабақ | (sabaq) | lesson |
| сабан | (saban) | straw |
| сабын | (sabın) | soap |
| сабырлы | (sabırlı) | patient |
| сағат | (saghat) | clock, hour |
| сағат жөндеуші | (saghat zhöndewshi) | watchmaker |
| садақ | (sadaq) | bow |
| сайла- | (sayla-) | elect |
| сайлау | (saylaw) | election |
| сақал | (saqal) | beard |
| сақта- | (saqta-) | keep |
| сақтан | (saqtan) | precaution |
| сақтан- | (saqtan-) | prevent |
| сақтандыру | (saqtandıruw) | insurance |

| | | |
|---|---|---|
| салат | (salat) | lettuce, salad |
| салқын | (salqın) | cool |
| салмақты | (salmaqtı) | serious |
| салфетка | (salfetka) | napkin |
| салық | (salıq) | tax |
| салыстыру | (salıstıruw) | comparison |
| самолёт | (samolyot) | airplane, plane |
| сан | (san) | amount, number, thigh |
| сана- | (sana-) | count |
| сапа | (sapa) | quality |
| сапар | (sapar) | journey |
| сарай | (saray) | palace |
| сары | (sarı) | yellow |
| сары май | (sarı may) | butter |
| сарымсақ | (sarımsaq) | garlic |
| сат- | (sat-) | sell |
| сату | (satuw) | sale |
| сатушы | (satuwshı) | salesperson, seller |
| саты | (satı) | ladder, stairs |
| сатып ал- | (satıp al-) | buy, shop |
| сатып алушы | (satıp aluwshı) | buyer, customer |
| сау | (saw) | healthy |
| сауатты | (sawattı) | literate |
| саусақ | (sawsaq) | finger |
| сауық кеші | (sawıq keshi) | party |
| сахна | (sakhna) | stage |
| саясат | (sayasat) | politics |
| саяхат | (sayakhat) | travel |
| сәбіз | (säbiz) | carrot |
| сәлем | (sälem) | hello |
| сәрсенбі | (särsenbi) | Wednesday |
| сәттілік | (sättilik) | luck |
| сәуле | (säwlye) | ray |
| сәулетші | (säwletshi) | architect |
| светофор | (svetofor) | traffic light |
| свитер | (sviter) | sweater |
| себеп | (sebep) | cause, reason |
| сегіз | (segiz) | eight |
| сез- | (sez-) | feel |
| сезім | (sezim) | feeling |
| сейсенбі | (seysenbi) | Tuesday |
| секретарь | (sekretar') | secretary |
| сексен | (seksen) | eighty |
| секта | (sekta) | sect |
| секунд | (sekund) | second |
| секция | (sektsiya) | section |
| секір- | (sekir-) | jump |
| селдерей | (selderey) | celery |
| семья | (sem'ya) | family |
| семіз | (semiz) | fat |
| сен | (sen) | you |
| сен- | (sen-) | believe |
| сенбі | (senbi) | Saturday |
| сенікі | (seniki) | yours |
| сенім | (senim) | belief, confidence, faith |
| сенің | (sening) | your |
| серуенде- | (seruwende-) | stroll |
| серік | (serik) | partner |
| серіппе | (serippe) | spring |
| символ | (simvol) | symbol |
| сиқыр | (siyqır) | magic, spell |
| сипа- | (siypa-) | stroke |
| сиыр | (siyır) | cow |
| сиыр еті | (siyır yeti) | beef |
| сия | (siya) | ink |
| сияқты | (siyaqtı) | as if, like |
| скульптура | (skul'ptura) | sculpture |
| соғыс | (soghıs) | war |
| соқа | (soqa) | plow |
| соқыр | (soqır) | blind |
| соқырлық | (soqırlıq) | blindness |
| сол | (sol) | left, that |
| сол уақытта | (sol waqıtta) | then |
| солтүстік | (soltüstik) | north |
| сонан кейін | (sonan keyin) | then |
| сонда | (sonda) | there |
| сондықтан | (sondıqtan) | because, therefore |
| соң | (song) | after, end |
| соңғы | (songghı) | last |
| сорпа | (sorpa) | soup |
| сот | (sot) | court, judge |
| сөз | (söz) | speech, word |
| сөздік | (sözdik) | dictionary |
| сөйле- | (söyle-) | speak |
| сөйлем | (söylem) | sentence |
| сөмке | (sömke) | bag |
| сөре | (söre) | shelf |
| спорт | (sport) | sport |
| станция | (stantsiya) | station |
| стол | (stol) | table |
| студент | (student) | student |
| су | (suw) | water |
| су ағыны | (suw aghını) | flood |
| сулы | (suwlı) | wet |

| | | |
|---|---|---|
| сурет | (suwret) | painting, picture |
| суретте- | (suwrette-) | describe |
| суреттеу | (suwrettew) | description |
| суретші | (suwretshi) | artist |
| суффикс | (suffiks) | suffix |
| суық | (suwıq) | cold |
| сұйықтық | (suyıqtıq) | liquid |
| сұлулық | (suluwlıq) | beauty |
| сұр | (sur) | grey |
| сұра- | (sura-) | ask |
| сұрақ | (suraq) | question |
| сүзгіш | (süzgish) | strainer |
| сүй- | (süy-) | love |
| сүйек | (süyek) | bone |
| сүйен- | (süyen-) | rely |
| сүйкімді | (süykimdi) | pretty |
| сүйіс- | (süyis-) | kiss |
| сүлгі | (sülgi) | towel |
| сүңгі- | (sünggi-) | dive |
| сүңгуір қайық | (süngguwir qayıq) | submarine |
| сүт | (süt) | milk |
| сызғыш | (sızghısh) | ruler |
| сызу | (sızuw) | drawing |
| сызық | (sızıq) | line |
| сыйла- | (sıyla-) | present |
| сылтау | (sıltaw) | excuse |
| сым | (sım) | wire |
| сын есім | (sın yesim) | adjective |
| сына- | (sına-) | test |
| сындыр- | (sındır-) | break |
| сынық | (sınıq) | broken |
| сыпыр- | (sıpır-) | sweep |
| сыпырғыш | (sıpırghısh) | broom |
| сыра | (sıra) | beer |
| сыртында | (sırtında) | outside |
| сіз | (siz) | you |
| сіздер | (sizder) | you |
| сіздікі | (sizdiki) | yours |
| сіздің | (sizding) | your |
| сій- | (siy-) | urinate |
| сілк- | (silk-) | shake |
| сіңлі | (singli) | sister |
| сірке суы | (sirke suwı) | vinegar |
| сіріңке | (siringke) | match |
| -та, -те | (-ta, -te) | at, in |
| таб- | (tab-) | find |
| таба | (taba) | pan |
| табақ | (tabaq) | dish, plate |
| табақша | (tabaqsha) | saucer |
| табиғат | (tabiyghat) | nature |
| табиғи | (tabiyghiy) | natural |
| таблетка | (tabletka) | pill |
| табыну | (tabınuw) | worship |
| табыс | (tabıs) | success |
| табысқа жет- | (tabısqa zhet-) | succeed |
| тағайындау | (taghayındaw) | appointment |
| тағдыр | (taghdır) | fate |
| тағы да | (taghı da) | also, too |
| таз | (taz) | bald |
| таза | (taza) | clean, pure |
| тазала- | (tazala-) | clean |
| тай- | (tay-) | slip |
| тайғақ | (tayghaq) | slippery |
| такси | (taksi) | cab, taxi |
| тақырып | (taqırıp) | subject |
| тал | (tal) | willow |
| тала- | (tala-) | plunder |
| талас | (talas) | argument |
| талас- | (talas-) | argue |
| талқылау | (talqılaw) | discussion |
| талып қал- | (talıp qal-) | faint |
| тамақ | (tamaq) | dish, throat |
| таможня | (tamozhnya) | customs |
| тамшы | (tamshı) | drop |
| тамыз | (tamız) | August |
| тамыр | (tamır) | root |
| -тан, -тен | (-tan, -ten) | from |
| таны- | (tanı-) | know, recognize |
| таныстыр- | (tanıstır-) | introduce |
| таң | (tang) | dawn |
| таңда- | (tangda-) | choose, select |
| таңдан- | (tangdan-) | admire |
| таңертең | (tangyerteng) | morning |
| таңертеңгі ас | (tangyertenggi as) | breakfast |
| тапошке | (taposhke) | slipper |
| тапсыр- | (tapsır-) | order |
| тапсырма | (tapsırma) | assignment |
| тар | (tar) | narrow, tight |
| тара- | (tara-) | comb |
| таразы | (tarazı) | scale |
| тарақ | (taraq) | comb |
| тарих | (tariykh) | history |
| тарихшы | (tariykhshı) | historian |
| тарт- | (tart-) | pull |
| тартымдылық | (tartımdılıq) | attraction |
| тас | (tas) | stone |

| | | |
|---|---|---|
| тасбақа | (tasbaqa) | tortoise |
| тасушы | (tasuwshı) | porter |
| тасы- | (tası-) | carry |
| тау | (taw) | mountain |
| тауық | (tawıq) | hen |
| тауық еті | (tawıq yeti) | chicken |
| таяз | (tayaz) | shallow |
| тәжірибе | (täzhiriybe) | experience |
| тәртіп | (tärtip) | behavior |
| тәтті | (tätti) | sweet |
| тәтті тағам | (tätti tagham) | dessert |
| тәуелсіздік | (täwelsizdik) | independence |
| театр | (teatr) | theater |
| тегін | (tegin) | free |
| тез | (tez) | quick |
| тез-тез | (tez-tez) | often |
| телевизор | (televizor) | television |
| телеграмма | (telegramma) | telegram |
| телефон | (telefon) | telephone |
| телефон автомат | (telefon avtomat) | phone booth, public phone |
| телефон нөмірі | (telefon nömiri) | phone number |
| темекі | (temeki) | cigarette, tobacco |
| темекі шег- | (temeki sheg-) | smoke |
| температура | (temperatura) | temperature |
| темір | (temir) | iron |
| темір жол | (temir zhol) | railroad |
| тең | (teng) | equal |
| теңіз | (tengiz) | sea |
| теория | (teoriya) | theory |
| теп- | (tep-) | kick |
| терезе | (tereze) | window |
| терек | (terek) | poplar |
| терең | (tereng) | deep |
| терендік | (terengdik) | depth |
| тергеу | (tergew) | investigation |
| терле- | (terle-) | sweat |
| термометр | (termometr) | thermometer |
| тері | (teri) | fur, leather, skin |
| тесік | (tesik) | hole |
| ти- | (tiy-) | touch |
| тираж | (tirazh) | circulation |
| тиын | (tiyın) | coin |
| тиін | (tiyin) | squirrel |
| тоғай | (toghay) | wood |
| тоғыз | (toghız) | nine |
| тозақ | (tozaq) | hell |
| тоқсан | (toqsan) | ninety |
| тоқта- | (toqta-) | stop |
| тоқтат- | (toqtat-) | stop |
| тоқыма | (toqıma) | textile |
| толқын | (tolqın) | wave |
| толтыр- | (toltır-) | fill |
| толы | (tolı) | full |
| толықтауыш | (tolıqtawısh) | object |
| тоң- | (tong-) | freeze |
| тоңазытқыш | (tongazıtqısh) | refrigerator |
| топырақ | (topıraq) | earth, soil |
| торғай | (torghay) | sparrow |
| торт | (tort) | cake |
| төбе | (töbe) | ceiling, hill, roof |
| төле- | (töle-) | pay |
| төмен | (tömen) | down, low |
| төменде | (tömende) | below, underneath |
| төңкеріс | (töngkeris) | revolution |
| төрт | (tört) | four |
| төсек | (tösek) | mattress |
| трамвай | (tramvay) | tram |
| транспорт ағымы | (transport aghımı) | traffic |
| тротуар | (trotuar) | sidewalk |
| туған күн | (tuwghan kün) | birthday |
| тура | (tuwra) | correct, straight |
| туралы | (tuwralı) | about |
| туризм | (turizm) | tourism |
| турист | (turist) | tourist |
| туыл- | (tuwıl-) | born: be born |
| туылу | (tuwıluw) | birth |
| туысқан | (tuwısqan) | relative |
| тұз | (tuz) | salt |
| тұман | (tuman) | fog |
| тұмау | (tumaw) | cold |
| тұмсық | (tumsıq) | beak |
| тұр- | (tur-) | get up, live, stand |
| тұт | (tut) | mulberry |
| тұтқа | (tutqa) | handle |
| тұтынушы | (tutınuwshı) | consumer |
| түбек | (tübek) | peninsula |
| түгел | (tügel) | complete |
| түзет- | (tüzet-) | correct |
| түйе | (tüye) | camel |
| түйме | (tüyme) | button |
| түйін | (tüyin) | knot |
| түкір- | (tükir-) | spit |

| | | |
|---|---|---|
| түлкі | (tülki) | fox |
| түн | (tün) | night |
| түн ортасы | (tün ortası) | midnight |
| түр | (tür) | kind |
| түрме | (türme) | jail, prison |
| түс | (tüs) | afternoon, color, dream, noon |
| түс- | (tüs-) | get off |
| түскі ас | (tüski as) | lunch |
| түсін- | (tüsin-) | understand |
| түсіндір- | (tüsindir-) | explain |
| түсіндіру | (tüsindiruw) | explanation |
| тый- | (tıy-) | forbid |
| тынық | (tınıq) | calm |
| тыныш | (tınısh) | quiet |
| тыныштал- | (tınıshtal-) | quiet: be quiet |
| тыныштық | (tınıshtıq) | silence |
| тыңайтқыш | (tıngaytqısh) | fertilizer |
| тыңда- | (tıngda-) | listen |
| тырнақ | (tırnaq) | nail |
| тырыс- | (tırıs-) | try |
| тышқан | (tıshqan) | mouse |
| тіг- | (tig-) | sew |
| тігінші | (tiginshi) | tailor |
| тізе | (tize) | knee |
| тіл | (til) | language, tongue |
| тіл білімі | (til bilimi) | linguistics |
| тіле- | (tile-) | wish |
| тілек | (tilek) | wish |
| тіпті | (tipti) | even |
| тірі | (tiri) | alive |
| тіркеу | (tirkew) | registration |
| тіс | (tis) | tooth |
| тіс ауруы | (tis awruwı) | toothache |
| тіс дәрігері | (tis därigeri) | dentist |
| тіс пастасы | (tis pastası) | toothpaste |
| тіс шөткесі | (tis shötkesi) | toothbrush |
| тісте- | (tiste-) | bite |
| у | (uw) | poison |
| уақыт | (waqıt) | date, time |
| уәде бер- | (wäde ber-) | promise |
| уқала- | (uqala-) | rub |
| улы | (uwlı) | poisonous |
| универмаг | (univermag) | department store |
| университет | (universitet) | university |
| ұзын | (uzın) | long |
| ұзын бойлы | (uzın boylı) | tall |
| ұзындық | (uzındıq) | length |
| ұйғар- | (uyghar-) | decide |
| ұйқы | (uyqı) | sleep |
| ұйық | (uyıq) | sock |
| ұйықта- | (uyıqta-) | sleep |
| ұйықтайтын бөлме | (uyıqtaytın bölme) | bedroom |
| ұқса- | (uqsa-) | resemble |
| ұқсас | (uqsas) | alike, similar |
| ұл | (ul) | son |
| ұл бала | (ul bala) | boy |
| ұлас- | (ulas-) | continue |
| ұлт | (ult) | nation |
| ұлтшылдық | (ultshıldıq) | nationalism |
| ұмыт- | (umıt-) | forget |
| ұн | (un) | flour |
| ұнат- | (unat-) | like |
| ұр- | (ur-) | hit |
| ұрла- | (urla-) | steal |
| ұры | (urı) | thief |
| ұрық | (urıq) | grain, seed |
| ұрыс | (urıs) | battle |
| ұста- | (usta-) | catch, hold |
| ұстара | (ustara) | razor |
| ұсын- | (usın-) | offer, recommend |
| ұсыныс | (usınıs) | suggestion |
| ұш- | (ush-) | fly |
| ұял- | (uyal-) | ashamed: be ashamed |
| ұялшақ | (uyalshaq) | shy |
| үгіт- | (ügit-) | grind |
| үй | (üy) | home, house |
| үй тонаушы | (üy tonawshı) | burglar |
| үйлен- | (üylen-) | marry |
| үйлену | (üylenuw) | marriage |
| үйрек | (üyrek) | duck |
| үйрен- | (üyren-) | learn |
| үйреніп кет- | (üyrenip ket-) | used: be used to |
| үкі | (üki) | owl |
| үкім | (ükim) | verdict |
| үкімет | (ükimet) | government |
| үлкен | (ülken) | big, great, huge |
| үміт | (ümit) | hope |

| | | |
|---|---|---|
| үміттен- | (ümitten-) | hope |
| үстеу | (üstew) | adverb |
| үстінде | (üstinde) | above, on, over |
| үтік | (ütik) | iron |
| үтір | (ütir) | comma |
| үш | (üsh) | three |
| үшбұрыш | (üshburısh) | triangle |
| үшін | (üshin) | for |
| фабрика | (fabrika) | factory |
| фамилия | (familiya) | surname |
| фармацевт | (farmatsevt) | pharmacist |
| ферма | (ferma) | farm |
| физика | (fizika) | physics |
| фильм | (fil'm) | movie |
| фольклор | (fol'klor) | folklore |
| фонтан | (fontan) | fountain |
| форма | (forma) | shape |
| фотоаппарат | (fotoapparat) | camera |
| фотография | (fotografiya) | photo |
| футбол | (futbol) | soccer |
| хабарландыру | (khabarlandıruw) | advertisement |
| халық | (khalıq) | people, population |
| халықаралық | (khalıqaralıq) | international |
| ханым | (khanım) | lady |
| хат | (khat) | letter |
| хирургия | (khirurgiya) | surgery |
| христиан | (khristiyan) | Christian |
| цемент | (tsement) | cement |
| цензура | (tsenzura) | censorship |
| цирк | (tsirk) | circus |
| чек | (chek) | check |
| чемодан | (chemodan) | suitcase |
| шабдалы | (shabdalı) | peach |
| шабуыл | (shabuwıl) | attack |
| шабуылда- | (shabuwılda-) | attack |
| шай | (shay) | tea |
| шай пұл | (shay pul) | tip |
| шайна- | (shayna-) | chew |
| шайтан | (shaytan) | Satan |
| шақыр- | (shaqır-) | call, invite, summon |
| шақыру | (shaqıruw) | invitation |
| шалбар | (shalbar) | pants |
| шамамен | (shamamen) | about |

| | | |
|---|---|---|
| шана | (shana) | sled |
| шанышқы | (shanıshqı) | fork |
| шаң | (shang) | dust |
| шаңғы | (shangghı) | skiing |
| шапалақта- | (shapalaqta-) | clap |
| шарап | (sharap) | wine |
| шарбақ | (sharbaq) | fence |
| шарт | (shart) | condition |
| шаруа | (sharuwa) | peasant |
| шарф | (sharf) | scarf |
| шаршаған | (sharshaghan) | tired |
| шаршы | (sharshı) | square |
| шахмат | (shakhmat) | chess |
| шаш | (shash) | hair |
| шаш- | (shash-) | scatter |
| шаштараз | (shashtaraz) | hairdresser |
| шәйнек | (shäynek) | teapot |
| шеберлік | (sheberlik) | skill |
| шеге | (shege) | nail |
| шегіртке | (shegirtke) | grasshopper |
| шек қой- | (shek qoy-) | restrict |
| шекара | (shekara) | border |
| шелек | (shelek) | bucket |
| шеңбер | (shengber) | circle |
| шет | (shet) | edge |
| шет елдік | (shet yeldik) | foreigner |
| шеш- | (shesh-) | solve |
| шешім | (sheshim) | decision |
| шие | (shiye) | cherry |
| шикі | (shiyki) | raw |
| шин | (shiyn) | tire |
| шиша | (shiysha) | bottle |
| шкаф | (shkaf) | cupboard |
| шорт | (short) | shorts |
| шофёр | (shofyor) | driver |
| шошқа | (shoshqa) | pig |
| шошқа еті | (shoshqa yeti) | pork |
| шөл | (shöl) | desert |
| шөлдеген | (shöldegen) | thirsty |
| шөп | (shöp) | grass |
| шпинат | (shpiynat) | spinach |
| шу | (shuw) | noise |
| шұлық | (shulıq) | stocking |
| шыбын | (shıbın) | fly |
| шығ- | (shıgh-) | exit |
| шығанақ | (shıghanaq) | bay |
| шығарма | (shıgharma) | composition |
| шығын | (shıghın) | expense |
| шығыс | (shıghıs) | east |
| шығу | (shıghuw) | exit |

| | | | | | |
|---|---|---|---|---|---|
| шын | (shın) | real, true | ізге түс- | (izge tüs-) | chase |
| шындық | (shındıq) | truth | іл- | (il-) | hang |
| шынтақ | (shıntaq) | elbow | ілгіш | (ilgish) | hanger |
| шыны | (shını) | glass | іні | (ini) | brother |
| шыныаяқ | (shınıayaq) | cup | інжір | (inzhir) | fig |
| шыңғыр- | (shıngghır-) | scream | ірі | (iri) | large |
| шырақ | (shıraq) | candle | ірімшік | (irimshik) | cheese |
| шырша | (shırsha) | fir | іс | (is) | business |
| шырын | (shırın) | fruit juice | іс- | (is-) | swell |
| шілде | (shilde) | July | іскер | (isker) | businessman |
| шір- | (shir-) | rot | ісік | (isik) | swelling |
| шіркеу | (shirkew) | church | іш- | (ish-) | drink |
| | | | іш қату | (ish qatuw) | constipation |
| щётка | (shchyotka) | brush | іш өткізетін дәрі | (ish ötkizetin däri) | laxative |
| ыдыс жуғыш | (ıdıs zhuwghısh) | dishwasher | іш өту | (ish ötuw) | diarrhea |
| ықыласты | (ıqılastı) | diligent | іш тарлық | (ish tarlıq) | envy |
| ылғал | (ılghal) | moist | ішек | (ishek) | intestine |
| ымырт | (ımırt) | dusk | ішімдік | (ishimdik) | beverage, drink |
| ыңғайлы | (ıngghaylı) | comfortable | ішінде | (ishinde) | inside |
| ыстакан | (ıstakan) | glass | | | |
| ыстық | (ıstıq) | hot | экономика | (ekonomika) | economics |
| ыстықтық | (ıstıqtıq) | heat | экран | (ekran) | screen |
| | | | электр | (elektr) | electricity |
| із | (iz) | trace | эпик | (epik) | epic |
|ізде- | (izde-) | look for, search, seek | юбка | (yubka) | skirt |

# KYRGYZ - ENGLISH INDEX

| | | |
|---|---|---|
| аары | (aarı) | bee |
| аба | (aba) | air |
| аба жолу | (aba jolu) | airline |
| аба ырайы | (aba ırayı) | climate, weather |
| аба-ырай маалыматы | (aba-ıray maalımatı) | weather report |
| абайла | (abayla) | careful |
| абстрактуу | (abstraktuu) | abstract |
| авария | (avariya) | accident |
| август | (avgust) | August |
| авиапочта | (aviapochta) | airmail |
| автобус | (avtobus) | bus |
| автомобиль | (avtomobil') | automobile |
| автономия | (avtonomiya) | autonomy |
| автор | (avtor) | author |
| ага | (aga) | brother |
| адабий | (adabiy) | literary |
| адабий эмгек | (adabiy emgek) | literary work |
| адабият | (adabiyat) | literature |
| адам | (adam) | human being, person |
| адат | (adat) | habit |
| адептүү | (adeptüü) | diligent |
| адилдик | (adildik) | justice |
| адрес | (adres) | address |
| ажыраш- | (ajırash-) | divorce |
| ажырашуу | (ajırashuu) | divorce |
| аз | (az) | few |
| азай- | (azay-) | decrease |
| азил | (azil) | joke |
| азчылык | (azchılık) | minority |
| азыр | (azır) | now |
| ай | (ay) | month, moon |
| айбан | (ayban) | animal |
| айва | (ayva) | quince |
| айда- | (ayda-) | drive |
| айдоочу | (aydoochu) | driver |
| айкел | (aykel) | statue |
| айнек | (aynek) | glass |
| айран | (ayran) | yogurt |
| айрыкча | (ayrıkcha) | especially |
| айт- | (ayt-) | say, tell |
| айыл | (ayıl) | countryside, village |
| айым | (ayım) | lady |
| айырма | (ayırma) | difference |
| ак | (ak) | white |
| ак куу | (ak kuu) | swan |
| ак- | (ak-) | flow |
| аким | (akim) | mayor |
| акмак | (akmak) | stupid |
| акча | (akcha) | currency, money |
| акыл | (akıl) | mind |
| акылдуу | (akılduu) | clever |
| акын | (akın) | poet |
| акыркы | (akırkı) | last |
| акырын | (akırın) | slow |
| ал | (al) | he, it, she |
| ал тургай | (al turgay) | even |
| ал- | (al-) | take |
| алар | (alar) | they, those |
| аларды | (alardı) | them |
| алардын | (alardın) | their |
| албетте | (albette) | course: of course |
| алга | (alga) | forward |
| алгебра | (algebra) | algebra |
| алда- | (alda-) | lie |
| алдында | (aldında) | front: in front of |
| алып кел- | (alıp kel-) | bring |
| алыс | (alıs) | far |
| али | (ali) | still, yet |
| алкыш | (alkısh) | gratitude |
| алма | (alma) | apple |
| алмурут | (almurut) | pear |
| алты | (altı) | six |
| алтымыш | (altımısh) | sixty |
| алтын | (altın) | gold |
| алуу | (aluu) | subtraction |
| алфавит | (alfavit) | alphabet |
| амандаш- | (amandash-) | greet |
| анан | (anan) | then |
| анар | (anar) | pomegranate |
| анархия | (anarkhiya) | anarchy |
| андан соң | (andan song) | then |
| ант бер- | (ant ber-) | swear |
| антенна | (antenna) | antenna |
| аны | (anı) | her, him |
| аныык | (anık) | obvious |
| аныкы | (anıkı) | hers, his, its |
| анын | (anın) | her, his, its |
| аң | (ang) | game |
| аң уула- | (ang uula-) | hunt |
| аңгеме | (anggeme) | story |
| аңгемелеш- | (anggemelesh-) | talk |
| апельсин | (apel'sin) | orange |
| апрель | (aprel') | April |

| | | |
|---|---|---|
| ар | (ar) | any, conscience, every |
| ар дайым | (ar dayım) | always |
| ар жерде | (ar jerde) | everywhere |
| ар ким | (ar kim) | everybody, anybody |
| араа | (araa) | saw |
| араба | (araba) | cart |
| аракет | (araket) | attempt |
| арал | (aral) | island |
| аралашкан | (aralashkan) | messy |
| аралаштыр- | (aralashtır-) | mix |
| аралык | (aralık) | distance |
| арасында | (arasında) | between |
| арзан | (arzan) | cheap |
| арзандатуу | (arzandatuu) | discount, sale |
| арип | (arip) | letter |
| арка | (arka) | back |
| аркалуу | (arkaluu) | by |
| армия | (armiya) | army |
| арпа | (arpa) | barley |
| арстан | (arstan) | lion |
| артиллерия | (artilleriya) | artillery |
| артта | (artta) | behind |
| артык көр- | (artık kör-) | prefer |
| архитектор | (arkhitektor) | architect |
| арча | (archa) | cherry |
| арыз | (arız) | complaint |
| арыздан- | (arızdan-) | complain |
| асан-үсөн | (asan-üsön) | rainbow |
| аска | (aska) | rock |
| аскер | (asker) | soldier |
| аспап | (aspap) | instrument, tool |
| астында | (astında) | under, underneath |
| ат | (at) | horse, name, title |
| ат атооч | (at atooch) | pronoun |
| ата | (ata) | father |
| ата-эне | (ata-ene) | parents |
| атаандаштык | (ataandashtık) | competition |
| атайын | (atayın) | official |
| атактуу | (ataktuu) | famous |
| атыр | (atır) | perfume |
| ач | (ach) | hungry |
| ач- | (ach-) | discover, open |
| ачарчылык | (acharchılık) | famine |

| | | |
|---|---|---|
| ачкыч | (achkıch) | wrench |
| ачтык | (achtık) | hunger |
| ачуу | (achuu) | anger, bitter |
| ачуулуу | (achuuluu) | angry |
| ачык | (achık) | open |
| ашыгуу | (ashıguu) | haste |
| ашык- | (ashık-) | hurry |
| ашказан | (ashkazan) | stomach |
| ашкана | (ashkana) | dining room, kitchen |
| ашпоз | (ashpoz) | cook |
| аэропорт | (aeroport) | airport |
| аяк | (ayak) | foot |
| аял | (ayal) | wife, woman |
| аялдама | (ayaldama) | stop |
| аянт | (ayant) | square |
| аюу | (ayuu) | bear |
| баа | (baa) | price |
| баалуу | (baaluu) | valuable |
| баары | (baarı) | all, everything |
| багын- | (bagın-) | obey |
| багынуу | (bagınuu) | surrender |
| багыт | (bagıt) | direction |
| бадыраң | (badırang) | cucumber |
| бажыкана | (bajıkana) | customs |
| базар | (bazar) | market |
| бай | (bay) | rich |
| байге | (bayge) | prize |
| байке | (bayke) | uncle |
| байла- | (bayla-) | tie |
| байланыш | (baylanısh) | communication |
| байлык | (baylık) | wealth |
| байпак | (baypak) | sock, stocking |
| бака | (baka) | frog |
| баклажан | (baklajan) | eggplant |
| бактылуу | (baktıluu) | happy |
| бактысыз | (baktısız) | unhappy |
| бакча | (bakcha) | garden |
| бакчы | (bakchı) | gardener |
| бал | (bal) | honey |
| бал ай | (bal ay) | honeymoon |
| бала | (bala) | child |
| балаты | (balatı) | fir |
| балет | (balet) | ballet |
| балка | (balka) | hammer |
| балким | (balkim) | perhaps, probably |
| балкон | (balkon) | balcony |

| Kyrgyz | Transcription | English |
|---|---|---|
| балмуздак | (balmuzdak) | ice cream |
| балта | (balta) | axe |
| балык | (balık) | fish |
| балыкчы | (balıkchı) | fisherman |
| банан | (banan) | banana |
| банк | (bank) | bank |
| банка | (banka) | jar |
| банкет | (banket) | banquet |
| бар- | (bar-) | visit |
| бара бара | (bara bara) | gradually |
| барлык | (barlık) | existence |
| барометр | (barometr) | barometer |
| баруу | (baruu) | visit |
| бас- | (bas-) | press, print |
| баскетбол | (basketbol) | basketball |
| басма | (basma) | publishing house |
| басма сөз | (basma söz) | press |
| басмакана | (basmakana) | printing press |
| бассейн | (basseyn) | pool |
| бат- | (bat-) | sink |
| батир | (batir) | apartment |
| баткак | (batkak) | mud |
| батыш | (batısh) | west |
| баш | (bash) | head |
| баш ооруу | (bash ooruu) | headache |
| башка | (bashka) | another, besides, different, other |
| башкаруучу | (bashkaruuchu) | manager |
| башта- | (bashta-) | begin, start |
| бейиш | (beyish) | paradise |
| бейшемби | (beyshembi) | Thursday |
| бекер | (beker) | free |
| бекит- | (bekit-) | fasten |
| бел боо | (bel boo) | belt |
| бензин | (benzin) | gasoline |
| бер- | (ber-) | give |
| бери | (beri) | since |
| бет | (bet) | cheek, face, page |
| беш | (besh) | five |
| биз | (biz) | we |
| бизди | (bizdi) | us |
| биздики | (bizdiki) | ours |
| биздин | (bizdin) | our |
| бизнес | (biznes) | business |
| бийчи | (biychi) | dancer |
| бийик | (biyik) | high, tall |
| бийиктик | (biyiktik) | height |
| бийле- | (biyle-) | dance |
| бил- | (bil-) | know |
| билек | (bilek) | wrist |
| билет | (bilet) | ticket |
| билим | (bilim) | education, knowledge |
| бинт | (bint) | bandage |
| бир | (bir) | one |
| бир аз | (bir az) | little, some |
| бир нерсе | (bir nerse) | anything |
| бир нече | (bir neche) | several |
| бир түрлүү | (bir türlüü) | strange |
| бирге | (birge) | together |
| бирок | (birok) | but |
| бирөө | (biröö) | anybody |
| бит | (bit) | louse |
| бланк | (blank) | form |
| боё- | (boyo-) | dye, paint |
| бойго жеткен | (boygo jetken) | adult |
| бол- | (bol-) | be, become |
| болжо- | (boljo-) | guess |
| болот | (bolot) | steel |
| болуп кал- | (bolup kal-) | happen |
| бомбу | (bombu) | bomb |
| бооз | (booz) | pregnant |
| боор | (boor) | liver |
| борбор | (borbor) | capital, center |
| бороон | (boroon) | storm |
| бош | (bosh) | empty, loose |
| бош эмес | (bosh emes) | busy |
| бошот- | (boshot-) | empty, release |
| бою узун | (boyu uzun) | tall |
| бөбөк | (böbök) | baby |
| бөгөт | (bögöt) | dam |
| бөйрөк | (böyrök) | kidney |
| бөл- | (böl-) | distribute, divide, separate |
| бөлмө | (bölmö) | room |
| бөлөк | (bölök) | separate |
| бөлү | (bölü) | division |
| бөлүм | (bölüm) | department, part |
| бөлүн- | (bölün-) | separated: be separated |
| бөлчөк | (bölchök) | fraction |

| | | |
|---|---|---|
| бөтөлкө | (bötölkö) | bottle |
| бугу | (bugu) | deer |
| буз- | (buz-) | disturb |
| буйрук бер- | (buyruk ber-) | command, order |
| бука | (buka) | bull |
| бул | (bul) | this |
| бул жерде | (bul jerde) | here |
| булар | (bular) | these |
| булуң | (bulung) | bay |
| булут | (bulut) | cloud |
| булчуң | (bulchung) | muscle |
| бура- | (bura-) | twist |
| бурагыч | (buragıch) | screwdriver |
| бургу | (burgu) | drill |
| бурул- | (burul-) | turn |
| бурч | (burch) | angle, corner |
| бут | (but) | leg |
| бут кийим | (but kiyim) | shoe |
| бутак | (butak) | branch |
| бутерброд | (buterbrod) | sandwich |
| буудай | (buuday) | wheat |
| буурчак | (buurchak) | bean, pea |
| буюм | (buyum) | goods |
| бүгүн | (bügün) | today |
| бүргө | (bürgö) | flea |
| бүркүт | (bürküt) | eagle |
| бүтүн | (bütün) | whole |
| бүтүр- | (bütür-) | finish |
| бычак | (bıchak) | knife |
| быш- | (bısh-) | cook |
| бышыр- | (bıshır-) | cook |
| бышкан | (bıshkan) | ripe |
| бюджет | (byudjet) | budget |
| | | |
| ванна | (vanna) | bathroom |
| варенье | (varen'e) | jam |
| велосипед | (velosiped) | bicycle |
| вертолёт | (vertolyot) | helicopter |
| видео | (video) | video |
| вилка | (vilka) | fork |
| | | |
| -га, -ге, -го, -гө | (-ga, -ge, -go, -gö) | to |
| гавань | (gavan') | harbor |
| газ | (gaz) | gas |
| галстук | (galstuk) | tie |
| гараж | (garaj) | garage |
| гармония | (garmoniya) | harmony |
| гезит | (gezit) | newspaper |

| | | |
|---|---|---|
| география | (geografiya) | geography |
| геология | (geologiya) | geology |
| геометрия | (geometriya) | geometry |
| горизонт | (gorizont) | horizon |
| горчица | (gorchitsa) | mustard |
| гөңкө | (göngkö) | bakery |
| градус | (gradus) | degree |
| граждан | (grajdan) | citizen |
| графин | (grafin) | pitcher |
| грипп | (gripp) | flu |
| гүл | (gül) | flower |
| | | |
| -да, -де, -до, -дө | (-da, -de, -do, -dö) | at, in |
| -дан, -ден, -дон, -дөн | (-dan, -den, don, -dön) | from |
| да | (da) | too |
| да ... да | (da ... da) | both ... and |
| даам тат- | (daam tat-) | taste |
| даамдуу | (daamduu) | delicious, tasty |
| даараткана | (daaratkana) | toilet |
| дабыш | (dabısh) | sound |
| дагы да | (dagı da) | also |
| дайындоо | (dayındoo) | appointment |
| далил | (dalil) | proof |
| далилде- | (dalilde-) | represent |
| дан | (dan) | grain |
| дарбаза | (darbaza) | gate |
| дарбыз | (darbız) | watermelon |
| дароо | (daroo) | immediately |
| дары | (darı) | drug, medicine |
| дарыгер | (darıger) | doctor |
| дарыкана | (darıkana) | pharmacy |
| дарыла- | (darıla-) | cure |
| дарыя | (darıya) | river |
| дасторкон | (dastorkon) | tablecloth |
| дата | (data) | date |
| даяр | (dayar) | ready |
| даярда- | (dayarda-) | prepare |
| декабрь | (dekabr') | December |
| дем | (dem) | breath |
| дем алыш | (dem alısh) | holiday, rest, vacation |
| демократия | (demokratiya) | democracy |
| демон | (demon) | demon |
| демонстрация | (demonstratsiya) | demonstration |
| ден соолук | (den sooluk) | health |
| дене | (dene) | body |

| деңгээл | (denggeel) | level |
|---------|-----------|-------|
| деңиз | (dengiz) | sea |
| дептер | (depter) | notebook |
| дин | (din) | religion |
| диний | (diniy) | religious |
| диний майрам | (diniy mayram) | religious holiday |
| диний секта | (diniy sekta) | sect |
| диплом | (diplom) | diploma |
| дирилде- | (dirilde-) | tremble |
| добуш | (dobush) | voice, vote |
| добуш бер- | (dobush ber-) | vote |
| доор | (door) | era |
| дос | (dos) | friend |
| достук | (dostuk) | friendship |
| дөбө | (döbö) | hill |
| дөңгөлөк | (dönggölök) | round, tire, wheel |
| дөө | (döö) | giant |
| драма | (drama) | drama |
| драматург | (dramaturg) | playwright |
| дубал | (dubal) | wall |
| дубал саат | (dubal saat) | clock |
| дудук | (duduk) | mute |
| духовка | (dukhovka) | oven |
| душ | (dush) | shower |
| душмандык | (dushmandık) | enmity |
| дүйнө | (düynö) | world |
| дүйшөмбү | (düyshömbü) | Monday |
| дүкөн | (dükön) | shop, store |
| дүлөй | (dülöy) | deaf |
| дүлөйлүк | (dülöylük) | deafness |
| дыйкан | (dıykan) | peasant |
| дыйканчылык | (dıykanchılık) | agriculture |
| дээрлик | (deerlik) | almost |
| еврей | (evrey) | Jew |
| жаа- | (jaa-) | precipitate |
| жабык | (jabık) | closed |
| жабыш- | (jabısh-) | stick |
| жагдай | (jagday) | condition, situation |
| жадатма | (jadatma) | boring |
| жаз | (jaz) | spring |
| жаз- | (jaz-) | write |
| жаза | (jaza) | punishment |
| жазала- | (jazala-) | punish |
| жаздык | (jazdık) | pillow |
| жаздык кап | (jazdık kap) | pillowcase |

| жазуу | (jazuu) | writing |
|--------|---------|--------|
| жазуучу | (jazuuchu) | writer |
| жай | (jay) | summer |
| жай- | (jay-) | spread |
| жайыт | (jayıt) | meadow |
| жак | (jak) | side, way |
| жак- | (jak-) | burn |
| жака | (jaka) | collar |
| жакет | (jaket) | jacket |
| жактыр- | (jaktır-) | like |
| жакшы | (jakshı) | fine, good, nice, OK, well |
| жакшыраак | (jakshıraak) | better |
| жакын | (jakın) | near |
| жакында | (jakında) | near, soon |
| жакында- | (jakında-) | approach |
| жалбыз | (jalbız) | mint |
| жалбырак | (jalbırak) | leaf |
| жалган | (jalgan) | false, lie |
| жалгыз | (jalgız) | alone |
| жалдоо | (jaldoo) | rent |
| жалкоо | (jalkoo) | lazy |
| жалкоолук | (jalkooluk) | laziness |
| жалпы | (jalpı) | general |
| жалын | (jalın) | flame |
| жаман | (jaman) | bad |
| жамгыр | (jamgır) | rain |
| жан- | (jan-) | burn |
| жана | (jana) | and |
| жанында | (janında) | near |
| жаңгак | (janggak) | walnut |
| жаңы | (jangı) | fresh, new |
| Жаңы Жыл | (Jangı Jıl) | New Year |
| жаңылык | (jangılık) | news |
| жап- | (jap-) | close, cover, shut |
| жапайы | (japayı) | wild |
| жар- | (jar-) | split |
| жара | (jara) | wound |
| жарамдуу | (jaramduu) | convenient |
| жараш- | (jarash-) | suit |
| жардам | (jardam) | help |
| жардамдаш- | (jardamdash-) | assist |
| жаркылда- | (jarkılda-) | shine |
| жарык | (jarık) | bright, light |
| жарым | (jarım) | half |
| жарым ай | (jarım ay) | crescent |
| жарым арал | (jarım aral) | peninsula |
| жарыш | (jarısh) | race |

| | | |
|---|---|---|
| жарыя | (jarıya) | advertisement |
| жаса- | (jasa-) | make |
| жасалма | (jasalma) | artificial |
| жастык | (jastık) | cushion |
| жасымык | (jasımık) | lentil |
| жат- | (jat-) | lie (down) |
| жата турган бөлмө | (jata turgan bölmö) | bedroom |
| жаш | (jash) | age, young |
| жаша- | (jasha-) | live |
| жашик | (jashik) | box |
| жаштык | (jashtık) | youth |
| жашыл | (jashıl) | green |
| жашылча | (jashılcha) | vegetable |
| жашыр- | (jashır-) | hide |
| жашырын | (jashırın) | secret |
| же | (je) | or |
| же ... же | (je ... je) | neither ... nor |
| же ... же | (je ... je) | either ... or |
| же- | (je-) | eat |
| жебе | (jebe) | arrow |
| жез | (jez) | copper |
| жек көр- | (jek kör-) | hate |
| жекшемби | (jekshembi) | Sunday |
| жел | (jel) | wind |
| жел кайык | (jel kayık) | sailboat |
| желек | (jelek) | flag |
| желим | (jelim) | glue |
| жемиш | (jemish) | fruit |
| жең- | (jeng-) | defeat, win |
| жеңил | (jengil) | light |
| жеңилүү | (jengilüü) | defeat |
| жеңиш | (jengish) | victory |
| жер титирөө | (jer titiröö) | earthquake |
| жер | (jer) | earth |
| жергиликтүү өкмөт | (jergiliktüü ökmöt) | municipality |
| жет- | (jet-) | arrive, reach |
| жети | (jeti) | seven |
| жетилген | (jetilgen) | perfect |
| жетимиш | (jetimish) | seventy |
| жетишээрлик | (jetisheerlik) | sufficient |
| жеткиликтүү | (jetkiliktüü) | enough |
| жибек | (jibek) | silk |
| жибер- | (jiber-) | send |
| жийиркенүү | (jiyirkenüü) | disgust |
| жинди | (jindi) | crazy |
| жиндилик | (jindilik) | insanity |
| жогол- | (jogol-) | disappear |
| жогорудо | (jogorudo) | above |
| жогот- | (jogot-) | lose |
| жок | (jok) | no |
| жол | (jol) | road, way |
| жол кире | (jol kire) | fare |
| жолборс | (jolbors) | tiger |
| жолдун кыйылычы | (joldung kıyılıchı) | crosswalk |
| жомок | (jomok) | folktale |
| жоо | (joo) | enemy |
| жоомарт | (joomart) | generous |
| жоон | (joon) | thick |
| жооп | (joop) | answer, reply |
| жооп бер- | (joop ber-) | answer, reply |
| жөндө- | (jöndö-) | mend |
| жөнөкөй | (jönököy) | simple |
| жөө | (jöö) | pedestrian |
| жөргөмүш | (jörgömüsh) | spider |
| жөрмөлөп чык- | (jörmölöp chık-) | climb |
| жөтөл | (jötöl) | cough |
| жука | (juka) | fine, thin |
| жума | (juma) | Friday, week |
| жумуртка | (jumurtka) | egg |
| жумушчу | (jumushchu) | worker |
| жумшак | (jumshak) | soft |
| журнал | (jurnal) | magazine |
| жуу- | (juu-) | wash |
| жууркан | (juurkan) | blanket |
| жүгөрү | (jügörü) | corn |
| жүгүр- | (jügür-) | run |
| жүз | (jüz) | hundred |
| жүзүм | (jüzüm) | grape |
| жүк | (jük) | baggage, cargo |
| жүк ташуучу машине | (jük tashuuchu mashine) | truck |
| жүн | (jün) | wool |
| жүр- | (jür-) | walk |
| жүргүнчү | (jürgünchü) | passenger |
| жүрөк | (jürök) | heart |
| жыгач | (jıgach) | tree |
| жыйна- | (jıyna-) | collect |
| жыйын | (jıyın) | meeting |
| жыйырма | (jıyırma) | twenty |
| жыл | (jıl) | year |
| жылан | (jılan) | snake |
| жыланач | (jılangach) | bare |
| жылдыз | (jıldız) | star |
| жылдык | (jıldık) | anniversary |

| | | |
|---|---|---|
| жылуу | (jıluu) | lukewarm, warm |
| жылып өт- | (jılıp öt-) | slide |
| жымый- | (jımıy-) | smile |
| жырт- | (jırt-) | tear |
| жыт | (jıt) | smell |
| жыт- | (jıt-) | smell |
| жытта- | (jıtta-) | smell |
| жээк | (jeek) | coast |
| | | |
| залал | (zalal) | harm |
| замбирек | (zambirek) | cannon |
| заңчы | (zangchı) | lawyer |
| зарыл | (zarıl) | necessary |
| зат | (zat) | matter, thing |
| зат атооч | (zat atooch) | noun |
| зеендүү | (zeendüü) | intelligent |
| зейтун | (zeytun) | olive |
| зергер | (zerger) | jeweler |
| зерик- | (zerik-) | bored: be bored |
| зым | (zım) | wire |
| зыян | (zıyan) | damage, loss |
| зыяндуу | (zıyanduu) | harmful |
| зоопарк | (zoopark) | zoo |
| | | |
| ибадаткана | (ibadatkana) | temple |
| идиома | (idioma) | idiom |
| идиш жуугуч | (idish juuguch) | dishwasher |
| из | (iz) | trace |
| изге түш- | (izge tüsh-) | chase |
| изде- | (izde-) | look for, search, seek |
| изилдөө | (izildöö) | research |
| ий- | (iy-) | bend |
| ийгилик | (iygilik) | success |
| ийин | (iyin) | shoulder |
| ийне | (iyne) | needle |
| ил- | (il-) | hang |
| илгич | (ilgich) | hanger |
| илим | (ilim) | scientist |
| инженер | (injener) | engineer |
| инжир | (injir) | fig |
| ини | (ini) | brother |
| интелигент | (inteligent) | intellectual |
| инфекция | (infektsiya) | infection |
| инфляция | (inflyatsiya) | inflation |
| информация | (informatsiya) | information |
| ири | (iri) | large |
| искусство | (iskusstvo) | art |

| | | |
|---|---|---|
| иг | (it) | dog |
| итер- | (iter-) | push |
| ич катуу | (ich katuu) | constipation |
| ич өткөрүүчү дары | (ich ötkörüüchü darı) | laxative |
| ич өтүү | (ich ötüü) | diarrhea |
| ич- | (ich-) | drink |
| ичеги | (ichegi) | intestine |
| ичи тардык | (ichi tardık) | envy |
| ичимдик | (ichimdik) | drink |
| ичинде | (ichinde) | inside |
| ичке | (ichke) | slim |
| иш | (ish) | business, job |
| иш таштоо | (ish tashtoo) | strike |
| ишемби | (ishembi) | Saturday |
| ишен- | (ishen-) | believe |
| ишеним | (ishenim) | belief, confidence, faith |
| ишкер | (ishker) | businessman |
| иште- | (ishte-) | work |
| июль | (iyul') | July |
| июнь | (iyun') | June |
| | | |
| -ка, -ке, -ко, -кө | (-ka, -ke, -ko, -kö) | to |
| каала- | (kaala-) | want |
| каалоо | (kaaloo) | desire |
| кабарла- | (kabarla-) | inform |
| кабарчы | (kabarchı) | journalist |
| кабат | (kabat) | storey |
| кабык | (kabık) | bark |
| кабыл ал- | (kabıl al-) | accept |
| кагаз | (kagaz) | paper |
| кагаз кол аарчы | (kagaz kol aarchı) | napkin |
| кадам | (kadam) | step |
| кажет | (kajet) | necessity, need |
| | | |
| каз | (kaz) | goose |
| каз- | (kaz-) | dig |
| казына | (kazına) | treasure |
| казыркы | (kazırkı) | present |
| кай жерге | (kay jerge) | where |
| кайгылан- | (kaygılan-) | worry |
| кайгылуу | (kaygıluu) | sad, sorry |
| кайда | (kayda) | where |
| каймак | (kaymak) | cream |
| кайна- | (kayna-) | boil |

| | | |
|---|---|---|
| кайраттану | (kayrattanu) | courage |
| кайраттуу | (kayrattuu) | brave, courageous |
| кайрымдуу | (kayrımduu) | kind |
| кайсы | (kaysı) | which |
| кайт- | (kayt-) | return |
| кайтадан | (kaytadan) | again |
| кайтала- | (kaytala-) | repeat |
| кайчы | (kaychı) | scissors |
| кайык | (kayık) | boat |
| кал- | (kal-) | remain, stay |
| калем | (kalem) | pen |
| калемпир | (kalempir) | carnation |
| календарь | (kalendar') | calendar |
| калктын саны | (kalktın sanı) | population |
| калпак | (kalpak) | hat |
| калың | (kalıng) | thick |
| калың эл | (kalıng el) | crowd |
| камсыздоо | (kamsızdoo) | insurance |
| кан | (kan) | blood |
| кан басымы | (kan basımı) | blood pressure |
| кана- | (kana-) | bleed |
| канал | (kanal) | canal, channel |
| канат | (kanat) | wing |
| кандай | (kanday) | how |
| канжар | (kanjar) | dagger |
| кант | (kant) | sugar |
| канча | (kancha) | how much, how much |
| капитан | (kapitan) | captain |
| капкак | (kapkak) | lid |
| капуста | (kapusta) | cabbage |
| капчык | (kapchık) | purse, wallet |
| кар | (kar) | snow |
| кара | (kara) | black |
| кара мал | (kara mal) | cattle |
| кара өрүк | (kara örük) | plum |
| кара- | (kara-) | look |
| карагай | (karagay) | pine |
| карай | (karay) | towards |
| карама-каршы | (karama-karshı) | opposite |
| карандаш | (karandash) | pencil |
| караңгы | (karanggı) | dark |
| караңгылык | (karanggılık) | darkness |
| карга | (karga) | crow |
| каржыландыруу | (karjılandıruu) | investment |
| карикатура | (karikatura) | cartoon |
| карлыгач | (karlıgach) | swallow |
| карма- | (karma-) | catch, hold |
| кармалуу | (karmaluu) | delay |
| карта | (karta) | map, playing card |
| картөшкө | (kartöshkö) | potato |
| каршы | (karshı) | against |
| кары | (karı) | old |
| карыз | (karız) | debt, loan |
| карыз ал- | (karız al-) | borrow |
| карын | (karın) | belly |
| карышкыр | (karıshkır) | wolf |
| касапчы | (kasapchı) | butcher |
| кассет | (kasset) | cassette |
| кассир | (kassir) | cashier |
| кастрюля | (kastrulya) | saucepan |
| кат | (kat) | letter |
| ката | (kata) | fault, mistake, wrong |
| катаал | (kataal) | cruel |
| катар | (katar) | row |
| катта- | (katta-) | fold |
| каттоо | (kattoo) | registration |
| катуу | (katuu) | hard, loud |
| кафе | (kafe) | café |
| кач- | (kach-) | escape, flee, run away |
| качан | (kachan) | when |
| каш | (kash) | eyebrow |
| кашаа | (kashaa) | fence |
| каштан | (kashtan) | chestnut |
| кашык | (kashık) | spoon |
| квитанция | (kvitantsiya) | receipt |
| кедей | (kedey) | poor |
| кее бир | (kee bir) | some |
| кездеме | (kezdeme) | textile |
| кездеш- | (kezdesh-) | meet |
| кездешүү | (kezdeshüü) | appointmen |
| кел- | (kel-) | arrive, come, visit |
| келерки | (kelerki) | next |
| келечек | (kelechek) | future |
| келин | (kelin) | bride |
| келишим | (kelishim) | agreement |
| келүү | (kelüü) | arrival, visit |
| кеме | (keme) | ship |
| кемпут | (kemput) | candy |

|  |  |  |
|---|---|---|
| кеӊ | (keng) | broad, loose, spacious, wide |
| кеӊеш | (kengesh) | advice |
| керебет | (kerebet) | bed |
| керек бол- | (kerek bol-) | need |
| керектөөчү | (kerektööchü) | consumer |
| кес- | (kes-) | cut |
| кесе | (kese) | bowl |
| кесип | (kesip) | occupation |
| кет- | (ket-) | depart, go, leave |
| кетүү | (ketüü) | departure |
| кеч | (kech) | evening, late |
| кечээ | (kechee) | yesterday |
| кечир- | (kechir-) | forgive |
| кечирим | (kechirim) | apology |
| кечирим сура- | (kechirim sura-) | apologize |
| кечки тамак | (kechki tamak) | dinner |
| кий- | (kiy-) | put on, wear |
| кийим | (kiyim) | clothes, dress |
| кийин | (kiyin) | after |
| кийинкиге калтыр- | (kiyinkige kaltır-) | postpone |
| килем | (kilem) | carpet |
| килит | (kilit) | key |
| ким | (kim) | who |
| кино | (kino) | cinema, movie |
| кир | (kir) | dirty |
| кир- | (kir-) | enter, scrape |
| киреше | (kireshe) | income |
| кириш сөз | (kirish söz) | preface |
| кирпик | (kirpik) | eyelash |
| кирүү | (kirüü) | entrance |
| китеп | (kitep) | book |
| китеп дүкөнү | (kitep dükönü) | bookshop |
| китеп сатуучу | (kitep satuuchu) | bookseller |
| китепкана | (kitepkana) | library |
| кичине | (kichine) | small |
| кичине табак | (kichine tabak) | saucer |
| кичинекей | (kichinekey) | little |
| киши | (kishi) | person |
| класс | (klass) | classroom |
| клуб | (klub) | club |
| коён | (koyon) | rabbit |
| кожоюн | (kojoyun) | host |
| козгол- | (kozgol-) | move |
| козу | (kozu) | lamb |
| козу карын | (kozu karın) | mushroom |
| кой | (koy) | sheep |
| кой эти | (koy eti) | mutton |
| кой- | (koy-) | put |
| кол | (kol) | arm, hand |
| кол аарчы | (kol aarchı) | handkerchief |
| кол жуугуч | (kol juuguch) | sink |
| кол кап | (kol kap) | glove |
| кол кой- | (kol koy-) | sign |
| кол саат | (kol saat) | watch |
| кол сөмкө | (kol sömkö) | handbag |
| кол сун- | (kol sun-) | reach |
| кол тамга | (kol tamga) | signature |
| кол чап- | (kol chap-) | clap |
| кол чатыр | (kol chatır) | umbrella |
| колбаса | (kolbasa) | sausage |
| колдон- | (koldon-) | use |
| комедия | (komediya) | comedy |
| компания | (kompaniya) | company, firm |
| композитор | (kompozitor) | composer |
| компьютер | (komp'yuter) | computer |
| конверт | (konvert) | envelope |
| конок | (konok) | guest |
| концерт | (kontsert) | concert |
| коӊгуроо | (kongguroo) | bell |
| коӊшу | (kongshu) | neighbor, neighborhood |
| коом | (koom) | society |
| коон | (koon) | melon |
| коопсуз | (koopsuz) | safe |
| копол | (kopol) | rude |
| корго- | (korgo-) | defend, protect |
| коргонуу | (korgonuu) | defense |
| коргошун | (korgoshun) | lead |
| корзина | (korzina) | basket |
| корк- | (kork-) | afraid: be afraid |
| коркок | (korkok) | coward |
| коркоктук | (korkoktuk) | cowardice |
| коркунуч | (korkunuch) | danger |
| коркунучтуу | (korkunuchtuu) | dangerous |
| коркуу | (korkuu) | fear |
| короз | (koroz) | rooster |
| король | (korol') | king |
| короо | (koroo) | courtyard |

| | | |
|---|---|---|
| коррупция | (korruptsiya) | corruption |
| космос | (kosmos) | space |
| костюм | (kostyum) | suit |
| котор- | (kotor-) | translate |
| котормо | (kotormo) | translation |
| кофе | (kofe) | coffee |
| кош бойлук | (kosh boyluk) | pregnancy |
| кош болуңуз | (kosh bolunguz) | bye-bye |
| кош келипсиз | (kosh kelipsiz) | welcome |
| кош- | (kosh-) | add |
| кошуу | (koshuu) | addition |
| көбөй- | (köböy-) | increase |
| көбөйтүү | (köböytüü) | multiplication |
| көбүрөөк | (köbüröök) | more |
| көгүчкөн | (kögüchkön) | pigeon |
| көз | (köz) | eye |
| көз айнек | (köz aynek) | glasses |
| көйнөк | (köynök) | blouse, shirt |
| көк | (kök) | blue, sky |
| көк кытан | (kök kıtan) | stork |
| көкүрөк | (kökürök) | chest |
| көл | (köl) | lake |
| көлөкө | (kölökö) | shade, shadow |
| көм- | (köm-) | bury |
| көмөк | (kömök) | assistance |
| көмөктөш- | (kömöktösh-) | help |
| көмүр | (kömür) | coal |
| көңүл ач- | (köngül ach-) | enjoy |
| көп | (köp) | many, much |
| көпөлөк | (köpölök) | butterfly |
| көпүрө | (köpürö) | bridge |
| көпчүлүк | (köpchülük) | majority |
| көр- | (kör-) | see |
| көргөзмө | (körgözmö) | exhibition |
| көрпө | (körpö) | quilt |
| көрпөчө | (körpöchö) | mattress |
| көрсөт- | (körsöt-) | show |
| көрүн- | (körün-) | appear |
| көрүстөн | (körüstön) | cemetery |
| көтөр- | (kötör-) | lift, raise |
| көтөрүлүш | (kötörülüsh) | rebellion |
| көчө | (köchö) | street |
| кран | (kran) | faucet |
| кредит | (kredit) | credit |
| крокодил | (krokodil) | crocodile |
| кубаныч | (kubanıch) | joy |
| кудай | (kuday) | God |
| куй- | (kuy-) | pour |
| куйрук | (kuyruk) | tail |
| кула- | (kula-) | fall |
| кулак | (kulak) | ear |
| кулпу | (kulpu) | lock |
| кулпунay | (kulpunay) | strawberry |
| култивация | (kultivatsiya) | cultivation |
| кум | (kum) | sand |
| кумура | (kumura) | jug |
| кумурска | (kumurska) | ant |
| куну | (kunu) | cost |
| кур- | (kur-) | build |
| курал | (kural) | equipment, weapon |
| курал-жарак | (kural-jarak) | gun |
| курга- | (kurga-) | dry |
| кургак | (kurgak) | dry |
| кургакчылык | (kurgakchılık) | drought |
| курма | (kurma) | date |
| курмандык | (kurmandık) | sacrifice |
| курт | (kurt) | worm |
| курт-кумурска | (kurt-kumurska) | insect |
| курулуш | (kurulush) | building |
| курча- | (kurcha-) | surround |
| курчоо | (kurchoo) | siege |
| кус- | (kus-) | vomit |
| куткар- | (kutkar-) | rescue |
| куттукта- | (kuttukta-) | congratulate |
| куттуктоо | (kuttuktoo) | congratulation |
| куур- | (kuur-) | roast |
| кучакта- | (kuchakta-) | embrace |
| куш | (kush) | bird |
| куш канаты | (kush kanatı) | feather |
| күбө | (kübö) | witness |
| күз | (küz) | autumn |
| күзгү | (küzgü) | mirror |
| күйөө | (küyöö) | bridegroom, husband |
| күл | (kül) | ash |
| күл- | (kül-) | laugh |
| күлгүн | (külgün) | purple |
| күмүш | (kümüsh) | silver |
| күн | (kün) | day, sun |
| күн батыш | (kün batısh) | sunset |
| күн карама | (kün karama) | sunflower |
| күн күркүрөө | (kün kürküröö) | thunder |
| күн чыгыш | (kün chıgısh) | sunrise |
| күндүз | (kündüz) | daytime |

| КҮНӨӨКӨР | (künöökör) | guilty |
|---|---|---|
| КҮНӨӨСҮЗ | (künöösüz) | innocent |
| КҮНӨӨСҮЗДҮК | (künöösüzdük) | innocence |
| КҮРӨК | (kürök) | shovel, spade |
| КҮРӨҢ | (küröng) | brown |
| КҮРӨШ | (kürösh) | wrestling |
| КҮРӨШ- | (kürösh-) | fight |
| КҮРП | (kürp) | turkey |
| КҮРҮЧ | (kürüch) | rice |
| КҮТ- | (küt-) | wait |
| КҮТПӨГӨН | (kütpögön | sudden |
| ЖЕРДЕН | jerden) | |
| КҮҮГҮМ | (küügüm) | dusk |
| КҮЧ | (küch) | force, power, |
| | | strength |
| КҮЧСҮЗ | (küchsüz) | weak |
| КҮЧТҮҮ | (küchtüü) | powerful, |
| | | strong |
| КЫЗ | (kız) | daughter, girl |
| КЫЗГАЛДАК | (kızgaldak) | tulip |
| КЫЗГАН- | (kızgan-) | envy |
| КЫЗГАНЧААК | (kızganchaak) | jealous |
| КЫЗГЫЛТ | (kızgılt) | pink |
| КЫЗМАТКЕР | (kızmatker) | servant |
| КЫЗЫГУУ | (kızıguu) | interest |
| КЫЗЫК | (kızık) | interesting |
| КЫЗЫЛ | (kızıl) | red |
| КЫЙКЫР- | (kıykır-) | scream, shout |
| КЫЙРАТ- | (kıyrat-) | destroy |
| КЫЙЫН | (kıyın) | difficult, hard |
| КЫК | (kık) | fertilizer |
| КЫЛ- | (kıl-) | do |
| КЫЛМЫШ | (kılmısh) | crime |
| КЫЛМЫШКЕР | (kılmıshker) | criminal |
| КЫЛЫМ | (kılım) | century |
| КЫЛЫЧ | (kılıch) | sword |
| КЫМБАТ | (kımbat) | expensive |
| КЫМБАТТУУ | (kımbattuu) | dear |
| КЫРК | (kırk) | forty |
| КЫСКА | (kıska) | short |
| КЫЧКЫЛ | (kıchkıl) | sour |
| КЫШ | (kısh) | brick, winter |
| КЭЭДЕ | (keede) | sometimes |
| ЛАМПА | (lampa) | lamp |
| ЛЕКЦИЯ | (lektsiya) | lecture |
| ЛИМОН | (limon) | lemon |
| ЛИНГВИСТ | (lingvist) | linguist |
| ЛИФТ | (lift) | elevator |
| ЛЫЖА | (lıja) | skiing |

| маалымат | (maalımat) | data |
|---|---|---|
| маанилүү | (maanilüü) | important |
| магнитофон | (magnitofon) | tape recorder |
| маданият | (madaniyat) | culture |
| май | (may) | butter, fat, |
| | | May, oil |
| майда акча | (mayda akcha) | change |
| майдала- | (maydala-) | grind |
| маймыл | (maymıl) | monkey |
| майрам | (mayram) | holiday |
| майрамда- | (mayramda-) | celebrate |
| майрамдоо | (mayramdoo) | celebration |
| макал | (makal) | proverb |
| макала | (makala) | article |
| максат | (maksat) | purpose |
| макта- | (makta-) | praise |
| мактан- | (maktan-) | boast |
| мактаныч | (maktanıch) | pride |
| макулдау | (makuldau) | approval |
| макулдаш- | (makuldash-) | agree |
| мамлекет | (mamleket) | state |
| манжа | (manja) | finger |
| маңдай | (mangday) | forehead |
| марка | (marka) | stamp |
| март | (mart) | March |
| мас | (mas) | drunk |
| математика | (matematika) | mathematics |
| материал | (material) | material |
| матч | (match) | match |
| махаббат | (makhabbat) | love |
| машина | (mashina) | car, machine |
| машинка | (mashinka) | typewriter |
| маяна | (mayana) | salary |
| медицина | (meditsina) | medicine |
| медсестра | (medsestra) | nurse |
| мезгил | (mezgil) | season |
| меймандостук | (meymandostuk) | hospitality |
| мейманкана | (meymankana) | hotel |
| мектеп | (mektep) | school |
| мен | (men) | I |
| менен | (menen) | by, with |
| мени | (meni) | me |
| меники | (meniki) | mine |
| менин | (menin) | my |
| меню | (menyu) | menu |
| металл | (metall) | metal |
| метро | (metro) | subway |
| мечит | (mechit) | mosque |
| меш | (mesh) | stove |

| | | |
|---|---|---|
| мыйзам | (mıyzam) | law |
| мык | (mık) | nail, screw |
| мылтык | (mıltık) | rifle |
| мында | (mında) | here |
| мырза | (mırza) | gentleman |
| мышык | (mıshık) | cat |
| милдет | (mildet) | duty |
| милиция | (militsiya) | policeman |
| миллиард | (milliard) | billion |
| миллион | (million) | million |
| мин- | (min-) | get on, ride |
| миндаль | (mindal') | almond |
| министр | (ministr) | minister |
| миӊ | (ming) | thousand |
| мисал | (misal) | example |
| мискей | (miskey) | pan |
| мифология | (mifologiya) | mythology |
| мода | (moda) | fashion |
| момент | (moment) | moment |
| мор | (mor) | chimney |
| мотор | (motor) | engine |
| мотоцикл | (mototsikl) | motorcycle |
| моюн | (moyun) | neck |
| моюн орогуч | (moyun oroguch) | scarf |
| мөндүр | (möndür) | hail |
| мугалим | (mugalim) | teacher |
| муз | (muz) | ice |
| муздаткыч | (muzdatkıch) | refrigerator |
| музей | (muzey) | museum |
| музоо эти | (muzoo eti) | veal |
| музыка | (muzıka) | music |
| музыкант | (muzıkant) | musician |
| мунара | (munara) | tower |
| мурда | (murda) | ago, before |
| мурун | (murun) | nose |
| мурут | (murut) | mustache |
| мурч | (murch) | pepper |
| мусулман | (musulman) | Muslim |
| мүйүз | (müyüz) | horn |
| мүмкүн | (mümkün) | possible, probably |
| мүмкүн эмес | (mümkün emes) | impossible |
| мүмкүндүк | (mümkündük) | possibility |
| мүнөт | (münöt) | minute |
| мүчө | (müchö) | member, suffix |
| мээ | (mee) | brain |

| | | |
|---|---|---|
| наабайчы | (naabaychı) | baker |
| назар | (nazar) | attention |
| назик | (nazik) | gentle |
| найза | (nayza) | spear |
| нак акча | (nak akcha) | cash |
| намаз оку- | (namaz oku-) | pray |
| намыс | (namıs) | honor |
| нан | (nan) | bread |
| нарк | (nark) | value |
| натыйжа | (natıyja) | result |
| небере | (nebere) | grandchild |
| негизги | (negizgi) | main |
| нерв | (nerv) | nerve |
| нерсе | (nerse) | any |
| нефть | (neft') | oil |
| ниет | (niet) | intention |
| ноябрь | (noyabr') | November |
| нөл | (nöl) | zero |
| нымдуу | (nımduu) | damp |
| обон | (obon) | tune |
| озуп кет- | (ozup ket-) | surpass |
| ой | (oy) | idea, thought |
| ойгон- | (oygon-) | awake, wake |
| ойгот- | (oygot-) | awake, wake |
| ойло- | (oylo-) | think |
| ойно- | (oyno-) | play |
| океан | (okean) | ocean |
| октябрь | (oktyabr') | October |
| оку- | (oku-) | read |
| оку изилде- | (oku izilde-) | study |
| окут- | (okut-) | teach |
| окуу акысы | (okuu akısı) | tuition |
| окууну бүтүрүү | (okuunu bütürüü) | graduation |
| окуучу | (okuuchu) | reader |
| окуя | (okuya) | event |
| окшо- | (oksho-) | resemble |
| окшош | (okshosh) | alike, same, similar |
| олтургуч | (olturguch) | stool |
| омуртка | (omurtka) | spine |
| он | (on) | ten |
| он алты | (on altı) | sixteen |
| он беш | (on besh) | fifteen |
| он бир | (on bir) | eleven |
| он жети | (on jeti) | seventeen |
| он сегиз | (on segiz) | eighteen |
| он тогуз | (on toguz) | nineteen |
| он төрт | (on tört) | fourteen |

| | | |
|---|---|---|
| он үч | (on üch) | thirteen |
| он эки | (on eki) | twelve |
| он эки дана | (on eki dana) | dozen |
| оң | (ong) | right |
| оңдо- | (ongdo-) | repair |
| оңой | (ongoy) | easy |
| ооба | (ooba) | yes |
| ооз | (ooz) | mouth |
| оор | (oor) | heavy |
| оору | (ooru) | illness, pain |
| оорукана | (oorukana) | hospital |
| ооруу | (ooruu) | ill, sick |
| опера | (opera) | opera |
| операция | (operatsiya) | operation |
| оптик | (optik) | optician |
| оптому менен сатуу | (optomu menen satuu) | wholesale |
| ормон жаңгак | (ormon janggak) | hazelnut |
| орнош- | (ornosh-) | situated: be situated |
| оро- | (oro-) | wrap |
| орок | (orok) | sickle |
| орозо | (orozo) | fast |
| орто | (orto) | medium, middle |
| орток | (ortok) | partner |
| орун | (orun) | place, seat |
| орундук | (orunduk) | chair |
| оруу | (oruu) | harvest |
| от | (ot) | fire |
| открытка | (otkrıtka) | postcard |
| отор | (otor) | herd |
| отставкага чык- | (otstavkaga chık-) | retire |
| отуз | (otuz) | thirty |
| отур- | (otur-) | sit |
| отургуч | (oturguch) | armchair |
| отуруш | (oturush) | party |
| офицер | (ofitser) | officer |
| официант | (ofitsiant) | waiter |
| оффис | (offis) | office |
| ошондой | (oshondoy) | such |
| ошондуктан | (oshonduktan) | because, therefore |
| оюн | (oyun) | game |
| оюн шоок | (oyun shook) | entertainment |
| оюнчук | (oyunchuk) | toy |
| өгөө | (ögöö) | file |
| өгүз | (ögüz) | ox |
| өзгөрт- | (özgört-) | change |
| өзү | (özü) | herself, himself, itself |
| өзүм | (özüm) | myself |
| өзүмүз | (özümüz) | ourselves |
| өзүн алып жүр- | (özün alıp jür-) | behave |
| өзүң | (özüng) | yourself |
| өзүңүз | (özüngüz) | yourselves |
| өкмөт | (ökmöt) | government |
| өкүм | (öküm) | verdict |
| өкүнүч | (ökünüch) | regret |
| өл- | (öl-) | die |
| өлтүр- | (öltür-) | kill |
| өлүк | (ölük) | dead |
| өлүм | (ölüm) | death |
| өлчөм | (ölchöm) | measure |
| өмүр | (ömür) | life |
| өндүр- | (öndür-) | produce |
| өнүгүү | (önügüü) | development |
| өп- | (öp-) | kiss |
| өпкө | (öpkö) | lung |
| өрдөк | (ördök) | duck |
| өрөөн | (öröön) | valley |
| өрт | (ört) | fire |
| өрүк | (örük) | apricot |
| өс- | (ös-) | grow |
| өсүмдүк | (ösümdük) | plant |
| өсүү | (ösüü) | growth |
| өт- | (öt-) | pass |
| өткөн | (ötkön) | last |
| өткүр | (ötkür) | sharp |
| өтө | (ötö) | very |
| өтүк | (ötük) | boot |
| өтүкчү | (ötükchü) | shoemaker |
| өтүн- | (ötün-) | apply |
| өтүнүч | (ötünüch) | suggestion |
| өч алуу | (öch aluu) | revenge |
| өчүр- | (öchür-) | erase, extinguish, put out |
| өчүргүч | (öchürgüch) | eraser |
| пайгамбар | (paygambar) | prophet |
| пайда | (payda) | benefit, interest, profit |
| пайдалуу | (paydaluu) | useful |

| | | |
|---|---|---|
| палоо | (paloo) | rice |
| пальто | (pal'to) | overcoat |
| пар | (par) | pair |
| параграф | (paragraf) | paragraph |
| парад | (parad) | parade |
| паралич | (paralich) | paralysis |
| парда | (parda) | curtain |
| парк | (park) | park |
| парта | (parta) | desk |
| партия | (partiya) | party |
| паспорт | (pasport) | passport |
| пахта | (pakhta) | cotton |
| пациент | (patsient) | patient |
| periшte | (perishte) | angel |
| петрушка | (petrushka) | parsley |
| печенье | (pechen'ye) | cookie |
| пиво | (pivo) | beer |
| пижама | (pijama) | pajamas |
| пикир | (pikir) | opinion |
| пил | (pil) | elephant |
| писте | (piste) | pistachio |
| пияз | (piyaz) | onion |
| планета | (planeta) | planet |
| пластинка | (plastinka) | record |
| платформа | (platforma) | platform |
| плащ | (plashch) | raincoat |
| пленка | (plenka) | film |
| пляж | (plyaj) | beach |
| поезд | (poezd) | train |
| пол | (pol) | floor |
| помидор | (pomidor) | tomato |
| поп | (pop) | priest |
| посылка | (posilka) | parcel |
| почто | (pochto) | post office |
| почто жашиги | (pochto jashigi) | mailbox |
| почто чыгындары | (pochto chigindari) | postage |
| почточу | (pochtochu) | mailman |
| поэзия | (poeziya) | poetry |
| президент | (prezident) | president |
| премьер-министр | (prem'er-ministr) | prime minister |
| проблема | (problema) | problem |
| провинция | (provintsiya) | province |
| программа | (programma) | program |
| проза | (proza) | prose |
| проспект | (prospekt) | avenue |
| пулемет | (pulemet) | machine gun |
| пьеса | (p'esa) | play |

| | | |
|---|---|---|
| радио | (radio) | radio |
| размер | (razmer) | size |
| рак | (rak) | cancer |
| рамка | (ramka) | frame |
| расмий | (rasmiy) | official |
| реализм | (realizm) | realism |
| резервация | (reservatsiya) | reservation |
| рейс | (reys) | flight |
| республика | (respublika) | republic |
| ресторан | (restoran) | restaurant |
| рецепт | (retsept) | prescription |
| роза | (roza) | rose |
| роман | (roman) | novel |
| ромашка | (romashka) | daisy |
| ромб | (romb) | diamond |
| рух | (rukh) | spirit |
| саадак | (saadak) | bow |
| саат ондоочу | (saat ongdoochu) | watchmaker |
| саат | (saat) | hour |
| сабак | (sabak) | lesson |
| сабаттуу | (sabattuu) | literate |
| сабиз | (sabiz) | carrot |
| сакал | (sakal) | beard |
| сахна | (sakhna) | stage |
| сакта- | (sakta-) | keep |
| сактан- | (saktan-) | prevent |
| сактануу | (saktanuu) | precaution |
| салам | (salam) | hello |
| салат | (salat) | lettuce, salad |
| салык | (salik) | tax |
| салыштыруу | (salishtiruu) | comparison |
| салкын | (salkin) | cool |
| салмактуу | (salmaktuu) | serious |
| салтанат | (saltanat) | ceremony |
| саман | (saman) | straw |
| самын | (samin) | soap |
| самолёт | (samolyot) | airplane, plane |
| сан | (san) | amount, number, quantity, thigh |
| сана- | (sana-) | count |
| сапар | (sapar) | journey |
| сапат | (sapat) | quality |
| сарай | (saray) | palace |
| саргылт | (sargilt) | orange |

| | | |
|---|---|---|
| сары | (sarı) | yellow |
| сарымсак | (sarımsak) | garlic |
| сарпта- | (sarpta-) | spend |
| сат- | (sat-) | sell |
| сатып ал- | (satıp al-) | buy, shop |
| сатып алуучу | (satıp aluuchu) | buyer, customer |
| саттуу | (sattuu) | luck |
| сатуу | (satuu) | sale |
| сатуучу | (satuuchu) | salesperson, seller |
| саякат | (sayakat) | travel |
| саясат | (sayasat) | politics |
| сайу | (sayu) | shot |
| саз | (saz) | swamp |
| светофор | (svetofor) | traffic light |
| свитер | (sviter) | sweater |
| себеп | (sebep) | cause, reason |
| сегиз | (segiz) | eight |
| секир- | (sekir-) | jump |
| секретарь | (sekretar') | secretary |
| сексен | (seksen) | eighty |
| секция | (sektsiya) | section |
| секунда | (sekunda) | second |
| селдерей | (selderey) | celery |
| семиз | (semiz) | fat |
| сен, сиз | (sen, siz) | you |
| сеники, сиздики | (seniki, sizdiki) | yours |
| сенин, силердин | (senin, silerdin) | your |
| сентябрь | (sentyabr') | September |
| серпилме зым | (serpilme zım) | spring |
| серүүндө- | (serüündö-) | stroll |
| сейрек | (seyrek) | seldom |
| сез- | (sez-) | feel |
| сезим | (sezim) | feeling |
| силер, сиздер | (siler, sizder) | you |
| символ | (simvol) | symbol |
| сий- | (siy-) | urinate |
| синди | (singdi) | sister |
| скелет | (skelet) | skeleton |
| скульптура | (skulptura) | sculpture |
| согуш | (sogush) | war |
| соко | (soko) | plow |
| сокур | (sokur) | blind |
| сокурлук | (sokurluk) | blindness |
| сол | (sol) | left |
| сомке | (somke) | bag |

| | | |
|---|---|---|
| соңку | (songku) | end |
| соо | (soo) | healthy |
| сот | (sot) | court, judge |
| союз | (soyuz) | union |
| сөөк | (söök) | bone |
| сөз | (söz) | speech, word |
| сөздүк | (sözdük) | dictionary |
| спорт | (sport) | sport |
| станция | (stantsiya) | station |
| студент | (student) | student |
| су агымы | (su agımı) | flood |
| сулуу | (suluu) | beautiful |
| сулуулук | (suluuluk) | beauty |
| сунуш кыл- | (sunush kıl-) | recommend |
| сунуш- | (sunush-) | offer |
| сур | (sur) | grey |
| сура- | (sura-) | ask, request |
| суроо | (suroo) | question |
| суу астында сүзүүчү кеме | (suu astında süzüüchü keme) | submarine |
| суу | (suu) | moist, water |
| суук | (suuk) | cold |
| суулу | (suulu) | wet |
| суусундук | (suusunduk) | beverage |
| сүюк | (suyuk) | liquid |
| сүлгү | (sülgü) | towel |
| сүңгү- | (sünggü-) | dive |
| сүрөт | (süröt) | painting, picture |
| сүрөтчү | (sürötchü) | artist |
| сүрөттө- | (süröttö-) | describe |
| сүрөттөө | (süröttöö) | description |
| сүт | (süt) | milk |
| сүй- | (süy-) | love |
| сүйкүмдүү | (süykümdüü) | handsome, pretty |
| сүйкүмдүүлүк | (süykümdüülük) | attraction |
| сүйлө- | (süylö-) | speak |
| сүйлөм | (süylöm) | sentence |
| сүйөн- | (süyön-) | rely |
| сүз- | (süz-) | swim |
| сүзгүч | (süzgüch) | strainer |
| сүзүү | (süzüü) | swimming |
| сын атооч | (sın atooch) | adjective |
| сына- | (sına-) | test |
| сындыр- | (sındır-) | break |
| сынык | (sınık) | broken |
| сыноо | (sınoo) | examination |
| сыпайы | (sıpayı) | polite |

| | | |
|---|---|---|
| сыр | (sır) | cheese |
| сырдоочуу | (sırdoochu) | painter |
| сыя | (sıya) | ink |
| сыяктуу | (sıyaktuu) | as if, like |
| сыйынуу | (sıyınuu) | prayer |
| сыйкыр | (sıykır) | spell |
| сыйкырдуу | (sıykırduu) | magic |
| сыйла- | (sıyla-) | present |
| сыйпала- | (sıypala-) | stroke |
| сызгыч | (sızgıch) | ruler |
| сызык | (sızık) | line |
| сызуу | (sızuu) | drawing |
| | | |
| -та, -те, -то, -тө | (-ta, -te, -to, -tö) | at, in |
| тааны- | (taanı-) | know, recognize |
| тааныштыр- | (taanıshtır-) | introduce |
| таасир | (taasir) | effect, influence |
| табигый | (tabigıy) | natural |
| табият | (tabiyat) | nature |
| таблетка | (tabletka) | pill |
| табынуу | (tabınuu) | worship |
| табышка жет- | (tabıshka jet-) | succeed |
| тагдыр | (tagdır) | fate |
| тажрыйба | (tajrıyba) | experience |
| таз | (taz) | bald |
| таза | (taza) | clean, pure |
| тазала- | (tazala-) | clean |
| тай- | (tay-) | slip |
| тай эже | (tay eje) | aunt |
| тайгак | (taygak) | slippery |
| тайыз | (tayız) | shallow |
| так | (tak) | concrete |
| такси | (taksi) | cab, taxi |
| тактay | (taktay) | wood |
| тактооч | (taktooch) | adverb |
| тал | (tal) | willow |
| тала- | (tala-) | plunder |
| талаа | (talaa) | field |
| талаш- | (talash-) | argue |
| талаш-тартыш | (talash-tartısh) | argument |
| талкылоо | (talkıloo) | discussion |
| талып кал- | (talıp kal-) | faint |
| тамак | (tamak) | dish, throat |
| тамак-аш | (tamak-ash) | food |
| тамеки | (tameki) | cigarette, tobacco |
| тамеки тарт- | (tameki tart-) | smoke |
| тамчы | (tamchı) | drop |
| тамыр | (tamır) | root |
| -тан, -тен, -тон, -төн | (-tan, -ten, -ton, tön) | from |
| тан- | (tan-) | deny |
| танда- | (tanda-) | choose, select |
| таң | (tang) | dawn |
| таң эртең | (tang erteng) | morning |
| таңдан- | (tangdan-) | admire |
| таңкы аш | (tangkı ash) | breakfast |
| тап- | (tap-) | find |
| тапичке | (tapichke) | slipper |
| тапшыр- | (tapshır-) | order |
| тапшырма | (tapshırma) | assignment |
| тар | (tar) | narrow, tight |
| тара- | (tara-) | comb |
| тараза | (taraza) | scale |
| тарак | (tarak) | comb |
| тарелка | (tarelka) | dish, plate |
| тарт- | (tart-) | pull |
| тартип | (tartip) | behavior |
| тарых | (tarıkh) | history |
| тарыхчы | (tarıkhchı) | historian |
| таш | (tash) | stone |
| ташбака | (tashbaka) | tortoise |
| таштанды | (tashtandı) | trash |
| ташуучу | (tashuuchu) | porter |
| ташы- | (tashı-) | carry |
| таттуу | (tattuu) | sweet |
| таттуу тамак | (tattuu tamak) | dessert |
| таяке | (tayake) | uncle |
| театр | (teatr) | theater |
| тегерек | (tegerek) | circle |
| тегирмен | (tegirmen) | mill |
| тез | (tez) | fast, quick, speedy |
| тез жардам | (tez jardam) | ambulance |
| тез-тез | (tez-tez) | often |
| текче | (tekche) | bookcase, shelf |
| телевизор | (televizor) | television |
| телеграмма | (telegramma) | telegram |
| телефон | (telefon) | telephone |
| телефон автомат | (telefon avtomat) | phone booth, public phone |

| | | |
|---|---|---|
| телефон номуру | (telefon nomuru) | phone number |
| тема | (tema) | subject |
| темир | (temir) | iron |
| темир жол | (temir jol) | railroad |
| температура | (temperatura) | fever, temperature |
| тең | (teng) | equal |
| теория | (teoriya) | theory |
| теп- | (tep-) | kick |
| тергөө | (tergöö) | investigation |
| терде- | (terde-) | sweat |
| терезе | (tereze) | window |
| терек | (terek) | poplar |
| терең | (tereng) | deep |
| терендик | (terengdik) | depth |
| тери | (teri) | fur, leather, skin |
| термометр | (termometr) | thermometer |
| тешик | (teshik) | hole |
| тиги | (tigi) | that, that |
| тиги жерде | (tigi jerde) | there |
| тизе | (tize) | knee |
| тий- | (tiy-) | touch |
| тик- | (tik-) | sew |
| тикмечи | (tikmechi) | tailor |
| тил | (til) | language, tongue |
| тил илими | (til ilimi) | linguistics |
| тиле- | (tile-) | wish |
| тилек | (tilek) | wish |
| тинт- | (tint-) | seek |
| тираж | (tiraj) | circulation |
| тиричилик | (tirichilik) | excuse |
| тиш | (tish) | tooth |
| тиш дарыгери | (tish darıgeri) | dentist |
| тиш оору | (tish ooru) | toothache |
| тиш паста | (tish pasta) | toothpaste |
| тиш щётка | (tish shchyotka) | toothbrush |
| тиште- | (tishte-) | bite |
| тогуз | (toguz) | nine |
| тозок | (tozok) | hell |
| токой | (tokoy) | forest |
| токойчо | (tokoycho) | wood |
| токсон | (tokson) | ninety |
| токто- | (tokto-) | stop |
| токтот- | (toktot-) | stop |
| толкун | (tolkun) | wave |

| | | |
|---|---|---|
| толкундоо | (tolkundoo) | excitement |
| толо | (tolo) | full |
| толтур- | (toltur-) | fill |
| толуктооч | (toluktooch) | object |
| томоло- | (tomolo-) | roll |
| тоң | (tong) | frost |
| тоң- | (tong-) | freeze |
| тоо | (too) | mountain |
| тоок | (took) | hen |
| тоок эти | (took eti) | chicken |
| топ | (top) | ball |
| топурак | (topurak) | clay, earth, soil |
| торгой | (torgoy) | sparrow |
| торт | (tort) | cake |
| төлө- | (tölö-) | pay |
| төмөн | (tömön) | down, low |
| төмөндө | (tömöndö) | below |
| төңкөрүш | (töngkörüsh) | revolution |
| төө | (töö) | camel |
| төрт | (tört) | four |
| трамвай | (tramvay) | tram |
| транспорт | (transport) | traffic |
| тротуар | (trotuar) | sidewalk |
| туз | (tuz) | salt |
| туман | (tuman) | fog |
| тумоо | (tumoo) | cold |
| тумшук | (tumshuk) | beak |
| тур- | (tur-) | get up, stand |
| туризм | (turizm) | tourism |
| турист | (turist) | tourist |
| тутка | (tutka) | handle |
| тууган | (tuugan) | relative |
| туул- | (tuul-) | born: be born |
| туулган күн | (tuulgan kün) | birthday |
| туулуш | (tuulush) | birth |
| туура | (tuura) | correct, straight |
| тууралуу | (tuuraluu) | about |
| түбөлүк | (tübölük) | eternity |
| түгөл | (tügöl) | complete |
| түз | (tüz) | plain |
| түзөт- | (tüzöt-) | correct |
| түймө | (tüymö) | button |
| түйүн | (tüyün) | knot |
| түктүү килем | (tüktüü kilem) | rug |
| түкүр- | (tükür-) | spit |
| түлкү | (tülkü) | fox |
| түн | (tün) | night |

| | | |
|---|---|---|
| түн ортосу | (tün ortosu) | midnight |
| түндүк | (tündük) | north |
| түр | (tür) | kind |
| түрмө | (türmö) | jail, prison |
| түрү суук | (türü suuk) | ugly |
| түрүү | (türüü) | alive |
| түс | (tüs) | color |
| түш | (tüsh) | afternoon, dream, noon |
| түш- | (tüsh-) | get off |
| түшкү тамак | (tüshkü tamak) | lunch |
| түштүк | (tüshtük) | south |
| түшүн- | (tüshün-) | understand |
| түшүндүр- | (tüshündür-) | explain |
| түшүндүрүү | (tüshündürüü) | explanation |
| тый- | (tıy-) | forbid |
| тыйын | (tıyın) | coin |
| тыйын чычкан | (tıyın chıchkan) | squirrel |
| тынч | (tınch) | calm, quiet |
| тынчсыздандыр- | (tınchsızdandır-) | bother |
| тынчтык | (tınchtık) | peace, silence |
| тынчы- | (tınchı-) | quiet: be quiet |
| тыңда- | (tıngda-) | listen |
| тырмак | (tırmak) | nail |
| тырыш- | (tırısh-) | try |
| тыт | (tıt) | mulberry |
| тышкарыда | (tıshkarıda) | outside |
| | | |
| убада бер- | (ubada ber-) | promise |
| убакыт | (ubakıt) | time |
| узун | (uzun) | long |
| узундук | (uzunduk) | length |
| уй | (uy) | cow |
| уй эти | (uy eti) | beef |
| уйкала- | (uykala-) | rub |
| уйку | (uyku) | sleep |
| ук- | (uk-) | hear |
| уксус | (uksus) | vinegar |
| укта- | (ukta-) | sleep |
| уламыш | (ulamısh) | legend |
| улан- | (ulan-) | continue |
| улут | (ulut) | nation |
| улутчулдук | (ulutchulduk) | nationalism |
| ун | (un) | flour |
| универмаг | (univermag) | department store |
| университет | (universitet) | university |

| | | |
|---|---|---|
| унут- | (unut-) | forget |
| ур- | (ur-) | hit |
| урмат | (urmat) | respect |
| урматта- | (urmatta-) | respect |
| урп-адат | (urp-adat) | custom |
| урук | (uruk) | grain, seed |
| уруксат ет- | (uruksat et-) | permit |
| уруш | (urush) | battle |
| устара | (ustara) | razor |
| уу | (uu) | poison |
| уул | (uul) | son |
| уулуу | (uuluu) | poisonous |
| уурда- | (uurda-) | steal |
| ууру | (uuru) | thief |
| уч- | (uch-) | fly |
| уял- | (uyal-) | ashamed: be ashamed |
| уялчаак | (uyalchaak) | shy |
| | | |
| үгүт-насыят | (ügüt-nasıyat) | propaganda |
| үй | (üy) | home, house |
| үй тоноочу | (üy tonoochu) | burglar |
| үй-бүлө | (üy-bülö) | family |
| үйлөн- | (üylön-) | marry |
| үйлөнүү | (üylönüü) | marriage |
| үйрөн- | (üyrön-) | learn, used: be used to |
| үкү | (ükü) | owl |
| үмүт | (ümüt) | hope |
| үмүт кыл- | (ümüt kıl-) | hope |
| үндүү | (ündüü) | vowel |
| үнсүз тыбыш | (ünsüz tıbısh) | consonant |
| үстөл | (üstöl) | table |
| үстүндө | (üstündö) | above, on, over |
| үтүк | (ütük) | iron |
| үтүр | (ütür) | comma |
| үч | (üch) | three |
| үч бурчтук | (üch burchtuk) | triangle |
| үчүн | (üchün) | for |
| | | |
| фабрика | (fabrika) | factory |
| фамилия | (familiya) | surname |
| фармацевт | (farmatsevt) | pharmacist |
| февраль | (fevral') | February |
| ферма | (ferma) | farm |
| фестиваль | (festival') | festival |
| физика | (fizika) | physics |
| фольклор | (fol'klor) | folklore |

| | | |
|---|---|---|
| фонтан | (fontan) | fountain |
| форма | (forma) | shape |
| фотоаппарат | (fotoapparat) | camera |
| фотография | (fotografiya) | photo |
| футбол | (futbol) | soccer |
| хирургия | (khirurgiya) | surgery |
| христиан | (khristian) | Christian |
| цемент | (tsement) | cement |
| цензура | (tsenzura) | censorship |
| цирк | (tsirk) | circus |
| чабуул | (chabuul) | attack |
| чабуул кой- | (chabuul koy-) | attack |
| чагылган | (chagılgan) | lightning |
| чай | (chay) | tea |
| чай пулу | (chay pulu) | tip |
| чайка- | (chayka-) | shake |
| чайна- | (chayna-) | chew |
| чайнек | (chaynek) | teapot |
| чака | (chaka) | bucket |
| чакыр- | (chakır-) | call, invite, summon |
| чакыруу | (chakıruu) | invitation |
| чамасы менен | (chaması menen) | about |
| чана | (chana) | sled |
| чаң | (chang) | dust |
| чаңкаган | (changkagan) | thirsty |
| чарчаган | (charchagan) | tired |
| чарчы | (charchı) | square |
| чатыр | (chatır) | roof |
| чач | (chach) | hair |
| чачтарач | (chachtarach) | hairdresser |
| чачырат- | (chachırat-) | scatter |
| чеберлик | (cheberlik) | skill |
| чегиртке | (chegirtke) | grasshopper |
| чейин | (cheyin) | until |
| чек | (chek) | check |
| чек ара | (chek ara) | border |
| чек кой- | (chek koy-) | restrict |
| чекит | (chekit) | period |
| чемодан | (chemodan) | suitcase |
| черт- | (chert-) | play |
| чет | (chet) | edge |
| чет элдик | (chet eldik) | foreigner |
| чеч- | (chech-) | decide, solve |
| чечим | (chechim) | decision |
| чийки | (chiyki) | raw |
| чири- | (chiri-) | rot |
| чиркей | (chirkey) | mosquito |
| чиркөө | (chirköö) | church |
| чочко | (chochko) | pig |
| чочко эти | (chochko eti) | pork |
| чоң | (chong) | big, great, huge |
| чоң ата | (chong ata) | grandfather |
| чоң эне | (chong ene) | grandmother |
| чөгүп кет- | (chögüp ket-) | drown |
| чөл | (chöl) | desert |
| чөнтөк | (chöntök) | pocket |
| чөп | (chöp) | grass |
| чыдамдуу | (chıdamduu) | patient |
| чыгарма | (chıgarma) | composition |
| чыгуу | (chıguu) | exit |
| чыгым | (chıgım) | expense |
| чыгыш | (chıgısh) | east |
| чык- | (chık-) | exit |
| чыканак | (chıkanak) | elbow |
| чымын | (chımın) | fly |
| чын | (chın) | real, true |
| чындык | (chındık) | truth |
| чынчыл | (chınchıl) | honest |
| чыны аяк | (chını ayak) | cup |
| чычкан | (chıchkan) | mouse |
| шаар | (shaar) | city, town |
| шаардын чети | (shaardın cheti) | suburb |
| шабдалы | (shabdalı) | peach |
| шайла- | (shayla-) | elect |
| шайлоо | (shayloo) | election |
| шайтан | (shaytan) | ghost, Satan |
| шам | (sham) | candle |
| шарап | (sharap) | wine |
| шаршемби | (sharshembi) | Wednesday |
| шарт | (shart) | condition |
| шаты | (shatı) | ladder, stairs |
| шахмат | (shakhmat) | chess |
| шедевр | (shedevr) | masterpiece |
| шейшемби | (sheyshembi) | Tuesday |
| шейшеп | (sheyshep) | sheet |
| шектенүү | (shektenüü) | doubt |
| шире | (shire) | fruit juice |
| ширеңке | (shirengke) | match |
| шиши- | (shishi-) | swell |
| шишик | (shishik) | swelling |
| шкаф | (shkaf) | cupboard |
| шоола | (shoola) | ray |

| | | |
|---|---|---|
| шорпо | (shorpo) | soup |
| шорт | (short) | shorts |
| шпинат | (shpinat) | spinach |
| шым | (shım) | pants |
| шып | (shıp) | ceiling |
| шыпыр- | (shıpır-) | sweep |
| шыпыргы | (shıpırgı) | broom |
| | | |
| щётка | (shchyotka) | brush |
| | | |
| ызы-чуу | (ızı-chuu) | noise |
| ыйла- | (ıyla-) | cry, weep |
| ылдамдык | (ıldamdık) | speed |
| ыңгайлуу | (ınggayluu) | comfortable |
| ыр | (ır) | poem, song |
| ыраазы | (ıraazı) | glad |
| ыракмат айт- | (ırakmat ayt-) | thank |
| ыракым этиңиз | (ırakım etingiz) | please |
| ырахат | (ırakhat) | pleasure |
| ырда- | (ırda-) | sing |
| ыргыт- | (ırgıt-) | throw |
| ырчы | (ırchı) | singer |
| ыстакан | (ıstakan) | glass |
| ысык | (ısık) | hot |
| ысыктык | (ısıktık) | heat |
| | | |
| эгерде | (egerde) | if |
| эгиз | (egiz) | twin |
| эгин | (egin) | crop |
| эже | (eje) | aunt, sister |
| эз- | (ez-) | crush |
| эзүү | (ezüü) | oppression |
| эк- | (ek-) | plant, sow |
| эки | (eki) | two |
| экономика | (ekonomika) | economics |
| экран | (ekran) | screen |
| эл | (el) | people |
| эл аралык | (el aralık) | international |
| электр | (elektr) | electricity |
| элүү | (elüü) | fifty |
| элчи | (elchi) | ambassador |
| эм | (em) | cure |
| эм чөп | (em chöp) | herb |
| эм- | (em-) | suck |
| эмгек акы | (emgek akı) | wage |
| эмен | (emen) | oak |
| эмерек | (emerek) | furniture |
| эмес | (emes) | not |
| эмкана | (emkana) | clinic |
| эмне | (emne) | what |
| эмне үчүн | (emne üchün) | why |
| эмчек | (emchek) | breast |
| эне | (ene) | mother |
| эң жакшы | (eng jakshı) | best |
| эң көп | (eng köp) | most |
| эпик | (epik) | epic |
| эри- | (eri-) | melt |
| эрин | (erin) | lip |
| эркек | (erkek) | man |
| эркек бала | (erkek bala) | boy |
| эркин | (erkin) | free |
| эркиндик | (erkindik) | freedom, independence |
| эрте | (erte) | early |
| эртең | (erteng) | tomorrow |
| эс | (es) | memory |
| эсеп | (esep) | account, bill |
| эсепте- | (esepte-) | calculate |
| эске түшүр- | (eske tüshür-) | remember |
| эске түшүрт- | (eske tüshürt-) | remind |
| эски | (eski) | old |
| эсте- | (este-) | yawn |
| эстелик | (estelik) | monument |
| эт | (et) | meat |
| эт дүкөнү | (et dükönü) | butcher shop |
| этиш | (etish) | verb |
| эч жерде | (ech jerde) | nowhere |
| эч качан | (ech kachan) | never |
| эч ким | (ech kim) | nobody |
| эч нерсе | (ech nerse) | nothing |
| эчки | (echki) | goat |
| эшек | (eshek) | donkey |
| эшик | (eshik) | door |
| ээ | (ee) | subject |
| ээк | (eek) | chin |
| ээрчи- | (eerchi-) | follow |
| | | |
| юбка | (yubka) | skirt |
| | | |
| январь | (yanvar') | January |

# TATAR - ENGLISH INDEX

| | | | | | |
|---|---|---|---|---|---|
| абрикос | (abrikos) | apricot | акыл | (akıl) | mind |
| абстракт | (abstrakt) | abstract | акылдан язган | (akıldan yazgan) | crazy |
| абый | (abıy) | brother, uncle | акыллы | (akıllı) | clever, intelligent |
| авария | (avariya) | accident | ал- | (al-) | take |
| август | (avgust) | August | алар | (alar) | they |
| авиапочта | (aviapochta) | airmail | аларны | (alarnı) | them |
| автобус | (avtobus) | bus | аларның | (alarnıng) | their |
| автомат | (avtomat) | machine gun | алга | (alga) | forward |
| автомобиль | (avtomobil') | automobile | алга барыш | (alga barısh) | development |
| автор | (avtor) | author | алгебра | (algebra) | algebra |
| авыз | (avız) | mouth | алда | (alda) | front: in front of |
| авыл | (avıl) | village | | | |
| авыл хуҗалыгы | (avıl khujalıgı) | agriculture | алдагы | (aldagı) | next |
| | | | алла | (alla) | God |
| авыр | (avır) | difficult, hard, heavy | алма | (alma) | apple |
| авырту | (avırtu) | pain | алмашлык | (almashlık) | pronoun |
| авыру | (aviru) | ill, illness, sick | алсу | (alsu) | pink |
| | | | алтмыш | (altmısh) | sixty |
| ага | (aga) | uncle | алты | (altı) | six |
| агач | (agach) | tree, wood | алтын | (altın) | gold |
| агу | (agu) | poison | алу | (alu) | subtraction |
| агулы | (agulı) | poisonous | алып кил- | (alıp kil-) | bring |
| адвокат | (advokat) | lawyer | ана | (ana) | mother |
| адрес | (adres) | address | анар | (anar) | pomegranate |
| адым | (adım) | step | анархия | (anarkhiya) | anarchy |
| адәм | (adäm) | human being | анда | (anda) | there |
| аер- | (ayer-) | separate | андый | (andıy) | such |
| аеруча | (ayerucha) | especially | аннан соң | (annan song) | then |
| аерыл- | (ayeril-) | divorce, separated: be separated | ансат | (ansat) | easy |
| | | | ант ит- | (ant it-) | swear |
| | | | антенна | (antenna) | antenna |
| аерылышу | (ayerılıshu) | divorce | аны | (anı) | her, him |
| аерым | (ayerım) | separate | аныk | (anık) | concrete |
| аерымлык | (aerımlık) | difference | аныкы | (anıkı) | hers, his, its |
| аз | (az) | few | аның | (anıng) | her, his, its |
| азчылык | (azchılık) | minority | апа | (apa) | aunt, sister |
| ай | (ay) | month, moon | апельсин | (apel'sin) | orange |
| айва | (ayva) | quince | апрель | (aprel') | April |
| ак | (ak) | white | аптека | (apteka) | pharmacy |
| ак чәчәк | (ak chächäk) | daisy | аптекачы | (aptekachı) | pharmacist |
| ак- | (ak-) | flow | ара | (ara) | distance |
| аккош | (akkosh) | swan | арасында | (arasında) | between |
| акрын | (akrın) | slow | арба | (arba) | cart |
| акрынлап | (akrınlap) | gradually | аренда | (arenda) | rent |
| акча | (akcha) | currency, money | арзан | (arzan) | cheap |
| | | | арка | (arka) | back |
| акча янчыгы | (akcha yanchıgı) | purse | аркылы | (arkılı) | by |
| | | | армут | (armut) | pear |

| | | |
|---|---|---|
| арпа | (arpa) | barley |
| арт- | (art-) | increase |
| артиллерия | (artilleriya) | artillery |
| артта | (artta) | behind |
| артыграк | (artıgrak) | more |
| артыннан бар- | (artınnan bar-) | follow |
| архитектор | (arkhitektor) | architect |
| ары | (arı) | there |
| арыган | (arıgan) | tired |
| арык | (arık) | slim |
| арыслан | (arıslan) | lion |
| ас- | (as-) | hang |
| астында | (astında) | under, underneath |
| ат | (at) | horse |
| ата | (ata) | father |
| ата-ана | (ata-ana) | parents |
| атаклы | (ataklı) | famous |
| атна | (atna) | week |
| ау | (au) | game |
| аула- | (aula-) | hunt |
| ач | (ach) | hungry |
| ач- | (ach-) | discover, open |
| ачкыч | (achkıch) | key |
| ачлык | (achlık) | famine |
| ачу | (achu) | anger |
| ачулы | (achulı) | angry |
| ачы | (achı) | bitter |
| ачыгу | (achıgu) | hunger |
| ачык | (achık) | obvious, open |
| ачыкла- | (achıkla-) | explain |
| аш | (ash) | food |
| аш бүлмәсе | (ash bülmäse) | dining room |
| аш пешерүче | (ash pesherüche) | cook |
| аш өе | (ash öye) | kitchen |
| аша- | (asha-) | eat |
| ашамлык | (ashamlık) | dish |
| ашказан | (ashkazan) | stomach |
| ашлык | (ashlık) | grain |
| ашъяулык | (ash'yaulık) | tablecloth |
| ашыгу | (ashıgu) | haste |
| ашык- | (ashık-) | hurry |
| аэропорт | (aeroport) | airport |
| аю | (ayu) | bear |
| аяк | (ayak) | foot, leg |
| аяк киеме | (ayak kiyeme) | shoe |
| аңгыра | (anggıra) | stupid |
| аңла- | (angla-) | understand |
| аңлатма | (anglatma) | explanation |
| бабай | (babay) | grandfather |
| бавыр | (bavır) | liver |
| багланыш | (baglanısh) | communication |
| бадам | (badam) | almond |
| базар | (bazar) | market |
| бай | (bay) | rich |
| байлык | (baylık) | wealth |
| байрак | (bayrak) | flag |
| бака | (baka) | frog |
| баклажан | (baklazhan) | eggplant |
| бакча | (bakcha) | garden |
| бакчачы | (bakchachı) | gardener |
| бакыр | (bakır) | copper |
| бал | (bal) | honey |
| бал корты | (bal kortı) | bee |
| бала | (bala) | child |
| балет | (balet) | ballet |
| балкон | (balkon) | balcony |
| балта | (balta) | axe |
| балчык | (balchık) | clay |
| балык | (balık) | fish |
| балыкчы | (balıkchı) | fisherman |
| банан | (banan) | banana |
| банк | (bank) | bank |
| банка | (banka) | jar |
| банкет | (banket) | banquet |
| бар- | (bar-) | go |
| барлык | (barlık) | all, existence |
| бармак | (barmak) | finger |
| барометр | (barometr) | barometer |
| бас- | (bas-) | print |
| баскетбол | (basketbol) | basketball |
| баскыч | (baskıch) | ladder, stairs |
| бассейн | (basseyn) | pool |
| бат- | (bat-) | drown, sink |
| баткак | (batkak) | mud |
| батыр | (batır) | brave, courageous |
| баш | (bash) | head |
| баш авыруы | (bash avıruı) | headache |
| башка | (bashka) | another, besides, different, other |

|  |  |  |
|-------|-----------------|---------|
| башкала | (bashkala) | capital |
| башла- | (bashla-) | begin, start |
| без | (bez) | we |
| безне | (bezne) | us |
| безнеке | (bezneke) | ours |
| безнең | (bezneng) | our |
| бел- | (bel-) | know |
| белдер- | (belder-) | inform |
| белем | (belem) | knowledge |
| белəзек сөяге | (beläzek söyage) | wrist |
| белəн | (belän) | by, with |
| бензин | (benzin) | gasoline |
| бер | (ber) | one |
| бер төрле | (ber törle) | same |
| бераз | (beraz) | little |
| бергə | (bergä) | together |
| берничə | (bernichä) | several, some |
| берəр нəрсə | (berär närsä) | anything |
| бет | (bet) | louse |
| бетер- | (beter-) | finish |
| бетергеч | (betergech) | eraser |
| би- | (bi-) | dance |
| биек | (biyek) | high, tall |
| биеклек | (biyeklek) | height |
| бизнесмен | (biznesmen) | businessman |
| бик | (bik) | very |
| бик зур | (bik zur) | huge |
| билбау | (bilbau) | belt |
| билет | (bilet) | ticket |
| бина | (bina) | building |
| бинт | (bint) | bandage |
| бир- | (bir-) | give |
| бирелү | (birelü) | surrender |
| бирем | (birem) | assignment |
| бирле | (birle) | since |
| бистə | (bistä) | suburb |
| бит | (bit) | face, page |
| биш | (bish) | five |
| биюче | (biyuche) | dancer |
| биялəй | (biyaläy) | glove |
| бланк | (blank) | form |
| блуза | (bluza) | blouse |
| боерык бир- | (boyerık bir-) | command, order |
| боз | (boz) | hail, ice |
| бозау ите | (bozau ite) | veal |
| бодай | (boday) | wheat |
| болан | (bolan) | deer |
| болар | (bolar) | these |
| болыт | (bolıt) | cloud |
| бомба | (bomba) | bomb |
| бор- | (bor-) | twist |
| борау | (borau) | drill |
| борча | (borcha) | flea |
| борчак | (borchak) | pea |
| борчыл- | (borchıl-) | worry |
| борыл- | (borıl-) | turn |
| борын | (borın) | before, faucet, nose |
| борыч | (borıch) | pepper |
| бот | (bot) | thigh |
| ботак | (botak) | branch |
| бритва | (britva) | razor |
| бу | (bu) | this |
| буа | (bua) | dam |
| буйга җиткəн | (buyga jitkän) | adult |
| буйсын- | (buysın-) | obey |
| букча | (bukcha) | handbag |
| бул- | (bul-) | be, become, happen |
| буран | (buran) | storm |
| бурыч | (burıch) | debt, duty, loan |
| бурычка ал- | (burıchka al-) | borrow |
| буталчык | (butalchık) | messy |
| бутерброд | (buterbrod) | sandwich |
| буш | (bush) | empty, loose |
| бушат- | (bushat-) | empty, release |
| буя- | (buya-) | dye, paint |
| буяучы | (buyauchı) | painter |
| бəби | (bäbi) | baby |
| бəгъзе | (bäg'ze) | some |
| бəйлə- | (bäylä-) | fasten, tie |
| бəйрəм | (bäyräm) | holiday |
| бəйрəм ит- | (bäyräm it-) | celebrate |
| бəлеш | (bälesh) | cake |
| бəлки | (bälki) | perhaps |
| бəрəнге | (bärängge) | potato |
| бəти | (bäti) | lamb |
| бəхетсез | (bäkhetsez) | unhappy |
| бəхəс | (bäkhäs) | argument |
| бəхəслəш- | (bäkhäsläsh-) | argue |
| бəя | (bäya) | price |
| бөер | (böyer) | kidney |
| бөк- | (bök-) | fold |
| бөркет | (börket) | eagle |

| | | | | | |
|---|---|---|---|---|---|
| бөтен | (böten) | whole | гасыр | (gasır) | century |
| бөтнек | (bötnek) | mint | гафу ит- | (gafu it-) | forgive |
| бөжәк | (böjäk) | insect | гафу сора- | (gafu sora-) | apologize |
| бүген | (bügen) | today | гаҗәп | (gajäp) | strange |
| бүл- | (bül-) | distribute, divide | география | (geografiya) | geography |
| | | | геология | (geologiya) | geology |
| бүлек | (bülek) | department | геометрия | (geometriya) | geometry |
| бүлмә | (bülmä) | room | гомуми | (gomumi) | general |
| бүләк | (büläk) | prize | гореф-гадәт | (goref-gadät) | custom |
| бүлү | (bülü) | division | горурлык | (gorurlık) | pride |
| бүре | (büre) | wolf | горчица | (gorchitsa) | mustard |
| бюджет | (byudzhet) | budget | градус | (gradus) | degree |
| бюро | (byuro) | office | граждан | (grazhdan) | citizen |
| | | | графин | (grafin) | pitcher |
| вак акча | (vak akcha) | change | грипп | (gripp) | flu |
| вакланма | (vaklanma) | fraction | груша | (grusha) | pear |
| вакыйга | (vakıyga) | event | гыйбадәт | (gıybadät) | worship |
| вакыт | (vakıt) | time | гыйбадәтханә | (gıybadätkhanä) | temple |
| ванна | (vanna) | bathroom | гыйнвар | (gıynvar) | January |
| варенье | (varen'ye) | jam | гәүдә | (gäüdä) | body |
| ватылган | (vatılgan) | broken | гөл | (göl) | flower |
| велосипед | (velosiped) | bicycle | гөлчәчәк | (gölchächäk) | rose |
| вертолёт | (vertolyot) | helicopter | гөмбә | (gömbä) | mushroom |
| видео | (video) | video | гөнаһсызлык | (gönahsızlık) | innocence |
| визит | (vizit) | visit | гөрелте | (görelte) | noise |
| винт | (vint) | screw | гүя(ки) | (güya[ki]) | as if |
| вәгъдә бир- | (väg'dä bir-) | promise | гүзәл әсәр | (güzäl äsär) | masterpiece |
| вәкиле бул- | (väkile bul-) | represent | | | |
| вөҗдан | (vöjdan) | conscience | -да, -дә | (-da, -dä) | at, in |
| | | | да, дә | (da, dä) | also, too |
| -га, -гә | (-ga, -gä) | to | -дан, -дән | (-dan, -dän) | from |
| гавань | (gavan') | harbor | дару | (daru) | drug, medicine |
| гадаләт | (gadalät) | justice | | | |
| гади | (gadi) | simple | дару үләне | (daru üläne) | herb |
| гадәт | (gadät) | habit | дастан | (dastan) | epic |
| гадәтлән- | (gadätlän-) | used: be used to | декабрь | (dekabr') | December |
| | | | демократия | (demokratiya) | democracy |
| гаепле | (gayeple) | guilty | демонстрация | (demonstratsiya) | demonstration |
| гаепсез | (gayepsez) | innocent | десерт | (desert) | dessert |
| газ | (gaz) | gas | дикъкать | (dik'kat') | attention |
| газета | (gazeta) | newspaper | дин | (din) | faith, religion |
| газиз | (gaziz) | dear | дини | (dini) | religious |
| гаилә | (gailä) | family | дини бәйрәм | (dini bäyräm) | religious holiday |
| гайка ачкычы | (gayka achkıchı) | wrench | диплом | (diplom) | diploma |
| галим | (galim) | scientist | дию | (diyu) | giant |
| галстук | (galstuk) | tie | диярлек | (diyarlek) | almost |
| гараж | (garazh) | garage | диңгез | (dinggez) | sea |
| гармония | (garmoniya) | harmony | дога | (doga) | prayer |
| гаскәр | (gaskär) | army | доктор | (doktor) | doctor |

| дошман | (doshman) | enemy |
|---|---|---|
| дошман күр- | (doshman kür-) | hate |
| дошманлык | (doshmanlık) | enmity |
| драма | (drama) | drama |
| драматург | (dramaturg) | playwright |
| дулкын | (dulkın) | wave |
| дулкынлану | (dulkınlanu) | excitement |
| дус | (dus) | friend |
| дуслык | (duslık) | friendship |
| духовка | (dukhovka) | oven |
| душ | (dush) | shower |
| дуңгыз | (dunggız) | pig |
| дымлы | (dımlı) | damp |
| дюжина | (dyuzhina) | dozen |
| дәвала- | (dävala-) | cure |
| дәвалау | (dävalau) | cure |
| дәвам ит- | (dävam it-) | continue |
| дәлил | (dälil) | proof |
| дәрес | (däres) | lesson |
| дәрәҗә | (däräjä) | level |
| дәфтәр | (däftär) | notebook |
| дәүләт | (däülät) | state |
| дөге | (döge) | rice |
| дөнья | (dön'ya) | world |
| дөрес | (döres) | correct |
| дөя | (döya) | camel |
| дүрт | (dürt) | four |
| дүшәмбе | (düshämbe) | Monday |
| | | |
| еврей | (yevrey) | Jew |
| егерме | (yegerme) | twenty |
| елга | (yelga) | river |
| ел | (yel) | year |
| ела- | (yela-) | cry, weep |
| елан | (yelan) | snake |
| еллык | (yellık) | anniversary |
| ерак | (yerak) | far |
| ерт- | (yert-) | tear |
| ефәк | (yefäk) | silk |
| еш-еш | (yesh-yesh) | often |
| | | |
| жакет | (zhaket) | jacket |
| журнал | (zhurnal) | magazine |
| журналист | (zhurnalist) | journalist |
| | | |
| заказ бир- | (zakaz bir-) | order |
| зар | (zar) | complaint |
| зарар | (zarar) | harm |
| зарарлы | (zararlı) | harmful |

| звонок | (zvonok) | bell |
|---|---|---|
| зиярәт кыл- | (ziyarät kıl-) | visit |
| золым | (zolım) | oppression |
| зонтик | (zontik) | umbrella |
| зоопарк | (zoopark) | zoo |
| зур | (zur) | big, great, large |
| зыян | (zıyan) | damage, loss |
| зәйтүн | (zäytün) | olive |
| зәркән | (zärkän) | jeweler |
| зәңгәр | (zänggär) | blue |
| | | |
| иблис | (iblis) | demon |
| игезәкләр | (igezäklär) | twin |
| игенче | (igenche) | peasant |
| игәү | (igäü) | file |
| идарә итүче | (idarä itüche) | manager |
| идиома | (idioma) | idiom |
| идән | (idän) | floor |
| из- | (iz-) | crush |
| ий- | (iy-) | bend |
| ике | (ike) | two |
| икмәк | (ikmäk) | bread |
| икмәк кибете | (ikmäk kibete) | bakery |
| икмәк пешерүче | (ikmäk pesherüche) | baker |
| илле | (ille) | fifty |
| илче | (ilche) | ambassador |
| им- | (im-) | suck |
| имза | (imza) | signature |
| имза куй- | (imza kuy-) | sign |
| имтихан | (imtikhan) | examination |
| имчәк | (imchäk) | breast |
| имән | (imän) | oak |
| инженер | (inzhener) | engineer |
| инкыйлап | (inkıylap) | revolution |
| инкярь ит- | (inkyar' it-) | deny |
| инфекция | (infektsiya) | infection |
| инфляция | (inflyatsiya) | inflation |
| информация | (informatsiya) | information |
| инжир | (injir) | fig |
| иптәш | (iptäsh) | partner |
| ир | (ir) | husband, man |
| ир бала | (ir bala) | boy |
| ирен | (iren) | lip |
| иркен | (irken) | free |
| иркенлек | (irkenlek) | freedom |

| | | |
|---|---|---|
| иртə | (irtä) | early, morning |
| иртəгə | (irtägä) | tomorrow |
| иртəнге аш | (irtänge ash) | breakfast |
| ис | (is) | smell |
| ис чык- | (is chık-) | smell |
| исем | (isem) | name, noun, title |
| исерек | (iserek) | drunk |
| исерткеч эчемлек | (isertkech echemlek) | drink |
| иске | (iske) | old |
| иске төшер- | (iskä tösher-) | remind |
| ислемай | (islemay) | perfume |
| иснə- | (isnä-) | smell, yawn |
| исəнлəш- | (isänläsh-) | greet |
| исəнмесез | (isänmesez) | hello |
| исəп | (isäp) | account |
| ит | (it) | meat |
| ит кибете | (it kibete) | butcher shop |
| итек | (itek) | boot |
| итекче | (itekche) | shoemaker |
| итче | (itche) | butcher |
| итəк | (itäk) | skirt |
| ихтимал | (ikhtimal) | probably |
| ихтыяҗ | (ikhtıyaj) | necessity, need |
| ишегалды | (ishegaldı) | courtyard |
| ишек | (ishek) | door |
| ишет- | (ishet-) | hear |
| ишəк | (ishäk) | donkey |
| июль | (iyul') | July |
| июнь | (iyun') | June |
| ияк | (iyak) | chin |
| иң күп | (ing küp) | most |
| иң яхшы | (ing yakhshı) | best |
| иңбаш | (ingbash) | shoulder |
| йогырт | (yogırt) | yogurt |
| йогыш | (yogısh) | infection |
| йозак | (yozak) | lock |
| йокла- | (yokla-) | sleep |
| йокы | (yokı) | sleep |
| йокы бүлмəсе | (yokı bülmäse) | bedroom |
| йолдыз | (yoldız) | star |
| йомшак | (yomshak) | soft |
| йомшак күңелле | (yomshak küngelle) | kind |
| йомырка | (yomırka) | egg |
| йон | (yon) | wool |
| йорт | (yort) | house |
| йөгер- | (yöger-) | run |
| йөз | (yöz) | hundred |
| йөз- | (yöz-) | swim |
| йөзем | (yözem) | grape |
| йөзү | (yözü) | swimming |
| йөк | (yök) | baggage, cargo |
| йөк машинасы | (yök mashinası) | truck |
| йөкле | (yökle) | pregnant |
| йөклелек | (yöklelek) | pregnancy |
| йөкче | (yökche) | porter |
| йөр- | (yör-) | stroll, walk |
| йөрт- | (yört-) | drive |
| йөрəк | (yöräk) | heart |
| йөрəклелек | (yöräklelek) | courage |
| -ка, -кə | (-ka, -kä) | to |
| каберлек | (kaberlek) | cemetery |
| кабул ит- | (kabul it-) | accept |
| кабык | (kabık) | bark |
| кавын | (kavın) | melon |
| кадак | (kadak) | nail |
| кадəр | (kadär) | until |
| каек | (kayek) | boat |
| каз | (kaz) | goose |
| каз- | (kaz-) | dig |
| кайгылы | (kaygılı) | sorry |
| кайда | (kayda) | where |
| каймак | (kaymak) | cream |
| кайна- | (kayna-) | boil |
| кайсы | (kaysı) | which |
| кайт- | (kayt-) | return |
| кайчакта | (kaychakta) | sometimes |
| кайчан | (kaychan) | when |
| кайчы | (kaychı) | scissors |
| кал- | (kal-) | remain, stay |
| календарь | (kalendar') | calendar |
| калкулык | (kalkulık) | hill |
| калтыра- | (kaltıra-) | tremble |
| калын | (kalın) | thick |
| калəм | (kaläm) | feather, pencil |
| камау | (kamau) | siege |
| кан | (kan) | blood |
| кан басымы | (kan basımı) | blood pressure |
| кана- | (kana-) | bleed |

| | | |
|---|---|---|
| канал | (kanal) | canal, channel |
| канат | (kanat) | wing |
| канун | (kanun) | law |
| канәгать | (kanägat') | glad |
| канәфер чәчәк | (kanäfer chächäk) | carnation |
| капитал салу | (kapital salu) | investment |
| капитан | (kapitan) | captain |
| капка | (kapka) | gate |
| капкач | (kapkach) | lid |
| капма-каршы | (kapma-karshı) | opposite |
| капчык | (kapchık) | wallet |
| кар | (kar) | snow |
| кара | (kara) | black, ink |
| кара җимеш | (kara jimesh) | plum |
| кара- | (kara-) | look |
| карават | (karavat) | bed |
| карак | (karak) | burglar, thief |
| карандаш | (karandash) | pencil |
| карар | (karar) | decision |
| карар ит- | (karar it-) | decide |
| караңгы | (karanggı) | dark |
| караңгылык | (karanggılık) | darkness |
| карбыз | (karbız) | watermelon |
| карга | (karga) | crow |
| карикатура | (karikatura) | cartoon |
| карлыгач | (karlıgach) | swallow |
| карт | (kart) | old |
| карта | (karta) | map, playing card |
| каршы | (karshı) | against |
| кассета | (kasseta) | cassette |
| кассир | (kassir) | cashier |
| кастрюль | (kastryul') | saucepan |
| касә | (kasä) | bowl |
| кат | (kat) | storey |
| каты | (katı) | loud |
| катыштыр- | (katıshtır-) | mix |
| кафе | (kafe) | café |
| кач- | (kach-) | escape, flee, run away |
| каш | (kash) | eyebrow |
| кашык | (kashık) | spoon |
| кая | (kaya) | where |
| квадрат | (kvadrat) | square |
| квартал | (kvartal) | neighborhood |
| квартира | (kvartira) | apartment |
| квитанция | (kvitantsiya) | receipt |
| келәм | (keläm) | carpet |
| кем | (kem) | who |
| кемдер | (kemder) | anybody |
| кер- | (ker-) | enter |
| керфек | (kerfek) | eyelash |
| керү | (kerü) | entrance |
| кесә | (kesä) | pocket |
| кечкенә | (kechkenä) | little, small |
| кечкенә әрҗә | (kechkenä ärjä) | box |
| ки | (ki) | that |
| кибет | (kibet) | shop, store |
| кием | (kiyem) | clothes |
| кием элгеч | (kiyem elgech) | hanger |
| кий- | (kiy-) | put on, wear |
| кил- | (kil-) | arrive, come |
| килен | (kilen) | bride |
| килер | (kiler) | income |
| килешү | (kileshü) | agreement |
| киләчәк | (kilächäk) | future |
| килү | (kilü) | arrival |
| ким- | (kim-) | decrease |
| кинотеатр | (kinoteatr) | cinema |
| кирпеч | (kirpech) | brick |
| кирәкле | (kiräkle) | necessary |
| кис- | (kis-) | cut |
| кит- | (kit-) | depart |
| китап | (kitap) | book |
| китап кибете | (kitap kibete) | bookshop |
| китап сатучысы | (kitap satuchısı) | bookseller |
| китапханә | (kitapkhanä) | library |
| киту | (kitü) | departure |
| кич | (kich) | evening |
| кичектер- | (kichekter-) | postpone |
| кичерү | (kicherü) | apology |
| кичке аш | (kichke ash) | dinner |
| кичә | (kichä) | yesterday |
| кишер | (kisher) | carrot |
| киштә | (kishtä) | shelf |
| кияү | (kiyaü) | bridegroom |
| киң | (king) | broad, loose, spacious, wide |
| класс | (klass) | classroom |
| климат | (klimat) | climate |

| Tatar | Transcription | English |
|---|---|---|
| клиника | (klinika) | clinic |
| клуб | (klub) | club |
| кой- | (koy-) | pour |
| койма | (koyma) | fence |
| койрык | (koyrık) | tail. |
| колак | (kolak) | ear |
| колбаса | (kolbasa) | sausage |
| ком | (kom) | sand |
| комедия | (komediya) | comedy |
| компания | (kompaniya) | company, firm |
| композитор | (kompozitor) | composer |
| композиция | (kompozitsiya) | composition |
| компьютер | (komp'yuter) | computer |
| конверт | (konvert) | envelope |
| концерт | (kontsert) | concert |
| кор- | (kor-) | build, dry |
| корабль | (korabl') | ship |
| корал | (koral) | gun, tool, weapon |
| корбан | (korban) | sacrifice |
| король | (korol') | king |
| корт | (kort) | worm |
| коры | (korı) | dry |
| корылык | (korılık) | drought |
| корыч | (korıch) | steel |
| кос- | (kos-) | vomit |
| космос | (kosmos) | space |
| костюм | (kostyum) | suit |
| коткар- | (kotkar-) | rescue |
| котла- | (kotla-) | congratulate |
| котлау | (kotlau) | celebration, congratulation |
| кофе | (kofe) | coffee |
| кочакла- | (kochakla-) | embrace |
| кош | (kosh) | bird |
| кояш | (koyash) | sun |
| кояш бату | (koyash batu) | sunset |
| кояш чыгу | (koyash chıgu) | sunrise |
| кран | (kran) | faucet |
| кредит | (kredit) | credit |
| кресло | (kreslo) | armchair |
| крокодил | (krokodil) | crocodile |
| ку- | (ku-) | chase |
| куй- | (kuy-) | put |
| кукуруз | (kukuruz) | corn |
| кул | (kul) | arm, hand |
| кул суз- | (kul suz-) | reach |

| Tatar | Transcription | English |
|---|---|---|
| кул сәгате | (kul sägate) | watch |
| кул чап- | (kul chap-) | clap |
| кулда булган акча | (kulda bulgan akcha) | cash |
| куллан- | (kullan-) | use |
| кулланучы | (kullanuchı) | consumer |
| култык | (kultık) | bay |
| культивацияләу | (kultivatsiyaläü) | cultivation |
| кулъяулык | (kul'yaulık) | handkerchief |
| кунак | (kunak) | guest |
| кунакханә | (kunakkhanä) | hotel |
| кунакчыллык | (kunakchıllık) | hospitality |
| кургаш(ын) | (kurgash[ın]) | lead |
| курк- | (kurk-) | afraid: be afraid |
| куркак | (kurkak) | coward |
| куркаклык | (kurkaklık) | cowardice |
| курку | (kurku) | fear |
| кухня | (kukhnya) | kitchen |
| куш- | (kush-) | add |
| кушу | (kushu) | addition |
| кушымча | (kushımcha) | suffix |
| куян | (kuyan) | rabbit |
| кыз | (kız) | daughter |
| кыз бала | (kız bala) | girl |
| кызгылт көрән | (kızgılt körän) | brown |
| кызгылт сары | (kızgılt sarı) | orange |
| кыздыр- | (kızdır-) | roast |
| кызу | (kızu) | heat |
| кызык- | (kızık-) | envy |
| кызыклы | (kızıklı) | interesting |
| кызыксыз | (kızıksız) | boring |
| кызыксыну | (kızıksınu) | interest |
| кызыл | (kızıl) | red |
| кыйммәт | (kıymmät) | cost, expensive, value |
| кыйммәтле | (kıymmätle) | valuable |
| кыл- | (kıl-) | do |
| кыл иләк | (kıl iläk) | strainer |
| кылыч | (kılıch) | sword |
| кыр | (kır) | countryside, field |
| кыр- | (kır-) | scrape |
| кыргый | (kırgıy) | wild |
| кырмыска | (kırmıska) | ant |
| кырык | (kırık) | forty |
| кыска | (kıska) | short |

| | | |
|---|---|---|
| кычкыр- | (kıchkır-) | scream, shout |
| кыш | (kısh) | winter |
| кыя | (kıya) | rock |
| кыяр | (kıyar) | cucumber |
| кәбестә | (käbestä) | cabbage |
| кәгазь | (kägaz') | paper |
| кәнфит | (känfit) | candy |
| кәнәфи | (känäfi) | armchair |
| кәрҗин | (kärjin) | basket |
| кәстәнә | (kästänä) | chestnut |
| кәҗә | (käjä) | goat |
| көз | (köz) | autumn |
| көзге | (közge) | mirror |
| көй | (köy) | tune |
| көл | (köl) | ash |
| көл- | (köl-) | laugh, smile |
| көмеш | (kömesh) | silver |
| көн | (kön) | day |
| көнбагыш | (könbagısh) | sunflower |
| көнбатыш | (könbatısh) | west |
| көндез | (köndez) | daytime |
| көнче | (könche) | jealous |
| көнчелек | (könchelek) | envy |
| көнчыгыш | (könchıgısh) | east |
| көньяк | (kön'yak) | south |
| көрәк | (köräk) | shovel, spade |
| көрәш | (köräsh) | wrestling |
| көрәш- | (köräsh-) | fight |
| көт- | (köt-) | wait |
| көтелмәгән | (kötelmägän) | sudden |
| көтү | (kötü) | herd |
| көтүлек | (kötülek) | meadow |
| көч | (köch) | force, power, strength |
| көчле | (köchle) | powerful, strong |
| көчсез | (köchsez) | weak |
| күбәләк | (kübäläk) | butterfly |
| күгәрчен | (kügärchen) | pigeon |
| күз | (küz) | eye |
| күзлек | (küzlek) | glasses |
| күк | (kük) | sky |
| күкрәк | (kükräk) | chest |
| күкрәү | (kükräü) | thunder |
| күл | (kül) | lake |
| күлмәк | (külmäk) | dress, shirt |
| күләгә | (külägä) | shade, shadow |
| күләм | (küläm) | quantity |
| күм- | (küm-) | bury |
| күмер | (kümer) | coal |
| күмәртәләп (сату) | (kümärtäläp [satu]) | wholesale |
| күп | (küp) | many, much |
| күпер | (küper) | bridge |
| күпчелек | (küpchelek) | majority |
| күр- | (kür-) | see |
| күргәзмә | (kürgäzmä) | exhibition |
| күрен- | (küren-) | appear |
| күркә | (kürkä) | turkey |
| күркәм | (kürkäm) | handsome |
| күрсәт- | (kürsät-) | show |
| күрше | (kürshe) | neighbor |
| күтәр- | (kütär-) | lift, raise |
| лалә | (lalä) | tulip |
| лампа | (lampa) | lamp |
| лекция | (lektsiya) | lecture |
| лимон | (limon) | lemon |
| лифт | (lift) | elevator |
| ләззәтлән- | (läzzätlän-) | enjoy |
| ләкләк | (läkläk) | stork |
| магазин | (magazin) | store |
| магнитофон | (magnitofon) | tape recorder |
| май | (may) | fat, May, oil |
| маймыл | (maymıl) | monkey |
| максат | (maksat) | purpose |
| макта- | (makta-) | praise |
| мактан- | (maktan-) | boast |
| мал-туар | (mal-tuar) | cattle |
| мамык | (mamık) | cotton |
| манара | (manara) | tower |
| марка | (marka) | stamp |
| март | (mart) | March |
| матбугат | (matbugat) | press |
| матбугат йорты | (matbugat yortı) | printing press |
| матдә | (matdä) | matter |
| математика | (matematika) | mathematics |
| материал | (material) | material |
| матрас | (matras) | mattress |
| матур | (matur) | beautiful, pretty |
| матурлык | (maturlık) | beauty |
| матч | (match) | match |
| машина | (mashina) | car, machine |
| маңгай | (manggay) | forehead |
| медицина | (meditsina) | medicine |
| мен- | (men-) | ride |

| | | |
|---|---|---|
| мендәр | (mendär) | cushion, pillow |
| меню | (menyu) | menu |
| металл | (metall) | metal |
| метро | (metro) | subway |
| мех | (mekh) | fur |
| мең | (meng) | thousand |
| ми | (mi) | brain |
| микъдар | (mik'dar) | amount |
| милиционер | (militsioner) | policeman |
| миллиард | (milliard) | billion |
| миллион | (million) | million |
| милләт | (millät) | nation |
| милләтчелек | (millätchelek) | nationalism |
| мин | (min) | I |
| мине | (mine) | me |
| минеке | (mineke) | mine |
| минем | (minem) | my |
| министр | (ministr) | minister |
| минут | (minut) | minute |
| мисал | (misal) | example |
| мифология | (mifologiya) | mythology |
| мич | (mich) | stove |
| мода | (moda) | fashion |
| момент | (moment) | moment |
| моназара | (monazara) | discussion |
| монда | (monda) | here |
| мондый | (mondıy) | such |
| моржа | (morja) | chimney |
| мотор | (motor) | engine |
| мотоцикл | (mototsikl) | motorcycle |
| мохтаҗ бул- | (mokhtaj bul-) | need |
| моңлы | (monglı) | sad |
| муен | (muyen) | neck |
| музей | (muzey) | museum |
| музыка | (muzıka) | music |
| музыка остасы | (muzıka ostası) | musician |
| музыкаль инструмент | (muzıkal' instrument) | instrument |
| музыкант | (muzıkant) | musician |
| муниципалитет | (munitsipalitet) | municipality |
| мускул | (muskul) | muscle |
| мыек | (mıyek) | mustache |
| мылтык | (mıltık) | rifle |
| мэр | (mer) | mayor |
| мәгълүматлар | (mäg'lümatlar) | data |
| мәгълүматлы | (mäg'lümatlı) | literate |
| мәдәният | (mädäniyat) | culture |
| мәзһәп | (mäzhäp) | sect |
| мәйдан | (mäydan) | square |
| мәкаль | (mäkal') | proverb |
| мәкалә | (mäkalä) | article |
| мәктәп | (mäktäp) | school |
| мәрхәмәтсез | (märkhämätsez) | cruel |
| мәслихәт | (mäslikhät) | advice |
| мәсьәлә | (mäs'älä) | problem |
| мәхәббәт | (mähäbbät) | love |
| мәчет | (mächet) | mosque |
| мәшгуль | (mäshgul') | busy |
| мәҗлес | (mäjles) | party |
| мәңгелек | (mänggelek) | eternity |
| мөгез | (mögez) | horn |
| мөкәммәл | (mökämmäl) | perfect |
| мөмкин | (mömkin) | possible |
| мөмкинлек | (mömkinlek) | possibility |
| мөрәҗәгать ит- | (möräjägat' it-) | apply |
| мөселман | (möselman) | Muslim |
| мөстәкыйльлек | (möstäkıyl'lek) | independence |
| мөһим | (möhim) | important |
| назлы | (nazlı) | gentle |
| намаз укы- | (namaz ukı-) | pray |
| намус | (namus) | honor |
| намуслы | (namuslı) | honest |
| -нан, -нән | (-nan, -nän) | from |
| нарат | (narat) | pine |
| начар | (nachar) | bad |
| нерв | (nerv) | nerve |
| нефть | (neft') | oil |
| ни ... ни | (ni ... ni) | neither ... nor |
| нигә | (nigä) | why |
| ничә | (nichä) | how much |
| ничек | (nichek) | how |
| ният | (niyat) | intention |
| нокта | (nokta) | period |
| ноль | (nol') | zero |
| ноябрь | (noyabr') | November |
| нур | (nur) | ray |
| нык | (nık) | hard |
| нәрсә | (närsä) | thing, what |
| нәтижә | (nätijä) | result |
| нәфрәт | (näfrät) | disgust |
| нәшрият | (näshriyat) | publishing house |
| оборона | (oborona) | defense |
| оек | (oyek) | stocking |
| оекбаш | (oyekbash) | sock |

| | | |
|---|---|---|
| озакламый | (ozaklamıy) | soon |
| озын | (ozın) | long |
| озын буйлы | (ozın buylı) | tall |
| озынлык | (ozınlık) | length |
| океан | (okean) | ocean |
| октябрь | (oktyabr') | October |
| он | (on) | flour |
| оныкъ | (onık) | grandchild |
| оныт- | (onıt-) | forget |
| опера | (opera) | opera |
| операция | (operatsiya) | operation |
| оптик | (optik) | optician |
| орлык | (orlık) | grain, seed |
| отвёртка | (otvyortka) | screwdriver |
| открытка | (otkrıtka) | postcard |
| отставкага чык- | (otstavkaga chık-) | retire |
| офицер | (ofitser) | officer |
| официант | (ofitsiant) | waiter |
| офык | (ofık) | horizon |
| охша- | (okhsha-) | resemble |
| охшаш | (okhshash) | alike, like, similar |
| оч- | (och-) | fly |
| очкыч | (ochkıch) | airplane, plane |
| очраш- | (ochrash-) | meet |
| очрашу | (ochrashu) | appointment |
| оял- | (oyal-) | ashamed: be ashamed |
| оялчан | (oyalchan) | shy |
| | | |
| пальто | (pal'to) | overcoat |
| пар | (par) | pair |
| параграф | (paragraf) | paragraph |
| парад | (parad) | parade |
| паралич | (paralich) | paralysis |
| парикмахер | (parikmakher) | hairdresser |
| парта | (parta) | desk |
| партия | (partiya) | party |
| партнёр | (partnyor) | partner |
| паспорт | (pasport) | passport |
| пассажир | (passazhir) | passenger |
| пациент | (patsient) | patient |
| пелəш | (peläsh) | bald |
| персик | (persik) | peach |
| песи | (pesi) | cat |
| пестə | (pestä) | pistachio |
| петрушка | (petrushka) | parsley |
| печенье | (pechen'ye) | cookie |

| | | |
|---|---|---|
| пеш- | (pesh-) | cook |
| пешер- | (pesher-) | cook |
| пешкəн | (peshkän) | ripe |
| пижама | (pizhama) | pajamas |
| пирог | (pirog) | cake |
| планета | (planeta) | planet |
| пластинка | (plastinka) | record |
| платформа | (platforma) | platform |
| плащ | (plashch) | raincoat |
| плёнка | (plyonka) | film |
| пляж | (plyazh) | beach |
| поезд | (poyezd) | train |
| помидор | (pomidor) | tomato |
| посылка | (posılka) | parcel |
| почмак | (pochmak) | angle, corner |
| почта | (pochta) | post office |
| почта чыгымы | (pochta chıgımı) | postage |
| почта ящигы | (pochta yashchigı) | mailbox |
| почтальон | (pochtal'on) | mailman |
| президент | (prezident) | president |
| прививка | (privivka) | shot |
| программа | (programma) | program |
| проза | (proza) | prose |
| пропаганда | (propaganda) | propaganda |
| проспект | (prospekt) | avenue |
| простыня | (prostınya) | sheet |
| процент | (protsent) | interest |
| пружина | (pruzhina) | spring |
| пылау | (pılau) | rice |
| пычак | (pıchak) | knife |
| пычкы | (pıchkı) | saw |
| пычрак | (pıchrak) | dirty |
| пыяла | (pıyala) | glass |
| пьеса | (p'yesa) | play |
| пəйгамбəр | (päygambär) | prophet |
| пəнжешəмбе | (pänjeshämbe) | Thursday |
| пəрдə | (pärdä) | curtain |
| | | |
| радио | (radio) | radio |
| рак | (rak) | cancer |
| рамка | (ramka) | frame |
| реализм | (realizm) | realism |
| регистрация | (registratsiya) | registration |
| резервта саклау | (rezervta saklau) | reservation |
| рейс | (reys) | flight |
| реклама | (reklama) | advertisement |
| республика | (respublika) | republic |

| | | |
|---|---|---|
| ресторан | (restoran) | restaurant |
| рецепт | (retsept) | prescription |
| риваять | (rivayat') | legend |
| риза бул- | (riza bul-) | agree |
| ришвәтчелек | (rishvätchelek) | corruption |
| роза | (roza) | rose |
| роман | (roman) | novel |
| ромб | (romb) | diamond |
| рух | (rukh) | spirit |
| рухани | (rukhani) | priest |
| ручка | (ruchka) | pen |
| рәвеш | (rävesh) | adverb |
| рәсем | (räsem) | painting, picture |
| рәсми | (räsmi) | official |
| рәссам | (rässam) | artist |
| рәт | (rät) | row |
| рәхим итегез | (räkhim itegez) | please |
| рәхмәт | (räkhmät) | gratitude |
| рәхәт | (räkhät) | pleasure |
| рөхсәт ит- | (rökhsät it-) | permit |
| сабан | (saban) | plow |
| сабын | (sabın) | soap |
| сабырлы | (sabırlı) | patient |
| савыт юучы машина | (savıt yuuchı mashina) | dishwasher |
| саз(лык) | (saz[lık]) | swamp |
| сай | (say) | shallow |
| сайла- | (sayla-) | choose, elect, select |
| сайлау | (saylau) | election |
| сак | (sak) | careful |
| сакал | (sakal) | beard |
| сакла- | (sakla-) | defend, keep, protect |
| саклык | (saklık) | precaution |
| салават күпере | (salavat küpere) | rainbow |
| салам | (salam) | straw |
| салат | (salat) | lettuce, salad |
| салкын | (salkın) | cool |
| салым | (salım) | tax |
| самолёт | (samolyot) | airplane, plane |
| сан | (san) | number |
| сана- | (sana-) | count |
| сап | (sap) | handle |
| сарай | (saray) | palace |
| сары | (sarı) | yellow |
| сары май | (sarı may) | butter |
| сарык | (sarık) | sheep |
| сарык ите | (sarık ite) | mutton |
| сарымсак | (sarımsak) | garlic |
| сарыф ит- | (sarıf it-) | spend |
| сат- | (sat-) | sell |
| сатып ал- | (satıp al-) | buy, shop |
| сатып алучы | (satıp aluchı) | buyer, customer |
| сату | (satu) | sale |
| сатучы | (satuchı) | salesperson, seller |
| сау | (sau) | healthy |
| саулык | (saulık) | health |
| саф | (saf) | pure |
| саңгырау | (sanggırau) | deaf |
| саңгыраулык | (sanggıraulık) | deafness |
| светофор | (svetofor) | traffic light |
| свитер | (sviter) | sweater |
| себер- | (seber-) | sweep |
| себерке | (seberke) | broom |
| сез | (sez) | you |
| сезнеке | (sezneke) | yours |
| сезнең | (sezneng) | your |
| секретарь | (sekretar') | secretary |
| секунд | (sekund) | second |
| секция | (sektsiya) | section |
| селкет- | (selket-) | shake |
| сельдерей | (sel'derey) | celery |
| сентябрь | (sentyabr') | September |
| серкә | (serkä) | vinegar |
| серле | (serle) | secret |
| сеңел | (sengel) | sister |
| си- | (si-) | urinate |
| сигарет | (sigaret) | cigarette |
| сигез | (sigez) | eight |
| сиз- | (siz-) | feel |
| сикер- | (siker-) | jump |
| сиксән | (siksän) | eighty |
| символ | (simvol) | symbol |
| син | (sin) | you |
| синеке | (sineke) | yours |
| синең | (sineng) | your |
| сирәк | (siräk) | seldom |
| сихер | (sikher) | magic |
| сишәмбе | (sishämbe) | Tuesday |
| скелет | (skelet) | skeleton |
| скульптура | (skul'ptura) | sculpture |
| слива | (sliva) | plum |

| | | |
|---|---|---|
| сокланып карап тор- | (soklanıp karap tor-) | admire |
| солдат | (soldat) | soldier |
| сора- | (sora-) | ask, request |
| сорау | (sorau) | question |
| сорт | (sort) | kind |
| соры | (sorı) | grey |
| союз | (soyuz) | union |
| соң | (song) | after, end, late |
| соңа калу | (songa kalu) | delay |
| соңгы | (songgı) | last |
| спорт | (sport) | sport |
| стакан | (stakan) | glass |
| станция | (stantsiya) | station |
| стена | (stena) | wall |
| стена сәгате | (stena sägate) | clock |
| страховка | (strakhovka) | insurance |
| студент | (student) | student |
| су | (su) | fruit juice, water |
| су асты көймәсе | (su astı köymäse) | submarine |
| субъект | (sub'yekt) | subject |
| суган | (sugan) | onion |
| сугыш | (sugısh) | battle, war |
| суд | (sud) | court |
| судья | (sud'ya) | judge |
| сузык | (suzık) | vowel |
| сук- | (suk-) | hit |
| сукыр | (sukır) | blind |
| сукырлык | (sukırlık) | blindness |
| сул | (sul) | left |
| сумка | (sumka) | bag, handbag |
| суык | (suık) | cold, frost |
| суыткыч | (suıtkıch) | refrigerator |
| счёт | (schyot) | bill |
| сыеклык | (sıyeklık) | liquid |
| сыер | (sıyer) | cow |
| сыер ите | (sıyer ite) | beef |
| сызгыч | (sızgıch) | ruler |
| сызык | (sızık) | line |
| сызым | (sızım) | drawing |
| сыйфат | (sıyfat) | adjective, quality |
| сык- | (sık-) | press |
| сылтау | (sıltau) | excuse |
| сын | (sın) | statue |
| сындыр- | (sındır-) | break |

| | | |
|---|---|---|
| сыпыр- | (sıpır-) | stroke |
| сыр | (sır) | cheese |
| сыра | (sıra) | beer |
| сәбәп | (säbäp) | cause, reason |
| сәгать | (sägat') | hour |
| сәгать остасы | (sägat' ostası) | watchmaker |
| сәнгать | (sängat') | art |
| сәхнә | (säkhnä) | stage |
| сәясәт | (säyasät) | politics |
| сәяхәт | (säyakhät) | journey, tourism, travel |
| сәяхәтче | (säyakhätche) | tourist |
| сәүдә | (säüdä) | business |
| сәүдәгәр | (säüdägär) | businessman |
| сөйкемлелек | (söykemlelek) | attraction |
| сөйләш- | (söyläsh-) | speak, talk |
| сөйләшү | (söyläshü) | speech |
| сөлге | (sölge) | towel |
| сөрт- | (sört-) | erase |
| сөт | (söt) | milk |
| сөяк | (söyak) | bone |
| сөңге | (söngge) | spear |
| сүз | (süz) | word |
| сүз башы | (süz bashı) | preface |
| сүзлек | (süzlek) | dictionary |
| сүндер- | (sünder-) | extinguish, put out |
| -та, -тә | (-ta, -tä) | at, in |
| таба | (taba) | pan, towards |
| табигать | (tabigat') | nature |
| табигый | (tabigıy) | natural |
| таблетка | (tabletka) | pill |
| тавык | (tavık) | hen |
| тавык ите | (tavık ite) | chicken |
| тавыш | (tavısh) | sound, voice, vote |
| тавыш бир- | (tavısh bir-) | vote |
| тагы(н) | (tagı[n]) | again |
| таза | (taza) | clean |
| тазарт- | (tazart-) | clean |
| тай- | (tay-) | slip |
| тайгалак | (taygalak) | slippery |
| такси | (taksi) | cab, taxi |
| тал | (tal) | willow |
| тала- | (tala-) | plunder |
| тамак | (tamak) | throat |
| таможня | (tamozhnya) | customs |

| Tatar | Transcription | English |
|---|---|---|
| тамчы | (tamchı) | drop |
| тамыр | (tamır) | root |
| -тан, -тэн | (-tan, -tän) | from |
| тантана | (tantana) | ceremony |
| таны- | (tanı-) | know, recognize |
| таныштыр- | (tanıshtır-) | introduce |
| тап- | (tap-) | find |
| тапкырлау | (tapkırlau) | multiplication |
| тар | (tar) | narrow, tight |
| тара- | (tara-) | comb |
| тарак | (tarak) | comb |
| тарат- | (tarat-) | spread |
| тарих | (tarikh) | date, history |
| тарихчы | (tarikhchı) | historian |
| тарт- | (tart-) | grind, pull |
| тартык | (tartık) | consonant |
| тасвирла- | (tasvirla-) | describe |
| тасвирлау | (tasvirlau) | description |
| тастымал | (tastımal) | napkin |
| тат- | (tat-) | taste |
| татлы | (tatlı) | sweet, tasty |
| тау | (tau) | mountain |
| таш | (tash) | stone |
| ташбака | (tashbaka) | tortoise |
| ташкын | (tashkın) | flood |
| ташла- | (tashla-) | leave, throw |
| ташы- | (tashı-) | carry |
| таң | (tang) | dawn |
| театр | (teatr) | theater |
| тегермэн | (tegermän) | mill |
| тегүче | (tegüche) | tailor |
| тез | (tez) | knee |
| тек- | (tek-) | sew |
| тел | (tel) | language, tongue |
| тел белеме | (tel beleme) | linguistics |
| телевизор | (televizor) | television |
| телеграмма | (telegramma) | telegram |
| телефон | (telefon) | telephone |
| телефон автомат | (telefon avtomat) | public phone |
| телефон буткасы | (telefon butkası) | phone booth |
| телефон номеры | (telefon nomerı) | phone number |
| телсез | (telsez) | mute |
| телче | (telche) | linguist |
| телэ- | (telä-) | want, wish |
| телэк | (teläk) | desire, wish |
| телэсэ нинди | (teläsä nindi) | any |
| тема | (tema) | subject |
| температура | (temperatura) | fever, temperature |
| теория | (teoriya) | theory |
| термометр | (termometr) | thermometer |
| терсэк | (tersäk) | elbow |
| теш | (tesh) | tooth |
| теш врачы | (tesh vrachı) | dentist |
| теш авыруы | (tesh avıruı) | toothache |
| теш чистарту пастасы | (tesh chistartu pastası) | toothpaste |
| теш щёткасы | (tesh shchyotkası) | toothbrush |
| тешлэ- | (teshlä-) | bite |
| ти- | (ti-) | touch |
| тигезлек | (tigezlek) | plain |
| тиен | (tiyen) | squirrel |
| тиз | (tiz) | fast, quick, speedy |
| тиз ярдэм күрсэту машинасы | (tiz yardäm kürsätü mashinası) | ambulance |
| тизлек | (tizlek) | speed |
| тикшер- | (tiksher-) | test |
| тикшеру | (tiksherü) | investigation |
| тилелек | (tilelek) | insanity |
| тимер | (timer) | iron |
| тимер чыбык | (timer chıbık) | wire |
| тимер юл | (timer yul) | railroad |
| тип- | (tip-) | kick |
| тираж | (tirazh) | circulation |
| тире | (tire) | leather, skin |
| тирес | (tires) | fertilizer |
| тирлэ- | (tirlä-) | sweat |
| тирэк | (tiräk) | poplar |
| тирэн | (tirän) | deep |
| тирэнлек | (tiränlek) | depth |
| тишек | (tishek) | hole |
| тиң | (ting) | equal |
| товар | (tovar) | goods |
| тоз | (toz) | salt |
| тойгы | (toygı) | feeling |
| томан | (toman) | fog |
| томау | (tomau) | cold |
| томшык | (tomshık) | beak |
| тор- | (tor-) | get up, stand |

| | | | | | | |
|---|---|---|---|---|---|
| тормыш | (tormısh) | life | тәмамлык | (tämamlık) | object |
| тот- | (tot-) | catch, hold | тәмле | (tämle) | delicious |
| трамвай | (tramvay) | tram | тәмугъ | (tämug') | hell |
| тротуар | (trotuar) | sidewalk | тәмәке | (tämäke) | tobacco |
| ту- | (tu-) | born: be born | тәмәке тарт- | (tämäke tart-) | smoke |
| туган | (tugan) | relative | тәрбия | (tärbiya) | education |
| туган көн | (tugan kön) | birthday | тәрәзә | (täräzä) | window |
| тугыз | (tugız) | nine | тәрҗемә | (tärjemä) | translation |
| тузан | (tuzan) | dust | тәрҗемә ит- | (tärjemä it-) | translate |
| туксан | (tuksan) | ninety | тәтәй | (tätäy) | aunt |
| тукта- | (tukta-) | stop | тәэсир | (täesir) | effect, |
| туктaлыш | (tuktalısh) | stop | | | influence |
| туктат- | (tuktat-) | stop | тәҗрибә | (täjribä) | experience |
| тукыма | (tukıma) | textile | тәңкә | (tängkä) | coin |
| тулы | (tulı) | complete, full | төзәт- | (tözät-) | correct, |
| туп | (tup) | ball, cannon | | | mend, repair |
| тупас | (tupas) | rude | төймә | (töymä) | button |
| туры | (turı) | straight | төкер- | (töker-) | spit |
| туры кил- | (turı kil-) | suit | төлке | (tölke) | fox |
| тут | (tut) | mulberry | төн | (tön) | night |
| тутыр- | (tutır-) | fill | төн уртасы | (tön urtası) | midnight |
| туу | (tuu) | birth | төньяк | (tön'yak) | north |
| туфрак | (tufrak) | earth, soil | төп | (töp) | main |
| туң- | (tung-) | freeze | төр | (tör) | kind |
| туңдырма | (tungdırma) | ice cream | төрмә | (törmä) | jail, prison |
| тыгыз | (tıgız) | thick | төс | (tös) | color |
| тый- | (tıy-) | forbid | төш | (tösh) | dream |
| тылсым | (tılsım) | spell | төш вакыты | (tösh vakıtı) | noon |
| тын | (tın) | breath | төш- | (tösh-) | fall, get off |
| тынлык | (tınlık) | silence | төшем | (töshem) | profit |
| тыныч | (tınıch) | calm, quiet | төшеру | (tösherü) | discount, sale |
| тынычлан- | (tınıchlan-) | quiet: be | төшке аш | (töshke ash) | lunch |
| | | quiet | төштән соңгы | (töshtän | afternoon |
| тынычлык | (tınıchlık) | peace | вакыт | songgı | |
| тынычсызла- | (tınıchsızla-) | bother, | | vakıt) | |
| | | disturb | түбә | (tübä) | roof |
| тырнак | (tırnak) | nail | түбән | (tübän) | down, low |
| тырыш- | (tırısh-) | try | түбәндә | (tübändä) | below |
| тырышу | (tırıshu) | attempt | түгел | (tügel) | not |
| тычкан | (tıchkan) | mouse | түгәрәк | (tügäräk) | circle, round |
| тышта | (tıshta) | outside | түлә- | (tülä-) | pay |
| тыңла- | (tıngla-) | listen | түләу | (tüläü) | fare |
| тәвсия ит- | (tävsiya it-) | recommend | түләусез | (tüläüsez) | free |
| тәгаенләу | (tägayenläü) | appointment | түшәк | (tüshäk | sheet |
| тәгәрмәч | (tägärmäch) | wheel | җәймәсе | jäymäse) | |
| тәгәрәт- | (tägärät-) | roll | түшәм | (tüshäm) | ceiling |
| тәкрар ит- | (täkrar it-) | repeat | | | |
| тәкъдим | (täk'dim) | suggestion | уен | (uyen) | game |
| тәкъдим ит- | (täk'dim it-) | offer, present | уенчык | (uyenchık) | toy |
| тәлинкә | (tälinkä) | dish, plate | уй | (uy) | thought |

| | | |
|---|---|---|
| уйла- | (uyla-) | guess, think |
| уйна- | (uyna-) | play |
| ук | (uk) | arrow |
| укуны бетеру | (ukunı beterü) | graduation |
| укучы | (ukuchı) | reader |
| укы- | (ukı-) | read |
| укымышлы | (ukımıshlı) | intellectual |
| укыт- | (ukıt-) | teach |
| укыту акчасы | (ukıtu akchası) | tuition |
| укытучы | (ukıtuchı) | teacher |
| ул | (ul) | he, it, she, son |
| ул вакытта | (ul vakıtta) | then |
| умыртка баганасы | (umırtka baganası) | spine |
| ун | (un) | ten |
| уналты | (unaltı) | sixteen |
| унбер | (unber) | eleven |
| унбиш | (unbish) | fifteen |
| ундурт | (undürt) | fourteen |
| универмаг | (univermag) | department store |
| университет | (universitet) | university |
| унике | (unike) | twelve |
| унсигез | (unsigez) | eighteen |
| унтугыз | (untugız) | nineteen |
| уноч | (unöch) | thirteen |
| унҗиде | (unjide) | seventeen |
| ура- | (ura-) | wrap |
| ураза | (uraza) | fast |
| урак | (urak) | sickle |
| урам | (uram) | street |
| урам хәрәкәте | (uram khäräkäte) | traffic |
| уратып ал- | (uratıp al-) | surround |
| урла- | (urla-) | steal |
| урман | (urman) | forest, wood |
| урнаш- | (urnash-) | situated: be situated |
| урта | (urta) | medium, middle |
| уру | (uru) | harvest |
| урын | (urın) | bed, place, seat |
| урындык | (urındık) | chair, stool |
| ут | (ut) | fire |
| утрау | (utrau) | island |
| утыз | (utız) | thirty |
| утыр- | (utır-) | get on, sit |
| утырт- | (utırt-) | plant, sow |
| уян- | (uyan-) | awake, wake |
| уят- | (uyat-) | awake, wake |
| уң | (ung) | right |
| уңайлы | (ungaylı) | comfortable, convenient |
| уңыш | (ungısh) | crop, luck, success |
| уңышка иреш- | (ungıshka iresh-) | succeed |
| фабрика | (fabrika) | factory |
| файда | (fayda) | benefit |
| файдалы | (faydalı) | useful |
| фамилия | (familiya) | surname |
| фасоль | (fasol') | bean |
| фасыл | (fasıl) | season |
| фатир | (fatir) | apartment |
| февраль | (fevral') | February |
| ферма | (ferma) | farm |
| фестиваль | (festival') | festival |
| фетнә | (fetnä) | rebellion |
| фигыль | (figıl') | verb |
| физика | (fizika) | physics |
| фикер | (fiker) | idea, opinion |
| фил | (fil) | elephant |
| фильм | (fil'm) | movie |
| фольклор | (fol'klor) | folklore |
| фонтан | (fontan) | fountain |
| форма | (forma) | shape |
| фотоаппарат | (fotoapparat) | camera |
| фотография | (fotografiya) | photo |
| фундук | (funduk) | hazelnut |
| футбол | (futbol) | soccer |
| фәнни хезмәт | (fänni khezmät) | research |
| фәрештә | (färeshtä) | angel |
| хайван | (khayvan) | animal |
| хаким | (khakim) | judge |
| хакыйкать | (khakıykat') | truth |
| хакыйкый | (khakıykıy) | true |
| хакында | (khakında) | about |
| халык | (khalık) | people |
| халык саны | (khalık sanı) | population |
| халык төркеме | (khalık törkeme) | crowd |
| халык әкияте | (khalık äkiyate) | folktale |

|  |  |  |
|---|---|---|
| халыкара | (khalıkara) | international |
| ханым | (khanım) | lady |
| хат | (khat) | letter |
| хат ташучы | (khat tashuchı) | mailman |
| хата | (khata) | fault, mistake |
| хатын | (khatın) | wife, woman |
| хезмәт сөючән | (khezmät söyuchän) | diligent |
| хезмәткәр | (khezmätkär) | official |
| хезмәтче | (khezmätche) | servant |
| хикәя | (khikäya) | story |
| хирургия | (khirurgiya) | surgery |
| хисапла- | (khisapla-) | calculate |
| холык | (kholık) | behavior |
| христиан | (khristian) | Christian |
| хуплау | (khuplau) | approval |
| хуш | (khush) | bye-bye |
| хуш килдегез | (khush kildegez) | welcome |
| хушыгыз | (khushıgız) | bye-bye |
| хуҗа | (khuja) | host |
| хәбәр | (khäbär) | news |
| хәвефсез | (khävefsez) | safe |
| хәзер | (khäzer) | now, present |
| хәзер үк | (khäzer ük) | immediately |
| хәзинә | (khäzinä) | treasure |
| хәл | (khäl) | condition, situation |
| хәл ит- | (khäl it-) | solve |
| хәнҗәр | (khänjär) | dagger |
| хәреф | (khäref) | letter |
| хәрәкәтлән- | (khäräkätlän-) | move |
| хәтер | (khäter) | memory |
| хәтерлә- | (khäterlä-) | remember |
| хәтта | (khätta) | even |
| хәтфә келәм | (khätfä keläm) | rug |
| хәтәр | (khätär) | danger |
| хәтәрле | (khätärle) | dangerous |
| хөкем | (khökem) | verdict |
| хөкүмәт | (khökümät) | government |
| хөкүмәт башлыгы | (khökümät bashlıgı) | prime minister |
| хөрмә | (khörmä) | date |
| хөрмәт | (khörmät) | respect |
| хөрмәтлә- | (khörmätlä-) | respect |
| цемент | (tsement) | cement |
| цензура | (tsenzura) | censorship |
| цирк | (tsirk) | circus |
| чабата | (chabata) | slipper |
| чагыштыру | (chagıshtıru) | comparison |
| чакыр- | (chakır-) | call, invite, summon |
| чакыру | (chakıru) | invitation |
| чалбар | (chalbar) | pants |
| чамасы | (chaması) | about |
| чана | (chana) | sled |
| чарасыз | (charasız) | impossible |
| чаңгы спорты | (changgı sportı) | skiing |
| чебен | (cheben) | fly |
| чек | (chek) | check |
| чемодан | (chemodan) | suitcase |
| чер- | (cher-) | rot |
| черки | (cherki) | mosquito |
| чи | (chi) | raw |
| чик | (chik) | border |
| чикерткә | (chikertkä) | grasshopper |
| чиклә- | (chiklä-) | restrict |
| чикләвек | (chiklävek) | walnut |
| чиләк | (chiläk) | bucket |
| чиркәү | (chirkäü) | church |
| чит | (chit) | edge |
| чит ил кешесе | (chit il keshese) | foreigner |
| чия | (chiya) | cherry |
| чум- | (chum-) | dive |
| чучка ите | (chuchka ite) | pork |
| чыгу | (chıgu) | exit |
| чыгым | (chıgım) | expense |
| чык- | (chık-) | exit |
| чын | (chın) | real |
| чынаяк | (chınayak) | cup |
| чыпчык | (chıpchık) | sparrow |
| чыршы | (chırshı) | fir |
| чәй | (chäy) | tea |
| чәй тәлинкәсе | (chäy tälinkäse) | saucer |
| чәйлек | (chäylek) | tip |
| чәйнек | (chäynek) | teapot |
| чәйнә- | (chäynä-) | chew |
| чәнечке | (chänechke) | fork |
| чәршәмбе | (chärshämbe) | Wednesday |
| чәч | (chäch) | hair |
| чәч- | (chäch-) | scatter |
| чөнки | (chönki) | because |

| | | |
|---|---|---|
| чукеч | (chükech) | hammer |
| чул | (chül) | desert |
| чулмәк | (chülmäk) | jug |
| чүп-чар | (chüp-char) | trash |
| шагыйрь | (shagıyr') | poet |
| шайтан | (shaytan) | Satan |
| шарт | (shart) | condition |
| шарф | (sharf) | scarf |
| шат | (shat) | happy |
| шатлык | (shatlık) | joy |
| шахмат | (shakhmat) | chess |
| шаярту | (shayartu) | joke |
| шаһит | (shahit) | witness |
| шеш | (shesh) | swelling |
| шеш- | (shesh-) | swell |
| шешә | (sheshä) | bottle |
| шигърият | (shig'riyat) | poetry |
| шигырь | (shigır') | poem |
| шикаять ит- | (shikayat' it-) | complain |
| шикәр | (shikär) | sugar |
| шимбә | (shimbä) | Saturday |
| шина | (shina) | tire |
| ширбәт ае | (shirbät aye) | honeymoon |
| шифаханә | (shifakhanä) | hospital |
| шкаф | (shkaf) | cupboard |
| шорт | (short) | shorts |
| шофер | (shofyer) | driver |
| шпинат | (shpinat) | spinach |
| шу- | (shu-) | slide |
| шул | (shul) | that |
| шулар | (shular) | those |
| шулпа | (shulpa) | soup |
| шунлыктан | (shunlıktan) | therefore |
| шырпы | (shırpı) | match |
| шәм | (shäm) | candle |
| шәмәхә | (shämäkhä) | purple |
| шәраб | (shärab) | wine |
| шәфкать туташы | (shäfkat' tutashı) | nurse |
| шәфталу | (shäftalu) | peach |
| шәхес | (shäkhes) | person |
| шәһәр | (shähär) | city, town |
| шөбһә | (shöbhä) | doubt |
| шөкер кыл- | (shöker kıl-) | thank |
| шөреп | (shörep) | screw |
| шөреп боргыч | (shörep borgıch) | screwdriver |
| щётка | (shchyotka) | brush |
| ышан- | (ıshan-) | believe, rely |
| ышану | (ıshanu) | belief |
| ышаныч | (ıshanıch) | confidence |
| ышк- | (ıshk-) | rub |
| эз | (ez) | trace |
| эзлә- | (ezlä-) | look for, search, seek |
| экономика | (ekonomika) | economics |
| экран | (ekran) | screen |
| элек | (elek) | ago |
| электричество | (elektrichestvo) | electricity |
| эне | (ene) | brother |
| энә | (enä) | needle |
| эпос | (epos) | epic |
| эра | (era) | era |
| эре- | (ere-) | melt |
| эссе | (esse) | hot |
| эт | (et) | dog |
| этажерка | (etazherka) | bookcase |
| этәр- | (etär-) | push |
| эч | (ech) | belly |
| эч йомшарткыч | (ech yomshartkıch) | laxative |
| эч кату | (ech katu) | constipation |
| эч китү | (ech kitü) | diarrhea |
| эч- | (ech-) | drink |
| эчемлек | (echemlek) | beverage |
| эчтә | (echtä) | inside |
| эчәк | (echäk) | intestine |
| эчәсе килгән | (echäse kilgän) | thirsty |
| эш | (esh) | job |
| эш ташлау | (esh tashlau) | strike |
| эш хакы | (esh khakı) | salary, wage |
| эшлә- | (eshlä-) | work |
| эшләп чыгар- | (eshläp chıgar-) | produce |
| эшләпә | (eshläpä) | hat |
| эшче | (eshche) | worker |
| эңгер-меңгер | (engger-mengger) | dusk |
| ю- | (yu-) | wash |
| юан | (yuan) | fat |
| юаныч | (yuanıch) | entertainment |
| юбка | (yubka) | skirt |
| югал- | (yugal-) | disappear |
| югалт- | (yugalt-) | lose |

| | | |
|---|---|---|
| югарыда | (yugarıda) | above |
| юеш | (yuesh) | moist, wet |
| юк | (yuk) | no |
| юка | (yuka) | fine, thin |
| юл | (yul) | road, way |
| юл куйма- | (yul kuyma-) | prevent |
| юл чаты | (yul chatı) | crosswalk |
| юлбарыс | (yulbarıs) | tiger |
| юмарт | (yumart) | generous |
| юрган | (yurgan) | blanket, quilt |
| ютәл | (yutäl) | cough |
| юыну бүлмәсе | (yuınu bülmäse) | bathroom |
| юынгыч | (yuıngıch) | sink |
| | | |
| я ... я | (ya ... ya) | either ... or |
| ябалак | (yabalak) | owl |
| ябык | (yabık) | closed |
| ябыш- | (yabısh-) | stick |
| яз | (yaz) | spring |
| яз- | (yaz-) | write |
| язмыш | (yazmısh) | fate |
| язу | (yazu) | writing |
| язу машинкасы | (yazu mashinkası) | typewriter |
| язучы | (yazuchı) | writer |
| як | (yak) | direction, side, way |
| яка | (yaka) | collar |
| яки | (yaki) | or |
| яклаучы | (yaklauchı) | lawyer |
| якты | (yaktı) | bright |
| яктылык | (yaktılık) | light |
| якшәмбе | (yakshämbe) | Sunday |
| якын | (yakın) | near |
| якында | (yakında) | near |
| якынлаш- | (yakınlash-) | approach |
| ял | (yal) | holiday, rest, vacation |
| ял паркы | (yal parkı) | park |
| ялан | (yalan) | bare |
| ялган | (yalgan) | lie |
| ялган сөйлә- | (yalgan söylä-) | lie |
| ялгыз | (yalgız) | alone |
| ялгыш | (yalgısh) | wrong |
| ялкау | (yalkau) | lazy |
| ялкаулык | (yalkaulık) | laziness |
| ялкын | (yalkın) | flame |
| ялтыра- | (yaltıra-) | shine |

| | | |
|---|---|---|
| ямансула- | (yamansula-) | bored: be bored |
| ямьсез | (yam'sez) | ugly |
| ян- | (yan-) | burn |
| янгын | (yangın) | fire |
| яндыр- | (yandır-) | burn |
| янында | (yanında) | beside |
| яп- | (yap-) | close, cover, shut |
| яр- | (yar-) | split |
| яр буе | (yar buye) | coast |
| яра | (yara) | wound |
| ярат- | (yarat-) | like, love |
| ярдәм | (yardäm) | assistance, help |
| ярдәм бир- | (yardäm bir-) | help |
| ярдәм ит- | (yardäm it-) | assist |
| ярлы | (yarlı) | poor |
| ярты | (yartı) | half |
| ярый | (yarıy) | OK |
| ярымутрау | (yarımutrau) | peninsula |
| ярыш | (yarısh) | race |
| ярышучылык | (yarıshuchılık) | competition |
| яса- | (yasa-) | make |
| ясалма | (yasalma) | artificial, false |
| ясмык | (yasmık) | lentil |
| ястык тышлыгы | (yastık tıshlıgı) | pillowcase |
| ят- | (yat-) | lie |
| яу- | (yau-) | precipitate |
| яфрак | (yafrak) | leaf |
| яхшы | (yakhshı) | better, fine, well |
| яхшырак күр- | (yakhshırak kür-) | prefer |
| яшел | (yashel) | green |
| яшелчә | (yashelchä) | vegetable |
| яшен | (yashen) | lightning |
| яшер- | (yasher-) | hide |
| яшь | (yash') | age, young |
| яшьлек | (yash'lek) | youth |
| яшә- | (yashä-) | live |
| яңа | (yanga) | fresh, new |
| яңа ай | (yanga ay) | crescent |
| яңа ел | (yanga yel) | New Year |
| яңа туган бала | (yanga tugan bala) | baby |
| яңак | (yangak) | cheek |
| яңгыр | (yanggır) | rain |

| | | |
|---|---|---|
| әби | (äbi) | grandmother |
| әгъза | (äg'za) | member |
| әгәр | (ägär) | if |
| әдәби | (ädäbi) | literary |
| әдәби әсәр | (ädäbi äsär) | literary work |
| әдәбият | (ädäbiyat) | literature |
| әдәпле | (ädäple) | polite |
| әзер | (äzer) | ready |
| әзерлә- | (äzerlä-) | prepare |
| әйбәт | (äybät) | good, nice |
| әйе | (äye) | yes |
| әйт- | (äyt-) | say, tell |
| әлбәттә | (älbättä) | course: of course |
| әле | (äle) | yet |
| әлегәчә | (älegächä) | still |
| әлифба | (älifba) | alphabet |
| әмма | (ämma) | but |
| әни | (äni) | mother |
| әти | (äti) | father |
| әтәч | (ätäch) | rooster |
| әфәнде | (äfände) | gentleman |
| әчи | (ächi) | sour |
| әҗәтханә | (äjätkhanä) | toilet |
| өй | (öy) | home |
| өйлән- | (öylän-) | marry |
| өйләнү | (öylänü) | marriage |
| өйрән- | (öyrän-) | learn, study |
| өлеш | (ölesh) | part |
| өлкә | (ölkä) | province |
| өмет | (ömet) | hope |
| өметлән- | (ömetlän-) | hope |
| өрек | (örek) | apricot |
| өрәк | (öräk) | ghost |
| өстендә | (östendä) | above, on, over |
| өстәл | (östäl) | table |
| өтер | (öter) | comma |
| өч | (öch) | three |
| өчен | (öchen) | for |
| өчпочмак | (öchpochmak) | triangle |
| үгез | (ügez) | bull, ox |
| үзе | (üze) | herself, himself, itself |
| үзебез | (üzebez) | ourselves |
| үзегез | (üzegez) | yourselves |
| үзем | (üzem) | myself |

| | | |
|---|---|---|
| үзен тот- | (üzen tot-) | behave |
| үзең | (üzeng) | yourself |
| үзгәрт- | (üzgärt-) | change |
| үзидарә | (üzidarä) | autonomy |
| үзәк | (üzäk) | center |
| үзән | (üzän) | valley |
| үкенеч | (ükenech) | regret |
| үл- | (ül-) | die |
| үле | (üle) | dead |
| үлем | (ülem) | death |
| үлчәм | (ülchäm) | measure, size |
| үлчәү | (ülchäü) | scale |
| үлән | (ülän) | grass |
| үп- | (üp-) | kiss |
| үпкә | (üpkä) | lung |
| үрдәк | (ürdäk) | duck |
| үрмәкүч | (ürmäküch) | spider |
| үрмәләп мен- | (ürmäläp men-) | climb |
| үс- | (üs-) | grow |
| үсемлек | (üsemlek) | plant |
| үсү | (üsü) | growth |
| үт- | (üt-) | pass |
| үтер- | (üter-) | kill |
| үткен | (ütken) | sharp |
| үткән | (ütkän) | last |
| үтүк | (ütük) | iron |
| үч | (üch) | revenge |
| җавап | (javap) | answer, reply |
| җавап бир- | (javap bir-) | answer, reply |
| җанлы | (janlı) | alive |
| җибәр- | (jibär-) | send |
| җиде | (jide) | seven |
| җил | (jil) | wind |
| җилем | (jilem) | glue |
| җилкәнле көймә | (jilkänle köymä) | sailboat |
| җимер- | (jimer-) | destroy |
| җимеш | (jimesh) | fruit |
| җинаять | (jinayat') | crime |
| җинаятьче | (jinayat'che) | criminal |
| җир | (jir) | earth |
| җир тетрәү | (jir teträü) | earthquake |
| җир җиләге | (jir jiläge) | strawberry |
| җит- | (jit-) | arrive, reach |
| җитди | (jitdi) | serious |
| җитмеш | (jitmesh) | seventy |
| җитәрлек | (jitärlek) | enough, sufficient |

| җиң- | (jing-) | defeat, surpass, win |
| җиңел | (jingel) | light |
| җиңелү | (jingelü) | defeat |
| җиңеш | (jingesh) | victory |
| җиһаз | (jihaz) | furniture |
| җиһазлар | (jihazlar) | equipment |
| җомга | (jomga) | Friday |
| җы- | (jı-) | collect |
| җыелыш | (jıyelısh) | meeting |
| җылы | (jılı) | lukewarm, warm |
| җыр | (jır) | song |
| җырла- | (jırla-) | sing |
| җырчы | (jırchı) | singer |
| җәза | (jäza) | punishment |
| җәзала- | (jäzala-) | punish |
| җәй | (jäy) | summer |
| җәмгыять | (jämgıyat') | society |
| җәннәт | (jännät) | paradise |
| җәя | (jäya) | bow |
| җәяүле | (jäyaüle) | pedestrian |
| җөй | (jöy) | knot |
| җөмлә | (jömlä) | sentence |
| һава | (hava) | air, weather |

| һава торышы турында прогноз | (hava torıshı turında prognoz) | weather report |
| һава юлы | (hava yulı) | airline |
| һичвакыт | (hichvakıt) | never |
| һичкайда | (hichkayda) | nowhere |
| һичкем | (hichkem) | nobody |
| һични | (hichni) | nothing |
| һуштан яз- | (hushtan yaz-) | faint |
| һәйкәл | (häykäl) | monument |
| һәм | (häm) | and |
| һәм ... һәм | (häm ... häm) | both ... and |
| һәммә | (hämmä) | all |
| һәр | (här) | every |
| һәрвакыт | (härvakıt) | always |
| һәркайда | (härkayda) | everywhere |
| һәркем | (härkem) | anybody, everybody |
| һәрнәрсә | (härnärsä) | everything |
| һөнәр | (hönär) | occupation, skill |
| һөҗүм | (höjüm) | attack |
| һөҗүм ит- | (höjüm it-) | attack |

# TURKISH - ENGLISH INDEX

| | | | |
|---|---|---|---|
| -a, -e | to | altta | underneath |
| abla | sister | ama | but |
| acayip | strange | ambulans | ambulance |
| acele | haste | amca | uncle |
| acele et- | hurry | ameliyat | operation |
| acı | bitter | an | moment |
| aç | hungry | ana | main |
| aç- | open | ana baba | parents |
| açı | angle | anahtar | key |
| açık | open | anarşi | anarchy |
| açıkla- | explain | anıt | monument |
| açıklama | explanation | ani | sudden |
| açlık | famine, hunger | anla- | understand |
| ad | name | anne | mother |
| ada | island | anten | antenna |
| adalet | justice | apartman dairesi | apartment |
| adet | habit | aptal | stupid |
| adım | step | ara- | look for, search, seek |
| adres | address | araba | car |
| affet- | forgive | aralık | December |
| ağaç | tree | arasında | between |
| ağır | heavy | araştırma | investigation, research |
| ağız | mouth | arı | bee |
| ağla- | cry, weep | arkada | behind |
| ağrı | pain | arkadaş | friend |
| ağustos | August | arkadaşlık | friendship |
| aile | family | armut | pear |
| ak- | flow | arpa | barley |
| akciğer | lung | art- | increase |
| akıl | mind | arzu | desire |
| akıllı | clever | as- | hang |
| akraba | relative | asansör | elevator |
| akşam | evening | asker | soldier |
| akşam karanlığı | dusk | askı | hanger |
| akşam yemeği | dinner | asla | never |
| al- | take | aslan | lion |
| alçak | low | aşağı | down |
| alet | tool | aşağıda | below |
| alev | flame | aşçı | cook |
| alfabe | alphabet | aşı | shot |
| alıcı | buyer | aşk | love |
| alın | forehead | at | horse |
| alış- | used: be used to | at arabası | cart |
| alışveriş et- | shop | at- | throw |
| alkışla- | clap | atama | appointment |
| allahaısmarladık | bye-bye | atasözü | proverb |
| altı | six | ateş | fever, fire |
| altın | gold | av | game |
| altında | under, underneath | avla- | hunt |
| altmış | sixty | avlu | courtyard |

| | | | |
|---|---|---|---|
| avukat | lawyer | bas- | print |
| ay | month, moon | basın | press |
| ayak | foot | basit | simple |
| ayakkabı | shoe | basketbol | basketball |
| ayakkabıcı | shoemaker | baş | head |
| ayakta dur- | stand | baş ağrısı | headache |
| ayçiçeği | sunflower | baş vur- | apply |
| aydın | intellectual | başar- | succeed |
| aydınlık | bright | başarı | success |
| ayı | bear | başbakan | prime minister |
| ayır- | separate | başka | another, besides |
| ayna | mirror | başkent | capital |
| aynı | same | başla- | begin, start |
| ayrı | separate | başlık | title |
| ayrıl- | separated: be separated | bat- | sink |
| ayva | quince | bataklık | swamp |
| az | few | batı | west |
| azal- | decrease | battaniye | blanket |
| azınlık | minority | bavul | suitcase |
| | | bayıl- | faint |
| baba | father | baykuş | owl |
| baca | chimney | bayrak | flag |
| bacak | leg | bayram | holiday |
| badem | almond | bazen | sometimes |
| bağımsızlık | independence | bazı | some |
| bağır- | scream, shout | bebek | baby |
| bağırsak | intestine | bedava | free |
| bağla- | fasten, tie | beden | body |
| bahane | excuse | bekle- | wait |
| bahçe | garden | bel | spade |
| bahçıvan | gardener | belediye | municipality |
| bahşiş | tip | belediye başkanı | mayor |
| bak- | look | belki | perhaps |
| bakan | minister | ben | I |
| bakır | copper | beni | me |
| baklava biçimi | diamond | benim | my |
| bal | honey | benimki | mine |
| balayı | honeymoon | benze- | resemble |
| bale | ballet | benzer | alike, similar |
| balık | fish | benzin | gasoline |
| balıkçı | fisherman | berber | hairdresser |
| balkon | balcony | beri | since |
| balta | axe | besbelli | obvious |
| banka | bank | beste | composition |
| banliyö | suburb | besteci | composer |
| banyo | bathroom | beş | five |
| baraj | dam | beyaz | white |
| bardak | glass | beyin | brain |
| barış | peace | bezelye | pea |
| barometre | barometer | bıçak | knife |

| | | | |
|---|---|---|---|
| bırak- | release | bulaşık makinesi | dishwasher |
| bıyık | mustache | bulut | cloud |
| bil- | know | bulvar | avenue |
| bilek | wrist | bundan dolayı | therefore |
| bilet | ticket | bunlar | these |
| bilgi | information, knowledge | burada | here |
| bilgisayar | computer | buraya | here |
| bilim adamı | scientist | burun | nose |
| bin | thousand | but | thigh |
| bin- | get on, ride | buz | ice |
| bina | building | buzdolabı | refrigerator |
| bir | one | bük- | twist |
| bira | beer | büro | office |
| biraz | little, some | bütçe | budget |
| birkaç | several | bütün | all, whole |
| birlikte | together | büyü | spell |
| bisiklet | bicycle | büyü- | grow |
| bit | louse | büyük | big, great, large |
| bitir- | finish | büyük mağaza | department store |
| bitki | herb, plant | büyüme | growth |
| biz | we | | |
| bizi | us | cam | glass |
| bizim | our | cami | mosque |
| bizimki | ours | canlı | alive |
| bluz | blouse | cazibe | attraction |
| boğa | bull | cebir | algebra |
| boğaz | throat | cehennem | hell |
| boğul- | drown | ceket | jacket |
| bol | loose | cennet | paradise |
| bomba | bomb | cep | pocket |
| borç | debt, loan | cerrahlık | surgery |
| boş | empty | cesaret | courage |
| boşalt- | empty | cesur | brave, courageous |
| boşan- | divorce | cetvel | ruler |
| boşanma | divorce | cevap | answer, reply |
| boya- | dye, paint | cevap ver- | answer, reply |
| boyacı | painter | ceviz | walnut |
| boynuz | horn | ceza | punishment |
| boyun | neck | ceza ver- | punish |
| bozuk para | change | ciddi | serious |
| böbrek | kidney | coğrafya | geography |
| böcek | insect | cömert | generous |
| böl- | divide | cuma | Friday |
| bölme | division | cumartesi | Saturday |
| bölüm | department, section | cumhurbaşkanı | president |
| böyle | such | cumhuriyet | republic |
| bu | this | cümle | sentence |
| bugün | today | cüzdan | purse |
| buğday | wheat | | |
| bul- | find | çabuk | quick |

| | | | |
|---|---|---|---|
| çağır- | call, summon | çöp | trash |
| çal- | play, steal | çöz- | solve |
| çalgı aleti | instrument | çünkü | because |
| çalış- | study, try, work | çürü- | rot |
| çalışkan | diligent | | |
| çam ağacı | pine | -da, -de | at, in |
| çamur | mud | da, de | also, too |
| çanta | bag | dağ | mountain |
| çarpma | multiplication | daha çok | more |
| çarşaf | sheet | daha iyi | better |
| çarşamba | Wednesday | daima | always |
| çatal | fork | daire | circle |
| çatı | roof | dakika | minute |
| çay | tea | daktilo | typewriter |
| çaydanlık | teapot | dal | branch |
| çek | check | dal- | dive |
| çek- | pull | dalga | wave |
| çekiç | hammer | damla | drop |
| çekirge | grasshopper | -dan, -den | from |
| çelik | steel | dana eti | veal |
| çene | chin | dans et- | dance |
| çerçeve | frame | dansör | dancer |
| çeşit | kind | dansöz | dancer |
| çeşme | fountain | dar | narrow |
| çık- | exit | davet | invitation |
| çıkarma | subtraction | davet et- | invite |
| çıkış | exit | davran- | behave |
| çılgın | crazy | davranış | behavior |
| çıplak | bare | dayı | uncle |
| çiçek | flower | de- | say |
| çift | pair | dede | grandfather |
| çiftçi | peasant | defter | notebook |
| çiftlik | farm | değil | not |
| çiğ | raw | değirmen | mill |
| çiğne- | chew | değiştir- | change |
| çilek | strawberry | delik | hole |
| çimen | grass | delil | proof |
| çimento | cement | delilik | insanity |
| çirkin | ugly | demir | iron |
| çit | fence | demiryolu | railroad |
| çivi | nail | demokrasi | democracy |
| çizgi | line | deniz | sea |
| çizim | drawing | denizaltı | submarine |
| çizme | boot | deprem | earthquake |
| çocuk | child | derece | degree |
| çoğunluk | majority | dergi | magazine |
| çok | many, much, very | deri | leather, skin |
| çorap | sock, stocking | derin | deep |
| çorba | soup | derinlik | depth |
| çöl | desert | ders | lesson |

| | | | |
|---|---|---|---|
| destan | epic | don | frost |
| dev | giant | don- | freeze |
| devam et- | continue | dondurma | ice cream |
| deve | camel | dök- | pour |
| devir | era | dön- | turn |
| devlet | state | dört | four |
| devrim | revolution | döşeme | floor |
| deyim | idiom | dua | prayer |
| dışarıda | outside | dua et- | pray |
| diğer | other | dudak | lip |
| dik- | plant, sew | dur- | stop |
| dikkat | attention | durak | stop |
| dikkatli | careful | durdur- | stop |
| dil | language, tongue | durum | situation |
| dilbilim | linguistics | duş | shower |
| dilci | linguist | dut | mulberry |
| dile- | wish | duvar | wall |
| dilek | wish | duvar saati | clock |
| dilsiz | mute | duy- | hear |
| din | religion | duygu | feeling |
| dinî | religious | düğme | button |
| dinî bayram | religious holiday | düğüm | knot |
| dinle- | listen | dükkân | shop |
| dinlenme | rest | dün | yesterday |
| diploma | diploma | dünya | earth, world |
| dirsek | elbow | dürüst | honest |
| diş | tooth | düş- | fall |
| diş ağrısı | toothache | düşman | enemy |
| diş fırçası | toothbrush | düşmanlık | enmity |
| diş macunu | toothpaste | düşün- | think |
| dişçi | dentist | düşünce | thought |
| diz | knee | düz | straight |
| doğ- | born: be born | düzelt- | correct |
| doğa | nature | düzine | dozen |
| doğal | natural | | |
| doğru | correct, towards | ebediyet | eternity |
| doğu | east | eczacı | pharmacist |
| doğum | birth | eczane | pharmacy |
| doğum günü | birthday | edebi | literary |
| doksan | ninety | edebi eser | literary work |
| doktor | doctor | edebiyat | literature |
| dokuma | textile | efendi | gentleman |
| dokun- | touch | efsane | legend |
| dokuz | nine | eğ- | bend |
| dolap | cupboard | eğe | file |
| doldur- | fill | eğer | if |
| dolu | full, hail | eğitim | education |
| domates | tomato | eğlence | entertainment |
| domuz | pig | ek- | plant |
| domuz eti | pork | ekim | October |

| | | | |
|---|---|---|---|
| ekin | crop | farklı | different |
| ekle- | add | fasulye | bean |
| ekmek | bread | fayda | benefit |
| ekonomi | economics | faydalı | useful |
| ekran | screen | felç | paralysis |
| ekşi | sour | fındık | hazelnut |
| el | hand | fırça | brush |
| el çantası | handbag | fırın | bakery, oven |
| elbette | course: of course | fırıncı | baker |
| elbise | clothes, dress | fırtına | storm |
| elçi | ambassador | fiil | verb |
| eldiven | glove | fikir | idea, opinion |
| elektrik | electricity | fil | elephant |
| elli | fifty | film | film, movie |
| elma | apple | fincan | cup |
| elverişli | convenient | fincan tabağı | saucer |
| em- | suck | fiyat | price |
| emekliye ayrıl- | retire | fizik | physics |
| emin | safe | folklor | folklore |
| emret- | command, order | form | form |
| en çok | most | fotoğraf | photo |
| en iyi | best | fotoğraf makinası | camera |
| enfeksiyon | infection | futbol | soccer |
| enflasyon | inflation | | |
| eri- | melt | gaga | beak |
| erik | plum | garaj | garage |
| erkek | man | garson | waiter |
| erkek kardeş | brother | gaz | gas |
| erken | early | gazete | newspaper |
| ertele- | postpone | gazeteci | journalist |
| eski | old | gece | night |
| esne- | yawn | gece yarısı | midnight |
| eşarp | scarf | gecikme | delay |
| eşek | donkey | geç | late |
| eşit | equal | geç- | pass, surpass |
| et | meat | geçen | last |
| etek | skirt | gel- | arrive, come |
| etki | effect, influence | gelecek | future, next |
| ev | home, house | gelenek | custom |
| ev sahibi | host | gelin | bride |
| evet | yes | gelir | income |
| evlen- | marry | gelişme | development |
| evlilik | marriage | gemi | ship |
| eylül | September | genç | young |
| ez- | crush | gençlik | youth |
| | | genel | general |
| fabrika | factory | geniş | broad, spacious, wide |
| faiz | interest | geometri | geometry |
| fakir | poor | gerçek | real |
| fark | difference | gerçekçilik | realism |

| | | | |
|---|---|---|---|
| gerekli | necessary | gürültü | noise |
| geri dön- | return | güven | confidence |
| getir- | bring | güven- | rely |
| gevşek | loose | güvercin | pigeon |
| geyik | deer | güvey | bridegroom |
| gezegen | planet | güzel | beautiful, fine, pretty |
| gezin- | stroll | güzellik | beauty |
| gibi | like | | |
| gider | expense | haber | news |
| gir- | enter | haber ver- | inform |
| giriş | entrance | hafıza | memory |
| git- | go | hafif | light |
| giy- | put on, wear | hafta | week |
| gizli | secret | hakikat | truth |
| göğüs | breast, chest | hakiki | true |
| gök gürlemesi | thunder | hakkında | about |
| gökkuşağı | rainbow | hal | condition |
| gökyüzü | sky | hala | aunt |
| göl | lake | halı | carpet, rug |
| gölge | shade, shadow | halk | people |
| göm- | bury | halk hikâyesi | folktale |
| gömlek | shirt | hamal | porter |
| gönder- | send | hamile | pregnant |
| gör- | see | hamilelik | pregnancy |
| görev | duty | hançer | dagger |
| görün- | appear | hangi | which |
| göster- | show | hanım | lady |
| gösteri | demonstration | hap | pill |
| göz | eye | hapishane | jail, prison |
| gözlük | glasses | harca- | spend |
| gözlükçü | optician | hardal | mustard |
| grev | strike | hareket et- | move |
| gri | grey | harf | letter |
| grip | flu | harita | map |
| gurur | pride | hasat | harvest |
| gübre | fertilizer | haset | envy |
| güç | force, power, strength | hasta | ill, patient, sick |
| güçlü | powerful, strong | hastabakıcı | nurse |
| gül | rose | hastalık | illness |
| gül- | laugh | hastane | hospital |
| gülümse- | smile | hata | fault, mistake |
| gümrük | customs | hatırla- | remember |
| gümüş | silver | hatırlat- | remind |
| gün | day | hatta | even |
| gün doğuşu | sunrise | hava | air, weather |
| günbatımı | sunset | hava raporu | weather report |
| gündüz | daytime | hava yolu | airline |
| güneş | sun | havaalanı | airport |
| güney | south | havlu | towel |
| güreş | wrestling | havuç | carrot |

| | | | |
|---|---|---|---|
| havuz | pool | hürmet et- | respect |
| hayat | life | | |
| hayır | no | ılık | lukewarm, warm |
| hayran ol- | admire | ısı | heat |
| hayvan | animal | ısır- | bite |
| hayvanat bahçesi | zoo | ıslak | wet |
| hazır | ready | ısmarla- | order |
| hazırla- | prepare | ıspanak | spinach |
| hazine | treasure | ışık | light |
| haziran | June | ışın | ray |
| hâlâ | still | ibadet | worship |
| helikopter | helicopter | iç- | drink |
| hem ... hem | both ... and | içecek | beverage |
| hemen | immediately | içeride | inside |
| hemen hemen | almost | için | for |
| henüz | yet | içki | drink |
| hepsi | all | idareci | manager |
| her | every | iğne | needle |
| her yerde | everywhere | ihtiyaç | necessity, need |
| herhangi | any | iki | two |
| herhangi bir şey | anything | ikiz | twin |
| herkes | anybody, everybody | iklim | climate |
| herşey | everything | ilaç | drug, medicine |
| hesap | account, bill | ile | by, with |
| hesapla- | calculate | ileri | forward |
| heyecan | excitement | iletişim | communication |
| heykel | statue | ilgi | interest |
| heykeltıraşlık | sculpture | ilginç | interesting |
| Hıristiyan | Christian | ilkbahar | spring |
| hırsız | burglar, thief | imkân | possibility |
| hıyar | cucumber | imkânsız | impossible |
| hız | speed | imza | signature |
| hızlı | fast, speedy | imzala- | sign |
| hiç kimse | nobody | in- | get off |
| hiçbir yerde | nowhere | inan- | believe |
| hiçbir şey | nothing | inanç | belief |
| hikâye | story | ince | fine, slim, thin |
| hilal | crescent | incir | fig |
| hindi | turkey | indirim | discount, sale |
| hisset- | feel | inek | cow |
| hizmetçi | servant | ingiliz anahtarı | wrench |
| horoz | rooster | inkar et- | deny |
| hoş | nice | insan | human being |
| hoş geldin[iz] | welcome | inşa et- | build |
| hurma | date | ipek | silk |
| hücum | attack | irtikâp | corruption |
| hücum et- | attack | ishal | diarrhea |
| hükûmet | government | isim | noun |
| hüküm | verdict | iskambil kağıdı | playing card |
| hüner | skill | iskelet | skeleton |

| | | | |
|---|---|---|---|
| istasyon | station | kaplumbağa | tortoise |
| iste- | want | kaptan | captain |
| isyan | rebellion | kar | snow |
| iş | business, job | karabiber | pepper |
| iş adamı | businessman | karaciğer | liver |
| işçi | worker | karanfil | carnation |
| işe- | urinate | karanlık | dark, darkness |
| itaat et- | obey | karar | decision |
| itikat | faith | karar ver- | decide |
| ittir- | push | kare | square |
| iyi | good, well | karga | crow |
| iz | trace | karı | wife |
| izle- | follow | karın | belly |
| | | karınca | ant |
| jeoloji | geology | karıştır- | mix |
| | | karikatür | cartoon |
| kaba | rude | karmakarışık | messy |
| kabızlık | constipation | karpuz | watermelon |
| kabuk | bark | karşı | against |
| kabul et- | accept | karşılaş- | meet |
| kaç- | escape, flee, run away | karşılaştırma | comparison |
| kaça | how much | kartal | eagle |
| kadar | until | kartpostal | postcard |
| kader | fate | kas | muscle |
| kadın | woman | kasaba | town |
| kafeterya | café | kasap | butcher |
| kahvaltı | breakfast | kasap dükkânı | butcher shop |
| kahve | coffee | kaset | cassette |
| kahverengi | brown | kasım | November |
| kal- | remain, stay | kaş | eyebrow |
| kalabalık | crowd | kaşık | spoon |
| kaldır- | lift, raise | kat | storey |
| kaldırım | sidewalk | katı | hard |
| kalın | thick | katla- | fold |
| kalite | quality | kavak | poplar |
| kalk- | depart, get up | kavanoz | jar |
| kalkış | departure | kavga et- | fight |
| kalp | heart | kavun | melon |
| kamyon | truck | kay- | slide, slip |
| kan | blood | kaya | rock |
| kana- | bleed | kayak | skiing |
| kanal | canal, channel | kaybet- | lose |
| kanat | wing | kaybol- | disappear |
| kanser | cancer | kaygan | slippery |
| kanun | law | kaygılan- | worry |
| kapa- | close, shut | kayık | boat |
| kapak | lid | kayısı | apricot |
| kapalı | closed | kayıt | registration |
| kapı | door, gate | kaymak | cream |
| kaplan | tiger | kayna- | boil |

| | | | |
|---|---|---|---|
| kaz | goose | kibar | polite |
| kaz- | dig | kibrit | ch |
| kaza | accident | kil | clay |
| kazak | sweater | kilise | church |
| kazan- | win | kilit | lock |
| kazı- | scrape | kim | who |
| kâfi | sufficient | kimse | anybody |
| kâğıt | paper | kira | rent |
| kâr | profit | kiraz | cherry |
| kâse | bowl | kirli | dirty |
| keçi | goat | kirpik | eyelash |
| kedi | cat | kitap | book |
| kel | bald | kitapçı | bookseller, bookshop |
| kelebek | butterfly | kitaplık | bookcase |
| kelime | word | klinik | clinic |
| kemer | belt | klüp | club |
| kemik | bone | koca | husband |
| kenar | edge | kocaman | huge |
| kendim | myself | kok- | smell |
| kendimiz | ourselves | kokla- | smell |
| kendin | yourself | koku | smell |
| kendiniz | yourselves | kol | arm |
| kendisi | herself, himself, itself | kol saati | watch |
| kereviz | celery | kolay | easy |
| kes- | cut | koltuk | armchair |
| kesir | fraction | komedi | comedy |
| keskin | sharp | komşu | neighbor |
| kestane | chestnut | konferans | lecture |
| keşfet- | discover | konser | concert |
| kılıç | sword | konu | subject |
| kır | countryside | konukseverlik | hospitality |
| kır- | break | konuş- | speak, talk |
| kırık | broken | konuşma | speech |
| kırk | forty | kork- | afraid: be afraid |
| kırlangıç | swallow | korkak | coward |
| kırmızı | red | korkaklık | cowardice |
| kısa | short | korku | fear |
| kısım | part | koru | wood |
| kısıtla- | restrict | koru- | protect |
| kıskan- | envy | koş- | run |
| kıskanç | jealous | kova | bucket |
| kış | winter | kovala- | chase |
| kıymet | value | koy- | put |
| kıymetli | valuable | koyun | sheep |
| kız | daughter, girl | koyun eti | mutton |
| kızak | sled | kök | root |
| kızart- | roast | köknar | fir |
| kızgın | angry | kömür | coal |
| kızkardeş | sister | köpek | dog |
| ki | that | köprü | bridge |

| | | | |
|---|---|---|---|
| kör | blind | lâle | tulip |
| körfez | bay | leylek | stork |
| körlük | blindness | lezzetli | delicious, tasty |
| köşe | corner | liman | harbor |
| kötü | bad | limon | lemon |
| köy | village | lokanta | restaurant |
| kral | king | lütfen | please |
| kravat | tie | | |
| kredi | credit | maaş | salary |
| kuaför | hairdresser | maç | match |
| kucakla- | embrace | madde | matter |
| kuğu | swan | madeni para | coin |
| kulak | ear | mağaza | store |
| kule | tower | mahalle | neighborhood |
| kullan- | use | mahkeme | court |
| kum | sand | makale | article |
| kurabiye | cookie | makas | scissors |
| kuraklık | drought | makbuz | receipt |
| kuram | theory | makina | machine |
| kurbağa | frog | makinalı tüfek | machine gun |
| kurban | sacrifice | maksat | purpose |
| kurşun | lead | mal | goods |
| kurşun kalem | pencil | malzeme | material |
| kurt | wolf, worm | mantar | mushroom |
| kurtar- | rescue | mart | March |
| kuru | dry | marul | lettuce |
| kuru- | dry | masa | table |
| kus- | vomit | masa örtüsü | tablecloth |
| kuş | bird | masumiyet | innocence |
| kuşat- | surround | matbaa | printing press |
| kuşatma | siege | matematik | mathematics |
| kuştüyü | feather | matkap | drill |
| kutla- | celebrate | mavi | blue |
| kutlama | celebration | maydanoz | parsley |
| kutu | box | mayıs | May |
| kuyruk | tail | maymun | monkey |
| kuyumcu | jeweler | mektup | letter |
| kuzey | north | melek | angel |
| kuzu | lamb | memnun | glad |
| küçük | little, small | memur | official |
| kül | ash | mendil | handkerchief |
| kültür | culture | mercimek | lentil |
| kürek | shovel | merdiven | ladder, stairs |
| kürk | fur | merhaba | hello |
| kütüphane | library | merkez | center |
| | | mesafe | distance |
| lahana | cabbage | meslek | occupation |
| lamba | lamp | meşe ağacı | oak |
| lastik | tire | meşgul | busy |
| lavabo | sink | meşhur | famous |

| | | | |
|---|---|---|---|
| metal | metal | | |
| metro | subway | nadiren | seldom |
| mevsim | season | nağme | tune |
| meydan | square | nakit | cash |
| meyva suyu | fruit juice | nane | mint |
| meyve | fruit | nar | pomegranate |
| mezarlık | cemetery | nasıl | how |
| mezhep | sect | nazik | gentle, kind |
| mezuniyet | graduation | ne | what |
| mısır | corn | ne ... ne [de] | neither ... nor |
| mızrak | spear | ne kadar | how much |
| mide | stomach | ne zaman | when |
| miktar | amount, quantity | nefes | breath |
| millet | nation | nefret | disgust |
| milliyetçilik | nationalism | nefret et- | hate |
| milyar | billion | nemli | |
| milyon | million | nemli | damp, moist |
| mimar | architect | nerede | where |
| minder | cushion | nereye | where |
| minnettarlık | gratitude | nesir | prose |
| misafir | guest | nesne | object |
| mitoloji | mythology | niçin | why |
| mobilya | furniture | nine | grandmother |
| moda | fashion | nisan | April |
| mor | purple | niyet | intention |
| motor | engine | nokta | period |
| motosiklet | motorcycle | nüfus | population |
| muhtaç ol- | need | | |
| muhtemelen | probably | o | he, it, she, that |
| mum | candle | o zaman | then |
| Musevi | Jew | ocak | January |
| musluk | faucet | oda | room |
| mutfak | kitchen | oğlan | boy |
| mutlu | happy | oğul | son |
| mutsuz | unhappy | ok | arrow |
| muz | banana | okşa- | stroke |
| mühendis | engineer | oku- | read |
| mükemmel | perfect | okul | school |
| mümkün | possible | okul parası | tuition |
| münakaşa | argument | okur | reader |
| mürekkep | ink | okur yazar | literate |
| mürekkepli kalem | pen | okyanus | ocean |
| müsade et- | permit | ol- | be, become, happen |
| müshil | laxative | olay | event |
| Müslüman | Muslim | olgun | ripe |
| müşteri | customer | omurga | spine |
| müzakere | discussion | omuz | shoulder |
| müze | museum | on | ten |
| müzik | music | on altı | sixteen |
| müzisyen | musician | on beş | fifteen |

| | | | |
|---|---|---|---|
| on bir | eleven | öğren- | learn |
| on dokuz | nineteen | öğrenci | student |
| on dört | fourteen | öğret- | teach |
| on iki | twelve | öğretmen | teacher |
| on sekiz | eighteen | öğüt | advice |
| on üç | thirteen | öğüt- | grind |
| on yedi | seventeen | öksürük | cough |
| onar- | mend, repair | öküz | ox |
| onaylama | approval | öl- | die |
| ondan sonra | then | ölçü | measure, size |
| onlar | they, those | öldür- | kill |
| onları | them | ölü | dead |
| onların | their | ölüm | death |
| onun | her, his, its, her, him | önce | ago, before |
| onunki | hers, his, its | önemli | important |
| opera | opera | öneri | suggestion |
| orada | there | önle- | prevent |
| orak | sickle | önsöz | preface |
| oraya | there | önünde | front: in front of |
| ordu | army | öp- | kiss |
| orman | forest | ördek | duck |
| orta | medium, middle | örnek | example |
| ortak | partner | ört- | cover |
| oruç | fast | örümcek | spider |
| ot | herb | öv- | praise |
| ot | grass | övün- | boast |
| otel | hotel | özellikle | especially |
| otlak | meadow | özerklik | autonomy |
| otobüs | bus | özgür | free |
| otomobil | automobile | özgürlük | freedom |
| otur- | sit | özne | subject |
| otuz | thirty | özür | apology |
| ov- | rub | özür dile- | apologize |
| ova | plain | | |
| oy | vote | paha | cost |
| oy ver- | vote | pahalı | expensive |
| oyna- | play | paket | parcel |
| oyun | game, play | palto | overcoat |
| oyun yazarı | playwright | pamuk | cotton |
| oyuncak | toy | pantolon | pants |
| | | papatya | daisy |
| öç | revenge | papaz | priest |
| öde- | pay | para | currency, money |
| ödev | assignment | para cüzdanı | wallet |
| ödül | prize | paragraf | paragraph |
| ödünç al- | borrow | parfüm | perfume |
| öfke | anger | park | park |
| öğle | noon | parla- | shine |
| öğle yemeği | lunch | parmak | finger |
| öğleden sonra | afternoon | parti | party |

| | | | |
|---|---|---|---|
| pasaport | passport | resmigeçit | parade |
| pasta | cake | ressam | artist |
| patates | potato | rica et- | request |
| patlıcan | eggplant | roman | novel |
| paylaştır- | distribute | ruh | ghost, spirit |
| pazar | market, Sunday | rüya | dream |
| pazartesi | Monday | rüzgâr | wind |
| peçete | napkin | | |
| pembe | pink | saat | hour |
| pencere | window | saatçi | watchmaker |
| perde | curtain | sabah | morning |
| peron | platform | saban | plow |
| perşembe | Thursday | sabırlı | patient |
| petrol | oil | sabun | soap |
| peygamber | prophet | saç | hair |
| peynir | cheese | saç- | scatter |
| pijama | pajamas | saf | pure |
| pilav | rice | sağ | right |
| pire | flea | sağır | deaf |
| pirinç | rice | sağırlık | deafness |
| piş- | cook | sağlık | health |
| pişir- | cook | sağlıklı | healthy |
| pişmanlık | regret | sahil | coast |
| piyes | drama | sahne | stage |
| plaj | beach | sahte | false |
| plak | record | sakal | beard |
| polis | policeman | sakin | calm |
| portakal | orange | sakla- | hide |
| portakal rengi | orange | salata | salad |
| posta kutusu | mailbox | salı | Tuesday |
| posta ücreti | postage | salla- | shake |
| postacı | mailman | saman | straw |
| postane | post office | sanat | art |
| program | program | sandalye | chair |
| propaganda | propaganda | sandviç | sandwich |
| pul | stamp | saniye | second |
| | | sanki | as if |
| radyo | radio | sansür | censorship |
| raf | shelf | sap | handle |
| rahat | comfortable | sar- | wrap |
| rahatsız et- | bother, disturb | saray | palace |
| randevu | appointment | sargı bezi | bandage |
| razı ol- | agree | sarhoş | drunk |
| reçel | jam | sarı | yellow |
| reçete | prescription | sarmısak | garlic |
| rekabet | competition | sat- | sell |
| reklam | advertisement | satıcı | salesperson, seller |
| renk | color | satın al- | buy |
| resim | painting, picture | satış | sale |
| resmî | official | satranç | chess |

| | | | |
|---|---|---|---|
| savaş | battle, war | sına- | test |
| savun- | defend | sınav | examination |
| savunma | defense | sınıf | classroom |
| say- | count | sınır | border |
| sayfa | page | sıra | desk, row |
| saygı | respect | sırt | back |
| sayı | number | sıvı | liquid |
| sebep | cause, reason | sigara | cigarette |
| sebze | vegetable | sigara iç- | smoke |
| seç- | choose, elect, select | sigorta | insurance |
| seçim | election | sihir | magic |
| sekiz | eight | sil- | erase |
| sekreter | secretary | silah | gun, weapon |
| seksen | eighty | silgi | eraser |
| sel | flood | sincap | squirrel |
| selamlaş- | greet | sinek | fly |
| sembol | symbol | sinema | cinema |
| siz | you | sinir | nerve |
| sendika | union | sirk | circus |
| senin | your | sirke | vinegar |
| seninki | yours | sis | fog |
| sepet | basket | sivrisinek | mosquito |
| serçe | sparrow | siyah | black |
| sergi | exhibition | siyaset | politics |
| serin | cool | siz | you |
| ses | sound, voice | sizin | your |
| sessiz | quiet | sizinki | yours |
| sessiz ol- | quiet: be quiet | soba | stove |
| sessizlik | silence | soğan | onion |
| sev- | like, love | soğuk | cold |
| sevgi | love | soğuk algınlığı | cold |
| sevgili | dear | sokak | street |
| sevinç | joy | sol | left |
| seviye | level | somut | concrete |
| seyahat | travel | son | end, last |
| sıcak | hot | sonbahar | autumn |
| sıcaklık | temperature | sonek | suffix |
| sıçan | mouse | sonra | after |
| sıçra- | jump | sonuç | result |
| sıfat | adjective | sor- | ask |
| sıfır | zero | soru | question |
| sığ | shallow | sorun | problem |
| sığır | cattle | sosis | sausage |
| sığır eti | beef | soyadı | surname |
| sık | thick | soyut | abstract |
| sık sık | often | söğüt | willow |
| sık- | press | söndür- | extinguish, put out |
| sıkı | tight | söyle- | tell |
| sıkıcı | boring | söz ver- | promise |
| sıkıl- | bored: bc bored | sözleşme | agreement |

| | | | |
|---|---|---|---|
| sözlük | dictionary | şişman | fat |
| spor | sport | şort | shorts |
| su | water | şöyle | such |
| subay | officer | şubat | February |
| suç | crime | şüphe | doubt |
| suçlu | criminal, guilty | | |
| suçsuz | innocent | -ta, -te | at, in |
| sun- | present | tabak | dish, plate |
| susamış | thirsty | tabure | stool |
| süpür- | sweep | tahmin et- | guess |
| süpürge | broom | tahminen | about |
| sür- | drive | tahrip et- | destroy |
| sürahi | pitcher | tahta | wood |
| sürü | herd | takım elbise | suit |
| sürücü | driver | taksi | cab, taxi |
| süt | milk | takvim | calendar |
| süzgeç | strainer | tam | complete |
| | | tamam | OK |
| şaheser | masterpiece | -tan, -ten | from |
| şahıs | person | tan | dawn |
| şahit | witness | tane | grain |
| şair | poet | tanı- | know, recognize |
| şaka | joke | tanıştır- | introduce |
| şam fıstığı | pistachio | Tanrı | God |
| şans | luck | tansiyon | blood pressure |
| şapka | hat | tapınak | temple |
| şarap | wine | tara- | comb |
| şarkı | song | tarafından | by |
| şarkı söyle- | sing | tarak | comb |
| şarkıcı | singer | tarım | agriculture, cultivation |
| şart | condition | tarif et- | describe |
| şeftali | peach | tarih | date, history |
| şehir | city | tarihçi | historian |
| şeker | candy, sugar | tarla | field |
| şekil | shape | tartış- | argue |
| şemsiye | umbrella | tasvir | description |
| şenlik | festival | taş | stone |
| şeref | honor | taşı- | carry |
| şey | thing | tat- | taste |
| şeytan | demon, Satan | tatil | holiday, vacation |
| şiir | poem, poetry | tatlı | dessert, sweet |
| şikâyet | complaint | tava | pan |
| şikâyet et- | complain | tavan | ceiling |
| şimdi | now | tavsiye et- | recommend |
| şimdiki zaman | present | tavşan | rabbit |
| şimşek | lightning | tavuk | hen |
| şirket | company, firm | tavuk eti | chicken |
| şiş | swelling | taze | fresh |
| şiş- | swell | tebrik | congratulation |
| şişe | bottle | tebrik et- | congratulate |

| | | | |
|---|---|---|---|
| tecrübe | experience | tiraj | circulation |
| teçhizat | equipment | titre- | tremble |
| tedavi | cure | tiyatro | theater |
| tedavi et- | cure | tohum | grain, seed |
| tedbir | precaution | tohum ek- | sow |
| tedricen | gradually | top | artillery, ball, cannon |
| tehlike | danger | topla- | collect |
| tehlikeli | dangerous | toplama | addition |
| tekerlek | wheel | toplantı | meeting |
| teklif et- | offer | toplum | society |
| tekmele- | kick | toprak | earth, soil |
| tekrar | again | toptan satış | wholesale |
| tekrar et- | repeat | tornavida | screwdriver |
| tel | wire | torun | grandchild |
| telefon | telephone | toz | dust |
| telefon kulübesi | phone booth | tören | ceremony |
| telefon numarası | phone number | trafik | traffic |
| televizyon | television | trafik ışığı | traffic light |
| telgraf | telegram | tramvay | tram |
| tembel | lazy | tren | train |
| tembellik | laziness | tuğla | brick |
| temiz | clean | turist | tourist |
| temizle- | clean | turizm | tourism |
| temmuz | July | tut- | hold, keep |
| temsil et- | represent | tuvalet | toilet |
| tencere | saucepan | tuz | salt |
| tepe | hill | tüfek | rifle |
| terazi | scale | tüketici | consumer |
| tercih et- | prefer | tükür- | spit |
| tercüme | translation | tütün | tobacco |
| tercüme et- | translate | | |
| tereyağı | butter | ucuz | cheap |
| terk et- | leave | uç- | fly |
| terle- | sweat | uçak | airplane, plane |
| terlik | slipper | uçak postası | airmail |
| termometre | thermometer | uçuş | flight |
| terzi | tailor | ufuk | horizon |
| teslim olma | surrender | ulaş- | reach |
| testere | saw | uluslararası | international |
| testi | jug | um- | hope |
| teşebbüs | attempt | umumî telefon | public phone |
| teşekkür et- | thank | umut | hope |
| teyp | tape recorder | un | flour |
| teyze | aunt | unut- | forget |
| tıp | medicine | ustura | razor |
| tırman- | climb | utan- | ashamed: be ashamed |
| tırnak | nail | utangaç | shy |
| ticaret | business | uyan- | awake, wake |
| tilki | fox | uyandır- | awake, wake |
| timsah | crocodile | uygun ol- | suit |

| | | | |
|---|---|---|---|
| uyku | sleep | yağmurluk | raincoat |
| uyu- | sleep | yak- | burn |
| uyum | harmony | yaka | collar |
| uzak | far | yakala- | catch |
| uzan- | reach | yakın | near |
| uzay | space | yakında | near, soon |
| uzun | long | yakınında | near |
| uzun boylu | tall | yakışıklı | handsome |
| uzunluk | length | yaklaş- | approach |
| | | yalan | lie |
| ücret | wage | yalan söyle- | lie |
| üç | three | yalnız | alone |
| üçgen | triangle | yan | side |
| üniversite | university | yan- | burn |
| ünlü | vowel | yanak | cheek |
| ünsüz | consonant | yangın | fire |
| üret- | produce | yanında | beside |
| üstünde | above, on | yanlış | wrong |
| ütü | iron | yap- | do, make |
| üye | member | yapay | artificial |
| üzerinde | over | yapış- | stick |
| üzgün | sad, sorry | yaprak | leaf |
| üzüm | grape | yar- | split |
| | | yara | wound |
| vadi | valley | yardım | assistance, help |
| vahşi | wild | yardım et- | assist, help |
| var- | arrive | yargıç | judge |
| varış | arrival | yarım | half |
| varlık | existence | yarımada | peninsula |
| vatandaş | citizen | yarın | tomorrow |
| ve | and | yarış | race |
| ver- | give | yasakla- | forbid |
| vergi | tax | yastık | pillow |
| veri | data | yastık kılıfı | pillowcase |
| veya | or | yaş | age |
| veznedar | cashier | yaşa- | live |
| vicdan | conscience | yaşlı | old |
| vida | screw | yat- | lie |
| video | video | yatak | bed, mattress |
| vilayet | province | yatak odası | bedroom |
| virgül | comma | yatırım | investment |
| vur- | hit | yavaş | slow |
| | | yay | bow, spring |
| -ya, -ye | to | yay- | spread |
| ya ... ya [da] | either ... or | yaya | pedestrian |
| yabancı | foreigner | yaya geçidi | crosswalk |
| yağ | fat, oil | yayınevi | publishing house |
| yağ- | precipitate | yaz | summer |
| yağmala- | plunder | yaz- | write |
| yağmur | rain | yazar | author, writer |

| | | | |
|---|---|---|---|
| yazı | writing | yuvarla- | roll |
| ye- | eat | yuvarlak | round |
| yedi | seven | yük | baggage, cargo |
| yelkenli gemi | sailboat | yüksek | high, tall |
| yemek | dish | yüksek (ses) | loud |
| yemek listesi | menu | yükseklik | height |
| yemek odası | dining room | yün | wool |
| yemin et- | swear | yürü- | walk |
| yen- | defeat | yüz | face, hundred |
| yeni | new | yüz- | swim |
| yeni yıl | New Year | yüzme | swimming |
| yenilgi | defeat | yüzyıl | century |
| yer | place, seat | | |
| yer ayırtma | reservation | zafer | victory |
| yerleş- | situated: be situated | zalim | cruel |
| yeşil | green | zaman | time |
| yeteri kadar | enough | zamir | pronoun |
| yetişkin | adult | zamk | glue |
| yetmiş | seventy | zarar | harm |
| yıka- | wash | zararlı | harmful |
| yıl | year | zarf | adverb, envelope |
| yılan | snake | zayıf | weak |
| yıldız | star | zehir | poison |
| yıldönümü | anniversary | zehirli | poisonous |
| yırt- | tear | zeki | intelligent |
| yirmi | twenty | zengin | rich |
| yiyecek | food | zenginlik | wealth |
| yoğurt | yogurt | zevk | pleasure |
| yol | road, way | zevk al- | enjoy |
| yol parası | fare | zeytin | olive |
| yolcu | passenger | zıt | opposite |
| yolculuk | journey | zil | bell |
| yorgan | quilt | ziyafet | banquet |
| yorgun | tired | ziyan | damage, loss |
| yön | direction, way | ziyaret | visit |
| yönetici | manager | ziyaret et- | visit |
| yukarıda | above | zor | difficult, hard |
| yumurta | egg | zulüm | oppression |
| yumuşak | soft | | |

# TURKMEN - ENGLISH INDEX

| Turkmen | Latin | English |
|---|---|---|
| -a | -a | to |
| абстракт | abstrakt | abstract |
| ав | aw | game |
| авария | awariýa | accident |
| август | awgust | August |
| авиапочта | awiapoçta | airmail |
| авла- | awla- | hunt |
| автобус | awtobus | bus |
| автономия | awtonomiýa | autonomy |
| автор | awtor | author |
| ага | aga | uncle |
| агач | agaç | tree, wood |
| агза | agza | member |
| агла- | agla- | cry, weep |
| аграс | agras | serious |
| агтар- | agtar- | search |
| агтык | agtyk | grandchild |
| агшам | agşam | evening |
| агшамлык нахар | agşamlyk nahar | dinner |
| агыз | agyz | mouth |
| агыр | agyr | heavy |
| агыры | agyry | pain |
| ада | ada | island |
| адалат | adalat | justice |
| адам | adam | person |
| адат | adat | habit |
| адрес | adres | address |
| ажы | ajy | bitter |
| аз | az | few |
| азажык | azajyk | little |
| азал | azal | plow |
| азал- | azal- | decrease |
| азат | azat | free |
| азатлык | azatlyk | freedom |
| азлык | azlyk | minority |
| ай | aý | month, moon |
| айдым | aýdym | song |
| айдым айт- | aýdym aýt- | sing |
| айдымчы | aýdymçy | singer |
| айлаг | aýlag | bay |
| айлан- | aýlan- | turn |
| айлык | aýlyk | salary, wage |
| айна | aýna | glass, mirror |
| айра | aýra | separate |
| айрыл- | aýryl- | separated: be separated |
| айрылма | aýrylma | divorce |
| айрылыш- | aýrylyş- | divorce |
| айт- | aýt- | tell |
| айы | aýy | bear |
| айыр- | aýyr- | separate |
| айырмак | aýyrmak | subtraction |
| ак | ak | white |
| ак- | ak- | flow |
| акыл | akyl | mind |
| акыллы | akylly | clever, intelligent |
| ал- | al- | take |
| алгебра | algebra | algebra |
| алда- | alda- | lie |
| алма | alma | apple |
| алтмыш | altmyş | sixty |
| алты | alty | six |
| алыжы | alyjy | buyer, consumer |
| алым | alym | scientist |
| аматлы | amatly | convenient |
| -ан | -an | that |
| анархия | anarhiýa | anarchy |
| анна | anna | Friday |
| ант ич- | ant iç- | swear |
| антенна | antenna | antenna |
| анык | anyk | obvious |
| аңсат | añsat | easy |
| апельсин | apelsin | orange |
| апрель | aprel | April |
| аптека | apteka | pharmacy |
| аптекарь | aptekar | pharmacist |
| ар | ar | revenge |
| араба | araba | cart |
| арагатнашык | aragatnaşyk | communication |
| аралык | aralyk | distance |
| арасса | arassa | clean |
| арассала- | arassala- | clean |
| арасында | arasynda | between |
| арвах | arwah | ghost |
| арза бер- | arza ber- | apply |
| арзан | arzan | cheap |
| арзанладып сатыш | arzanladyp satyş | sale |
| арзанлатма | arzanlatma | discount |
| арзув | arzuw | desire |
| арзув эт- | arzuw et- | wish |
| арка | arka | back |
| аркада | arkada | behind |
| армыт | armyt | pear |
| арпа | arpa | barley |
| аррык | arryk | slim |
| арт- | art- | increase |

| артиллерия | artilleriýa | artillery |
|---|---|---|
| архитектор | arhitektor | architect |
| ас- | as- | hang |
| асман | asman | sky |
| асыл | asyl | never |
| асыр | asyr | century |
| ат | at | horse, name, noun, title |
| ата | ata | grandfather |
| ата-эне | ata-ene | parents |
| атыр | atyr | perfume |
| ач | aç | hungry |
| ач- | aç- | open |
| ачар | açar | key |
| ачлык | açlyk | famine, hunger |
| ачык | açyk | open |
| ашагында | aşagynda | under, underneath |
| ашак | aşak | down |
| ашакда | aşakda | below, underneath |
| ашгазан | aşgazan | stomach |
| ашпез | aşpez | cook |
| аэропорт | aeroport | airport |
| аяз | aýaz | frost |
| аяк | aýak | foot, leg |
| аякгап | aýakgap | shoe |
| аял | aýal | wife, woman |
| аял доган | aýal dogan | sister |
| аял көйнеги | aýal köynegi | dress |
| баг | bag | garden |
| багана | bagana | fur |
| багбан | bagban | gardener |
| багт | bagt | luck |
| багтлы | bagtly | happy |
| багтсыз | bagtsyz | unhappy |
| багыр | bagyr | liver |
| багышла- | bagyşla- | forgive |
| бадам | badam | almond |
| бадамжан | badamjan | eggplant |
| базар | bazar | market |
| бай | baý | rich |
| байгуш | baýguş | owl |
| байдак | baýdak | flag |
| байлык | baýlyk | wealth |
| байрак | baýrak | prize |
| байрам | baýram | holiday |
| байрам эт- | baýram et- | celebrate |
| байрам этме | baýram etme | celebration |
| байрамчылык | baýramçylyk | festival |
| бак- | bak- | look |
| бакжа | bakja | garden |
| бал | bal | honey |
| бал айы | bal aýy | honeymoon |
| бал арысы | bal arysy | bee |
| балак | balak | pants |
| балет | balet | ballet |
| балкон | balkon | balcony |
| балык | balyk | fish |
| балыкчы | balykçy | fisherman |
| банан | banan | banana |
| банк | bank | bank |
| банка | banka | jar |
| банкет | banket | banquet |
| бар- | bar- | arrive |
| бар болмаклык | bar bolmaklyk | existence |
| барада | barada | about |
| бармак | barmak | finger |
| барометр | barometr | barometer |
| баскетбол | basketbol | basketball |
| бат- | bat- | sink |
| батга | batga | swamp |
| батыр | batyr | brave, courageous |
| баха | baha | cost, price, value |
| бахана | bahana | excuse |
| бахар | bahar | spring |
| башга | başga | another |
| башга-да | başga-da | besides |
| башла- | başla- | begin, start |
| бегенч | begenç | joy |
| беден | beden | body |
| бедре | bedre | bucket |
| бежер- | bejer- | cure |
| бейи | beýi | quince |
| бейик | beýik | high, tall |
| бейиклик | beýiklik | height |
| бейле | beýle | such |
| бейлеки | beýleki | other |
| бейни | beýni | brain |
| белка | belka | squirrel |
| белки | belki | perhaps |
| беллеме | belleme | appointment |
| беневше | benewşe | purple |
| бензин | benzin | gasoline |
| бент | bent | dam |

| бер- | ber- | give |
| берги | bergi | debt |
| берк | berk | perfect |
| беян эт- | beÿan et- | describe |
| бигүнә | bigünä | innocent |
| бигүнәлик | bigünälik | innocence |
| биз | biz | we |
| бизи | bizi | us |
| бизиң | biziň | our |
| бизиңки | biziňki | ours |
| бизнесмен | biznesmen | businessman |
| бил- | bil- | know |
| бил багла- | bil bagla- | rely |
| биле | bile | together |
| билен | bilen | by, with |
| билет | bilet | ticket |
| билим | bilim | education, knowledge |
| бина | bina | building |
| бинт | bint | bandage |
| бир | bir | one |
| бираз | biraz | some |
| бирден | birden | sudden |
| бирнәче | birnäçe | several |
| бит | bit | louse |
| биш- | biş- | cook |
| бишен | bişen | ripe |
| бишир- | bişir- | cook |
| биынжалык эт- | biynjalyk et- | bother |
| бланка | blanka | form |
| блузка | bluzka | blouse |
| богаз | bogaz | throat |
| боз- | boz- | erase |
| бозгуч | bozguç | eraser |
| бол- | bol- | be, become, happen |
| бомба | bomba | bomb |
| бош | boş | empty |
| бошат- | boşat- | empty |
| боюн | boÿun | neck |
| боюн бол- | boÿun bol- | obey |
| боюн эгме | boÿun egme | surrender |
| боя- | boÿa- | dye, paint |
| бөврек | böwrek | kidney |
| бөк- | bök- | jump |
| бөл- | böl- | divide |
| бөлмек | bölmek | division |
| бөлүм | bölüm | department, part, section |
| бу | bu | this |
| бу гүн | bu gün | today |
| бу ерде | bu ÿerde | here |
| буга | buga | bull |
| бугдай | bugdaÿ | wheat |
| буз | buz | ice |
| буйрук бер- | buÿruk ber- | command, order |
| букжа | bukja | envelope |
| булар | bular | these |
| булашык | bulaşyk | messy |
| булут | bulut | cloud |
| бурав | buraw | drill |
| бурун | burun | nose |
| бурч | burç | angle, corner, pepper |
| бут | but | thigh |
| бутерброд | buterbrod | sandwich |
| бутхана | buthana | church |
| буюр- | buÿur- | order |
| бүргүт | bürgüt | eagle |
| бүре | büre | flea |
| бычгы | byçgy | saw |
| бәбек | bäbek | baby |
| бәгүл | bägül | rose |
| бәри | bäri | since |
| бәсдешлик | bäsdeşlik | competition |
| бәш | bäş | five |
| бюжет | büuʃet | budget |
| вагт | wagt | time |
| вагырды | wagyrdy | noise |
| вакцина | waktsina | shot |
| ванна отагы | wanna otagy | bathroom |
| васп этме | wasp etme | description |
| ве | we | and |
| везипе | wezipe | duty |
| векиллик эт- | wekillik et- | represent |
| велаят | welaÿat | province |
| велосипед | welosiped | bicycle |
| вертолёт | wertolÿot | helicopter |
| вешалка | weşalka | hanger |
| визит | wizit | visit |
| видео | wideo | video |
| вилка | wilka | fork |
| врач | wraç | doctor |
| выждан | wyʃdan | conscience |
| габав | gabaw | siege |
| габанжаң | gabanjaň | jealous |

| габык | gabyk | bark |
| гавун | gawun | melon |
| гадаган эт- | gadagan et- | forbid |
| газ | gaz | gas, goose |
| газ- | gaz- | dig |
| газа- | gaza- | scrape |
| газан | gazan | saucepan |
| газет | gazet | newspaper |
| гайка ачары | gaÿka açary | wrench |
| гаймак | gaÿmak | cream |
| гайна- | gaÿna- | boil |
| гайра гой- | gaÿra goÿ- | postpone |
| гайт- | gaÿt- | return |
| гайтала- | gaÿtala- | repeat |
| гайчы | gaÿçy | scissors |
| гайык | gaÿyk | boat |
| гайыш | gaÿyş | leather |
| гал- | gal- | remain, stay |
| галам | galam | pencil |
| галдыр- | galdyr- | leave |
| галстук | galstuk | tie |
| гама | gama | dagger |
| ган | gan | blood |
| гана- | gana- | bleed |
| ганат | ganat | wing |
| гант | gant | sugar |
| гапак | gapak | lid |
| гап-гач ювма машыны | gap-gaç ÿuwma maşyny | dishwasher |
| гапдал | gapdal | side |
| гапжык | gapjyk | purse, wallet |
| гаплаң | gaplañ | tiger |
| гапы | gapy | door |
| гар | gar | snow |
| гара | gara | black |
| гара мал | gara mal | cattle |
| гараж | garaʃ | garage |
| гаралы | garaly | plum |
| гараңкы | garañky | dark |
| гараңкылык | garañkylyk | darkness |
| гараш- | garaş- | wait |
| гарашсызлык | garaşsyzlyk | independence |
| гарга | garga | crow |
| гарк бол- | gark bol- | drown |
| гарлавач | garlawaç | swallow |
| гарпыз | garpyz | watermelon |
| гарры | garry | old |
| гаршы | garşy | against, opposite |
| гарын | garyn | belly |
| гарындаш | garyndaş | relative |
| гарынжа | garynja | ant |
| гарып | garyp | poor |
| гарышдыр- | garyşdyr- | mix |
| гассап | gassap | butcher |
| гаты | gaty | hard |
| гаты [сес] | gaty [ses] | loud |
| гатык | gatyk | yogurt |
| гахар | gahar | anger |
| гахарлы | gaharly | angry |
| гач- | gaç- | flee, run away |
| гачып гит- | gaçyp git- | escape |
| гаш | gaş | eyebrow |
| гвоздика | gwozdika | carnation |
| гезмеле- | gezmele- | stroll |
| гей- | geÿ- | put on, wear |
| гел- | gel- | arrive, come |
| гелжек | geljek | future |
| гелиш | geliş | arrival |
| гелиш- | geliş- | suit |
| гелшиксиз | gelşiksiz | ugly |
| геӊ | geñ | strange |
| география | geografiÿa | geography |
| геология | geologiÿa | geology |
| геометрия | geometriÿa | geometry |
| гепле- | geple- | speak, talk |
| геплеме | gepleme | speech |
| герек бол- | gerek bol- | need |
| гермев | germew | fence |
| гетир- | getir- | bring |
| геч- | geç- | pass |
| гечелге | geçelge | crosswalk |
| гечен | geçen | last |
| гечи | geçi | goat |
| гиже | gije | night |
| гизле- | gizle- | hide |
| гизлин | gizlin | secret |
| гиӊ | giñ | broad, large, loose, spacious, wide |
| гир- | gir- | enter |
| гирдежи | girdeji | income |
| гирелге | girelge | entrance |
| гит- | git- | go |
| гитме | gitme | departure |
| гич | giç | late |
| говур- | gowur- | roast |
| говшак | gowşak | loose |

| говы | gowy | good, well |
|---|---|---|
| говы гөр- | gowy gör- | prefer |
| говырак | gowyrak | better |
| гозгалаң | gozgalañ | rebellion |
| гой- | goý- | put |
| гойбер- | goýber- | release |
| гол | gol | arm, signature |
| гол чек- | gol çek- | sign |
| голай | golaý | near |
| голайда | golaýda | near |
| голайында | golaýynda | near |
| гоңур | goñur | brown |
| гоңшы | goñşy | neighbor |
| гора- | gora- | defend, protect |
| горанма | goranma | defense |
| горизонт | gorizont | horizon |
| горк- | gork- | afraid: be afraid |
| горкак | gorkak | coward |
| горкаклык | gorkaklyk | cowardice |
| горкы | gorky | fear |
| горчица | gorçitsa | mustard |
| гош- | goş- | add |
| гошар | goşar | wrist |
| гошгы | goşgy | poem |
| гошма | goşma | addition |
| гошулма | goşulma | suffix |
| гошун | goşun | army |
| гоюн | goýun | sheep |
| гоюн эти | goýun eti | mutton |
| гөврели | göwreli | pregnant |
| гөврелилик | göwrelilik | pregnancy |
| гөвус | göwüs | breast |
| гөдек | gödek | rude |
| гөз | göz | eye |
| гөзден гайып бол- | gözden gaýyp bol- | disappear |
| гөзел | gözel | pretty |
| гөзи гит- | gözi git- | envy |
| гөзле- | gözle- | look for, seek |
| гөк | gök | blue |
| гөк гүррүлдиси | gök gürrüldisi | thunder |
| гөк нохут | gök nohut | pea |
| гөк өнүм | gök önüm | vegetable |
| гөле эти | göle eti | veal |
| гөм- | göm- | bury |
| гөни | göni | straight |

| гөр- | gör- | see |
|---|---|---|
| гөреш | göreş | wrestling |
| гөриплик | göriplik | envy |
| гөркез- | görkez- | present, show |
| гөрмәге бар- | görmäge bar- | visit |
| гөрмегей | görmegeý | handsome |
| гөрмегейлик | görmegeýlik | attraction |
| гөрнүш | görnüş | shape |
| гөрүн- | görün- | appear |
| гөтер- | göter- | lift, raise |
| градус | gradus | degree |
| граждан | graſdan | citizen |
| графин | grafin | pitcher |
| грип | grip | flu |
| гув | guw | swan |
| гуванч | guwanç | pride |
| гужакла- | gujakla- | embrace |
| гузы | guzy | lamb |
| гуй- | guý- | pour |
| гуйрук | guýruk | tail |
| гулак | gulak | ear |
| гулп | gulp | lock |
| гур- | gur- | build |
| гура- | gura- | dry |
| гуракчылык | gurakçylyk | drought |
| гурал | gural | tool |
| гурбага | gurbaga | frog |
| гурбан | gurban | sacrifice |
| гурчук | gurçuk | worm |
| гурша- | gurşa- | surround |
| гуршун | gurşun | lead |
| гуры | gury | dry |
| гус- | gus- | vomit |
| гутар- | gutar- | finish |
| гутла- | gutla- | congratulate |
| гутлама | gutlama | congratulation |
| гуты | guty | box |
| гуш | guş | bird |
| гушак | guşak | belt |
| гүйз | güýz | autumn |
| гүйменме | güýmenme | entertainment |
| гүйч | güýç | force, power, strength |
| гүйчли | güýçli | powerful, strong |
| гүл | gül | flower |
| гүл- | gül- | laugh |
| гүлгүн | gülgün | pink |
| гүмрүк | gümrük | customs |
| гүн | gün | day, sun |

| гүнбатар | günbatar | west |
|---|---|---|
| гүндиз | gündiz | daytime |
| гүндогар | gündogar | east |
| гүнебакар | günebakar | sunflower |
| гүнорта | günorta | south |
| гүнорта нахары | günorta nahary | lunch |
| гүнортан | günortan | noon |
| гүнүң догмагы | günüň dogmagy | sunrise |
| гүнүң яшмагы | günüň ýaşmagy | sunset |
| гүнә | günä | crime |
| гүнәкәр | günäkär | guilty |
| гүнәли | günäli | criminal |
| гүр | gür | thick |
| гыгыр- | gygyr- | shout |
| гыз | gyz | daughter, girl |
| гызгын | gyzgyn | fever |
| гызыклы | gyzykly | interesting |
| гызыл | gyzyl | gold, red |
| гылык | gylyk | behavior |
| гылыч | gylyç | sword |
| гыммат | gymmat | expensive |
| гымматлы | gymmatly | valuable |
| гымылда- | gymylda- | move |
| гынанчлы | gynançly | sad, sorry |
| гыра | gyra | edge |
| гысга | gysga | short |
| гыш | gyş | winter |
| гәми | gämi | ship |
| | | |
| -да, -де | -da, -de | at, in |
| да, де | da, de | also, too |
| дабара | dabara | ceremony |
| дава | dawa | argument |
| давалаш- | dawalaş- | argue |
| давление | dawleniýe | blood pressure |
| даг | dag | mountain |
| дайза | daýza | aunt |
| дайхан | daýhan | peasant |
| дайы | daýy | uncle |
| дамжа | damja | drop |
| -дан, -ден | -dan, -den | from |
| даң | daň | dawn |
| даң- | daň- | fasten, tie |
| дар | dar | narrow, tight |
| дара- | dara- | comb |
| дарак | darak | comb |

| даргат- | dargat- | scatter |
|---|---|---|
| дат- | dat- | taste |
| даш | daş | far, rock, stone |
| дашарда | daşarda | outside |
| дашары юртлы | daşary ýurtly | foreigner |
| дег- | deg- | touch |
| дегирмен | degirmen | mill |
| дегишме | degişme | joke |
| декабрь | dekabr | December |
| деллек | dellek | hairdresser |
| дем | dem | breath |
| демир | demir | iron |
| демир ёл | demir ýol | railroad |
| демиргазык | demirgazyk | north |
| демократия | demokratiýa | democracy |
| демонстрация | demonstratsiýa | demonstration |
| дең | deň | equal |
| деңешдирме | deňeşdirme | comparison |
| дениз | deňiz | sea |
| деп- | dep- | kick |
| депдер | depder | notebook |
| депе | depe | hill |
| дервезе | derweze | gate |
| дере | dere | valley |
| дереже | dereje | level |
| дерек | derek | poplar |
| дери | deri | skin |
| дерле- | derle- | sweat |
| дерман | derman | drug, medicine |
| дерман өсүмлиги | derman ösümligi | herb |
| дерңев | derňew | investigation |
| деррев | derrew | immediately |
| деря | derýa | river |
| десерт | desert | dessert |
| дессан | dessan | epic |
| дешик | deşik | hole |
| дивар | diwar | wall |
| дивар сагады | diwar sagady | clock |
| диен ялы | diýen ýaly | almost |
| дий- | diý- | say |
| дил | dil | language, tongue |
| дилег | dileg | wish |
| дилчи | dilçi | linguist |
| дин | din | religion |
| дини | dini | religious |

| | | |
|---|---|---|
| дини байрам | dini baÿram | religious holiday |
| диңле- | diñle- | listen |
| диплом | diplom | diploma |
| дири | diri | alive |
| диш | diş | tooth |
| диш агыры | diş agyry | toothache |
| диш догторы | diş dogtory | dentist |
| диш пастасы | diş pastasy | toothpaste |
| диш чотгасы | diş çotgasy | toothbrush |
| дишле- | dişle- | bite |
| довам эт- | dowam et- | continue |
| довзах | dowzah | hell |
| дога | doga | prayer |
| дога ока- | doga oka- | pray |
| доган | dogan | brother |
| доглан гүн | doglan gün | birthday |
| догручыл | dogruçyl | honest |
| догры | dogry | correct |
| догул- | dogul- | born: be born |
| догулма | dogulma | birth |
| додак | dodak | lip |
| докма | dokma | textile |
| докуз | dokuz | nine |
| дола- | dola- | wrap |
| долдур- | doldur- | fill |
| долдургыч | doldurgyç | object |
| долы | doly | complete, full, hail |
| доң- | doñ- | freeze |
| доңуз | doñuz | pig |
| доңуз эти | doñuz eti | pork |
| дост | dost | friend |
| достлук | dostluk | friendship |
| дөв | döw | giant |
| дөв- | döw- | break |
| дөвлет | döwlet | state |
| дөвук | döwük | broken |
| дөкун | dökün | fertilizer |
| дөрт | dört | four |
| дөш | döş | chest |
| драматург | dramaturg | playwright |
| дробь | drob | fraction |
| дуб | dub | oak |
| дуз | duz | salt |
| дуй- | duÿ- | feel |
| дуйгы | duÿgy | feeling |
| думан | duman | fog |
| дур- | dur- | stop |
| дуралга | duralga | stop |
| дурмуш | durmuş | life |
| дурмуша чык- | durmuşa çyk- | marry |
| дурмуша чыкма | durmuşa çykma | marriage |
| дурмуша чыкян гыз | durmuşa çykÿan gyz | bride |
| дуруз- | duruz- | stop |
| духовка | duhowka | oven |
| душ | duş | shower |
| душенбе | duşenbe | Monday |
| душман | duşman | enemy |
| душманчы-лык | duşmançylyk | enmity |
| душуш- | duşuş- | meet |
| душушык | duşuşyk | appointment |
| дувун | düwün | knot |
| дуе | düye | camel |
| дузет- | düzet- | correct |
| дузлук | düzlük | plain |
| дуйн | düÿn | yesterday |
| дуйш | düÿş | dream |
| дукан | dükan | shop |
| думев | dümew | cold |
| дунйә | dünyä | world |
| душ- | düş- | get off |
| душек | düşek | mattress |
| душун- | düşün- | understand |
| душундир- | düşündir- | explain |
| душундириш | düşündiriş | explanation |
| дыз | dyz | knee |
| дынч алма | dynç alma | rest |
| дынч алыш | dynç alyş | holiday |
| дырмаш- | dyrmaş- | climb |
| дырнак | dyrnak | nail |
| дәл | däl | not |
| дәли | däli | crazy |
| дәлилик | dälilik | insanity |
| дәне | däne | grain |
| дәп-дессур | däp-dessur | custom |
| еврей | ÿewreÿ | Jew |
| еди | ÿedi | seven |
| еке | ÿeke | alone |
| екшенбе | ÿekşenbe | Sunday |
| ел | ÿel | wind |
| елек | ÿelek | feather |
| елим | ÿelim | glue |
| елкенли гәми | ÿelkenli gämi | sailboat |

| | | | | | |
|---|---|---|---|---|---|
| елмеш- | ÿelmeş- | stick | зат | zat | thing |
| ене | ÿene | again | зат ал- | zat al- | shop |
| ең- | ÿeñ- | defeat, win | зейтун | zeÿtun | olive |
| еңил | ÿeñil | light | зелелли | zelelli | harmful |
| еңиш | ÿeñiş | victory | землияника | zemliÿanika | strawberry |
| еңлиш | ÿeñliş | defeat | зергәр | zergär | jeweler |
| ер | ÿer | earth, place, seat | зерур | zerur | necessary |
| | | | зерурлык | zerurlyk | necessity, need |
| ер титремеси | ÿer titremesi | earthquake | | | |
| ерлеш- | ÿerleş- | situated: be situated | зибил | zibil | trash |
| | | | зоопарк | zoopark | zoo |
| ет- | ÿet- | reach | зулум | zulum | oppression |
| етерлик | ÿeterlik | enough | зыян | zyÿan | damage, harm |
| етерлик[ли] | ÿeterlik[li] | sufficient | зәхер | zäher | poison |
| етмиш | ÿetmiş | seventy | зәхерли | zäherli | poisonous |
| | | | | | |
| ёгын | ÿogyn | thick | ибер- | iber- | send |
| ёк | ÿok | no | иге | ige | file |
| ёкарда | ÿokarda | above | идиома | idioma | idiom |
| ёл | ÿol | road, way | ий- | iÿ- | eat |
| ёл кирейи | ÿol kireÿi | fare | иймит | iÿmit | food |
| ёлагчы | ÿolagçy | passenger | ики | iki | two |
| ёлбарс | ÿolbars | lion | илат | ilat | population |
| ёлбашчы | ÿolbaşçy | manager | илик | ilik | button |
| ёрган | ÿorgan | quilt | илчи | ilçi | ambassador |
| | | | иман | iman | faith |
| журнал | ʃurnal | magazine | индики | indiki | next |
| журналист | ʃurnalist | journalist | индюк | indÿuk | turkey |
| | | | инженер | inʃener | engineer |
| жады | jady | magic | инжир | injir | fig |
| жайлы | jaÿly | comfortable | инкәр эт- | inkär et- | deny |
| жаң | jañ | bell | интеллектуал | intellektual | intellectual |
| жеза | jeza | punishment | инфекция | infektsiÿa | infection |
| жеза бер- | jeza ber- | punish | инфляция | inflÿatsiÿa | inflation |
| жемгыет | jemgyÿet | society | информация | informatsiÿa | information |
| жемгыетчилик телефоны | jemgyÿetçilik telefony | public phone | инче | inçe | fine, thin |
| | | | иң говы | iñ gowy | best |
| женаят | jenaÿat | crime | иң көп | iñ köp | most |
| женаятчы | jenaÿatçy | criminal | инне | iññe | needle |
| женнет | jennet | paradise | инрик | iñrik | dusk |
| жентльмен | jentlmen | gentleman | ир | ir | early |
| жогап | jogap | answer, reply | ир- | ir- | bored: be bored |
| жогап бер- | jogap ber- | answer, reply | | | |
| жорап | jorap | sock, stocking | иргинч | irginç | boring |
| жошгун | joşgun | excitement | исле- | isle- | want |
| жүби | jübi | pocket | ислендик | islendik | any |
| жүбүт | jübüt | pair | ит | it | dog |
| | | | ит- | it- | push |
| заказ бер- | zakaz ber- | order | ич- | iç- | drink |
| залым | zalym | cruel | ичгечме | içgeçme | diarrhea |

| | | |
|---|---|---|
| ичги | içgi | beverage, drink |
| ичеге | içege | intestine |
| ичерде | içerde | inside |
| ичиң гатама | içiň gatama | constipation |
| ичиңи сүрйән дерман | içiňi sürýän derman | laxative |
| иш | iş | job |
| иш кабинети | iş kabineti | office |
| иш ташлайыш | iş taşlaýyş | strike |
| ишгәр | işgär | worker |
| ишле- | işle- | work |
| ишлик | işlik | verb |
| июль | iýul | July |
| июнь | iýun | June |
| | | |
| йигрен- | ýigren- | hate |
| йигренч | ýigrenç | disgust |
| йигрими | ýigrimi | twenty |
| йитги | ýitgi | loss |
| йити | ýiti | sharp |
| йитир- | ýitir- | lose |
| йөнекей | ýönekeý | simple |
| йөре- | ýöre- | walk |
| йүз | ýüz | face, hundred |
| йүз тут- | ýüz tut- | apply |
| йүз- | ýüz- | swim |
| йүзме | ýüzme | swimming |
| йүк | ýük | baggage, cargo |
| йүк машыны | ýük maşyny | truck |
| йүң | ýüň | wool |
| йүпек | ýüpek | silk |
| йүрек | ýürek | heart |
| йыгна- | ýygna- | collect |
| йыгнак | ýygnak | meeting |
| йык- | ýyk- | destroy |
| йыкыл- | ýykyl- | fall |
| йыл | ýyl | year |
| йылан | ýylan | snake |
| йылгыр- | ýylgyr- | smile |
| йылдыз | ýyldyz | star |
| йылдырым | ýyldyrym | lightning |
| йылы | ýyly | lukewarm, warm |
| йылылык | ýylylyk | heat |
| йырт- | ýyrt- | tear |
| -йән | -ýän | that |

| | | |
|---|---|---|
| кабул эт- | kabul et- | accept |
| кагыз | kagyz | paper |
| кака | kaka | father |
| календарь | kalendar | calendar |
| канал | kanal | canal, channel |
| каникул | kanikul | vacation |
| канун | kanun | law |
| капитан | kapitan | captain |
| карар | karar | decision |
| карара гел- | karara gel- | decide |
| карз | karz | loan |
| карз ал- | karz al- | borrow |
| карикатура | karikatura | cartoon |
| карт | kart | playing card |
| карта | karta | map |
| картошка | kartoşka | potato |
| касета | kaseta | cassette |
| кассир | kassir | cashier |
| кафе | kafe | café |
| каштан | kaştan | chestnut |
| квадрат | kwadrat | square |
| квартира | kwartira | apartment |
| квитанция | kwitantsiýa | receipt |
| кебелек | kebelek | butterfly |
| кейик | keýik | deer |
| кейп | keýp | pleasure |
| келем | kelem | cabbage |
| келлагыры | kellagyry | headache |
| келле | kelle | head |
| кепдери | kepderi | pigeon |
| кер | ker | deaf |
| керлик | kerlik | deafness |
| керпич | kerpiç | brick |
| кес- | kes- | cut |
| кесел | kesel | illness |
| кеселхана | keselhana | hospital |
| ким | kim | who |
| кинотеатр | kinoteatr | cinema |
| кирей | kireý | rent |
| кирпик | kirpik | eyelash |
| китап | kitap | book |
| китап магазини | kitap magazini | bookshop |
| китап сатыжысы | kitap satyjysy | bookseller |
| китап шкафы | kitap şkafy | bookcase |
| китапхана | kitaphana | library |
| кичи | kiçi | little, small |

| клас | klas | classroom |
| климат | klimat | climate |
| клиника | klinika | clinic |
| клуб | klub | club |
| ковала- | kowala- | chase |
| комедия | komediÿa | comedy |
| композитор | kompozitor | composer |
| компьютер | kompÿuter | computer |
| конкрет | konkret | concrete |
| концерт | kontsert | concert |
| король | korol | king |
| коррупция | korruptsiÿa | corruption |
| космос | kosmos | space |
| костюм | kostÿum | suit |
| кофе | kofe | coffee |
| көйнек | köÿnek | shirt |
| көк | kök | root |
| көке | köke | cookie |
| көл | köl | lake |
| көлеге | kölege | shade, shadow |
| көмек бер- | kömek ber- | assist |
| көмелек | kömelek | mushroom |
| көмүр | kömür | coal |
| көне | köne | old |
| көп | köp | many, much |
| көпелтмек | köpeltmek | multiplication |
| көпрәк | köpräk | more |
| көпри | köpri | bridge |
| көпчүлик | köpçülik | majority |
| көр | kör | blind |
| көрлүк | körlük | blindness |
| көче | köçe | street |
| көшк | köşk | palace |
| кравать | krawat | bed |
| кран | kran | faucet |
| кредит | kredit | credit |
| кресло | kreslo | armchair |
| крокодил | krokodil | crocodile |
| кувватсыз | kuwwatsyz | weak |
| куртка | kurtka | jacket |
| кухня | kuhnÿa | kitchen |
| күйзе | küÿze | jug |
| күл | kül | ash |
| күмүш | kümüş | silver |
| күрек | kürek | shovel |
| күшт | küşt | chess |
| кын | kyn | difficult, hard |
| кырк | kyrk | forty |
| кәбир | käbir | some |
| кәвагт | käwagt | sometimes |
| кән | kän | many |
| кәр | kär | occupation |
| кәшир | käşir | carrot |
| лал | lal | mute |
| лампа | lampa | lamp |
| легенда | legenda | legend |
| леглек | leglek | stork |
| лекция | lektsiÿa | lecture |
| лимон | limon | lemon |
| лингвистика | lingwistika | linguistics |
| линейка | lineÿka | ruler |
| лифт | lift | elevator |
| ломай совда | lomaÿ sowda | wholesale |
| лыжа | lyʃa | skiing |
| ләле | läle | tulip |
| магазин | magazin | store |
| маглуматлар | maglumatlar | data |
| магнитофон | magnitofon | tape recorder |
| мадда | madda | matter |
| мазарчылык | mazarçylyk | cemetery |
| май | maÿ | May |
| маймын | maÿmyn | monkey |
| макала | makala | article |
| максат | maksat | purpose |
| макуллама | makullama | approval |
| мама | mama | grandmother |
| маңлай | mañlaÿ | forehead |
| маргаритка | margaritka | daisy |
| марка | marka | stamp |
| мароженое | maroʃenoÿe | ice cream |
| март | mart | March |
| маслахат | maslaxat | advice |
| маслахатлашма | maslahatlaşma | discussion |
| математика | matematika | mathematics |
| материал | material | material |
| машгала | maşgala | family |
| машын | maşyn | automobile, car, machine |
| машынка | maşynka | typewriter |
| мая гоюш | maÿa goÿuş | investment |
| мебель | mebel | furniture |
| медениет | medeniÿet | culture |
| медицина | meditsina | medicine |
| медсестра | medsestra | nurse |
| межме | mejme | dish |
| мезхеп | mezhep | sect |
| мейдан | meÿdan | field, square |

| | | |
|---|---|---|
| мекгежөвен | mekgejöwen | corn |
| мекдеп | mekdep | school |
| мен | men | I |
| менежер | menejer | manager |
| мени | meni | me |
| мениң | meniň | my |
| мениңки | meniňki | mine |
| меню | menýu | menu |
| meнзe- | meňze- | resemble |
| меңзеш | meňzeş | alike, similar |
| мердиван | merdiwan | ladder, stairs |
| мержимек | merjimek | lentil |
| меркез | merkez | center |
| меселе | mesele | problem |
| месге яг | mesge ýag | butter |
| метал | metal | metal |
| метбугат | metbugat | press |
| метжит | metjit | mosque |
| метро | metro | subway |
| мешгул | meşgul | busy |
| мешхур | meşhur | famous |
| миве | miwe | fruit |
| миве сувы | miwe suwy | fruit juice |
| микрорайон | mikroraýon | neighborhood |
| милиция | militsiýa | policeman |
| миллет | millet | nation |
| миллетчилик | milletçilik | nationalism |
| миллиард | milliard | billion |
| миллион | million | million |
| минара | minara | tower |
| министр | ministr | minister |
| миннетдарлык | minnetdarlyk | gratitude |
| минут | minut | minute |
| мис | mis | copper |
| мифология | mifologiýa | mythology |
| мода | moda | fashion |
| мотор | motor | engine |
| мотоцикл | mototsikl | motorcycle |
| мөжек | möjek | wolf |
| мөй | möÿ | spider |
| мөр-мөжек | mör-möjek | insect |
| мөхүм | möhüm | important |
| мугаллым | mugallym | teacher |
| мугт | mugt | free |
| музей | muzeÿ | museum |
| мукдар | mukdar | amount, quantity |
| мурт | murt | mustache |
| мусулман | musulman | Muslim |
| мүмкин | mümkin | possible |
| мүмкин дәл | mümkin däl | impossible |
| мүмкинчилик | mümkinçilik | possibility |
| мүн- | mün- | get on, ride |
| мүң | müň | thousand |
| мүрепбе | mürepbe | jam |
| мүшдери | müşderi | customer |
| мысал | mysal | example |
| мыхман | myhman | guest |
| мыхмансөерлик | myhmansöÿerlik | hospitality |
| мыхманхана | myhmanhana | hotel |
| мышца | myştsa | muscle |
| мэр | mer | mayor |
| мәмиши | mämişi | orange |
| мәреке | märeke | crowd |
| мәхирли | mähirli | gentle, kind |
| | | |
| нагт | nagt | cash |
| найза | naýza | spear |
| накыл | nakyl | proverb |
| нар | nar | pomegranate |
| нарпыз | narpyz | mint |
| нахар | nahar | dish |
| нахар ийилйән отаг | nahar iÿilýän otag | dining room |
| не... не(-де) | ne... ne [-de] | neither ... nor |
| небит | nebit | oil |
| непис иш | nepis iş | masterpiece |
| нерв | nerw | nerve |
| нетиже | netije | result |
| неширят | neşirýat | publishing house |
| ниет | niÿet | intention |
| нире | nire | where |
| ниреде | nirede | where |
| нойба | noÿba | bean |
| нокат | nokat | period |
| ноль | nol | zero |
| ноябрь | noÿabr | November |
| нурбат | nurbat | screw |
| нәме | näme | what |
| нәме үчин | näme üçin | why |
| нәхили | nähili | how |
| нәче | näçe | how much, how much |
| о | o | he, it, she, that |
| оба | oba | village |
| оба ери | oba ÿeri | countryside |

| Turkmen (Cyrillic) | Turkmen (Latin) | English |
|---|---|---|
| оба хоҗалыгы | oba hojalygy | agriculture |
| овадан | owadan | beautiful |
| оваданлык | owadanlyk | beauty |
| овнук пул | ownuk pul | change |
| оврат- | owrat- | crush |
| оглан | oglan | boy |
| огры | ogry | burglar, thief |
| огул | ogul | son |
| огурла- | ogurla- | steal |
| огша- | ogşa- | kiss |
| о-да шейле | o-da şeýle | same |
| одеял | odeýal | blanket |
| озал | ozal | ago |
| ой-пикир | oý-pikir | opinion |
| ойлан- | oýlan- | think |
| ойна- | oýna- | play |
| ойнавач | oýnawaç | toy |
| ока- | oka- | read |
| окара | okara | bowl |
| океан | okean | ocean |
| окла- | okla- | throw |
| октябрь | oktýabr | October |
| окув гутарма | okuw gutarma | graduation |
| окув төлеги | okuw tölegi | tuition |
| окыҗы | okyjy | reader |
| ол | ol | he, it, she, that |
| ол ерде | ol ýerde | there |
| ол ере | ol ýere | there |
| олар | olar | they, those |
| олары | olary | them |
| оларың | olaryň | their |
| он | on | ten |
| он алты | on alty | sixteen |
| он бәш | on bäş | fifteen |
| он бир | on bir | eleven |
| он докуз | on dokuz | nineteen |
| он дөрт | on dört | fourteen |
| он еди | on ýedi | seventeen |
| он ики | on iki | dozen, twelve |
| он секиз | on sekiz | eighteen |
| он үч | on üç | thirteen |
| онда | onda | then |
| онуң | onuň | her, his, its |
| онуңкы | onuňky | hers, his, its |
| оны | ony | her, him |
| оңар- | oňar- | mend, repair |
| оңат | oňat | fine, nice |
| оңурга | oňurga | spine |
| опера | opera | opera |
| операция | operatsiýa | operation |
| оптик | optik | optician |
| ораза | oraza | fast |
| орак | orak | harvest, sickle |
| орта | orta | medium, middle |
| от | ot | fire, grass |
| отаг | otag | room |
| отвёртка | otwýortka | screwdriver |
| открытка | otkrytka | postcard |
| отлучөп | otluçöp | match |
| отлы | otly | train |
| отуз | otuz | thirty |
| отур | otur | comma |
| отур- | otur- | sit |
| отурылышык | oturylyşyk | party |
| офицер | ofitser | officer |
| официант | ofitsiant | waiter |
| оюн | oýun | game, match |
| оян- | oýan- | awake, wake |
| ояр- | oýar- | awake, wake |
| оят- | oýat- | awake, wake |
| өв- | öw- | praise |
| өврен- | öwren- | learn, study |
| өврет- | öwret- | teach |
| өвсүн | öwsün | spell |
| өвүн- | öwün- | boast |
| өзи | özi | herself, himself, itself |
| өзүм | özim | myself |
| өзүмиз | özümiz | ourselves |
| өзүнден гит- | özünden git- | faint |
| өзүң | özüň | yourself |
| өзүңи алып бар- | özüňi alyp bar- | behave |
| өзүңиз | özüňiz | yourselves |
| өй | öý | home, house |
| өй эеси | öý eýesi | host |
| өйкен | öýken | lung |
| өйле | öýle | afternoon |
| өйлен- | öýlen- | marry |
| өйленйән йигит | öýlenýän ýigit | bridegroom |
| өйленме | öýlenme | marriage |
| өкүз | öküz | ox |
| өкүнме | ökünme | regret |

| | | |
|---|---|---|
| өл | öl | moist, wet |
| өл- | öl- | die |
| өлдүр- | öldür- | kill |
| өли | öli | dead |
| өлүм | ölüm | death |
| өлчег | ölçeg | measure, size |
| өндүр- | öndür- | produce |
| өң | öň | before |
| өңе | öňe | forward |
| өңүнде | öňünde | front: in front of |
| өңүни ал- | öňüni al- | prevent |
| өрдек | ördek | duck |
| өрт- | ört- | cover |
| өрән | örän | very |
| өс- | ös- | grow |
| өсүмлик | ösümlik | plant |
| өсүш | ösüş | development, growth |
| өтүнч сора- | ötünç sora- | apologize |
| өтүнч сорама | ötünç sorama | apology |
| | | |
| пагта | pagta | cotton |
| пайла- | paýla- | distribute |
| пайтагт | paýtagt | capital |
| палав | palaw | rice |
| палла- | palla- | yawn |
| палта | palta | axe |
| пальто | palto | overcoat |
| палчык | palçyk | mud |
| папак | papak | hat |
| параграф | paragraf | paragraph |
| парад | parad | parade |
| паралич | paraliç | paralysis |
| парахатчылык | parahatçylyk | peace |
| парк | park | park |
| парта | parta | desk |
| партия | partiýa | party |
| паспорт | pasport | passport |
| пасыл | pasyl | season |
| пейда | peýda | benefit, profit |
| пейдалы | peýdaly | useful |
| пейнир | peýnir | cheese |
| пенсия чык- | pensiýa çyk- | retire |
| пеншенбе | penşenbe | Thursday |
| перде | perde | curtain |
| перишде | perişde | angel |
| пес | pes | low |
| петрушка | petruşka | parsley |
| печь | peç | stove |

| | | |
|---|---|---|
| пиво | piwo | beer |
| пижама | piʃama | pajamas |
| пикир | pikir | idea, thought |
| пил | pil | elephant, spade |
| писсе | pisse | pistachio |
| пихта | pihta | fir |
| пишик | pişik | cat |
| планета | planeta | planet |
| пластинка | plastinka | record |
| платформа | platforma | platform |
| плащ | plaşç | raincoat |
| плёнка | plÿonka | film |
| пляж | plÿaʃ | beach |
| пол | pol | floor |
| полат | polat | steel |
| полотенце | polotentse | towel |
| помидор | pomidor | tomato |
| порт | port | harbor |
| посылка | posylka | parcel |
| потолок | potolok | ceiling |
| почта | poçta | post office |
| почта | poçta | postage |
| чыкдажысы | çykdajysy | |
| почта ящиги | poçta ÿaşçigi | mailbox |
| почтальон | poçtalon | mailman |
| поэзия | poeziÿa | poetry |
| пөкги | pökgi | ball |
| президент | prezident | president |
| премьер | premÿer | prime |
| министр | ministr | minister |
| проблема | problema | problem |
| программа | programma | program |
| проза | proza | prose |
| пропаганда | propaganda | propaganda |
| проспект | prospekt | avenue |
| простын | prostyn | sheet |
| профсоюз | profsoÿuz | union |
| процент | protsent | interest |
| пружин | pruʃin | spring |
| пул | pul | currency, money |
| пулемёт | pulemÿot | machine gun |
| пыгамбер | pygamber | prophet |
| пычак | pyçak | knife |
| пышбага | pyşbaga | tortoise |
| пыяда | pyÿada | pedestrian |
| пьеса | piÿesa | drama, play |
| пәки | päki | razor |

| радио | radio | radio |
|---|---|---|
| рак | rak | cancer |
| раковина | rakowina | sink |
| рамка | ramka | frame |
| реализм | realizm | realism |
| революция | rewolÿutsiÿa | revolution |
| регистрирлеме | registrirleme | registration |
| резервация | rezerwatsiÿa | reservation |
| рейс | reÿs | flight |
| реклама | reklama | advertisement |
| ренк | reñk | color |
| ресми | resmi | official |
| ресми адам | resmi adam | official |
| республика | respublika | republic |
| ресторан | restoran | restaurant |
| рецепт | retsept | prescription |
| роман | roman | novel |
| ромб | romb | diamond |
| ругсат бер- | rugsat ber- | permit |
| рух | ruh | spirit |
| руханы | ruhany | priest |
| ручка | ruçka | pen |
| | | |
| сабын | sabyn | soap |
| сабырлы | sabyrly | patient |
| саг | sag | right |
| саг бол айт- | sag bol aÿt- | thank |
| сагат | sagat | healthy, hour, watch |
| сагатчы | sagatçy | watchmaker |
| саглык | saglyk | health |
| саз | saz | music |
| саз гуралы | saz guraly | instrument |
| саз әсери | saz eseri | composition |
| сазанда | sazanda | musician |
| сазлашма | sazlaşma | harmony |
| сай | saÿ | shallow |
| сайла- | saÿla- | choose, elect, select |
| сайлав | saÿlaw | election |
| сакгал | sakgal | beard |
| сакла- | sakla- | keep |
| сал- | sal- | build |
| салам | salam | hello |
| саламлаш- | salamlaş- | greet |
| салат | salat | lettuce, salad |
| салгыт | salgyt | tax |
| салкын | salkyn | cool |
| салфетка | salfetka | napkin |
| салым | salym | moment |

| саман | saman | straw |
|---|---|---|
| самсык | samsyk | stupid |
| сан | san | number |
| сана- | sana- | count |
| сани | sani | sled |
| сап | sap | handle, pure |
| сапак | sapak | lesson |
| сары | sary | yellow |
| сарымсак | sarymsak | garlic |
| сат- | sat- | sell |
| сатув | satuw | sale |
| сатыжы | satyjy | salesperson, seller |
| сатын ал- | satyn al- | buy |
| сахна | sahna | stage |
| сахы | sahy | generous |
| сахыпа | sahypa | page |
| сач | saç | hair |
| сачак | saçak | tablecloth |
| саяван | saÿawan | umbrella |
| светофор | swetofor | traffic light |
| свитер | switer | sweater |
| себет | sebet | basket |
| себәп | sebäp | cause, reason |
| сегсен | segsen | eighty |
| сейрек | seÿrek | seldom |
| секиз | sekiz | eight |
| секретарь | sekretar | secretary |
| секта | sekta | sect |
| секунд | sekund | second |
| селдерей | seldereÿ | celery |
| семиз | semiz | fat |
| сен | sen | you |
| сене | sene | date |
| сенин | seniñ | your |
| сенинки | seniñki | yours |
| сентябрь | sentÿabr | September |
| серги | sergi | exhibition |
| серхет | serhet | border |
| серхош | serhoş | drunk |
| серче | serçe | sparrow |
| сес | ses | sound, voice, vote |
| сес бер- | ses ber- | vote |
| сиз | siz | you |
| сизин | siziñ | your |
| сизинки | siziñki | yours |
| сий- | siÿ- | urinate |
| силк- | silk- | shake |
| сим | sim | wire |

| символ | simwol | symbol |
|---|---|---|
| сиңек | siñek | fly |
| сирке | sirke | vinegar |
| сишенбе | sişenbe | Tuesday |
| скелет | skelet | skeleton |
| соватлы | sowatly | literate |
| совук | sowuk | cold |
| соган | sogan | onion |
| соңкы | soňky | last |
| соңра | soňra | after, then |
| соңы | soňy | end |
| сора- | sora- | ask |
| сораг | sorag | question |
| сосиска | sosiska | sausage |
| сосна | sosna | pine |
| сөвда | söwda | business |
| сөвеш | söweş | battle |
| сөвут | söwüt | willow |
| сөз | söz | word |
| сөз бер- | söz ber- | promise |
| сөзбашы | sözbaşy | preface |
| сөзлем | sözlem | sentence |
| сөзлук | sözlük | dictionary |
| сөй- | söÿ- | like, love |
| сөйги | söÿgi | love |
| сөндур- | söndür- | extinguish, put out |
| спорт | sport | sport |
| стакан | stakan | glass |
| станция | stantsiÿa | station |
| стол | stol | table |
| страхование | strahowaniÿe | insurance |
| студент | student | student |
| стул | stul | chair |
| субутнама | subutnama | proof |
| сув | suw | water |
| сув дашгыны | suw daşgyny | flood |
| сувасты | suwasty | submarine |
| сувсан | suwsan | thirsty |
| сувук | suwuk | liquid |
| суд | sud | court |
| судья | sudÿa | judge |
| сумка | sumka | bag |
| сунгат | sungat | art |
| сурат | surat | painting, picture |
| сурат чекме | surat çekme | drawing |
| сүбсе | sübse | broom |
| сүзгуч | süzgüç | strainer |
| сүйжи | süÿji | candy, sweet |
| сүйт | süÿt | milk |
| сүңк | süñk | bone |
| супур- | süpür- | sweep |
| сур- | sür- | drive |
| сури | süri | herd |
| сурт- | sürt- | rub |
| сурч- | sürç- | slip |
| счёт | sçÿot | bill |
| сыгыр | sygyr | cow |
| сыгыр эти | sygyr eti | beef |
| сык- | syk- | press |
| сыла- | syla- | respect |
| сына- | syna- | test |
| сынанышык | synanyşyk | attempt |
| сыпала- | sypala- | stroke |
| сыпат | sypat | adjective |
| сыркав | syrkaw | ill, patient, sick |
| сычан | syçan | mouse |
| сыя | syÿa | ink |
| сыясат | syÿasat | politics |
| сыяхат | syÿahat | journey, travel |
| таба | taba | pan |
| табажык | tabajyk | saucer |
| табуретка | taburetka | stool |
| табшырык | tabşyryk | assignment |
| тагамлы | tagamly | delicious, tasty |
| тайяр | taÿÿar | ready |
| тайярла- | taÿÿarla- | prepare |
| такмынан | takmynan | about |
| такси | taksi | cab, taxi |
| такыр келле | takyr kelle | bald |
| тал | tal | willow |
| тала- | tala- | plunder |
| тамың усти | tamyñ üsti | roof |
| тана- | tana- | know, recognize |
| танс эт- | tans et- | dance |
| тансчы | tansçy | dancer |
| танышдыр- | tanyşdyr- | introduce |
| таңры | tañry | God |
| тап- | tap- | discover, find |
| тапавут | tapawut | difference |
| тарапа | tarapa | towards |
| тарапындан | tarapyndan | by |
| тарелка | tarelka | plate |

| | | |
|---|---|---|
| тарых | taryh | history |
| тарыхчы | taryhçy | historian |
| театр | teatr | theater |
| тебигат | tebigat | nature |
| тебигы | tebigy | natural |
| тегелек | tegelek | circle, round |
| теджрибе | tejribe | experience |
| текже | tekje | shelf |
| теклип | teklip | suggestion |
| телевизор | telewizor | television |
| телеграмма | telegramma | telegram |
| телефон | telefon | telephone |
| телефон кабинасы | telefon kabinasy | phone booth |
| телефон номери | telefon nomeri | phone number |
| тема | tema | subject |
| теммэки | temmäki | tobacco |
| температура | temperatura | temperature |
| теория | teoriýa | theory |
| терези | terezi | scale |
| терджиме | terjime | translation |
| терджиме эт- | terjime et- | translate |
| термометр | termometr | thermometer |
| тигир | tigir | wheel |
| тигирле- | tigirle- | roll |
| тиз | tiz | quick |
| тиз көмек машыны | tiz kömek maşyny | ambulance |
| тиз-тизден | tiz-tizden | often |
| тизлик | tizlik | speed |
| тик- | tik- | sew |
| тикинчи | tikinçi | tailor |
| тилки | tilki | fox |
| тираж | tiraſ | circulation |
| тирсек | tirsek | elbow |
| титре- | titre- | tremble |
| товла- | towla- | twist |
| товук | towuk | hen |
| товук эти | towuk eti | chicken |
| товшан | towşan | rabbit |
| тогалак дерман | togalak derman | pill |
| тогсан | togsan | ninety |
| тозан | tozan | dust |
| токай | tokaý | forest, wood |
| толкун | tolkun | wave |
| томус | tomus | summer |
| топ | top | ball, cannon |
| топрак | toprak | earth, soil |
| торт | tort | cake |
| тохум | tohum | grain, seed |
| тоюн | toýun | clay |
| төле- | töle- | pay |
| трамвай | tramwaý | tram |
| тротуар | trotuar | sidewalk |
| тупан | tupan | storm |
| тур- | tur- | get up |
| туризм | turizm | tourism |
| турист | turist | tourist |
| туруп дур- | turup dur- | stand |
| туршы | turşy | sour |
| тут | tut | mulberry |
| тут- | tut- | catch, hold |
| тутуш | tutuş | whole |
| тәви | tüwi | rice |
| түйкүр- | tüýkür- | spit |
| түпең | tüpeñ | rifle |
| түрме | türme | jail, prison |
| түссечыкар | tüsseçykar | chimney |
| тып- | typ- | slide |
| тыпанчак | typançak | slippery |
| тәзе | täze | fresh, new |
| тәзе йыл | täze ýyl | New Year |
| тәсин гал- | täsin gal- | admire |
| тәсир | täsir | effect, influence |
| угра- | ugra- | depart |
| уграма | ugrama | departure |
| угур | ugur | direction, way |
| узын | uzyn | long, tall |
| узынлык | uzynlyk | length |
| укла- | ukla- | sleep |
| укы | uky | sleep |
| улан- | ulan- | use |
| улы | uly | big, great, large |
| умумы | umumy | general |
| умыт | umyt | hope |
| умыт эт- | umyt et- | hope |
| ун | un | flour |
| универмаг | univermag | department store |
| университет | uniwersitet | university |
| унут- | unut- | forget |
| ур- | ur- | hit |
| уруш | uruş | war |
| уруш- | uruş- | fight |

| утан- | utan- | ashamed: be ashamed |
|---|---|---|
| утанҗаң | utanjañ | shy |
| уч- | uç- | fly |
| учар | uçar | airplane, plane |
| уя | uýa | sister |
| уял- | uýal- | ashamed: be ashamed |
| үве- | üwe- | grind |
| үзүм | üzüm | grape |
| үйтгет- | üýtget- | change |
| үйтгешик | üýtgeşik | different |
| үлҗе | ülje | cherry |
| үмсүм | ümsüm | quiet |
| үмсүмлик | ümsümlik | silence |
| үмүр | ümür | fog |
| үнс | üns | attention |
| үсгүлевүк | üsgülewük | cough |
| үстүн чык- | üstün çyk- | surpass |
| үстүнде | üstünde | above, on, over |
| үстүнлик | üstünlik | success |
| үстүнлик газан- | üstünlik gazan- | succeed |
| үтүк | ütük | iron |
| үч | üç | three |
| үчбурчлук | üçburçluk | triangle |
| үчин | üçin | for |
| фабрик | fabrik | factory |
| фамилия | familiýa | surname |
| февраль | fewral | February |
| ферма | ferma | farm |
| физика | fizika | physics |
| фильм | film | movie |
| фирма | firma | company, firm |
| фольклор | folklor | folklore |
| фонтан | fontan | fountain |
| фото | foto | photo |
| фотоаппарат | fotoapparat | camera |
| фундук хозы | funduk hozy | hazelnut |
| футбол | futbol | soccer |
| хабар | habar | news |
| хабар бер- | habar ber- | inform |
| хава | hawa | yes |
| хаҗыса | hadysa | event |

| хаҗатхана | hajathana | toilet |
|---|---|---|
| хазына | hazyna | treasure |
| хайван | haýwan | animal |
| хайсы | haýsy | which |
| хайсы хем болса бир зат | haýsy hem bolsa bir zat | anything |
| хайыш эдйәрин | haýyş edyärin | please |
| хайыш эт- | haýyş et- | request |
| хакыкат | hakykat | truth |
| хакыкы | hakyky | real, true |
| хал | hal | adverb |
| халас эт- | halas et- | rescue |
| халк | halk | people |
| халк дессаны | halk dessany | folktale |
| халкара | halkara | international |
| халы | haly | carpet |
| халыча | halyça | rug |
| хамала | hamala | as if |
| хаммал | hammal | porter |
| ханым | hanym | lady |
| хапа | hapa | dirty |
| хараҗат | harajat | expense |
| харчла- | harçla- | spend |
| харп | harp | letter |
| харытлар | harytlar | goods |
| хасап | hasap | account |
| хасапла- | hasapla- | calculate |
| хат | hat | letter |
| хатар | hatar | row |
| хатда | hatda | even |
| хачан | haçan | when |
| хезил эт- | hezil et- | enjoy |
| хейкел | heýkel | sculpture, statue |
| хекая | hekaýa | story |
| хем | hem | also, too |
| хем... хем | hem... hem | both ... and |
| хемише | hemişe | always |
| хеммеси | hemmesi | all |
| хениз | heniz | still |
| хең | heñ | tune |
| хепде | hepde | week |
| хер | her | every |
| хер ерде | her ýerde | everywhere |
| хер зат | her zat | everything |
| хер ким | her kim | anybody, everybody |

| хереует | hereket | traffic |
|---|---|---|
| хич ерде | hiç ÿerde | nowhere |
| хич зат | hiç zat | nothing |
| хич ким | hiç kim | nobody |
| хил | hil | kind, quality |
| хирургия | hirurgiÿa | surgery |
| хова | howa | air, weather |
| хова ёлы | howa ÿoly | airline |
| хова маглуматы | howa maglumaty | weather report |
| ховлук- | howluk- | hurry |
| ховлукмачлык | howlukmaçlyk | haste |
| ховлы | howly | courtyard |
| ховп | howp | danger |
| ховплы | howply | dangerous |
| ховпсуз | howpsuz | safe |
| ховуз | howuz | pool |
| хоз | hoz | walnut |
| холодильник | holodilnik | refrigerator |
| хораз | horaz | rooster |
| хормат | hormat | honor, respect |
| хош | hoş | bye-bye |
| хош гелдин[из] | hoş geldiñ[iz] | welcome |
| хөвес | höwes | interest |
| хөдурле- | hödürle- | offer, recommend |
| хөкум | höküm | verdict |
| хөкумет | hökümet | government |
| христиан | hristian | Christian |
| художник | hudo⌐nik | artist, painter |
| хурма | hurma | date |
| хужум | hüjüm | attack |
| хунəр | hünär | skill |
| хызматкəр | hyzmatkär | servant |
| хыяр | hyÿar | cucumber |
| хəзир | häzir | now |
| хəзирки | häzirki | present |
| цемент | tsement | cement |
| цензура | tsenzura | censorship |
| цирк | tsirk | circus |
| чага | çaga | child |
| чагыр- | çagyr- | call, invite, summon |
| чай | çaÿ | tea |
| чай пулы | çaÿ puly | tip |
| чайник | çaÿnik | teapot |

| чакла- | çakla- | guess |
|---|---|---|
| чакылык | çakylyk | invitation |
| чакыр | çakyr | wine |
| чал | çal | grey |
| чал- | çal- | play |
| чалт | çalt | fast, speedy |
| чалыш- | çalyş- | try |
| чалышма | çalyşma | pronoun |
| чап эт- | çap et- | print |
| чапхана | çaphana | printing press |
| чаршенбе | çarşenbe | Wednesday |
| чашка | çaşka | cup |
| чейне- | çeÿne- | chew |
| чек | çek | check |
| чек- | çek- | carry, pull |
| чекимли | çekimli | vowel |
| чекимсиз | çekimsiz | consonant |
| чекиртге | çekirtge | grasshopper |
| чекич | çekiç | hammer |
| чемелеш- | çemeleş- | approach |
| чемедан | çemedan | suitcase |
| чемче | çemçe | spoon |
| ченли | çenli | until |
| чеп | çep | left |
| чиг | çig | raw |
| чилим | çilim | cigarette |
| чилим чек- | çilim çek- | smoke |
| чиш | çiş | swelling |
| чиш- | çiş- | swell |
| чоз- | çoz- | attack |
| чорба | çorba | soup |
| чотга | çotga | brush |
| чөз- | çöz- | solve |
| чөл | çöl | desert |
| чөрек | çörek | bread |
| чөрекчи | çörekçi | baker |
| чөрекхана | çörekhana | bakery |
| чунлук | çuñluk | depth |
| чуннур | çuññur | deep |
| чуй | çüÿ | nail |
| чуйре- | çüÿre- | rot |
| чуйше | çüÿşe | bottle |
| чум- | çüm- | dive |
| чунки | çünki | because |
| чунк | çüñk | beak |
| чыбын | çybyn | mosquito |
| чыглы | çygly | damp |
| чыгыр- | çygyr- | scream |
| чызык | çyzyk | line |
| чык- | çyk- | exit |

| | | |
|---|---|---|
| чыкалга | çykalga | exit |
| чыкдажы | çykdajy | expense |
| чәге | çäge | sand |
| чәклендир- | çäklendir- | restrict |
| | | |
| шайы пул | şaÿy pul | coin |
| шарф | şarf | scarf |
| шат | şat | glad |
| шах | şah | horn |
| шаха | şaha | branch |
| шахыр | şahyr | poet |
| шаят | şaÿat | witness |
| шейле | şeÿle | such |
| шейтан | şeÿtan | demon, Satan |
| шекер | şeker | sugar |
| шем | şem | candle |
| шенбе | şenbe | Saturday |
| шерт | şert | condition |
| шетдалы | şetdaly | peach |
| шикаят | şikaÿat | complaint |
| шикаят эт- | şikaÿat et- | complain |
| шин | şin | tire |
| шкаф | şkaf | cupboard |
| шонуӊ үчин | şonuñ üçin | therefore |
| шорт | şort | shorts |
| шофёр | şofÿor | driver |
| шөхле | şöhle | ray |
| шүбхе | şübhe | doubt |
| шыпбык | şypbyk | slipper |
| шәрикдеш | şärikdeş | partner |
| шәхер | şäher | city, town |
| шәхер эдарасы | şäher edarasy | municipality |
| шәхер әтеги | şäher etegi | suburb |
| | | |
| ыбадат | ybadat | worship |
| ыбадатхана | ybadathana | temple |
| ыз | yz | trace |
| ызарла- | yzarla- | follow |
| ыкбал | ykbal | fate |
| ылалаш- | ylalaş- | agree |
| ылалашык | ylalaşyk | agreement |
| ылайта-да | ylaÿta-da | especially |
| ылга- | ylga- | run |
| ылмы иш | ylmy iş | research |
| ынам | ynam | confidence |
| ынан- | ynan- | believe |
| ынанч | ynanç | belief |
| ынжалыксызлан- | ynjalyksyzlan- | worry |
| ынжалыксызландыр- | ynjalyksyzlandyr- | disturb |

| | | |
|---|---|---|
| ынсан | ynsan | human being |
| ыс | ys | smell |
| ыс бер- | ys ber- | smell |
| ысга- | ysga- | smell |
| ысманак | ysmanak | spinach |
| ыссы | yssy | hot |
| ыхласлы | yhlasly | diligent |
| ышык | yşyk | light |
| | | |
| -ә | -e | to |
| әбедилик | ebedilik | eternity |
| әг- | eg- | bend |
| әгер | eger | if |
| әгин | egin | shoulder |
| әгин-әшик | egin-eşik | clothes |
| әгленме | eglenme | delay |
| әдеби | edebi | literary |
| әдеби әсер | edebi eser | literary work |
| әдебият | edebiÿat | literature |
| әдепли | edepli | polite |
| әдерменлик | edermenlik | courage |
| әе | eÿe | subject |
| әже | eje | mother |
| әжеке | ejeke | aunt, sister |
| әзиз | eziz | dear |
| әк- | ek- | plant, sow |
| әкзамен | ekzamen | examination |
| әкиз | ekiz | twin |
| әкин | ekin | crop |
| әкин әкме | ekin ekme | cultivation |
| әкономика | ekonomika | economics |
| әкран | ekran | screen |
| әл | el | hand |
| әл етир- | el ÿetir- | reach |
| әл сумкасы | el sumkasy | handbag |
| әл чарп- | el çarp- | clap |
| әл яглык | el ÿaglyk | handkerchief |
| әлбетде | elbetde | course: of course |
| әлектрик тогы | elektrik togy | electricity |
| әлипбий | elipbiÿ | alphabet |
| әлли | elli | fifty |
| әллик | ellik | glove |
| әм | em | cure |
| әм- | em- | suck |
| әмма | emma | but |
| -ән | -en | that |
| әндик эт- | endik et- | used: be used to |

| эне | ene | grandmother |
| энҗамлар | enjamlar | equipment |
| энтек | entek | yet |
| эңек | eñek | chin |
| эпле- | eple- | fold |
| эра | era | era |
| эрбет | erbet | bad |
| эре- | ere- | melt |
| эрик | erik | apricot |
| эркек | erkek | man |
| эртир | ertir | morning, tomorrow |
| эртирлик | ertirlik | breakfast |
| эсасы | esasy | main |
| эсгер | esger | soldier |
| эт | et | meat |
| эт дүканы | et dükany | butcher shop |
| эт- | et- | do, make |
| этаж | etaſ | storey |
| эшек | eşek | donkey |
| эшит- | eşit- | hear |
| | | |
| әгирт улы | ägirt uly | huge |
| әдик | ädik | boot |
| әдикчи | ädikçi | shoemaker |
| әдим | ädim | step |
| әйнек | äÿnek | glasses |
| әлемгошар | älemgoşar | rainbow |
| әпишге | äpişge | window |
| әр | är | husband |
| әтиячлы | ätiÿaçly | careful |
| әтиячлык | ätiÿaçlyk | precaution |
| әхли | ähli | all |
| әхтимал | ähtimal | probably |
| | | |
| юбилей | ÿubileÿ | anniversary |
| юбка | ÿubka | skirt |
| юв- | ÿuw- | wash |
| юваш | ÿuwaş | calm, slow |
| юваш бол- | ÿuwaş bol- | quiet: be quiet |
| юваш - ювашдан | ÿuwaş- ÿuwaşdan | gradually |
| юмуртга | ÿumurtga | egg |
| юмшак | ÿumşak | soft |
| юрист | ÿurist | lawyer |
| я | ÿa | or |
| я... я(-да) | ÿa... ÿa [-da] | either ... or |
| я-да | ÿa-da | or |

| ябаны | ÿabany | wild |
| яг | ÿag | fat, oil |
| яг- | ÿag- | precipitate |
| ягдай | ÿagdaÿ | condition, situation |
| ягты | ÿagty | bright |
| ягшы | ÿagşy | OK |
| ягын | ÿagyn | rain |
| ягыш | ÿagyş | rain |
| яда сал- | ÿada sal- | remind |
| ядав | ÿadaw | tired |
| ядыгәрлик | ÿadygärlik | monument |
| яз | ÿaz | spring |
| яз- | ÿaz- | write |
| язув | ÿazuw | writing |
| языҗы | ÿazyjy | writer |
| яй | ÿaÿ | bow |
| яйла | ÿaÿla | meadow |
| яйрат- | ÿaÿrat- | spread |
| яйың окы | ÿaÿyñ oky | arrow |
| як- | ÿak- | burn |
| яка | ÿaka | coast, collar |
| якында | ÿakynda | soon |
| ялан | ÿalan | lie |
| яландан | ÿalandan | false |
| ялаңач | ÿalañaç | bare |
| ялдыра- | ÿaldyra- | shine |
| ялңыш | ÿalñyş | mistake, wrong |
| ялңышлык | ÿalñyşlyk | fault |
| ялта | ÿalta | lazy |
| ялталык | ÿaltalyk | laziness |
| ялы | ÿaly | like |
| ялын | ÿalyn | flame |
| -ян | -ÿan | that |
| ян- | ÿan- | burn |
| январь | ÿanwar | January |
| янгын | ÿangyn | fire |
| янында | ÿanynda | beside |
| яңак | ÿañak | cheek |
| яп- | ÿap- | close, shut |
| япрак | ÿaprak | leaf |
| япык | ÿapyk | closed |
| яр- | ÿar- | split |
| яра | ÿara | wound |
| яраг | ÿarag | gun, weapon |
| ярдам | ÿardam | assistance, help |
| ярдам эт- | ÿardam et- | help |
| яры гиже | ÿary gije | midnight |

| ярым | ÿarym | half | ят- | ÿat- | lie |
| ярымада | ÿarymada | peninsula | ятла- | ÿatla- | remember |
| ярымай | ÿarymaÿ | crescent | ятылян отаг | ÿatylÿan otag | bedroom |
| ярыш | ÿaryş | race | яш | ÿaş | age, young |
| ясама | ÿasama | artificial | яша- | ÿaşa- | live |
| яссык | ÿassyk | cushion, pillow | яшлык | ÿaşlyk | youth |
| яссык дашы | ÿassyk daşy | pillowcase | яшы етен | ÿaşy ÿeten | adult |
| ят | ÿat | memory | яшыл | ÿaşyl | green |

# UIGHUR - ENGLISH INDEX

| | | | | | |
|---|---|---|---|---|---|
| ئابزاس | (abzas) | paragraph | ئادۋوكات | (advokat) | lawyer |
| ئابستراكت | (abstrakt) | abstract | ئارال | (aral) | island |
| ئاپتاپپەرەس | (aptappäräs) | sunflower | ئارپا | (arpa) | barley |
| ئاپتوبۇس | (aptobus) | bus | ئارخىتېكتور | (arkhetektor) | architect |
| ئاپتور | (aptor) | author | ئارزۇ | (arzu) | desire, wish |
| ئاپتوموبىل | (aptomobil) | automobile | ئارقىدا | (arqida) | behind |
| ئاپرېل | (aprel) | April | ئارمىيە | (armiyä) | army |
| ئات | (at) | name, horse | ئارىسىدا | (arisida) | between |
| ئات_ | (at-) | throw | ئارىلاشتۇر_ | (arilashtur-) | mix |
| ئاتا_ئانا | (ata-ana) | parents | ئارىلىق | (ariliq) | distance |
| ئاتكرىتكا | (atkiritka) | postcard | ئاز | (az) | few |
| ئاتمىش | (atmish) | sixty | ئاز سانلىق | (az sanliq) | minority |
| ئاجراش_ | (ajrash-) | divorce | ئازاي_ | (azay-) | decrease |
| ئاجرال_ | (ajral-) | separated: be separated | ئاس_ | (as-) | hang |
| ئاجرىشىش | (ajrishish) | divorce | ئاساسىي | (asasiy) | main |
| ئاجىز | (ajiz) | weak | ئاسان | (asan) | easy |
| ئاچ | (ach) | hungry | ئاستا | (asta) | slow |
| ئاچ_ | (ach-) | open | ئاستىدا | (astida) | underneath |
| ئاچا | (acha) | sister | ئاسمان | (asman) | sky |
| ئاچارچىلىق | (acharchiliq) | famine | ئاشپەز | (ashpäz) | cook |
| ئاچچىق | (achchiq) | bitter | ئاشخانا ئۆي | (ashkhana öy) | kitchen |
| ئاچچىقسۇ | (achchiqsu) | vinegar | ئاشقازان | (ashqazan) | stomach |
| ئاچقۇچ | (achquch) | key | ئاشكۆكى | (ashköki) | parsley |
| ئاچلىق | (achliq) | hunger | ئاشلىق | (ashliq) | grain |
| ئاخشام | (akhsham) | evening | ئاغرىق | (aghriq) | pain |
| ئاخىر | (akhir) | end | ئاق | (aq) | white |
| ئاخىرقى | (akhirqi) | last | ئاق_ | (aq-) | flow |
| ئادالەت | (adalät) | justice | ئاق قارىغاي | (aq qarighay) | fir |
| ئادەت | (adät) | custom, habit | ئاق قۇ | (aq qu) | swan |
| ئادەتلەن_ | (adätlän-) | used: be used to | ئاكا | (aka) | brother |
| ئادەم | (adäm) | human being | ئاڭلا_ | (angla-) | hear, listen |
| ئادەملەر توپى | (adämlär topi) | crowd | ئال_ | (al-) | take |
| ئاددىي | (addiy) | simple | ئالەم بوشلۇقى | (aläm boshluqi) | space |
| ئادرېس | (adres) | address | ئالتە | (altä) | six |
| | | | ئالتۇن | (altun) | gold |

|  |  |  |
|---|---|---|
| ئالد ىدا | (aldida) | front: in front of |
| ئالد ىرا_ | (aldira-) | hurry |
| ئالد ىراش | (aldirash) | busy |
| ئالد ىراشلىق | (aldirashliq) | haste |
| ئالد ىنى ئال_ | (aldini al-) | prevent |
| ئالغا | (algha) | forward |
| ئالگېبرا | (algebra) | algebra |
| ئالما | (alma) | apple |
| ئالماس | (almas) | diamond |
| ئالماش | (almash) | pronoun |
| ئالىم | (alim) | scientist |
| ئامەت | (amät) | luck |
| ئاممىۋى تېلېفون | (ammivi telefon) | public phone |
| ئامۇت | (amut) | pear |
| ئانا | (ana) | mother |
| ئانار | (anar) | pomegranate |
| ئانارخىزم | (anarkhizm) | anarchy |
| ئانتېننا | (antenna) | antenna |
| ئاندىن كېيىن | (andin keyin) | then |
| ئاھاڭداشلىق | (ahangdashliq) | harmony |
| ئاۋارە قىل_ | (avarä qil-) | bother, disturb |
| ئاۋاز | (avaz) | voice, vote |
| ئاۋاز بەر_ | (avaz bär-) | vote |
| ئاۋغۇست | (avghust) | August |
| ئائىلە | (a'ilä) | family |
| ئاي | (ay) | month, moon |
| ئاياغ | (ayagh) | shoe |
| ئايال | (ayal) | wife |
| ئاياللار كىيىمى | (ayallar kiyimi) | dress |
| ئايروپورت | (ayroport) | airport |
| ئايروپىلان | (ayropilan) | airplane, plane |
| ئايرى_ | (ayri-) | separate |
| ئايرىم | (ayrim) | separate |
| ئايلان_ | (aylan-) | stroll |
| ئەپەندى | (äpändi) | gentleman |
| ئەپسانىشۇناسلىق | (äpsanishunasliq) | mythology |
| ئەپسۇن | (äpsun) | spell |
| ئەپۇ | (äpu) | apology |
| ئەتە | (ätä) | tomorrow |
| ئەتۆرگۈچ | (ätvirkä) | screwdriver |
| ئەتىر | (ätir) | perfume |
| ئەتىرگۈل | (ätirgül) | rose |
| ئەتىگەن | (ätigän) | early, morning |
| ئەتىگەنلىك تاماق | (ätigänlik tamaq) | breakfast |
| ئەتىياز | (ätiyaz) | spring |
| ئەخلەت | (äkhlät) | trash |
| ئەدەپلىك | (ädäblik) | polite |
| ئەدەبى | (ädäbiy) | literary |
| ئەدەبى ئەسەر | (ädäbiy äsär) | literary work |
| ئەدەبىيات | (ädäbiyat) | literature |
| ئەدىيال | (ädiyal) | blanket |
| ئەر | (är) | husband, man |
| ئەرزان | (ärzan) | cheap |
| ئەركىن | (ärkin) | free |
| ئەركىنلىك | (ärkinlik) | freedom |
| ئەز_ | (äz-) | crush |
| ئەزا | (äza) | member |
| ئەس | (äs) | memory |
| ئەسكەر | (äskär) | soldier |
| ئەسلە_ | (äslä-) | remember |
| ئەسلەت_ | (äslät-) | remind |
| ئەسنە_ | (äsnä-) | yawn |
| ئەسۋاب | (äsvab) | tool |
| ئەسىر | (äsir) | century |
| ئەقىل | (äqil) | mind |
| ئەقىللىق | (äqillliq) | clever, intelligent |
| ئەگ_ | (äg-) | bend |

| | | | | | |
|---|---|---|---|---|---|
| ئەگەر | (ägär) | if | باشقۇرغۇچى | (bashqurghuchi) manager | |
| ئەگەش_ | (ägäsh-) | follow | باشلا_ | (bashla-) | begin, start |
| ئەڭ كۆپ | (äng köp) | most | باغچە | (baghchä) | garden, park |
| ئەڭ ياخشى | (äng yakhshi) | best | باغلا_ | (baghla-) | fasten, tie |
| ئەلچى | (älchi) | ambassador | باغۋەن | (baghvän) | gardener |
| ئەللىك | (ällik) | fifty | بالا | (bala) | child |
| ئەلۋەتتە | (älvättä) | course: of course | بالكون | (balkon) | balcony |
| ئەم_ | (äm-) | suck | بالېت | (balet) | ballet |
| ئەمەس | (ämäs) | not | بانان | (banan) | banana |
| ئەمما | (ämma) | but | بانكا | (banka) | bank |
| ئەنجۈر | (änjür) | fig | باها | (baha) | cost, price |
| ئەۋەت_ | (ävät-) | send | باهاسىنى چۈشۈرۈش | (bahasini chüshürüsh) | discount, sale |
| ئەۋزەل كۆر_ | (ävzäl kör-) | prefer | باهانە | (bahanä) | excuse |
| ئەينەك | (äynäk) | glass, mirror | باي | (bay) | rich |
| ئەينۇلا | (äynula) | plum | بايراق | (bayraq) | flag |
| ئەيىب | (äyib) | fault | بايرام | (bayram) | festival, holiday |
| ئەيىبدار | (äyibdar) | guilty | بايلىق | (bayliq) | treasure, wealth |
| ئەيىبسىز | (äyibsiz) | innocent | | | |
| ئەيىبسىزلىك | (äyibsizlik) | innocence | بەت | (bät) | page |
| | | | بەختسىز | (bäkhtsiz) | unhappy |
| باج | (baj) | tax | بەختىيار | (bäkhtiyar) | happy |
| بادام | (badam) | almond | بەدەن | (bädän) | body |
| بار_ | (bar-) | go | بەر_ | (bär-) | give |
| بارا_بارا | (bara-bara) | gradually | بەزى | (bäzi) | some |
| بارلىق | (barliq) | all | بەزىدە | (bäzidä) | sometimes |
| بارماق | (barmaq) | finger | بەش | (bäsh) | five |
| بارومېتر | (barometr) | barometer | بەلباغ | (bälbagh) | belt |
| بازار | (bazar) | market | بوتۇلكا | (botulka) | bottle |
| باس_ | (bas-) | print | بوران | (boran) | storm |
| باش | (bash) | head | بوش | (bosh) | empty, loose |
| باش ئاغرىقى | (bash aghriqi) | headache | بوشات_ | (boshat-) | empty, release |
| باش كىيىم | (bash kiyim) | hat | بول_ | (bol-) | be, become |
| باش مىنىستىر | (bash ministir) | prime minister | بولقا | (bolqa) | hammer |
| باشقا | (bashqa) | another, other | بومبا | (bomba) | bomb |
| | | | بوۋا | (bova) | grandfather |

| | | | | | |
|---|---|---|---|---|---|
| بوۋاق | (bovaq) | baby | بۆرگە | (bürgä) | flea |
| بويا_ | (boya-) | dye | بۈگۈن | (bügün) | today |
| بويسۇن_ | (boysun-) | obey | بېرى | (beri) | since |
| بويۇن | (boyun) | neck | بېغىش | (beghish) | wrist |
| بويى ئېگىز | (boyi egiz) | tall | بېكەت | (bekät) | stop |
| بويىغا يەتكەن ئادەم | (boyigha yätkän adäm) | adult | بېلەت | (belät) | ticket |
| | | | بېلىق | (beliq) | fish |
| بۇ | (bu) | this | بېلىقچى | (beliqchi) | fisherman |
| بۇ يەردە | (bu yärdä) | here | بېنزىن | (benzin) | gasoline |
| بۇدجېت | (budjet) | budget | بېھى | (behi) | quince |
| بۇرا_ | (bura-) | twist | بىخەتەر | (bikhätär) | safe |
| بۇرغا | (burgha) | drill | بىر | (bir) | one |
| بۇرما مىخ | (burma mikh) | screw | بىر ئاز | (bir az) | little, some |
| بۇرۇت | (burut) | mustache | بىر كىم | (bir kim) | anybody |
| بۇرۇل_ | (burul-) | turn | بىرەر نەرسە | (birär närsä) | anything |
| بۇرۇن | (burun) | ago, before, nose | بىرەۋ | (biräv) | anybody |
| | | | بىرگە | (birgä) | together |
| بۇز_ | (buz-) | destroy | بىرنەچچە | (birnächchä) | several |
| بۇغا | (bugha) | deer | بىز | (biz) | we |
| بۇغداي | (bughday) | wheat | بىزنى | (bizni) | us |
| بۇقا | (buqa) | bull | بىزنىڭ | (bizning) | our |
| بۇلار | (bular) | these | بىزنىڭكى | (bizningki) | ours |
| بۇلاڭچىلىق قىل_ | (bulangchiliq qil-) | plunder | بىل_ | (bil-) | know |
| بۇلۇت | (bulut) | cloud | بىلەك | (biläk) | arm |
| بۇلۇڭ | (bulung) | angle, corner | بىلەن | (bilän) | by, with |
| | | | بىلىم | (bilim) | knowledge |
| بۇنداق | (bundaq) | such | بىنا | (bina) | building |
| بۇيرۇ_ | (buyru-) | command, order | بىنا ئۆي | (bina öy) | apartment |
| بۇيرۇت_ | (buyrut-) | order | پات ئارىدا | (pat arida) | soon |
| بۆرە | (börä) | wolf | پات_پات | (pat-pat) | often |
| بۆرەك | (böräk) | kidney | پاتقاق | (patqaq) | mud |
| بۆل_ | (böl-) | divide | پاتېفون تەخسىسى | (patefon täkhsisi) | record |
| بۆلجۈرگەن | (böljürgän) | strawberry | | | |
| بۆلۈش | (bölüsh) | division | پاختا | (pakhta) | cotton |
| بۆلۈم | (bölüm) | department | پادا | (pada) | herd |
| بۈركۈت | (bürküt) | eagle | پادىشاھ | (padishah) | king |

| | | | | | |
|---|---|---|---|---|---|
| پارات | (parat) | parade | پروزا | (proza) | prose |
| پاراخوت | (parakhot) | ship | پروگرامما | (programma) | program |
| پارتا | (parta) | desk | پرېزىدېنت | (prezident) | president |
| پارتىيە | (partiyä) | party | پلاتفورما | (platforma) | platform |
| پارچە پۇل | (parchä pul) | change | پوپ | (pop) | priest |
| پاسپورت | (pasport) | passport | پوپايكا | (popayka) | sweater |
| پاسكىنا | (paskina) | dirty | پوچتا ھەققى | (pochta häqqi) | postage |
| پاشا | (pasha) | mosquito | پوچتا ساندۇقى | (pochta sanduqi) | mailbox |
| پاقا | (paqa) | frog | پوچتىخانا | (pochtikhana) | post office |
| پاقلان | (paqlan) | lamb | پوچتىكەش | (pochtikäsh) | mailman |
| پاڭ | (pang) | deaf | پورت | (port) | harbor |
| پاڭلىق | (pangliq) | deafness | پورتمال | (portmal) | purse |
| پالەچلىك | (palächlik) | paralysis | پورتمان | (portman) | wallet |
| پالەك | (paläk) | spinach | پوسۇلكا | (posulka) | parcel |
| پالتا | (palta) | axe | پول | (pol) | floor |
| پايپاق | (paypaq) | sock, stocking | پولات | (polat) | steel |
| پايتەخت | (paytäkht) | capital | پولۇ | (polu) | rice |
| پايدا | (payda) | benefit, profit | پويىز | (poyiz) | train |
| پايدىلىق | (paydiliq) | useful | پۇت | (put) | foot, leg |
| پەردە | (pärdä) | curtain | پۇتبول | (putbol) | soccer |
| پەرق | (pärq) | difference | پۇرا_ | (pura-) | smell |
| پەرقسىز | (pärqsiz) | same | پۇراق | (puraq) | smell |
| پەرقلىك | (pärqlik) | different | پۇرچاق | (purchaq) | bean, pea |
| پەرىشتە | (pärishtä) | angel | پۇرژىنا | (purzhina) | spring |
| پەس | (päs) | low | پۇل | (pul) | currency, money |
| پەسىل | (päsil) | season | پۇل پاخاللىقى | (pul pakhalliqi) | inflation |
| پەش | (päsh) | comma | پۇلسىز | (pulsiz) | free |
| پەلەمپەي | (pälämpäy) | stairs | پۈتتۈر_ | (püttür-) | finish |
| پەلەي | (päläy) | glove | پۈتۈن | (pütün) | whole |
| پەلتو | (pälto) | overcoat | پېشانە | (peshanä) | forehead |
| پەمىدۇر | (pämidur) | tomato | پېنسىيىگە چىق_ | (pensiyigä chiq-) | retire |
| پەي | (päy) | feather | پېئىل | (pe'il) | verb |
| پەيدا بول_ | (päyda bol-) | appear | پېت | (pit) | louse |
| پەيشەنبە | (päyshänbä) | Thursday | پىچاق | (pichaq) | knife |
| پەيغەمبەر | (päyghämbär) | prophet | | | |

| | | | | | |
|---|---|---|---|---|---|
| پرهٔ نك | (piränik) | cookie | تاشپاقا | (tashpaqa) | tortoise |
| پسته | (pistä) | pistachio | تاشقىرى | (tashqiri) | besides |
| پش۔ | (pish-) | cook | تاغ | (tagh) | mountain |
| پششق | (pishshiq) | ripe | تاغا | (tagha) | uncle |
| پشلاق | (pishlaq) | cheese | تاقىر | (taqir) | bald |
| پشۇر۔ | (pishur-) | cook | تاڭ | (tang) | dawn |
| پكىر | (pikir) | opinion, suggestion | تالاش۔تارتش | (talash-tartish) | argument |
| پل | (pil) | elephant | تالاش۔تارتش قل۔ | (talash-tartish qil-) | argue |
| پلىموت | (pilimot) | machine gun | | | |
| پىۋا | (piva) | beer | تاللا۔ | (talla-) | choose, select |
| پىياده ماڭغۇچى | (piyadä mangghuchi) | pedestrian | تالون | (talon) | receipt |
| پىيادىلەر ئۆتش يولى | (piyadilär ötish yoli) | crosswalk | تام | (tam) | wall |
| | | | تام سائتى | (tam sa'iti) | clock |
| پىيادىلەر يولى | (piyadilär yoli) | sidewalk | تاماق تزملكى | (tamaq tizimliki) | menu |
| پىياز | (piyaz) | onion | تاماق يەيدىغان ئۆي | (tamaq yeyidighan öy) | dining room |
| پىيالە | (piyalä) | cup | | | |
| | | | تاماكا | (tamaka) | cigarette, tobacco |
| ۔تا، ۔تە | (-ta, -tä) | at, in | تاماكا چەك۔ | (tamaka chäk-) | smoke |
| تائام | (ta'am) | dish | | | |
| تابلىتكا | (tabletka) | pill | تامچە | (tamchä) | drop |
| تاپ۔ | (tap-) | find | تاموژنا | (tamozhna) | customs |
| تاپشۇرۇق | (tapshuruq) | assignment | تاۋا | (tava) | pan |
| تاتلق | (tatliq) | sweet | تاۋۇز | (tavuz) | watermelon |
| تاتلق يەمەكلك | (tatliq yemäklik) | dessert | تاۋۇش | (tavush) | sound |
| تار | (tar) | narrow | تەبرىك | (täbrik) | congratulation |
| تارا۔ | (tara-) | comb | تەبرىكلە۔ | (täbriklä-) | celebrate, congratulate |
| تارازا | (taraza) | scale | تەبىئەت | (täbi'ät) | nature |
| تارت۔ | (tart-) | grind, pull | تەبىئىي | (täbi'iy) | natural |
| تارغاق | (targhaq) | comb | تەپ۔ | (täp-) | kick |
| تارىخ | (tarikh) | history | تەتقىقات | (tätqiqat) | research |
| تارىخشۇناس | (tarikhshunas) | historian | تەتىل | (tätil) | holiday |
| تازا | (taza) | clean | تەجرىبە | (täjribä) | experience |
| تازىلا۔ | (tazila-) | clean | تەخسە | (täkhsä) | dish, plate, saucer |
| تاسادىپىي | (tasadipiy) | sudden | | | |
| تاش | (tash) | rock, stone | تەخمىن قل۔ | (täkhmin qil-) | guess |

| | | | | | |
|---|---|---|---|---|---|
| تەخمىنەن | (täkhminän) | about | تەييارلا_ | (täyyarla-) | prepare |
| تەدبىر | (tädbir) | precaution | ترامۋاي | (tramvay) | tram |
| تەرەپ | (täräp) | side, way | توپ | (top) | ball |
| تەرەپكە | (täräpkä) | towards | توپا | (topa) | soil |
| تەرجىمە | (tärjimä) | translation | توختا_ | (tokhta-) | stop |
| تەرجىمە قىل_ | (tärjimä qil-) | translate | توختات_ | (tokhtat-) | stop |
| تەرخەمەك | (tärkhämäk) | cucumber | توخۇ گۆشى | (tokhu göshi) | chicken |
| تەرلە_ | (tärlä-) | sweat | تورت | (tort) | cake |
| تەرىپىدىن | (täripidin) | by | تورۇس | (torus) | ceiling |
| تەس | (täs) | difficult, hard | توسما | (tosma) | dam |
| تەسلىم بولۇش | (täslim bolush) | surrender | توشقان | (toshqan) | rabbit |
| | | | توشۇ_ | (toshu-) | carry |
| تەسۋىر | (täsvir) | description | توغرا | (toghra) | correct |
| تەسۋىرلە_ | (täsvirlä-) | describe | توغرىلا_ | (toghrila-) | correct |
| تەسىر | (täsir) | effect, influence | توق سېرىق | (toq seriq) | orange |
| تەشۋىقات | (täshviqat) | propaganda | توقسان | (toqsan) | ninety |
| تەقدىر | (täqdir) | fate | توققۇز | (toqquz) | nine |
| تەقدىم قىل_ | (täqdim qil-) | offer, present | تونگلا_ | (tongla-) | freeze |
| تەقسىم قىل_ | (täqsim qil-) | distribute | تولدۇر_ | (toldur-) | fill |
| تەكرارلا_ | (täkrarla-) | repeat | تولدۇرغۇچى | (toldurghuchi) | object |
| تەكشۈرۈش | (täkshürüsh) | censorship, investigation | تولۇق | (toluq) | complete, full |
| تەكلىپ | (täklip) | invitation | تونۇ_ | (tonu-) | know, recognize |
| تەكلىپ قىل_ | (täklip qil-) | invite | تونۇشتۇر_ | (tonushtur-) | introduce, recommend |
| تەگ_ | (täg-) | touch | توي قىل_ | (toy qil-) | marry |
| تەڭ | (täng) | equal | تۇپراق | (tupraq) | earth |
| تەڭرى | (tängri) | God | تۇت | (tut) | mulberry |
| تەڭگە | (tänggä) | coin | تۇت_ | (tut-) | catch, hold |
| تەلۋە | (tälvä) | crazy | تۇخۇم | (tukhum) | egg |
| تەلىم-تەربىيە | (tälim-tärbiyä) | education | تۇر_ | (tur-) | get up, stand |
| تەملىك | (tämlik) | delicious, tasty | تۇرخۇن | (turkhun) | chimney |
| تەنتەنە | (täntänä) | ceremony | تۇز | (tuz) | salt |
| تەنھەرىكەت | (tänhärikät) | sport | تۇغقان | (tughqan) | relative |
| تەيىنلەش | (täyinläsh) | appointment | تۇغۇت | (tughut) | birth |
| تەييار | (täyyar) | ready | تۇغۇل_ | (tughul-) | born: be born |

| | | | | | |
|---|---|---|---|---|---|
| توغۇلغان كۈن | (tughulghan kün) | birthday | تېلېفون | (telefon) | telephone |
| تۇمان | (tuman) | fog | تېلېفون بوتكىسى | (telefon botkisi) | phone booth |
| تۇمشۇق | (tumshuq) | beak | تېلېفون نومۇرى | (telefon nomuri) | phone number |
| تۇيغۇ | (tuyghu) | feeling | تېلېگرامما | (telegramma) | telegram |
| تۆت | (töt) | four | تېلېۋىزور | (televizor) | television |
| تۆشۈك | (töshük) | hole | تېمپېراتۇرا | (temperatura) | temperature |
| تۆگە | (tögä) | camel | تېيىز | (teyiz) | shallow |
| تۆلە- | (tölä-) | pay | تېيىل- | (teyil-) | slide, slip |
| تۆمۈر | (tömür) | iron | تېيىلغاق | (teyilghaq) | slippery |
| تۆمۈريول | (tömüryol) | railroad | تىترە- | (titrä-) | tremble |
| تۆۋەن | (tövän) | down | تىراژ | (tirazh) | circulation |
| تۆۋەندە | (tövändä) | below | تىرناق | (tirnaq) | nail |
| تۈرمە | (türmä) | jail, prison | تىرىش- | (tirish-) | try |
| تۈز | (tüz) | straight | تىرىشچان | (tirishchan) | diligent |
| تۈزه ت- | (tüzät-) | mend, repair | تىرىشىش | (tirishish) | attempt |
| تۈزلەڭلىك | (tüzlänglik) | plain | تىرىك | (tirik) | alive |
| تۈكۈر- | (tükür-) | spit | تىز | (tiz) | knee |
| تۈگمە | (tügmä) | button | تىزىملاشتۇرۇش | (tizimlashturush) | registration |
| تۈگمەن | (tügmän) | mill | تىك ئۇچار ئايروپىلان | (tik uchar ayropilan) | helicopter |
| تۈگۈن | (tügün) | knot | | | |
| تۈلكە | (tülkä) | fox | تىك- | (tik-) | plant, sew |
| تۈن | (tün) | night | تىل | (til) | language, tongue |
| تۈن يېرىمى | (tün yerimi) | midnight | | | |
| تۈنۈگۈن | (tünügün) | yesterday | تىلە- | (tilä-) | wish |
| تېتى- | (teti-) | taste | تىلشۇناس | (tilshunas) | linguist |
| تېخى | (tekhi) | still, yet | تىلشۇناسلىق | (tilshunasliq) | linguistics |
| تېرە | (terä) | fur, skin | تىمساھ | (timsah) | crocodile |
| تېرەك | (teräk) | poplar | -تىن | (-tin) | from |
| تېرمومېتر | (termometr) | thermometer | تىنچ | (tinch) | calm, quiet |
| تېرى- | (teri-) | sow | تىنچلىق | (tinchliq) | peace |
| تېرىقچىلىق | (teriqchiliq) | cultivation | تىنچى- | (tinchi-) | quiet: be quiet |
| تېز | (tez) | fast, quick, speedy | تىياتىرخانا | (tiyatirkhana) | theater |
| تېزلىك | (tezlik) | speed | تىيىن | (tiyin) | squirrel |
| تېگىدە | (tegidä) | under, underneath | جاراھەت | (jarahät) | wound |
| تېڭىق | (tengiq) | bandage | | | |

| | | |
|---|---|---|
| جازا | (jaza) | punishment, shelf |
| جازالا_ | (jazala-) | punish |
| جاسارەت | (jasarät) | courage |
| جاۋاب | (javab) | answer, reply |
| جاۋاب بەر_ | (javab bär-) | answer, reply |
| جاي | (jay) | place |
| جايلاش_ | (jaylash-) | situated: be situated |
| جەسۇر | (jäsur) | brave, courageous |
| جەڭ | (jäng) | battle |
| جەلپ | (jälp) | attraction |
| جەمئىيەت | (jäm'iyät) | society |
| جەننەت | (jännät) | paradise |
| جەنۇب | (jänub) | south |
| جەينەك | (jäynäk) | elbow |
| جوزا | (joza) | table |
| جۇغراپىيە | (jughrapiyä) | geography |
| جۇمھۇرىيەت | (jumhuriyät) | republic |
| جۈپ | (jüp) | pair |
| جۈزە | (jüzä) | orange |
| جۈمە | (jümä) | Friday |
| جۈمەك | (jümäk) | faucet |
| جۈملە | (jümlä) | sentence |
| جىددىي | (jiddiy) | serious |
| جىگەر | (jigär) | liver |
| جىمجىتلىق | (jimjitliq) | silence |
| جىن | (jin) | ghost |
| جىنايەت | (jinayät) | crime |
| جىنايەتچى | (jinayätchi) | criminal |
| چاپان | (chapan) | jacket |
| چاپلاش_ | (chaplash-) | stick |
| چاچ | (chach) | hair |
| چاچ_ | (chach-) | scatter |
| چارشەنبە | (charshänbä) | Wednesday |
| چاسا | (chasa) | square |
| چاشقان | (chashqan) | mouse |
| چاق | (chaq) | tire, wheel |
| چاقچاق | (chaqchaq) | joke |
| چاقماق | (chaqmaq) | lightning |
| چاقىر_ | (chaqir-) | call, summon |
| چاڭ توزان | (chang-tozan) | dust |
| چاڭغا تېيىلىش | (changgha teyilish) | skiing |
| چال_ | (chal-) | play |
| چالغۇ ئەسۋابلىرى | (chalghu äsvabliri) | instrument |
| چامادان | (chamadan) | suitcase |
| چانا | (chana) | sled |
| چاۋاق چال_ | (chavaq chal-) | clap |
| چاي | (chay) | tea |
| چاي پۇلى | (chay puli) | tip |
| چاينا_ | (chayna-) | chew |
| چەت | (chät) | edge |
| چەت ئەللىك | (chät ällik) | foreigner |
| چەك | (chäk) | check |
| چەكلە_ | (chäklä-) | restrict |
| چەيزە | (chäyzä) | eggplant |
| چەينەك | (chäynäk) | teapot |
| چوتكا | (chotka) | brush |
| چوشقا | (choshqa) | pig |
| چوشقا گۆشى | (choshqa göshi) | pork |
| چوڭ | (chong) | big |
| چوڭ كوچا | (chong kocha) | avenue |
| چوڭقۇر | (chongqur) | deep |
| چوڭقۇرلۇق | (chongqurluq) | depth |
| چۆچەك | (chöchäk) | folktale |
| چۆك_ | (chök-) | drown, sink |
| چۆل_باياۋان | (chöl-bayavan) | desert |
| چۈچۈك | (chüchük) | sour |

| چۈش | (chüsh) | dream, noon | خاپا | (khapa) | angry |
|---|---|---|---|---|---|
| چۈش | (chüsh-) | fall, get off | خاتا | (khata) | wrong |
| چۈشەن | (chüshän-) | understand | خاتالىق | (khataliq) | mistake |
| چۈشەندۈر | (chüshändür-) | explain | خاتىره مۇنارىسى | (khatirä munarisi) | monument |
| چۈشتىن كېيىن | (chüshtin keyin) | afternoon | خالا | (khala-) | want |
| چۈشلۈك تاماق | (chüshlük tamaq) | lunch | خالتا | (khalta) | bag |
| چۈمۈله | (chümülä) | ant | خام | (kham) | raw |
| چۈنكى | (chünki) | because | خانىم | (khanim) | lady |
| چېركاۋ | (cherkav) | church | خەت | (khät) | letter |
| چېكەتكە | (chekätkä) | grasshopper | خەت بېسىش ماشنىسى | (khät besish mashinisi) | typewriter |
| چېكىت | (chekit) | period | خەتەر | (khätär) | danger |
| چېگرا | (chegra) | border | خەتەرلىك | (khätärlik) | dangerous |
| چېلەك | (cheläk) | bucket | خەجلە | (khäjlä-) | spend |
| چېلىش | (chelish) | wrestling | خەرىتە | (khäritä) | map |
| چىت | (chit) | fence | خەلق | (khälq) | people |
| چىراغ | (chiragh) | lamp | خەلقئارا | (khälq'ara) | international |
| چىراي | (chiray) | face | خەنجەر | (khänjär) | dagger |
| چىرايلىق | (chirayliq) | beautiful, pretty | خەۋەر | (khävär) | news |
| چىرقىرا | (chirqira-) | scream | خەير—خوش | (khäyr-khosh) | bye-bye |
| چىرى | (chiri-) | rot | خرىستىئان | (khristi'an) | Christian |
| چىرىكلىشىش | (chiriklishish) | corruption | خوپ | (khop) | OK |
| چىش | (chish) | tooth | خوتۇن | (khotun) | woman |
| چىش ئاغرىغى | (chish aghriqi) | toothache | خوراز | (khoraz) | rooster |
| چىش پاستىسى | (chish pastisi) | toothpaste | خورما | (khorma) | date |
| چىش چوتكىسى | (chish chotkisi) | toothbrush | خۇددى | (khuddi) | as if |
| چىش دوختۇرى | (chish dokhturi) | dentist | خۇسۇسەن | (khususän) | especially |
| چىشلە | (chishlä-) | bite | خۇش كەپسىز | (khush käpsiz) | welcome |
| چىق | (chiq-) | exit, get on | خۇشال | (khushal) | glad |
| چىقىش | (chiqish) | exit | خۇشاللىق | (khushalliq) | joy |
| چىڭ | (ching) | tight | خېرىدار | (kheridar) | buyer, customer |
| چىڭسەي | (chingsäy) | celery | خىراجەت | (khirajät) | expense |
| چىۋىن | (chivin) | fly | خىزمەتچى | (khizmätchi) | official, servant |
| | | | خىش | (khish) | brick |

| خىل | (khil) | kind |
| ـدا، ـده | (-da, -dä) | at, in |
| دادا | (dada) | father |
| داستان | (dastan) | epic |
| داستىخان | (dastikhan) | tablecloth |
| دان | (dan) | grain |
| داۋالا_ | (davala-) | cure |
| داۋالاش | (davalash) | cure |
| داۋام قىل_ | (davam qil-) | continue |
| دائىره | (da'irä) | circle |
| ـده | (dä-) | say |
| دەپ | (däp) | that |
| دەپتەر | (däptär) | notebook |
| دەرەخ | (däräkh) | tree |
| دەرەخلىك | (däräkhlik) | wood |
| دەرس | (därs) | lesson |
| دەرھال | (därhal) | immediately |
| دەرۋازا | (därvaza) | gate |
| دەريا | (därya) | river |
| دەزمال | (däzmal) | iron |
| دەستارگۈل | (dästargül) | daisy |
| دەلىل | (dälil) | proof |
| دەم | (däm) | moment |
| دەم ئېلىش | (däm elish) | rest, vacation |
| دەۋر | (dävr) | era |
| دراما | (drama) | drama |
| دراما يازغۇچىسى | (drama yazghuchisi) | playwright |
| دوختۇر | (dokhtur) | doctor |
| دوختۇرخانا | (dokhturkhana) | clinic, hospital |
| دوختۇرلۇق | (dokhturluq) | medicine |
| دورا | (dora) | drug, medicine |
| دورا ئۆسۈملۈكلەر | (dora ösümlüklär) | herb |
| دورىخانا | (dorikhana) | pharmacy |
| دورىگەر | (dorigär) | pharmacist |
| دوزاخ | (dozakh) | hell |
| دوژنا | (dozhna) | dozen |
| دوست | (dost) | friend |
| دوستلۇق | (dostluq) | friendship |
| دولقۇن | (dolqun) | wave |
| دومىلا ت_ | (domilat-) | roll |
| دۇئا | (du'a) | prayer |
| دۇئا قىل_ | (du'a qil-) | pray |
| دۇب دەرىخى | (dub därikhi) | oak |
| دۇخوپكا | (dukhupka) | oven |
| دۇش | (dush) | shower |
| دۇكان | (dukan) | shop |
| دۇنيا | (dunya) | world |
| دۆت | (döt) | stupid |
| دۆڭ | (döng) | hill |
| دۆلەت | (dölät) | state |
| دۈشەنبە | (düshänbä) | Monday |
| دۈشمەن | (düshmän) | enemy |
| دۈشمەنلىك | (düshmänlik) | enmity |
| دۈگىلەك | (dügiläk) | round |
| دۈمبە | (dümbä) | back |
| دېرىزە | (derizä) | window |
| دېكابر | (dekabr) | December |
| دېڭىز | (dengiz) | sea |
| دېڭىز بويى | (dengiz boyi) | beach |
| دېڭىز قولتۇقى | (dengiz qoltuqi) | bay |
| دېڭىز قىرغىقى | (dengiz qirghiqi) | coast |
| دېموكراتىيە | (demokratiyä) | democracy |
| دېھقان | (dehqan) | peasant |
| دېھقانچىلىق مەيدانى | (dehqanchiliq mäydani) | farm |
| دېيەرلىك | (deyärlik) | almost |
| دىپلوم | (diplom) | diploma |
| دىققەت | (diqqät) | attention |

| | | |
|---|---|---|
| ــدىن | (-din) | from |
| دىن | (din) | religion |
| دىنى | (diniy) | religious |
| دىۋە | (divä) | giant |
| رادىئو | (radi'o) | radio |
| راست | (rast) | real |
| راك | (rak) | cancer |
| رامكا | (ramka) | frame |
| راھەتلىك | (rahätlik) | comfortable |
| راۋاجلىنىش | (ravajlinish) | development |
| رەسسام | (rässam) | artist |
| رەسمى | (räsmiy) | official |
| رەسىم | (räsim) | drawing, painting, picture |
| رەسىملىك لېنتا | (räsimlik lenta) | video |
| رەڭ | (räng) | color |
| رەنجىگەن | (ränjigän) | sorry |
| رەھمەت ئېيت- | (rähmät eyt-) | thank |
| رەھىمسىز | (rähimsiz) | cruel |
| رەۋىش | (rävish) | adverb |
| روزا | (roza) | fast |
| رومان | (roman) | novel |
| روھ | (roh) | spirit |
| رۇخسەت بەر- | (rukhsät bär-) | permit |
| رېئالىزم | (re'alizm) | realism |
| رېتسېپ | (retsep) | prescription |
| رېستوران | (restoran) | restaurant |
| رىقابەت | (riqabät) | competition |
| رىۋايەت | (rivayät) | legend |
| زاۋۇت | (zavut) | factory |
| زەرەر | (zärär) | harm |
| زەرگەر | (zärgär) | jeweler |
| زەمبىرەك | (zämbiräk) | artillery, cannon |
| زەھەر | (zähär) | poison |
| زەھەرلىك | (zähärlik) | poisonous |
| زەيتۇن | (zäytun) | olive |
| زور | (zor) | large |
| زور ئەسەر | (zor äsär) | masterpiece |
| زۇكام | (zukam) | cold |
| زۇلۇم | (zulum) | oppression |
| زۆرۈر | (zörür) | necessary |
| زېرىك- | (zerik-) | bored: be bored |
| زېرىكەرلىك | (zerikärlik) | boring |
| زىياپەت | (ziyapät) | banquet |
| زىيارەت | (ziyarät) | visit |
| زىيارەت قىل- | (ziyarät qil-) | visit |
| زىيالى | (ziyaliy) | intellectual |
| زىيان | (ziyan) | damage, loss |
| زىيانلىق | (ziyanliq) | harmful |
| ژۇرنال | (zhurnal) | magazine |
| سائەت | (sa'ät) | hour |
| سائەتچى | (saätchi) | watchmaker |
| ساپ | (sap) | handle, pure |
| سات- | (sat-) | sell |
| ساتقۇچى | (satquchi) | salesperson, seller |
| ساتىراش | (satirash) | hairdresser |
| ساختا | (sakhta) | false |
| سارغلىق | (sarangliq) | insanity |
| ساراي | (saray) | palace |
| سازلىق | (sazliq) | swamp |
| ساغلام | (saghlam) | healthy |
| ساقال | (saqal) | beard |
| ساقچى | (saqchi) | policeman |
| ساقلا- | (saqla-) | keep |
| ساقلاپ قويۇش | (saqlap qoyush) | reservation |
| سالاد | (salad) | salad |

| Uighur | Transcription | English |
|--------|--------------|---------|
| سالام بەر_ | (salam ber-) | greet |
| سالامەتلىك | (salamätlik) | health |
| سالقىن | (salqin) | cool |
| سامان | (saman) | straw |
| سامساق | (samsaq) | garlic |
| سان | (san) | number |
| سانا_ | (sana-) | count |
| ساۋاتلىق | (savatliq) | literate |
| ساياهەت | (sayahät) | travel |
| ساياهەتچى | (sayahätchi) | tourist |
| ساياهەتچىلىك | (sayahätchilik) | tourism |
| سايە | (sayä) | shade, shadow |
| سايلا_ | (sayla-) | elect |
| سايلام | (saylam) | election |
| سەپەر | (säpär) | journey |
| سەت | (sät) | ugly |
| سەرەڭگە | (säränggä) | match |
| سەرلەۋھە | (särlävhä) | title |
| سەكرە_ | (säkrä-) | jump |
| سەكسەن | (säksän) | eighty |
| سەككىز | (säkkiz) | eight |
| سەل | (säl) | flood |
| سەمىمى | (sämimiy) | honest |
| سەن | (sän) | you |
| سەنئەت | (sän'ät) | art |
| سەھرا | (sähra) | countryside |
| سەھنە | (sähnä) | stage |
| سەھنە ئەسىرى | (sähnä äsiri) | play |
| سەۋەب | (säväb) | cause, reason |
| سەۋرچان | (sävrchan) | patient |
| سەۋىيە | (säviyä) | level |
| سەۋزە | (sävzä) | carrot |
| سەيپۇڭ | (säypung) | tailor |
| سەيشەنبە | (säyshänbä) | Tuesday |
| سەييارە | (säyyarä) | planet |
| سوئال | (so'al) | question |
| سوپۇن | (sopun) | soap |
| سوت مەھكىمىسى | (sot mähkimisi) | court |
| سوتچى | (sotchi) | judge |
| سودا | (soda) | business |
| سودا ساراي | (soda saray) | department store |
| سودىگەر | (sodigär) | businessman |
| سورا_ | (sora-) | ask |
| سوزۇق تاۋۇش | (sozuq tavush) | vowel |
| سوزۇل_ | (sozul-) | reach |
| سوغۇق | (soghuq) | cold |
| سوقا | (soqa) | plow |
| سوقۇش_ | (soqush-) | fight |
| سول | (sol) | left |
| سۇ | (su) | water |
| سۇ ئاستى كېمىسى | (su asti kemisi) | submarine |
| سۇ ئۈز_ | (su üz-) | swim |
| سۇ ئۈزۈش كۆلى | (su üzüsh köli) | pool |
| سۇغۇرتا | (sughurta) | insurance |
| سۇندۇر_ | (sundur-) | break |
| سۇنۇق | (sunuq) | broken |
| سۇيۇقلۇق | (suyuqluq) | liquid |
| سۆز | (söz) | word |
| سۆزلە_ | (sözlä-) | speak, talk |
| سۆسۈن | (sösün) | purple |
| سۆگەت | (sögät) | willow |
| سۆڭەك | (söngäk) | bone |
| سۆي_ | (söy-) | kiss, love |
| سۈپەت | (süpät) | adjective, quality |
| سۈپۈر_ | (süpür-) | sweep |
| سۈپۈرگە | (süpürgä) | broom |
| سۈت | (süt) | milk |
| سۈر_ | (sür-) | rub |
| سۈرگە | (sürgä) | laxative |

| | | | | | |
|---|---|---|---|---|---|
| سۈزگۈچ | (süzgüch) | strainer | سىيا | (siya) | ink |
| سۈنئى | (sün'iy) | artificial | سىياست | (siyasät) | politics |
| سبتش | (setish) | sale | شاپتۇل | (shaptul) | peach |
| سبتـۋال_ | (setival-) | buy, shop | شاخ | (shakh) | branch |
| سبخي | (sekhiy) | generous | شارپا | (sharpa) | scarf |
| سبرك | (serk) | circus | شام | (sham) | candle |
| سبرق | (seriq) | yellow | شامال | (shamal) | wind |
| سبرق ماي | (seriq may) | butter | شاهمات | (shahmat) | chess |
| سبسترا | (sestra) | nurse | شائىر | (sha'ir) | poet |
| سبغىز لاي | (seghiz lay) | clay | شەخس | (shäkhs) | person |
| سبكۇنت | (sekunt) | second | شەرەپ | (shäräp) | honor |
| سبلىشتۇرۇش | (selishturush) | comparison | شەرت | (shärt) | condition |
| سبمونت | (semont) | cement | شەرق | (shärq) | east |
| سبمىز | (semiz) | fat | شەكىل | (shäkil) | shape |
| سبنىڭ | (sening) | your | شەنبە | (shänbä) | Saturday |
| سبنىڭكى | (seningki) | yours | شەهەر | (shähär) | city |
| سبنتەبر | (sentäbr) | September | شەهەر ئەتراپى | (shähär ätrapi) | suburb |
| سبهىر | (sehir) | magic | شەهەر باشلىقى | (shähär bashliqi) | mayor |
| سبۋەت | (sevät) | basket | شەهەرچە | (shähärchä) | town |
| سىرتىدا | (sirtida) | outside | شەهەرلىك هۆكۈمەت | (shähärlik hökümät) | municipality |
| سىرچى | (sirchi) | painter | | | |
| سىرلا_ | (sirla-) | paint | شەيتان | (shäytan) | demon, Satan |
| سىز | (siz) | you | شوپۇر | (shopur) | driver |
| سىزغۇچ | (sizghuch) | ruler | شوتا | (shota) | ladder |
| سىزنىڭ | (sizning) | your | شورپا | (shorpa) | soup |
| سىزنىڭكى | (sizningki) | yours | شۇ چاغدا | (shu chaghda) | then |
| سىزىق | (siziq) | line | شۇڭغۇ_ | (shungghu-) | dive |
| سىق_ | (siq-) | press | شۇنداق | (shundaq) | such |
| سىڭگىل | (singil) | sister | شۇنىڭ ئۈچۈن | (shuning üchün) | therefore |
| سىلا_ | (sila-) | stroke | شېرىك | (sherik) | partner |
| سىلەر | (silär) | you | شېرىن ئاي | (sherin ay) | honeymoon |
| سىم | (sim) | wire | شېئىر | (she'ir) | poem, poetry |
| سىمۋول | (simvol) | symbol | شىر | (shir) | lion |
| سىنا_ | (sina-) | test | | | |
| سىنىپ | (sinip) | classroom | | | |
| سىي_ | (siy-) | urinate | | | |

| | | | | | |
|---|---|---|---|---|---|
| شـركـت | (shirkät) | company, firm | قاچا يۇيۇش ماشىنسى | (qacha yuyush mashinisi) | dishwasher |
| شـرنه | (shirnä) | fruit juice | قاچان | (qachan) | when |
| شكايـت | (shikayät) | complaint | قار | (qar) | snow |
| شكايـت قىلـ | (shikayät qil-) | complain | قارا | (qara) | black |
| شـم | (shim) | pants | قارا_ | (qara-) | look |
| شمال | (shimal) | north | قارا مال | (qara mal) | cattle |
| | | | قارار | (qarar) | decision |
| ـغا، ـگه | (-gha, -gä) | to | قارار قىلـ | (qarar qil-) | decide |
| غاز | (ghaz) | goose | قاراڭغۇ | (qarangghu) | dark |
| غـهرب | (ghärb) | west | قاراڭغۇلۇق | (qarangghuluq) | darkness |
| غـهزهپ | (ghäzäp) | anger | قارتا | (qarta) | playing card |
| غـهلبه | (ghälibä) | victory | قارشى | (qarshi) | against |
| غـهلتـه | (ghälitä) | strange | قارلىغاچ | (qarlighach) | swallow |
| غهم قىلـ | (ghäm qil-) | worry | قارغاي | (qarighay) | pine |
| ـغىچه | (-ghichä) | until | قارغۇ | (qarighu) | blind |
| | | | قارغۇلۇق | (qarighuluq) | blindness |
| فامىله | (familä) | surname | قارمۇ قارشى | (qarimu qarshi) | opposite |
| فوتو | (foto) | photo | | | |
| فوتو ئاپپارات | (foto apparat) | camera | قارمۇچ | (qarimuch) | pepper |
| فولكلور | (folklor) | folklore | قاز_ | (qaz-) | dig |
| فونتان | (fontan) | fountain | قازا | (qaza) | accident |
| فېۋرال | (fevral) | February | قازان | (qazan) | saucepan |
| فىزىكا | (fizika) | physics | قاسساپ | (qassap) | butcher |
| | | | قاش | (qash) | eyebrow |
| ـقا، ـقه | (-qa, -qä) | to | قاغا | (qagha) | crow |
| قاپقاق | (qapqaq) | lid | قالـ | (qal-) | remain, stay |
| قاتار | (qatar) | row | قالايمىقان | (qalaymiqan) | messy |
| قاتتـق | (qattiq) | hard, loud | قان | (qan) | blood |
| قاتلا_ | (qatla-) | fold | قان بېسىمى | (qan besimi) | blood pressure |
| قاتناش | (qatnash) | communication, traffic | قانا_ | (qana-) | bleed |
| قاتناش چىرىقى | (qatnash chiriqi) | traffic light | قانات | (qanat) | wing |
| قاچ_ | (qach-) | escape, flee, run away | قانال | (qanal) | canal, channel |
| قاچا | (qacha) | bowl | قانچه | (qanchä) | how much |
| | | | قانداق | (qandaq) | how |
| | | | قانۇن | (qanun) | law |

| | | | | | |
|---|---|---|---|---|---|
| قايت ــ | (qayt-) | return | توشۇق | (qoshuq) | spoon |
| قايچا | (qaycha) | scissors | توشۇلـ | (qoshul-) | agree |
| قايسى | (qaysi) | which | توشۇمچ | (qoshumchä) | suffix |
| قايغۇلۇق | (qayghuluq) | sad | توغداـ | (qoghda-) | protect |
| قايماق | (qaymaq) | cream | توغلاـ | (qoghla-) | chase |
| قاينا ـ | (qayna-) | boil | قوغۇشۇن | (qoghushun) | lead |
| قايىل بول ـ | (qayil bol-) | admire | قوغۇن | (qoghun) | melon |
| قەدەم | (qädäm) | step | توڭغۇراق | (qongghuraq) | bell |
| قەدىر | (qädir) | value | توڭۇر | (qongur) | brown |
| قەدىرلىك | (qädirlik) | dear | قول | (qol) | hand |
| قەرز | (qärz) | debt, loan | قول سائىتى | (qol sa'iti) | watch |
| قەسەم قىلـ | (qäsäm qil-) | swear | قول سومكىسى | (qol somkisi) | handbag |
| قەغەز | (qäghäz) | form, paper | قول قوي ـ | (qol qoy-) | sign |
| قەلەم | (qäläm) | pen | قول ياغلىق | (qol yaghliq) | handkerchief |
| قەلەمپۇر | (qälämpur) | carnation | قوناق | (qonaq) | corn |
| قەنت | (qänt) | sugar | قوۋزاق | (qovzaq) | bark |
| قەھۋە | (qähvä) | coffee | قوي | (qoy) | sheep |
| قەھۋەخانا | (qähväkhana) | café | قوي ـ | (qoy-) | put |
| قەۋەت | (qävät) | storey | قوي گۆشى | (qoy göshi) | mutton |
| قەيەردە | (qäyärdä) | where | قويۇق | (qoyuq) | thick |
| قەيەرگە | (qäyärgä) | where | قۇتا | (quta) | box |
| قوبۇل قىلـ | (qobul qil-) | accept | قۇتقۇز ـ | (qutquz-) | rescue |
| قوپال | (qopal) | rude | قۇتقۇزۇش ماشىنىسى | (qutquzush mashinisi) | ambulance |
| قورال | (qoral) | gun, weapon | | | |
| قورال سايمان | (qoral-sayman) | equipment | قۇتلۇقلاش | (qutluqlash) | celebration |
| قورساق | (qorsaq) | belly | قۇچاقلا ـ | (quchaqla-) | embrace |
| قورشاـ | (qorsha-) | surround | قۇر ـ | (qur-) | build |
| قورق ـ | (qorq-) | afraid: be afraid | قۇربان | (qurban) | sacrifice |
| | | | قۇرت | (qurt) | worm |
| قورقاق | (qorqqaq) | coward | قۇرت ـ قوڭغۇز | (qurt-qongghuz) | insect |
| قورقاقلىق | (qorqqaqliq) | cowardice | | | |
| قوش ـ | (qosh-) | add | قۇرغاقچىلىق | (qurghaqchiliq) | drought |
| قوشقان سەرمايە | (qoshqan särmayä) | investment | قۇرۇ ـ | (quru-) | dry |
| | | | قۇرۇق | (quruq) | dry |
| قوشكېزەك | (qoshkezäk) | twin | قۇس ـ | (qus-) | vomit |
| قوشنا | (qoshna) | neighbor | قۇش | (qush) | bird |
| قوشۇش | (qoshush) | addition | قۇشقاچ | (qushqach) | sparrow |

| | | | | | |
|---|---|---|---|---|---|
| قۇلاق | (qulaq) | ear | كاشتان | (kashtan) | chestnut |
| قۇلۇپ | (qulup) | lock | كالا | (kala) | cow, ox |
| قۇم | (qum) | sand | كالا گۆشى | (kala göshi) | beef |
| قۇي_ | (quy-) | pour | كالپۇك | (kalpuk) | lip |
| قۇيرۇق | (quyruq) | tail | كالتە شىم | (kaltä shim) | shorts |
| قېتىق | (qetiq) | yogurt | كاللەكبەسەي | (kalläkbäsäy) | cabbage |
| قېرى | (qeri) | old | كالېندار | (kalendar) | calendar |
| قېرىنداش | (qerindash) | pencil | كاۋاپ قىل_ | (kavap qil-) | roast |
| قېلىن | (qelin) | thick | كەپتەر | (käptär) | pigeon |
| قېيىق | (qeyiq) | boat | كەت_ | (kät-) | leave |
| _قىچە | (-qichä) | until | كەچ | (käch) | late |
| قىچا | (qicha) | mustard | كەچكى تاماق | (kächki tamaq) | dinner |
| قىچقار_ | (qichqar-) | shout | كەچۈر_ | (kächür-) | forgive |
| قىر_ | (qir-) | scrape | كەچۈرۈم سورا_ | (kächürüm sora-) | apologize |
| قىراۋ | (qirav) | frost | كەس_ | (käs-) | cut |
| قىرىق | (qiriq) | forty | كەسىپ | (käsip) | occupation |
| قىز | (qiz) | daughter, girl | كەسىر | (käsir) | fraction |
| قىزىتما | (qizitma) | fever | كەش | (käsh) | slipper |
| قىزىق | (qiziq) | interesting | كەشپ قىل_ | (käshp qil-) | discover |
| قىزىقىش | (qiziqish) | interest | كەڭ | (käng) | broad, loose, spacious, wide |
| قىزىل | (qizil) | red | | | |
| قىسقا | (qisqa) | short | كەل_ | (käl-) | arrive, come |
| قىسىم | (qisim) | part, section | كەلگۈسى | (kälgüsi) | future |
| قىش | (qish) | winter | كەمبەغەل | (kämbäghäl) | poor |
| قىل_ | (qil-) | do | كەمپۈت | (kämpüt) | candy |
| قىلىچ | (qilich) | sword | كرېدىت | (kredit) | credit |
| قىممەت | (qimmät) | expensive | كوچا | (kocha) | street |
| قىممەتلىك | (qimmätlik) | valuable | كوزا | (koza) | jug, pitcher |
| | | | كولباسا | (kolbasa) | sausage |
| _ك، _كا | (-ka, -kä) | to | كومپوزىتور | (kompozitor) | composer |
| كاپىتان | (kapitan) | captain | كومېدىيە | (komediyä) | comedy |
| كاتتا | (katta) | great | كونا | (kona) | old |
| كاتىپ | (katip) | secretary | كونسېرت | (konsert) | concert |
| كارىۋات | (karivat) | bed | كونكرېت | (konkret) | concrete |
| كاستۇم | (kastum) | suit | كونۋېرت | (konvert) | envelope |
| كاسسىر | (kassir) | cashier | | | |

| كۆلۆب | (kulub) | club | كۆز | (küz) | autumn |
|---|---|---|---|---|---|
| كۆلۆچ | (kuluch) | wrench | كۆل | (kül) | ash |
| كۆپ | (köp) | many, much | كۆلـ | (kül-) | laugh |
| كۆپ سانلىق | (köp sanliq) | majority | كۆلرەڭ | (külräng) | grey |
| كۆپەيـ | (köpäy-) | increase | كۆلۆمسىرەـ | (külümsirä-) | smile |
| كۆپەيتىش | (köpäytish) | multiplication | كۆمۈش | (kümüsh) | silver |
| كۆپرەك | (köpräk) | more | كۈن | (kün) | day, sun |
| كۆتۈرـ | (kötür-) | lift, raise | كۈنپەتىش | (künpetish) | sunset |
| كۆرـ | (kör-) | see | كۈنچىقىش | (künchiqish) | sunrise |
| كۆرپە | (körpä) | cushion | كۈندۈز | (kündüz) | daytime |
| كۆرسەتـ | (körsät-) | show | كۈنلۈك | (künlük) | umbrella |
| كۆرگەزمە | (körgäzmä) | exhibition | كۈي | (küy) | tune |
| كۆز | (köz) | eye | كۈيوغۇل | (küyoghul) | bridegroom |
| كۆزەينەك | (közäynäk) | glasses | كېپىنەك | (kepinäk) | butterfly |
| كۆزەينەك ساتغۇچى | (közäynäk satghuchi) | optician | كېچىكتۈرـ | (kechiktür-) | postpone |
| | | | كېچىكىش | (kechikish) | delay |
| كۆك | (kök) | blue | كېرەك بولـ | (keräk bol-) | need |
| كۆكتات | (köktat) | vegetable | كېسەل | (kesäl) | ill, patient, sick |
| كۆكرەك | (kökräk) | chest | | | |
| كۆكس | (köks) | breast | كېسەللىك | (kesällik) | illness |
| كۆڭلەك | (köngläk) | blouse, shirt | كېلەر | (kelär) | next |
| كۆل | (köl) | lake | كېلىش | (kelish) | arrival |
| كۆمـ | (köm-) | bury | كېلىشكەن | (kelishkän) | handsome |
| كۆمۈر | (kömür) | coal | كېلىشىم | (kelishim) | agreement |
| كۆن | (kön) | leather | كېلىن | (kelin) | bride |
| كۆۋرۈك | (kövrük) | bridge | كېيىن | (keyin) | after |
| كۆيـ | (köy-) | burn | ـكىچە | (-kichä) | until |
| كۆيدۈرـ | (köydür-) | burn | كىتاب | (kitab) | book |
| كۈتـ | (küt-) | wait | كىتاب جازىسى | (kitab jazisi) | bookcase |
| كۈتكۈچى | (kütküchi) | waiter | كىتابپۇرۇش | (kitabpurush) | bookseller |
| كۈتۈپخانا | (kütüpkhana) | library | كىتابخان | (kitabkhan) | reader |
| كۈچ | (küch) | force, power, strength | كىتابخانا | (kitabkhana) | bookshop |
| | | | كىچىك | (kichik) | little, small |
| كۈچلۈك | (küchlük) | powerful, strong | كىچىك گىلەم | (kichik giläm) | rug |
| كۈرەك | (küräk) | shovel | كىرـ | (kir-) | enter |
| كۈركە | (kürkä) | turkey | كىرا ماشىنىسى | (kira mashinisi) | cab, taxi |

| | | | | | |
|---|---|---|---|---|---|
| كىرپىك | (kirpik) | eyelash | گىلاس | (gilas) | cherry |
| كىرلىك | (kirlik) | sheet | گىلەم | (giläm) | carpet |
| كىرىش | (kirish) | entrance | لالە | (lalä) | tulip |
| كىرىش سۆز | (kirish söz) | preface | لەززەت | (läzzät) | pleasure |
| كىرىم | (kirim) | income | لەيلەك | (läyläk) | stork |
| كىم | (kim) | who | لۇغەت | (lughät) | dictionary |
| كىنو | (kino) | movie | لۆڭگە | (lönggä) | towel |
| كىنوخانا | (kinokhana) | cinema | لېكسىيە | (leksiyä) | lecture |
| كىي | (kiy-) | put on, wear | لېنتا | (lenta) | film |
| كىيىم | (kiyim) | clothes | لىفت | (lift) | elevator |
| كىيىم ئاسقۇچ | (kiyim asquch) | hanger | لىڭشىت | (lingshit-) | shake |
| | | | لىمون | (limon) | lemon |
| گاچا | (gacha) | mute | مائاش | (ma'ash) | salary |
| گاراژ | (garazh) | garage | ماتراس | (matras) | mattress |
| گاز | (gaz) | gas | ماتور | (mator) | engine |
| گال | (gal) | throat | ماتېرىيال | (materiyal) | material |
| گالستۇك | (galstuk) | tie | ماتېماتىكا | (matematika) | mathematics |
| گەزمال | (gäzmal) | textile | ماختا | (makhta-) | praise |
| گرادۇس | (gradus) | degree | ماختان | (makhtan-) | boast |
| گراژدان | (grazhdan) | citizen | ماددا | (madda) | matter |
| گۇمان | (guman) | doubt | مارت | (mart) | March |
| گۇۋاھچى | (guvahchi) | witness | ماركا | (marka) | stamp |
| گۆش | (gösh) | meat | مارۇژنى | (marozhni) | ice cream |
| گۆش دۇكانى | (gösh dukani) | butcher shop | مازارلىق | (mazarliq) | cemetery |
| گۆشنان | (göshnan) | sandwich | ماشىنا | (mashina) | car, machine |
| گۈرجەك | (gürjäk) | spade | ماقال | (maqal) | proverb |
| گۈرۈچ | (gürüch) | rice | ماقالە | (maqalä) | article |
| گۈزەللىك | (güzällik) | beauty | ماقۇللاش | (maqullash) | approval |
| گۈگۈم | (gügüm) | dusk | ماگىزىن | (magizin) | store |
| گۈل | (gül) | flower | ماڭ | (mang-) | walk |
| گۈلدۈرماما | (güldürmama) | thunder | مال | (mal) | goods |
| گېزىت | (gezit) | newspaper | ماھارەت | (maharät) | skill |
| گېئولوگىيە | (ge'ologiyä) | geology | ماۋزۇ | (mavzu) | subject |
| گېئومېترىيە | (ge'ometriyä) | geometry | ماي | (may) | May |
| ـگىچە | (-gichä) | until | | | |

|  |  |  |
|---|---|---|
| مايلىق | (mayliq) | napkin |
| مايمۇن | (maymun) | monkey |
| مەتبەئە | (mätbä'ä) | printing press |
| مەتبۇئات | (mätbu'at) | press |
| مەخپىي | (mäkhpiy) | secret |
| مەدەنىيەت | (mädäniyät) | culture |
| مەركەز | (märkäz) | center |
| مەرھەمەت | (märhämät) | please |
| مەزھەپ | (mäzhäp) | sect |
| مەست | (mäst) | drunk |
| مەسچىت | (mäschit) | mosque |
| مەسىلە | (mäsilä) | problem |
| مەش | (mäsh) | stove |
| مەشھۇر | (mäshhur) | famous |
| مەغلۇبىيەت | (mäghlubiyät) | defeat |
| مەقسەت | (mäqsät) | purpose |
| مەكتەپ | (mäktäp) | school |
| مەڭز | (mängz) | cheek |
| مەڭگۈلۈك | (mänggülük) | eternity |
| مەلۇمات | (mälumat) | data, information |
| مەن | (män) | I |
| مەنئى قىل_ | (män'i qil-) | forbid |
| مەھەللە | (mähällä) | neighborhood |
| مەۋجۇدىيەت | (mävjudiyät) | existence |
| مەيدان | (mäydan) | square |
| موتسىكلىت | (motsiklit) | motorcycle |
| مودا | (moda) | fashion |
| موزاي گۆشى | (mozay göshi) | veal |
| موزدوز | (mozduz) | shoemaker |
| موگۇ | (mogu) | mushroom |
| موما | (moma) | grandmother |
| _مۇ | (-mu) | too, also |
| مۇخبىر | (mukhbir) | journalist |
| مۇختارىيەت | (mukhtariyät) | autonomy |
| مۇداپىئە | (mudapi'ä) | defense |
| مۇداپىئە قىل_ | (mudapi'ä qil-) | defend |
| مۇراببا | (murabba) | jam |
| مۇز | (muz) | ice |
| مۇزاكىرە | (muzakirä) | discussion |
| مۇزلاتقۇ | (muzlatqu) | refrigerator |
| مۇزېي | (muzey) | museum |
| مۇزىكا | (muzika) | composition, music |
| مۇزىكانت | (muzikant) | musician |
| مۇسابىقە | (musabiqä) | match, race |
| مۇستەقىللىك | (mustäqillik) | independence |
| مۇسكۇل | (muskul) | muscle |
| مۇسۇلمان | (musulman) | Muslim |
| مۇشۇ يەردە | (mushu yärdä) | here |
| مۇكاپات | (mukapat) | prize |
| مۇكەممەل | (mukämmäl) | perfect |
| مۇمكىن | (mumkin) | possible |
| مۇمكىن بولمىغان | (mumkin bolmighan) | impossible |
| مۇمكىنچىلىك | (mumkinchilik) | possibility |
| مۇنار | (munar) | tower |
| مۇنچا | (muncha) | bathroom |
| مۇھاسىرە | (muhasirä) | siege |
| مۇھەببەت | (muhäbbät) | love |
| مۇھىم | (muhim) | important |
| مۇۋەپپەقىيەت | (muväppäqiyät) | success |
| مۇۋەپپەقىيەت قازان_ | (muväppäqiyät qazan-) | succeed |
| مۆڭگۈز | (mönggüz) | horn |
| مۆلدۈر | (möldür) | hail |
| مۈرە | (mürä) | shoulder |
| مۈشۈك | (müshük) | cat |
| مۈشۈك ياپىلاق | (müshük yapilaq) | owl |
| مېتال | (metal) | metal |
| مېترو | (metro) | subway |
| مېكىيان | (mekiyan) | hen |

| مېڭ | (mengä) | brain | نەپەس | (näpäs) | breath |
|---|---|---|---|---|---|
| مېنى | (meni) | me | نەپرەت | (näprät) | disgust |
| مېنىڭ | (mening) | my | نەپرەتلەن_ | (näprätlän-) | hate |
| مېنىڭكى | (meningki) | mine | نەتىجە | (nätijä) | result |
| مېھرىبان | (mehriban) | kind | نەچچە | (nächchä) | how much |
| مېھمان | (mehman) | guest | نەرسە | (närsä) | thing |
| مېھمانخانا | (mehmankhana) | hotel | نەزەرىيە | (näzäriyä) | theory |
| مېھماندوستلۇق | (mehmandostluq) | hospitality | نەسىھەت | (näsihät) | advice |
| مېۋە | (mevä) | fruit | نەشرىيات | (näshriyat) | publishing house |
| مىخ | (mikh) | nail | نەق پۇل | (näq pul) | cash |
| مىس | (mis) | copper | نەم | (näm) | damp, moist |
| مىسال | (misal) | example | نەۋرە | (nävrä) | grandchild |
| مىقدار | (miqdar) | amount, quantity | نەيزە | (näyzä) | spear |
| مىڭ | (ming) | thousand | نوپۇس | (nopus) | population |
| مىلتىق | (miltiq) | rifle | نويابىر | (noyabir) | November |
| مىللەت | (millät) | nation | نۇتۇق | (nutuq) | speech |
| مىللەتچىلىك | (millätchilik) | nationalism | نۇر | (nur) | ray |
| مىليارد | (milyard) | billion | نۆل | (nöl) | zero |
| مىليون | (milyon) | million | نېرۋا | (nerva) | nerve |
| مىن_ | (min-) | ride | نېفىت | (nefit) | oil |
| مىننەتدارلىق | (minnätdarliq) | gratitude | نېمە | (nemä) | what |
| مىنۇت | (minut) | minute | نېمە ئۈچۈن | (nemä üchün) | why |
| مىنىستىر | (ministir) | minister | نىكاھ | (nikah) | marriage |
| | | | نىيەت | (niyät) | intention |
| ناخشا | (nakhsha) | song | | | |
| ناخشا ئوقۇ_ | (nakhsha oqu-) | sing | ھاجەتخانا | (hajätkhana) | toilet |
| ناخشىچى | (nakhshichi) | singer | ھاراق | (haraq) | drink |
| نامايىش | (namayish) | demonstration | ھارغىن | (harghin) | tired |
| نان | (nan) | bread | ھارۋا | (harva) | cart |
| ناھايىتى | (nahayiti) | very | ھازىر | (hazir) | now, present |
| ناھايىتى ئاز | (nahayiti az) | seldom | ھال | (hal) | condition |
| ناھايىتى چوڭ | (nahayiti chong) | huge | ھالرەڭ | (halräng) | pink |
| ناۋاي | (navay) | baker | ھامما | (hamma) | aunt |
| ناۋايخانا | (navaykhana) | bakery | ھاممال | (hammal) | porter |
| نە...نە | (nä ... nä) | neither ... nor | ھامىلىدار | (hamilidar) | pregnant |

| | | |
|---|---|---|
| هامىلىدارلىق | (hamilidarliq) | pregnancy |
| هاۋا | (hava) | air, weather |
| هاۋا پوچتىسى | (hava pochtisi) | airmail |
| هاۋا يولى | (hava yoli) | airline |
| هاۋادىن مەلۇمات | (havadin mälumat) | weather report |
| هايات | (hayat) | life |
| هاياجان | (hayajan) | excitement |
| هايۋان | (hayvan) | animal |
| هايۋانات باغچىسى | (hayvanat baghchisi) | zoo |
| هەئە | (hä'ä) | yes |
| هەپتە | (häptä) | week |
| هەتتا | (hätta) | even |
| هەجۋىي رەسىم | (häjviy räsim) | cartoon |
| هەر | (här) | every |
| هەر بىر نەرسە | (här bir närsä) | everything |
| هەركىم | (här kim) | everybody |
| هەر يەردە | (här yärdä) | everywhere |
| هەرە | (härä) | bee, saw |
| هەرپ | (härp) | letter |
| هەرقانداق | (härqandaq) | any |
| هەرىكەتلەن‌ | (härikätlän-) | move |
| هەسەتخور | (häsätkhor) | jealous |
| هەسەتخورلۇق | (häsätkhorluq) | envy |
| هەسەتخورلۇق قىل‌ | (häsätkhorluq qil-) | envy |
| هەسەل | (häsäl) | honey |
| هەسەن-هۈسەن | (häsän-hüsän) | rainbow |
| هەققىدە | (häqqidä) | about |
| هەقىقەت | (häqiqät) | truth |
| هەقىقىي | (häqiqiy) | true |
| هەل قىل‌ | (häl qil-) | solve |
| هەم ... هەم | (häm ... häm) | both ... and |
| هەممە | (hämmä) | all |
| هەمىشە | (hämishä) | always |
| هەيدە‌ | (häydä-) | drive |
| هەيكەل | (häykäl) | statue |
| هەيكەلتىراشلىق | (häykältrashliq) | sculpture |
| هوسۇل | (hosul) | crop, harvest |
| هويلا | (hoyla) | courtyard |
| هۇجۇم | (hujum) | attack |
| هۇجۇم قىل‌ | (hujum qil-) | attack |
| هۇرۇن | (hurun) | lazy |
| هۇرۇنلۇق | (hurunluq) | laziness |
| هۇزۇرلان‌ | (huzurlan-) | enjoy |
| هۇشىدىن كەت‌ | (hushidin kät-) | faint |
| هۆكۈم | (höküm) | verdict |
| هۆكۈمەت | (hökümät) | government |
| هۆل | (höl) | wet |
| هۈرمەت | (hürmät) | respect |
| هۈرمەتلە‌ | (hürmätlä-) | respect |
| هېچقاچان | (hechqachan) | never |
| هېچكىم | (hechkim) | nobody |
| هېچنېمە | (hechnemä) | nothing |
| هېچيەردە | (hechyärdä) | nowhere |
| هېس قىل‌ | (hes qil-) | feel |
| هېسابات | (hesabat) | account, bill |
| هېسابلا‌ | (hesabla-) | calculate |
| هېسابلاش ماشىنىسى | (hesablash mashinisi) | computer |
| هېكايە | (hekayä) | story |
| هېيت | (heyt) | religious holiday |
| ئوپېرا | (opera) | opera |
| ئوپېراتسىيە | (operatsiyä) | operation, surgery |
| ئوت | (ot) | fire, grass |
| ئوتتۇرا | (ottura) | medium, middle |
| ئوتتۇز | (ottuz) | thirty |
| ئوتلاق | (otlaq) | meadow |

| | | | | | |
|---|---|---|---|---|---|
| ئوچۇق | (ochuq) | open | ئون بىر | (on bir) | eleven |
| ئوخشا_ | (okhsha-) | resemble | ئون توققۇز | (on toqquz) | nineteen |
| ئوخشاش | (okhshash) | alike, like, similar | ئون تۆت | (on töt) | fourteen |
| ئورا_ | (ora-) | wrap | ئون سەككىز | (on säkkiz) | eighteen |
| ئورغاق | (orghaq) | sickle | ئون ئۈچ | (on üch) | thirteen |
| ئورمان | (orman) | forest | ئون ئىككى | (on ikki) | twelve |
| ئورمان ياڭگىقى | (orman yangiqi) | hazelnut | ئون يەتتە | (on yättä) | seventeen |
| ئورۇق | (oruq) | slim | ئوۋ | (ov) | game |
| ئورۇن | (orun) | seat | ئوۋلا_ | (ovla-) | hunt |
| ئورۇندۇق | (orunduq) | chair, stool | ئوي | (oy) | idea, thought |
| ئوغرى | (oghri) | burglar, thief | ئويغات_ | (oyghat-) | awake, wake |
| ئوغرىلا_ | (oghrila-) | steal | ئويغان_ | (oyghan-) | awake, wake |
| ئوغۇت | (oghut) | fertilizer | ئويلا_ | (oyla-) | think |
| ئوغۇل | (oghul) | son | ئوينا_ | (oyna-) | play |
| ئوغۇل بالا | (oghul bala) | boy | ئويۇن | (oyun) | game |
| ئوفىتسېر | (ofitser) | officer | ئويۇن_تاماشا | (oyun-tamasha) | entertainment |
| ئوق | (oq) | arrow | ئويۇنچۇق | (oyunchuq) | toy |
| ئوقۇ_ | (oqu-) | read | | | |
| ئوقۇت_ | (oqut-) | teach | ئۇ | (u) | he, it, she, that |
| ئوقۇتقۇچى | (oqutquchi) | teacher | ئۇ يەردە | (u yärdä) | there |
| ئوقۇش بەدەلى | (oqush bädäli) | tuition | ئۇ يەرگە | (u yärgä) | there |
| ئوقۇشنى پۈتۈرۈش | (oqushni pütürüsh) | graduation | ئۇپۇق | (upuq) | horizon |
| ئوقۇغۇچى | (oqughuchi) | student | ئۇچ_ | (uch-) | fly |
| ئوكۇل | (okul) | shot | ئۇچراش_ | (uchrash-) | meet |
| ئوكيان | (okyan) | ocean | ئۇچرىشىش | (uchrishish) | appointment |
| ئوڭ | (ong) | right | ئۇچۇش | (uchush) | flight |
| ئوڭگاي | (ongay) | convenient | ئۇخلا_ | (ukhla-) | sleep |
| ئولتۇر_ | (oltur-) | sit | ئۇخلاش كىيىمى | (ukhlash kiyimi) | pajamas |
| ئولتۇرۇش | (olturush) | party | ئۇر_ | (ur-) | hit |
| ئومۇرتقا | (omurtqa) | spine | ئۇرۇش | (urush) | war |
| ئومۇمىي | (omumiy) | general | ئۇرۇق | (uruq) | seed |
| ئومۇۋالنىك | (omuvalnik) | sink | ئۇزاق | (uzaq) | far |
| ئون | (on) | ten | ئۇزۇن | (uzun) | long |
| ئون ئالتە | (on altä) | sixteen | ئۇزۇنلۇق | (uzunluq) | length |
| ئون بەش | (on bäsh) | fifteen | ئۇستۇرا | (ustura) | razor |

| | | |
|---|---|---|
| ئۇستىخان | (ustikhan) | skeleton |
| ئۇسسۇز | (ussuz) | thirsty |
| ئۇسسۇل ئويناـ | (ussul oyna-) | dance |
| ئۇسسۇلچى | (ussulchi) | dancer |
| ئۇقتۇرـ | (uqtur-) | inform |
| ئۇكا | (uka) | brother |
| ئۇلار | (ular) | they, those |
| ئۇلارنى | (ularni) | them |
| ئۇلارنىڭ | (ularning) | their |
| ئۇن | (un) | flour |
| ئۇنتۇـ | (untu-) | forget |
| ئۇنى | (uni) | her, him |
| ئۇنىڭ | (uning) | her, his, its |
| ئۇنىڭكى | (uningki) | hers, his, its |
| ئۇنىۋېرسىتېت | (universitet) | university |
| ئۇياتچان | (uyatchan) | shy |
| ئۇيالـ | (uyal-) | ashamed: be ashamed |
| ئۇيقۇ | (uyqu) | sleep |
| ئۇيۇشما | (uyushma) | union |
| ئۆپكە | (öpkä) | lung |
| ئۆتـ | (öt-) | pass |
| ئۆتكەن | (ötkän) | last |
| ئۆتنە ئالـ | (ötnä al-) | borrow |
| ئۆتۈك | (ötük) | boot |
| ئۆچكە | (öchkä) | goat |
| ئۆچۈرـ | (öchür-) | erase, extinguish, put out |
| ئۆچۈرگۈچ | (öchürgüch) | eraser |
| ئۆردەك | (ördäk) | duck |
| ئۆرۈك | (örük) | apricot |
| ئۆزگەرتـ | (özgärt-) | change |
| ئۆزلىرى | (özliri) | yourself |
| ئۆزۈڭ | (özüng) | yourself |
| ئۆزى | (özi) | herself, himself, itself |
| ئۆزىڭىز | (özingiz) | yourselves |
| ئۆزىم | (özim) | myself |
| ئۆزىمىز | (özimiz) | ourselves |
| ئۆزىنى تۇتـ | (özini tut-) | behave |
| ئۆسـ | (ös-) | grow |
| ئۆسۈم | (ösüm) | growth, interest |
| ئۆسۈملۈك | (ösümlük) | plant |
| ئۆكتەبىر | (öktäbir) | October |
| ئۆكۈنچ | (ökünch) | regret |
| ئۆگەنـ | (ögän-) | learn, study |
| ئۆگزە | (ögzä) | roof |
| ئۆلـ | (öl-) | die |
| ئۆلتۈرـ | (öltür-) | kill |
| ئۆلچەم | (ölchäm) | measure, size |
| ئۆلكە | (ölkä) | province |
| ئۆلۈك | (ölük) | dead |
| ئۆلۈم | (ölüm) | death |
| ئۆمۈچۈك | (ömüchük) | spider |
| ئۆي | (öy) | home, house, room |
| ئۆي جاھازلىرى | (öy jahazliri) | furniture |
| ئۆي ئىگىسى | (öy igisi) | host |
| ئۈچ | (üch) | three |
| ئۈچ بۇلۇڭ | (üch bulung) | triangle |
| ئۈچەي | (üchäy) | intestine |
| ئۈچۈن | (üchün) | for |
| ئۈزۈش | (üzüsh) | swimming |
| ئۈزۈك تاۋۇش | (üzük tavush) | consonant |
| ئۈزۈم | (üzüm) | grape |
| ئۈزۈم ھارىقى | (üzüm hariqi) | wine |
| ئۈستىدە | (üstidä) | above, on, over |
| ئۈلگۈجە سېتىش | (ülgüjä setish) | wholesale |
| ئۈمىد | (ümid) | hope |

| | | |
|---|---|---|
| ئۇمىد قىل_ | (ümid qil-) | hope |
| ئۈنئالغۇ | (ün'alghu) | tape recorder |
| ئۈنئالغۇ لېنتىسى | (ün'alghu lentisi) | cassette |
| ژادى | (vadi) | valley |
| ژاراڭ_چۇرۇڭ | (varang-churung) | noise |
| ژاسكېتبول | (vasketbol) | basketball |
| ژاقىت | (vaqit) | date, time |
| ژە | (vä) | and |
| ژەدە بەر_ | (vädä bär-) | promise |
| ژەزىپە | (väzipä) | duty |
| ژەزىيەت | (väziyät) | situation |
| ژەقە | (väqä) | event |
| ژەكىللىك قىل_ | (väkillik qil-) | represent |
| ژەھىمە | (vähimä) | fear |
| ژېلىسىپىت | (velisipit) | bicycle |
| ژىجدان | (vijdan) | conscience |
| ژىلكا | (vilka) | fork |
| ئېتىز | (etiz) | field |
| ئېتىقاد | (etiqad) | faith |
| ئېرى_ | (eri-) | melt |
| ئېشەك | (eshäk) | donkey |
| ئېشىپ كەت_ | (eship ket-) | surpass |
| ئېغىر | (eghir) | heavy |
| ئېغىز | (eghiz) | mouth |
| ئېكەك | (ekäk) | file |
| ئېكران | (ekran) | screen |
| ئېگىز | (egiz) | high, tall |
| ئېگىزلىك | (egizlik) | height |
| ئېڭەك | (engäk) | chin |
| ئېلان | (elan) | advertisement |
| ئېلېكتر | (elektr) | electricity |
| ئېلىپ كەل_ | (elip käl-) | bring |
| ئېلىپبە | (elipbä) | alphabet |
| ئېلىش | (elish) | subtraction |
| ئېنىق | (eniq) | obvious |
| ئېھتىمال | (ehtimal) | perhaps, probably |
| ئېھتىياتچان | (ehtiyatchan) | careful |
| ئېھتىياج | (ehtiyaj) | necessity, need |
| ئېيت_ | (eyt-) | tell |
| ئېيىق | (eyiq) | bear |
| ئىبادەت | (ibadät) | worship |
| ئىبادەتخانا | (ibadätkhana) | temple |
| ئىپتىخار | (iptikhar) | pride |
| ئىت | (it) | dog |
| ئىتتەر_ | (ittär-) | push |
| ئىتتىك | (ittik) | sharp |
| ئىجارە | (ijarä) | rent |
| ئىچ قېتىش | (ich qetish) | constipation |
| ئىچ سۈرۈش | (ich sürüsh) | diarrhea |
| ئىچ_ | (ich-) | drink |
| ئىچىدە | (ichidä) | inside |
| ئىچىملىك | (ichimlik) | beverage |
| ئىدىش | (idish) | jar |
| ئىدئوم | (idi'om) | idiom |
| ئىز | (iz) | trace |
| ئىزاھات | (izahat) | explanation |
| ئىزدە_ | (izdä-) | look for, search, seek |
| ئىستاكان | (istakan) | glass |
| ئىستانسا | (istansa) | station |
| ئىستېمالچى | (istemalchi) | consumer |
| ئىسسىق | (issiq) | hot |
| ئىسسىقلىق | (issiqliq) | heat |
| ئىسىم | (isim) | noun |
| ئىسيان | (isyan) | rebellion |
| ئىش | (ish) | job |
| ئىش تاشلاش | (ish tashlash) | strike |

| | | |
|---|---|---|
| ئـش ھەققى | (ish häqqi) | wage |
| ئـشـەنـ | (ishän-) | believe, rely |
| ئـشـەنـچ | (ishänch) | belief, confidence |
| ئـشـچـى | (ishchi) | worker |
| ئـشـخـانـا | (ishkhana) | office |
| ئـشـشـ | (ishshi-) | swell |
| ئـشـشـق | (ishshiq) | swelling |
| ئـشـكـاپ | (ishkap) | cupboard |
| ئـشـلـە | (ishlä-) | work |
| ئـشـلـەپ چـقـار | (ishläp chiqar-) | produce |
| ئـشـلـە تـ | (ishlät-) | use |
| ئـشـك | (ishik) | door |
| ئـقـتـسـاد | (iqtisad) | economics |
| ئـقـلـم | (iqlim) | climate |
| ئـكـكـى | (ikki) | two |
| ئـگـ | (igä) | subject |
| ئـلـتـمـاس قـلـ | (iltimas qil-) | apply, request |
| ئـمـتـهـان | (imtihan) | examination |
| ئـمـزا | (imza) | signature |
| ئـنـتـقـام | (intiqam) | revenge |
| ئـنـچـكـه | (inchikä) | fine, thin |
| ئـنـژبـنـر | (inzhener) | engineer |
| ئـنـقـلـاب | (inqilab) | revolution |
| ئـنـكـار قـلـ | (inkar qil-) | deny |
| ئـيـزل | (iyul) | July |
| ئـيـؤن | (iyun) | June |
| يا | (ya) | bow |
| يا(كى)...يا(كى) | (ya[ki] ... ya[ki]) | either ... or |
| يـاپـ | (yap-) | close, cover, shut |
| يـاتـ | (yat-) | lie |
| يـاتـاق ئـۆيـى | (yataq öyi) | bedroom |
| يـاخـشـى | (yakhshi) | fine, good, nice, well |
| يـاخـشـى كـۆر | (yakhshi kör-) | like |
| يـاخـشـراق | (yakhshiraq) | better |
| يـاخـشـمـۇسـز | (yakhshimusiz) | hello |
| يـار | (yar-) | split |
| يـاراشـ | (yarash-) | suit |
| يـاردەم | (yardäm) | assistance, help |
| يـاردەم قـلـ | (yardäm qil-) | assist, help |
| يـاز | (yaz) | summer |
| يـازـ | (yaz-) | write |
| يـازغـۇچـى | (yazghuchi) | writer |
| يـاسـا | (yasa-) | make |
| يـاسـتـۇق | (yastuq) | pillow |
| يـاسـتـۇق قـبـى | (yastuq qepi) | pillowcase |
| يـاش | (yash) | age, young |
| يـاشـا | (yasha-) | live |
| يـاشـلـق | (yashliq) | youth |
| يـاغ | (yagh) | fat, oil |
| يـاغـ | (yagh-) | precipitate |
| يـاغـاچ | (yaghach) | wood |
| يـاق | (yaq) | no |
| يـاقـا | (yaqa) | collar |
| يـاكـى | (yaki) | or |
| يـاڭـاق | (yangaq) | walnut |
| يـاڭـيـۇ | (yangyu) | potato |
| يـالـپـۇز | (yalpuz) | mint |
| يـالـغـان سـۆزلـە | (yalghan sözlä-) | lie |
| يـالـغـان گـەپ | (yalghan gäp) | lie |
| يـالـغـۇز | (yalghuz) | alone |
| يـالـقـۇن | (yalqun) | flame |
| يـالـلـۇغ | (yallugh) | infection |
| يـالـڭـاچ | (yalingach) | bare |
| يـامـاشـ | (yamash-) | climb |
| يـامـان | (yaman) | bad |
| يـامـغـۇر | (yamghur) | rain |
| يـامـغـۇرلـۇق | (yamghurluq) | raincoat |

| | | | | | |
|---|---|---|---|---|---|
| يانچۇق | (yanchuq) | pocket | يۇقىرىدا | (yuqirida) | above |
| يانغىن | (yanghin) | fire | يۇڭ | (yung) | wool |
| يانۋار | (yanvar) | January | يۇلتۇز | (yultuz) | star |
| ياۋاش | (yavash) | gentle | يۇمشاق | (yumshaq) | soft |
| ياۋايى | (yavayi) | wild | يۆتەل | (yötäl) | cough |
| ياي‑ | (yay-) | spread | يۆلەنچۈكلۈك ئورۇندۇق | (yölänchük-lük orunduq) | armchair |
| يە‑ | (yä-) | eat | | | |
| يەت‑ | (yät-) | arrive, reach | يۆنىلىش | (yönilish) | direction |
| يەتتە | (yättä) | seven | يۈرەك | (yüräk) | heart |
| يەتمىش | (yätmish) | seventy | يۈرۈش‑تۇرۇش | (yürüsh-turush) | behavior |
| يەر تەۋرەش | (yär tävräsh) | earthquake | يۈز | (yüz) | hundred |
| يەر شارى | (yär shari) | earth | يۈز بەر‑ | (yüz bär-) | happen |
| يەكشەنبە | (yäkshänbä) | Sunday | يۈك | (yük) | cargo |
| يەڭ‑ | (yäng-) | defeat, win | يۈك‑تاق | (yük-taq) | baggage |
| يەلكەنلىك كېمە | (yälkänlik kemä) | sailboat | يۈك ماشىنىسى | (yük mashinisi) | truck |
| يەنە | (yänä) | again | يۈگۈر‑ | (yügür-) | run |
| يەھۇدىي | (yähudiy) | Jew | يېپىق | (yepiq) | closed |
| يوپكا | (yopka) | skirt | يېتەرلىك | (yetärlik) | enough, sufficient |
| يوپۇرماق | (yopurmaq) | leaf | يېرىم | (yerim) | half |
| يوتا | (yota) | thigh | يېرىم ئارال | (yerim aral) | peninsula |
| يوتقان | (yotqan) | quilt | يېزا | (yeza) | village |
| يورۇ‑ | (yoru-) | shine | يېزا ئىگىلىكى | (yeza igiliki) | agriculture |
| يورۇق | (yoruq) | bright | يېزىق | (yeziq) | writing |
| يورۇقلۇق | (yoruqluq) | light | يېسىموق | (yesimuq) | lentil |
| يوشۇر‑ | (yoshur-) | hide | يېشىل | (yeshil) | green |
| يوقات‑ | (yoqat-) | lose | يېقىن | (yeqin) | near |
| يوقال‑ | (yoqal-) | disappear | يېقىنلاش‑ | (yeqinlash-) | approach |
| يول | (yol) | road, way | يېقىنىدا | (yeqinida) | near |
| يول ھەققى | (yol häqqi) | fare | يېڭى | (yengi) | fresh, new |
| يولغا چىق‑ | (yolgha chiq-) | depart | يېڭى ئاي | (yengi ay) | crescent |
| يولغا چىقىش | (yolgha chiqish) | departure | يېڭى يىل | (yengi yil) | New Year |
| يولۇچى | (yoluchi) | passenger | يېلىم | (yelim) | glue |
| يولۋاس | (yolvas) | tiger | يېمەك | (yemäk) | food |
| يۇ‑ | (yu-) | wash | يېنىدا | (yenida) | beside |
| يۇقۇملۇق زۇكام | (yuqumluq zukam) | flu | يېنىق | (yeniq) | light |

| | | | | | |
|---|---|---|---|---|---|
| يىپەك | (yipäk) | silk | يىڭنە | (yingnä) | needle |
| يىرت_ | (yirt-) | tear | يىل | (yil) | year |
| يىغـ | (yigh-) | collect | يىلان | (yilan) | snake |
| يىغلا_ | (yighla-) | cry, weep | يىلتىز | (yiltiz) | root |
| يىغىن | (yighin) | meeting | يىللىق | (yilliq) | anniversary, lukewarm, warm |
| يىگىرمە | (yigirmä) | twenty | | | |

# UZBEK - ENGLISH INDEX

| авария | avariya | accident |
| аввал | avval | ago |
| август | avgust | August |
| авиапочта | aviapochta | airmail |
| автобус | avtobus | bus |
| автомат | avtomat | machine gun |
| автомобиль | avtomobil' | automobile |
| агар | agar | if |
| адабиёт | adabiyot | literature |
| адабий | adabiy | literary |
| адабий асар | adabiy asar | literary work |
| адвокат | advokat | lawyer |
| адёл | adyol | blanket |
| адолат | adolat | justice |
| адрес | adres | address |
| аёл | ayol | woman |
| ажойиб | ajoyib | nice |
| ажрал- | ajral- | separated: be separated |
| ажралиш | ajralish | divorce |
| ажрат- | ajrat- | separate |
| ажраш- | ajrash- | divorce |
| азиз | aziz | dear |
| айб | ayb | fault |
| айбдор | aybdor | guilty |
| айириш | ayirish | subtraction |
| айиқ | ayiq | bear |
| айни | ayni | same |
| айниқса | ayniqsa | especially |
| айт- | ayt- | tell |
| ака | aka | brother |
| аланга | alanga | flame |
| албатта | albatta | course: of course |
| алгебра | algebra | algebra |
| алда- | alda- | lie |
| алифбо | alifbo | alphabet |
| аломат | alomat | symbol |
| алоқа | aloqa | communication |
| алоҳида | alohida | separate |
| амаки | amaki | uncle |
| амма | amma | aunt |
| анархия | anarxiya | anarchy |
| анжир | anjir | fig |
| аниқ | aniq | concrete, obvious |
| анор | anor | pomegranate |
| антенна | antenna | antenna |
| апельсин | apel'sin | orange |
| апрель | aprel' | April |
| арава | arava | cart |
| аралаштир- | aralashtir- | mix |
| арвоҳ | arvoh | ghost |
| арзон | arzon | cheap |
| арзонлаштириш | arzonlashtirish | discount, sale |
| ари | ari | bee |
| арпа | arpa | barley |
| арра | arra | saw |
| артиллерия | artilleriya | artillery |
| асаб | asab | nerve |
| асал | asal | honey |
| асал ойи | asal oyi | honeymoon |
| асбоб | asbob | instrument, tool |
| асбоб-ускуна | asbob-uskuna | equipment |
| аскар | askar | soldier |
| асосий | asosiy | main |
| аср | asr | century |
| аста-секин | asta-sekin | gradually |
| атир | atir | perfume |
| атиргул | atirgul | rose |
| афзал кўр- | afzal ko'r- | prefer |
| афсона | afsona | legend |
| афсун | afsun | spell |
| ахлат | axlat | trash |
| аччиқ | achchiq | bitter |
| ашула айт- | ashula ayt- | sing |
| аъзо | a'zo | member |
| ақл | aql | mind |
| ақлли | aqlli | clever, intelligent |
| ағдар-тўнтар | ag'dar-to'ntar | messy |
| аҳамиятли | ahamiyatli | important |
| аҳвол | ahvol | condition |
| аҳён-аҳён | ahyon-ahyon | seldom |
| аҳмоқ | ahmoq | stupid |
| аҳоли | aholi | population |
| бадан | badan | body |
| байрам | bayram | holiday |
| байроқ | bayroq | flag |
| баланд | baland | high, tall |
| баланд [овоз] | baland [ovoz] | loud |
| баландлик | balandlik | height |
| балет | balet | ballet |
| балиқ | baliq | fish |

| | | |
|---|---|---|
| балиқчи | baliqchi | fisherman |
| балки | balki | probably |
| балкон | balkon | balcony |
| балоғатга | balog'atga | adult |
| етган одам | yetgan odam | |
| балчиқ | balchiq | mud |
| банан | banan | banana |
| банд | band | busy |
| банк | bank | bank |
| банка | banka | jar |
| барг | barg | leaf |
| бармоқ | barmoq | finger |
| барометр | barometr | barometer |
| баскетбол | basketbol | basketball |
| бассейн | basseyn | pool |
| бастакор | bastakor | composer |
| бахтиёр | baxtiyor | happy |
| бахтсиз | baxtsiz | unhappy |
| баъзан | ba'zan | sometimes |
| баъзи | ba'zi | some |
| бақир- | baqir- | shout |
| бақлажон | baqlajon | eggplant |
| баҳона | bahona | excuse |
| баҳор | bahor | spring |
| баҳс | bahs | argument |
| баҳслаш- | bahslash- | argue |
| бегуноҳ | begunoh | innocent |
| бегуноҳлик | begunohlik | innocence |
| безовта қил- | bezovta qil- | disturb |
| бекат | bekat | stop |
| белкурак | belkurak | spade |
| бемор | bemor | patient |
| бензин | benzin | gasoline |
| бер- | ber- | give |
| бери | beri | since |
| беш | besh | five |
| беҳи | behi | quince |
| биз | biz | we |
| бизни | bizni | us |
| бизники | bizniki | ours |
| бизнинг | bizning | our |
| бил- | bil- | know |
| билак | bilak | wrist |
| билан | bilan | by, with |
| билет | bilet | ticket |
| билим | bilim | knowledge |
| бинафша ранг | binafsha rang | purple |
| бино | bino | building |
| бинт | bint | bandage |
| бир | bir | one |
| бир неча | bir necha | several, some |
| бир оз | bir oz | little |
| бирга | birga | together |
| бирор нарса | biror narsa | anything |
| бироқ | biroq | but |
| бит | bit | louse |
| битим | bitim | agreement |
| бланка | blanka | form |
| блуза | bluza | blouse |
| бобо | bobo | grandfather |
| бодом | bodom | almond |
| бодринг | bodring | cucumber |
| божхона | bojxona | customs |
| бозор | bozor | market |
| бой | boy | rich |
| бойлик | boylik | wealth |
| бойўғли | boyo'g'li | owl |
| бола | bola | child |
| болта | bolta | axe |
| болға | bolg'a | hammer |
| бомба | bomba | bomb |
| бор- | bor- | go |
| бос- | bos- | print |
| ботқоқ | botqoq | swamp |
| бош | bosh | head |
| бош оғриғи | bosh og'rig'i | headache |
| бошла- | boshla- | start |
| бошла(н)- | boshla[n]- | begin |
| бошқа | boshqa | another, other |
| бошқарувчи | boshqaruvchi | manager |
| боғ | bog' | garden |
| боғбон | bog'bon | gardener |
| боғла- | bog'la- | fasten, tie |
| бу | bu | this |
| бу ерга | bu yerga | here |
| бу ерда | bu yerda | here |
| буви | buvi | grandmother |
| бугун | bugun | today |
| буз- | buz- | destroy |
| бузоқ гўшти | buzoq go'shti | veal |
| буйрак | buyrak | kidney |
| буйруқ бер- | buyruq ber- | command |
| бук- | buk- | bend |
| букла- | bukla- | fold |
| булар | bular | these |
| булут | bulut | cloud |
| бундай | bunday | such |
| бура- | bura- | twist |

| бурама мих | burama mix | screw |
| бурга | burga | flea |
| бургут | burgut | eagle |
| бурил- | buril- | turn |
| бурун | burun | nose |
| бурч | burch | duty |
| бурчак | burchak | angle, corner |
| бутерброд | buterbrod | sandwich |
| бутун | butun | whole |
| буюр- | buyur- | order |
| буюрт- | buyurt- | order |
| бюджет | byudjet | budget |
| буқа | buqa | bull |
| буғдой | bug'doy | wheat |
| буғу | bug'u | deer |
| бўёқчи | bo'yoqchi | painter |
| бўйин | bo'yin | neck |
| бўйсун- | bo'ysun- | obey |
| бўл- | bo'l- | be, become, divide |
| бўлим | bo'lim | department, section |
| бўлиш | bo'lish | division |
| бўри | bo'ri | wolf |
| бўрон | bo'ron | storm |
| бўш | bo'sh | empty, loose |
| бўшат- | bo'shat- | empty, release |
| бўя- | bo'ya- | dye, paint |
| ва | va | and |
| вазир | vazir | minister |
| вазифа | vazifa | assignment |
| вазият | vaziyat | situation |
| вакил бўл- | vakil bo'l- | represent |
| ванна | vanna | bathroom |
| ваъда бер- | va'da ber- | promise |
| вақт | vaqt | time |
| велосипед | velosiped | bicycle |
| вергуль | vergul' | comma |
| вертолёт | vertolyot | helicopter |
| видео | video | video |
| виждон | vijdon | conscience |
| виждонли | vijdonli | honest |
| вилоят | viloyat | province |
| вино | vino | wine |
| водий | vodiy | valley |
| воқеа | voqea | event |

| -га | -ga | to |
| газ | gaz | gas |
| газета | gazeta | newspaper |
| газмол | gazmol | textile |
| гайка калити | gayka kaliti | wrench |
| галстук | galstuk | tie |
| гап | gap | sentence |
| гапир- | gapir- | speak |
| гаплаш- | gaplash- | talk |
| гараж | garaj | garage |
| гаранг | garang | deaf |
| гаранглик | garanglik | deafness |
| -гача | -gacha | until |
| геология | geologiya | geology |
| геометрия | geometriya | geometry |
| гилам | gilam | carpet |
| гиламча | gilamcha | rug |
| графин | grafin | pitcher |
| грипп | gripp | flu |
| гувоҳ | guvoh | witness |
| гугурт | gugurt | match |
| гул | gul | flower |
| гурунч | gurunch | rice |
| гўзаллик | go'zallik | beauty |
| гўшт | go'sht | meat |
| гўшт дўкони | go'sht do'koni | butcher shop |
| -да | -da | at, in |
| давлат | davlat | state |
| давола- | davola- | cure |
| даволаш | davolash | cure |
| давом эт- | davom et- | continue |
| давр | davr | era |
| дазмол | dazmol | iron |
| дала | dala | field |
| далил | dalil | proof |
| дам олиш | dam olish | holiday, rest |
| -дан | -dan | from |
| дангаса | dangasa | lazy |
| дангасалик | dangasalik | laziness |
| даража | daraja | degree |
| дарахт | daraxt | tree |
| дарвоза | darvoza | gate |
| дарё | daryo | river |
| даромад | daromad | income |
| дарс | dars | lesson |
| дарҳол | darhol | immediately |
| дасторгул | dastorgul | daisy |
| дастур | dastur | program |
| дастурхон | dasturxon | tablecloth |

| | | | | | |
|---|---|---|---|---|---|
| дафтар | daftar | notebook | е- | ye- | eat |
| дақиқа | daqiqa | minute | елим | yelim | glue |
| де- | de- | say | елка | yelka | shoulder |
| дев | dev | giant | елканли кема | yelkanli kema | sailboat |
| девор | devor | wall | енгил | yengil | light |
| девор соати | devor soati | clock | ер | yer | earth |
| декабрь | dekabr' | December | ер қимирлаш | yer qimirlash | earthquake |
| демократия | demokratiya | democracy | ет- | yet- | reach |
| денгиз | dengiz | sea | етарли | yetarli | enough, |
| денгиз соҳили | dengiz sohili | coast | | | sufficient |
| дераза | deraza | window | етиб бор- | yetib bor- | arrive |
| деярли | deyarli | almost | етмиш | yetmish | seventy |
| деҳқон | dehqon | peasant | етти | yetti | seven |
| деҳқончилик | dehqonchilik | cultivation | | | |
| дин | din | religion | ё ... ё | yo ... yo | either ... or |
| диний | diniy | religious | ёввойи | yovvoyi | wild |
| диний байрам | diniy bayram | religious | ёдгорлик | yodgorlik | monument |
| | | holiday | ёз | yoz | summer |
| диплом | diplom | diploma | ёз- | yoz- | write |
| диққат | diqqat | attention | ёзув | yozuv | writing |
| доим | doim | always | ёзувчи | yozuvchi | writer |
| доира | doira | circle | ёй- | yoy- | spread |
| доктор | doktor | doctor | ёки | yoki | or |
| дон | don | grain | ёлғиз | yolg'iz | alone |
| дори | dori | drug, | ёлғон | yolg'on | lie |
| | | medicine | ёмон | yomon | bad |
| доривор | dorivor | herb | ёмғир | yomg'ir | rain |
| ўсимлик | o'simlik | | ён- | yon- | burn |
| доригар | dorigar | pharmacist | ёнида | yonida | beside |
| дорихона | dorixona | pharmacy | ёноқ | yonoq | cheek |
| достон | doston | epic | ёнғин | yong'in | fire |
| драма | drama | drama | ёнғоқ | yong'oq | walnut |
| драматург | dramaturg | playwright | ёп- | yop- | close, cover, |
| дум | dum | tail | | | shut |
| думалат- | dumalat- | roll | ёпиқ | yopiq | closed |
| думалоқ | dumaloq | round | ёпиш- | yopish- | stick |
| дунё | dunyo | world | ёр- | yor- | split |
| дуо | duo | prayer | ёрдам | yordam | assistance, |
| духовка | duxovka | oven | | | help |
| душ | dush | shower | ёрдамлаш- | yordamlash- | help |
| душанба | dushanba | Monday | ёруғлик | yorug'lik | light |
| душман | dushman | enemy | ёрқин | yorqin | bright |
| душманлик | dushmanlik | enmity | ёстиқ | yostiq | pillow |
| дюжина | dyujina | dozen | ёстиқ жилди | yostiq jildi | pillowcase |
| дўзах | do'zax | hell | ёт- | yot- | lie |
| дўкон | do'kon | shop, store | ётоқхона | yotoqxona | bedroom |
| дўл | do'l | hail | ёш | yosh | age, young |
| дўст | do'st | friend | ёшлик | yoshlik | youth |
| дўстлик | do'stlik | friendship | ёқ- | yoq- | burn |
| | | | ёқа | yoqa | collar |

| | | |
|---|---|---|
| ёқимли | yoqimli | handsome |
| ёқтир- | yoqtir- | like |
| ёғ | yog' | fat, oil |
| ёғ- | yog'- | precipitate |
| ёғоч | yog'och | wood |
| жавоб | javob | answer, reply |
| жавоб бер- | javob ber- | answer, reply |
| жазо | jazo | punishment |
| жазола- | jazola- | punish |
| жамият | jamiyat | society |
| жамоат телефони | jamoat telefoni | public phone |
| жанг | jang | battle |
| жаннат | jannat | paradise |
| жаноб | janob | gentleman |
| жануб | janub | south |
| жарроҳлик | jarrohlik | surgery |
| жасур | jasur | courageous |
| жаҳл | jahl | anger |
| жаҳли чиққан | jahli chiqqan | angry |
| жигар | jigar | liver |
| жигар ранг | jigar rang | brown |
| жиддий | jiddiy | serious |
| жилмай- | jilmay- | smile |
| жинни | jinni | crazy |
| жиннилик | jinnilik | insanity |
| жиноят | jinoyat | crime |
| жиноятчи | jinoyatchi | criminal |
| жиҳоз | jihoz | furniture |
| жозиба | joziba | attraction |
| жой | joy | place |
| жойлаш- | joylash- | situated: be situated |
| жойни олдиндан банд қилиш | joyni oldindan band qilish | reservation |
| жуда | juda | very |
| жума | juma | Friday |
| жун | jun | wool |
| журнал | jurnal | magazine |
| журналист | jurnalist | journalist |
| жуфт | juft | pair |
| жўнаб кет- | jo'nab ket- | depart |
| жўнаб кетиш | jo'nab ketish | departure |
| жўнат- | jo'nat- | send |
| жўнатма ҳақи | jo'natma haqi | postage |
| жўғрофия | jo'g'rofiya | geography |

| | | |
|---|---|---|
| завод | zavod | factory |
| заём | zayom | loan |
| зайтун | zaytun | olive |
| зарар | zarar | harm |
| зарарли | zararli | harmful |
| заргар | zargar | jeweler |
| зарур | zarur | necessary |
| зарурият | zaruriyat | necessity, need |
| заҳар | zahar | poison |
| заҳарли | zaharli | poisonous |
| зерик- | zerik- | bored: be bored |
| зериктирадиган | zeriktiradigan | boring |
| зиёли | ziyoli | intellectual |
| зиён | ziyon | damage, loss |
| зиёрат | ziyorat | visit |
| зиёфат | ziyofat | banquet |
| зинапоя | zinapoya | stairs |
| зич | zich | thick |
| зулм | zulm | oppression |
| иблис | iblis | demon |
| ибодат | ibodat | worship |
| ибодат қил- | ibodat qil- | pray |
| ибодатхона | ibodatxona | temple |
| ибора | ibora | idiom |
| игна | igna | needle |
| идиш | idish | dish |
| идиш ювадиган машина | idish yuvadigan mashina | dishwasher |
| ижара ҳақи | ijara haqi | rent |
| из | iz | trace |
| икки | ikki | two |
| илгак | ilgak | hanger |
| илдиз | ildiz | root |
| илиқ | iliq | lukewarm, warm |
| иложсиз | ilojsiz | impossible |
| илон | ilon | snake |
| илтимос қил- | iltimos qil- | request |
| имзо | imzo | signature |
| имконият | imkoniyat | possibility |
| имтиҳон | imtihon | examination |
| ингичка | ingichka | fine |
| инкор қил- | inkor qil- | deny |
| инфекция | infektsiya | infection |
| инфляция | inflyatsiya | inflation |

| инқилоб | inqilob | revolution |
| ипак | ipak | silk |
| исён | isyon | rebellion |
| иситма | isitma | fever |
| исм | ism | name |
| исмалоқ | ismaloq | spinach |
| иссиқ | issiq | hot |
| иссиқлик | issiqlik | heat |
| истеъмолчи | iste'molchi | consumer |
| истироҳат боғи | istirohat bog'i | park |
| ит | it | dog |
| итар- | itar- | push |
| ифлос | iflos | dirty |
| ифтихор | iftixor | pride |
| ич- | ich- | drink |
| ич кетиш | ich ketish | diarrhea |
| ичак | ichak | intestine |
| ичимлик | ichimlik | beverage |
| ичкарида | ichkarida | inside |
| иш | ish | business, job |
| иш ҳақи | ish haqi | wage |
| ишбилармон | ishbilarmon | businessman |
| ишла- | ishla- | work |
| ишлаб чиқар- | ishlab chiqar- | produce |
| ишлат- | ishlat- | use |
| ишон- | ishon- | believe, rely |
| ишонч | ishonch | belief, confidence |
| ишташлаш | ishtashlash | strike |
| ишхона | ishxona | office |
| ишчи | ishchi | worker |
| ишқала- | ishqala- | rub |
| июль | iyul' | July |
| июнь | iyun' | June |
| ияк | iyak | chin |
| иқлим | iqlim | climate |
| иқтисод | iqtisod | economics |
| йигирма | yigirma | twenty |
| йил | yil | year |
| йиллик | yillik | anniversary |
| йирт- | yirt- | tear |
| йиқил- | yiqil- | fall |
| йиғ- | yig'- | collect |
| йиғла- | yig'la- | cry, weep |
| йўл | yo'l | road, way |
| йўл ҳаракати | yo'l harakati | traffic |
| йўл ҳақи | yo'l haqi | fare |
| йўлбарс | yo'lbars | tiger |

| йўлка | yo'lka | sidewalk |
| йўловчи | yo'lovchi | passenger |
| йўналиш | yo'nalish | direction |
| йўтал | yo'tal | cough |
| йўқ | yo'q | no |
| йўқол- | yo'qol- | disappear |
| йўқот- | yo'qot- | lose |
| каби | kabi | like |
| кал | kal | bald |
| календарь | kalendar' | calendar |
| калит | kalit | key |
| кам | kam | few |
| камай- | kamay- | decrease |
| камалак | kamalak | rainbow |
| камар | kamar | belt |
| камбағал | kambag'al | poor |
| камзул | kamzul | jacket |
| камон | kamon | bow |
| канал | kanal | canal, channel |
| капалак | kapalak | butterfly |
| капитан | kapitan | captain |
| каптар | kaptar | pigeon |
| каравот | karavot | bed |
| карам | karam | cabbage |
| карикатура | karikatura | cartoon |
| картошка | kartoshka | potato |
| касал | kasal | ill, sick |
| касаллик | kasallik | illness |
| касалхона | kasalxona | hospital |
| касб | kasb | occupation |
| каср | kasr | fraction |
| кассета | kasseta | cassette |
| кассир | kassir | cashier |
| катта | katta | big, great, large |
| каттакон | kattakon | huge |
| кафе | kafe | café |
| каштан | kashtan | chestnut |
| кашф қил- | kashf qil- | discover |
| квадрат | kvadrat | square |
| квартира | kvartira | apartment |
| квитанция | kvitantsiya | receipt |
| кейин | keyin | after, then |
| кел- | kel- | arrive, come |
| келажак | kelajak | future |
| келгуси | kelgusi | next |
| келин | kelin | bride |
| келиш | kelish | arrival |

| кема | kema | ship |
|---|---|---|
| кенг | keng | broad, loose, spacious, wide |
| керак бўл- | kerak bo'l- | need |
| кес- | kes- | cut |
| кеч | kech | late |
| кеча | kecha | yesterday |
| кечиктир- | kechiktir- | postpone |
| кечиктириш | kechiktirish | delay |
| кечир- | kechir- | forgive |
| кечки овқат | kechki ovqat | dinner |
| ки | ki | that |
| кий- | kiy- | put on, wear |
| кийим-кечак | kiyim-kechak | clothes |
| ким | kim | who |
| кинотеатр | kinoteatr | cinema |
| киприк | kiprik | eyelash |
| кир- | kir- | enter |
| кириш | kirish | entrance |
| китоб | kitob | book |
| китоб дўкони | kitob do'koni | bookshop |
| китоб жавони | kitob javoni | bookcase |
| китоб сотувчи | kitob sotuvchi | bookseller |
| кичик | kichik | little, small |
| клиника | klinika | clinic |
| клуб | klub | club |
| ковла- | kovla- | dig |
| колбаса | kolbasa | sausage |
| комедия | komediya | comedy |
| композитор | kompozitor | composer |
| композиция | kompozitsiya | composition |
| компьютер | komp'yuter | computer |
| конверт | konvert | envelope |
| конфет | konfet | candy |
| концерт | kontsert | concert |
| коса | kosa | bowl |
| костюм | kostyum | suit |
| котиб | kotib | secretary |
| кран | kran | faucet |
| кресло | kreslo | armchair |
| куёв | kuyov | bridegroom |
| куз | kuz | autumn |
| кул | kul | ash |
| кул ранг | kul rang | grey |
| кул- | kul- | laugh |
| кумуш | kumush | silver |
| кун | kun | day |
| кунгабоқар | kungaboqar | sunflower |
| кундуз | kunduz | daytime |

| курак | kurak | shovel |
|---|---|---|
| кураш | kurash | wrestling |
| кураш- | kurash- | fight |
| курка | kurka | turkey |
| курси | kursi | chair, stool |
| кут- | kut- | wait |
| кутубхона | kutubxona | library |
| куч | kuch | force, strength |
| куч-қувват | kuch-quvvat | power |
| кучли | kuchli | powerful, strong |
| кучсиз | kuchsiz | weak |
| кўз | ko'z | eye |
| кўза | ko'za | jug |
| кўзгу | ko'zgu | mirror |
| кўзойнак | ko'zoynak | glasses |
| кўзойнак мутахассиси | ko'zoynak mutahassisi | optician |
| кўйлак | ko'ylak | dress, shirt |
| кўк | ko'k | blue |
| кўкрак | ko'krak | breast, chest |
| кўл | ko'l | lake |
| кўм- | ko'm- | bury |
| кўмаклаш- | ko'maklash- | assist |
| кўмир | ko'mir | coal |
| кўп | ko'p | many, much |
| кўпай- | ko'pay- | increase |
| кўпайтириш | ko'paytirish | multiplication |
| кўприк | ko'prik | bridge |
| кўпроқ | ko'proq | more |
| кўпчилик | ko'pchilik | majority |
| кўр | ko'r | blind |
| кўр- | ko'r- | see |
| кўргазма | ko'rgazma | exhibition |
| кўрлик | ko'rlik | blindness |
| кўрпа | ko'rpa | quilt |
| кўрпача | ko'rpacha | cushion |
| кўрсат- | ko'rsat- | show |
| кўрфаз | ko'rfaz | bay |
| кўтар- | ko'tar- | lift, raise |
| кўтара (савдо) | ko'tara (savdo) | wholesale |
| кўч- | ko'ch- | move |
| кўча | ko'cha | street |
| лаб | lab | lip |
| лайлак | laylak | stork |
| лекция | lektsiya | lecture |
| лимон | limon | lemon |

| | | |
|---|---|---|
| лифт | lift | elevator |
| ловия | loviya | bean |
| лой | loy | clay |
| лола | lola | tulip |
| луғат | lug'at | dictionary |
| мавжудлик | mavjudlik | existence |
| мавзу | mavzu | subject |
| мавхум | mavhum | abstract |
| магнитофон | magnitofon | tape recorder |
| маданият | madaniyat | culture |
| мажлис | majlis | meeting |
| мазали | mazali | delicious, tasty |
| мазхаб | mazhab | sect |
| май | may | May |
| майда пул | mayda pul | change |
| майдала- | maydala- | grind |
| майдон | maydon | square |
| маймун | maymun | monkey |
| маккажўхори | makkajo'xori | corn |
| мактаб | maktab | school |
| ман эт- | man et- | forbid |
| мангулик | mangulik | eternity |
| маош | maosh | salary |
| мард | mard | brave |
| мардлик | mardlik | courage |
| марка | marka | stamp |
| марказ | markaz | center |
| март | mart | March |
| мархамат | marhamat | please |
| масала | masala | problem |
| масжид | masjid | mosque |
| маслахат | maslahat | advice |
| масофа | masofa | distance |
| маст | mast | drunk |
| матбаа | matbaa | printing press |
| матбуот | matbuot | press |
| математика | matematika | mathematics |
| материал | material | material |
| машина | mashina | car, machine |
| машинка | mashinka | typewriter |
| машхур | mashhur | famous |
| маълумот | ma'lumot | data |
| мақол | maqol | proverb |
| мақола | maqola | article |
| мақсад | maqsad | purpose |
| мақта- | maqta- | praise |
| мақтан- | maqtan- | boast |
| мағлубият | mag'lubiyat | defeat |
| махалла | mahalla | neighborhood |
| мева | meva | fruit |
| медицина | meditsina | medicine |
| мезбон | mezbon | host |
| мен | men | I |
| мени | meni | me |
| меники | meniki | mine |
| менинг | mening | my |
| металл | metall | metal |
| метро | metro | subway |
| меъмор | me'mor | architect |
| мехмон | mehmon | guest |
| мехмондўстлик | mehmondo'stlik | hospitality |
| мехмонхона | mehmonxona | hotel |
| мехрибон | mehribon | kind |
| миллат | millat | nation |
| миллатчилик | millatchilik | nationalism |
| миллиард | milliard | billion |
| миллион | million | million |
| милтиқ | miltiq | rifle |
| мин- | min- | ride |
| минг | ming | thousand |
| миннатдорчилик | minnatdorchilik | gratitude |
| миннатдорчи- лик билдир- | minnatdorchi- lik bildir- | thank |
| минора | minora | tower |
| мис | mis | copper |
| мисол | misol | example |
| мифология | mifologiya | mythology |
| мих | mix | nail |
| мия | miya | brain |
| миқдор | miqdor | amount, quantity |
| мода | moda | fashion |
| модда | modda | matter |
| мол | mol | goods |
| мол гўшти | mol go'shti | beef |
| момақалдироқ | momaqaldiroq | thunder |
| мос кел- | mos kel- | suit |
| мотор | motor | engine |
| мотоцикл | mototsikl | motorcycle |
| мохирлик | mohirlik | skill |
| муаллиф | muallif | author |
| муваффақият | muvaffaqiyat | success |
| муваффақият қозон- | muvaffaqiyat qozon- | succeed |
| мудофаа | mudofaa | defense |
| муз | muz | ice |

| | | |
|---|---|---|
| музей | muzey | museum |
| музиқачи | muzikachi | musician |
| музла- | muzla- | freeze |
| музлатгич | muzlatgich | refrigerator |
| музокара | muzokara | discussion |
| музқаймоқ | muzqaymoq | ice cream |
| мукаммал | mukammal | perfect |
| мумкин | mumkin | possible |
| мураббо | murabbo | jam |
| мурожаат қил- | murojaat qil- | apply |
| мурч | murch | pepper |
| мусиқа | musiqa | music |
| мускул | muskul | muscle |
| мусобақа | musobaqa | race |
| мустақиллик | mustaqillik | independence |
| мусулмон | musulmon | Muslim |
| мухандис | muxandis | engineer |
| мухторият | muxtoriyat | autonomy |
| мушук | mushuk | cat |
| муҳаббат | muhabbat | love |
| мўйлов | mo'ylov | mustache |
| мўйна | mo'yna | fur |
| мўри | mo'ri | chimney |
| | | |
| на ... на | na ... na | neither ... nor |
| назария | nazariya | theory |
| назм | nazm | poetry |
| найза | nayza | spear |
| нам | nam | damp, moist, wet |
| намойиш | namoyish | demonstration |
| нарвон | narvon | ladder |
| нарса | narsa | thing |
| нарх | narx | cost, price |
| наср | nasr | prose |
| натижа | natija | result |
| нафас | nafas | breath |
| нафрат | nafrat | disgust |
| нафратлан- | nafratlan- | hate |
| нашриёт | nashriyot | publishing house |
| нақд пул | naqd pul | cash |
| невара | nevara | grandchild |
| нефт | neft | oil |
| неча | necha | how much |
| нима | nima | what |
| нима учун | nima uchun | why |
| нишонла- | nishonla- | celebrate |
| нишонлаш | nishonlash | celebration |

| | | |
|---|---|---|
| ният | niyat | intention |
| новвой | novvoy | baker |
| новвойхона | novvoyxona | bakery |
| новча | novcha | tall |
| нозик | nozik | gentle |
| нок | nok | pear |
| ноль | nol' | zero |
| нон | non | bread |
| нонушта | nonushta | breakfast |
| нордон | nordon | sour |
| нотўгри | noto'g'ri | wrong |
| ноябрь | noyabr' | November |
| нур | nur | ray |
| нутқ | nutq | speech |
| нуқта | nuqta | period |
| нўхат | no'xat | pea |
| | | |
| об-ҳаво | ob-havo | weather |
| об-ҳаво маълумоти | ob-havo ma'lumoti | weather report |
| ов | ov | game |
| овла- | ovla- | hunt |
| овоз | ovoz | voice, vote |
| овоз бер- | ovoz ber- | vote |
| одам | odam | human being |
| одат | odat | habit |
| одатлан- | odatlan- | used: be used to |
| оддий | oddiy | simple |
| оёқ | oyoq | foot, leg |
| озиқ-овқат | oziq-ovqat | food |
| озчилик | ozchilik | minority |
| оила | oila | family |
| ой | oy | month, moon |
| океан | okean | ocean |
| октябрь | oktyabr' | October |
| ол- | ol- | take |
| олдида | oldida | front: in front of |
| олдин | oldin | before |
| олдини ол- | oldini ol- | prevent |
| олиб кел- | olib kel- | bring |
| олим | olim | scientist |
| олма | olma | apple |
| олмахон | olmaxon | squirrel |
| олмош | olmosh | pronoun |
| оломон | olomon | crowd |
| олти | olti | six |
| олтин | oltin | gold |
| олтмиш | oltmish | sixty |

| олхўри | olxo'ri | plum |
|---|---|---|
| олча | olcha | cherry |
| олға | olg'a | forward |
| омад | omad | luck |
| омоч | omoch | plow |
| он | on | moment |
| она | ona | mother |
| опа | opa | sister |
| опера | opera | opera |
| операция | operatsiya | operation |
| орасида | orasida | between |
| орзу | orzu | wish |
| ориқ | oriq | slim |
| орол | orol | island |
| орқа | orqa | back |
| орқада | orqada | behind |
| орқали | orqali | by |
| ос- | os- | hang |
| осмон | osmon | sky |
| осойишта | osoyishta | calm |
| осон | oson | easy |
| от | ot | horse, noun |
| ота | ota | father |
| ота-она | ota-ona | parents |
| отвертка | otvertka | screwdriver |
| откритка | otkritka | postcard |
| офицер | ofitser | officer |
| официант | ofitsiant | waiter |
| охир | oxir | end |
| охирги | oxirgi | last |
| оч | och | hungry |
| оч- | och- | open |
| очарчилик | ocharchilik | famine |
| очиқ | ochiq | open |
| очлик | ochlik | hunger |
| ош | osh | rice |
| ошпаз | oshpaz | cook |
| ошхона | oshxona | dining room, kitchen |
| ошқозон | oshqozon | stomach |
| оқ | oq | white |
| оқ- | oq- | flow |
| оқшом | oqshom | dusk, evening |
| оққуш | oqqush | swan |
| оғиз | og'iz | mouth |
| оғир | og'ir | heavy |
| оғриқ | og'riq | pain |
| оҳанг | ohang | tune |

| пайдо бўл- | paydo bo'l- | appear |
|---|---|---|
| пайпоқ | paypoq | sock, stocking |
| пайшанба | payshanba | Thursday |
| пайғамбар | payg'ambar | prophet |
| пальто | pal'to | overcoat |
| панжара | panjara | fence |
| параграф | paragraf | paragraph |
| парад | parad | parade |
| парда | parda | curtain |
| пармадаста | parmadasta | drill |
| парта | parta | desk |
| партия | partiya | party |
| паспорт | pasport | passport |
| паст | past | down, low |
| пастда | pastda | below |
| пат | pat | feather |
| пахта | paxta | cotton |
| пашша | pashsha | fly |
| пенсияга чиқ- | pensiyaga chiq- | retire |
| петрушка | petrushka | parsley |
| печенье | pechen'ye | cookie |
| печка | pechka | stove |
| пешана | peshana | forehead |
| пиво | pivo | beer |
| пиёда | piyoda | pedestrian |
| пиёз | piyoz | onion |
| пиёла | piyola | cup |
| пижама | pijama | pajamas |
| пирожное | pirojnoye | cake |
| писта | pista | pistachio |
| пичоқ | pichoq | knife |
| пиш- | pish- | cook |
| пишган | pishgan | ripe |
| пишир- | pishir- | cook |
| пишлоқ | pishloq | cheese |
| планета | planeta | planet |
| пластинка | plastinka | record |
| платформа | platforma | platform |
| плаш | plash | raincoat |
| плёнка | plyonka | film |
| пляж | plyaj | beach |
| пода | poda | herd |
| поезд | poyezd | train |
| пойтахт | poytaxt | capital |
| пол | pol | floor |
| полиция | politsiya | policeman |
| помидор | pomidor | tomato |
| порахўрлик | poraxo'rlik | corruption |

| порт | port | harbor |
| посилка | posilka | parcel |
| почта | pochta | post office |
| почта қутиси | pochta qutisi | mailbox |
| почтачи | pochtachi | mailman |
| президент | prezident | president |
| пружина | prujina | spring |
| пул | pul | currency, money |
| пушти | pushti | pink |
| пьеса | p'yesa | play |
| пўлат | po'lat | steel |
| пўстлоқ | po'stloq | bark |
| равиш | ravish | adverb |
| радио | radio | radio |
| размер | razmer | size |
| рак | rak | cancer |
| рамка | ramka | frame |
| ранг | rang | color |
| расм | rasm | painting, picture |
| расмий | rasmiy | official |
| рассом | rassom | artist |
| рақобат | raqobat | competition |
| рақсга туш- | raqsga tush- | dance |
| рақкос(а) | raqqos(a) | dancer |
| рахмсиз | rahmsiz | cruel |
| реализм | realizm | realism |
| рейс | reys | flight |
| реклама | reklama | advertisement |
| республика | respublika | republic |
| ресторан | restoran | restaurant |
| рецепт | retsept | prescription |
| ривожланиш | rivojlanish | development |
| рози бўл- | rozi bo'l- | agree |
| роман | roman | novel |
| ромб | romb | diamond |
| рохат | rohat | pleasure |
| рохатлан- | rohatlan- | enjoy |
| рухсат бер- | ruxsat ber- | permit |
| ручка | ruchka | pen |
| рух | ruh | spirit |
| рухоний | ruhoniy | priest |
| рўза | ro'za | fast |
| рўмолча | ro'molcha | handkerchief |
| сабаб | sabab | cause, reason |
| сабзавот | sabzavot | vegetable |
| сабзи | sabzi | carrot |
| сабрли | sabrli | patient |
| сават | savat | basket |
| савдо | savdo | business |
| савия | saviya | level |
| саводли | savodli | literate |
| саёз | sayoz | shallow |
| саёхат | sayohat | tourism, travel |
| сайёх | sayyoh | tourist |
| сайла- | sayla- | elect |
| сайлов | saylov | election |
| сайр қил- | sayr qil- | stroll |
| саккиз | sakkiz | eight |
| сакра- | sakra- | jump |
| саксон | sakson | eighty |
| салат | salat | lettuce, salad |
| салом | salom | hello |
| саломлаш- | salomlash- | greet |
| салфетка | salfetka | napkin |
| салқин | salqin | cool |
| сана | sana | date |
| сана- | sana- | count |
| санчқи | sanchqi | fork |
| санъат | san'at | art |
| сариёғ | sariyog' | butter |
| саримсоқ | sarimsoq | garlic |
| сариқ | sariq | yellow |
| сарлавха | sarlavha | title |
| сарой | saroy | palace |
| сартарош | sartarosh | hairdresser |
| сарфла- | sarfla- | spend |
| сафар | safar | journey |
| сахий | saxiy | generous |
| сақла- | saqla- | keep |
| сахифа | sahifa | page |
| сахна | sahna | stage |
| светофор | svetofor | traffic light |
| свитер | sviter | sweater |
| сев- | sev- | love |
| секин | sekin | slow |
| секунд | sekund | second |
| сельдерей | sel'derey | celery |
| семиз | semiz | fat |
| сен | sen | you |
| сеники | seniki | yours |
| сенинг | sening | your |
| сентябрь | sentyabr' | September |
| сешанба | seshanba | Tuesday |

| | | |
|---|---|---|
| сехр | sehr | magic |
| сигарет | sigaret | cigarette |
| сигир | sigir | cow |
| сиёсат | siyosat | politics |
| сиёх | siyoh | ink |
| сиз | siz | you |
| сизники | sizniki | yours |
| сизнинг | sizning | your |
| сий- | siy- | urinate |
| сила- | sila- | stroke |
| силкит- | silkit- | shake |
| сим | sim | wire |
| сина- | sina- | test |
| сингил | singil | sister |
| синдир- | sindir- | break |
| синиқ | siniq | broken |
| синф | sinf | classroom |
| сирка | sirka | vinegar |
| сирпанчиқ | sirpanchiq | slippery |
| сирған- | sirg'an- | slide |
| сифат | sifat | adjective, quality |
| сичқон | sichqon | mouse |
| сиқ- | siq- | press |
| скелет | skelet | skeleton |
| соат | soat | hour |
| соатсоз | soatsoz | watchmaker |
| соврин | sovrin | prize |
| совун | sovun | soap |
| совуқ | sovuq | cold, frost |
| сокин | sokin | quiet |
| солиқ | soliq | tax |
| сомон | somon | straw |
| сон | son | number, thigh |
| соп | sop | handle |
| сот- | sot- | sell |
| сотиб ол- | sotib ol- | buy |
| сотиш | sotish | sale |
| сотувчи | sotuvchi | salesperson, seller |
| соф | sof | pure |
| соч | soch | hair |
| соч- | soch- | scatter |
| сочиқ | sochiq | towel |
| соя | soya | shade, shadow |
| соябон | soyabon | umbrella |
| соқов | soqov | mute |
| соқол | soqol | beard |

| | | |
|---|---|---|
| соғлик | sog'lik | health |
| соғлом | sog'lom | healthy |
| спиртли ичимлик | spirtli ichimlik | drink |
| спорт | sport | sport |
| стакан | stakan | glass |
| станция | stantsiya | station |
| стол | stol | table |
| сув | suv | water |
| сув ости кемаси | suv osti kemasi | submarine |
| сув тошқини | suv toshqini | flood |
| суд | sud | court |
| судья | sud'ya | judge |
| сузг- | suz- | swim |
| сузгич | suzgich | strainer |
| сузиш | suzish | swimming |
| сукунат | sukunat | silence |
| сумка | sumka | bag |
| сумкача | sumkacha | handbag |
| сунъий | sun'iy | artificial |
| супур- | supur- | sweep |
| супурги | supurgi | broom |
| сурат | surat | photo |
| сурги | surgi | laxative |
| сут | sut | milk |
| суюқлик | suyuqlik | liquid |
| суяк | suyak | bone |
| суғурта | sug'urta | insurance |
| сўз | so'z | word |
| сўз боши | so'z boshi | preface |
| сўр- | so'r- | suck |
| сўра- | so'ra- | ask |
| сўроқ | so'roq | question |
| табиат | tabiat | nature |
| табиий | tabiiy | natural |
| табрикла- | tabrikla- | congratulate |
| табриклаш | tabriklash | congratulation |
| тавсия қил- | tavsiya qil- | recommend |
| тагида | tagida | under, underneath |
| тадбир | tadbir | precaution |
| тадқиқот | tadqiqot | research |
| тажриба | tajriba | experience |
| тайёр | tayyor | ready |
| тайёра | tayyora | airplane, plane |
| тайёрагох | tayyoragoh | airport |
| тайёрла- | tayyorla- | prepare |

| | | |
|---|---|---|
| тайинлаш | tayinlash | appointment |
| таклиф | taklif | invitation, suggestion |
| таклиф эт- | taklif et- | offer |
| таклиф қил- | taklif qil- | invite |
| такрорла- | takrorla- | repeat |
| такси | taksi | cab, taxi |
| тала- | tala- | plunder |
| тамаки | tamaki | tobacco |
| танга | tanga | coin |
| тани- | tani- | know, recognize |
| таништир- | tanishtir- | introduce |
| танла- | tanla- | choose, select |
| тантана | tantana | ceremony |
| таом | taom | dish |
| таомнома | taomnoma | menu |
| тара- | tara- | comb |
| тараф | taraf | side |
| тарвуз | tarvuz | watermelon |
| тарелка | tarelka | plate |
| таржима | tarjima | translation |
| таржима қил- | tarjima qil- | translate |
| тарих | tarix | history |
| тарихчи | tarixchi | historian |
| тарози | tarozi | scale |
| тароқ | taroq | comb |
| тасвирла- | tasvirla- | describe |
| тасвирлаш | tasvirlash | description |
| тасдиқлаш | tasdiqlash | approval |
| таслим бўлиш | taslim bo'lish | surrender |
| татиб кўр- | tatib ko'r- | taste |
| тахминан | taxminan | about |
| ташаббус | tashabbus | investment |
| ташвишлан- | tashvishlan- | worry |
| ташвишландир- | tashvishlandir- | bother |
| ташвиқот | tashviqot | propaganda |
| таши- | tashi- | carry |
| ташла- | tashla- | throw |
| (ташлаб) кет- | [tashlab] ket- | leave |
| ташна | tashna | thirsty |
| ташриф буюр- | tashrif buyur- | visit |
| ташқари | tashqari | besides |
| ташқарида | tashqarida | outside |
| таълим | ta'lim | education |
| таъсир | ta'sir | effect, influence |
| таътил | ta'til | vacation |
| тақдир | taqdir | fate |
| тақсимла- | taqsimla- | distribute |
| тақсимча | taqsimcha | saucer |
| театр | teatr | theater |
| тег- | teg- | touch |
| тегирмон | tegirmon | mill |
| тез | tez | fast, quick, speedy |
| тез орада | tez orada | soon |
| тез тиббий ёрдам машинаси | tez tibbiy yordam mashinasi | ambulance |
| тез-тез | tez-tez | often |
| тезлик | tezlik | speed |
| текин | tekin | free |
| текислик | tekislik | plain |
| текшириш | tekshirish | investigation |
| телевизор | televizor | television |
| телеграмма | telegramma | telegram |
| телефон | telefon | telephone |
| телефон будкаси | telefon budkasi | phone booth |
| телефон номери | telefon nomeri | phone number |
| темир | temir | iron |
| темирйўл | temiryo'l | railroad |
| тенг | teng | equal |
| теп- | tep- | kick |
| тепа | tepa | hill |
| терак | terak | poplar |
| тери | teri | leather, skin |
| терла- | terla- | sweat |
| термометр | termometr | thermometer |
| тешик | teshik | hole |
| тизза | tizza | knee |
| тик- | tik- | sew |
| тикувчи | tikuvchi | tailor |
| тил | til | language, tongue |
| тила- | tila- | wish |
| тилшунос | tilshunos | linguist |
| тилшунослик | tilshunoslik | linguistics |
| тимсох | timsoh | crocodile |
| тинчлан- | tinchlan- | quiet: be quiet |
| тинчлик | tinchlik | peace |
| тираж | tiraj | circulation |
| тирик | tirik | alive |
| тиришқоқ | tirishqoq | diligent |
| тирмашиб чиқ- | tirmashib chiq- | climb |

| Cyrillic | Latin | English |
|---|---|---|
| тирноқ | tirnoq | nail |
| тирсак | tirsak | elbow |
| тиш | tish | tooth |
| тиш доктори | tish doktori | dentist |
| тиш оғриғи | tish og'rig'i | toothache |
| тиш пастаси | tish pastasi | toothpaste |
| тиш чўткаси | tish cho'tkasi | toothbrush |
| тишла- | tishla- | bite |
| това | tova | pan |
| товуш | tovush | sound |
| товуқ | tovuq | hen |
| товуқ гўшти | tovuq go'shti | chicken |
| тоза | toza | clean |
| тозала- | tozala- | clean |
| тойиб кет- | toyib ket- | slip |
| токча | tokcha | shelf |
| тол | tol | willow |
| том | tom | roof |
| томон | tomon | way |
| томонга | tomonga | towards |
| томоша | tomosha | entertainment |
| томоқ | tomoq | throat |
| томчи | tomchi | drop |
| тонг | tong | dawn |
| топ- | top- | find |
| тор | tor | narrow, tight |
| тор-мор қил- | tor-mor qil- | defeat |
| торт- | tort- | pull |
| тош | tosh | stone |
| тошбақа | toshbaqa | tortoise |
| тоғ | tog' | mountain |
| тоға | tog'a | uncle |
| трамвай | tramvay | tram |
| тугал | tugal | complete |
| тугат- | tugat- | finish |
| тугатиш | tugatish | graduation |
| тугма | tugma | button |
| тугун | tugun | knot |
| туз | tuz | salt |
| тузат- | tuzat- | mend, repair |
| тулки | tulki | fox |
| туман | tuman | fog |
| тумшуқ | tumshuq | beak |
| тун | tun | night |
| тупроқ | tuproq | earth, soil |
| тупур- | tupur- | spit |
| тур- | tur- | get up, stand |
| турли | turli | different |
| турмушга чиқ- | turmushga chiq- | marry |
| турмушга чиқиш | turmushga chiqish | marriage |
| тусмолла- | tusmolla- | guess |
| тут | tut | mulberry |
| тут- | tut- | catch |
| туфли | tufli | shoe |
| тухум | tuxum | egg |
| туш | tush | dream, noon |
| туш- | tush- | fall, get off |
| тушки пайт | tushki payt | afternoon |
| тушлик | tushlik | lunch |
| тушун- | tushun- | understand |
| тушунтир- | tushuntir- | explain |
| тушунтириш | tushuntirish | explanation |
| туя | tuya | camel |
| туғил- | tug'il- | born: be born |
| туғилган кун | tug'ilgan kun | birthday |
| туғилиш | tug'ilish | birth |
| тўла | to'la | full |
| тўла- | to'la- | pay |
| тўлдир- | to'ldir- | fill |
| тўлдирувчи | to'ldiruvchi | object |
| тўлқин | to'lqin | wave |
| тўп | to'p | ball, cannon |
| тўрт | to'rt | four |
| тўсатдан | to'satdan | sudden |
| тўхта- | to'xta- | stop |
| тўхтат- | to'xtat- | stop |
| тўшак | to'shak | mattress |
| тўқ сариқ | to'q sariq | orange |
| тўқсон | to'qson | ninety |
| тўққиз | to'qqiz | nine |
| тўғон | to'g'on | dam |
| тўғри | to'g'ri | correct, straight |
| тўғрила- | to'g'rila- | correct |
| у | u | he, it, she, that |
| у вақтда | u vaqtda | then |
| у ерга | u yerga | there |
| у ерда | u yerda | there |
| узоқ | uzoq | far |
| узр | uzr | apology |
| узр сўра- | uzr so'ra- | apologize |
| узум | uzum | grape |
| узун | uzun | long |
| узунлик | uzunlik | length |
| уй | uy | home, house |

| уйланиш | uylanish | marriage |
| уйқу | uyqu | sleep |
| уйғон- | uyg'on- | awake, wake |
| уйғот- | uyg'ot- | awake, wake |
| ука | uka | brother |
| улар | ular | they, those |
| уларни | ularni | them |
| уларнинг | ularning | their |
| умид | umid | hope |
| умид қил- | umid qil- | hope |
| умумий | umumiy | general |
| умуртқа | umurtqa | spine |
| ун | un | flour |
| ундош | undosh | consonant |
| уни | uni | her, him |
| универмаг | univermag | department store |
| университет | universitet | university |
| уники | uniki | hers, his, its |
| унинг | uning | her, his, its |
| унли | unli | vowel |
| унут- | unut- | forget |
| ур- | ur- | hit |
| уруш | urush | war |
| урф-одат | urf-odat | custom |
| уруғ | urug' | seed |
| устара | ustara | razor |
| устида | ustida | above, on, over |
| устун кел- | ustun kel- | surpass |
| уфқ | ufq | horizon |
| ухла- | uxla- | sleep |
| уч | uch | three |
| уч- | uch- | fly |
| учбурчак | uchburchak | triangle |
| учраш- | uchrash- | meet |
| учрашув | uchrashuv | appoinment |
| учун | uchun | for |
| ушла- | ushla- | hold |
| уюшма | uyushma | union |
| уял- | uyal- | ashamed: be ashamed |
| уятчан | uyatchan | shy |
| фазо | fazo | space |
| фалаж | falaj | paralysis |
| фамилия | familiya | surname |
| фаришта | farishta | angel |
| фарқ | farq | difference |
| фасл | fasl | season |

| февраль | fevral' | February |
| фестиваль | festival' | festival |
| феъл | fe'l | verb |
| физика | fizika | physics |
| фикр | fikr | opinion, thought |
| фил | fil | elephant |
| фильм | fil'm | movie |
| фойда | foyda | benefit, interest, profit |
| фойдали | foydali | useful |
| фольклор | fol'klor | folklore |
| фонтан | fontan | fountain |
| фотоаппарат | fotoapparat | camera |
| футбол | futbol | soccer |
| фуқаро | fuqaro | citizen |
| хабар | xabar | information, news |
| хабар қил- | xabar qil- | inform |
| хавф | xavf | danger |
| хавфли | xavfli | dangerous |
| хавфсиз | xavfsiz | safe |
| хазина | xazina | treasure |
| хайр | xayr | bye-bye |
| халқ | xalq | people |
| халқ эртаги | xalq ertagi | folktale |
| халқаро | xalqaro | international |
| ханжар | xanjar | dagger |
| хантал | xantal | mustard |
| хапдори | xapdori | pill |
| харажат | xarajat | expense |
| харид қил- | xarid qil- | shop |
| харидор | xaridor | buyer, customer |
| харита | xarita | map |
| хат | xat | letter |
| хато | xato | mistake |
| хиёбон | xiyobon | avenue |
| хизматкор | xizmatkor | servant |
| хизматчи | xizmatchi | official |
| хил | xil | kind |
| хола | xola | aunt |
| хом | xom | raw |
| хона | xona | room |
| хоним | xonim | lady |
| хотин | xotin | wife |
| хотира | xotira | memory |
| хоҳиш | xohish | desire |

| | | | | | |
|---|---|---|---|---|---|
| хохла- | xohla- | want | чой | choy | tea |
| христиан | xristian | Christian | чойнак | choynak | teapot |
| худди | xuddi | as if | чойшаб | choyshab | sheet |
| худо | xudo | God | чойчақа | choychaqa | tip |
| хулқ | xulq | behavior | чорраҳа | chorraha | crosswalk |
| хунук | xunuk | ugly | чоршанба | chorshanba | Wednesday |
| хурмо | xurmo | date | чумоли | chumoli | ant |
| хурсанд | xursand | glad | чумчуқ | chumchuq | sparrow |
| хуш келибсиз | xush kelibsiz | welcome | чунки | chunki | because |
| хушдан кет- | xushdan ket- | faint | чуқур | chuqur | deep |
| хушмуомала | xushmuomala | polite | чуқурлик | chuqurlik | depth |
| хўжалик | xo'jalik | farm | чўзил- | cho'zil- | reach |
| хўп | xo'p | OK | чўк- | cho'k- | drown, sink |
| хўроз | xo'roz | rooster | чўл | cho'l | desert |
| | | | чўнтак | cho'ntak | pocket |
| цемент | tsement | cement | чўтка | cho'tka | brush |
| цензура | tsenzura | censorship | чўчқа | cho'chka | pig |
| цирк | tsirk | circus | чўчқа гўшти | cho'chqa go'shti | pork |
| чайна- | chayna- | chew | | | |
| чал- | chal- | play | шайтон | shayton | Satan |
| чамадон | chamadon | suitcase | шакл | shakl | shape |
| чана | chana | sled | шам | sham | candle |
| чанг | chang | dust | шамол | shamol | wind |
| чаноқ | chanoq | sink | шамоллаш | shamollash | cold |
| чанғи спорти | chang'i sporti | skiing | шанба | shanba | Saturday |
| чап | chap | left | шараф | sharaf | honor |
| чапак чал- | chapak chal- | clap | шарбат | sharbat | fruit juice |
| чақалоқ | chaqaloq | baby | шароит | sharoit | condition |
| чақир- | chaqir- | call, summon | шарф | sharf | scarf |
| чақмоқ | chaqmoq | lightning | шарқ | sharq | east |
| чегара | chegara | border | шафтоли | shaftoli | peach |
| чек | chek | check | шахмат | shaxmat | chess |
| чек- | chek- | smoke | шахс | shaxs | person |
| чекла- | chekla- | restrict | шаҳар | shahar | city |
| челак | chelak | bucket | шаҳар атрофи | shahar atrofi | suburb |
| черков | cherkov | church | шаҳар хокимияти | shahar hokimiyati | municipality |
| чет эллик | chet ellik | foreigner | | | |
| чивин | chivin | mosquito | шаҳарча | shaharcha | town |
| чигиртка | chigirtka | grasshopper | шер | sher | lion |
| чизиқ | chiziq | line | шерик | sherik | partner |
| чизиш | chizish | drawing | шеър | she'r | poem |
| чизғич | chizg'ich | ruler | шикоят | shikoyat | complaint |
| чиннигул | chinnigul | carnation | шикоят қил- | shikoyat qil- | complain |
| чири- | chiri- | rot | шим | shim | pants |
| чиройли | chiroyli | beautiful, pretty | шимол | shimol | north |
| | | | шина | shina | tire |
| чироқ | chiroq | lamp | шип | ship | ceiling |
| чиқ- | chiq- | exit, get on | шиппак | shippak | slipper |
| чиқиш | chiqish | exit | ширин | shirin | sweet |

| | | | | | |
|---|---|---|---|---|---|
| ширинлик | shirinlik | dessert | этик | etik | boot |
| ширкат | shirkat | company, firm | этикдўз | etikdo'z | shoemaker |
| шиш | shish | swelling | эчки | echki | goat |
| шиш- | shish- | swell | эшак | eshak | donkey |
| шиша | shisha | bottle, glass | эшик | eshik | door |
| шкаф | shkaf | cupboard | эшит- | eshit- | hear, listen |
| шляпа | shlyapa | hat | эътиқод | e'tiqod | faith |
| шовқин | shovqin | noise | эҳтиёткор | ehtiyotkor | careful |
| шодлик | shodlik | joy | эҳтимол | ehtimol | perhaps |
| шоир | shoir | poet | | | |
| шорт | short | shorts | юбка | yubka | skirt |
| шох | shox | branch, horn | юв- | yuv- | wash |
| шошил- | shoshil- | hurry | югур- | yugur- | run |
| шошиш | shoshish | haste | юз | yuz | face, hundred |
| шох асар | shoh asar | masterpiece | юз бер- | yuz ber- | happen |
| шубҳа | shubha | doubt | юк | yuk | baggage, cargo |
| шунинг учун | shuning uchun | therefore | | | |
| шундай | shunday | such | юк машинаси | yuk mashinasi | truck |
| шўнғи- | sho'ng'i- | dive | юлдуз | yulduz | star |
| шўрва | sho'rva | soup | юмшоқ | yumshoq | soft |
| | | | юпқа | yupqa | thin |
| эг- | eg- | bend | юр- | yur- | walk |
| эга | ega | subject | юрак | yurak | heart |
| эгизак | egizak | twin | юқорида | yuqorida | above |
| эгов | egov | file | | | |
| эз- | ez- | crush | яйлов | yaylov | meadow |
| эк- | ek- | plant, sow | якшанба | yakshanba | Sunday |
| экран | ekran | screen | яланг | yalang | bare |
| электр | elektr | electricity | ялпиз | yalpiz | mint |
| эллик | ellik | fifty | ялтира- | yaltira- | shine |
| элчи | elchi | ambassador | яна | yana | again |
| эман | eman | oak | январь | yanvar' | January |
| эмас | emas | not | янги | yangi | fresh, new |
| эмлаш | emlash | shot | янги йил | yangi yil | New Year |
| энг кўп | eng ko'p | most | яра | yara | wound |
| энг яхши | eng yaxshi | best | ярим | yarim | half |
| эр | er | husband | ярим орол | yarim orol | peninsula |
| эргаш- | ergash- | follow | ярим тун | yarim tun | midnight |
| эри- | eri- | melt | яса- | yasa- | make |
| эркак | erkak | man | ясмиқ | yasmiq | lentil |
| эркин | erkin | free | яхши | yaxshi | fine, good, well |
| эркинлик | erkinlik | freedom | | | |
| эрта | erta | early | яхшироқ | yaxshiroq | better |
| эртага | ertaga | tomorrow | яша- | yasha- | live |
| эрталаб | ertalab | morning | яшил | yashil | green |
| эсга сол- | esga sol- | remind | яшир- | yashir- | hide |
| эски | eski | old | яширин | yashirin | secret |
| эсла- | esla- | remember | яқин | yaqin | near |
| эсна- | esna- | yawn | яқинида | yaqinida | near |

| | | |
|---|---|---|
| яқинлаш- | yaqinlash- | approach |
| яҳудий | yahudiy | Jew |
| | | |
| ўзгартир- | o'zgartir- | change |
| ўзи | o'zi | herself, himself, itself |
| ўзим | o'zim | myself |
| ўзимиз | o'zimiz | ourselves |
| ўзинг | o'zing | yourself |
| ўзингиз | o'zingiz | yourselves |
| ўзини тут- | o'zini tut- | behave |
| ўй | o'y | idea |
| ўйин | o'yin | game, match |
| ўйинчоқ | o'yinchoq | toy |
| ўйла- | o'yla- | think |
| ўйлан- | o'ylan- | marry |
| ўйна- | o'yna- | play |
| ўкиниш | o'kinish | regret |
| ўл- | o'l- | die |
| ўлдир- | o'ldir- | kill |
| ўлик | o'lik | dead |
| ўлим | o'lim | death |
| ўлчов | o'lchov | measure |
| ўн | o'n | ten |
| ўн беш | o'n besh | fifteen |
| ўн бир | o'n bir | eleven |
| ўн етти | o'n yetti | seventeen |
| ўн икки | o'n ikki | twelve |
| ўн олти | o'n olti | sixteen |
| ўн саккиз | o'n sakkiz | eighteen |
| ўн тўрт | o'n to'rt | fourteen |
| ўн тўққиз | o'n to'qqiz | nineteen |
| ўн уч | o'n uch | thirteen |
| ўнг | o'ng | right |
| ўп- | o'p- | kiss |
| ўпка | o'pka | lung |
| ўра- | o'ra- | wrap |
| ўрган- | o'rgan- | learn, study |
| ўргат- | o'rgat- | teach |
| ўргимчак | o'rgimchak | spider |
| ўрдак | o'rdak | duck |
| ўрик | o'rik | apricot |
| ўрин | o'rin | seat |
| ўрмон | o'rmon | forest, wood |
| ўрмон ёнғоғи | o'rmon yong'og'i | hazelnut |
| ўроқ | o'roq | sickle |
| ўрта | o'rta | middle |
| ўртача | o'rtacha | medium |

| | | |
|---|---|---|
| ўс- | o's- | grow |
| ўсимлик | o'simlik | plant |
| ўсиш | o'sish | growth |
| ўт | o't | fire, grass |
| ўт- | o't- | pass |
| ўтган | o'tgan | last |
| ўтир- | o'tir- | sit |
| ўтириш | o'tirish | party |
| ўткир | o'tkir | sharp |
| ўттиз | o'ttiz | thirty |
| ўхша- | o'xsha- | resemble |
| ўхшаш | o'xshash | alike, similar |
| ўчир- | o'chir- | erase, extinguish, put out |
| ўчиргич | o'chirgich | eraser |
| ўқ | o'q | arrow |
| ўқи- | o'qi- | read |
| ўқитувчи | o'qituvchi | teacher |
| ўқиш учун тўланган пул | o'qish uchun to'langan pul | tuition |
| ўқувчи | o'quvchi | reader, student |
| ўғил | o'g'il | son |
| ўғил бола | o'g'il bola | boy |
| ўғирла- | o'g'irla- | steal |
| ўғит | o'g'it | fertilizer |
| ўғри | o'g'ri | burglar, thief |
| қабзият | qabziyat | constipation |
| қабристон | qabriston | cemetery |
| қабул қил- | qabul qil- | accept |
| қават | qavat | storey |
| қадам | qadam | step |
| қаерга | qayerga | where |
| қаерда | qayerda | where |
| қайд қилиш | qayd qilish | registration |
| қайиқ | qayiq | boat |
| қаймоқ | qaymoq | cream |
| қайна- | qayna- | boil |
| қайси | qaysi | which |
| қайт- | qayt- | return |
| қайчи | qaychi | scissors |
| қайғули | qayg'uli | sorry |
| қалам | qalam | pencil |
| қалбаки | qalbaki | false |
| қалдирғоч | qaldirg'och | swallow |
| қалин | qalin | thick |
| қалтира- | qaltira- | tremble |

| | | | | | |
|---|---|---|---|---|---|
| қамал | qamal | siege | қичқир- | qichqir- | scream |
| қамоқхона | qamoqxona | jail, prison | қиш | qish | winter |
| қанд | qand | sugar | қишлоқ | qishloq | village |
| қандай | qanday | how | қишлоқ жой | qishloq joy | countryside |
| қанот | qanot | wing | қишлоқ хўжалиги | qishloq xo'jaligi | agriculture |
| қанча | qancha | how much | | | |
| қара- | qara- | look | қовун | qovun | melon |
| қарама-қарши | qarama-qarshi | opposite | қовур- | qovur- | roast |
| | | | қозонча | qozoncha | saucepan |
| қарағай | qarag'ay | pine | қойил қол- | qoyil qol- | admire |
| қарз | qarz | credit, debt, loan | қол- | qol- | remain, stay |
| | | | қон | qon | blood |
| қарз ол- | qarz ol- | borrow | қон босими | qon bosimi | blood pressure |
| қари | qari | old | | | |
| қариндош | qarindosh | relative | қона- | qona- | bleed |
| қарор | qaror | decision | қонун | qonun | law |
| қарор қил- | qaror qil- | decide | қопқоқ | qopqoq | lid |
| қарта | qarta | playing card | қор | qor | snow |
| қарши | qarshi | against | қора | qora | black |
| қарға | qarg'a | crow | қорамол | qoramol | cattle |
| қасам ич- | qasam ich- | swear | қорақарағай | qoraqarag'ay | fir |
| қасос | qasos | revenge | қорин | qorin | belly |
| қассоб | qassob | butcher | қоронғи | qorong'i | dark |
| қатиқ | qatiq | yogurt | қоронғилик | qorong'ilik | darkness |
| қатор | qator | row | қочиб кет- | qochib ket- | escape, run away |
| қаттиқ | qattiq | hard | | | |
| қачон | qachon | when | қочиб қутул- | qochib qutul- | flee |
| қаҳва | qahva | coffee | қош | qosh | eyebrow |
| қидир- | qidir- | look for, search, seek | қошиқ | qoshiq | spoon |
| | | | қоя | qoya | rock |
| | | | қоғоз | qog'oz | paper |
| қиёслаш | qiyoslash | comparison | қув(ла)- | quv[la]- | chase |
| қиз | qiz | daughter, girl | қуён | quyon | rabbit |
| | | | қуёш | quyosh | sun |
| қизил | qizil | red | қуёш ботиши | quyosh botishi | sunset |
| қизиқарли | qiziqarli | interesting | | | |
| қизиқиш | qiziqish | interest | қуёш чиқиши | quyosh chiqishi | sunrise |
| қийин | qiyin | difficult, hard | | | |
| | | | қуй- | quy- | pour |
| қиймат | qiymat | value | қулай | qulay | comfortable, convenient |
| қил- | qil- | do | | | |
| қилич | qilich | sword | қулоқ | quloq | ear |
| қиммат | qimmat | expensive | қулупнай | qulupnay | strawberry |
| қимматли | qimmatli | valuable | қулф | qulf | lock |
| қир- | qir- | scrape | қум | qum | sand |
| қирол | qirol | king | қур- | qur- | build |
| қирра | qirra | edge | қурбақа | qurbaqa | frog |
| қирқ | qirq | forty | қурбон | qurbon | sacrifice |
| қисм | qism | part | қури- | quri- | dry |
| қисқа | qisqa | short | қурол | qurol | gun, weapon |

| | | |
|---|---|---|
| қурт | qurt | worm |
| қурша- | qursha- | surround |
| қуруқ | quruq | dry |
| қурғоқчилик | qurg'oqchilik | drought |
| қус- | qus- | vomit |
| қути | quti | box |
| қутқар- | qutqar- | rescue |
| қучоқла- | quchoqla- | embrace |
| қуш | qush | bird |
| қўзичоқ | qo'zichoq | lamb |
| қўзиқорин | qo'ziqorin | mushroom |
| қўй | qo'y | sheep |
| қўй гўшти | qo'y go'shti | mutton |
| қўй- | qo'y- | put |
| қўл | qo'l | arm, hand |
| қўл соати | qo'l soati | watch |
| қўл қўй- | qo'l qo'y- | sign |
| қўлқоп | qo'lqop | glove |
| қўнғироқ | qo'ng'iroq | bell |
| қўпол | qo'pol | rude |
| қўрқ- | qo'rq- | afraid: be afraid |
| қўрқоқ | qo'rqoq | coward |
| қўрқоқлик | qo'rqoqlik | cowardice |
| қўрқув | qo'rquv | fear |
| қўрғошин | qo'rg'oshin | lead |
| қўш- | qo'sh- | add |
| қўшимча | qo'shimcha | suffix |
| қўшин | qo'shin | army |
| қўшиш | qo'shish | addition |
| қўшиқ | qo'shiq | song |
| қўшиқчи | qo'shiqchi | singer |
| қўшни | qo'shni | neighbor |
| ғалаба | g'alaba | victory |
| ғалаба қил- | g'alaba qil- | win |
| ғалати | g'alati | strange |
| ғамгин | g'amg'in | sad |
| ғарб | g'arb | west |
| ғилдирак | g'ildirak | wheel |
| ғишт | g'isht | brick |
| ғоз | g'oz | goose |
| ҳа | ha | yes |
| ҳаво | havo | air |
| ҳаво йўли | havo yo'li | airline |
| ҳавола қил- | havola qil- | present |
| ҳаёт | hayot | life |
| ҳазил | hazil | joke |
| ҳайвон | hayvon | animal |
| ҳайвонот боғи | hayvonot bog'i | zoo |
| ҳайда- | hayda- | drive |
| ҳайдовчи | haydovchi | driver |
| ҳайкал | haykal | statue |
| ҳайкалтарошлик | haykaltaroshlik | sculpture |
| ҳал қил- | hal qil- | solve |
| ҳали | hali | yet |
| ҳали ҳам | hali ham | still |
| ҳам | ham | also, too |
| ҳам ... ҳам | ham ... ham | both ... and |
| ҳамён | hamyon | purse, wallet |
| ҳамма | hamma | all, anybody |
| ҳаммол | hammol | porter |
| ҳамоҳанглик | hamohanglik | harmony |
| ҳамшира | hamshira | nurse |
| ҳар | har | every |
| ҳар ерда | har yerda | everywhere |
| ҳар ким | har kim | anybody, everybody |
| ҳар нарса | har narsa | everything |
| ҳар қандай | har qanday | any |
| ҳаракат қил- | harakat qil- | try |
| ҳаракат қилиш | harakat qilish | attempt |
| ҳарорат | harorat | temperature |
| ҳарф | harf | letter |
| ҳасад | hasad | envy |
| ҳасад қил- | hasad qil- | envy |
| ҳасадчи | hasadchi | jealous |
| ҳатто | hatto | even |
| ҳафта | hafta | week |
| ҳашарот | hasharot | insect |
| ҳаяжон | hayajon | excitement |
| ҳақида | haqida | about |
| ҳақиқат | haqiqat | truth |
| ҳақиқий | haqiqiy | real, true |
| ҳеч ким | hech kim | nobody |
| ҳеч нарса | hech narsa | nothing |
| ҳеч қаерда | hech qayerda | nowhere |
| ҳеч қачон | hech qachon | never |
| ҳид | hid | smell |
| ҳид тарат- | hid tarat- | smell |
| ҳидла- | hidla- | smell |
| ҳикоя | hikoya | story |
| ҳилол | hilol | crescent |
| ҳимоя қил | himoya qil- | defend, protect |
| ҳис | his | feeling |
| ҳис қил- | his qil- | feel |
| ҳисоб | hisob | account |

| ҳисоб-китоб варақаси | hisob-kitob varaqasi | bill |
| ҳисобла- | hisobla- | calculate |
| ҳовли | hovli | courtyard |
| ҳожатхона | hojatxona | toilet |
| ҳозир | hozir | now, present |
| ҳоким | hokim | mayor |
| ҳомиладор | homilador | pregnant |
| ҳомиладорлик | homiladorlik | pregnancy |
| ҳорғин | horg'in | tired |
| ҳосил | hosil | crop, harvest |

| ҳужум | hujum | attack |
| ҳужум қил- | hujum qil- | attack |
| ҳукм | hukm | verdict |
| ҳукумат | hukumat | government |
| ҳукумат бошлиғи | hukumat boshlig'i | prime minister |
| ҳурмат | hurmat | respect |
| ҳурматла- | hurmatla- | respect |
| ҳўкиз | ho'kiz | ox |

Printed in the United Kingdom
by Lightning Source UK Ltd.
122180UK00001B/39/A